Interpersonal Communication

Relating to Others

Interpersonal Communication

Relating to Others

EIGHTH EDITION

Steven A. Beebe
Texas State University

Susan J. Beebe
Texas State University

Mark V. Redmond
Iowa State University

PEARSON

Boston   Columbus   Indianapolis   New York   San Francisco   Amsterdam
Cape Town   Dubai   London   Madrid   Milan   Munich   Paris   Montreal   Toronto   Delhi
Mexico City   São Paulo   Sydney   Hong Kong   Seoul   Singapore   Taipei   Tokyo

Publisher, Communication: Karon Bowers
Program Manager: Anne Ricigliano
Project Manager: Maria Piper
Development Editor: Ellen Keohane
Editorial Assistant: Nikki Toner
Product Marketing Manager: Becky Rowland
Senior Field Marketing Manager: Blair Zoe Tuckman
Senior Managing Editor: Melissa Feimer
Procurement Manager: Mary Fischer

Senior Procurement Specialist: Mary Ann Gloriande
Associate Creative Director: Blair Brown
Senior Art Director: Maria Lange
Cover Designer: Maria Lange
Cover Credit: Laurent Renault/Fotolia
Digital Media Specialist: Sean Silver
Full-Service Project Management and Composition: Integra Software Services
Printer/Binder: RR Donnelley
Cover Printer: Phoenix Color/Hagerstown

Library of Congress Cataloging-in-Publication Data
Beebe, Steven A.,
   Interpersonal communication : relating to others/Steven A. Beebe, Susan J. Beebe,
Mark V. Redmond. — Eighth edition.
    pages cm
   ISBN 978-0-13-420203-7 — ISBN 0-13-420203-1 1. Interpersonal communication.
I. Beebe, Susan J., author. II. Redmond, Mark V., 1949- author. III. Title.
   BF637.C45B43 2016
   153.6—dc23

2015025487

Student Edition:
ISBN-13: 978-0-13-420203-7
ISBN-10:   0-13-420203-1

Books à la Carte:
ISBN-13: 978-0-13-420421-5
ISBN-10:   0-13-420421-2

Dedicated to Our Families

Mark and Matthew Beebe
Peggy, Nicholas, and Eric Redmond, and Beth Maroney

Contents

PART 3

Interpersonal
Communication
in Relationships   241

Special Features

#communicationandtechnology

Preface

The world does not revolve around you. This un-profound observation has profound implications for the study of interpersonal communication: **At the heart of quality interpersonal relationships is an emphasis on others.** A focus on others rather than on oneself has been the hallmark of most volunteer, community, and faith movements in the world for millennia. Yet this book is not about religion or philosophy. It's about how to enhance the quality of your interpersonal communication with others.

The importance of being other-oriented was the foundation of the first seven well-received editions of *Interpersonal Communication: Relating to Others,* and it continues to be the central theme of the eighth edition.

What's New in the Eighth Edition REVEL™

Educational technology designed for the way today's students read, think, and learn

When students are engaged deeply, they learn more effectively and perform better in their courses. This simple fact inspired the creation of REVEL: an immersive learning experience designed for the way today's students read, think, and learn. Built in collaboration with educators and students nationwide, REVEL is the newest, fully digital way to deliver respected Pearson content.

REVEL enlivens course content with media interactives and assessments—integrated directly within the authors' narrative—that provide opportunities for students to read about and practice course material in tandem. This immersive educational technology boosts student engagement, which leads to better understanding of concepts and improved performance throughout the course.

Learn more about REVEL

http://www.pearsonhighered.com/revel/

SPECIAL FEATURES FOR COMMUNICATION STUDENTS
REVEL is a dynamic learning experience that offers students a way to study the content and topics relevant to communication in a whole new way. Rather than simply offering opportunities to read about and study interpersonal communication, REVEL facilitates deep, engaging interactions with the concepts that matter most. For example, in Chapter 5, students are presented with a self-assessment that scores their skill in empathizing with others, allowing them to examine their level of empathy and consider how they could improve on it. Interactive text and figures on topics like "What You Do with Your Communication Time" are designed to capture student's attention and engage them in the text. In addition, students are presented with video examples throughout the book on topics like listening styles, social media, nonverbal communication, perception barriers, and personal space. A wealth of student and instructor resources and interactive materials can be found within REVEL. Some of our favorites include the following:

- **Audio Excerpts**
  Students can listen to audio clips while they read, bringing examples to life in a way that a printed text cannot. Throughout the book, dialogue excerpts highlight effective as well as ineffective ways to communicate. These audio examples reinforce learning and add dimension to the printed text.

- **Self-Assessments**
  Self-assessment instruments allow students to analyze their own communication styles, enabling them to learn and grow over the duration of the course. A variety of self-assessments are offered, including ones on topics such as testing your empathy and strategies for improving intercultural competence.

- **Videos and Video Self-Checks**
  Video clips appear throughout the narrative to boost mastery, and many videos are bundled with correlating self-checks, enabling students to test their knowledge.

- **Interactive Figures**
  Animated figures help students understand hard-to-grasp concepts, such as the model of relational development, through interactive visualizations.

- **Integrated Writing Opportunities**
  To help students connect chapter content with personal meaning, each chapter offers two varieties of writing prompts: the Journal prompt, which elicits free-form, topic-specific responses addressing content at the module level, and the Shared Writing prompt, which encourages students to share and respond to each other's brief responses to high-interest topics in the chapter.

For more information about all the tools and resources in REVEL and access to your own REVEL account for *Interpersonal Communication: Relating to Others*, Eighth Edition go to www.pearsonhighered.com/revel.

Chapter Updates

In addition to the abundance of in-chapter interactive and media materials you'll find in REVEL, we have worked to retain the strengths of the text that readers seem to value most—an easily accessible style, our other-oriented approach, and a balance of theory and skills. This new edition adds fresh examples and new research throughout. Here are some reasons to give this new edition a close look:

- **Chapter 1**, *"Introduction to Interpersonal Communication,"* includes additional discussion, research, and examples about social media. In addition, newly titled **#communicationandtechnology** boxes, which are included in each chapter, discuss the influence of new technology on interpersonal communication.

- **Chapter 2**, *"Interpersonal Communication and Self,"* presents additional research on the material self, attachment styles, and self-disclosure, among other topics. More social media examples have also been added to the chapter.

- **Chapter 3**, *"Interpersonal Communication and Perception,"* contains a new discussion on active and passive perception. New research on stereotyping and fundamental attribution error has also been added to the chapter.

- **Chapter 4**, *"Interpersonal Communication and Diversity: Adapting to Others,"* includes an expanded discussion on discrimination and new content on the cultural dimensions of happiness.

- **Chapter 5**, *"Listening and Responding Skills,"* contains new research on social media and listening goals. The chapter features a new **#communicationandtechnology** box about being "listened to" by our Facebook friends.

A **Relating to Diverse Others** box also explores the updated topic, "Who Listens Better: Men or Women?"

- **Chapter 6**, *"Verbal Communication Skills,"* features a new section on how to have a conversation with others. The chapter also includes a new discussion on online relationships.

- **Chapter 7**, *" Nonverbal Communication Skills,"* includes new research on how our vocal cues provide clues about our relationships and how physical appearance can influence perception.

- **Chapter 8**, *"Conflict Management Skills,"* has been reorganized so that the content on conflict triggers appears before the discussion of conflict as a process. A new **Communication and Emotion** box covering "hot button" issues has also been added. The discussion of power negotiation has been streamlined.

- **Chapter 9**, *"Understanding Interpersonal Relationships,"* contains new research on how intimate relationships enhance our self-esteem and confidence, and how our use of Facebook changes as relationships escalate. Additional examples about online dating and speed dating have also been added to the chapter.

- **Chapter 10**, *"Managing Relationship Challenges,"* features a new discussion on addressing grief and delivering bad news. Coverage of cyberbullying has been increased, and Facebook surveillance has been added.

- **Chapter 11**, *"Interpersonal Relationships: Friendship and Romance,"* includes more social media examples and research. The discussion on romantic relationships, including dating, has been expanded with new examples and research.

- **Chapter 12**, *"Interpersonal Relationships: Family and Workplace,"* has additional coverage on the dark side of workplace communication, nontraditional families, and the adoption of communication technology in the workplace. New studies, data, and examples have been added throughout the chapter.

Unique Features
An Other-Oriented Approach

Becoming other-oriented is a collection of skills and principles that are designed to increase your sensitivity to and understanding of others. Being other-oriented doesn't mean you abandon your own thoughts, ignore your feelings, and change your behavior only to please others; that would not only be unethical, it would also be an ineffective approach to developing genuine, honest relationships with others. An other-oriented person is self-aware in addition to being aware of others. True empathy, emotional intelligence, and sensitivity are possible only when we feel secure about our own identities.

Becoming other-oriented is a mindful process of considering the thoughts, needs, feelings, and values of others, rather than focusing exclusively on oneself. This process involves all the classic principles and skills typically taught in interpersonal communication courses—listening, feedback, conflict management skills, and verbal and nonverbal skills—and places additional emphasis on the importance of the perceptions, thoughts, attitudes, beliefs, values, and emotions of others.

> **BEING Other-ORIENTED**
>
> It's important to know your own preferred listening style, but it's also important to understand the listening style of your communication partner. How can you do this? Look for clues that help you identify your partner's listening style. Relational listeners want to hear stories and anecdotes about others. Analytical listeners will be interested in facts. Critical listeners will be more focused on errors, inconsistencies, and discrepancies when listening. Task-oriented listeners will be focused on verbs; they want to know what to do with the information they hear.

BEING OTHER-ORIENTED   **Being Other-Oriented** boxes appear throughout the book and connect the other-orientation theme to specific discussions, often presenting thought-provoking questions to get students thinking about how other-oriented their own communication is.

> ## Applying an Other-Orientation
> ### to Listening and Responding Skills
>
> It's impossible to be other-oriented without listening and observing others. Listening to comprehend information, empathize, or critically evaluate what others say is the quintessential other-oriented skill. The following poem by an anonymous author, simply called "Listen," nicely summarizes the reason listening is such an important interpersonal skill.
>
> **Listen**
>
> When I ask you to listen to me and you start giving advice, you have not done what I asked.
> When I ask you to listen to me and you begin to tell me why I shouldn't feel that way, you are trampling on my feelings.
> When I ask you to listen to me and you feel you have to do something to solve my problems, you have failed me, strange as that may seem.
> Listen! All I asked was that you listen. Not talk or do—just hear
>
> And I can do for myself; I'm not helpless. Maybe discouraged and faltering, but not helpless.
> When you do something for me that I can and need to do for myself, you contribute to my fear and weakness.
> But when you accept as a simple fact that I do feel what I feel, no matter how irrational, then I quit trying to convince you and can get about the business of understanding what's behind this irrational feeling.
> And when that's clear, the answers are obvious and I don't need advice.
> Irrational feelings make sense when we understand what's behind them.
> Perhaps that's why prayer works, sometimes, for some people—because God is mute, and doesn't give advice or try to fix things.

APPLYING AN OTHER-ORIENTATION   At the end of each chapter, the summary section **Applying an Other-Orientation** discusses essential applications and specifically applies the other-orientation to the chapter content.

A Balance of Principles and Skills

This book provides a clear overview of interpersonal communication theory and principles to help students understand how they communicate, balanced with strategies to help students improve their interpersonal communication skill. Every chapter includes both classic and contemporary research conclusions that document essential interpersonal communication principles. Theory that helps explain the interpersonal communication behavior of others also helps students predict how best to enhance their own interpersonal communication. The research-based skills and practical suggestions throughout will show students how to apply the principles and improve such skills as listening, conflict management, and verbal and nonverbal communication.

An Emphasis on Diversity

Inherent in our other-oriented approach is the understanding that people differ in significant ways, such as culture, age, gender, sexual orientation, religion, political perspectives, and other points of view. It is because of these differences that we need skills and principles that allow us to develop links to other people and encourage us to establish meaningful interpersonal relationships with them.

Communication occurs when people find commonalities in meaning that transcend their differences. Using a competency-based approach, this book presents practical, research-based strategies for increasing understanding when interacting with those who are different from us. Using examples, illustrations, and research conclusions woven throughout each chapter, we identify ways to become other-oriented despite differences we encounter in people of the other gender or of other cultures, ethnicities, or ideologies.

INTERPERSONAL COMMUNICATION AND DIVERSITY: ADAPTING TO OTHERS   This in-depth chapter (Chapter 4) not only identifies barriers to competent intercultural communication but also presents strategies to bridge the chasm of differences that still too often divide rather than unite people.

RELATING TO DIVERSE OTHERS   This feature, included in every chapter, presents research findings as well as communication strategies for understanding differences.

> ### Relating to Diverse Others
> **Who Listens Better: Men or Women?**
>
> Research provides no clear-cut answer to the question "Who listens better, men or women?" There is evidence, however, that men and women may listen somewhat differently. The following general patterns have emerged from research, but are not necessarily applicable to all men and women.[31]
>
> Men tend to listen to
> - solve a problem.
> - accomplish a task.
> - look for a new structure in a message.
> - focus on one element in a message.
>
> Women tend to listen to
> - search for relationships among pieces of information in the message.
>
> - enhance a relationship.
> - reinforce the existing structure in a message.
> - understand multiple elements in a message.
>
> These differences have been summarized with this statement: *Men listen to report while women listen to establish rapport.* Yet even this broad distinction between the ways men and women may process information is controversial. Communication researchers Stephanie Sargent and James Weaver suggest that pop psychology, which alleges dramatic "Mars" and "Venus" differences between the way men
>
> and women listen, may simply be perpetuating stereotypes based on the way men and women think they are supposed to listen.[32] Additionally, although there may be some differences, the distinctions may not be based on a person's biological sex; they more likely reflect differences in gender (socially constructed, cultural, or co-cultural learned behavior).[33] As we have stressed, an other-oriented approach to interpersonal communication focuses on the individual needs or perspectives of the other person, rather than relying on stereotypes to make definitive judgments

An Emphasis on Technology

The line between face-to-face and electronically mediated communication has become increasingly blurred as we text, e-mail, and Skype with our friends and share the latest news and views via Facebook, LinkedIn, Twitter, and blogs. This text explores the ever-increasing role of technology in interpersonal communication and the implications of technology for our daily communication and our relationships with others. Throughout the book we have included the latest research findings about how our electronic connections affect our face-to-face interactions.

#communicationandtechnology   The **#communicationandtechnology** feature box focuses on research conclusions about the ways in which technology is changing how we relate to and interact with others and offers practical applications relating to the impact of such technologies as Skype, Instagram, Facebook, and Twitter on establishing and maintaining interpersonal relationships.

> ### #communicationandtechnology
> **Being "Listened to" by our Facebook Friends**
>
> Listening to others is a way to show our support and express our affection toward them, especially if the other person is having a difficult time. When we have a difficult day or have had a disappointment, research suggests that we expect our friends to be there for us and support us.
>
> There is evidence that we increasingly turn to Facebook and other social media to seek a "listening ear" when life gets tough.[58] Although we may have many close friends in whom we can confide, Facebook provides us with a broader audience of acquaintances as well as good, close friends who can ... our concerns and life challenges. Research ...
>
> that if we are fearful of being judged by close friends or we feel at risk disclosing something personal that would invite a detailed response, we may turn to Facebook to seek support in the form of a quick "like"—enough for us to know that someone "hears" us and that we don't have to provide lengthy explanations.[59]
>
> How do you enhance your empathic listening skills? First, think about what the ... by social ...

An Emphasis on Relationships

As the book's subtitle *Relating to Others* suggests, we highlight the importance of enhancing interpersonal relationships by developing an increased awareness of and sensitivity to how we relate to others. Relationship chapters focus first on fundamental interpersonal theory and skills directly related to relationships and on theories of the stages of relationship development. While we emphasize the positive nature of relationships, we also provide a glimpse into the challenging "dark side" of relating to others, including such issues as deception, jealousy, and the influence of technology on our interactions and communication. A wide range of relationship types is then explored in detail, including relationships with friends, romantic partners, family members, and coworkers, as well as strategies for managing these relationships.

COMMUNICATION AND EMOTION   Revised **Communication and Emotion** boxes throughout help students see how emotions affect their relationships with others.

> ### Communication and Emotion
> **What's Your Emotional Intelligence Level and Why Does It Matter?**
>
> You've undoubtedly heard about emotional intelligence, perhaps on TV or in the media. Researchers have found it is an important factor in how you relate to others.
>
> **What Is Emotional Intelligence?**
> **Emotional intelligence (EI)** is the ability to be empathic and aware of your own emotions as well as the emotions of others. Emotionally intelligent people are also able to manage their own emotions. It has been almost twenty-five years since Daniel Goleman's book *Emotional Intelligence: Why It Can Matter More than IQ* was published. That book, along with a *Time* magazine cover story about emotional intelligence—sometimes referred to as EQ, for "emo-... to popularize the ...
>
> voices and paying attention to facial expressions, posture, and other cues.
>
> *EI Helps You Think and Work More Effectively*
> Emotional intelligence can help you with other cognitive tasks. For example, if you know you are usually in a more productive, positive mood in the morning than in the evening, you will use the morning hours for tasks (such as writing) that require focused concentration.
>
> *EI Helps You Express Emotions*
> An emotionally intelligent person is able to express his or her own ... use words accura...
>
> emotions, but also the emotions of others. A skilled public speaker, for example, knows how to use motivational appeals to persuade or motivate others. Of course, using one's emotional intelligence to manipulate others is unethical, just as it is unethical to use one's cognitive intelligence to be deceptive and trick others. Many thieves and con artists are quite emotionally intelligent, but they focus this intelligence on duping their victims. Emotional intelligence, like cognitive intelligence, is a gift that can be used for either good or bad purposes.

A Partnership with Students and Instructors

To use a music metaphor, we have provided the "notes," but the instructor is the one who makes the music, in concert with the student reader. We provide the melody line, but the instructor adds harmony, texture, and color to make the instructional message sing.

Built into the book is a vast array of pedagogical features:

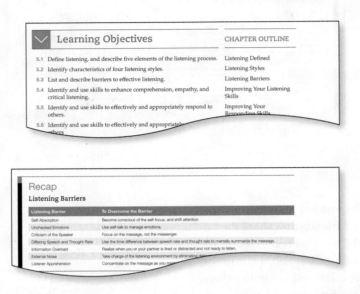

- **Learning Objectives** appear at the beginning of each chapter and are additionally highlighted in their related sections. Then, using the **learning objectives** as an organizing framework, our **Study Guide** feature at the end of each chapter gives students the opportunity to review, apply, and assess key chapter concepts through critical thinking questions, and classroom and group activities.

- **Chapter-opening sections** highlight the one-to-one correspondence of the learning objectives and chapter outlines.

- Student-friendly **Recap** feature boxes periodically summarize key concepts and terms.

- **Improving Your Communication Skills** boxes throughout offer practical strategies for applying chapter content.

- **Key terms** are defined in a full end-of-book **glossary**. Key term definitions also appear in the margins.

In addition to the learning resources built into the book, we provide a wide array of instructional resources and student supplements.

Resources in Print and Online

Key instructor resources include an Instructor's Manual (ISBN 0-13-420422-0), Test Bank (ISBN 0-13-420419-0), and PowerPoint Presentation Package (ISBN 0-13-420420-4). These supplements are available at www.pearsonhighered.com/irc (access code required). MyTest online test generating software (ISBN 0-13-420417-4) is available at www.pearsonmytest.com (access code required).

For a complete listing of the instructor and student resources available with this text, please visit the Interpersonal Communication e-Catalog page at www.pearsonhighered.com.

Pearson MediaShare

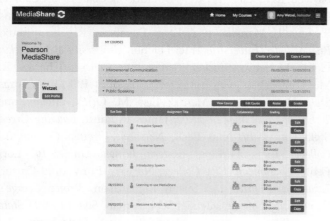

Pearson's comprehensive media upload tool allows students to post video, images, audio, or documents for instructor and peer viewing, time-stamped commenting, and assessment. MediaShare is an easy, mobile way for students and professors to interact and engage with speeches, presentation aids, group projects, and other files. MediaShare gives professors the tools to provide contextual feedback to demonstrate how students can improve their skills.

Structured like a social networking site, MediaShare helps promote a sense of community among students. In face-to-face and online course settings, MediaShare saves instructors valuable time and enriches the student learning experience by providing contextual feedback.

- Use MediaShare to assign or view speeches, outlines, presentation aids, video-based assignments, role-plays, group projects, and more in a variety of formats including video, Word, PowerPoint, and Excel.

- Assess students using customizable, Pearson-provided rubrics or create your own around classroom goals, learning outcomes, or department initiatives.

- Set up assignments for students with options for full-class viewing and commenting, private comments between you and the student, peer groups for reviewing, or as collaborative group assignments.

- Record video directly from a tablet, phone, or other webcam (including a batch upload option for instructors) and tag submissions to a specific student or assignment.

- Set up Learning Objectives tied to specific assignments, rubrics, or quiz questions to track student progress.

- Embed video from YouTube to incorporate current events into the classroom experience.

- Set up quiz questions on video assignments to ensure students master concepts and interact and engage with the media.

- Sync slides to media submissions for more robust presentation options.

- Import grades into most learning management systems.

- Ensure a secure learning environment for instructors and students through robust privacy settings.

- Upload videos, comment on submissions, and grade directly from our new MediaShare app, available free from the iTunes store and GooglePlay; search for Pearson MediaShare.

Pearson MediaShare is available as a standalone product, as part of MyCommunicationLab, or in a package with REVEL.

Acknowledgments

This book is not only a collaboration among the three of us, but also a collaboration with a host of others. Without the research conclusions of the talented, creative scholars who have studied interpersonal communication and published their results, a book of this scope would not be possible. We also thank our students, who are a constant source of questions, ideas, inspiration, and challenges that enrich our teaching and writing.

We are especially thankful for the continuing outstanding editorial support and leadership that kept our multi-author team collaborating with aplomb. Publisher for *Communication*, Karon Bowers, who has worked with us for more than a decade, continues to be a source of inspiration and unwavering support. Our talented development editor, Ellen Keohane, provided the perfect balance of attention to details while also helping us keep the larger issues and goals in focus. We also appreciate the dozens of gifted interpersonal communication instructors and scholars who read the manuscript and offered suggestions that have made this a better book. We thank the following people for sharing their information, ideas, and ingenuity with us as they reviewed this edition or previous editions of the book.

Eighth Edition Reviewers

Paula Casey, *Colorado Mesa University*; Linda Kalfayan, *SUNY Westchester Community College*; Christa Tess Kalk, *Minneapolis Community and Technical College*; Jeffrey Lawrence, *Ivy Tech Community College*; Narissa Punyanunt-Carter, *Texas Tech University*; Elizabeth Ribarsky, *University of Illinois, Springfield*; Dennis Sutton, *Grand Rapids Community College*; Lindsay Timmerman, *University of Wisconsin–Milwaukee*; Zuoming Wang, *University of North Texas*; Michael Wittig, *Waukesha County Technical College*; Denise Woolsey, *Yavapai College*.

Reviewers of Previous Editions

Rebecca Anderson, *Johnson County Community College*; Leonard Barchak, *McNeese University*; Cameron Smith Basquiat, *Community College of Southern Nevada*; Judyth Betz-Gonzales, *Delta College*; Marion Boyer, *Kalamazoo Community College*; Mark Bruner, *University of Alaska–Anchorage*; Scott E. Caplan, *University of Delaware*; Carolyn Clark, *Salt Lake Community College*; Norman Clark, *Appalachian State University*; Carolyn P. DeLeCour, *Palo Alto College*; Carol Z. Dolphin, *University of Wisconsin–Waukesha*; Terrence Doyle, *Northern Virginia Community College*; Rebecca E. Dunn, *Westmoreland County Community College*; Reginald E. Ecarma, *Campbellsville University*; David L. Edwards, *South Central Technical College*; Janie Harden Fritz, *Duquesne University*; Neva Gronert, *Arapahoe Community College*;

Patricia M. Harris-Jenkinson, *Sacramento City College*; Sherry J. Holmen, *Albuquerque Technical Vocational Institute*; Adna G. Howell, *Delta College*; David D. Hudson, *Golden West College*; Diana K. Ivy, *Texas A&M University–Corpus Christi*; Thomas E. Jewell, *Marymount College*; Elizabeth R. Lamoureux, *Buena Vista University*; Traci Letcher, *University of Kentucky*; Heidi McGrew, *Sinclair Community College*; Charles R. McMahan, *Vincennes University*; Timothy P. Mottet, *Texas State University–San Marcos*; Lisa M. Orick, *Albuquerque Technical Vocational Institute*; James R. Pauff, *Bowling Green State University*; Nan Peck, *Northern Virginia Community College*; Terry Perkins, *Eastern Illinois University*; Lori Petite, *Sacramento City College*; Narissra Punyanunt-Carter, *Texas Tech University*; Susan Richardson, *Prince George's Community College*; Michael Schliessman, *South Dakota State University*; Xiaowei Shi, *Middle Tennessee State University*; Cheri Simonds, *Illinois State University*; Anntarie Lanita Sims, *Trenton State College*; Heather A. Smith, *Santa Monica College*; Vincent Scott Smithson, *Purdue University North Central*; Dickie Spurgeon, *Southern Illinois University*; Glen H. Stamp, *Ball State University*; R. Weylin Sternglanz, *Nova Southeastern University*; Douglas H. Stewart, *Lake Washington Technical College*; Pamela Stovall, *University of New Mexico–Gallup*; Claire Sullivan, *University of Maine*; Dennis Sutton, *Grand Rapids Community College*; James J. Tolhuizen, *Indiana University Northwest*; Sally Vogl-Bauer, *University of Wisconsin–Whitewater*; Mary Walker, *South Texas College*; Sheryl L. Williams, *University of Wisconsin–Whitewater*; Bethany Winkler, *Central Texas College*; Lori Wisdom-Whitley, *Everett Community College*; Richard L. Wiseman, *California State University–Fullerton*.

We are blessed with the support and ideas of our many colleagues and friends, as well as the ongoing love and encouragement given to us by our families:

From Sue and Steve: We thank Thompson Biggers, a valued friend and colleague who helped conceptualize this book. Mary Jeanette Smythe, Tom Willett, Tim Mottet, and Diana Ivy are long-time educators and friends who inspired us with their knowledge and gift of friendship. Phil Salem, Lee Williams, Cathy Fleuriet, and Maureen Keeley are friends and colleagues at Texas State University who have positively influenced our work. John Masterson, a valued friend and colleague, also greatly influenced our teaching and writing about interpersonal communication. Special thanks go to the late Michael Argyle at Oxford University, Oxford, England, who sponsored Steve as a Visiting Scholar at Oxford's Wolfson College and generously shared his research findings. Thanks, too, to Peter and Jill Collett, friends and colleagues from Oxford, for their assistance, support, and friendship. Thane McCollough, now president of Gonzaga University, also provided valuable support for this project.

We have outstanding support from many people. Sue Hall, senior administrative assistant in the Department of

Communication Studies at Texas State, continues to be an invaluable assistant and friend. Bob Hanna and Chelsea Stockton are also valued colleagues and staff members who provided skilled support. We thank our good friend Kosta Tovstiadi for his skillful research assistance in helping us secure the most contemporary research we could find about interpersonal communication.

We want especially to thank our parents, Russell and Muriel Beebe, who are beginning their seventy-fifth year of marriage, and Jane and the late Herb Dye, who were married for more than sixty years. These humble, loving, and dedicated parental mentors were our first and finest teachers of interpersonal communication. We also thank our son Mark, who continues to teach us that the power of love can overcome life's challenges, and our son Matt, who teaches us about the importance of finding music and beauty in days filled with both sunshine and clouds.

From Mark: I have used the textbook for many years in teaching the introduction to interpersonal communication course at Iowa State and I owe a debt to hundreds of students, both for their feedback on the text and for teaching me through their own interpersonal experiences. For example, it was my students who first introduced me to the term and meaning of "friends with benefits." My Iowa State colleagues Denise Vrchota, Tina Coffelt, Stacy Tye-Williams, Racheal Ruble, Todd Jenks, and David Vogel continue to provide their support, encouragement, and friendship. I would also like to acknowledge and thank a group of colleagues I met years ago when we were all graduate students at the University of Denver and with whom I have developed lifelong treasured friendships: Rich Arthur, John Masterson, Diane Ritzdorf, Marc Routhier, the late Jim Tolhuizen, and especially Phil Backlund at Central Washington University.

I am particularly thankful to my parents, the late Jack and Alice Redmond; my brother, Jack; and my sisters, Ruthann, Mary Lynn, and Tina, who helped shape a family environment that planted the seeds for studying and appreciating interpersonal communication. Those seeds have been nurtured into a full-grown fascination with how communication shapes our lives and personal development by my wife, Peggy; my daughter, Beth; my son Nicholas and his wife, Kimberlee; and my son Eric and his wife, Amy. On a practical level, I owe a lot of my understanding of the Internet and Facebook to my kids.

Steven A. Beebe
Susan J. Beebe
Mark V. Redmond

About the Authors

Steven A. Beebe is Regents' and University Distinguished Professor in the Department of Communication Studies at Texas State University. He served as Chair of his department at Texas State for twenty-eight years and concurrently as Associate Dean for twenty-five years. Steve is the author or co-author of twelve widely used communication books, most of which have been through multiple editions (including Russian and Chinese editions), as well as numerous articles, book chapters, and conference presentations. He has been a Visiting Scholar at both Oxford University and Cambridge University in England. He made international headlines when conducting research at Oxford; he discovered a manuscript that was the partial opening chapter of a book that was to be co-authored with J. R. R. Tolkien and C. S. Lewis called *Language and Human Nature*. Steve has traveled widely in Europe and Asia, and has played a leadership role in establishing new communication curricula in Russian universities. He has received his university's highest awards for research and twice for service, has been recognized as Honors Professor of the year, and was named Outstanding Communication Professor by the National Speaker's Association. In 2013 he served as President of the National Communication Association, the largest professional communication association in the world. His passions include his family and a lifelong love of music; he is a pianist and organist and a struggling cellist.

Susan J. Beebe's professional interests and expertise encompass both oral and written communication. Sue has co-authored three books and has published a number of articles and teaching materials in both English and communication studies. She has received the Texas State University Presidential Awards for Excellence in Teaching and in Service and the College of Liberal Arts Awards for Excellence in Scholarly/ Creative Activities, in Teaching, and in Service. After serving as Director of Lower-Division Studies in English for eleven years, Sue retired in 2014 from the Department of English at Texas State. An active volunteer in the community of San Marcos, Texas, Sue was the founding coordinator of the San Marcos Volunteers in Public Schools Program and has served on the San Marcos School Board and the Education Foundation Board. In 1993 she was named the statewide Friend of Education by the Texas Classroom Teachers' Association; in 2000 the San Marcos school district presented her with its Lifetime Achievement Award. Sue enjoys reading, traveling, and caring for the Beebe family cats, Luke and Bouncer. Sue and Steve have two sons: Mark, a graduate of Rice University; and Matt, a graduate of Southwestern University and a middle school teacher in nearby Austin.

Mark V. Redmond is an Associate Professor of Communication Studies at Iowa State University. In 2012 he received the College of Liberal Arts and Sciences award for Outstanding Achievement in Teaching. Besides this book, Mark has authored an introductory text on communication theory and research, edited an upper-level text in interpersonal communication, and co-authored a public speaking text. His research focuses on social decentering (taking into account another person's thoughts, feelings, perspectives, etc.), one of the themes incorporated in this text. His research studies include expectations associated with male–female relationships, social decentering's impact in marriage, initial interactions between strangers, adaptation in interpersonal interactions, and intercultural communication competence. He is a Cyclone sports fan with an avocation for playing basketball at least three times a week (despite an aging hook shot). An unaccomplished piano and guitar player, he loves composing and writing songs and vows to someday complete the musical he's been working on for twenty years. Mark and his wife Peggy have three children: Beth, a graduate of the University of Iowa and Mount Mercy University; Nicholas, a graduate of Iowa State University and McCormick Theological Seminary; and Eric, a graduate of Iowa State University and Northwest Missouri State University.

Chapter 1
Introduction to Interpersonal Communication

"Communication is to a relationship what breathing is to maintaining life."

Virginia Satir

Learning Objectives

1.1 Compare and contrast definitions of communication, human communication, and interpersonal communication.

1.2 Explain why it is useful to study interpersonal communication.

1.3 Describe the key components of the communication process, including communication as action, interaction, and transaction.

1.4 Discuss five principles of interpersonal communication.

1.5 Discuss the role of electronically mediated communication in developing and maintaining interpersonal relationships.

1.6 Identify strategies that can improve your communication competence.

CHAPTER OUTLINE

Interpersonal Communication Defined

Interpersonal Communication's Importance to Your Life

Interpersonal Communication and the Communication Process

Interpersonal Communication Principles

Interpersonal Communication and Social Media

Interpersonal Communication Competence

1

Interpersonal communication is like breathing; it is a requirement for life. And, like breathing, interpersonal communication is inescapable. Unless you live in isolation, you communicate interpersonally every day. Listening to your roommate, talking to a teacher, texting a friend, and talking to your parents or your spouse in person or via Skype are all examples of interpersonal communication. Like many people, you probably use a wide range of social media applications to develop, maintain, and redefine *social* relationships with others. You may find yourself seamlessly toggling between e-conversations and "realspace" interactions. Research suggests that online conversations mirror the same kinds of topics and issues that occur during face-to-face (FtF) interactions.[1] You may well be one of a growing number of people who turn to online dating sites to seek and develop relationships. More than 40 million Americans look for love online, which is rapidly becoming a primary means of establishing relationships with others.[2]

Whether on- or offline, it is impossible *not* to communicate with others.[3] Even before we are born, we respond to movement and sound, and we continue to communicate until we draw our last breath. Without interpersonal communication, a special form of human communication that occurs as we manage our relationships, people suffer and even die. Recluses, hermits, and people isolated in solitary confinement dream and hallucinate about talking with others face to face.

Human communication is at the core of our existence. Most people spend between 80 and 90 percent of their waking hours communicating with others.[4] Think of the number of times you communicated with someone today, as you worked, ate, studied, shopped, or experienced your other daily activities. The younger you are, the more likely you communicated via text message today. Young adults ages 18 to 24 send an average of 110 text messages a day—20 times more than someone 65 years old.[5] It is through these interactions with others, both on and offline, that we develop interpersonal relationships.[6]

Because relationships are so important to our lives, later chapters will focus on the communication skills and principles that explain and predict how we develop, sustain, and sometimes end relationships. We'll explore such questions as the following:

- Why do we like some people and not others?
- How can we interpret other people's unspoken messages with greater accuracy?
- Why do some relationships blossom and others deteriorate?
- How can we better manage disagreements with others?
- How does social media influence making, maintaining, and ending relationships?

other-oriented

To be aware of the thoughts, needs, experiences, personality, emotions, motives, desires, culture, and goals of your communication partners while still maintaining your own integrity.

As we address essential questions about how you relate to others, we will emphasize the importance of being **other-oriented**. Being other-oriented requires awareness of the thoughts, needs, experiences, personality, emotions, motives, desires, culture, and goals of your communication partners while still maintaining your own integrity. Becoming other-oriented is not a single skill, but a collection of skills and principles that are designed to increase your sensitivity to and understanding of others. In general, research has found that we are becoming less empathic and other-oriented.[7]

This chapter charts the course ahead, addressing key questions about what interpersonal communication is and why it is important. We will begin by seeing how our understanding of the interpersonal communication process has evolved. And we will conclude by examining how we initiate and sustain relationships through interpersonal communication.

Interpersonal Communication Defined

1.1 Compare and contrast definitions of communication, human communication, and interpersonal communication.

To understand interpersonal communication, we must begin by understanding how it relates to two broader categories: communication in general and human communication. Scholars have attempted to arrive at a general definition of communication for decades, yet experts cannot agree on a single one. One research team counted more than 126 published definitions.[8] In the broadest sense, **communication** is the process of acting on information.[9] Someone does or says something, and others think or do something in response to the action or the words as they understand them.

To refine our broad definition, we can say that **human communication** is the process of making sense out of the world and sharing that sense with others by creating meaning through the use of verbal and nonverbal messages.[10] We learn about the world by listening, observing, tasting, touching, and smelling; then we share our conclusions with others. Human communication encompasses many media: speeches, e-mail, songs, radio and television broadcasts, podcasts, online discussion groups, letters, books, articles, poems, and advertisements.

Interpersonal communication is *a distinctive, transactional form of human communication involving mutual influence, usually for the purpose of managing relationships*. The three essential elements of this definition differentiate the unique nature of interpersonal communication from other forms of human communication.[11]

Interpersonal Communication Is a Distinctive Form of Communication

For years, many scholars defined interpersonal communication simply as communication that occurs when two people interact face to face. This limited definition suggests that if two people are interacting, they are engaging in interpersonal communication. Today, interpersonal communication is defined not only by the number of people who communicate, but also by the quality of the communication. Interpersonal communication occurs when you treat the other person as a unique human being.[12]

Increasingly, people are relating via Twitter, Facebook, LinkedIn, Instagram, Vine, Pinterest, Google+, and Skype. Research confirms that many of us think of the various electronic means we use to connect to others as natural ways to establish and maintain relationships.[13] With a smartphone in our pocket, we are almost always within easy reach of our friends, family, and colleagues. Although sometimes our tweets and Facebook posts more closely resemble mass communication (sending a message to a large group of people at the same time), we nonetheless also use social media to enrich personal relationships with individuals.[14]

INTERPERSONAL VERSUS IMPERSONAL COMMUNICATION Think of all human communication, whether mediated or face-to-face, as ranging on a continuum from impersonal to interpersonal communication. **Impersonal communication** occurs when you treat others as objects or respond to their roles rather than to who they are as unique persons. When you ask a server in a restaurant for a glass of water, you are interacting with the role, not necessarily with the individual. You're having an impersonal conversation rather than an interpersonal one.

I–IT AND I–THOU RELATIONSHIPS Philosopher Martin Buber influenced our thinking about the distinctiveness of interpersonal communication when he described communication as consisting of two different qualities of relationships: an "I–It" relationship or an "I–Thou" relationship.[15] He described an "I–It" relationship as an impersonal one, in which the other person is viewed as an "It" rather than as an authentic, genuine person. For every communication transaction to be a personal, intimate dialogue would be unrealistic and inappropriate. It's possible to go through an entire day communicating with others but not be involved in interpersonal communication.

An "I–Thou" relationship, on the other hand, occurs when you interact with another person as a unique, authentic individual rather than as an object or an "It." In this kind of relationship, true, honest dialogue results in authentic communication. An "I–Thou" relationship is not self-centered. The communicators

communication
Process of acting on information.

human communication
Process of making sense out of the world and sharing that sense with others by creating meaning through the use of verbal and nonverbal messages.

interpersonal communication
A distinctive, transactional form of human communication involving mutual influence, usually for the purpose of managing relationships.

impersonal communication
Process that occurs when we treat others as objects or respond to their roles rather than to who they are as unique persons.

are patient, kind, and forgiving. They have developed an attitude toward each other that is honest, open, spontaneous, nonjudgmental, and based on equality rather than superiority.[16] However, although interpersonal communication is more intimate and reveals more about the people involved than does impersonal communication, not all interpersonal communication involves sharing closely guarded personal information.

INTERPERSONAL VERSUS OTHER FORMS OF COMMUNICATION   In this book, we define interpersonal communication as a unique form of human communication. There are other forms of communication, as well.

mass communication

Process that occurs when one person issues the same message to many people at once; the creator of the message is usually not physically present, and listeners have virtually no opportunity to respond immediately to the speaker.

public communication

Process that occurs when a speaker addresses an audience.

small group communication

Process that occurs when a group of three to fifteen people meet to interact with a common purpose and mutually influence one another.

intrapersonal communication

Communication with yourself; thinking.

- **Mass communication** occurs when one person communicates the same message to many people at once, but the creator of the message is usually not physically present, and listeners have virtually no opportunity to respond immediately to the speaker. Messages communicated via radio and TV are examples of mass communication. Tweets and Facebook posts can resemble mass communication messages since a large number of people usually view those messages.
- **Public communication** occurs when a speaker addresses an audience.
- **Small group communication** occurs when a group of three to fifteen people meet to interact with a common purpose and mutually influence one another. The purpose of the gathering can be to solve a problem, make a decision, learn, or just have fun. While communicating with others in a small group, it is also possible to communicate interpersonally with one or more individuals in the group.
- **Intrapersonal communication** is communication with yourself. Thinking is perhaps the best example of intrapersonal communication. In our discussion of self and communication in Chapter 2, we discuss the relationships between your thoughts and your interpersonal communication with others.

Interpersonal Communication Involves Mutual Influence Between Individuals

Every interpersonal communication transaction influences us. Mutual influence means that *all* partners in the communication are affected by a transaction that may or may not involve words. The degree of mutual influence varies a great deal from transaction to transaction. You probably would not be affected a great deal by a brief smile that you received from a traveling companion on a bus, but you would be greatly affected by your lover telling you he or she was leaving you. Sometimes interpersonal communication changes our lives dramatically, sometimes in small

Recap

The Continuum Between Interpersonal Communication and Impersonal Communication

Interpersonal Communication ⟷ Impersonal Communication

- People are treated as unique individuals.
- People communicate in an "I–Thou" relationship. Each person is treated as special, and there is true dialogue and honest sharing of self with others.
- Interpersonal communication often involves communicating with someone you care about, such as a good friend or cherished family member.

- People are treated as objects.
- People communicate in an "I–It" relationship. Each person has a role to perform.
- There is mechanical, stilted interaction, rather than honest sharing of feelings.
- Impersonal communication involves communicating with people such as sales clerks and servers—you have no history with them, and you expect no future with them.

ways. Long-lasting interpersonal relationships are sustained not by one person giving and another taking, but by a spirit of mutual equality. Both you and your partner listen and respond with respect for each other. There is no attempt to manipulate others.

Buber's concept of an "I–Thou" relationship includes the quality of being fully "present" when communicating with another person.[17] To be present is to give your full attention to the other person. The quality of interpersonal communication is enhanced when both you and your partner are simultaneously present and focused on each other.

Interpersonal Communication Helps Individuals Manage Their Relationships

Question: What is neither you nor I, but always you and I? Answer: A relationship.[18] A **relationship** is a connection established when you communicate with another person. When two individuals are in a relationship, what one person says or does influences the other person. As in dancing, people in relationships are affected by the beat of the music (that is, the situation in which they are communicating), their ability to interpret the music and move accordingly (the personal skills they possess), and the moves and counter-moves of their partner.

You initiate and form relationships by communicating with others whom you find attractive in some way. You seek to increase your interactions with people with whom you wish to develop relationships, and you continually communicate interpersonally to maintain the relationship. You also use interpersonal communication to end or redefine relationships that you have decided are no longer viable or need to be changed. In essence, to relate to someone is to "dance" with them. You dance with them in a specific time and place, with certain perceptions and expectations. Over time, this dance becomes an ongoing interpersonal relationship.

You are increasingly likely to use social media to connect with friends and manage your relationships. Research has found that instant messages (including text messages) have an overall positive effect on your relationships. E-mail, texting, and other forms of instant messages appear to be primarily used to maintain *existing* relationships, although they certainly play a role in establishing initial contact with others. Additional research has found that people first perceive online and instant messages as lower quality than face-to-face interactions, but over time they are judged just as positively.[19] So whether it occurs on- or offline, interpersonal communication helps you manage your relationships.

In face-to-face encounters, we simultaneously exchange both verbal and nonverbal messages that result in shared meanings. Through this kind of interrelation, we build relationships with others.

relationship
Connection established when one person communicates with another.

Interpersonal Communication's Importance to Your Life

1.2 **Explain why it is useful to study interpersonal communication.**

Why learn about interpersonal communication? Because it touches every aspect of our lives. It is not only pleasant or desirable to develop quality interpersonal relationships with others, it is vital for our well-being. We have a strong need to communicate interpersonally with others, whether face to face or through social media. Learning how to understand and improve interpersonal communication can enhance our relationships with family, loved ones, friends, and colleagues, and can enrich the quality of our physical and emotional health.[20]

Improved Relationships with Family

Relating to family members can be a challenge. The divorce statistics in the United States document the difficulties that can occur when people live in relationships with others: About half of all marriages end in divorce. We don't claim that you will avoid all family conflicts or that your family relationships will always be harmonious if you learn principles and skills of interpersonal communication. You can, however, develop more options for responding when family communication challenges come your way. You will be more likely to develop creative, constructive solutions to family conflict if you understand what's happening and can promote true dialogue with your spouse, partner, child, parent, brother, or sister. Furthermore, family communication author Virginia Satir calls family communication "the largest single factor determining the kinds of relationships [people make] with others."[21] Being able to have conversations with family members and loved ones is the fundamental way of establishing close, personal relationships with them and with others.

Improved Relationships with Friends and Romantic Partners

For unmarried people, developing friendships and falling in love are the top-rated sources of satisfaction and happiness in life.[22] Conversely, losing a relationship is among life's most stressful events. Most people between the ages of nineteen and twenty-four report that they have had five to six romantic relationships and have been "in love" once or twice.[23] Studying interpersonal communication may not unravel all the mysteries of romantic love and friendship, but it can offer insight into behaviors.[24] Increasingly, people use Facebook and other social media to develop their relationships with friends and loved ones.[25]

Improved Relationships with Colleagues

In many ways, colleagues at work are like family members. Although you choose your friends and romantic partners, you don't always have the same flexibility in choosing those with whom or for whom you work. Understanding how relationships develop on the job can help you avoid conflict and stress, and increase your sense of satisfaction. In addition, your success or failure in a job often hinges on how well you get along with supervisors and peers.

Several surveys document the importance of quality interpersonal relationships in contributing to success at work.[26] The abilities to listen to others, manage conflict, and develop quality interpersonal relationships with others are usually at the top of the skills list employers seek in today's job applicants.[27]

Improved Physical and Emotional Health

Positive interpersonal relationships with others have direct benefits for your overall health and happiness. Research has shown that the lack or loss of a close relationship can lead to ill health and even death. Physicians have long observed that patients who are widowed or divorced experience more medical problems such as heart disease, cancer, pneumonia, and diabetes than married people.[28] Grief-stricken spouses are more likely than others to die prematurely, especially around the time of the departed spouse's birthday or near their wedding anniversary.[29] Being childless can also shorten one's life. One study found that middle-aged, childless wives were almost two-and-one-half times more likely to die in a given year than those who had at least one child.[30] Terminally ill patients with a limited number of friends or no social support die sooner than those with stronger ties.[31] Without companions and close friends, opportunities for intimacy and stress-minimizing interpersonal communication are diminished. Although being involved in intimate interpersonal relationships can lead to conflict and feelings of anger and frustration, researchers suggest that when all is said and done, having close relationships with others is a major source of personal happiness.[32] Studying how to enhance the quality of your communication with others can make life more enjoyable and enhance your overall well-being.[33]

Interpersonal Communication and the Communication Process

1.3 **Describe the key components of the communication process, including communication as action, interaction, and transaction.**

Interpersonal communication is a complex process of creating meaning in the context of an interpersonal relationship. To better understand interpersonal communication as a distinct form of communication, it is useful to examine the basic communication process.[34]

Elements of the Communication Process

The most basic components of communication include these elements: source, message, channel, receiver, noise, feedback, and context. Understanding each of these elements can help you analyze your own communication with others as you relate to them in interpersonal situations as well as other communication contexts. Let's explore these elements in greater detail.

- *Source.* The **source** of a message is the originator of the ideas and feelings expressed. The source puts a message into a code, a process called **encoding**. The opposite of encoding is the process of **decoding**, which occurs when the receiver interprets the words or nonverbal cues.
- *Message.* **Messages** are the written, spoken, and unspoken elements of communication to which people assign meaning. You can send a message intentionally (talking to a professor before class) or unintentionally (falling asleep during class); verbally ("Hi. How are you?"), nonverbally (a smile and a handshake), or in written form (this book).
- *Channel.* The **channel** is the means by which the message is expressed to the receiver. You probably receive messages through a variety of channels including mediated channels such as text messaging, e-mail, phone, video conference, Facebook, or Twitter.
- *Receiver.* The **receiver** of the message is the person or persons who interpret the message and ultimately determine whether your message was understood and appropriate. As we emphasize in this book, effective communicators are other-oriented; they understand that the listener ultimately makes sense of the message they express.
- *Noise.* **Noise** is anything that interferes with the message being interpreted as it was intended. Noise happens. If there were no noise, all of our messages would be interpreted accurately. But noise is always present. It can be literal (e.g., beeps coming from an iPad or iPhone that signal incoming e-mail or text messages) or it can be psychological (e.g., competing thoughts, worries, and feelings that capture our attention).
- *Feedback.* **Feedback** is the response to the message. Think of a Ping-Pong game. Like a Ping-Pong ball, messages bounce back and forth. We talk; someone listens and responds; we listen and respond to this response. This perspective can be summarized using the following physical principle: For every action, there is a reaction.

source
Originator of a thought or emotion, who puts it into a code that can be understood by a receiver.

encode
To translate ideas, feelings, and thoughts into code.

decode
To interpret ideas, feelings, and thoughts that have been translated into a code.

message
Written, spoken, and unspoken elements of communication to which people assign meaning.

channel
Pathway through which messages are sent.

receiver
Person who decodes a message and attempts to make sense of what the source has encoded.

noise
Anything literal or psychological that interferes with accurate reception of a message.

feedback
Response to a message.

Without feedback, communication is rarely effective. When your roommate says, "Would you please pick up some milk at the store?" you may say, "What kind—1 percent, 2 percent, organic, or chocolate?" Your quest for clarification is feedback. Further feedback may seek additional information, or simply confirm that the message has been interpreted: "Oh, some 1 percent organic milk would be good." Like other messages, feedback can be intentional (your mother gives you a hug when you announce your engagement) or unintentional (you yawn as you listen to your uncle tell his story about bears again); verbal ("That's a pepperoni pizza, right?") or nonverbal (blushing after being asked to dance). Feedback happens not only face to face, but also online. Your responses (feedback) to what you have purchased on Amazon.com and other shopping sites often result in directed, customized messages crafted just for you.[35]

context

Physical and psychological environment for communication.

- *Context.* **Context** is the physical and psychological environment for communication. All communication takes place in some context. As the cliché goes, "Everyone has to be somewhere." A conversation on the beach with your good friend would likely differ from a conversation the two of you might have in a funeral home. Context encompasses not only the physical environment but also the people present and their relationships with the communicators, the communication goal, and the culture of which the communicators are a part.[36]

Models of the Communication Process

The elements of the communication process are typically arranged in one of three communication models, showing communication as action, as interaction, or as transaction. Let's review each model in more detail to see how expert thinking about human communication has evolved.

COMMUNICATION AS ACTION: MESSAGE TRANSFER The oldest and simplest model, shown in Figure 1.1, is *communication as action*—a transferring of meaning. "Did you get my message?" This sentence reflects the communication-as-action approach to human communication. Communication takes place when a message is sent and received. Period.

COMMUNICATION AS INTERACTION: MESSAGE EXCHANGE The perspective of communication as interaction adds two elements to the action model: feedback and context. As shown in Figure 1.2, the interaction model is more realistic than the action perspective, but it still has limitations. Although it emphasizes feedback and context, the interaction model does not quite capture the complexity of simultaneous human communication. The interaction model of communication still views communication as a linear, step-by-step process. But in interpersonal situations, both the source and the receiver send and receive messages at the same time.

COMMUNICATION AS TRANSACTION: MESSAGE CREATION Today, the most sophisticated and realistic model views communication as transaction, in which each element influences all of the other elements in the process at the same time. This perspective acknowledges that when you talk to another person face to face, you are

Figure 1.1 A Simple Model of Human Communication as Action

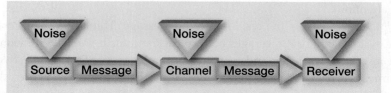

Figure 1.2 A Model of Communication as Interaction

Interaction models of communication include feedback as a response to a message sent by the communication source and context as the environment for communication.

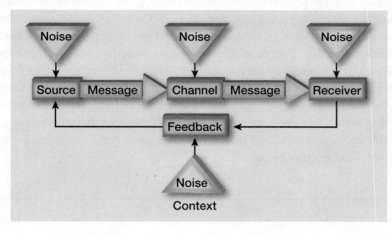

Figure 1.3 A Model of Communication as Transaction

The source and receiver of a message experience communication simultaneously.

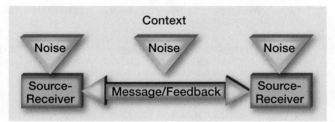

constantly reacting to your partner's responses. In this model, all the components of the communication process are simultaneous. As Figure 1.3 indicates, even as you talk, you are also interpreting your partner's nonverbal and verbal responses.

The transactional approach to communication is based on **systems theory**. A system is a set of interconnected elements in which a change in one element affects all of the other elements. Key elements of any system include *inputs* (all of the variables that go into the system), *throughputs* (all of the things that make communication a process), and *outputs* (what the system produces). From a systems theory point of view, each element of communication is connected to all other elements of

systems theory

Theory that describes the interconnected elements of a system in which a change in one element affects all of the other elements.

Relating to Diverse Others

The World Is Here

The title of Ishmael Reed's essay "The World Is Here" reminds us that America is not a one-dimensional culture.[37] You need not travel to far-off places to develop interpersonal relationships with people from other cultures, races, or ethnic backgrounds. It takes skill and sensitivity to develop quality interpersonal relationships with others whose religion, race, ethnicity, age, gender, or sexual orientation differ from your own. Throughout this text, we include boxes like this one to help you develop your sensitivity to important issues related to cultural diversity. As you embark on your study of interpersonal communication, consider

these questions, either individually or with a group of your classmates:

1. What are the implications of living in a melting pot or tossed salad culture for your study of interpersonal communication?
2. Is there too much emphasis on being politically correct on college campuses today? Support your answer.
3. What specific interpersonal skills will help you communicate effectively with others from different cultural and ethnic traditions?

communication. From a transactional communication perspective, a change in any aspect of the communication system (source, message, channel, receiver, noise, context, feedback) potentially influences all the other elements of the system.

A transactional approach to communication suggests that no single cause explains why you interpret messages the way you do. In fact, it is inappropriate to point to a single factor to explain how you are making sense of the messages of others; communication is messier than that. The meaning of messages in interpersonal relationships evolves from the past, is influenced by the present, and is affected by visions of the future.

One researcher says that interpersonal communication is "the coordinated management of meaning" through **episodes**: a sequence of interactions between individuals during which the message of one person influences the message of another.[38] Technically, only the sender and receiver of those messages can determine where one episode ends and another begins.

episode

Sequence of interactions between individuals, during which the message of one person influences the message of another.

Recap

An Evolving Model for Interpersonal Communication

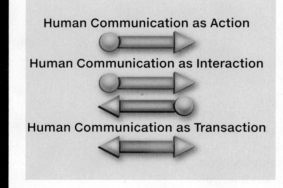

Human Communication as Action

Human communication is linear, with meaning sent or transferred from source to receiver.

Human Communication as Interaction

Human communication occurs as the receiver of the message responds to the source through feedback. This interactive model views communication as a linear action–reaction sequence of events within a specific context.

Human Communication as Transaction

Human communication is mutually interactive. Meaning is created based on a concurrent sharing of ideas and feelings. This transaction model most accurately describes human communication.

Interpersonal Communication Principles

1.4 Discuss five principles of interpersonal communication.

Underlying our current understanding of interpersonal communication are five principles: Interpersonal communication connects us to others, is irreversible, is complicated, is governed by rules, and involves both content and relationship dimensions. Without a clear understanding of interpersonal communication principles, people may rely on untrue characterizations of communication, which can increase communication problems. So in addition to presenting interpersonal communication principles, we will also correct some of the misunderstandings people have about interpersonal communication and suggest why these myths persist.

Interpersonal Communication Connects Us to Others

Unless you are a living in a cave or have become a cloistered monk, you interact with others every day. We agree with author H. D. Duncan, who said, "We do not relate and then talk, but relate in talk." Fundamental to an understanding of interpersonal communication is the assumption that the quality of interpersonal relationships stems from the quality of communication with others. As we noted earlier, people can't *not* communicate. Because people often don't *intend* to express ideas or feelings, this perspective is debated among communication scholars. However, there is no question that interpersonal communication is inescapable and that communication connects us to others.

As important as communication is in connecting us to others, it's a myth that all interpersonal relationship problems are communication problems. "You don't understand me!" shouts Paul to his exasperated partner, Chris. "We just can't communicate anymore!" Paul seems to think that the problem he and Chris are having is a communication problem. But Paul and Chris may understand each other perfectly; they may be self-centered or grumpy, or they may just disagree. The problem in the relationship may not be communication, but a non–other-oriented, self-absorbed communicator.

The ever-present nature of interpersonal communication doesn't mean others will always *accurately* decode your messages; it does mean that others will draw inferences about you and your behavior—conclusions based on available information, which may be right or wrong. As you silently stand in a crowded elevator, you avoid eye contact with fellow passengers. When a friend sends you a text, you wait two days to reply. Your unspoken messages, even when you are asleep, provide cues that others interpret. Remember: *People judge you by your behavior, not your intent.* Even in well-established interpersonal relationships, you may be evoking an unintended response by your behavior.

Interpersonal Communication Is Irreversible

"Disregard that last statement made by the witness," instructs the judge. Yet the clever lawyer knows that once her client has told the jury her husband gave her a black eye during an argument, the client cannot really "take it back," and the jury cannot really disregard it. This principle applies to all forms of communication. We may try to modify the meaning of a spoken message by saying something like "Oh, I really didn't mean it." But in most cases, the damage has been done. Once created, communication has the physical property of matter; it can't be uncreated. As the helical model in Figure 1.4 suggests, once interpersonal communication begins, it never loops back on itself. Instead, it continues to be shaped by the events, experiences, and thoughts of the communication partners. A Russian proverb nicely summarizes the point: "Once a word goes out of your mouth, you can never swallow it again."

Because interpersonal communication is irreversible, it's a myth to assume that messages can be taken back like erasing information from a page or hitting the delete key on your computer.

Figure 1.4 Interpersonal Communication Is Irreversible

This helical model shows that interpersonal communication never loops back on itself. Once it begins, it expands infinitely as the communication partners contribute their thoughts and experiences to the exchange.

COPYRIGHT © F. E. X. Dance in *Human Communication Theory*, Holt, Rinehart and Winston, 1967, 294.

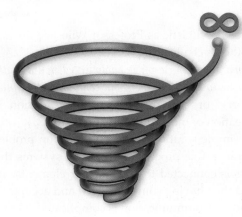

"How many times do I have to tell you not to surf the Internet while you're on the job?" "Can't you read? It's in the syllabus." "Are you deaf? I've already told you that I love you a hundred times!" Each of these exasperated communicators seems to believe that information is the same thing as communication. But information is *not* communication. Presenting information doesn't make people "get" your meaning. Like the proverbial tree that falls silently in the forest because no one is there to hear it, a message is not necessarily communication just because you've expressed it. So you can't take a message back simply because you erased it—the meaning already has been created.

Interpersonal Communication Is Complicated

No form of communication is simple. If any were, we would know how to reduce the number of misunderstandings and conflicts in our world. One of the purposes of communication, according to communication theorists, is to reduce our uncertainty about what is happening at any given moment.[39] Because of the variables involved in interpersonal exchanges, even simple requests are extremely complex. Additionally, communication theorists have noted that whenever you communicate with another person, at least six "people" are actually involved: (1) who you think you are; (2) who you think the other person is; (3) who you think the other person thinks you are; (4) who the other person thinks he or she is; (5) who the other person thinks you are; and (6) who the other person thinks you think he or she is.[40] Whew! And when you add more people to the interaction, it becomes even more involved.

symbol

Word, sound, or visual image that represents something else, such as a thought, concept, or object.

Moreover, when humans communicate, they interpret information from others as symbols. A **symbol** is a word, sound, or visual image that represents something else, such as a thought, concept, or object; it can have various meanings and interpretations. Language is a system of symbols. In English, for example, the word (symbol) for *cow* does not look at all like a cow; someone, somewhere, decided that *cow* should mean a beast that chews its cud and gives milk. The reliance on symbols to communicate poses a communication challenge; you are often misinterpreted. Sometimes you don't know the code. Only if you are up to date on contemporary slang will you know, for example, that "throwing shade" means that you're expressing a negative attitude, "wikidemia" is a term paper entirely researched on Wikipedia.org, and "brodown" is a boys' night out.

Messages are not always interpreted as we intend them. Osmo Wiio, a Scandinavian communication scholar, points out the messiness of communicating with others when he suggests the following maxims:

> If communication can fail, it will.
>
> If a message can be understood in different ways, it will be understood in just that way which does the most harm.
>
> There is always somebody who knows better than you what you meant by your message.
>
> The more communication there is, the more difficult it is for communication to succeed.[41]

Although we are not as pessimistic as Professor Wiio, we do suggest that the task of understanding each other is challenging.

Because interpersonal communication is complicated, it's a myth to assume that there are always simple solutions to every interpersonal communication problem. Yes, sometimes simply saying "I'm sorry" or "I forgive you" can melt tension. But because multiple factors result in the creation of meaning in people's minds, it's not accurate to assume that there are always simple solutions to communication problems. As we've noted, communication is a transactive process anchored in systems theory, in which every element in the process is connected to all the other elements. Taking time to clearly express a message and then having someone listen and accurately respond is a multifaceted, multistep process. Communication is complicated.

Interpersonal Communication Is Governed by Rules

According to communication researcher Susan Shimanoff, a **rule** is a "followable prescription that indicates what behavior is obligated, preferred, or prohibited in certain contexts."[42] The rules that help define appropriate and inappropriate communication in any given situation may be *explicit* or *implicit*. For your interpersonal communication class, explicit rules are probably spelled out in your syllabus. But your instructor has other rules that are more implicit. They are not written or verbalized, because you learned them long ago: Only one person speaks at a time; you raise your hand to be called on; you do not send text messages during class.

Interpersonal communication rules are developed by the people involved in the interaction and by the culture in which the individuals are communicating. Many times, we learn communication rules from experience, by observing and interacting with others.

British researcher Michael Argyle and his colleagues asked people to identify general rules for relationship development and maintenance and then rate their importance. The study yielded the following most important rules:[43]

> Respect each other's privacy.
>
> Don't reveal each other's secrets.
>
> Look the other person in the eye during conversation.
>
> Don't criticize the other person publicly.

Although communication is governed by rules, it's a myth that the rules are always clear and that one person determines the rules and can modify the meaning of a relationship. Although rules are always present, they may not be clear to each person in the relationship. You thought it was OK to bring your dog to a casual pizza date. Your partner thought it was crude and thoughtless. It takes communication to uncover rules and expectations. Few of us learn relationship rules by copying them from a book. Most of us learn these rules from experience, through observing and interacting with family members and friends. Individuals who grow up in environments in which these rules are not observed may not know how to behave in close relationships. In addition, relationships have both implicit and explicit rules that involve more than one person in the relationship. The rules of interpersonal relationships are *mutually* defined and agreed on. Expectations and rules are continually renegotiated as the relationship unfolds. So although rules exist, they may not be clear or shared by the individuals in the relationship.

For many of us, friendships are vital to our personal well-being. By improving our interpersonal communication skills, we can learn how to improve our friendships.

rule

Followable prescription that indicates what behavior is obligated, preferred, or prohibited in certain contexts.

Interpersonal Communication Involves Both Content and Relationship Dimensions

What you say (your words) and how you say it (your tone of voice, amount of eye contact, facial expression, and posture) can reveal much about the true meaning of your message. If one of your roommates loudly and abruptly bellows, "HEY, DORK! CLEAN THIS ROOM!" and another roommate uses the same verbal message but more gently and playfully says, "Hey, dork. Clean this room," both are communicating a message aimed at achieving the same outcome. But the two messages have different relationship cues. The shouted message suggests that roommate number one may be frustrated that the room is still full of leftovers from last night's pizza party, whereas roommate number two's teasing request suggests he or she may be fondly amused by your untidiness. What you say and how you say it provide information not only about content but also about the relationship you have with the other person.

content

Information, ideas, or suggested actions that a speaker wishes to share.

CONTENT MESSAGE The **content** of a communication message consists of the information, ideas, or suggested action that the speaker wishes to share. You may think that your messages to others are primarily about content, but that's not the whole story. You also provide clues about your relationship with others.

relationship dimension

The implied aspect of a communication message, which conveys information about emotions, attitudes, power, and control.

RELATIONSHIP MESSAGE The **relationship dimension** of a communication message offers cues about the emotions, attitudes, and amount of power and control the speaker feels with regard to the other person. This distinction between the content of a message (what is said) and relationship cues (how the message is expressed) explains why a printed transcript can seem to reveal quite a different meaning from a spoken message.

metacommunication

Verbal or nonverbal communication about communication.

METACOMMUNICATION MESSAGE Because messages have both content and relationship dimensions, one dimension can modify or even contradict the other dimension. Communication theorists have a word that describes how we can communicate about our communication: *metacommunication*. Stated in the simplest way, **metacommunication** is verbal or nonverbal communication about communication. Accurately decoding metamessages helps you understand what people really mean and can help you "listen between the lines" of what someone is expressing. [44]

You can express an idea nonverbally (for example, by smiling to communicate that you are pleased), and you can also express your positive feeling verbally (for example, by saying, "I'm happy to be here"). But sometimes your nonverbal communication can contradict your verbal message. You can say "Oh, that's just great" and use your voice to indicate the opposite of what the verbal content of the message means. The sarcasm communicated by the tone of your voice (a relationship cue) modifies the meaning of your verbal message (the content of your message).

In addition to nonverbal cues, which provide communication about communication, you can also use words to talk explicitly about your message. For example, when you can ask, "Is what I'm saying bothering you?" you are using a metamessage to check on how your message is being understood. Here's another example of verbal metacommunication: "I'd like to talk with you about the way we argue." Again, you are using communication to talk about communication. Talking about the way you talk can help clarify misunderstandings. Being aware of the metamessage, in both its verbal and nonverbal forms, can help improve the accuracy of your interpretations of the meaning of message content, as well as enhance the quality of your relationships with others.

Recap

Understanding Interpersonal Communication Principles Can Help Overcome Interpersonal Myths

Principle	Myth	Reality
Interpersonal communication connects us to others.	All interpersonal relationship problems are always communication problems.	We may understand what people mean and feel connected to them, but we may still disagree with them.
Interpersonal communication is irreversible.	A message can be taken back because when information has been presented, communication has occurred.	We can't simply hit "delete" and erase communication. Communication is more than the information in a message; it creates meaning for others.
Interpersonal communication is complicated.	There are always simple solutions to all communication problems.	Because of the complicated nature of how meaning is created, untangling communication problems often takes time, skill, and patience to enhance human understanding.
Interpersonal communication is governed by rules.	One person can resolve interpersonal communication problems.	The communication rules are developed *mutually* between all people in the relationship. Understanding how the rules are developed and interpreted can help minimize misunderstandings.
Interpersonal communication involves both content and relationship dimensions.	Meanings are in words and gestures.	Meanings reside within a person based on the interpretation of both the content and the relationship dimensions of a message and how the metamessage is interpreted.

Because meaning is created in the heart and mind of the communicator, it's a myth to think that meaning resides in a word. Given the potential for miscommunication as the content and relationship dimensions of a message create meaning, it is important to remember that the ultimate meaning for a word or expression is not in the word or gesture but within the person who creates the meaning. Being aware of the metamessage can help you better interpret a message and derive meaning from it. Simply because you said something doesn't mean your partner understood you. Your vocal inflection, facial expression, or gesture may have created a different interpretation of what you intended. Meaning is in people, not in words or gestures.

Interpersonal Communication and Social Media

1.5 **Discuss the role of electronically mediated communication in developing and maintaining interpersonal relationships.**

Can you really communicate *interpersonally* with people on a smartphone or the Internet without meeting them face to face? Yes, of course. You probably relate to others through such media every day, to both initiate and maintain relationships. When you go on Facebook, Instagram, or Twitter, or text friends and family members, you are using **social media**, the vast array of technological applications that serve as channels to help you relate to others. Social media applications are also sometimes called **electronically mediated communication (EMC)**, which includes e-mail, text or any other electronic method of communication. As social media expert Sherry Turkle has noted, "Those little devices in our pockets don't only change what we do, they change who we are."[45]

Mediated communication is not new; people have been communicating for centuries without being face to face; sending letters and other written messages is an age-old human way of relating to others. And even before written communication was widespread, humans used smoke signals and drum beats to communicate via long distances. What's new is that there are so many different ways of *immediately* connecting with someone, such as using a smartphone, social networking applications (such as Twitter and Instagram), text messages, e-mail, instant messaging, video messages on YouTube, Vine, or Skype, and a host of other Internet-based ways of communicating that constantly shift in their popularity. E-mail was once the hot new way of connecting; then came instant messaging (IM). Today, as noted in the #communicationandtechnology box, texting and connecting via Facebook, Twitter, or Instagram are among the most used EMC technologies.[46] What's also new is how the very presence of technology affects our face-to-face conversations. Researchers have found that the presence of a visible smartphone when two people are talking diminishes the quality of the conversation. Why? Because we are checking to see if anyone else wants to communicate with us, even as we're having a pleasant chat with the person right in front of us.[47]

Social media has transformed the way we make, maintain, and dissolve relationships in the twenty-first century. We frequently use our technology to make and keep friends; to share information; and to listen and respond to, confirm, and support others.[48]

Interpersonal communication is only a click or a keystroke away. Mediated communication relationships can be as satisfying as face-to-face relationships; people seamlessly and easily switch from EMC to face-to-face context.[49] That's why throughout this book we'll discuss electronically mediated as well as face-to-face interpersonal communication. Our gadgets and EMC have a major impact on our real-life relationships.

social media
A variety of technological applications such as Facebook, Twitter, and Instagram that serve as channels to help people connect to one another.

electronically mediated communication (EMC)
Communication via a medium such as the Internet.

Communication and Emotion

The Role of Emotions in Our Relationships with Others

Your emotions and moods play an important role in how you communicate with others.

What is emotion? How do emotions work? What causes us to experience emotions?

One researcher described an emotion as a biological, cognitive, behavioral, and subjective affective reaction to an event.[50] A closer look suggests that an emotional reaction includes four things: biological or physiological responses (heart rate increases, breathing changes); cognitive responses (angry thoughts, happy thoughts); behavioral reactions to our thoughts and feelings (frowning, laughing); and subjective affective responses (mild or strong experiences of joy, panic, anger, pleasure, and the like).[51]

To have a better idea of the role emotions play in our relationships, consider the following general principles:

We are more likely to discuss our emotions in an *interpersonal* relationship than in an *impersonal* relationship. Research supports our common intuition: We are more likely to talk about our personal feelings with people we know, care about, and feel a unique relationship with (friends, romantic partners, and family members) than with people we don't know or don't particularly care about.[52]

We express our emotions both verbally and nonverbally, yet nonverbal messages often communicate our emotions more honestly. We sometimes explicitly tell people how we are feeling ("I'm feeling sad," "I'm angry with you," or "I love you"). But it's often through our nonverbal behavior (facial expression, tone of voice, or body posture) that our true feelings are communicated to others.

Our culture influences our emotional expression. It may seem that we express our feelings of happiness, joy, or sadness spontaneously, yet there is evidence that we learn what is and is not an appropriate expression of emotion.[53] The culture in which we are raised has a major influence on how we learn to both express emotions and respond to emotions expressed by others.[54]

Emotions are contagious. When you watch a funny movie in a crowded theatre, you are more likely to laugh when other people around you laugh. You are also more likely to cry when you see others experiencing sadness or pain. The process called **emotional contagion** occurs when we mimic the emotions of others.[55] So being around positive, upbeat people can have an impact on your emotions. And, in turn, your emotional expression can affect others.

---

emotional contagion

The process whereby people mimic the emotions of others after watching and hearing their emotional expressions.

hyperpersonal relationship

A relationship formed primarily through electronically mediated communication that becomes more personal than an equivalent face-to-face relationship because of the absence of distracting external cues, smaller amounts of personal information, and idealization of the communication partner.

Does communicating via social media have an affect on our face-to-face relationships? Some researchers say "yes," while others say "no." Nicole Michaeli found that spending too much time online, especially with social media applications like Facebook and Twitter, can have an overall negative effect on our interpersonal communication skills. With increased use of technology, we may deemphasize the importance of listening and being literally present when our friends are in need.[56] On the positive side, although EMC may have some negative implications for our face-to-face conversations, it makes us far more likely to interact with people we don't know than our parents did.[57]

Social media researcher Sook-Jung Lee found support for what he called the "Rich get richer" hypothesis: If you are already "rich" in terms of the quality of face-to-face interpersonal relationships, you will also experience enriched online interpersonal relationships. Some researchers have found that spending time online with friends does not necessarily result in the avoidance of "real time" friends.[58] Another research study found similar results: Spending time on Facebook does not mean that your face-to-face interpersonal relationships suffer. Rather, Facebook use is merely an extension of relationships, not a substitute for them.[59]

There is evidence that EMC messages can result in relationships becoming more intimate *in less time* than they would through face-to-face interpersonal communication. **Hyperpersonal relationships** are relationships formed primarily through EMC that become even *more personal* than equivalent face-to-face relationships, in part because of the absence of distracting external cues (such as physical qualities), an overdependence on just a few tidbits of personal information (which increases the importance of the information), and idealization of the partner.[60] Hyperpersonal relationships were first identified in a study in which pairs of students who were initially strangers interacted for up to an hour in a simulated instant-messaging situation, while another group of pairs met face to face for up to fifteen minutes. Those in EMC interactions skipped the typical superficial getting-acquainted questions and used more direct questioning and disclosure with their partners.[61] Online pairs engaged in more intimate probes and responses and reached a similar level of understanding and ability to predict their partners' behaviors as those in face-to-face interactions.

Researchers have explored questions about the type of person who is more likely to use EMC messages to initiate and maintain relationships. For example, researchers have asked whether people who spend a lot of time online generally have more or less personal contact with other people. A team of researchers led by Robert Kraut and Sara Kiesler made headlines when they published the results of their study, which concluded that the more people use the Internet, the *less* they will interact with others in person.[62] The researchers also found a correlation between claims of loneliness and Internet use. But other research contradicts this finding: Two follow-up studies found that people who use the Internet are *more likely* to have a greater number of friends, are more involved with community activities, and overall have greater levels of trust in other people. The most recent research seems to suggest that for some people—those who are already prone to being shy or introverted—there may be a link between Internet use and loneliness or feelings of social isolation. However, their isolation may not be the result of their use of the Internet, but simply because they are naturally less likely to make contact with others.[63] For those who are generally outgoing and who like to interact with others, the Internet is just another tool to reach out and make contact. If you're shy in person, you also may be less likely to tweet or instant message (IM); however, there are instances in which shy or introverted people may be more comfortable using IM.[64]

A comprehensive study that investigated whether instant messages and text messages are more like speech or writing concluded that instant messages contain elements of both, but nonetheless differ from speech in grammar, style, syntax, and other language factors. Text messages are more like writing than they are like spoken messages. There are also gender differences: Women's text and instant messages use more words, longer sentences, and more emoticons, and they discuss and include more social and relational information than men's messages.[65]

Differences Between EMC and Face-to-Face Communication

How is electronically mediated interpersonal communication different from live, face-to-face conversations? There are six key differences which have to do with (1) time shifting, (2) varying degrees of anonymity, (3) potential for deception, (4) availability of nonverbal cues, (5) role of the written word, and (6) distance.[66]

TIME SHIFTING When you interact with others using EMC, you can do so asynchronously. **Asynchronous messages** are not read, heard, or seen at the same time they are sent; there is a time delay between when you send such a message and when someone else receives it. A text message sent to a friend's phone, a post directed to someone who is not monitoring Facebook, or a voicemail message are examples of asynchronous messages.

Synchronous messages are sent and received instantly and simultaneously. Face-to-face conversations are synchronous—there is no time delay between when you send a message and when the other person receives it. A live video conference or a phone conversation are other examples of synchronous messages. Research has helped us understand phone etiquette. One study developed a scale to measure what the research referred to as "mobile communication competence." It confirmed what you'd expect: We don't like to overhear loud, personal conversations. And the

asynchronous message

A message that is not read, heard, or seen exactly when it is sent; there is a time delay between the sending of the message and its receipt.

synchronous message

A message that is sent and received simultaneously.

time and place of phone conversations are important variables that help determine whether we are using the phone competently or annoyingly.[67]

The more synchronous an interaction, the more similar it is to face-to-face interactions and the more social presence it creates. **Social presence** is the feeling we have when we act and think as if we're involved in an unmediated, face-to-face conversation. Technically, there is always some delay in sending and receiving messages (even in face-to-face interactions, sound takes time to travel). The key distinction among different forms of EMC and the degree of social presence we experience is whether we *feel* we are in a synchronous interaction. When we send text messages back and forth, or instant message, we create a shared sense of social or psychological co-presence with our partners. Receiving a tweet from a friend letting us know what he or she is doing at that moment gives us the feeling of being instantly connected to that person.

Another time difference between EMC and face-to-face messages is that it takes longer to tap out a typewritten message than to speak or convey a nonverbal message. The amount of delay (which corresponds to silence in face-to-face interactions) can have an impact on the interpretation of a message's meaning. When texting, participants may expect to see a response to their message very quickly. This is one reason text messages are often very short and concise. (Another reason is that it can be tricky to type on smaller keyboards with your thumbs—although some people are quite adept at using tiny keyboards.) A rapid succession of short messages fosters a sense of synchronicity and social presence.

Texting someone (as well as sending e-mail, instant messages, and tweets) allows you time to compose your message and craft it more carefully than you might in a face-to-face interaction. As a sender of text messages, you have more control over what you say and the impression you create; as the receiver of Internet messages, you no doubt realize that the other person has had the chance to shape his or her message carefully for its greatest impact on you.

VARYING DEGREES OF ANONYMITY   Maybe you've seen the now classic cartoon of a mutt sitting at a computer and saying to his companion, "On the Internet, nobody knows you're a dog." The cartoon canine communicator has a point: You may not always know precisely with whom you are communicating when you receive an e-mail message or are "friended" by someone you don't know. When you are friending someone on Facebook, that person may not know precisely who you are. (One study found seventeen Karl Marxes, seven Kermit the Frogs, four Anne Boleyns, and three people named Socrates of Athens who had Facebook pages.[68]) Because you can be anonymous, you may say things that are bolder, more honest, or even more outrageous than you would if your audience knew who you were. And being anonymous may also tempt you to say things that aren't true. Yet many of the EMC messages you send and receive are from people you know. So there are varying degrees of anonymity, depending on the technology that you are using and the honesty between you and your communication partners.

POTENTIAL FOR DECEPTION   Because with many forms of EMC you can't see or hear others, it's easy to lie. Here's evidence that people are deceptive when using EMC: 81 percent of people lied about their height, weight, or age in a dating profile.[69]

Online deception is almost as easy as typing. We say "almost," because you *can* assess the content of a written message for clues to deceit. In a study by Katherine Cornetto, college student respondents reported the most common indicator of deception was someone's making an implausible statement or bragging.[70] As friendships develop over the Internet, to detect deception, people come to depend on personal knowledge and impressions of their partners acquired over the course of their correspondence.[71] Interestingly, Cornetto's study found that those who reported lying frequently were most likely to suspect others of lying.[72] The ease with which someone can create a false persona means that you need to be cautious in forming relationships with strangers over the Internet. We apparently try to deceive not just people online we don't know well, but our family and close friends. Dariela Rodriguez and Megan

Wise found that undergraduate college students were *more* likely to send deceptive and untrue text messages to family and friends than to strangers.[73]

One researcher suggests looking for these top lying cues when reading online social media profiles:[74]

1. Liars often use fewer first-person pronouns (such as *I* or *me*).
2. Liars are more likely to use more negative terms like "not" and "never."
3. Liars use fewer negative words such as "sad" and "upset" to describe their emotions.
4. Liars write briefer online personal essays. The authors of the study suggested that it's easier not to get caught lying if you use fewer words.[75]

NONVERBAL CUES   Words and graphics become more important in EMC than in face-to-face interactions, because when communicating electronically, you must rely solely on words to carry nonverbal messages. Of course, a YouTube, Vine, or Skype video does include nonverbal messages, but even when using video some cues may be limited, such as the surrounding context and reactions from others.

There are some basic ways to add emotion to text messages, including CAPITALIZING THE MESSAGE (which is considered "yelling"), making letters **bold**, and inserting emoticons—such as a smiley face :-) or the now prevalent emoji 😳 😂 😠 available on a variety of social media applications. In face-to-face communication, we laugh and smile in direct response to what we or others are saying. In the EMC context, we use emoticons and emoji to provide emotional punctuation in our written messages. There are predictable places where we place a smiley face or a frowning face to underscore something we've just written.[76] The ability to tease or make sarcastic remarks is limited with EMC, because there is no tone of voice in the written message—so emoticons and emoji must provide information about the intended emotional tone of what is written. You can also write out an accompanying interpretation—for example, "Boy, am I insulted by that! (just kidding)" to compensate for the limited emotional cues.

There is also typically less emphasis on a person's physical appearance online than in face-to-face situations, unless you're using Facebook, Skype, or other video messages. In those forums, not only does your appearance in photos help determine how others react to you, but one study found that the physical attractiveness or unattractiveness of your "friends" rubs off on you. If you have Facebook friends who are perceived as attractive, you will be perceived as more popular and attractive.[77]

ROLE OF THE WRITTEN WORD   The reliance on the written word also affects EMC interpersonal relationships. One scholar suggests that a person's typing ability and writing skills affect the quality of any relationship that is developed.[78] Not everyone is able to encode thoughts quickly and accurately into written words. Writing skills not only affect your ability to express yourself and manage relationships, they also affect how others perceive you.

DISTANCE   Although we certainly can and do send text messages to people who live and work in the same building we're in (or even the same room), there is typically greater physical distance between people who are communicating using EMC. When using the Internet or a smartphone, we can just as easily send a text or a video message to someone on the other side of the globe as we can to someone on the other side of the room.

Understanding EMC

We've noted that EMC messages have both similarities to and differences from face-to-face messages. Which theories and models of electronically mediated messages help us understand how relationships are developed and make predictions about how we will use EMC messages?

The communication models that we've presented (communication as action, interaction, and transaction) are certainly applicable to EMC. There are times

People use electronically mediated communication (EMC) to share information that ranges from the dramatic to the routine. EMC can create a shared sense of social or psychological presence between two people, giving them the feeling of being instantly connected to each other.

when EMC is like the action model of communication. You post a message on a message board, blog, or Facebook wall and you get no immediate response from others. The communication is asynchronous—there's a time delay, so you're not really sure you've communicated with anyone. During some e-mail or text-message exchanges, your communication is more like the communication-as-interaction model; you send a text message and you wait for the response. There's a time delay, but sooner or later you get a response. And then there are instances when you can see and hear the other person simultaneously, such as in a live conversation with someone via a webcam— which is a synchronous interaction. In this instance the EMC resembles the transactional communication model, in that communicating this way is almost like being there in person because of the immediacy of the communication. Three theories have been developed to further explain and predict how EMC works.

CUES-FILTERED-OUT THEORY   One early theory of communication via the Internet was called **cues-filtered-out theory**. This theory suggested that emotional expression is severely restricted when we communicate using only text messages; nonverbal cues such as facial expression, gestures, and tone of voice are filtered out. The assumption was that text messages were best used for brief, task-oriented communication, such as sharing information or asking questions; text messages were assumed to be less effective in helping people establish meaningful relationships.[79] The cues-filtered-out theory also suggests that because of the lack of nonverbal cues and other social information, we'll be less likely to use EMC to manage relationships because of its limited ability to carry emotional and relational information. Although a venue like Facebook presents photos and ample personal information, communication through those forums is still not as rich as a face-to-face conversation.

MEDIA RICHNESS THEORY   Another theory helps us make predictions about which form of media we will use to send certain kinds of messages. We use different types of media depending on the richness of a medium—whether it allows us to express emotions and relational messages as well as send information. **Media richness theory** suggests that the richness of a communication channel is based on four criteria: (1) the amount of feedback that the communicator can receive, (2) the number of cues that the channel can convey and that can be interpreted by a receiver, (3) the variety of language that a communicator uses, and (4) the potential for expressing emotions and feelings.[80] Using these four criteria, researchers have developed a continuum of communication channels, from communication-rich to communication-lean. Figure 1.5 illustrates this continuum.

There is some evidence that those wishing to communicate a negative message, such as a message ending a relationship, may select a less rich communication medium—they may be more likely to send a letter or an e-mail rather than sharing the bad news face to face.[81] Similarly, people usually want to share good news in person, when they can enjoy the positive reaction to the message.

Both the cues-filtered-out theory and media richness theory suggest that the restriction of nonverbal cues, which provide information about the nature of the relationship between communicators, hampers the quality of relationships that can be established using EMC. But a newer perspective suggests that although EMC may communicate fewer relational cues, eventually we are able to discern relational information.

SOCIAL INFORMATION-PROCESSING THEORY   **Social information-processing theory** suggests that we *can* communicate relational and emotional messages via the Internet, *but it may take longer* to express messages that are typically communicated with facial expressions and tone of voice. A key difference between face-to-face and electronically mediated communication is the *rate* at which information reaches you. During an in-person conversation, you process a lot of information quickly; you process the words you hear as well as the many nonverbal cues you see (facial expression, gestures, and body posture) and hear (tone of voice and the use of pauses). During text-only interactions, there is less information to process (no audio cues or visual

---

cues-filtered-out theory

Theory that suggests that communication of emotions is restricted when people send messages to others via text messages because nonverbal cues such as facial expression, gestures, and tone of voice are filtered out.

media richness theory

Theory that identifies the richness of a communication medium based on the amount of feedback it allows, the number of cues receivers can interpret, the variety of language it allows, and the potential for emotional expression.

social information-processing theory

Theory that suggests people can communicate relational and emotional messages via the Internet, although such messages take longer to express without nonverbal cues.

Figure 1.5 A Continuum of Communication-Rich and Communication-Lean Channels

Adapted from L. K. Trevino, R. L. Draft, and R. H. Lengel, "Understanding Managers' Media Choices: A Symbolic Interactionist Perspective," in *Organizations and Communication Technology,* edited by J. Fulk and C. Steinfield (Newbury Park, CA: Sage, 1990), 71–94. Reprinted by permission of Sage Publications, Inc.

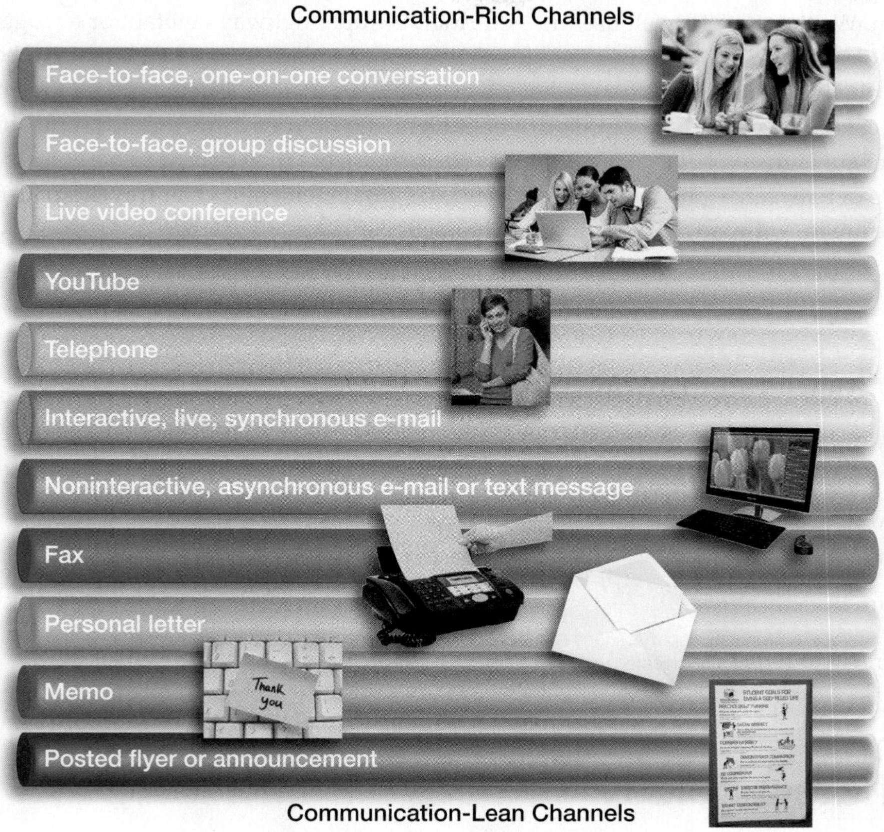

Communication-Rich Channels

Face-to-face, one-on-one conversation

Face-to-face, group discussion

Live video conference

YouTube

Telephone

Interactive, live, synchronous e-mail

Noninteractive, asynchronous e-mail or text message

Fax

Personal letter

Memo

Posted flyer or announcement

Communication-Lean Channels

nonverbal cues), so it takes a bit longer for the relationship to develop—but it does develop as you learn more about your partner's likes, dislikes, and feelings.

Social information-processing theory also suggests that if you expect to communicate with your electronic communication partner again, you will likely pay more attention to the relationship cues—expressions of emotions that are communicated directly (as when someone writes "I'm feeling bored today") or indirectly (as when an e-mail recipient responds to your long, chatty e-mail with only a sentence, which suggests he or she may not want to spend much time "talking" today).

In one study that supported social information-processing theory, communication researchers Joseph Walther and Judee Burgoon found that the kinds of relationships that developed between people who met face to face differed little from those between people who had computer-mediated interactions.[82] The general stages and patterns of communication were evident in both face-to-face and e-mail relationships. But over time, the researchers found that the electronically mediated communication actually developed into *more* socially rich relationships than face-to-face communication did. This finding reinforces the hypothesis that relationship cues *are* present in computer-mediated communication. It also supports the notion that we develop hyperpersonal relationships via EMC. So even though it may take more time for relationships to develop online, they can indeed develop and be just as satisfying as relationships nurtured through face-to-face conversation.

Research suggests that when using EMC, we ask questions and interact with others to enhance the quality of our relationship with them. A study by W. Scott Sanders found that people who communicated via Facebook enhanced the nature of the relationship and reduced their uncertainty about others by asking questions based on information that was already present on the other person's Facebook page.[83] Lisa

Tidwell and Joseph Walther found that people in computer-mediated conversations asked more direct questions, which resulted in respondents' revealing more information about themselves when online.[84]

Electronically mediated communication makes it possible for people to develop interpersonal relationships with others, whether they are miles away or in the next room. Walther and Tidwell use the "information superhighway" metaphor to suggest that EMC is not just a road for moving data from one place to another, but also a boulevard where people pass each other, occasionally meet, and decide to travel together. You can't see very much of other drivers unless you do travel together for some time. There are highway bandits, to be sure, who are not what they appear to be—one must drive defensively—and there are conflicts and disagreements when traveling, just as there are in "off-road," or face-to-face, interactions.[85]

Recap

Theories of Electronically Mediated Communication

Theory	Description
Cues-Filtered-Out Theory	The communication of emotion and relationship cues is restricted in e-mail or text messages because nonverbal cues, such as facial expression, gestures, and tone of voice, are filtered out.
Media Richness Theory	The richness or amount of information a communication medium has is based on the amount of feedback it permits, the number of cues in the channel, the variety of language used, and the potential for expressing emotions.
Social Information-Processing Theory	Emotional and relationship messages can be expressed via electronic means, although such messages take longer to be communicated without the immediacy of nonverbal cues.

#communicationandtechnology

Always On

The title of a book by Naomi Baron summarizes the impact of EMC on our lives: *Always On*.[86] Most of us are constantly connected to others via some electronic means.

We're online. In 2014, 87% of Americans used the Internet; and 97% of people between the ages of eighteen and twenty-seven were online.[87]

We're socially networked. 1.23 billion people used Facebook in 2014 and the number continues to rise.[88] In the Twitterverse, people are increasingly sending more tweets and using WhatsApp, Snapchat and iMessages with increasing frequency.

We've dramatically increased our use of text messages. We may even feel anxious if we're not receiving an e-bushel basket full of them.

We're less effective when talking with someone in person if we're also using our phone. Our conversation suffers if we take calls or check our phones for text updates while we are talking with someone. But apparently many of us still do it. One study found that almost 90 percent of people who owned a cellphone or smartphone said they used their phone in their last social situation.[89]

Consider these suggestions for text etiquette to help you be other-oriented when you text others.[90]

Don't text when you're with someone else, without apologizing.

Don't text if you've had too much to drink.
Don't text while driving.
Don't say anything in text you wouldn't say in person.
Don't send bad news by text.

In summary, although texting is easy and cheap, don't forget the joys of having a good face-to-face conversation with someone now and then.

Interpersonal Communication Competence

1.6   Identify strategies that can improve your communication competence.

Now that we have previewed the study of interpersonal communication, you may be saying to yourself, "Well, that's all well and good, but is it possible to improve my own interpersonal communication? Aren't some people just born with better interpersonal skills than others?" Just as some people have more musical talent or greater skill at throwing a football, evidence does suggest that some people may have an inborn, biological talent for communicating with others.[91]

To be a competent communicator is to express messages that are perceived to be both *effective* and *appropriate.*[92] You communicate effectively when your message is understood by others and achieves its intended effect. For example, if you want your roommate to stop using your hair dryer, and after you talk to him, he stops using your hair dryer, your message has been effective.

Competent communication should also be appropriate. By *appropriate,* we mean that the communicator should consider the time, place, and overall context of the message and should be sensitive to the feelings and attitudes of the listener. Who determines what is appropriate? Communication scholar Mary Jane Collier suggests that competence is a concept based on privilege; to label someone as competent means that another person has made a judgment as to what is appropriate or inappropriate behavior. Collier asks the following questions: "… competence and acceptance for whom? Who decides the criteria? Who doesn't? Competent or acceptable on the basis of what social and historical context?"[93] Collier points out that we have to be careful not to insist on one approach (our own approach) to interpersonal communication competence. *There is no single best way to communicate with others.* There are, however, avenues that can help you become both more effective and more appropriate when communicating with others.[94] We suggest a two-part strategy for becoming a more competent communicator. First, competent communicators are knowledgeable, skilled, and motivated.[95] Second, they draw on their knowledge, skill, and motivation to become other-oriented.

Become Knowledgeable, Skilled, and Motivated

Becoming a more effective communicator involves learning how communication works, developing skills such as listening, and motivating yourself to put what you've learned into practice.

BECOME KNOWLEDGEABLE   Effective communicators are knowledgeable. They know how communication works. They understand the components, principles, and rules of the communication process. By reading this chapter, you have already begun improving your interpersonal communication competence. As you read further in this book, you will learn theories, principles, concepts, and rules that will help you explain and predict how humans communicate interpersonally.

BECOME SKILLED   Effective communicators know how to translate knowledge into action.[96] You can memorize the characteristics of a good listener but still not listen well. To develop skill requires practice and helpful feedback from others who can confirm the appropriateness of your actions.[97] In this book, we examine the elements of complex skills (such as listening), offer activities that let you practice the skills, and provide opportunities for you to receive feedback and correct your application of the skills.[98]

PEANUTS © 1994 Peanuts Worldwide LLC. Dist. By UNIVERSAL UCLICK. Reprinted

BECOME MOTIVATED.   You need to be motivated to use your knowledge and skill. You must want to improve, and you must have a genuine desire to connect with others if you wish to become a competent communicator.

Become Other-Oriented

Lucy Van Pelt, in the Peanuts cartoon above, seems startled to learn that the world does not revolve around her. The signature concept for our study of interpersonal communication is the goal of becoming other-oriented in relationships. As noted earlier, to be an other-oriented communicator is to consider the thoughts, needs, experiences, personality, emotions, motives, desires, culture, and goals of your communication partners, while still maintaining your own integrity. The choices we make in forming our messages, in deciding how best to express those messages, and in deciding when and where to deliver those messages will be made more effectively when we consider the other person's thoughts and feelings. *To emphasize the importance of being an other-oriented communicator, throughout this book we will offer sidebar comments and questions to help you apply the concept of being other-oriented to your own interpersonal relationships.*

CONSIDER THE INTEREST OF OTHERS   Being other-oriented involves a conscious effort to consider the world from the point of view of those with whom you interact.[99] This effort occurs almost automatically when you are communicating with those you like or who are similar to you. Thinking about the thoughts and feelings of those you dislike or who are different from you is more difficult and requires more effort and commitment.

Sometimes, we are **egocentric communicators**; we create messages without giving much thought to the person who is listening. To be egocentric is to be self-focused and self-absorbed. Scholars of evolution might argue that our tendency to look out for Number One ensures the continuation of the human species and is therefore a good thing.[100] Yet, it is difficult to communicate effectively when we focus exclusively on ourselves. Research suggests that being egocentric is detrimental to developing healthy relationships with others.[101] If we fail to adapt our message to our listener, we may not be successful in achieving our intended communication goal. Other people can often perceive whether we're self-focused or other-oriented (especially if the person we're talking with is a sensitive, other-oriented communicator).

Are people more self-focused today than in the past? Sociologist Jean Twenge suggests that people today are increasingly more narcissistic (self-focused) than they have been in previous generations—she dubs today's narcissistic generation the "me generation." Her research found that "in the early 1950s, only 12 percent of teens aged fourteen to sixteen agreed with the statement 'I am an important person.' By the late

egocentric communicator

Person who creates messages without giving much thought to the person who is listening; a communicator who is self-focused and self-absorbed.

BEING Other-ORIENTED

Being other-oriented means focusing on the interests, needs, and goals of another person. Think about a person who is important to you—it could be a family member, close friend, lover, or colleague. Consider the other-oriented nature of the relationship you have with this person. Are there specific things you say, gifts you have given, or activities that you do with this person that demonstrate your focus on *his* or *her* interests, needs, and desires? What things does this person do that reflect his or her other-orientation towards you?

Improving Your Communication Skills

Practice Being Other-Oriented

At the heart of our study of interpersonal communication is the principle of becoming other-oriented. To be other-oriented means that you are aware of others' thoughts, feelings, goals, and needs and respond appropriately in ways that offer personal support. It does not mean that you abandon your own needs and interests or that you diminish your self-respect. To have integrity is to behave in a thoughtful, integrated way toward others while being true to your core beliefs and values. To be other-oriented is to have integrity; you don't just agree with others or give in to the demands of others in encounters with them.

Do you know a sycophant? A *sycophant* is a person who praises others only to manipulate emotions so that his or her needs are met. Sycophants may look as though they are focused on others, but their behavior is merely self-serving. A sycophant is not other-oriented. A person who is truly other-oriented is aware of the thoughts, feelings, and needs of others and then mindfully and honestly chooses to respond to those needs. To enhance your other-oriented awareness and skill takes practice. Throughout the book, we offer both principles and opportunities to practice the skill and mindset of being other-oriented.

To develop an awareness of being other-oriented with a communication partner, role-play the following interpersonal situations in two ways. First, role-play the scene as a communicator who is not other-oriented but rather self-focused. Then re-enact the same scene as a communicator who is other-oriented—someone who considers the thoughts and feelings of the other person while maintaining his or her own integrity.

Suggested situations:

- Return a broken DVD player to a department store salesperson.
- Correct a grocery store cashier who has scanned an item at the wrong price.
- Meet with a teacher who gave your son or daughter a failing grade.
- Ask your professor for a one-day extension on a paper that is due tomorrow.
- Ask someone for a donation to a worthy cause.
- Ask a professor for permission to get into a class that has reached its maximum enrollment.
- Accept an unappealing book as a gift from a friend.
- Remind your son or daughter that he or she needs to practice the cello.

1980s, an incredible 80 percent—almost seven times as many—claimed they were important."[102] Twenge and two of her colleagues found evidence for an increased self-focus among students in the twenty-first century.[103] Brain scans further suggest that the parts of our brains linked to self-oriented thought are more predominate during teenage years than adulthood.[104]

We may find ourselves speaking without considering the thoughts and feelings of our listener when we have a need to purge ourselves emotionally or to confirm our sense of self-importance, but doing so usually undermines our relationships with others. A self-focused communicator often alienates others. Research suggests that fortunately, almost by necessity, we adapt to our partner in order to carry on a conversation.[105]

EMPATHIZE How do you become other-oriented? Being other-oriented is really a collection of skills rather than a single skill. The practical information throughout this book will help you develop this collection of essential communication skills, including being self-aware, being aware of others, using and interpreting verbal messages, using and interpreting nonverbal messages, and listening and responding to others.[106] Being empathic—able to experience the feelings and emotions of others—is especially important in becoming other-oriented. After listening to and empathizing with others, someone who is other-oriented is able to appropriately adapt messages to them.

ADAPT To appropriately adapt messages to others is to be flexible. In this book, we do not identify tidy lists of sure-fire strategies that you can always use to win friends and influence people. The same set of skills is not effective in every situation, so other-oriented communicators do not assume that "one size fits all." Rather, they assess each unique situation and adapt their behavior to achieve the desired outcome.

Adaptation includes such things as simply asking questions in response to a communication partner's disclosures, finding topics of mutual interest to discuss, selecting words and examples that are meaningful to our partner, and avoiding topics that we don't feel comfortable discussing with another person. Adapting messages to others does *not* mean that we tell them only what they want to hear; that would be unethical.

ethics

The beliefs, values, and moral principles by which a person determines what is right or wrong.

BE ETHICAL   Other-oriented communicators are ethical. **Ethics** are the beliefs, values, and moral principles by which we determine what is right or wrong. To be an ethical communicator means to be sensitive to the needs of others, to give people choices rather than forcing them to act a certain way. Unethical communicators believe that they know what other people need, even without asking them for their preferences. Acting manipulative and forcing opinions on others usually results in a climate of defensiveness. Effective communicators seek to establish trust and reduce interpersonal barriers, rather than erect them. Ethical communicators keep confidences; they keep private information that others wish to be kept private. They also do not intentionally decrease others' feelings of self-worth. Another key element in being an ethical communicator is honesty. If you intentionally lie or distort the truth, then you are not communicating ethically or effectively. Ethical communicators also don't tell people only what they want to hear. At the end of each chapter, in our Study Guide section, we pose ethical questions to help you explore the ethics of interpersonal relationships.

In addition to appropriately and ethically adapting to others, being other-oriented includes developing positive, healthy attitudes about yourself and others. In 1951, Carl Rogers wrote a pioneering book called *Client-Centered Therapy*, which transformed the field of psychotherapy. In it, Rogers explains how genuine positive regard for another person and an open supportive communication climate lay the foundation for trusting relationships. But Rogers did not invent the concept of developing a positive, healthy regard for others. The core principles of every religion and faith movement in the last 5000 years include a focus on the needs of others. Our purpose is certainly not to promote a specific religion or set of spiritual beliefs. What we suggest is that becoming other-oriented, as evidenced through knowledge, skill, and motivation, can enhance your interpersonal communication competence and the quality of your life.

Applying an Other-Orientation

to Being a Competent Interpersonal Communicator

To be a competent interpersonal communicator is to be an other-oriented communicator—to focus on the needs, interests, values, and behaviors of others while being true to your own principles and ethical credo. In this chapter we've previewed some of the knowledge, provided a rationale for being motivated to master interpersonal competencies, and offered a glimpse of the skills that enhance an other-orientation.

Knowledge

When you view communication as a transactive process rather than as a simplistic action or even an interactive process, you gain realistic insight into the challenge of communicating with others and the potential for misunderstandings. Knowing the messiness and dynamic nature of communication, as well as the various components of the process (source, message, channel, receiver, context, and feedback) can help you better diagnose communication issues in your own relationships and improve your ability to accurately decode the messages of others.

Motivation

Why learn how to be other-oriented? As we've noted, learning about interpersonal communication has the potential to enhance both the quality of your relationships with others and your health. Developing your skill and knowledge of interpersonal communication can enhance your confidence to improve your relationships with family members, friends, romantic partners, and colleagues.

Skill

To be competently other-oriented takes more than knowledge of the elements and nature of communication (although that's a good start), and more than a strong motivation to enhance your abilities. It takes skill. As you begin your study of interpersonal communication, you can be confident that in the chapters ahead you will learn how to listen, respond, use, and interpret verbal messages, express and interpret emotional meanings of messages, more accurately use and interpret nonverbal messages, manage conflict, and adapt to human differences. To be other-oriented is to have the knowledge, nurture the motivation, and develop the skill to relate to others in effective and ethical ways.

STUDY GUIDE
Review, Apply, and Assess

Interpersonal Communication Defined

Objective 1.1 **Compare and contrast definitions of communication, human communication, and interpersonal communication.**

Key Terms

other-oriented
communication
human communication
interpersonal communication
impersonal communication

mass communication
public communication
small group communication
intrapersonal communication
relationship

Thinking Critically

Draw a relationship scale on a piece of paper, and label it "impersonal" at one end and "intimate" at the other. Place your family members, friends, and work colleagues on the scale. Why do some fall toward the "impersonal" end? What makes those relationships less personal than others? Discuss and compare your entries with those of classmates.

Assessing Your Skills

1. Briefly describe a recent interpersonal communication exchange that was *not* effective. Analyze the exchange. Write down some of the dialogue if you remember it. Did the other person understand you? Did your communication have the intended effect? Was your message ethical?
2. After reading Chapter 1, how would you rate your overall interpersonal communication skill on a scale of 1 to 10, with 10 being high and 1 being low? (At the end of the course, you'll want to make another assessment of your interpersonal communication skill and compare the result.)

Interpersonal Communication's Importance to Your Life

Objective 1.2 **Explain why it is useful to study interpersonal communication.**

Thinking Critically

Think of an example in which interpersonal communication was not a satisfying and positive experience between you and a family member, friend, lover, or colleague. How did the relationship suffer? What could you have done to improve the situation? After completing the course, answer the question again to see if you have new options for enhancing your interpersonal communication skill.

Assessing Your Skills

Select five people from your family or identify friends that you have known for a long time. Draw a line graph charting the quality of your relationship with these five people

for the past five years (the line goes up when you've had a positive relationship and down when the relationship has been less positive from your perspective). Use the current month to note the yearly benchmark for overall quality of the relationship. Identify the factors and experiences that influence you to rate a relationship as positive and/or negative for each relationship.

Interpersonal Communication and the Communication Process

Objective 1.3 **Describe the key components of the communication process, including communication as action, interaction, and transaction.**

Key Terms

source
encode
decode
message
channel
receiver

noise
feedback
context
systems theory
episode

Thinking Critically

Think of some recent interpersonal communication exchanges you've had. Which communication model best captures the nature of each exchange? Analyze each exchange, identifying the components of communication discussed in this section of the chapter. Was feedback an important component? Were you and your partner experiencing the communication simultaneously? What was the context? What were sources of internal and external noise? Did you or your partner have problems encoding or decoding each other's messages?

Assessing Your Skills

Working with a group of your classmates or individually, develop your own model of interpersonal communication. Include all of the components that are necessary to describe how communication between people works. Your model could be a drawing or an object that symbolizes the communication process. Share your model with the class, describing the decisions you made in developing it. Illustrate your model with a conversation between two people, pointing out how elements of the conversation relate to the model.

Interpersonal Communication Principles

Objective 1.4 **Discuss five principles of interpersonal communication.**

Key Terms

symbol
rule
content

relationship dimension
metacommunication

Thinking Critically

What rules govern your relationship with your mother? Your father? Your communication teacher? Your roommate? Your coach? Your spouse? Your siblings? Note the rules that are similar and those that are different.

Assessing Your Skills

The Recap box earlier in this chapter summarizes the principles of and myths about interpersonal communication. Identify other myths or common misunderstandings about the interpersonal communication process.

Interpersonal Communication and Social Media

Objective 1.5 Discuss the role of electronically mediated communication in developing and maintaining interpersonal relationships.

Key Terms

social media
electronically mediated communication (EMC)
emotional contagion
hyperpersonal relationship
asynchronous message
synchronous message
social presence
cues-filtered-out theory
media richness theory
social information-processing theory

Thinking Critically

Does electronically mediated communication make us more or less other-oriented than face-to-face communication? Explain. Think of the different types of EMC that you use in your daily life. How does each of these affect your social presence?

Assessing Your Skills

Keep a one-day log of your electronically mediated interactions (e.g., phone calls, Facebook messages, text messages, etc.). Select several messages and note whether there was a greater emphasis on the content or the relational elements of the messages you exchanged during the interaction.

Interpersonal Communication Competence

Objective 1.6 Identify strategies that can improve your interpersonal communication competence.

Key Terms

egocentric communicator   ethics

Thinking Critically

Think about your primary goal for this course. Is it to develop communication strategies to help you achieve personal goals? Is it to develop sensitivity to the needs of others? What is behind your goal? Is your purpose ethical?

Assessing Your Skills

1. Provide an assessment of your overall interpersonal knowledge, motivation, and skill. Which of these three areas do you most need to develop?
2. Make a list of the communication skills that could help you enhance your ability to be other-oriented. Rank order the skills in terms of importance and value to you.

Chapter 2
Interpersonal Communication and Self

"People tell themselves stories and then pour their lives into the stories they tell."

Anonymous

∨ Learning Objectives

2.1 Define self-concept and identify the factors that shape the development of your self-concept.

2.2 Define self-esteem and compare and contrast self-esteem with self-concept.

2.3 Define facework and discuss how you project your face and protect others' face.

2.4 Identify and describe seven strategies for improving your self-concept.

2.5 Identify the effects of your self-concept and self-esteem on your relationships with others.

CHAPTER OUTLINE

Self-Concept: Who You Think You Are

Self-Esteem: Your Self-Worth

Facework: Presenting Your Self-Image to Others

How to Improve Your Self-Esteem

Self and Interpersonal Relationships

Philosophers suggest that all people seek answers to three basic questions: (1) "Who am I?" (2) "Why am I here?" and (3) "Who are all these others?" In this chapter, we focus on these essential questions about the self as presented both online and face to face. We view these questions as progressive. Grappling with the question of who you are and seeking to define a purpose for your life are essential to understanding others and becoming other-oriented in your interpersonal communication and relationships.

Fundamentally, all your communication starts or ends with you. When you are the communicator, you intentionally or unintentionally code your thoughts and emotions to be interpreted by another. When you receive a message, you interpret the information through your own frame of reference. Your self-image and self-worth, as well as your needs, values, beliefs, and attitudes, serve as filters for your communication with others. As you establish and develop relationships, you may become more aware of these filters and perhaps want to alter them. A close relationship often provides the impetus for change.

To understand the role that self-concept plays in interpersonal communication, we will explore the first two basic questions—"Who am I?" and "Why am I here?"—in an effort to discover the meaning of self. We will examine the multifaceted dimensions of self-concept, learn how it develops, and compare self-concept to self-esteem. Then we will move to the third basic question, "Who are all these others?" What you choose to tell and not tell others about yourself reveals important clues about who you are, what you value, and how you relate to other people. In addition, focusing on the needs, wants, and values of other people while maintaining your own integrity is the basis of being other-oriented.

Self-Concept: Who You Think You Are

2.1 Define self-concept and identify the factors that shape the development of your self-concept.

You can begin your journey of self-discovery by doing the exercise in Improving Your Communication Skills: Who Are You? below.

Improving Your Communication Skills

Who Are You?

Consider this question: Who are you? More specifically, ask yourself this question ten times. Write your responses in the spaces provided here or on a separate piece of paper. It may be challenging to identify ten aspects of yourself. The Spanish writer Miguel de Cervantes said, "To know thyself … is the most difficult lesson in the world." Your answers will help you begin to explore your self-concept and self-esteem in this chapter.

I am
_____

I am
_____

I am
_____

I am
_____

I am
_____

I am
_____

I am
_____

I am
_____

I am
_____

I am
_____

How did you answer the question "Who are you?" Perhaps you listed activities in which you participate, or groups and organizations to which you belong. You may have listed some of the roles you assume, such as student, child, or parent. All these things are indeed a part of your self, the sum total of who you are. Psychologist Karen Horney defines **self** as "that central inner force, common to all human beings and yet unique in each, which is the deep source of growth."[1]

Your answers are also part of your **self-concept**. Your self-concept is a subjective description of who you *think* you are—it is filtered through your own perceptions. For example, you may have great musical talent, but you may not believe in it enough to think of yourself as a musician. Think of your self-concept as the labels you consistently use to describe yourself to others.

Although you may have used certain labels to describe yourself today, you may use different labels tomorrow or next week. A healthy self-concept is flexible. It may change depending upon new experiences you have and insights you gain from others. Yet although your self-concept is changeable, core elements will remain stable; otherwise, you'd be so adaptable that you or others wouldn't be able to recognize the essence of *you*.

Besides the issue of stability and change, people also vary in their level of self-awareness. Could you answer the "Who are you?" question quickly, or did you have to take some time to ponder it? You may be very conscious of who you are, and therefore able to quickly describe yourself. Or you may have required more time and effort to identify self labels. Reflection is one of the most powerful tools you can use to enhance self-awareness.

Attitudes, Beliefs, and Values Reflect Your Self-Concept

Who you are is anchored in the attitudes, beliefs, and values that you hold. You were not born with specific attitudes (what you like), beliefs (what you hold as true or false), or values (what you believe to be right or wrong). These are learned constructs that shape your behavior and self-image.

An **attitude** is a learned predisposition to respond to a person, object, or idea in a favorable or unfavorable way. Attitudes reflect what you like and what you don't like. If you like school, butter pecan ice cream, and your brother, you hold positive attitudes toward these things. You were not born with a fondness for butter pecan ice cream; you learned to like it, just as some people learn to enjoy the taste of snails, raw fish, or pureed turnips.

Beliefs are the ways in which you structure your understanding of reality—what is true and what is false for you. Most of your beliefs are based on previous experience. You believe that the sun will rise in the morning and that you will get burned if you put your hand on a hot stove.

How are attitudes and beliefs related? They often function quite independently of each other. You may have a favorable attitude toward something and still believe negative things about it. You may believe, for example, that your school football team will not win the national championship this year, although you may be a big fan. Or you may believe that God exists, yet you may not always like what you think God does or does not do. Beliefs have to do with what is true or not true, whereas attitudes reflect likes and dislikes.

Values are enduring concepts of good and bad, right and wrong. Your values are more resistant to change than either your attitudes or your beliefs. They are also more difficult for most people to identify. Values are so central to who you are that it is difficult to isolate them. For example, when you go to the supermarket, you may spend a few minutes deciding whether to buy regular or cream-style corn, but you probably

self
Sum total of who a person is; a person's central inner force.

self-concept
A person's subjective description of who he or she is.

attitude
Learned predisposition to respond to a person, object, or idea in a favorable or unfavorable way.

belief
Way in which you structure your understanding of reality–what is true and what is false for you.

value
Enduring concept of good and bad, right and wrong.

Figure 2.1 Values, Beliefs, and Attitudes in Relation to Self

do not spend much time deciding whether you will steal the corn or pay for it. Our values are instilled in us by our earliest interpersonal relationships; for almost all of us, our parents shape our values.

The model in Figure 2.1 illustrates that values are central to our behavior and concept of self and that what we believe to be true or false stems from our values; that's why values are in the center of the model. Attitudes are at the outer edge of the circle because they are the most likely to change. You may like your coworker today but not tomorrow, even though you *believe* the person will come to work every day and you still *value* the concept of friendship. Beliefs are between attitudes and values in the model because they are more likely to change than our core values but don't change as much as our attitudes (likes and dislikes).

Recap

Who You Are is Reflected in Your Attitudes, Beliefs, and Values

	Definition	Dimensions	Example
Attitude	Learned predisposition to respond favorably or unfavorably to something	Likes–Dislikes	You like ice cream, incense, and cats.
Belief	The way in which you structure reality	True–False	You believe that your parents love you.
Value	Enduring concepts of what is right and wrong	Good–Bad	You value honesty and truth.

Mindfulness: Being Consciously Aware

Do you know what you're doing right now? "Of course," you may think, "I'm reading this textbook." But are you *really* aware of all of the fleeting thoughts bouncing in your head, whether you're truly happy or sad, or even whether you may be twiddling a pencil, jiggling your leg, or in need of a snack? To be aware of who you are and what you may be thinking about is a more involved process than you may think. To be self-aware is to be mindful.

mindfulness

The ability to consciously think about what you are doing and experiencing.

Mindfulness is the ability to think consciously about what you are doing and experiencing, rather than responding out of habit or intuition.[2] If you've ever talked on the phone while driving (something illegal in many states), you may not have been mindful of, or consciously thinking about, where you were going. Researchers have described three ways of being mindfully self-aware, or conscious of who you are and what you are doing: subjective self-awareness, objective self-awareness, and symbolic self-awareness.[3]

SUBJECTIVE SELF-AWARENESS **Subjective self-awareness** is the ability to differentiate ourselves from our environment. You are a separate being apart from your surroundings. It is so basic an awareness that it may even seem not worth talking about. You know, for example, that you're not physically attached to the chair you may be sitting in. You are a separate entity from all that is around you.

subjective self-awareness
Ability to differentiate the self from the social and physical environment.

OBJECTIVE SELF-AWARENESS **Objective self-awareness** is the ability to be the object of our own thoughts and attention. You have the ability to think about your own thoughts as you are thinking about them. (Research suggests that some primates also have this ability.) Not only are you aware that you're separate from your environment (subjective self-awareness), but you can also ponder the distinct thoughts you are thinking about. Of course, objective self-awareness, like subjective self-awareness, can be "turned on" and "turned off." Sometimes you are aware of what you are thinking about and sometimes you're unaware of what you are thinking about or what you are focusing on.

objective self-awareness
Ability to be the object of one's own thoughts and attention–to be aware of one's state of mind and what one is thinking.

SYMBOLIC SELF-AWARENESS **Symbolic self-awareness**, unique to humans, is the ability not only to think about ourselves, but to use language (symbols) to represent ourselves to others. For example, you have the ability to think about how to make a good impression on others. In an effort to make a positive impression on someone, you may say, "Good evening, Mrs. Cleaver. You look nice this evening," rather than just saying, "Hi ya." You make conscious attempts to use symbols to influence the way you want to be perceived by others.

symbolic self-awareness
Uniquely human ability to think about oneself and use language (symbols) to represent oneself to others.

A four-stage model of how aware or unaware we are of what we are doing at any given moment has been attributed to psychologist Abraham Maslow. This framework has also been used to explain how individuals develop communication skills.

Stage 1: *Unconscious incompetence.* You are unaware of your own incompetence. You don't know what you don't know. For example, at one point in your life you didn't know how to ride a bicycle and you didn't even realize that you were missing this skill. You were unconsciously incompetent about your bicycle-riding skills.

Stage 2: *Conscious incompetence.* At this level, you become aware or conscious that you are not competent: You know what you don't know. Continuing our example, at some point you realized that others could ride a bike and you could not. You became conscious of your incompetence with regard to bicycle riding.

Stage 3: *Conscious competence.* You are aware that you know something, but applying it has not yet become a habit. When you first learned to ride a bike, if you're like most people, you had to concentrate on keeping your balance and focus on riding forward without falling over.

This artist sought to explore her self-dimensions by painting her self-portrait. What qualities does this self-portrait reveal about the artist?

Stage 4: *Unconscious competence.* At this level, your skills become second nature to you. Now you don't have to mentally review how to ride a bike every time you hop on one. You are unconsciously competent of how to ride a bicycle; you just get on and automatically start pedaling. The same could be said about tying your shoes; you don't have to think about how to tie your shoes; you just do it without thinking about each step.

These same four stages explain how you learn any skill, from riding a bike to enhancing the interpersonal communication skills we discuss in this book.

One or Many Selves?

Shakespeare's famous line "To thine own self be true" suggests that you have a single self to which you can be true. But do you have just one self? Or is there a more "real" you buried somewhere within? Most scholars conclude that each of us has a core set of behaviors, attitudes, beliefs, and values that constitutes our self—the sum total of who we are. But our *concept* of self can and does change, depending on circumstances and influences.

In addition, our self-concept is often different from the way others see us. We almost always behave differently in public than we do in private. Sociologist Erving Goffman suggests that, like actors and actresses, we have "on-stage" behaviors when others are watching and "backstage" behaviors when they are not.[4] Goffman writes that "often what talkers undertake to do is not to provide information to a recipient but to present dramas to an audience. Indeed, it seems that we spend most of our time not engaged in giving information but in giving shows."[5] With an audience present, whether it's one person or several, you adapt and "perform."

Perhaps the most enduring and widely accepted framework for describing who we are was developed by the philosopher William James. He identified three classic components of the self: the material self, the social self, and the spiritual self.[6]

material self

Concept of self as reflected in the total of all the tangible things you own.

THE MATERIAL SELF The **material self** is the total of all the tangible things you own: your body, your possessions, and your home. As you examine your list of responses to the question "Who are you?" note whether any of your statements refer to one of your physical attributes or something you own.

One element of the material self gets considerable attention in this culture: the body. Do you like the way you look? Most of us, if we're honest, would like to change something about our appearance. One study found that when asked, "What would you change about your body?" virtually all adults had one or more suggestions for modifying their physical appearance. But when children were asked the same question, they had no suggestions for enhancing their appearance. This suggests that we *learn* what aspects of our material self we find attractive.[7] When a discrepancy exists between our desired material self and our self-concept, we may respond to eliminate the discrepancy. We may try to lose weight, develop our muscles, or acquire hair in some places and lose hair in other places. The multibillion-dollar diet industry is just one of many businesses that profit from our collective desire to change our appearance.

social self

Concept of self as reflected in social interactions with others.

THE SOCIAL SELF Look at your "Who are you?" list once more. How many of your responses relate to your **social self**, the part of you that interacts with others? William James believed that you have many social selves—that, depending on the friend, family member, colleague, or acquaintance with whom you are interacting, you change the way you are. A person has, said James, as many social selves as there are people who recognize him or her. For example, when you talk to your best friend, you are willing to "let down your hair" and reveal more thoughts and feelings than you would in a conversation with your communication professor, or even your parents. Each relationship that you have with another person is unique because you bring to it a unique social self.

Do you find this list of variations on the Golden Rule from different world religions convincing evidence that being other-oriented is a universal value? Are there additional underlying values or principles, such as how the poor or the elderly should be treated, that should inform our interactions with others?

spiritual self

Concept of self based on thoughts and introspections about personal values, moral standards, and beliefs.

THE SPIRITUAL SELF Your **spiritual self** consists of all your thoughts and introspections about your values and moral standards. It does not depend on what you own or with whom you talk; it is the essence of who you *think* you are and your *feelings* about yourself, apart from external evaluations. It is an amalgam of your religious

Relating to Diverse Others

The "Golden Rule": Is Being Other-Oriented a Universal Value?

Cultural differences among the world's people include differences in language, food and housing preferences, and a host of other elements. Anthropologists and communication scholars who study intercultural communication, a topic we'll discuss in more detail in Chapter 4, teach the value of adapting to cultural differences in order to understand others better. But is it possible that despite our differences, a universally held principle influences the behavior of all people? The question is not a new one. Scholars, theologians, philosophers, and many others have debated for millennia whether there are any universal values that inform all human societies.

The importance of being other-oriented rather than self-absorbed is not a new idea. Most world religions emphasize some version of the same spiritual principle, known in Christianity as the Golden Rule: Do unto others as you would have others do unto you.[8]

Hinduism This is the sum of duty: Do nothing to others that would cause pain if done to you.

Buddhism One should seek for others the happiness one desires for one self.

Taoism Regard your neighbor's gain as your own gain, and your neighbor's loss as your loss.

Confucianism Is there one principle that ought to be acted on throughout one's whole life? Surely it is the principle of loving-kindness: do not unto others what you would not have them do unto you.

Zoroastrianism The nature alone is good that refrains from doing unto another whatsoever is not good for itself.

Judaism What is hateful to you, do not do to others. That is the entire law: all the rest is but commentary.

Islam No one of you is a believer until he desires for his brother that which he desires for himself.

Christianity Do unto others as you would have others do unto you.

beliefs and your sense of who you are in relationship to other forces in the universe. Whether you believe in intelligent design or Darwinian evolution (or both), your beliefs about the ultimate origins of the world (and about your own origins and ultimate destination) are embedded in your spiritual self. Your spiritual self is the part of you that answers the question "Why am I here?"

Recap

William James's Dimensions of Self

	Definition	Examples
Material Self	All the physical elements that reflect who you are	Body, clothes, car, home
Social Self	The self as reflected through your interactions with others; actually, a variety of selves that respond to changes in situations and roles	Your informal self interacting with your best friend; your formal self interacting with your professors
Spiritual Self	Introspections about values, morals, and beliefs	Belief or disbelief in God; regard for life in all its forms

How Your Self-Concept Develops

Some psychologists and sociologists have advanced theories that suggest you learn who you are through five basic means: (1) interactions with other individuals, (2) associations with groups, (3) roles you assume, (4) self-labels, and (5) your personality. Like James's framework, these five basic means do not cover every base in the study of self, but these constructs can provide some clues about how your own self-concept develops.

INTERACTION WITH INDIVIDUALS In 1902, Charles Horton Cooley first advanced the concept of the **looking-glass self**, which was his term for the notion that we form our self-concept by seeing ourselves in a kind of figurative looking glass: We

looking-glass self

Concept that suggests you learn who you are based on your interactions with others, who reflect your self back to you.

G Other-ORIENTED

of the ways we develop our self-concept is by interacting with others. Who are the others in your life who have had the most profound impact on who you are? Most people would say their parents and members of their family. Who else (besides family members) has helped to shape your concept of self? In what ways?

learn who we are by interacting with others, much as we look into a mirror and see our reflection.[9] Like Cooley, George Herbert Mead also believed that our sense of who we are is a consequence of our relationships with others.[10] And Harry Stack Sullivan theorized that from birth to death our selves change primarily because of how people respond to us.[11] One sage noted, "We are not only our brother's keeper; we are our brother's maker."

The process begins at birth. Our names, one of the primary ways we identify ourselves, are given to us by someone else. During the early years of our lives, our parents are the key individuals who reflect who we are. As we become less dependent on our parents, our friends become highly influential in shaping our attitudes, beliefs, and values. And as we grow older, friends continue to provide feedback on how well we perform certain tasks. This feedback, in turn, helps us shape our sense of identity as adults—we must acknowledge our talents in math, language, or art in our own minds before we say that we are mathematicians, linguists, or artists.

Fortunately, not *all* feedback affects our sense of who we think we are. We are likely to incorporate others' comments into our self-concept under three conditions: (1) How frequently the message is presented, (2) whether the message is perceived as credible, and (3) whether the message is consistent.

Frequent　We are more likely to believe another's statement if he or she repeats something we have heard several times. If one person casually tells you that you have a good singing voice, you are not likely to launch a search for an agent and a recording contract. But if several individuals tell you on many different occasions that you have a talent for singing, you may decide to do something about it.

Credible　We are more likely to value another's statements if we perceive him or her to be credible. If we believe the individual is competent, trustworthy, and qualified to make a judgment about us, then we are more likely to believe the person's assessment.

Consistent　We are likely to incorporate another's comments into our own concept of self if the comments are consistent with other comments and our own experience. If your boss tells you that you work too slowly, but for years people have been urging you to slow down, then your previous experience will probably encourage you to challenge your boss's evaluation.

attachment style

A style of relating to others that develops early in life, based on the emotional bond one forms with one's parents or primary caregiver.

ATTACHMENT STYLE　According to several researchers, you develop an **attachment style** based on how secure, anxious, or uncomfortable you felt in relating to one or both of your parents.[12] The emotional and relational bond that you developed early on with your parents—that is, how *attached* you felt to one or both of your parents or a primary caregiver—influenced your concept of self and continues to influence how you relate to others.[13] Why should you be interested in your attachment style? Your attachment style influences the nature of the friendships you develop, your motivation to "hook up" (be sexually active) with others, and overall patterns in how you relate to others.[14] Research suggests that you developed one of three different types of attachment styles: secure, anxious, or avoidant.[15]

secure attachment style

The style of relating to others that is characteristic of those who are comfortable giving and receiving affection, experiencing intimacy, and trusting other people.

Secure Attachment Style　You have a **secure attachment style** if you are comfortable giving and receiving affection, experiencing intimacy, and trusting other people. A secure attachment style likely reflects a strong, trusting, close, predictable, and positive emotional bond with your parents.[16]

Individuals with a secure attachment style experience greater overall feelings of hope and relationship satisfaction and tend to disclose more personal information about themselves.[17] Similar results have been found when couples with secure attachment styles are in romantic long-distance relationships—there's a greater feeling of closeness even when the partner is many miles away.[18] Research has also found that people with a secure attachment style are more likely to emerge as leaders[19] and to have improved memory and recognition of words with positive emotional connotations. About 60 percent of people develop a secure attachment style.[20]

Anxious Attachment Style   You may have developed an **anxious attachment style** if you received some affection, but not predictably enough to feel completely secure. As a result, you may experience some anxiety about intimacy and about giving and receiving affection. Individuals with an anxious attachment style report feeling more negative emotions and stress when interacting with others, especially a romantic partner.[21] They also report more Facebook jealousy and are more likely to keep tabs on others on Facebook.[22] About 10 percent of the population develops an anxious attachment style.[23]

anxious attachment style
The style of relating to others that is characteristic of those who experience anxiety in some intimate relationships and feel uncomfortable giving and receiving affection.

Avoidant Attachment Style   Finally, you may have an **avoidant attachment style** if you consistently received too little nurturing. People who had this type of upbringing may feel considerable discomfort and awkwardness when expressing or receiving intimacy. They may tend to fear and avoid relational intimacy (including sexual intimacy) with others, be more self-reliant, and have more doubts about romantic love.[24] Because of a lower preference for intimacy, individuals with an avoidant attachment style make fewer phone calls and send fewer text messages to their romantic partners.[25] They are also less likely to reach out for help to improve troubled relationships.[26] About 25 percent of the population fits this attachment style profile.[27]

avoidant attachment style
The style of relating to others that is characteristic of those who consistently experience discomfort and awkwardness in intimate relationships and who therefore avoid such relationships.

Your concept of yourself as someone who enjoys strong emotional connections with other people, or as someone who is anxious about or avoids relational intimacy, is thus influenced by the degree of attachment you felt during your formative years. One study found that when wives with anxious attachment styles were married to husbands with avoidant styles, these couples experienced more stress during times of marital conflict, as evidenced by their physiological responses to conflict.[28] You should neither blame nor congratulate your parents for *everything* about the way you relate to people today. But research suggests that early relationship connections with our parents do influence the way we relate to others.

ASSOCIATIONS WITH GROUPS   Reflect once more on your responses to the "Who are you?" question. How many responses associate you with a group? Religious, political, ethnic, social, study, occupational, and professional groups play important roles in determining your self-concept. Some of these groups you are born into; others you choose on your own. Either way, these group associations are significant parts of your identity.

Associating with groups is especially important for people who are not part of the dominant culture. Gays and lesbians, for example, find the support provided by associating with other gays and lesbians to be beneficial to their well-being. The groups you associate with provide not only information about your identity, but also needed social support.

ROLES YOU ASSUME   Look again at your answers to the "Who are you?" question. Perhaps you see words or phrases that signify a role you often assume. Father, aunt, sister, uncle, manager, salesperson, teacher, and student are labels that imply certain expectations for behavior, and they are important in shaping self-concept. Couples who live together before they marry often report that marriage alters their relationship. Before, they may have shared domestic duties such as doing dishes and laundry. But when they assume the labels of "husband" and "wife," they slip into traditional roles. Husbands don't do laundry. Wives don't mow the grass. These stereotypical gender role expectations learned long ago may require extensive discussion and negotiation. Couples who report the highest satisfaction with marriage agree on their expectations regarding roles ("We agree that I'll do laundry and you'll mow the grass").[29]

#communicationandtechnology

Comparing Your "Cyber Self" and Your "Realspace Self"

Perhaps you've heard the saying, "We are what we eat." New research provides another perspective: "We are what we blog." Researchers have found they can accurately identify our presentation of self by analyzing our blog entries, tweets, and Facebook posts.[30] But does your online presentation of yourself differ from your face-to-face presentation of self? Do you try to enhance your **electronically mediated communication (EMC)** "face" in ways that differ from the techniques you use when communicating face to face? The ease and prevalence of EMC have spurred communication researchers to investigate these and other questions about how we present ourselves online.[31]

What Are Key Differences Between "Online Self" and "Offline Self"?

Communication researchers Lisa Tidwell and Joseph Walther found that when people communicate via e-mail, they perceive themselves and others to be more "conversationally effective" because they exchange information more directly with each other. Perhaps people perceive their online communication as more effective because they can edit and revise what they write before sending it or posting it. E-mail conversation partners report feeling more confident when communicating online than in their face-to-face encounters.[32] Research also suggests that we are more likely to self-disclose information online than in face-to-face situations.[33] In addition, highly socially skilled individuals may use online communication channels less, while less communication-competent individuals may be more likely to use the Internet to meet their relational goals.[34]

How Honest Are We in Cyberspace?

We are likely to be less truthful about ourselves online than face-to-face. Two Internet researchers found strong evidence that people are much more likely to misrepresent themselves in cyberspace than in "realspace" relationships. As we noted in Chapter 1, we're more likely to lie about our age, weight, and personal appearance when communicating online.[35]

What's the Overall Tone and Quality of Our Cyberspace Relationships?

Research participants report that their face-to-face relationships are more serious in tone than their exclusively online relationships.[36] But we also work at keeping our online relationships strong by responding to Friends' posts, sending birthday greetings, and offering words of support.[37]

How Does Communication in Cyberspace Influence Our Sense of "Self"?

Our sense of self is influenced by the amount, kind, and quality of relationships we develop with people online. Canadian psychologist M. Kyle Matsuba found that the more clear college students are about their own identity (self-concept), the less likely they are to develop online relationships.[38] (Note that this phenomenon is a correlation rather than a cause-and-effect relationship.) Perhaps if we are not totally certain about who we are, we develop relationships with others online to help explore aspects of ourselves. Matsuba also found a strong correlation between being a heavy user of the Internet and reporting greater feelings of loneliness. (Again, he found a correlation rather than a cause-and-effect link; Internet use doesn't cause loneliness, but more people who feel lonely may use the Internet to connect with others.) Those of us who are generally apprehensive about communicating with others in realspace are also less likely to spend time on Facebook.[39] Another study found that the more narcissistic (self-centered) we are, the more likely we are to have more Facebook friends and to spend more time on Facebook and Twitter.[40]

Because we can control our online persona more readily than our realspace presentation of self, we're more confident about what we're saying about ourselves online. The Internet, which offers the opportunity to develop many relationships with others quickly and efficiently, especially on social networking sites, can help us explore facets of ourselves and clarify our self-concept.

---

electronically mediated communication (EMC)
Messages that are sent via some electronic channel such as the phone, e-mail, text, or the Internet.

One reason we assume traditional roles automatically is that our gender group asserts a powerful influence from birth on. As soon as parents know the sex of their children, many begin placing them in that gender group by following cultural rules. They paint the nursery pink for a girl, blue for a boy. Boys get catcher's mitts, train sets, or footballs for their birthdays; girls get dolls, frilly dresses, and tea sets. These cultural conventions and expectations play a major role in shaping our self-concept and behavior.

Although American culture is changing, it is still male-dominated. What we consider appropriate and inappropriate behavior is often different for males and for females. For example, in group and team meetings, task-oriented, male-dominated roles are valued more than relationship-building roles.[41] Some may applaud fathers who work sixty hours a week as diligent and hard-working but criticize mothers who do the same as neglectful and selfish.

Although our culture defines certain roles as masculine or feminine, we still exercise individual choices about our gender roles. One researcher developed an inventory designed to assess whether we play traditional masculine, feminine, or androgynous roles.[42] Because an **androgynous role** is both masculine and feminine, such a role encompasses a greater repertoire of actions and behaviors.

SELF-LABELS Although our self-concept is deeply affected by others, we are not blank slates for them to write on. Our own attitudes, beliefs, values, and actions also play a role in shaping our self-concept, as do our experiences. We interpret what we experience; we are self-reflexive. **Self-reflexiveness** is the human ability to be objectively self-aware—to think about what we are doing while we are doing it. We talk to ourselves about ourselves. We are both participants and observers in all that we do. This dual role encourages us to use labels to describe who we are.

When you were younger, perhaps you dreamed of becoming an all-star basketball player. Your coach may have told you that you were a great player, but as you matured, you probably began observing yourself more critically. You scored few points. So you self-reflexively decided that you were not, deep down, a basketball player, even though others may have labeled you as "talented." But through such self-observation, people sometimes discover strengths that encourage them to assume new labels. One woman we know never thought of herself as "heroic" until she went through seventy-two hours of labor before giving birth!

YOUR PERSONALITY AND BIOLOGY The concept of personality is central to **psychology**, the study of how your thinking and emotional responses influence the way you behave. According to psychologist Lester Lefton, your **personality** consists of a set of enduring behavioral characteristics and internal predispositions for reacting to your environment.[43] Understanding the forces that shape your personality is central to increasing your awareness of your self-concept and the way you relate to others.

Although numerous personality types have been described in research literature over several decades, psychologists today suggest that there are just five major personality traits. These **Big Five Personality Traits** include (1) extraversion, (2) agreeableness, (3) conscientiousness, (4) neuroticism, and (5) openness. Here's a brief summary of each:

> **Extraversion**: Outgoing, talkative, positive, and sociable
> **Agreeableness**: Friendly, compassionate, trusting, and cooperative
> **Conscientiousness**: Efficient, organized, self-disciplined, dutiful, and methodical
> **Neuroticism**: Nervous, insecure, emotionally distressed, and anxious
> **Openness**: Curious, imaginative, creative, adventurous, and inventive

According to psychologists, the combination of these five traits that you possess composes your overall personality.[44] Evidence suggests that your personality influences not only how you communicate in face-to-face situations but also how you relate to others on Facebook. If it is important for you to be liked by others, you will use Facebook to help achieve that goal.[45]

What shapes your personality? Are you *born* with the personality you have or do you *learn* behaviors by observing others? In other words, does nature or nurture play the predominant role in your personality? A growing body of research on what is called the **communibiological approach** to communication suggests that a major factor affecting how people communicate with others is their genetic makeup—their biology.[46] For example, perhaps someone you know was born an introvert—always

In American culture, behavior among girls is in many ways quite distinct from that among boys.

androgynous role
Gender role that includes both masculine and feminine qualities.

self-reflexiveness
Ability to think about what you are doing while you are doing it.

psychology
The study of how a person's thinking and emotional responses influence their behavior.

personality
A set of enduring behavioral characteristics and internal predispositions for reacting to your environment.

Big Five Personality Traits
Five personality traits that psychologists describe as constituting the major attributes of one's personality: extraversion, agreeableness, conscientiousness, neuroticism, and openness.

extraversion
A personality trait describing someone as outgoing, talkative, positive, and sociable.

agreeableness
A personality trait describing someone as friendly, compassionate, trusting, and cooperative.

conscientiousness
A personality trait describing someone as efficient, organized, self-disciplined, dutiful, and methodical.

neuroticism

A personality trait describing someone as nervous, insecure, emotionally distressed, and anxious.

openness

A personality trait describing someone as curious, imaginative, creative, adventurous, and inventive.

communibiological approach

Perspective that suggests that genetic and biological influences play a major role in influencing communication behavior.

social learning theory

A theory that suggests people can learn behavior that helps them adapt and adjust their behavior toward others.

shyness

A behavioral tendency not to talk or interact with others.

shy—and thus has more stage fright or anxiety when communicating with others.[47] In terms of the Big Five Personality Traits, he or she may have been born with a higher tendency toward neuroticism and is introverted (less likely to talk to others and more apt to gain energy from being alone) rather than extraverted. Other people, for as long as you have known them, just seem to be outgoing, ever cheerful, and open.

Although it's true that genes influence our communication behavior, proponents of **social learning theory** suggest that we can learn how to adapt and adjust our behavior toward others;[48] the way we behave is not solely dependent on our genetic makeup. By observing and interacting with others (hence the term *social learning*), we discover ways to change our behavior[49] and learn to enhance our interpersonal communication skills.

Some people just don't like to talk with others.[50] We may say such a person is shy. **Shyness** is the behavioral tendency to not talk with others. One study found that about 40 percent of adults reported they were shy.[51] In public-speaking situations, we say a person has stage fright; a better term to describe this feeling is **communication apprehension**, which according to James McCroskey and Virginia Richmond is "the fear or anxiety associated with either real or anticipated communication with another person or persons."[52] One study found that up to 80 percent of the population experience some degree of nervousness or apprehension when they speak in public.[53] Another study found that about 20 percent of people feel considerably anxious when they give a speech.[54]

Communication and Emotion

Self and Emotion: How We Influence How We Feel

In Chapter 1, we define an emotion as a biological, cognitive, behavioral, and subjective affective reaction to an event. Emotions are reactions to what we experience. What continues to be debated is the specific sequence of events that results in an emotional response. Are we in control of our emotions, or do our emotions control us? We present three different theories that describe the chain of events that cause us to experience emotions.

Commonsense Theory of Emotion: Emotions Happen

The commonsense approach is so named because it seems to describe the way many people would explain how emotions occur. The commonsense theory, shown in Figure 2.2, suggests the following order of emotional experience: (1) Something happens, (2) you have an affective (that is, an emotional) reaction to the event (you feel sad or happy), and finally, (3) you respond physiologically by blushing, experiencing an increased heart rate, or having another biological reaction to your emotion.[55] Here's an example: (1) You meet your new boss for the first time, (2) you feel nervous, and (3) your heart rate increases and you begin

to perspire. This sequence is typically the way many people think about emotions occurring—emotions just happen, and we really have no choice in how we feel. But there are other theories about what causes emotions.

James-Lange Theory of Emotion: Physiological Response Determines Emotional Response

Another theory of emotion, developed by psychologists William James and Carl Lange, is called the James-Lange theory of emotion.[56] Note the difference in the sequence of events in this theory in Figure 2.3: (1) Something happens, (2) you respond physiologically, and then (3) you experience an emotion. This theory suggests that we respond physiologically *before* we experience an emotion. The physiological responses tell us whether or not to experience an emotion. When you meet your new boss, you begin to perspire, and your heart starts beating more rapidly; this, in turn, *causes* you to feel nervous.

Figure 2.2 Commonsense Theory of Emotion

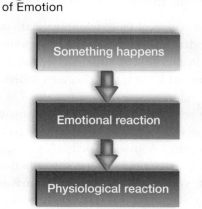

Figure 2.3 James-Lange Theory of Emotion

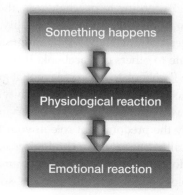

Appraisal Theory of Emotion: Labels Determine What Emotions Are Experienced

Yet a third view suggests that you are more in control of your emotions than you might think. You can change the emotion you are feeling by the way you decide to label or describe your experiences to yourself. This theory is called the *appraisal theory*, which means we appraise and label what we feel; the labels we use to describe what we experience have a major effect on what we feel as an emotional response.[57] Here's the suspected sequence according to this theory: (1) Something happens, (2) you respond physiologically, (3) you decide how you will react to what is happening to you, and then (4) you experience the emotion. (See Figure 2.4.) Do you see the difference in this last approach? *It suggests that you*

have control over how you feel, based in part on what you tell yourself about what you are experiencing.

According to the appraisal theory of emotion, you actively participate in determining what emotion you'll feel by labeling your experiences. For example, (1) you meet your new boss, (2) your heart rate increases and you start to perspire, (3) you tell yourself that this is an important and fear-inducing event, so (4) you feel nervous and anxious. Or you could tell yourself, "This is no big deal" and not feel nervous but enjoy the conversation with your new boss.

Although researchers continue to debate precisely how events trigger our emotions, we know that our emotional reaction to what we experience has a profound impact on how we relate to others.

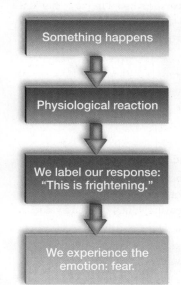

Figure 2.4 Appraisal Theory of Emotion

What makes some people apprehensive about communicating with others? Again, we get back to the nature–nurture issue. Heredity plays an important role in whether you are going to feel nervous or anxious when communicating with someone else. But your childhood experiences, such as whether you were reinforced for talking at a young age, also play an important role. Your overall **willingness to communicate** with others is a general way of summarizing the likelihood that you will talk with others in a variety of situations. If you are unwilling to communicate with others, you will be less comfortable in a career such as sales or customer service that forces you to interact with other people.

Understanding your overall comfort level in communicating with others as well as your interactions with individuals and groups, the roles you assume, your self-labels, your personality, and your biology can help you understand who you are and why you interact (or don't interact) with others. But it's not only who you are that influences your communication; it's also your overall sense of self-esteem or self-worth.

communication apprehension

Fear or anxiety associated with either real or anticipated communication with other people.

willingness to communicate

A behavioral trait that describes a person's comfortableness with and likelihood of initiating communication with other people.

Self-Esteem: Your Self-Worth

2.2 Define self-esteem and compare and contrast self-esteem with self-concept.

Your self-esteem is closely related to your self-concept. Your self-concept is a *description* of who you are. Your self-esteem is an *evaluation* of who you are. The term **self-worth** is often used interchangeably with *self-esteem.* Your overall feeling of self-worth is related to feeling and expressing positive messages toward others as well as being supportive of other people.[58] You feel better about yourself if you behave in ways that researchers call being *prosocial,* which means your behaviors benefit others. Research has also found a positive relationship between high self-esteem and happiness.[59] Although having high self-esteem doesn't mean you'll perform better in school or be more likely to be a leader, people with high self-esteem tend to speak up more in groups and share information with others.[60]

self-worth (self-esteem)

Your evaluation of your worth or value based on your perception of such things as your skills, abilities, talents, and appearance.

self-efficacy
A person's belief in his or her ability to perform a specific task in a particular situation.

Another term related to your sense of self-esteem and self-worth is the concept of **self-efficacy**. Researcher Albert Bandura suggests that self-efficacy is *your own belief* in your ability to perform a specific task in a particular situation.[61] If you believe you are a good karaoke singer, when it comes to belting out a song, you have high self-efficacy about karaoke singing. Your self-efficacy affects what you do and what you avoid. If you think you are good at karaoke singing, you will be more likely to step up to the microphone when the karaoke machine starts playing. Research offers additional evidence that you tend to do what you think you're good at: If you have high self-efficacy in sending and receiving text messages, you will be more likely to send frequent text messages.[62]

social comparison
Process of comparing yourself to others who are similar to you, to measure your worth and value.

People derive their sense of self-worth from comparing themselves to others, a process called **social comparison**. Social comparison helps people measure how well they think they are doing compared to others. I'm good at playing soccer (because I beat others); I can't cook (because others cook better than I do); I'm not good at meeting people (most people I know seem to be more comfortable interacting with others); I'm not handy (but my brothers and sisters can fix a leaky faucet). Each of these statements implies a judgment about how well or badly you can perform certain tasks, with implied references to how well others perform the same tasks. A belief that you cannot fix a leaky faucet or cook like a chef may not in itself lower your self-esteem. But if there are *several* things you can't do well or *many* important tasks that you cannot seem to master, these shortcomings may begin to color your overall sense of worth. At times you may need to be reminded that your value as a human being is not equivalent to your cooking ability, your grade-point average, or the kinds of clothes you wear. Your self-worth is more precious than money, grades, or fashion.

life position
Feelings of regard for self and others, as reflected in one's sense of worth and self-esteem.

Whether you base your self-esteem on others' perceptions of you or on your own self-perception, your self-esteem influences how you respond to feedback, especially criticism and negative feedback. One research team found that if your self-esteem is heavily influenced by what others think of you and you have a high need for approval, even a small amount of criticism is likely to further erode your self-esteem.[63] And, after receiving negative comments and criticism, subjects with low self-esteem found they wanted to take steps to increase their physical attractiveness (such as losing weight or buying a new wardrobe). Thus the source of our self-esteem, whether based on others or on our own interpretations of our behavior, influences how we respond to feedback. Evidence also suggests that we sometimes overinflate our importance and skills—especially our communication skill. It's called the self-efficacy bias: We think we are better than we are. One study found that most of us believe we are better at accurately communicating messages to people than we actually are.[64]

In the 1960s, psychologist Eric Berne developed the concept of a **life position** to describe people's overall sense of their own worth and that of others.[65] He identified four life positions: (1) "I'm OK, you're OK," or

"My self-esteem was so low I just followed her around everywhere she would go."

Bruce Eric Kaplan/The New Yorker Collection/The Cartoon Bank positive regard for self and others; (2) "I'm OK, you're not OK," or positive regard for self and low regard for others; (3) "I'm not OK, you're OK," or low self-regard and positive regard for others; and (4) "I'm not OK, you're not OK," or low regard for both self and others. Your life position is a driving force in your relationships with others. People in the "I'm OK, you're OK" position have the best chance for healthy relationships because they have discovered their own talents and also recognize that others have been given different talents.

Facework: Presenting Your Self-Image to Others

2.3 Define facework and discuss how you project your face and protect others' face.

Your face is important to you. Several times a day you may catch a fleeting glimpse of yourself as you pass a mirror or purposefully check to make sure you are looking your best. Your face is a focal point of your self-image. In addition, such common expressions as "in your face" or communicating "face-to-face" confirm that the face is a key part of everyone's identity. But *face* can refer to more than just the eyes, nose, and mouth. The aptly named Facebook is an important forum for many people to carefully (and sometimes not so carefully) craft and maintain their public face. Facebook can be especially important when people form early impressions of you or when you meet new people. For example, one research team found that students who transition from high school to college use Facebook to help maintain their public face with their "old" friends, while also presenting their "new face" to college friends.[66]

As a concept of interpersonal communication, **face** is an image of yourself you present to others for acceptance and confirmation.[67] A related term, **facework**, refers to using communication to maintain your own self-image and to seek approval of your face (your positive perception of who you are from others); you are also engaged in facework when you support, reinforce, or challenge someone else's face (or self-perception).

Projecting Your Face

The concept of *face* may have originated with the ancient Chinese, or perhaps the Chinese merely named a process that is a characteristic of being human. Like most people, you probably spend considerable effort projecting a **positive face**—a positive image of yourself to others. Most people want to be perceived as competent, respected, and valued. We also want to be included and connected to others. Facework helps us achieve these goals.[68]

You are using positive facework, for example, when you announce to your parents or friends that you made the dean's list during the recent college semester. By telling them the good news about your academic success, you're using communication to maintain a positive image of yourself and thus reinforce your own positive self-image. You are also using positive facework when you post flattering pictures of yourself on Facebook after you lose ten pounds. Even when the pounds find you again, you keep your "skinny picture" as your profile photo.

You use **preventative facework** to avoid developing a negative impression of yourself; in fact, you actively work to maintain and enhance your positive perception of yourself. For example, if you think you may be late for a meeting, you tell a

face
A person's positive perception of himself or herself in interactions with others.

facework
Using communication to maintain your own positive self-perception or to support, reinforce, or challenge someone else's self-perception.

positive face
An image of yourself that will be perceived as positive by others.

preventative facework
Efforts to maintain and enhance one's positive self-perceptions.

corrective facework

Efforts to correct what one perceives as a negative perception of oneself on the part of others.

coworker, "If I'm late, it's because of the heavy rush-hour traffic." Even before the event, you're trying to save face.

You engage in **corrective facework** when you "save face" by correcting what others may perceive as a negative perception of you, as when you might say, "Oh, I'm sorry I was late. I got stuck in heavy traffic."[69] Sociologist Erving Goffman suggests that saving face—a metaphor for instilling a positive perception of yourself in others—is important for most people.[70] The effort you expend to save face reflects the kind of perception you want others to have of you.

You are likely to feel embarrassed when you perceive that the face you'd like to project to others has been threatened or discredited, because of either something you did or something someone else initiated.[71] Research suggests that one response to embarrassment is simply not knowing what to say. Following an awkward silence, we may engage in facework to "save face" by apologizing, denying that the event occurred, lying, or using humor or other behaviors to distract from the embarrassing behavior that occurred.

What are strategies for projecting a positive face? One of the best ways is to simply be mindful of what you do to communicate positive information about yourself. Monitor how you talk to others, and consider the needs and expectations of others (be other-oriented) as you interact with them. In addition, make sure your words are consistent with your actions. If you tell your family that you're getting good grades, but your final grades don't correspond to your story, it's your actions, not your words, they will believe. Facebook and other social media applications are especially helpful in maintaining our self-image and presenting a positive face to our friends. Research suggests that women are more likely to use social media to maintain positive relationships online than men.[72]

Another way people save face is by purposefully manipulating how others perceive them. We can be deceitful and not reveal the complete truth to make ourselves "look good." Research has found that we are deceitful almost 25 percent of the time when we communicate about ourselves to others; we actively work to project a positive face but sometimes bend the truth a bit. This statistic has been found to be true whether we're communicating face-to-face, on the phone, or while sending e-mail or text messages.

Projecting a positive image of yourself—positive face—means being mindful of how you talk to and interact with others.

Others, not just you, will assess whether you have a positive image. By observing what others value, you can decide whether you want to conform to their expectations. This is always a delicate balance. If you know, for example, that your friend likes people to dress up when dining in a restaurant, you can accommodate your friend by dressing more formally than you typically do. We're not suggesting that you should *always* conform to the expectations of others, only that you should be aware of their expectations so that you can make a mindful decision about whether you will adapt to them.

Protecting Others' Face

Communication researchers Kathy Domenici and Stephen Littlejohn suggest several things you can do to actively help others maintain a positive face.[73] Underlying each of their prescriptions is the value of being other-oriented. For example, you can honor others by addressing them as they wish to be addressed. Some of your teachers want to be called "doctor" if they have a doctoral degree or "professor" if they hold that academic rank. Yet others may say, "Call me Steve."

Being polite is another way of enhancing the face of others. Saying "please," "thank you," or "excuse me" are common courtesies valued in virtually every culture. Being generous and supportive are other ways you enhance the face of others. Spending time with someone who enjoys your company, offering positive and affirming messages to the person, and interacting in appropriately attentive and supportive ways help to build face. An other-oriented communicator considers what the other person would like.

You engage in **face-threatening acts** when you communicate in a way that undermines or challenges someone's positive face.[74] You may not intend for something you say or do to threaten someone else's face (like posting on your Facebook page an unflattering photo of a friend that you found funny, but your friend, who is looking for a job at the moment, did not), but any interaction has the potential to be face-threatening to them. It's the other person, not you, who determines whether a statement or behavior is face-threatening. Being aware of how you may threaten someone's face can help you develop greater sensitivity toward others.

Social psychologists Penelope Brown and Stephen Levinson suggest that people from all cultures have a universal need to be treated politely.[75] Brown and Levinson developed **politeness theory**, which suggests not only that people have a tendency to promote a positive image of themselves (a positive face) but also that people will have a positive perception of others who treat them politely and respectfully. Politeness theory makes intuitive sense. Although people from different cultures have varying levels of need to be treated politely, what seems clear is that everyone wants to be valued and appreciated. Offering compliments, behaving respectfully, and showing concern for others are all ways of using politeness to help others project a positive face.

According to politeness theory, when we have a negative message to communicate, we make a choice regarding how much we threaten someone else's face. The statements in the following list are arranged from most face-threatening to least face-threatening.

1. Bluntly communicating a negative message: "Your office is a mess."
2. Delivering the negative message but also communicating a face-saving message: "Your office is a mess, but perhaps messy is the look you want."
3. Delivering the negative message but offering a counter-explanation to help the person save face: "Your office is a mess, but that's understandable, given how much work you do around here."
4. Communicating the negative message but doing so "off the record" or in such an indirect way that the other person saves face: "I'm not supposed to tell you this, but even though your office is a mess, the boss is impressed with how well you seem to find everything."
5. Finally, not communicating any message that would cause someone to lose face.

When someone threatens your face ("Because you were late to the meeting, I missed picking my daughter up from school"), you have choices to make. You can respond by defending yourself or by denying what the other person has said ("No, I wasn't late to the meeting yesterday"), or you can offer an explanation, an excuse, or an apology ("I'm so sorry. The elevator was broken so I had to walk up the stairs"). Or, by simply saying and doing nothing, you can communicate a range of responses. As researchers Dominici and Littlejohn suggest, being silent can mean (1) I'm thinking about what you said, (2) I'm ignoring what you said because it's not worth my time or effort, or (3) I'm simply not going to respond in kind to the way you've treated me.[76] The effort you expend to save face (to protect your positive image) reflects the kind of perception you want others to have of you. The more effort you expend to protect your face, the more you want others to have a positive perception of you.

face-threatening acts
Communication that undermines or challenges someone's positive face.

politeness theory
Theory that people have positive perceptions of others who treat them politely and respectfully.

BEING Other-ORIENTED
You have been taught from an early age to tell the truth and not tell lies. Yet, as research suggests, we often "bend the truth" to save face ("I studied until two in the morning") or to protect someone else's face ("Oh, yes, those jeans make you look much slimmer"). Is it really necessary to lie to others to protect their face? Is it other-oriented or simply deceitful to not tell the truth in order to protect others' face?

How to Improve Your Self-Esteem

2.4 Identify and describe seven strategies for improving your self-concept.

We have mentioned that low self-esteem can affect our own communication and interactions. In recent years, teachers, psychologists, ministers, rabbis, social workers, and even politicians have suggested that many societal problems stem from collective feelings of low self-esteem. Feelings of low self-worth may contribute to choosing the wrong partner; to becoming dependent on drugs, alcohol, or other substances; or to experiencing problems with eating or other vital activities. So people owe it to society, as well as to themselves, to maintain or develop a healthy self-esteem.

Although no simple list of tricks can easily transform low self-esteem into feelings of being valued and appreciated, you can improve how you think about yourself and interact with others. We'll explore seven proven techniques that have helped others.

Engage in Self-Talk

Just before she performs, singer Barbra Streisand, who gets extremely nervous singing in public when she can see people's faces, tells herself, "I can do this."[77] Both TV broadcaster Jane Pauley and on-air psychologist Dr. Phil McGraw describe themselves as somewhat shy and give themselves a mental message of encouragement before a broadcast.[78] Just like these well-known personalities, you, too, can use positive self-talk—reminding yourself that you have the necessary skills and ability to perform a task—to boost your confidence and improve your self-esteem.

Intrapersonal communication is communication within yourself—self-talk. Realistic, positive self-talk can have a reassuring effect on your level of self-worth and on your interactions with others.[79] Conversely, repeating negative messages about your lack of skill and ability can keep you from trying and achieving. If you think of yourself as apprehensive and unlikely to communicate well with others, these thoughts will likely influence your behavior—you will be less inclined to select a career that involves frequent communication with others. This behavior in turn will likely reinforce negative thinking that you are not a good speaker. Your thoughts affect your behavior, which then reinforces your thoughts. To break that cycle means changing your thoughts, altering your behavior, or both. But it's not always that simple: If you are by nature apprehensive or shy, then it will be more challenging to change your thoughts and behavior to become more outgoing.

Of course, blind faith without hard work won't succeed. Self-talk is not a substitute for effort; it can, however, keep you on track and help you ultimately to achieve your goal.

Visualize a Positive Image of Yourself

Visualization takes the notion of self-talk one step further. Besides just telling yourself that you can achieve your goal, you can actually try to "see" yourself conversing effectively with others, performing well on a project, or exhibiting some other desirable behavior. Being able to visualize completing a goal (thinking positively rather than thinking you won't achieve your goal) adds to your overall sense of happiness and well-being.[80] Recent research suggests that an apprehensive public speaker can manage his or her fears not only by developing skill in public speaking, but also by visualizing positive results when speaking to an audience.[81] The same technique can be used to boost your sense of self-worth about other tasks or skills. If, for example, you tend to get nervous when meeting people at a party, imagine yourself in a room

Although positive self-talk will never be able to make all of us become champion athletes, it can help us focus on our own goals and improve our performance levels.

intrapersonal communication
Communication within yourself; self-talk.

visualization
Technique of imagining that you are performing a particular task in a certain way; positive visualization can enhance self-esteem.

full of people, glibly introducing yourself to others with ease. Visualizing yourself performing well can yield positive results in changing long-standing feelings of inadequacy. Of course, your visualization should be realistic and coupled with a plan to achieve your goal.

Avoid Comparing Yourself with Others

Throughout our lives, we are compared with others. Rather than celebrating our uniqueness, these comparisons usually point up who is stronger, brighter, or more beautiful. Many of us have had the experience of being selected last to play on a sports team, being passed over for promotion, or standing unchosen against the wall at a dance. In North American culture, we may be tempted to compare our material possessions and personal appearance with those of others. If we know someone who has a newer car (or simply a car, if we rely on public transportation), a smaller waistline, or a higher grade point average, we may feel diminished. Comparisons such as "He has more money than I have" or "She looks better than I look" are likely to deflate our self-worth.

It's unrealistic to expect that you will *never* compare yourself to others. But you can be more mindful of how your comparisons may influence your self-esteem and learn not to rely on such comparisons to determine your own self-worth. Focus on the unique attributes that make you who you are.

Reframe Appropriately

Reframing is the process of redefining events and experiences from a different point of view. Just as reframing a work of art can give the picture a whole new look, reframing events that cause you to devalue your self-worth can change your perspective. For example, if you get a report from your supervisor that says you should improve one area of your performance, instead of listening to the negative self-talk saying you're bad at your job, reframe the event within a larger context: Tell yourself that one negative comment does not mean you are a hopeless employee.

Of course, not all negative experiences should be tossed away and left unexamined, because you can learn and profit from your mistakes. But it is important to remember that your worth as a human being does not depend on a single exam grade, a single response from a prospective employer, or a single play in a football game.

reframing
Process of redefining events and experiences from a different point of view.

Develop Honest Relationships

Having at least one other person who can help you objectively and honestly reflect on your virtues and vices can be extremely beneficial in fostering a healthy, positive self-image. A parent, spouse, mentor, or close friend who gives you honest feedback when you need it can help you determine when you need to work on specific ways to improve yourself. As we noted earlier, other people play a major role in shaping your self-concept and self-esteem. The more credible the source of information, the more likely you are to believe it. Later in the chapter, we discuss how honest relationships are developed through the process of self-disclosure. Honest, positive support can provide encouragement for a lifetime.

Let Go of the Past

Your self-concept was not implanted at birth to remain constant for the rest of your life. Things change. You change. Others change. Individuals with low self-esteem may be fixating on events and experiences that happened years ago and tenaciously refusing to let go of them. Perhaps you've heard religious and spiritual leaders say that it's important to forgive others who have hurt you in the past. Research also suggests it's important to your own mental health and sense of well-being to let go of old wounds and forgive others.[82] Someone once wrote, "The lightning bug is brilliant, but it hasn't much of a mind; it blunders through existence with its headlight on behind." Looking back at what we can't change only reinforces a sense of helplessness. Constantly replaying negative experiences in our mind makes our sense of worth more difficult to change. Becoming aware of the changes that have occurred and can occur in your life can help you develop a more realistic assessment of your value. Look past your past.

Seek Support

social support

Expression of empathy and concern for others that is communicated while listening to them and offering positive and encouraging words.

talk therapy

Technique in which a person describes his or her problems and concerns to a skilled listener in order to better understand the emotions and issues creating the problems.

You provide **social support** when you express care and concern as well as listen and empathize with others. Perhaps you just call it "talking with a friend." Having someone who will be socially supportive is especially important when we experience stress and anxiety or are faced with a vexing personal problem.[83] One study found that hearing positive, supportive messages from a friend is among the most helpful ways to restore self-esteem.[84] That support does not necessarily need to be received in a face-to-face conversation. Research has also found that seeking online support from others is an effective strategy to confirm and reinforce us.[85]

Social support from a friend or family member can be helpful, but some of your self-image problems may be so ingrained that you may need professional help. A trained counselor, clergy member, or therapist can help you sort through these problems. The technique of having a trained person listen as you verbalize your fears, hopes, and concerns is called **talk therapy**. You talk, and a skilled listener helps you sort out your feelings and problems. There is power in being able to put your emotions and thoughts, especially your negative thoughts, into words. By saying things out loud to an open, honest, empathic listener, we gain insight and can sometimes figure out why we experience the pain and difficulties that we do. If you are not sure to whom to turn for a referral, you can start with your school counseling services. Or, if you are near a medical-school teaching hospital, you can contact the counseling or psychotherapy office there for a referral.

Because you have spent your whole lifetime developing your self-esteem, it is not easy to make big changes. But talking through problems can make a difference. As communication researchers Frank E. X. Dance and Carl Larson see it, "Speech communication empowers each of us to share in the development of our own self-concept and the fulfillment of that self-concept."[86]

BEING Other-ORIENTED

We all need support and encouragement from others from time to time. When have other people helped you manage a difficult situation or period of your life? What are the qualities in others that you look for when you need social support? What talents and skills do you possess that will help you provide useful social support to others?

Recap

Strategies for Improving Your Self-Esteem

Engage in Self-Talk	If you're having a bad hair day, tell yourself that you have beautiful eyes and lots of friends who like you anyway.
Visualize	If you feel nervous before a meeting, visualize everyone in the room congratulating you on your great ideas.
Avoid Comparison	Focus on your positive qualities and on what you can do to enhance your own talents and abilities.
Reframe Appropriately	If you experience one failure, keep the larger picture in mind, rather than focusing on that isolated incident.
Develop Honest Relationships	Cultivate friends in whom you can confide and who will give you honest feedback about improving your skills and abilities.
Let Go of the Past	Talk yourself out of your old issues; focus on ways to enhance your abilities in the future.
Seek Support	Talk with professional counselors or find support online from friends who can help you identify your gifts and talents.

Self and Interpersonal Relationships

2.5 **Identify the effects of your self-concept and self-esteem on your relationships with others.**

Your self-concept and self-esteem filter every interaction with others. They determine how you approach, respond to, and interpret messages. Specifically, your self-concept and self-esteem affect your self-fulfilling prophecies, your interpretation of messages, your level of self-disclosure, your social needs, your typical communication style, and your ability to be sensitive to others.

Self and Interaction with Others

Your image of yourself and your sense of self-worth directly affect how you interact with others. Who you think you are affects how you communicate with other people.

We defined human communication as the way we make sense of the world and share that sense with others by creating meaning through verbal and nonverbal messages. **Symbolic interaction theory** is founded on the assumption that we make sense of the world through our interactions with others. At a basic level, we interpret what a word or symbol means based, in part, on how other people react to our use of that word or symbol. We learn, for example, that certain four-letter words have power because we see people react when they hear them. Even our understanding of who we think we are is influenced by what others tell us we are. For example, you may not think you're a good dancer, but after several friends compliment your dazzling dance moves, you start believing that you *do* have dancing talent. Central to understanding ourselves is realizing the importance of other people in shaping that self-understanding. Symbolic interaction theory has had a major influence on communication theory because of the pervasive way our communication with others influences our very sense of who we are.

George Herbert Mead is credited with the development of symbolic interaction theory, although Mead did not write extensively about his theory.[87] One of Mead's students, Herbert Blumer, actually coined the term *symbolic interaction* to describe the process through which our interactions influence our thoughts about others, our life experiences, and ourselves. Mead believed that we cannot have a self-identity without interactions with other people.

Because the influence of others on your life is so far reaching, it's sometimes hard to be consciously aware of how other people shape your thoughts. One of the ways to be more mindful of others' influence is to become increasingly other-oriented; this is essential for the development of quality relationships. Becoming other-oriented involves recognizing that your concept of self (who *you* think you are) is different from how others perceive you—even though it's influenced by others, as suggested by symbolic interaction theory. Mead suggests that we come to think of ourselves both as "I," based on our own perception of ourselves, and as "me," based on the collective responses we receive and interpret from others. Being aware of how your concept of self ("I") differs from the perceptions others have of you ("me") is an important first step in developing an other-orientation.

Although it may seem complicated, it's really quite simple: You affect others and others affect you. Your ability to predict how others will respond to you is based on your skill in understanding how your sense of the world is similar to and different from theirs. To enhance your skill in understanding this process, you need to know yourself well. But understanding yourself is only half the process; you also need to be other-oriented. One of the best ways to improve your ability to be other-oriented is to notice how others respond when you act on the predictions and assumptions you have made about them. If you assume that your friend, who is out of work and struggling to make ends meet, will like it if you pick up the check for lunch and she offers

symbolic interaction theory
Theory that people make sense of the world based on their interpretation of words or symbols used by others.

BEING Other-ORIENTED
By reflecting upon your past interactions with others, you may gain insights about whether you think of yourself as an "I"— an individual based primarily on your own self-generated thoughts—or a "me"—the reflection of how others see you. Think about the labels you give yourself and then consider: Are most of those labels self-generated (I messages) or do they come from others (*me* messages)? How powerful are others in influencing who you think you are?

BEING Other-ORIENTED
By becoming a detective, you can find clues in the behavior of others to determine if the assumptions you've made about them are accurate. Reflect on times when you have accurately identified the emotions of another person and compare those instances to other times when you weren't as accurate. What kinds of clues help you accurately predict others' moods and feelings?

You can increase your chances for success by having a positive mindset and high expectations of yourself and your abilities.

self-fulfilling prophecy
Prediction about future actions that is likely to come true because the person believes that it will come true.

an appreciative "Thank you so much," you have received confirmation that he or she appreciated your generosity and that your hunch about how your friend would react to your gesture was accurate.

Self and Your Future

What people believe about themselves often comes true because they expect it to happen. Their expectations become a **self-fulfilling prophecy**. If you think you will fail the math quiz because you have labeled yourself inept at math, then you must overcome not only your math deficiency, but also your low expectations of yourself. The theme of George Bernard Shaw's *Pygmalion* is "If you treat a girl like a flower girl, that's all she will ever be. If you treat her like a princess, she may be one." Research suggests that you can create your own obstacles to achieving your goals by being too critical of yourself.[88] Or you can increase your chances for success by having a more positive mindset.[89] Your attitudes, beliefs, and general expectations about your performance have a powerful and profound effect on your behavior.

The medical profession is learning the power that attitudes and expectations have for healing. Physician Howard Brody's research suggests that in many instances, just giving patients a placebo—a pill with no medicine in it—or telling patients that they have been operated on when they haven't had an operation can yield positive medical results. In his book *The Placebo Response*, Brody tells a story about a woman with debilitating Parkinson's disease who made a miraculous recovery after doctors told her that they had completed a medical procedure.[90] They hadn't. Yet before the "treatment," she could barely walk; now she can easily pace around the room. There is a clear link, suggests Dr. Brody, between mental state and physical health. Patients who believe they will improve are more likely to do so.

Self and Interpretation of Messages

Although it may have been many years since you've read A. A. Milne's classic children's stories about Winnie-the-Pooh, you probably remember his donkey friend Eeyore, who lives in the gloomiest part of the Hundred Acre Wood and has a self-image to match.[91]

Perhaps you know or have known an Eeyore—someone whose low self-esteem colors how he or she interprets messages and interacts with others. According to research, such people are more likely to[92]

- be more sensitive to criticism and negative feedback from others,
- be more critical of others,
- believe they are not popular or respected by others,
- expect to be rejected by others,
- prefer not to be observed while performing,
- feel threatened by people whom they feel are superior,
- expect to lose when competing with others,
- be overly responsive to praise and compliments, and
- evaluate their overall behavior as inferior to that of others.

The Pooh stories offer an antidote to Eeyore's gloom in the character of the optimistic Tigger, who assumes that everyone shares his exuberance for life.[93] If, like Tigger, your sense of self-worth is high, research suggests you will[94]

- have higher expectations for solving problems,
- think more highly of others,

- be more likely to accept praise and accolades from others without feeling embarrassed,
- be more comfortable having others observe you when you perform,
- be more likely to admit you have both strengths and weaknesses,
- prefer to interact with others who view themselves as highly competent,
- expect other people to accept you for who you are,
- be more likely to seek opportunities to improve skills that need improving, and
- evaluate your overall behavior more positively than would people with lower self-esteem.

Self and Interpersonal Needs

According to social psychologist Will Schutz, our concept of who we are, coupled with our need to interact with others, profoundly influences how we communicate with others. Schutz identifies three primary social needs that affect the degree of communication we have with others: the need for inclusion, the need for control, and the need for affection.[95]

INCLUSION Each of us has a **need for inclusion**—the desire to participate in activities with others and to experience human contact and fellowship. We need to be invited to join others. Of course, the level and intensity of this need differ from person to person, but even loners desire some social contact. Your personality and your genetic makeup, as discussed earlier, play a major role in your need for inclusion.

Not only do you have a need to be included, you also have a need to include others. Some people have a strong need to make sure no one is left out or that others are invited to social gatherings. Our need to include others and be included in activities may stem, in part, from our concept of ourselves as either a "party person" or a loner. Research has found that spending time on Facebook or other social media sites helps meet our need for inclusion.[96]

> **need for inclusion**
> Interpersonal need to be included and to include others in social activities.

CONTROL We also have a **need for control**. We need some degree of influence over the relationships we establish with others. Individuals with a high need for control are likely to seek leadership roles and generally be more directive in telling others what to do or how to behave. Again, your personality and your biology, as well as learned behaviors (as explained by the social learning theory), are factors that influence your need for control.

In addition to a need to control others, you may also have a need to *be* controlled because you desire some level of stability and comfort in your interactions with others. Sometimes you just want someone else to make the decisions; you don't want to be responsible or decide what to do. This need to be controlled is strong in some people, while others may prefer minimal control from others and resent being told what to do.

> **need for control**
> Interpersonal need for some degree of influence in our relationships, as well as the need to be controlled.

AFFECTION Finally, we each have a **need for affection**. We need to give and receive love, support, warmth, and intimacy, although the amounts we need vary enormously from person to person. Those individuals with a high need for affection seek compliments and are comfortable in relationships in which they feel highly supported, confirmed, and loved.[97]

And just as you have a need to receive affection, you also have a need to express affection toward others. Some people have a high need to express love and support, whereas others may have a low need to express affection.

The greater our interpersonal needs for inclusion, control, and affection, the more likely it is that we will actively seek others as friends and initiate communication with them.

> **need for affection**
> Interpersonal need to give and receive love, support, warmth, and intimacy.

Self and Disclosure to Others

self-disclosure

Purposefully providing information about yourself to others that they would not learn if you did not tell them.

When we interact with others, we reveal information about ourselves—we self-disclose. **Self-disclosure** occurs when we purposefully provide information to others about ourselves that they would not learn if we did not tell them. Self-disclosure ranges from revealing basic information about yourself, such as where you were born, to admitting your deepest fears and most private fantasies. Disclosing personal information not only provides a basis for another person to understand you better, it also conveys your level of trust and acceptance of the other person.

We are much more likely to self-disclose to someone whom we trust and feel close to, and we are less likely to self-disclose if we think we'll lose someone's respect and admiration.[98] When others self-disclose, you learn information about them and deepen your interpersonal relationships with them.[99] Another factor that has been found to influence the amount of self-disclosure is your overall mood. If you are feeling good about yourself and are in a positive mood, you are more likely to self-disclose. That's why someone who has consumed more alcohol than is advisable and is feeling mellow and "happy" (as well as having lowered inhibitions) may share more details about his or her life than you wish to hear. Someone who is sober and feeling less positive may be less likely to share intimate, personal information.[100]

We introduce the concept of self-disclosure in this chapter because it's an important element in helping us understand ourselves. If you have a Facebook profile, you may want to monitor your level of self-disclosure when posting photos and comments about your daily routine. Social media researcher Bradley Bond found that women are more likely to self-disclose more information on a wider range of topics on Facebook than men do.[101] Women are also "marginally more likely to report being sexually expressive on their profiles."[102] You might think that people self-disclose more on anonymous blogs. But researchers found a link between people who post a photo of themselves on their blogs and increased sharing of personal information.[103] Although social media apps such as Yik Yak provide a place for people to post anonymously, users of this app still tend to reveal very personal and frank comments about themselves and others. Because self-disclosure is the primary way we establish and maintain interpersonal relationships, we'll discuss self-disclosure in considerable detail in Chapter 9.

self-awareness

A person's conscious understanding of who he or she is.

In order to disclose personal information to others, you must first have **self-awareness**, an understanding of who you are. In addition to just thinking about who you are, asking others for information about yourself and then listening to what they tell you can enhance your self-awareness.

A variety of personality tests, such as the Myers-Briggs personality inventory, may give you additional insight into your interests, style, and ways of relating to others. Most colleges and universities have a career services office where you can take vocational aptitude tests to help you identify careers that fit who you are.

Johari Window model

Model of self-disclosure that summarizes how self-awareness is influenced by self-disclosure and information about yourself from others.

The **Johari Window model** nicely summarizes how your awareness of who you are is influenced by your own level of disclosure, as well as by how much information others share *about* you *with* you. (The name "Johari Window" sounds somewhat mystical and exotic, but it is simply a combination of the first names of the creators of the model, Joseph Luft and Harry Ingham.[104]) As Figure 2.5 shows, the model looks like a set of windows, and the windows represent your self. This self includes everything about you, including things even you don't yet see or realize. One axis is divided into what you have come to know about yourself and what you don't yet know about yourself. The other axis represents what someone else may know about you and not know about you. The intersection of these categories creates four windows, or quadrants.

OPEN: KNOWN TO SELF AND KNOWN TO OTHERS Quadrant 1 is an *open area.* The open area contains information that others know about you and that you are also aware of—such as your age, your occupation, and other things you might mention

Figure 2.5 Johari Window of Self-Disclosure

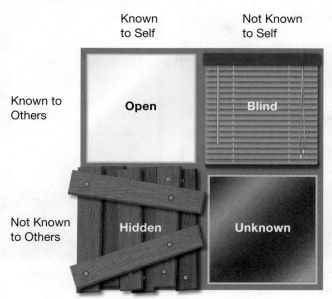

about yourself. At first glance, all four quadrants appear to be the same size. But that may not be the case (in fact, it probably isn't). In the case of quadrant 1, the more information that you reveal about yourself, the larger this quadrant will be. Put another way, the more you open up to others, the larger the open area will be.

BLIND: NOT KNOWN TO SELF BUT KNOWN TO OTHERS Quadrant 2 is a *blind area*. This window contains information that other people know about you, but that you do not know. Perhaps when you were in grade school, as a joke someone put a sign on your back that said, "Kick me." Everyone was aware of the sign but you. The blind window represents the same situation. For example, you may see yourself as generous, but others may see you as a tightwad. As you learn how others see you, the blind window gets smaller. Generally, the more accurately you know yourself and perceive how others see you, the better your chances are to establish open and honest relationships with others.

HIDDEN: KNOWN TO SELF BUT NOT KNOWN TO OTHERS Quadrant 3 is a *hidden area*. This area contains information that you know about yourself, but that others do not know about you. You can probably think of many facts, thoughts, feelings, and fantasies that you would not want anyone else to know. They may be feelings you have about another person or something you've done privately in the past that you'd be embarrassed to share with others. The point here is not to suggest you should share all information in the hidden area with others. However, it is useful to know that part of who you are is known by some people, but remains hidden from others.

UNKNOWN: NOT KNOWN TO SELF OR OTHERS Quadrant 4 is an *unknown area*. This area contains information that is unknown to both you and others. These are things you do not know about yourself *yet*. Perhaps you do not know how you will react under certain stressful situations. Maybe you are not sure what stand you will take on a certain issue next year or even next week. Other people may also not be aware of how you would respond or behave under certain conditions. Your personal potential, your untapped physical and mental resources, are unknown. You can assume that this area exists, because eventually some (though not necessarily all) of these things will become known to you, to others, or to both you and others. Because you can never know yourself completely, the unknown quadrant will always exist; you can only guess at its current size, because the information it contains is unavailable to you.

BEING Other-ORIENTED
Some things about ourselves we learn from others: elements of our personality (both positive and negative characteristics) and talents we have. What aspects of your personality or talents have you learned about from others but might not have known about if someone had not shared them with you? How have others helped you learn about yourself?

Figure 2.6 Variations on the Johari Window

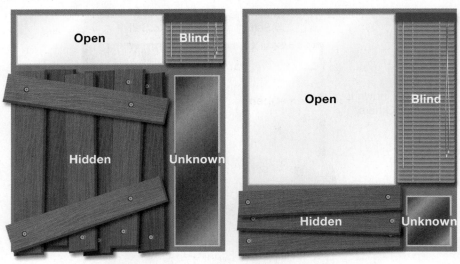

(A) A new relationship for someone who is very self-aware

(B) An intimate relationship

We can draw Johari Windows to represent each of our relationships (see Figure 2.6). Part A shows a new or restricted relationship for someone who knows himself or herself very well. The open and blind quadrants are small, but the unknown quadrant is also small. Part B shows a very intimate relationship, in which both individuals are open and disclosing.

Self and Communication Social Style

Over time we develop general patterns or styles of relating to others based on several factors, including our personality, self-concept, self-esteem, and what we choose to disclose to others. Our general style of relating to others is called our **communication social style**; it is an identifiable way of habitually communicating with others. The concept of communication social styles originates in the work of Carl Jung who, in his book *Psychological Types*, described people according to four types: thinkers, feelers, intuiters, and sensors.[105] (The Myers-Briggs personality inventory, which in part assesses ways of relating to others, is based on Jung's types.) Communication researchers built on Jung's pioneering work to identify communication social styles. The communication social style we develop helps others interpret our messages and predict how we will behave. As they get to know us, other people begin to expect us to communicate in a certain way, based on previous associations with us.[106]

According to communication researchers William Snavely and John McNeill, the notion of communication social style is based on four underlying assumptions about human behavior:

1. We develop consistent communication behavior patterns over time.
2. We form impressions of others based on their verbal and nonverbal behavior.
3. We interact with others based on our perceptions of them.
4. We develop our perceptions of others based primarily on two dimensions: assertiveness and responsiveness.[107]

A variety of different communication social style models have been developed during the past thirty years. Regardless of the specific model (some models describe four styles, others include just two), there is general agreement on the two

communication social style

An identifiable way of habitually communicating with others.

fundamental dimensions of assertiveness (which focuses on accomplishing a task) and responsiveness (which emphasizes concern for relationships) as anchoring elements in determining a person's social style.[108]

Assertiveness is the tendency to accomplish a task by making requests, asking for information, and generally looking out for one's own rights and best interests. An assertive style is sometimes called a "masculine" style. By masculine, we don't mean that only males can be assertive, but that in many cultures, males are expected to be assertive. You are assertive when you seek information if you are confused or direct others to help you get what you need.

Responsiveness is the tendency to focus on the dynamics of relationships with others by being sensitive to their needs. Being other-oriented and sympathetic to the feelings of others and placing others' feelings above your own are examples of being responsive. Researchers sometimes label responsiveness a "feminine" quality. Again, this does not mean that only women are or should be responsive, only that many cultures stereotype being responsive as a traditional and expected behavior of females.

To assess your style on the assertiveness and responsiveness dimensions, take the sociocommunicative orientation test by James McCroskey and Virginia Richmond in the Improving Your Communication Skills box. You may discover that you test higher on one dimension than on the other. It's also possible to be high on both or low on both.

Another way to identify your communication social style is to ask your friends, family members, and colleagues who know you best to help you assess your behavior by contributing their perceptions of you as assertive or nonassertive, responsive or nonresponsive.

assertiveness
Tendency to make requests, ask for information, and generally pursue one's own rights and best interests.

responsiveness
Tendency to be sensitive to the needs of others, including being sympathetic to others' feelings and placing the feelings of others above one's own feelings.

Improving Your Communication Skills

What's Your Communication Social Style?

Directions:

The following questionnaire lists twenty personality characteristics. Please indicate the degree to which you believe each of these characteristics applies to you, as you normally communicate with others, by marking whether you (5) strongly agree that it applies, (4) agree that it applies, (3) are undecided, (2) disagree that it applies, or (1) strongly disagree that it applies. There are no right or wrong answers. Work quickly; record your first impression.

- _____ **1.** helpful
- _____ **2.** defends own beliefs
- _____ **3.** independent
- _____ **4.** responsive to others
- _____ **5.** forceful
- _____ **6.** has strong personality
- _____ **7.** sympathetic
- _____ **8.** compassionate
- _____ **9.** assertive
- _____ **10.** sensitive to the needs of others

- _____ **11.** dominant
- _____ **12.** sincere
- _____ **13.** gentle
- _____ **14.** willing to take a stand
- _____ **15.** warm
- _____ **16.** tender
- _____ **17.** friendly
- _____ **18.** acts as a leader
- _____ **19.** aggressive
- _____ **20.** competitive

Scoring:

Items 2, 3, 5, 6, 9, 11, 14, 18, 19, and 20 measure assertiveness. Add the scores on these items to get your assertiveness score. Items 1, 4, 7, 8, 10, 12, 13, 15, 16, and 17 measure responsiveness. Add the scores on these items to get your responsiveness score. Scores range from 50 to 10. The higher your scores, the higher your orientation toward assertiveness and responsiveness.

SOURCE: McCroskey, James C., and Virgina P. Richmond. *Fundamentals of Human Communications: An Interpersonal Perspective*. Reprinted with permission of James C. McCroskey and Virgina P. Richmond.

Table 2.1 Identifying Assertive Behaviors in Others[109]

	More Assertive People Tend To	Less Assertive People Tend To
Speech	• Talk more • Talk faster • Talk loudly	• Talk less • Talk more slowly • Talk softly
Body	• Move faster • Appear more energetic • Lean forward	• Move more slowly • Appear less energetic • Lean backward

It's all well and good to understand your own communication social style and know how your self-concept, self-esteem, personality, and even your biology contribute to a predominant way of interacting with others. But as we've noted before: It's not always about you. At the heart of interpersonal communication is relating to others. Understanding your self in relationship to the style of other people can help you make mindful decisions about how to relate to them. This is not about manipulating people—it's about ethically and sensitively enhancing the quality of your communication with others.

How can you assess another person's communication social style? Although you're probably not going to have your friends, family members, colleagues, and acquaintances take a test to assess their communication style, you can look for behaviors that indicate their levels of assertiveness and responsiveness.

The longer you know someone, the more likely you are to be able to accurately identify another person's social style. Tables 2.1 and 2.2 list a few behaviors that may indicate assertiveness or responsiveness. The tables are based on research on the majority population of North Americans, so there are cultural and ethnic limitations to these lists. And we certainly don't claim that by observing these few cues, you can definitively determine someone's communication social style. But the tables will give you some initial ideas that you can use to later refine your impressions.

Experts who study and apply communication social style research suggest that the simplest way to adapt your style to enhance communication quality is to communicate in ways that more closely match the style of the other person. Keep the following principles in mind as you consider your communication social style and the social styles of others:

- Most people have a dominant communication social style (a primary way of interacting with others) that includes the two dimensions of assertiveness and responsiveness.
- No single communication social style is best for all situations—every style has advantages and disadvantages. Specific circumstances should help you determine whether you should be more assertive or more responsive toward others.
- To enhance interpersonal communication, it's useful to understand both your style and the style of the other person and then decide whether to adapt your communication social style.

Table 2.2 Identifying Responsive Behaviors in Others[110]

	More Responsive People Tend To	Less Responsive People Tend To
Speech	• Use more pitch variation • Take a brief time to respond • Use more vocal energy	• Use less pitch variation • Take a longer time to respond • Use less vocal energy
Body	• Show more facial animation when talking • Use more head nods • Use smoother, flowing gestures	• Show less facial animation when talking • Use fewer head nods • Use more hesitant, nonflowing gestures

Applying an Other-Orientation
to Self and Interpersonal Communication

"To thine own self be true." In this famous line from Act I, Scene iii of *Hamlet*, Polonius is providing advice to his son Laertes as Laertes prepares to travel abroad. Polonius gives Laertes a number of suggestions, and concludes with this wise fatherly advice: "This above all, to thine own self be true,/And it must follow, as the night the day,/Thou canst not then be false to any man."

In this chapter we've discussed the significance of self-perception and self-esteem and how they affect your relationships with others. Although we've emphasized the importance of being other-oriented, we conclude the chapter by echoing Polonius's advice to his son: *Be true to yourself*.

To be other-oriented doesn't mean only behaving in people-pleasing ways in order to ingratiate yourself with others. Rather, as an other-oriented communicator, you are aware of the thoughts and feelings of others, but remain true to your own ethics and beliefs. For example, if you object to watching violent movies and a group of your friends invites you to see a "slasher" film, you don't have to watch it with them. Nor do you have to make a self-righteous speech about your feelings about violent movies; you can simply excuse yourself after calmly saying you don't like those kinds of movies. You don't have to do what others do just to be popular. As your mother may have said when you were growing up, "If all of your friends jumped off a cliff, would you jump too?" In essence, your mother was echoing Polonius's counsel to be true to yourself rather than blindly following the herd.

The word credo means belief. What's your personal credo or set of beliefs? Being aware of your personal beliefs—whether about things philosophical or spiritual, about human nature, or about the political and social issues of the day—can serve as an anchoring point for your interactions with others. Without knowing where your "home" is—your personal credo—you won't know how far away from "home" you've traveled as you make your way in the world and relate to others.

Tension is sometimes evident between being true to yourself and being true to others. Consider drafting your own personal credo, your statement of core beliefs, so that you can more mindfully follow Polonius's advice to be true to yourself as you relate to others.

STUDY GUIDE
Review, Apply, and Assess

Self-Concept: Who You Think You Are

Objective 2.1 Define self-concept and identify the factors that shape the development of your self-concept.

Key Terms

self	electronically mediated
self-concept	communication (EMC)
attitude	androgynous role
belief	self-reflexiveness
value	psychology
mindfulness	personality
subjective self-awareness	Big Five Personality Traits
objective self-awareness	extraversion
symbolic self-awareness	agreeableness
material self	conscientiousness
social self	neuroticism
spiritual self	openness
looking-glass self	communibiological approach
attachment style	social learning theory
secure attachment style	shyness
anxious attachment style	communication apprehension
avoidant attachment style	willingness to communicate

Thinking Critically

1. What strategies might minimize the damage to your self-esteem that can result from comparing yourself with others?
2. Write a description of your self-concept (a description of your self) using the William James approach of noting your material self, social self, and spiritual self. Then describe your self-esteem (your self-worth). What insights did you gain about both your self-concept and self-worth by mindfully considering both of these concepts?

Assessing Your Skills

Rank the following list of values from 1 to 12 to reflect their importance to you. In a group with other students, compare your answers. Discuss how your ranking of these values influences your interactions with others.

_____	Honesty	_____	Good health
_____	Salvation	_____	Human rights
_____	Comfort	_____	Peace

_____ Justice	_____ Equality
_____ Wealth	_____ Freedom
_____ Beauty	_____ Mercy

Self-Esteem: Your Self-Worth

Objective 2.2 Define self-esteem and compare and contrast self-esteem with self-concept.

Key Terms

self-worth (self-esteem)   social comparison
self-efficacy   life position

Thinking Critically

Consider Shakespeare's line "To thine own self be true." Can you think of instances when you have not been true to yourself, in your actions, the role(s) you assumed, and/or your interactions with others? Did you know at the time that you were behaving in a way that was not compatible with your values? Do you think others were aware of this? Explain.

Assessing Your Skills

Using Eric Berne's four life positions discussed earlier in this chapter ("I'm OK, you're OK"; "I'm OK, you're not OK"; "I'm not OK, you're OK"; and "I'm not OK, you're not OK"), which life position best describes how you see yourself? What are steps you could take to maintain an "I'm OK, you're OK" life position?

Facework: Presenting Your Self-Image to Others

Objective 2.3 Define facework and discuss how you project your face and protect others' face.

Key Terms

face   corrective facework
facework   face-threatening acts
positive face   politeness theory
preventative facework

Thinking Critically

Reflect on the behaviors you engaged in during the past twenty-four hours where you used facework to promote a positive face. How conscious are you of the activities you engage in and the messages you send to promote your face? What strategies do you use to correct negative perceptions of your face? What are typical messages you might send to manage embarrassment and other situations that cast you in a negative light?

Assessing Your Skills

Think of a situation in which you have needed to communicate a negative message to others. Develop five face-threatening messages patterned after the five levels of communicating a face-threatening message described earlier in this chapter.

How to Improve Your Self-Esteem

Objective 2.4 Identify and describe seven strategies for improving your self-concept.

Key Terms

intrapersonal communication   social support
visualization   talk therapy
reframing

Thinking Critically

Describe a recent event or communication exchange that made you feel better or worse about yourself. What happened that made you feel good? Or, what made you feel bad—inadequate, embarrassed, or unhappy? In general, how do your communication exchanges influence your self-esteem? Explain. How might visualization or other strategies help?

Assessing Your Skills

1. Briefly describe an upcoming situation that makes you anxious, such as working on a group project, calling a prospective employer about a job, or competing in a sporting event. What strategies are you employing to deal with your nervousness? Describe how visualization might help. Share with your classmates or write in your journal a positive scenario, describing the successful outcome.

2. Evaluate your ability to comfortably use the strategies described earlier in this chapter to enhance your self-esteem. 1 = low; 10 = high.

   _____ Engage in self-talk
   _____ Visualize a positive image of yourself
   _____ Avoid comparing yourself with others
   _____ Reframe appropriately
   _____ Develop honest relationships
   _____ Let go of the past
   _____ Seek support

   Based on your self-analysis, which skills might you consider using to address issues of enhancing your self-esteem?

Self and Interpersonal Relationships

Objective 2.5 Identify the effects of your self-concept and self-esteem on your relationships with others.

Key Terms

symbolic interaction theory   self-awareness
self-fulfilling prophecy   Johari Window model
need for inclusion   communication social style
need for control   assertiveness
need for affection   responsiveness
self-disclosure

Thinking Critically

Provide an example of a recent communication exchange with a friend, classmate, family member, or work colleague that revealed that some aspect of your perception of yourself differed from the way the other person perceived you.

Why do you think the perceptions differed? Did knowing the other person's perception change your behavior and/or your own perceptions, or not? Explain.

Assessing Your Skills

1. Create a Johari Window that includes in square 3 ("hidden," or known to self but not to others) five or six adjectives that best describe your personality as you see it. Then ask a close friend to fill in square 2 ("blind," or known to others but not known to self) with five or six adjectives to describe your personality. Separately, ask a classmate you've just met to fill in square 2 as well. Compare and contrast these responses. Are the adjectives used by your close friend and the acquaintance you've just met similar or different? Is there any overlap? Now fill in square 1 ("open," or known to self and others) with any adjectives that both you and either of the other participants chose. What does this tell you about what you disclose about yourself to others?

2. Go through your music library and identify a song that best symbolizes you, based on either the lyrics or the music. Play the song for your classmates or write a journal entry about your selection. Describe why this music symbolizes you. Discuss how your music choice provides a glimpse of your attitudes and values, and why it's a vehicle for self-expression.

Chapter 3
Interpersonal Communication and Perception

"What you see and what you hear depends a good deal on where you are standing. It also depends on what sort of person you are."

C. S. Lewis

CHAPTER OUTLINE	Learning Objectives
Understanding Interpersonal Perception	**3.1** Define perception, and explain the three stages of interpersonal perception.
Forming Impressions of Others	**3.2** List and describe the strategies we use to form impressions of others.
Interpreting the Behavior of Others	**3.3** List and describe the strategies we use to interpret the behavior of others.
Identifying Barriers to Accurate Interpersonal Perception	**3.4** Identify the eight factors that distort the accuracy of interpersonal perception.
Improving Interpersonal Perception Skills	**3.5** Identify and apply five suggestions for improving interpersonal perception.

Look at the photo to the right. What is happening? What would you guess happened shortly before the photograph was taken? Do you see the boy as lost, running away from home, or in some kind of trouble? What might he be feeling? Why does he have the police officer's hat on? What do you think the officer is saying to the little boy? Do you see the officer as intimidating or providing comfort? Your interpretation of what is happening in the photograph reflects interpersonal perception, which we discuss in this chapter.

In Chapter 1, we defined human communication as the process of making sense of the world and sharing that sense with others by creating meaning through the use of verbal and nonverbal messages. In this chapter, we discuss the first half of that definition—the process of making sense of our world. As discussed in Chapter 2, how we make sense out of what we experience, filtered through our own sense of self, is the starting point for what we share with others. As human beings, we interpret and attribute meaning to what we observe or experience, particularly if what we are observing is other people. Increasingly, we develop perceptions of others based on their Facebook posts, tweets, or Instagram photos. We tend to make inferences about their motives, personalities, and other traits based on bits of information we observe. Those who are skilled at making observations and interpretations have a head start in developing effective interpersonal relationships. Those who are other-oriented, who are aware of and sensitive to the communication behaviors of others, will likely be better at accurately perceiving others, whether in person or online.

What do you think is happening in this photograph? Your interpretation reflects interpersonal perception.

Understanding Interpersonal Perception

3.1 **Define perception, and explain the three stages of interpersonal perception.**

Perception is the process of experiencing your world and then making sense out of what you experience. You experience your world through your five senses. Your perceptions of people, however, go beyond simple interpretations of sensory information.

Interpersonal perception is the process by which you decide what people are like and give meaning to their actions. It includes making judgments about their personalities and drawing inferences from what you observe.[1]

We perceive others either passively or actively. **Passive perception** occurs without effort, simply because our senses are operating. We see, hear, smell, taste, and feel things around us without any conscious attempt to do so. No one teaches you to be passively perceptive; you do it naturally and spontaneously.

Active perception, on the other hand, doesn't just happen. It is the process of purposely seeking specific information by intentionally observing and sometimes questioning others. We're engaged in active perception when we make a conscious effort to figure out what we are observing. Do you like to "people watch"? If you have some time on your hands while waiting for a friend, you may start looking at strangers and guessing what they do for a living; whether they are friendly, grumpy, peaceful, or petulant; where they are from; or whether they are in a committed relationship. When people watching, you are involved in active perception. You consciously make assumptions about the personalities and circumstances of those you observe.

When you engage in active perception, you *select* certain information to attend to: For example, you note that a person is female, speaks with a Southern accent, smiles, and uses a friendly tone of voice. You may also discover particular personal information (for example, you learn a woman is from Brownsville, Texas). You then *organize*

perception
Process of experiencing the world and making sense out of what you experience.

interpersonal perception
Process of selecting, organizing, and interpreting your observations of other people.

passive perception
Perception that occurs without conscious effort, simply in response to one's surroundings.

active perception
Perception that occurs because you seek out specific information through intentional observation and questioning.

the information into a category that is recognizable to you, such as "a friendly Texan." Then you *interpret* the organized perceptions: This woman is trustworthy, honest, hardworking, and likable.

Stage 1: Selecting

Sit for a minute after you read this passage and tune in to all the sensory input you are receiving. Consider the snugness of the socks on your feet, the pressure of the floor on your heels, or the feeling of furniture against your body as you sit. Listen to the sounds from various sources around you, such as the "white noise" from a refrigerator, personal computer, fluorescent lights, water in pipes, voices, passing traffic, or your own heartbeat or churning stomach. What do you smell? Without moving your eyes, turn your awareness to the images you see in the corner of your vision. What colors do you see? What shapes? What do you taste in your mouth? Now stop reading and consider all these sensations. Try to focus on all of them at the same time. You can't.

You are selective as you attempt to make sense out of the world around you. The number of sensations you can mindfully attend to at any given time is limited. For example, closing your eyes or sitting in the dark as you listen to music allows you to select more auditory sensations because you have eliminated visual cues.

WE PERCEIVE AND REMEMBER SELECTIVELY Why do we select certain sounds, images, and sensations and not others? Four principles frame the process of how we select what we see, hear, and experience: selective perception, selective attention, selective exposure, and selective recall.

Selective perception occurs when we see, hear, or make sense of the world around us based on a host of factors such as our personality, beliefs, attitudes, likes, dislikes, hopes, fears, and culture. We literally see and don't see things because of our tendency to perceive selectively. Our eyes are not cameras that record everything in the picture; our ears are not microphones that pick up every sound.

In a court of law, eyewitness testimony often determines whether someone is judged innocent or guilty of a crime. But a witness's powers of observation are not flawless. Many innocent people have been convicted because of what a witness thought he or she saw or heard. Again, our eyes are not cameras; our ears are not microphones. We perceive selectively.

Selective attention is the process of focusing on specific stimuli; we selectively lock on to some things in our environment and ignore others. As in the selective perception process, we are likely to attend to those things around us that relate to our needs and wants. When you're hungry, for example, and you're looking for a place to grab a quick bite of lunch, you'll probably be more attentive to fast-food advertising and less focused on ads for cars. We also attend to information that is moving, blinking, flashing, interesting, novel, or noisy. Online advertisement designers use many of these strategies to catch our attention.

Selective exposure is our tendency to put ourselves in situations that reinforce our attitudes, beliefs, values, or behaviors. The fact that we're selective about what we expose ourselves to means that we are more likely to be in places that make us feel comfortable and support the way we see the world than in places that make us uncomfortable. Who is usually at a Baptist church on Sunday mornings? Baptists. Who attends a Democratic Party convention? Democrats. If you perceive yourself to be a good student who does everything possible to get high grades, you will do your best to attend class. We expose ourselves to situations that reinforce how we make sense out of the world.

Selective recall occurs when we remember things we want to remember and forget or repress things that are unpleasant, uncomfortable, or unimportant to us. Not all that we see or hear is recorded in our memories so that we can easily retrieve it. Some

---

selective perception

Process of seeing, hearing, or making sense of the world around us based on such factors as our personality, beliefs, attitudes, hopes, fears, and culture, as well as what we like and don't like.

selective attention

Process of focusing on specific stimuli, locking on to some things in the environment and ignoring others.

selective exposure

Tendency to put ourselves in situations that reinforce our attitudes, beliefs, values, or behaviors.

selective recall

Process that occurs when we remember things we want to remember and forget or repress things that are unpleasant, uncomfortable, or unimportant to us.

experiences may simply be too painful to remember. Or we just don't remember some information because it's not relevant or needed (like the address of the web page you clicked on yesterday).

WE THIN SLICE   Have you ever gone to a grocery store and enjoyed the free samples that are sometimes offered to get you to buy various products? The grocer hopes that if you like the small sample, you'll want to purchase more. Perhaps after tasting a thin slice of cheese, you'll buy a pound of it. The concept of **thin slicing** in the perception process works the same way. You sample a little bit of someone's behavior and then generalize as to what the person may be like, based on the brief information you have observed. For example, when looking at the information and images posted on someone's Facebook page, you are likely to speculate about aspects of the person's life that aren't depicted or described there.

In journalist Malcolm Gladwell's popular book *Blink: The Power of Thinking Without Thinking*, he points to several examples of how people thin slice to make judgments of others.[2] For example, Gladwell reviewed research that found that a patient was less likely to sue a physician for malpractice if the doctor had effective "people skills." Doctors who took the time to listen, respond positively, empathize, and, in short, be other-oriented were less likely to be sued than doctors who were not other-oriented. As patients, we thin slice when we make a judgment about the overall credibility of a doctor based on just one aspect of the doctor's behavior—his or her bedside manner. Two researchers found support for the power of thin slicing when they noted that when subjects heard just a few seconds of someone's speech pattern—such as a southern drawl—they made judgments about the personality of the speaker.[3] When listeners *thought* the speaker had a pronounced speech dialect (even when there really wasn't one), they made stereotypical judgments about the speaker. So our ultimate judgment is based not only on what we hear, but also on what we think we are hearing.

Some people are better at thin slicing than others. There is evidence, for example, that women are better than men at interpreting nonverbal cues. Can you improve your ability to thin slice with accuracy? Yes. Learning how to be more perceptive and other-oriented can improve your ability to thin slice accurately. It also takes time and practice.

Stage 2: Organizing

Look at the four items in Figure 3.1. What does each of them mean to you? If you are like most people, you will perceive item A as a rabbit, item B as a telephone number, item C as the word *interpersonal,* and item D as a circle. Strictly speaking, none of those perceptions is correct. Let's see why by exploring the second stage of perception: organizing.

We organize our world by creating categories, linking together the categories we've created, and then seeking closure by filling in any missing gaps in what we perceive. Psychologists call the framework we use to organize and categorize our experiences a **cognitive schema**—a "mental basket" for sorting and identifying. Without cognitive schemas, we would have to constantly organize and label our experiences, which would be quite tedious.

WE CREATE CATEGORIES   One of the ways we create a cognitive schema is to **superimpose** a category or familiar structure on information we select. To superimpose is to use a framework we're already familiar with to interpret information that may, at first, look formless. We look for the familiar in the unfamiliar. For example, when you looked at item A in Figure 3.1, you saw the pattern of dots as a rabbit because rabbit is a concept you know and to which you attach various meanings. The set of dots would not have meaning for you in and of itself, nor would it be relevant

When we observe others, we gather information about them and ascribe motives and causes to their behaviors—sometimes incorrectly. What do you perceive about this couple's relationship? What might they be discussing?

BEING Other-ORIENTED

We are constantly selecting cues from our environment and then using those cues to help us perceive and form impressions of others. Are you aware of the behaviors that you typically notice about other people? What do you focus on when selecting information about other people and forming impressions of them?

thin slicing

Observing a small sample of someone's behavior and then making a generalization about what the person is like, based on the sample.

cognitive schema

A mental framework used to organize and categorize human experiences.

superimpose

To place a familiar structure on information you select.

Figure 3.1 What Do You See?

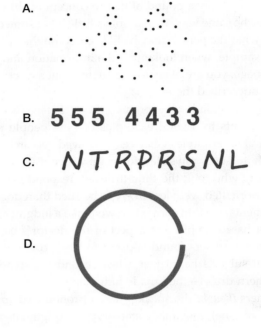

A.

B. **5 5 5 4 4 3 3**

C. **NTRPRSNL**

D.

---

for you to attend to each particular dot or to the dots' relationships to one another. For similar reasons, people have organized patterns of stars in the sky into the various constellations and have given them names that reflect their shapes, like the Bear, the Crab, and the Big and Little Dippers.

People also search for and apply patterns to their perceptions of other people. You might have a friend who jogs and works out at a gym. You put these activities together to create a pattern and label the friend as "athletic." That label represents a pattern of qualities you use in relating to your friend, a pattern that we discuss later in the chapter.

WE LINK CATEGORIES Once we have created cognitive schemas, we link them together as a way of further making sense of how we have chunked what we experience. We link the categories though punctuation. **Punctuation** is the process of making sense of stimuli by grouping, dividing, organizing, separating, and further categorizing information.[4]

Just as punctuation marks on this page tell you when a sentence ends, punctuation in the perception process makes it possible for you to see patterns in information. To many Americans, item B in Figure 3.1 looks like a telephone number because it has three numbers followed by four numbers. However, the digits could just as easily represent two totally independent numbers: five hundred fifty-five followed by the number four thousand, four hundred thirty-three. How we interpret the numbers depends on how we punctuate or separate them.

When it comes to punctuating relational events and behaviors, people develop their own separate sets of standards. You will sometimes experience difficulties and disagreements because of differences in how you and your communication partner choose to punctuate a conversational exchange or a shared sequence of events.[5] One classic example of relational problems resulting from differences in punctuation

punctuation

Process of making sense out of stimuli by grouping, dividing, organizing, separating, and categorizing information.

involves a husband who withdraws and a wife who nags.[6] The husband punctuates their interactions in such a way that he sees his withdrawing as a reaction to her nagging. The wife, in contrast, sees herself as nagging her husband because he keeps withdrawing. The husband and wife punctuate their perceptions differently because they each perceive different starting points for their interactions. Resolving such conflicts involves having the parties describe how they have punctuated the event and agree on a common punctuation.

WE SEEK CLOSURE   Another way we organize information is by seeking closure. **Closure** is the process of filling in missing information or gaps in what we perceive. Looking again at Figure 3.1, you can understand people's inclination to label the figure in item D a circle, even though circles are continuous lines without gaps. We apply the same principles in our interactions with people. When we have an incomplete picture of another human being, we impose a pattern or structure, classify the person on the basis of the information we do have, and fill in any missing information. For example, when you first meet someone who looks and acts like someone you already know, you may make assumptions about your new acquaintance, based on the characteristics of the person you already know. Of course, your assumptions may be wrong. But for many of us who are uncomfortable with uncertainty, creating closure is a way of helping us make better sense out of what is new and unfamiliar.

closure

Process of filling in missing information or gaps in what we perceive.

Stage 3: Interpreting

Once you have selected and organized stimuli, you next typically interpret the stimuli. You see your best friend across a crowded room at a party. He waves to you, and you say to yourself, "He wants to talk with me." Or you nervously wait as your British literature teacher hands back the results of the last exam. When the professor calls your name, she frowns ever so slightly; your heart sinks. You think, "I must have bombed the test." In both of these situations, you're trying to make sense of the information you hear or see. You're attempting to interpret the meaning of the verbal and nonverbal cues you experience. Sometimes even the most subtle cues can color how we interpret a person or situation. One study found that subjects were more likely to interpret someone's behavior as sexually alluring if they were exposed to words like "sex," "intercourse," and "hot" in word puzzles just before meeting the person. Merely being briefly exposed to provocative words resulted in provocative perceptions. Things we may not be conscious of may influence our interpretation of people.[7]

Recap

The Interpersonal Perception Process

Term	Explanation	Example
Selecting	The first stage in the perceptual process, in which we select certain sensations on which to focus awareness	Sitting in your apartment where you hear lots of traffic sounds and car horns, but attending to a particular rhythmic car honking that seems to be right outside your door
Organizing	The second stage in the perceptual process, in which we assemble stimuli into convenient and efficient patterns	Putting together the car honking with your anticipation of a friend's arrival to pick you up in her car to drive to a movie that starts in five minutes
Interpreting	The final stage in perception, in which we assign meaning to what we have observed	Deciding the car honking must be your friend signaling you to come out to the car quickly because she's running late

Forming Impressions of Others

impressions

Collection of perceptions about others that you maintain and use to interpret their behaviors.

impression formation theory

Theory that explains how you develop perceptions about people and how you maintain and use those perceptions to interpret their behaviors.

implicit personality theory

Your unique set of beliefs and hypotheses about what people are like.

construct

Bipolar quality or continuum used to classify people.

uncertainty reduction theory

Theory that claims people seek information in order to reduce uncertainty, thus achieving control and predictability.

3.2   List and describe the strategies we use to form impressions of others.

Impressions are collections of perceptions about others that we maintain and use to interpret their behaviors. Impressions tend to be very general: "She seems nice," "He was very friendly," or "What a nerd!" According to **impression formation theory**, we form these impressions based on our perceptions of physical qualities (what people look like), behavior (what people do), what people tell us, and what others tell us about them. When we first meet someone, we form a first impression without having much information, and we often hold on to this impression (even if it's an inaccurate one) throughout the relationship. So it's important to understand how we form impressions of others. Researchers have found that we often give special emphasis to the first things we see or the last things we observe about another person. We also generalize from specific positive or negative perceptions we hold.

We Develop Our Own Theories About Others

You don't need to read a book about interpersonal communication to develop your own theories about how you form impressions of others. You already have your own theories. **Implicit personality theory** consists of the personal assumptions you make about other people's personalities.[8] It encompasses your own ideas and expectations that influence how you make guesses about others' personalities. It's called *implicit* personality theory because the cues you use to interpret others' behavior are not explicitly evident but are instead implicit or indirect—whether you met someone ten minutes ago or ten years ago. And you may not always be aware that you have assumptions and biases when forming perceptions of others.

When making assumptions about others we develop specific categories, called *constructs*, for people. A **construct**, according to psychologist George Kelly, is a bipolar quality (that is, a quality with two opposite categories) or a continuum.[9] We may pronounce someone good or bad, athletic or nonathletic, warm or cold, funny or humorless, selfish or generous, beautiful or ugly, kind or cruel, and so on. But we don't necessarily classify people in these absolute terms; we usually categorize them in degrees.

To varying degrees, many people dislike or are uncomfortable with uncertainty. Some people just don't like surprises. **Uncertainty reduction theory** suggests that one of the primary reasons we communicate at all is to reduce our uncertainty about what we see and experience. Making guesses and assumptions about people reduces uncertainty. If we can reduce our uncertainty about other people, then we can predict their reactions and behaviors, adapt our behaviors and strategies, and therefore maximize the likelihood of fulfilling our own social needs.[10] Being able to reduce uncertainty and increase predictability gives us greater control when communicating with others. Although attaining greater control might sound calculating, it really isn't. If you enjoy outdoor activities such as camping and hiking, one of your goals in establishing social relationships is probably to find others who share your interest. So actively observing, questioning, and consciously processing information to determine a potential friend's interests can help you assess whether the relationship will meet your goals. And in the spirit of being other-oriented, you will also be able to assess whether you can meet the goals and interests of the other person. In Chapter 5, we discuss ways to improve your ability to gain information through more effective listening.

BEING Other-ORIENTED

By listening to and observing others, we reduce our uncertainty about how they will interact with us. Think about a person you met in school who is now a good friend. What type of active perception activities did you engage in to get to know this person better—to reduce your uncertainty about him or her? How would you assess your skill level in observing, questioning, and processing information to get to know other people?

Implicit assumptions and expectations color our impressions of others.

Now let's take a closer look at several typical ways most of us form impressions of others: drawing on social media, emphasizing what we see first or what we observe last when interacting with others, and generalizing from our perceptions of them as positive or negative.

We Form Impressions of Others Online: The Social Media Effect

Your online world affects your offline world. Increasingly, others evaluate you in interpersonal situations based upon what you have posted on Facebook. The photos you post, as well as the information you decide to include on your Facebook profile, provide both explicit and implicit cues about your interests, personality, and communication style. But there's evidence that what *others* say about you on Facebook, Twitter, or other social media applications is even more likely to have an effect on how others perceive you than what *you* post. Specifically, Sonia Utz found that what other people said about individuals on their Facebook pages had more impact on whether they were perceived positively or negatively than how the individuals described themselves.[11] Although some researchers have found that Facebook lurkers can gain accurate perceptions of your personality based only on your Facebook information, what others say about you has more credibility.[12]

People may also be making inferences about your popularity, personality, and sincerity simply by noting the number of friends you have on Facebook. One research team found that having too few or too many Facebook friends may seem unusual to others, thereby lowering their impression of your attractiveness or credibility.[13] Specifically, people with 102 friends were perceived as less socially attractive than people who had 302 friends. Yet if you have 502 or 1,000 friends, you are also perceived as less socially attractive. Thus there is a curvilinear relationship (think of an upside down "U" as charting the relationships) between the number of friends you have and how positively others perceive you. Having too few or too many friends is likely to lower your social attractiveness as perceived by others. Another study also found a positive relationship between how popular you appear to be based on the number of friends you have, and how attractive, extroverted, and approachable others perceive you to be.[14]

We Emphasize What Comes First: The Primacy Effect

There is evidence that when we form impressions of others, we pay more attention to our first impressions. The tendency to attend to the first pieces of information that we observe about another person is called the **primacy effect**. The primacy effect was documented in a famous study conducted by Solomon Asch.[15] Individuals were asked to evaluate two people based on two lists of adjectives. The list for the first person had the following adjectives: *intelligent, industrious, impulsive, critical, stubborn,* and *envious.* The list for the other person had the same adjectives, but in reverse order. Although the content was identical, respondents gave the first person a more positive evaluation than the second. One explanation for this is that the first words in each list created a first impression that respondents used to interpret the remaining adjectives. In a similar manner, the first impressions we form about someone often affect our interpretation of subsequent perceptions of that person.

Predicted outcome value theory (POV) helps to explain the primacy effect in our interpersonal relationships. This theory suggests that we make predictions about the future of a relationship based on how we size up people when we first interact with them. According to Michael Sunnafrank, who developed predicted outcome value theory, we will seek information about others to help us manage the uncertainty we experience when we first meet them.[16] Initial positive impressions can help us form

primacy effect

Tendency to attend to the first pieces of information observed about another person in order to form an impression.

predicted outcome value theory (POV)

People predict the future of a relationship based on how they size up someone during their first interaction.

more lasting positive impressions of people once we get to know them better. And early negative impressions increase the likelihood that we will diminish our contact with that person.

In support of predicted outcome value theory, one team of researchers found that if we learn early in an interaction that someone is HIV-positive or has cancer, our predictions about whether we will continue to have a relationship with that person are influenced by our knowledge of the presence of an illness.[17] The researchers also found that knowing that someone is HIV-positive is more of a negative stigma than knowing someone has cancer. Thus, when we first meet someone, we use our early knowledge (primacy effect) to help us make decisions about whether to continue or diminish the relationship.

We Emphasize What Comes Last: The Recency Effect

recency effect
Tendency to attend to the most recent information observed about another person in order to form or modify an impression.

Not only do we give more weight to our first impressions, we also give considerable attention to our most recent experiences and impressions. The tendency to put a lot of stock in the last thing we observe is called the **recency effect**.[18] For example, if you have thought for years that your friend is honest, but today you discover that she lied to you about something important, that lie will have a greater impact on your impression of her than the honest behavior she has displayed for years. Similarly, if, during a job interview, you skillfully answered all of the interviewer's questions yet your last answer to a question was not the answer the interviewer was looking for, you may not get the job.

We Generalize Positive Qualities to Others: The Halo Effect

halo effect
Attributing a variety of positive qualities to those you like.

One feature common to most of our implicit personality theories is the tendency to put people into one of two categories: people we like and people we don't like. Categorizing people as those we like often creates a **halo effect**, in which we attribute a variety of positive qualities to them without personally confirming the existence of these qualities. If you like me, you will add a "halo" to your impression of me and then apply to me those qualities from your implicit personality theory that apply to people you like, such as having a great sense of humor and being considerate, warm, caring, and fun to be with.

We Generalize Negative Qualities to Others: The Horn Effect

horn effect
Attributing a variety of negative qualities to those you dislike.

Just as we can use the halo effect to generalize about someone's positive qualities, the opposite can also happen. We sometimes make many negative assumptions about a person because of one unflattering perception. This is called the **horn effect**, named for the horns associated with medieval images of a devil. If you don't like the way someone looks, you might also decide that person is selfish or stingy and attribute a variety of negative qualities to that individual, using your implicit personality theory. As evidence of the horn effect, research suggests that during periods of conflict in our relationships, we are more likely to attribute negative behaviors to our feuding partner than we are to ourselves.[19] A little bit of negative information can affect how we perceive other attributes of a person. Communication researcher Jina Yoo found that sharing negative information about someone is much more likely to have an effect on the attitudes and perceptions of others in an interpersonal relationship than is sharing positive information.[20] We are also more likely to remember the negative information that we hear about someone, perhaps because a negative story about someone tends to have more information than a positive story, which leads to greater retention of the negative information.[21]

In support of the premise underlying the horn effect, researchers Dominic Infante and Andrew Rancer observed that some people have a tendency to see the worst in others, which causes them to lash out and be verbally aggressive.[22] There is also evidence that some people interpret any negative feedback they receive as a personal attack, no matter how carefully the feedback is worded.[23] For such people, there is no such thing as "constructive criticism." Like a sunburned sunbather, they perceive even a mild suggestion presented with a light touch as a stinging rebuke.

Interpreting the Behavior of Others

3.3   **List and describe the strategies we use to interpret the behavior of others.**

"I know why Alicia hasn't arrived at our meeting yet. She just doesn't like me. She is always late," says Cathy. "I'll bet she just wants people to think she's too busy to be on time for our little group meetings. She is so stuck up." Cathy seems not only to have formed a negative impression of Alicia, but also to harbor a hunch about why Alicia is typically late. Cathy is attributing meaning to Alicia's behavior. Even though Alicia could have just forgotten about the meeting, may have an earlier meeting that always runs overtime, or is from a culture in which meetings almost always start after the announced meeting time, Cathy thinks Alicia's absence is caused by feelings of superiority and contempt. Cathy's assumptions about Alicia can be explained by several theories about the way we interpret the behavior of others. Based on a small sample of someone's behavior, we develop our own explanations of why people do what they do. Attribution theory, standpoint theory, and intercultural communication theory offer perspectives on how we make sense of what we perceive.

We Attribute Motives to Others' Behavior: Attribution Theory

Attribution theory explains how we ascribe specific motives and causes to the behaviors of others. It helps us interpret what people do. For example, suppose the student sitting next to you in class gets up in the middle of the lecture and walks out. Why did the student leave? Did the student become angry at something the instructor said? It seems unlikely—the lecturer was simply describing types of cloud formations. Was the student sick? You remember noticing that the student looked a little flushed and occasionally winced. Maybe the student has an upset stomach. Or maybe the student is a bit of a rebel and often does strange things like leaving in the middle of a class.

Social psychologist Fritz Heider says that we are "naive psychologists," because we all seek to explain people's motives for their actions.[24] We are naive because we do not create these explanations in a systematic or scientific manner, but rather by applying common sense to our observations. Developing the most credible explanation for the behavior of others is the goal of the attribution process.

attribution theory

Theory that explains how you generate explanations for people's behaviors.

ZITS © 2000 Zits Partnership. Dist. by King Features Syndicate.

causal attribution theory
Theory of attribution that identifies the cause of a person's actions as circumstance, a stimulus, or the person himself or herself.

Causal attribution theory identifies three potential causes for any person's action: circumstance, a stimulus, or the person herself or himself.[25] Attributing behavior to *circumstance* means that you believe a person acts in a certain way because the situation leaves no choice. This way of thinking places responsibility for the action outside of the person. There is interesting research that suggests that during times when you feel lonely and isolated from others, you are more likely to attribute your feelings of loneliness to your specific circumstance rather than to any flaws in your personality.[26]

You would be attributing to circumstance if you believed the student quickly left the classroom because of an upset stomach. Concluding that the student left because the instructor said something inappropriate would be attributing the student's action to the *stimulus* (the instructor). But if you knew the instructor hadn't said anything out of line and that the student was perfectly healthy, you would place the responsibility for the action on the student. Attributing to the *person* means that you believe there is some quality about the person that caused the observed behavior.

To explore how attributions to a person affect us, interpersonal communication researchers Anita Vangelisti and Stacy Young investigated whether intentionally hurtful words inflict more pain than unintentionally hurtful comments.[27] As you might suspect, if we think someone intends to hurt us, spiteful words have more sting and bite than if we believe someone does not intend to hurt our feelings. Our attributions are factors in our impressions.

We Use Our Own Point of Reference About Power: Standpoint Theory

standpoint theory
Theory that a person's social position, power, or cultural background influences how the person perceives the behavior of others.

Standpoint theory is yet another framework that seeks to explain how we interpret the behavior of others. The theory is relatively simple: We each see the world differently because we're each viewing it from a different position. Some people have positions of power, and others do not; the resources that we have to help us make our way through life provide a lens through which we view the world and the people in it.

Standpoint theory explains why people with differing cultural backgrounds have different perceptions of others' behavior. In the early nineteenth century, German philosopher Georg Hegel noted this simple but powerful explanation of why people see and experience the world differently.[28] Hegel was especially interested in how one's standpoint was determined in part by one's power and influence. For example, people who have greater power and more influence in a particular culture may not be aware of their power and influence and how this power affects their perceptions of others. A person with less power (which in many cultures includes women and people of color) may be acutely aware of the power he or she doesn't have.

As evidence of standpoint theory, one team of researchers found that people who perceived that they were the victims of lying or cheating had an overall more negative view of the communication with their lying or cheating communication partner than with someone who they perceived did not lie or cheat.[29] This makes sense, doesn't it? If our point of view is that a certain person can't be trusted in one situation, we are less likely to trust the person in other situations. C. S. Lewis was right: What we see and hear depends a good deal on where we are standing.

We Draw on Our Own Cultural Background: Intercultural Communication Theory

When Cathy thought Alicia was rude and thoughtless because she always arrived at their meetings late, Cathy was attributing meaning to Alicia's behavior based on Cathy's cultural assumptions about when meetings usually begin. According to

Relating to Diverse Others
The Power of Being Other-Oriented

The more you can identify with the feelings and thoughts of others, the more empathy and understanding you will have toward them. As noted in our discussion of standpoint theory, where you stand makes a difference in what you see and how you interpret human behavior. Following the September 11, 2001, terrorist attacks on the United States, discussions about the perceptions of the power and influence of different cultural groups and countries became more common.

Men and women, Blacks and Whites, Jews and Christians, Muslims and Hindus, Hispanics and Asians, gay and straight individuals all experience life from their own cultural standpoints, which means they all have perceptions about their influence on others. To become more other-oriented is to become aware of your own perceived place in society and to be more sensitive to how that position of power or lack of power affects how you perceive others with a different standpoint.

To explore applications of standpoint theory in your life, consider the following questions:

1. How would you describe your standpoint in terms of power and influence in your school or at work, or in your family? Have you ever experienced rejection, alienation, or discrimination based on how others perceived you?
2. How would other people in your life (parents, siblings, children, coworkers, employer, or friends) describe your power and influence on them?
3. Identify a specific relationship with a teacher, coworker, or family member in which different standpoints influence the quality of the relationship in either positive or negative ways.
4. What can you do to become more aware of how your standpoint influences your interactions with others? How can your increased awareness enhance the quality of your interpersonal communication with others?

Cathy, if a meeting is supposed to start at 10:00 am, it's important to be prompt and ready to begin on time. But Alicia comes from a culture with a different approach to time; in Alicia's culture, meetings *never* begin on time. In fact, it's polite, according to Alicia, to be fashionably late so that the meeting leader can greet people and make any last-minute preparations for the meeting. To show up on time would be disrespectful. Both Alicia and Cathy are making sense out of their actions based on their own cultural framework. Alicia and Cathy aren't the only ones who interpret behavior through their cultural lens—we all do.

Culture is a learned system of knowledge, behaviors, attitudes, beliefs, values, and norms that is shared by a group of people. Our culture is reflected not only in our behavior but in every aspect of the way we live our lives. The categories of things and ideas that identify the most profound aspects of cultural influence are known as *cultural elements*. According to one research team, cultural elements include the following:[30]

culture

Learned system of knowledge, behavior, attitudes, beliefs, values, and norms shared by a group of people.

- Material culture: housing, clothing, automobiles, and other tangible things
- Social institutions: schools, governments, and religious organizations
- Belief systems: ideas about individuals and the universe
- Aesthetics: music, theatre, art, and dance
- Language: verbal and nonverbal communication systems

As you can see from the list, cultural elements are not only things we can see and hear, but also ideas and values. And because these elements are so prevalent, they have an effect on how we interpret all that we experience.

Our culture is like the air we breathe, in that we're often not aware that it's there—we simply go about our daily routines, usually not conscious that we are breathing. Because our culture is ever-present and is constantly influencing our thoughts and behavior, it has a profound impact on how we experience the world. If you come from a culture in which horsemeat is a delicacy, you'll likely savor each bite of your horse steak, because you've learned to enjoy it. Yet if eating horsemeat is not part of your cultural heritage, you will have a different perception if you're invited to chow down on filet of horse. So it is with how we interpret the behavior

Our own cultural framework has a profound effect on how we interpret everything we experience, including our interactions with others. Do people in your own culture typically behave like those in this photo? If not, what is your reaction to what you see here?

stereotype

To place a person or group of persons into an inflexible, all-encompassing category.

of other people who have different cultural expectations than we do. In some Asian countries, it's expected that when meeting someone you should politely bow as a sign of respect. And in some European or Latin American cultures, you may be kissed on the cheek when renewing an acquaintance. Yet in North America, these behaviors may be perceived differently because of different cultural expectations.

In a study investigating whether people from a variety of cultural backgrounds used their own culture to make sense out of the behavior of others, researchers found that *stereotyping*—making rigid judgments of others based on a small bit of information—is rampant in many cultures.[31] In this study, participants from Australia, Botswana, Canada, Kenya, Nigeria, South Africa, Zambia, Zimbabwe, and the United States all consistently formed stereotypical impressions of others. Culture strongly influences how we interpret the actions of others. Because culture is such a powerful influence on how we make sense of the world, we discuss the role of culture and cultural differences in more detail in the next chapter.

Identifying Barriers to Accurate Interpersonal Perception

3.4 Identify the eight factors that distort the accuracy of interpersonal perception.

Think about the most recent interaction you had with a stranger. Do you remember the person's age, sex, race, or physical description? Did the person have any distinguishing features, such as a beard, tattoos, or a loud voice? The qualities you recall will most likely serve as the basis for attributions you make about that person's behavior. But these attributions, based on your first impressions, might be wrong. Each person sees the world from his or her own unique perspective. That perspective is clouded by a number of distortions and barriers that contribute to inaccurate interpersonal perception.

We Stereotype

Preconceived notions about what they expect to find may keep people from seeing what's before their eyes and ears. We see what we want to see, hear what we want to hear. We stereotype others. To **stereotype** someone is to attribute a set of qualities to the person because of his or her membership in some category. The word *stereotype* was originally a printing term, referring to a metal plate that was cast from type set by a printer. The plate would print the same page of type over and over again. When we stereotype people, we place them into inflexible, all-encompassing categories. We "print" the same judgments on anyone placed in a given category.

Researchers have suggested that when we categorize and stereotype others, we do so to meet our own needs for power, authority, and structure.[32] It tends to be the minority group with less social and political power that gets marginalized and lost in the power shuffle.[33] There is clear evidence that this problem is especially acute for socially marginalized groups such as gays and lesbians and Blacks.[34] Being aware of the problem is the first step to solving it.

Although we've just advised you to be aware of stereotypes, that advice may contribute to the problem. Here's why: According to some researchers, awareness that we, along with others, have a tendency to stereotype people provides unspoken permission to stereotype. One research team found that if people know it's normal to

Recap

How We Organize and Interpret Interpersonal Perceptions

Theory	Description	Example
Impression Formation Theory	We form general impressions of others based on general physical qualities, behaviors, and disclosed information.	Categorizing people as nice, friendly, shy, or handsome.
Predicted Outcome Value Theory	We make predictions about the future of a relationship based on early information we learn.	"When I met Derek, I didn't like his messy appearance. I don't think he'd taken a shower in days. I decided then and there that I didn't think he was someone I wanted to hang out with."
Implicit Personality Theory	We use a personal set of assumptions to draw specific conclusions about someone's personality.	"If she is intelligent, then I believe she must be caring, too."
Attribution Theory	We develop reasons to explain the behaviors of others.	"I guess she didn't return my call because she doesn't like me." "He's just letting off steam because he had a bad week of exams."
Causal Attribution Theory	We ascribe a person's actions to circumstance, a stimulus, or the person himself or herself.	"He didn't go to class because his alarm didn't go off." "He didn't go to class because it was a makeup session." "He didn't go to class because he is bored by it."
Standpoint Theory	We interpret the behavior of others through the lens of our own social position, power, or cultural background.	"He won't join the fraternity because he doesn't understand how important that network can be to his professional career."
Intercultural Communication Theory	Our cultural experiences and backgrounds influence how we view the world.	"I don't understand why some people from Japan greet me by bowing. We don't do that in Missouri."

stereotype others, this knowledge provides implicit permission to join the crowd and stereotype as well.[35] So we are more likely to form and maintain stereotypes if we believe that the people with whom we typically interact also share them.[36] It's important to be aware of your own tendencies to stereotype others, but also whether other people around you do the same. With that awareness, mindfully work *not* to go along with the crowd.

When we stereotype others, we *overgeneralize*, or treat small amounts of information as if they were highly representative. This tendency leads people to draw inaccurate, prejudicial conclusions.[37] For example, a professor may talk to two students and then generalize an impression of them to the entire student population. In a similar way, most people tend to assume that a small sampling of another person's behavior is a valid representation of who that person is. As you saw in Figure 3.1, you might perceive a rabbit even when you have only a few dots on which to base your perception.

We Ignore Information

People sometimes don't focus on important information because they give too much weight to information that is obvious and superficial.[38] Why do we ignore important information that may be staring us in the face? It's because, as you learned in the discussion about attribution theory, we tend to explain a person's motives on the basis of what is most obvious rather than the in-depth information we might have. When meeting someone new, we perceive his or her physical qualities first: color of skin, body size and shape, age, sex, and other obvious characteristics. We overattribute to these qualities because they are so vivid and available, and we ignore other details. We have all been victims of these kinds of attributions, some of us more than others. Often, we are unaware that others are making biased attributions because they do not express them openly.

#communicationandtechnology

The SIDE Model: Forming Stereotypes Online

We use online cues to stereotype others, just as we do in face-to-face interactions. In fact, we may be *more* likely to stereotype others online than in person; when we are online, we have to make more inferences about the other person because there are fewer cues and it takes longer for relationship cues to emerge. This theory is called the **social identity model of deindividuation effects (SIDE)**.[39] We are more likely to reduce someone to a stereotype—or, to use a technical term, to *deindividuate* them—online because we have fewer cues to help us develop a clear impression.

One study found that Asian-American women were stereotypically perceived as shyer and more introverted, compared to African-American women, when communicating via e-mail but not when communicating by telephone.[40] The fewer cues available, the more likely stereotypical perceptions of the other person were to emerge. Since e-mail offers fewer cues than the telephone (the telephone is a richer medium), stereotyping is more likely in the media-lean e-mail context. Another study found that people make stereotypical judgments about another person's gender when communicating via e-mail when they aren't certain whether the person they are interacting with is a male or female.[41] We use whatever cues we have, such as language style and even topics discussed, to help us form a stereotypical impression of the other person.

Another interesting study found that if your friends appear to be attractive, *you* will be perceived as more attractive and will make a more positive impression on others than if your friends are perceived as less attractive.[42] In short, you look good if you have friends who look good.[43] This finding suggests that people form stereotypes not only on the basis of the qualities of other people, but also from context cues about those with whom others associate.[44]

Research Implications: So What?

How can we counter our tendency to oversimplify and stereotype others online? Consider these suggestions:

1. First, be mindful of the potential for developing inaccurate stereotypes online. Being aware of the problem is the first step in avoiding the problem.
2. Second, as you become aware that you may be making an inaccurate stereotype based on limited online information, be cautious of the conclusions you draw about others' personality and character.
3. Third, as you prepare *your* online profile on Facebook or other e-formats, look at your information with the other-oriented perspective of how others may perceive you online.

---

social identity model of deindividuation effects (SIDE)

Theory that people are more likely to stereotype others with whom they interact online, because such interactions provide fewer relationship cues and the cues take longer to emerge than they would in face-to-face interactions.

But sometimes we can tell by the way others react to us and treat us. We may even choose to ignore contradictory information that we receive directly from the other person. Instead of adjusting our impression of that person, we adjust our perception.[45] The halo and horn effects discussed earlier reflect this tendency. For example, if an instructor gets an excellent paper from a student whom the instructor has concluded is not particularly bright or motivated, she may tend to find errors and shortcomings that are not really there, or she may even accuse the student of plagiarism.

There is evidence that we make stereotypical judgments of others even when we may not be fully aware that we are making such judgments. Researchers have found that we hold *implicit attitudes* that affect how we perceive others.[46] Because implicit attitudes operate below our level of awareness, it's important to monitor our behavior and reactions to others to ensure that we are not unfairly, inaccurately, or inappropriately making stereotypical judgments of them.

We Impose Consistency

People overestimate the consistency and constancy of others' behaviors. When we organize our perceptions, we also tend to ignore fluctuation in people's behaviors and instead see them as consistent. We believe that if someone acted a certain way one day, he or she will continue to act that way in the future. Perhaps you have embarrassed yourself in front of a new acquaintance by acting silly. At another encounter with this new acquaintance, you realize that the person is continuing to see your behavior as foolish, even though you don't intend it to be seen that way. The other person is imposing consistency on your inconsistent behavior.

In fact, everyone's behavior varies from day to day. Some days, we are in a bad mood, and our behavior on those days does not represent what we are generally like. As intimacy develops in relationships, we interact with our partners in varying circumstances that provide a more complete picture of our true nature.

We Focus on the Negative

People give more weight to negative information than to positive information.[47] Job interviewers often ask you to describe your strengths and weaknesses. If you describe five strengths and one weakness, it is likely that the interviewer will attend more to the one weakness you mention than to the strengths. We seem to recognize this bias and compensate for it when we first meet someone by sharing only positive information about ourselves.

Stereotypes can help us make sense out of the wide range of stimuli we encounter every day. But we also need to be sure that we don't overuse stereotypes and thus fail to see people as individuals.

One piece of negative information can have a disproportionate effect on our impressions and negate the effect of several positive pieces of information. In another of Solomon Asch's experiments on impression formation, participants heard one of the following two lists of terms to describe a person: (1) *intelligent, skillful, industrious, warm, determined, practical, cautious;* or (2) *intelligent, skillful, industrious, cold, determined, practical, cautious.*[48] The only difference in these two lists is the use of *warm* in the first list and *cold* in the second. Despite the presence of six other common terms, those who heard the "cold" list had a much more negative impression of the person than those who heard the "warm" list. Perhaps you've noticed that following a near-flawless Olympic ice skating performance, the TV commentator, rather than focusing on the best executed leaps, twists, and turns, will first replay the one small error the skater made in the performance. In our own lives, we may have a tendency to do the same thing; we may focus on or even emphasize what we didn't do well rather than celebrate what we've done skillfully. Don't be too hard on yourself.

We Blame Others, Assuming They Have Control

People are more likely to believe that others are to blame when things go wrong than to believe that the problem was beyond their control. As we noted earlier, we attribute meaning and motives to the behavior of others (attribution theory). Often, however, we assume the worst rather than the best motives of others. Imagine, for example, that your parents were looking forward to celebrating their twenty-fifth wedding anniversary. They planned a quiet family celebration at a restaurant. You used an app on your iPad to remind you one week before the anniversary dinner to buy them a present. You hadn't anticipated, however, that you'd lose your iPad. When your phone rang and your mom asked, "Where are you?" it all came jarringly back to you: Today was their anniversary, and you'd forgotten it! Not only did you forget to buy them a present, you forgot to attend the dinner. Your parents were hurt. Your mother's quivering "How could you forget?" still sears your conscience. They think you just didn't care enough about them to remember such an important day. Rather than thinking that there might be an explanation for why you forgot their important day, they blame you for your thoughtlessness. Although they certainly have a right to be upset, their assumption that you don't care about them is an example of what researchers call the fundamental attribution error.

The **fundamental attribution error** occurs when we think that a person's behavior is influenced by his or her actions and choices rather than by external causes.[49]

fundamental attribution error
Error that arises from attributing another person's behavior to internal, controllable causes rather than to external, uncontrollable causes.

This driver may be making the fundamental attribution error—assuming that the other person's behavior was under his control, when in fact it may not have been.

The fundamental attribution error predicts that you're more likely to assume that the person who cuts you off in traffic is a jerk rather than to conclude he's trying to get out of the way of the truck that's tailgating him. One study found that when a teacher criticizes a student, he or she sometimes thinks that the problem lies with the instructor's judgment rather than with the student's poor performance. As a result of the fundamental attribution error, the student may offer a rebuttal to defend his or her behavior rather than think he or she needs to work harder and do a better job.[50]

You can avoid making the fundamental attribution error by honestly examining your role in the communication process. Simply being aware of our tendency to accuse others of purposeful misbehavior, rather than acknowledging the possibility of some outside cause, can help you avoid this tendency. Evidence also suggests that the more empathic or other-oriented you are, the less likely you are to blame the other person for any problem or mistake.[51] For example, if you can empathize with someone over the recent death of a loved one or a recent divorce, you may "cut that person some slack" and excuse behavior that otherwise might strike you as rude or self-centered. When you've made a mistake about a person's behavior, admit it. You can enhance the quality of your relationships when you own up to making perceptual errors.

We Avoid Responsibility

People are more likely to save face by believing that they are not the cause of a problem; people assume that other people or events are more than likely the source of problems or events that may put them in an unfavorable light. In one classic episode of *The Simpsons*, Bart Simpson created a popular catch phrase by saying, "I didn't do it" when he clearly was the cause of a calamity. Whether it was lighting Lisa's hair on fire or putting baby Maggie on the roof, Bart would simply say, "I didn't do it." We chuckle at Bart's antics and would never stoop to such juvenile pranks. Yet when we *do* cause a problem or make a mistake, we are more likely to blame someone else rather than ourselves. Bart's "I didn't do it" approach to life represents self-serving bias.

self-serving bias

Tendency to perceive our own behavior as more positive than others' behavior.

Self-serving bias is the tendency to perceive our own behavior as more positive than others' behavior and to avoid taking responsibility for our own errors and mistakes. Sociologist Erving Goffman was one of the first to note this tendency when he wrote his classic book *The Presentation of Self in Everyday Life*.[52] As the title of Goffman's book suggests, we work hard to actively present our own selves. We strive to preserve not only our physical existence, but our psychological health as well. We sometimes may try to present a positive image of ourselves by telling ourselves that we are skilled and effective. We are likely, for example, to attribute our own personal success to our hard work and effort rather than any to external, uncontrollable causes. You get an A on your anthropology paper because, you think, "I'm smart." When you get an F on your history paper, it's because your neighbor's loud party kept you up all night and you couldn't study. Self-serving bias is the tendency to take credit for the good things that happen to you and to say "I didn't do it" or "It's not my fault" when bad things happen to you.[53] Simply being aware of the self-serving bias may help you become more objective and accurate in identifying the causes of calamities in your own life.

Improving Your Communication Skills

Assuming the Best or the Worst About Others: Identifying Alternative Explanations

Do you give people the benefit of the doubt when they do something that irritates you or make a mistake, or do you tend to assume the worst about their intentions? The fundamental attribution error is the human tendency to believe that the cause of a problem or a personal slight is within the other person's control, rather than external to the person. This tendency to blame others rather than considering that there may be an alternative explanation for a problem or a behavior can result in developing a judgmental, negative attitude toward others. For each of the following, think about what your first explanation was when the event happened to you:

- A person not calling back after a first date
- A server giving you lousy service
- A customer service person breaking his or her promise that your car would be fixed by 5:00 pm
- A teacher being late for class
- A teacher not returning grades when he or she promised
- A student copying test answers from the student next to him
- A sales assistant ignoring you when you need help
- A friend not remembering your birthday

Now go back and generate several additional possible explanations for each behavior. How can you be sure which explanation is accurate? How often do you commit the fundamental attribution error? How often do you give someone the benefit of the doubt?

Recap

Barriers to Accurate Interpersonal Perception

Stereotyping	We allow our pre-existing rigid expectations about others to influence our perceptions.
Ignoring Information	We don't focus on important information because we give too much weight to obvious and superficial information.
Imposing Consistency	We overestimate the consistency and constancy of others' behavior.
Focusing on the Negative	We give more weight to negative information than to positive information.
Blaming Others by Assuming They Have Control	We are more likely to believe that others are to blame when things go wrong than to assume that the cause of the problem was beyond their control.
Avoiding Responsibility	We save face by believing that other people, not ourselves, are the cause of problems; when things go right, it's because of our own skills and abilities rather than help from others.

Improving Interpersonal Perception Skills

3.5 Identify and apply five suggestions for improving interpersonal perception.

With so many barriers to perceiving and interpreting other people's behavior accurately, what can you do to improve your perception skills? Increasing your awareness of the factors that lead to inaccuracy will help initially, and you will find additional suggestions in this section. Ultimately, your improvement will depend on your willingness to expand your experiences, to communicate about your perceptions with others, and to seek out and consider others' perceptions of you. Realize that you have had a lifetime to develop these barriers and that it will take time, commitment, and effort to overcome their effects.

Be Aware of Your Personal Perception Barriers

Don't get the idea that you (and everybody else) are automatically doomed to enact the various perception barriers that we've described. We presented them so that you can spot them and work to minimize them as you form impressions of, and interact with, others. But before you can minimize these perception barriers, you need to be aware of which ones are most likely to affect you. (Although also remember that being aware that others engage in behaviors such as stereotyping may implicitly lead us to stereotype others.)

What should you do to more accurately perceive others? Go back over the descriptions of the perception barriers and identify those that you've found yourself falling prey to most often. Specifically, which of the barriers are you most susceptible to? Do you tend to ignore information, to think in terms of stereotypes, or to blame others as your first response? After identifying the barrier or barriers that you most often experience, it may be helpful to think of a specific situation in which you perceived someone else inaccurately. What could you have done differently to gain additional information before drawing an inaccurate conclusion? Although making perceptual errors is a natural human tendency, by being aware of these barriers you can be on the lookout for them in your own interactions with others and more actively work to minimize their impact. Also realize that a variety of factors influence the accuracy of your perceptions of others. Stress and fatigue, for example, diminish your ability to perceive others accurately.[54]

Be Mindful of the Behaviors That Create Meaning for You

mindful

Being conscious of what you are doing, thinking, and sensing at any given moment.

To be **mindful** is to be conscious of what you are doing, thinking, and sensing at any given moment. In Chapter 2 we have noted that we are sometimes unconsciously incompetent—we may not even realize when we are making a perceptual error. A way to increase perceptual accuracy is to make an effort to be less on "automatic pilot" when making judgments of others and more aware of the conclusions that you draw. The opposite of being mindful is to be mindless—not attuned to what is happening to you. Have you ever walked into a room and then forgotten why you were going there? (Trust us: If this hasn't happened to you yet, it will happen when you get older.) Or have you ever misplaced your keys, even though you just had them in your hand minutes earlier? How could you forget what you were directly experiencing just moments ago? The answer is, you were mindless rather than mindful. We sometimes aren't paying attention to what we are doing. When you interact with others, try to identify one new thing to focus on and observe each time. Watch gestures, eyes, the wrinkles around eyes, and foot movements; listen to tone of voice. Try to notice as much detail as possible, but keep the entire picture in view, being mindful of what you are observing.

BEING Other-ORIENTED

Not only being willing to accept criticism from others, but also seeking it, can enhance a relationship if both people are sensitive when sharing and listening. Can you think of criticism that a close friend or family member has shared with you that strengthened the quality of your relationship with that person? Have you heard criticism that caused a relationship to deteriorate? What kind of shared information makes a relationship stronger? What kinds of criticism may be damaging to a relationship?

Link Details with the Big Picture

Any skilled detective knows how to use a small piece of information or evidence to reach a broader conclusion. Skilled perceivers keep the big picture in mind as they look for clues about a person. Just because someone may dress differently from you, or have a Facebook page or Twitter feed that includes misspellings and grammatical errors, don't rush to judgment about the person based on such small bits of information. Look and listen for other cues that can help you develop a more accurate understanding of who your new acquaintance is. Try not to use early information to form a quick or rigid judgment that may be inaccurate. Look at all the details you've gathered.

Become Aware of Others' Perceptions of You

The best athletes never avoid listening to criticism and observations from their coaches. Instead, they seek out as much feedback as they can about what they are doing right and wrong. It is difficult to be objective about our own behavior, so feedback from others can help us with our self-perceptions. The strongest relationships are those in which the partners are willing both to share their perceptions and to be receptive to the perceptions of the other.

Check Your Perceptions

Throughout this chapter we've encouraged you to be more mindful of your communication with others. It may seem like we're expecting you to be a mind reader—to look at someone and know precisely what he or she is thinking. Mind reading may be a good circus act, but it's not a well-documented way of enhancing your perception of others. What does seem to work is to check your perceptions of others. You can check the accuracy of your perceptions and attributions in two ways: indirectly and directly.

Indirect perception checking involves seeking additional information through passive perception, either to confirm or to refute your interpretations. If you suspect someone is angry at you but is not admitting it, for example, you could look for more cues in his or her tone of voice, eye contact, and body movements to confirm your suspicion. You could also listen more intently to the person's words and language.

Direct perception checking involves asking straight out whether your interpretation of what you perceive is correct. Asking someone to confirm a perception shows that you are committed to understanding his or her behavior. If your friend's voice sounds weary and her posture is sagging, you may assume that she is depressed or upset. If you ask, "I get the feeling from your tone of voice and the way you're acting that you are kind of down and depressed; what's wrong?" your friend can then either provide another interpretation: "I'm just tired; I had a busy week," or expand on your interpretation: "Yeah, things haven't been going very well…." Your observation might also trigger a revelation: "Really? I didn't realize I was acting that way. I guess I am a little down."

indirect perception checking
Seeking through passive perception, such as observing and listening, additional information to confirm or refute interpretations you are making.

direct perception checking
Asking for confirmation from the observed person of an interpretation or a perception about him or her.

> ### BEING Other-ORIENTED
> Being other-oriented may sound like a simple set of techniques that can solve all relationship problems. But it's not that simple. And we don't claim that if you are other-oriented, all your relational challenges will melt away. Can you think of situations in which you believed you were being other-oriented, yet the relationship continued to experience turbulence and challenges? What are the limitations of being other-oriented?

Become Other-Oriented

Effective interpersonal perception depends on the ability to understand where others are coming from, to get inside their heads, to see things from their perspectives. When people aren't other-oriented, their relationships tend to suffer. Research confirms that when we perceive that others are not responding appropriately or adapting thoughtfully to our message, we are likely to end the conversation, frown, or grimace to express disapproval, or just fake being pleasant even if we are not enjoying the conversation. If we think someone isn't being nice to us (*not* being other-oriented), then we are unlikely to be nice to them.[55] So our perception of others influences our response to them. Our advice: Be other-oriented. Seek to understand what others actually think and feel.

Becoming other-oriented involves a two-step process: social decentering (consciously *thinking* about another's thoughts and feelings) and empathizing (*responding emotionally* to another's feelings).[56] What does your boss think and feel when you arrive late for work? What would your

Do you think this father is using direct perception checking, indirect perception checking, or a combination of the two?

Communication and Emotion

How to Perceive the Emotions of Others More Accurately

Misreading someone's emotional response can impede effective and appropriate communication with that person. If, for example, you think your friend is angry with you because of something you did, but in reality he is upset because of his poor performance on a test, your misattribution of your friend's emotion could create relational turbulence between the two of you.

One way to improve your perceptions of others' emotions is to use the perception checking skills we've presented. You can try the indirect perception checking approach by simply withholding your interpretation until you spend more time observing your partner. Or you can check your perceptions directly by asking that person what she or he is feeling.

- Step one is to observe what someone is expressing nonverbally (the person's facial expression, tone of voice, movement, posture, and gestures).
- Step two is to make a mindful guess as to what the person may be feeling. But don't stop there.
- Step three is to ask a question to check whether your impression is accurate.

Besides using perception checking, it's useful to keep the following principles in mind when trying to accurately perceive others' emotions.

- Seek to interpret someone's emotion by considering the overall context of the communication.
- Don't consider just one bit of behavior, such as someone's facial expression or tone of voice in isolation; look for a variety of cues, both spoken and unspoken, to increase the accuracy of your perception of your partner's emotions.
- Consider how your partner has responded to information and events in the past to help you interpret emotional responses.

spouse think and feel if you brought a dog home as a surprise gift? Throughout this book we offer suggestions for becoming other-oriented, for reminding yourself that the world does not revolve around you. Being other-oriented enables you to increase your understanding of others and improve your ability to predict and adapt to what others do and say.

To improve your ability to socially decenter and empathize, strive for two key goals: (1) Gather as much information as possible about the circumstances that are affecting the other person; and (2) collect as much information as possible about the other person.

Applying an Other-Orientation

to Interpersonal Perception

We continue to stress the importance of considering the thoughts and feelings of others as a way to enhance the quality of your interpersonal relationships. When forming impressions of others and striving to perceive them accurately, it's especially important to consider what the other person may be thinking and feeling. To help you become more other-oriented, we offer several questions you could ask yourself. You don't need to ponder each question every time you meet someone new—that would be unrealistic. But in situations in which it's especially important to form an accurate impression of someone (whether you're interviewing the person for a job or thinking about asking the person out on a date), consider these questions:

- What factors or circumstances are affecting the other person right now?
- How can I determine whether there are factors I don't know about or don't fully understand about the other person? Should I ask specific questions?

- What do I know about this person that explains his or her behaviors?
- What might be going on in the other person's mind right now?
- What might the other person be feeling right now?
- What other possible explanations could there be for the person's actions?
- What would I be thinking if I were in the same situation as this person?
- How would I be feeling if I were in the same situation as this person?
- What would most other people think if they were in that situation?
- How would most other people feel if they were in that situation?

STUDY GUIDE
Review, Apply, and Assess

Understanding Interpersonal Perception

Objective 3.1   **Define perception, and explain the three stages of interpersonal perception.**

Key Terms

perception	thin slicing
interpersonal perception	cognitive schema
passive perception	superimpose
active perception	punctuation
selective perception	closure
selective attention	impressions
selective exposure	impression formation theory
selective recall	

Thinking Critically

Do you ever "people watch"? If so, do you find that you thin slice, or make judgments about the people you are observing? What cues do you tend to focus on?

Assessing Your Skills

Find a magazine ad or illustration, a photograph, or a painting that shows a group of people, and bring it to class. Form groups of four or five and pass around the pictures in your group. For each picture, write down a few words to describe your perceptions of what you see. What are the people doing? What is their relationship to one another? What is each person like? How is each person feeling? Why are they doing what they are doing? After you have finished, share what you wrote with the others in your group. Try to determine why people's descriptions differed. What factors influenced your perceptions?

Forming Impressions of Others

Objective 3.2   **List and describe the strategies we use to form impressions of others.**

Key Terms

implicit personality theory	predicted outcome value
construct	theory (POV)
uncertainty reduction	recency effect
theory	halo effect
primacy effect	horn effect

Thinking Critically

Describe a recent situation in which your first impression of someone turned out to be inaccurate, whether online or in person. What led you to form this initial impression? What were your initial perceptions? What then led you to change those perceptions?

Assessing Your Skills

Pair up with someone in class with whom you have not interacted before. Then, without saying anything to each other, write down ten words that you think apply to the other person based on your early impressions of them. Note: You will eventually reveal the words you write to your partner. After you've written your ten words, don't reveal the words just yet, but have a five-minute conversation getting to know the other person better. Following your conversation, make a second list of additional words that you now think apply to the person. In addition, cross out any words in the first list that you now think don't apply. Share both lists of words with each other. Discuss the reasons each of you chose each word noting what influenced your perceptions.

Interpreting the Behavior of Others

Objective 3.3   **List and describe the strategies we use to interpret the behavior of others.**

Key Terms

attribution theory	standpoint theory
causal attribution theory	culture

Thinking Critically

Think of a time when a friend or family member was late for an appointment or didn't attend a meeting as scheduled. Describe how you interpreted the absence or missed meeting. Which theory or theories mentioned in the chapter helped you interpret the behavior as you did?

Assessing Your Skills

Link the name of the theory with the accurate description of the theory.

Attribution
theory _____

A. We use a personal set of assumptions to draw specific conclusions about someone's personality.

Standpoint
theory _____

B. We ascribe a person's actions to circumstance, a stimulus, or the person himself or herself.

Causal attribution
theory _____

C. We interpret the behavior of others through the lens of our own social position, power, or cultural background.

Implicit personality
theory _____

D. We develop reasons to explain the behaviors of others.

Intercultural
communication
theory _____

E. People make predictions about the future of a relationship based on early impressions.

Predicted
outcome value
theory _____

F. Our different backgrounds, experiences, and culture influence how we interpret what we see and hear.

Check your answers by consulting the Recap box earlier in this chapter.

Identifying Barriers to Accurate Interpersonal Perception

Objective 3.4   **Identify the eight factors that distort the accuracy of interpersonal perception.**

Key Terms

stereotype
social identity model of
deindividuation effects (SIDE)

fundamental attribution error
self-serving bias

Thinking Critically

Think about some of your recent interpersonal conflicts. How would you describe your perception of the problem in each conflict? How do you think the others involved would describe their perceptions of the problem? What role did perception play in contributing to or resolving the conflict?

Assessing Your Skills

Make a list of between five and ten stereotypes of different groups or categories of people. Compare and contrast your list with those of your classmates. What factors contribute to the forming of these stereotypes?

Ask a classmate to make a list of adjectives that he or she would use to describe you. Then discuss with the classmate how many of these characteristics are based on stereotypes. How many are based on other perceptual barriers such as lack of information?

Improving Interpersonal Perception Skills

Objective 3.5   **Identify and apply five suggestions for improving interpersonal perception.**

Key Terms

mindful
indirect perception checking

direct perception checking

Thinking Critically

Describe a recent communication exchange in which you needed to be other-oriented. How did you "step back" to understand what the other person was thinking and feeling? Did you express empathy? Explain how you did so.

Assessing Your Skills

Think of a person in your life whose recent behavior and/or communication has puzzled or angered you. Put yourself in that person's place and analyze why he or she is behaving in this way. List the questions you need to ask yourself to help understand your perceptions and determine whether these perceptions are accurate. What perception-checking steps do you need to take? What, specifically, do you need to do to adjust your perceptions and have more effective communication with this person?

Chapter 4
Interpersonal Communication and Diversity: Adapting to Others

" Strangers, people different from us, stir up fear, discomfort, suspicion, and hostility. They make us lose our sense of security just by being 'other.'"

Henri J. M. Nouwen

⌄ Learning Objectives

4.1 Describe five human differences that influence communication.

4.2 Define culture and identify and describe the seven dimensions of culture.

4.3 List and describe barriers that inhibit effective intercultural communication.

4.4 Identify and apply strategies for developing knowledge, motivation, and skills that can improve intercultural competence.

CHAPTER OUTLINE

Understanding Diversity: Describing Our Differences

Understanding Culture: Dimensions of Our Mental Software

Barriers to Effective Intercultural Communication

Improving Intercultural Communication Competence

His Indonesian-American half sister attended along with her Chinese-Canadian husband. Another family member, the rabbi, was there, too. If all of the family members from his past could have attended, you would have heard English, Indonesian, French, Cantonese, German, Hebrew, Swahili, Luo, Igbo, and Gullah, a Creole dialect of South Carolina's Low Country.[1] His Black father from Kenya, who was a Muslim, and his White Methodist mother from Kansas, both of whom had passed away, would no doubt have been proud to attend. The event? The inauguration of the 44th President of the United States, Barack Obama.

Diversity is about differences. Diversity of culture, language, religion, and a host of other factors is increasingly commonplace in contemporary society. This diversity creates the potential for misunderstanding and even conflict stemming from the different ways we make sense out of the world and share that sense with others. In their book *Communicating with Strangers*, intercultural communication researchers William Gudykunst and Young Yun Kim point out that strangers are "people who are different and unknown."[2] As human beings we have many things in common. But through our interpersonal interactions with others it becomes obvious that many people look different and communicate in different ways from us.

In the first three chapters, we acknowledged the influence of diversity on interpersonal relationships. In this chapter, we examine in more detail the impact that people's differences have on their lives and suggest some communication strategies for bridging those differences in our interpersonal relationships. The premise of this chapter on diversity is that in order to live comfortably in the twenty-first century, people must learn to appreciate and understand our differences instead of ignoring them, suffering because of them, or wishing that they would disappear.

Some people may be weary of what they perceive as an overemphasis on diversity. One student overheard a classmate say, "I'm tired of all this politically correct nonsense. It seems like every textbook in every class is obsessed with it. Why don't they just teach us what we need to know and cut all of this diversity garbage?" Perhaps you've encountered this kind of "diversity backlash" among some of your classmates (or maybe you hold this attitude yourself). It may seem unsettling to some that textbooks emphasize cultural diversity. But this emphasis is not motivated by an irrational desire to be politically correct, but by the fact that the United States and other countries are becoming increasingly diverse.[3] With this diversity comes a growing awareness that learning about differences, especially cultural differences, can affect every aspect of people's lives in positive ways. You need not travel the world to interact with people who may seem different to you; the world is traveling to you.

A central goal of your study of interpersonal communication is to learn how you can better relate to others. Some differences that contribute to diversity and may interfere with developing relationships include age, learning style, gender, religion, ethnicity, sexual orientation, social class, and culture. We will emphasize the role of cultural differences and how they affect our interpersonal communication, while also noting a variety of ways in which we may seem strange to one another.

BEING Other-ORIENTED

Communicating with people who are different from you is something you probably do every day. Even your close friends and family members differ from you in many ways. Reflect on one or two interpersonal relationships you have, and note the similarities and differences between you and the other person. How have the differences (such as age, ethnicity, gender, religion, or culture) affected the way you interact with this person?

Understanding Diversity: Describing Our Differences

4.1 Describe five human differences that influence communication.

How are we different? Let us count the ways. No, let's not—that would take up too much space! There are an infinite number of ways in which we are different from one another. Unless you have an identical twin, you look different from everybody else, although you may have some things in common with a larger group of people (such as skin color, hair style, or clothing choice). Communication researchers have, however, studied several major differences that affect the way we interact with one another. To frame our discussion of diversity and communication, we'll note differences in gender, sexual orientation, ethnicity, age, and social class. Each of these differences—some

Relating to Diverse Others

A Diversity Almanac

1. Two-thirds of the immigrants on this planet come to the United States.[5]

2. In the United States, there are "minority majorities" (where minorities outnumber traditional European Americans) in Miami; Laredo, Texas; Gary, Indiana; Detroit; Washington, DC; Oakland, California; Atlanta; San Antonio; Los Angeles; Chicago; Baltimore; Houston; New York City; Memphis; San Francisco; Fresno, California; and San Jose, California.[6]

3. It is estimated that more than forty million US residents have a non-English first language, including eighteen million people whose first language is Spanish.[7]

4. Almost one-third of US residents under age thirty-five are members of minority groups, compared with one-fifth of those age thirty-five or older. According to US Bureau of the Census population projections, by the year 2025 nearly half of all young adults in this country will come from minority groups.[8]

5. If the current trend continues, by the year 2050 the percentage of the US population that is White will decrease to 53 percent, down from a current 79 percent. Asians will increase to 16 percent, up from 1.6 percent; Hispanics will more than triple their numbers to over 25 percent, up from just over 7.5 percent; and African Americans will increase their proportion slightly from the current 12 percent.[9]

6. More than 30 percent of graduate assistants teaching in universities in the United States are foreign born.[10]

7. Studies of gay and lesbian populations in the United States estimate that gay men make up from 1 to 9 percent of the general male population and lesbians make up from 1 to 5 percent of the general female population.[11]

8. There are more "Millennials" (people born between 1982 and 2002) in the US population than any other age group. In 2004 the US population included 100 million Millennials, 44 million Generation Xers (born 1961–1981), and 78 million Baby Boomers (born 1943–1960).[12]

9. One out of every eight US residents speaks a language other than English at home, and one-third of children in urban US public schools speak a first language other than English.[13]

10. Non-Hispanic Whites constitute a minority of the population in Texas, Hawaii, New Mexico, and California.[14]

11. Sixty percent of the residents of Miami are foreign-born.[15]

12. One in six marriages is between people of different ethnic groups.[16]

13. According to Census Bureau Director Louis Kincannon, "There are more minorities in this country (United States) today than there were people in the United States in 1910. In fact, the minority population in the United States is larger than the total population of all but eleven countries."[17]

learned, some based on biology, economic status, or simply on how long someone has lived—affects how you perceive others and interact with them.

One of the most significant problems that stems from focusing on people's differences is the tendency to discriminate and unfairly, inaccurately, or inappropriately ascribe stereotypes. **Discrimination** is the unfair or inappropriate treatment of other people based on their group membership.[4] One of the goals of learning about diversity and becoming aware of both differences and similarities among groups is to eliminate discrimination and stereotypes that cause people to rigidly and inappropriately prejudge others.

Following our discussion of some classic ways in which we are diverse, we'll turn our attention to cultural differences and the barriers they can create. We'll conclude the chapter by identifying strategies to enhance the quality of interpersonal communication with others, despite our differences.

discrimination

Unfair or inappropriate treatment of people based on their group membership.

Sex and Gender

Perhaps the most obvious form of human diversity is the existence of female and male human beings.[18] A person's **sex** is determined by biology; only men can impregnate; only women can menstruate, gestate, and lactate. In contrast to sex differences, *gender differences* reflect learned behavior that is culturally associated with being a man or a woman. Definitions of gender roles are flexible: A man can adopt behavior associated with a feminine role in a given culture, and vice versa. **Gender** refers to psychological and emotional characteristics that cause people to assume masculine, feminine, or androgynous (having a combination of both feminine and masculine traits) roles. Your gender is learned and socially reinforced by others, as well as by

sex

Biologically based differences that determine whether one is male or female.

gender

Socially learned and reinforced characteristics that include one's biological sex and psychological characteristics (femininity, masculinity, androgyny).

your life experiences and genetics. Some researchers prefer to study gender as a co-culture (a subset of the larger cultural group). We view gender as one of many basic elements of culture.

In the predominant culture of the United States, someone's sex and gender are both important things to know. Yet how different are men and women? John Gray, author of the popular book *Men Are from Mars, Women Are from Venus*, would have us believe that the sexes are so different from each other that we approach life as if we lived on two different planets.[19] Communication scholars have challenged many of Gray's stereotypical conclusions.[20] Although researchers have noted some differences in the way men and women interact (women tend to express their emotions directly, whereas men tend to manage and suppress their emotions),[21] to label *all* men and *all* women as acting in prototypical ways may cause us to assume differences that aren't really there. Sex and gender differences are complex and not easily classified into tidy categories of "male/masculine" and "female/feminine" behaviors.[22]

Deborah Tannen, author of several books on communication between the sexes, views men and women as belonging to different cultural groups.[23] She suggests that female–male communication is cross-cultural communication, with all of the challenges of communicating with people who are different from us.

Sex differences emerge in how we present ourselves online, as well as in our live-and-in-person presentation of self. Research has found that males are more likely than females to access the Internet in public places such libraries; some wonder whether this difference suggests a "digital divide" in which men access the Internet more than women.[24] Both men and women tend to present themselves online in stereotypical ways. According to observations made by a panel of men and women who reviewed Facebook pages, men were more likely to post photos of themselves in active, dominant, and independent roles. In contrast, women, were more likely to present themselves as more attractive and dependent in comparison to men.[25] Our desired online presence influences not only the photos we decide to post, but what we say about ourselves. One study found that when participating in online dating, men were more likely than women to include false or inaccurate information about their desire for a long-term relationship, as well as misleading information about their financial assets. Women were more likely to alter their weight when describing themselves online. The researchers speculated that these differences in what we're honest about can be linked to evolutionary psychology theory, which suggests that heterosexual men and women seek to make themselves more attractive to the opposite sex by adapting to the desires and expectations of others.[26]

Research conclusions can result in uncertainty about sex and gender differences. Are there really fundamental differences in the way men and women communicate? Yes, researchers have documented some differences. But these differences may have more to do with *why* we communicate than *how*. Men and those who adopt a masculine communication style tend to talk in order to accomplish something or complete a task. Women and those who identify with a feminine gender style are often more likely to use conversation to establish and maintain relationships. There is a short way of summarizing this difference: *Men often communicate to report; women often communicate to establish rapport.*[27] Research suggests that men tend to approach communication from a content orientation, meaning that they view the primary purpose of communication as an information exchange. You talk when you have something to say. Women tend to use communication for the purpose of relating or connecting to others. So the difference isn't in the way the sexes actually communicate, but in their motivations or reasons for communicating. Note, however, that although gender differences account for considerable variation in how men and women view the world and the assumptions they hold about the nature of relationships, cultural background is an even more powerful influence on some key assumptions about relationships.[28]

Sexual Orientation

During the past three decades, GLBTQ community members have become more assertive in expressing their rights within American society. Questions of whether gays and lesbians should participate in the military, the clergy, and the teaching profession have stirred the passions of many. Many, but not all US citizens, celebrated the Supreme Court's decision to legalize same-sex marriage in all 50 states. At the national and state levels of government, the judicial, executive, and legislative branches of government have increased legal rights for GLBTQ people—gay men, lesbian women, bisexual people, transgendered individuals (those who believe that their biological sex does not reflect their sexual identity psychologically), and those who identify as queer (people who are reluctant to place a label on their sexuality). Being GLBTQ is a source of pride for some, but it remains a social stigma for others who continue to conceal their sexual orientation due to fear of rejection or prejudice (homophobia). The incidence of suicide among gay and lesbian teenagers is significantly higher than among heterosexual teens.[29] Although GLBTQ individuals are gaining legal rights and protections, they are still subject to discriminatory laws and social intolerance. Yet GLBTQ communities are important co-cultures within the larger US culture.

GLBTQ individuals continue to be judged negatively based solely on their sexual orientation.[30] Research further suggests that heterosexuals who have negative perceptions of GLBTQ individuals are more likely to have rigid views about gender roles and to assume that their peers share these views.[31] In addition, those who hold negative attitudes toward gays and lesbians are less likely to have interpersonal communication with gays or lesbians.[32] Some gays and lesbians continue to conceal their sexual orientation because of the existence of these negative attitudes, as well as anti-gay violence and harassment.

An effective and appropriate interpersonal communicator is aware of and sensitive to issues and attitudes about sexual orientation in contemporary society. Homophobia, the irrational fear of, aversion to, or discrimination against homosexuality, continues to exist among many people. Just as people have been taught to avoid biased expressions that degrade someone's ethnicity, it is equally important to avoid using language that demeans a person's sexual orientation. Telling stories and jokes with points or punch lines that rely on cruelly ridiculing a person because of his or her sexual orientation lowers perceptions of the story. It also decreases the joke-teller's credibility among gay and lesbian people, as well as those who dislike any show of bias against gays and lesbians.

Although we may not intend anything negative, sometimes we unintentionally offend someone through more subtle use and misuse of language.[33] For example, gays and lesbians typically prefer to be referred to as "gay" or "lesbian" rather than "homosexual." In addition, the term *sexual orientation* is preferred over *sexual preference* when describing a person's sexual orientation. Our language should reflect and acknowledge the range of human relationships that exist. Our key point is this: Be sensitively other-oriented as you interact with those whose sexual orientation is different from your own.

Race and Ethnicity

Racial and ethnic differences are often discussed and sometimes debated. **Race** is a term that has evolved to include a group of people with a common cultural history, nationality, or geographical location, as well as genetically transmitted physical attributes.[34] A person's racial classification was historically based on visible physiological attributes—*phenotypes*—which include skin color, body type, hair color and texture, and facial attributes. Skin color and other physical characteristics affect our responses and influence the way people of different races interact.

race

A group of people with a common cultural history, nationality, or geographical location, as well as genetically transmitted physical attributes.

Although it may seem neat and tidy to classify individuals genetically as belonging to one race or another, it's not quite that simple. One geneticist has concluded that there is much more genetic variation *within* a given racial category than *between* one race and another.[35] There really aren't vast genetic differences among racial categories. That's why many scholars suggest that we think of race as a category that emphasizes biological or genetic characteristics, as well as cultural, economic, social, geographic, and historical elements.[36] The term *race,* therefore, is a fuzzy, somewhat controversial way of classifying people.

ethnicity

Social classification based on nationality, religion, language, and ancestral heritage, shared by a group of people who also share a common geographical origin.

Ethnicity is a related term, yet scholars suggest it is different from race. **Ethnicity** is a *social classification* based on a variety of factors, such as nationality, religion, language, and ancestral heritage (race), that are shared by a group of people who also share a common geographic origin. Simply stated, an ethnic group is a community of people who have labeled themselves based on a variety of factors that may or may not include race. In making distinctions between race and ethnicity, Brenda Allen suggests that ethnicity refers to "a common origin or culture based on shared activities and identity related to some mixture of race, religion, language and/or ancestry."[37] A key distinction between race and ethnicity is that one's ethnicity is a *socially constructed* category that emphasizes culture and a host of other factors rather than one's racial or genetic background. Not all Asians (race), for example, have the same cultural background (ethnicity).[38] Nationality and geographical location are especially important in defining an ethnic group. Those of Irish ancestry are usually referred to as an ethnic group rather than as a race. The same could be said of Britons, Norwegians, and Spaniards.

Different patterns in the ways people in various ethnic groups interact can be observed both in face-to-face communication situations and online. On Facebook profiles, for example, researchers found that members of some ethnic groups such as African Americans, Latinos, and American Indians displayed what researchers called a heavy "social" profile; they indicated their strong openness to interact with others. Profiles of individuals from these ethnic groups also included more information about ethnic ancestry and expressed the importance of belonging to an ethnic group more frequently than profiles of White or Vietnamese students. Specifically, students from African American, Latino, and American Indian ethnic groups were more likely to include inspirational quotations related to issues of injustice and equal rights for ethnic minorities when compared to White or Vietnamese students. It appears that your ethnic identity is important in how you present yourself and communicate with others online.[39]

Ethnicity, like race, fosters common bonds that affect communication patterns. On the positive side, ethnic groups bring vitality and variety to American society. On the negative side, members of these groups may experience persecution or rejection by members of other groups in society.

In 2015, President Obama along with thousands of others walked across this bridge in Selma, Alabama, to commemorate the civil rights demonstrations that took place there fifty years prior.

Age

Various generations tend to view life differently because of the cultural and historical events they have experienced in their lives. Today's explicit song lyrics may shock older Americans who grew up with "racy" lyrics like "makin' whoopee." The generation gap is real and has implications for the relationships we develop with others.

Generational differences have an effect not just on communication with your parents or other family members, but on a variety of relationships, including those with teachers, merchants, bosses, and mentors. There is considerable evidence that people hold stereotypical views of others based on their perceived age.[40] In addition, a person's age influences his or her communication with others. For example, one study found that older adults experience greater difficulty in accurately interpreting nonverbal messages than younger people do.[41] Older adults also don't like to be patronized or talked down to (who does?).[42] And younger people seem to value social support, empathic listening, and being mentored more than older people do.[43]

Authors Neil Howe and William Strauss, two researchers who have investigated the role of age and generation in society, define a generation as "a society-wide peer group, born over a period roughly the same length as the passage from youth to adulthood, who collectively possess a common persona."[44]

- *Baby Boomers* is the label for people born between 1943 and 1960. Perhaps your parents or grandparents are Boomers?
- *Generation X* is the term used for people born between 1961 and 1981.
- *Millennials* are those born between 1982 and 2002.[45]

Researchers Howe and Strauss suggest that as a group, "Millennials are unlike any other youth generation in living memory. They are more numerous, more affluent, better educated, and more ethnically diverse. More importantly, they are beginning to manifest a wide array of positive social habits that older Americans no longer associate with youth, including a focus on teamwork, achievement, modesty, and good conduct."[46] If you are a Millennial who is used to searching for information on the Internet and learning about things via tweets and texts, some researchers predict that you may need to develop critical analysis skills.[47] Research has found that even though Millennials access different contemporary media outlets than older individuals, political interest remains constant.[48] Do you know what "helicopter parents" are? They are parents who hover around their children to ensure they are safe, well-cared for, and get what they need. Millennials are more likely to have helicopter parents than are other age groups.[49] Therefore some (certainly not all) Millennials may harbor some expectation that their parents may rescue them from difficult or stressful situations. Table 4.1 summarizes labels for and common characteristics and values of several generational groups.

Table 4.1 Summary of Generational Characteristics

Generation Name	Birth Years	Typical Characteristics
Matures	1925–1942	• Work hard • Have a sense of duty • Are willing to sacrifice • Have a sense of what is right • Work quickly
Baby Boomers	1943–1960	• Value personal fulfillment and optimism • Crusade for causes • Buy now, pay later • Support equal rights for all • Work efficiently
Generation Xers	1961–1981	• Live with uncertainty • Consider balance important • Live for today • Save • Consider every job as a contract
Millennials	1982–2002	• Are close to their (sometimes "helicopter") parents • Feel "special" • Are goal-oriented • Are team-oriented • Focus on achievement

SOURCE: Data from N. Howe and W. Strauss, *Millennials Rising: The Next Great Generation* (New York: Vintage Books, 2000): 432.

Your generation has important implications for interpersonal communication, especially as you relate to others in both family and work situations. Each generation has developed its own set of values, which are anchored in social, economic, and cultural factors stemming from the times in which the generation has lived. Our values, core conceptualizations of what is fundamentally good or bad, or right or wrong, color our way of thinking about and responding to what we experience.

Generational and age differences may create barriers and increase the potential for conflict and misunderstanding.[50] For example, one team of researchers who investigated the role of generations in the workforce suggested that Generation X workers are paradoxically both more individualistic (self-reliant) and more team-oriented than Boomers are.[51] In contrast, Boomers are more likely to have a sense of loyalty to their employers, expect long-term employment, value a pension plan, and experience job burnout from overwork. Generation Xers, on the other hand, seek more of a balance between work and personal life, expect to have more than one job or career, value good working conditions over other job factors, and have a greater need to feel appreciated.[52] Another study found that younger people who rarely interact with older people were more likely to talk slowly and come across as patronizing to older individuals.[53] Of course, these are broad generalizations and do not apply to all people in these categories.

Social Class

The US Constitution declares that all people are created equal, but class differences do exist, and they affect communication patterns. Social psychologist Michael Argyle reports that the cues we use to identify class distinctions are (1) way of life, (2) family, (3) job, (4) money, and (5) education.[54] Brenda Allen suggests, "Social class encompasses a socially constructed category of identity that involves more than just economic factors; it includes an entire socialization process."[55] Such a socialization process influences the nature and quality of the interpersonal relationships we have with others. Class differences influence whom we talk with, whether we are likely to invite our neighbors over for coffee, and whom we choose as our friends and lovers. And research suggests that advertisers target sales pitches to specific types of people based on their social class.[56]

Some principles that describe how social classes emerge from society include the following:[57]

1. Virtually every organization or group develops a hierarchy that makes status distinctions.
2. We are more likely to interact with people from our own social class. There seems to be some truth to the maxim "Birds of a feather flock together."
3. People who interact with one another over time tend to communicate in similar ways; they develop similar speech patterns and use similar expressions.
4. Members of a social class develop ways of communicating class differences to others by the way they dress, the cars they drive, the homes they live in, and the schools they attend, as well as other visible symbols of social class.
5. It is possible to change one's social class through education, employment, and income.

Differences in social class and the attendant differences in education and lifestyle affect whom we talk with and even what we talk about.[58] These differences influence our overall cultural standpoint, from which we perceive the world.

Understanding Culture: Dimensions of Our Mental Software

4.2 **Define culture and identify and describe the seven dimensions of culture.**

We have noted ways that differences in sex, gender, sexual orientation, ethnicity, age, and social class contribute to an overall cultural perspective that influences how we relate to others. As we discussed in Chapter 3, **culture** is a learned system of knowledge, behaviors, attitudes, beliefs, values, and norms that is shared by a group of people. In the broadest sense, culture includes how people think, what they do, and how they use things to sustain their lives. Researcher Geert Hofstede describes culture as the "mental software" or "mental programming of the human mind" that touches every aspect of how we make sense of the world and share that sense with others.[59] Just like software installed on a computer, our culture influences how we process information. To interact with other people is to be touched by the influence of culture and cultural differences.

Your culture and your life experiences determine your **worldview**—the general cultural perspective on such key issues as death, God, and the meaning of life that shapes how you perceive and respond to what happens to you. Your cultural worldview shapes your thoughts, language, values, and actions; it permeates all aspects of how you interact with society. *You cannot avoid having a worldview*. Your personal worldview is so pervasive that you may not even be aware of it. Just as a goldfish may not be aware of the water in its bowl, you may not be aware of how your worldview influences every aspect of your life—how you see and what you think. Your worldview is one of the primary ways you make sense out of the world—it's how you interpret what happens to you. People from the rural United States, for example, are more likely to say "hello" to a stranger than are European city dwellers. Your cultural "software" influences with whom you initiate conversation. Cultural differences also predict how and where you send and receive text messages. One study found that people from India prefer private and semi-private places (such as their home) rather than public places (such as a restaurant or bar) to send and receive text messages.[60]

When we speak of culture, we may sometimes be referring to a co-culture. A **co-culture** is a distinct culture within a larger culture. The differences of gender, sexual orientation, ethnicity, age, and social class that we discussed earlier are co-cultures within the predominant culture. For example, about 72 percent of the population of the United States is classified as White, European, American, or Caucasian.[61] Members of minority groups such as African Americans, Latinos, and Asians develop a co-culture, or what is sometimes called a *microculture*. The Amish, Mennonite, Mormon, Islamic, and Jewish religious groups are additional examples of important religious co-cultures. Often, because they are in the minority, members of a co-culture not only *feel* marginalized, they *are* marginalized in employment, education, housing, and other aspects of society. To enhance their power and self-identity, members of co-cultures may develop their own rules and norms. For example, teens develop their own slang, wear certain kinds of clothing, value certain kinds of music, and engage in other behaviors that make it easier for them to be identified apart from the larger culture.

Researchers and scholars who study culture have identified various dimensions or elements of culture. These dimensions provide a framework to describe how our culture influences us. These cultural elements are not rooted in biology but are learned, passed on from parents to children.

Enculturation is the process of transmitting a group's culture from one generation to the next *from those within that culture* (such as parents, brothers, sisters, or

culture

Learned system of knowledge, behavior, attitudes, beliefs, values, and norms shared by a group of people.

worldview

Individual perceptions or perceptions by a culture or group of people about key beliefs and issues, such as death, God, and the meaning of life, which influence interaction with others.

co-culture

A microculture; a distinct culture within a larger culture (such as the gay and lesbian co-culture).

enculturation

The process of transmitting a group's culture from one generation to the next.

grandparents). This happens naturally through association and storytelling, as well as by example.

acculturation

The process of transmitting a host culture's values, ideas, and beliefs to someone from outside that culture.

Acculturation, a related concept, is the process of how people *from the new, host culture* transmit values, ideas, and beliefs to people outside the host culture. So when your parents teach you how to eat with chopsticks, that's *enculturation*. But when a teacher or friend shows you proper manners and etiquette, that's *acculturation*. Whether from within the culture or from a host culture, both processes describe how you learn about culture. You are not born with a certain taste in music, food, or automobiles. You *learn* to behave in accordance with the elements that characterize your culture. And you *learn* to appreciate the dimensions of your culture, just as you learn anything: through observing role models and receiving positive reinforcement from people within your own culture (enculturation) and from those outside your culture (acculturation).[62]

Researchers have identified seven dimensions that they say appear in all of the cultures they have studied. Think of these dimensions as general ways of describing how culture is expressed in the behavior of groups of people. The seven dimensions are (1) individualism (an emphasis on the individual) versus collectivism (an emphasis on the group); (2) an emphasis on the surrounding context, including nonverbal behaviors, versus little emphasis on context; (3) masculine values that emphasize accomplishment, versus feminine values that emphasize nurturing; (4) degree of tolerance for uncertainty; (5) approaches to power; (6) short- or long-term approaches to time; and (7) indulgence versus restraint.

Individualism: One and Many

One of the most prominent dimensions of a culture is that of individualism versus collectivism. Individualistic cultures such as those in North America value individual achievement and personal accomplishment. Collectivistic cultures, including many Asian cultures, value group and team achievement. One researcher summed up the American goal system this way:

> Chief among the virtues claimed … is self-realization. Each person is viewed as having a unique set of talents and potentials. The translation of these potentials into actuality is considered the highest purpose to which one can devote one's life.[63]

Individualism is a strong cultural dimension in the United States. Individual achievements are rewarded, often quite publicly.

Conversely, in a collectivistic culture, people strive to attain goals for all members of the family, group, or community. In collectivist Kenyan tribes, for example,

> [N]obody is an isolated individual. Rather, his [or her] uniqueness is a secondary fact… . Because of the emphasis on collectivity, harmony and cooperation among the group tends to be emphasized more than individual function and responsibility.[64]

Individualistic cultures tend to be more loosely knit socially; individuals feel responsible for taking care of themselves and their immediate families.[65] In collectivistic cultures, individuals expect more support from others; they also experience more loyalty to and from the community.[66] Because collectivistic cultures place more value on "we" than "I," teamwork approaches usually succeed better in their workplaces. US businesses have tried to adopt some of Japan's successful team strategies for achieving high productivity. There are not always clear-cut distinctions between individualistic and collectivistic cultures. Research suggests that within a given culture, such as a collectivistic culture, there are still variations and degrees of individualism and collectivism.[67] As with all categories, it's important not to make broad, sweeping generalizations but to acknowledge the considerable variation in cultural values.

Context: High and Low

Individuals from different cultures use cues from the **cultural context** to varying degrees to enhance messages and meaning. This insight led anthropologist Edward T. Hall to categorize cultures as either high- or low-context.[68] In **high-context cultures**, nonverbal cues are extremely important in interpreting messages. **Low-context cultures** rely more explicitly on language and use fewer contextual cues to send and interpret information. Individuals from high-context cultures may perceive people from low-context cultures as less attractive, knowledgeable, and trustworthy, because they violate unspoken rules of dress, conduct, and communication. Individuals from low-context cultures often are not skilled in interpreting unspoken, contextual messages.[69]

For example, Darrin is an exchange student who grew up in Tokyo, Japan, a high-context culture. If you grew up in Dallas, Texas, a low-context culture, you may want to tone down your gestures, facial expressions, and other overly expressive nonverbal cues when talking with Darrin. And Darrin may want to be more expressive when interacting with you. The challenge is to be aware of culture differences and preferences without going to extremes adapting to another person. As in all other-oriented conversations, before premeditating how you will adapt your communication style, you may want to observe and listen. You want to be appropriately sensitive without overadapting based on stereotypes or expectations.

cultural context
Aspects of the environment and/or nonverbal cues that convey information not explicitly communicated through language.

high-context culture
Culture in which people derive much information from nonverbal and environmental cues.

low-context culture
Culture in which people derive much information from the words of a message and less information from nonverbal and environmental cues.

Gender: Masculine and Feminine

Some cultures emphasize traditional male values, whereas others place greater value on female perspectives. These values are not really about biological sex differences but about overarching approaches to interacting with others.

People from **masculine cultures** tend to value more traditional roles for both men and women. Masculine cultures also value achievement, assertiveness, heroism, and material wealth. Research reveals that men tend to approach communication from a content orientation, meaning that they view communication as functioning primarily for information exchange. Men talk when they have something to say. This characteristic is also consistent with men's tendency to base their relationships, especially their male friendships, on sharing activities rather than talking.

Men and women from **feminine cultures** tend to value such things as caring for the less fortunate, being sensitive toward others, and enhancing the overall quality of life.[70] Feminine cultures tend to approach communication for the purpose of relating or connecting to others, and of extending themselves to other people in order to know them and be known by them.[71] What women talk about is less important than the fact that they're talking, because talking implies relationship.

Of course, rarely are cultures on the extreme end of the continuum; many are somewhere in between. For centuries, most countries in Europe, Asia, and the Americas have had masculine cultures. Men and their conquests dominate history books; men have been more prominent in leadership and decision making than women. But today many of these cultures are moving slowly toward the middle—legal and social rules encourage more gender balance and greater equality between masculine and feminine roles.

masculine culture
Culture in which people tend to value traditional roles for men and women, achievement, assertiveness, heroism, and material wealth.

feminine culture
Culture in which people tend to value caring, sensitivity, and attention to quality of life.

Uncertainty: High and Low Tolerance

Some cultures tolerate more ambiguity and uncertainty than others. Cultures in which people need certainty to feel secure are more likely to create and enforce rigid rules for behavior and to develop more elaborate codes of conduct. People from cultures with

Many cultures have traditionally put a high value on masculine domination of women, but today there is a gradual trend toward greater equality between male and female roles.

a greater tolerance for uncertainty have more relaxed, informal expectations for others. "Go with the flow" and "It will sort itself out" are phrases that describe the attitudes of people from cultures with greater tolerance. Research suggests that people from Portugal, Greece, Peru, Belgium, and Japan have high certainty needs, but people from Scandinavian countries tend to tolerate uncertainty.[72]

Power: Centralized and Decentralized

Some cultures value an equal, or decentralized, distribution of power, whereas others accept a concentration of hierarchical power in a centralized government and other organizations. In cultures in which people prefer a more centralized approach to power, hierarchical bureaucracies are common, and people expect some individuals to have more power than others. Russia, France, and China are all high on the concentrated power scale. Those that often strive for greater equality and distribution of power and control include many (but not all) citizens of Australia, Denmark, New Zealand, and Israel. People from these latter countries tend to minimize differences in power between people.

Time: Short-Term and Long-Term

A culture's orientation to time falls on a continuum between long-term and short-term.[73] People from a culture with a long-term orientation to time place an emphasis on the future and tend to value perseverance and thrift, because these are virtues that pay off over a long period of time. A long-term time orientation also implies a greater willingness to subordinate oneself for a larger purpose, such as the good of society or the group. In contrast, a culture that tends to have a short-term time orientation values spending rather than saving (because of a focus on the immediate rather than the future), tradition (because of the value placed on the present and the past), and preserving "face" of both self and others (making sure that an individual is respected and that his or her dignity is upheld). Short-term cultures also expect that results will soon follow the actions and effort expended on a task. These kinds of cultures place a high value on social and status obligations.

Cultures or societies with a long-term time orientation include many Asian cultures such as China, Hong Kong, Taiwan, and Japan. Short-term time orientation cultures include Pakistan, the Czech Republic, Nigeria, Spain, and the Philippines. Both Canada and the United States are closer to short-term rather than long-term time orientation, which suggests an emphasis on valuing quick results from projects and greater pressure toward spending rather than saving, as well as a respect for traditions.[74]

Happiness: Indulgent and Restrained

The newest cultural dimension added by intercultural researcher Geert Hofstede is the idea that some cultures indulge and focus on behaviors that make them happy more than other cultural groups. These more indulgent cultures desire and expect freedom and happiness. They also tend to value freedom of speech and place a high value on leisure activities and sports. Cultures that are more restrained do not necessarily expect to have all of their needs met to achieve happiness. They are less likely to remember positive emotions and have fewer expectations about participating in leisure activities, including sports.[75] The United States, Canada, Mexico, Brazil, and Australia are examples of more indulgent cultures.[76] In contrast, Russia, China, and much of Eastern Europe are more restrained cultures. In the United States, for example, we expect "the pursuit of happiness" in our personal lives, relationships, and work. As an American, if you are not happy with work or with a relationship, you are more likely than someone from a more restrained culture to leave and seek happiness somewhere else. But in restrained cultures where people don't necessarily assume everything will work out well or believe they have a right to be happy, people have greater tolerance for unhappiness and lower expectations about achieving specific goals. There is less data to support this newest cultural dimension, but Hofstede has been including it in his latest research results as yet another dimension of our mental software.[77]

Barriers to Effective Intercultural Communication

4.3 List and describe barriers that inhibit effective intercultural communication.

Intercultural communication occurs when individuals or groups from different cultures communicate. The greater the difference in culture between two people, the greater the potential for misunderstanding and mistrust. Research suggests that

intercultural communication
Communication between or among people who have different cultural traditions.

Recap

Understanding Culture: Dimensions of Our Mental Software

Cultural Dimension	Countries That Score Higher on This Cultural Dimension	Countries That Score Lower on This Cultural Dimension
Individualism: Societies that place greater emphasis on individualism generally value individual accomplishment more than societies that value collective or collaborative achievement.	United States, Australia, Great Britain, Canada, Netherlands, New Zealand, Italy, Belgium, Denmark, Sweden, France	Guatemala, Ecuador, Panama, Venezuela, Colombia, Indonesia, Pakistan, Costa Rica, Peru, Taiwan, South Korea
Context: High-context societies prefer to draw information from the surrounding context, including nonverbal messages. Low-context societies tend to prefer information to be presented explicitly, usually in words.	Japan, China, Saudi Arabia, Italy, Greece	Switzerland, Germany, Sweden, Denmark, Finland, United States, Australia
Gender: Societies with greater emphasis on masculinity value achievement, assertiveness, heroism, material wealth, and more clearly differentiated sex roles. People from less masculine (i.e., more feminine) cultures tend to value caring, sensitivity, and attention to quality of life.	Japan, Australia, Venezuela, Italy, Switzerland, Mexico, Ireland, Jamaica, Great Britain	Sweden, Norway, Netherlands, Denmark, Costa Rica, Finland, Chile, Portugal, Thailand
Uncertainty: People in societies with less tolerance for uncertainty generally like to know what will happen next. People in other societies are more comfortable with uncertainty.	Greece, Portugal, Guatemala, Uruguay, Belgium, Japan, Peru, France, Argentina, Chile	Singapore, Jamaica, Denmark, Sweden, Hong Kong, Ireland, Great Britain, Malaysia, India, Philippines, United States, Canada
Power: Societies with a more centralized power distribution generally value greater power differences between people; people in such societies are generally more accepting of fewer people having authority and power than are people from societies in which power is more decentralized.	Malaysia, Guatemala, Panama, Philippines, Mexico, Venezuela, Arab countries, Ecuador, Indonesia, India	Austria, Israel, Denmark, New Zealand, Ireland, Sweden, Norway, Finland, Switzerland, Great Britain
Time: People in societies with a long-term orientation to time tend to value perseverance and thrift. People in societies with a short-term orientation to time value both the past and the present, tradition, saving "face," and spending rather than saving.	China, Hong Kong, Taiwan, Japan, Vietnam, South Korea, Brazil, India, Thailand, Hungary, Singapore, Denmark, Netherlands	Pakistan, the Czech Republic, Nigeria, Spain, Philippines, Canada, Zimbabwe, Great Britain, United States, Portugal, New Zealand
Happiness: People in societies with a greater expectation of happiness desire and expect freedom and happiness. They also tend to value freedom of speech and place a high value on leisure activities and sports. Cultures that are more restrained do not necessarily expect to have all of their needs met to achieve happiness.	United States, Canada, Mexico, Brazil, Australia	Russia, China, much of Eastern Europe

culture shock
Feelings of stress and anxiety a person experiences when encountering a culture different from his or her own.

culture directly affects how we communicate with one another.[78] When we communicate with people from different cultural backgrounds than our own, we tend to share less information than we do with people who share our cultural heritage.[79]

Misunderstanding and miscommunication occur between people from different cultures because of different coding rules and cultural norms, which play a major role in shaping patterns of interaction. When you encounter a culture that has little in common with your own, you may experience **culture shock**, or a sense of confusion, anxiety, stress, and loss. If you are visiting or actually living in the new culture, it may take time for your uncertainty and stress to subside as you learn the values and codes that characterize the new culture. But if you are simply trying to communicate with someone from a background very different from your own—even on your home turf—you may find the suggestions in this section helpful in closing the communication gap.[80]

The first step to bridging differences between cultures is to find out what hampers effective communication. What keeps people from connecting with those from other cultures? Sometimes it is different meanings created by different languages or by different interpretations of nonverbal messages. Sometimes it is the inability to stop focusing on oneself and begin focusing on the other. We'll examine some of these barriers first, and then discuss strategies and skills for overcoming them.

Ethnocentrism

All good people agree,
And all good people say,
All nice people like Us, are We,
And everyone else is They.

#communicationandtechnology
Relating to Others Online in Intercultural Relationships

You don't have to travel the globe to communicate with people who live on the other side of the world. It's increasingly likely that you will interact online with others who have cultural or ethnic perspectives different from yours.

Research suggests that you or one or more of your work colleagues will work in an international location.[81] Social networking sites like Facebook or LinkedIn, as well as other online connections, make it easy to interact with international friends and colleagues. As more companies are outsourcing customer service to international venues, it's also increasingly likely that you may be speaking to someone in another country when you call for assistance about a problem with your computer or phone service. As online interaction increases, you are more likely to stereotype others inaccurately when connected via online channels than when communicating live and in person.

Here are some tips and strategies for enriching electronic intercultural connections with others:

- You may need to communicate more explicitly about your feelings and emotions, especially if you are using a "lean" communication channel such as e-mail or texting.

- Consider asking more questions than you normally would if you were interacting face-to-face, to clarify meanings and reduce uncertainty.

- Use "small talk" about the weather, your typical day, and other low-level disclosures to build a relationship. Then look for reciprocal responses from your communication partner that indicate a naturally evolving relationship.

- Summarize and paraphrase messages that you receive more often than you might normally, in order to increase the accuracy of message content.

- Keep in mind that international outreach attracts international friends. When interacting on Facebook, the more international friends you have, the more likely it is that other international individuals will "friend" you.[82]

- Remember and respect the difference between your time zone and the other person's time zone.

- If you find a relationship is awkward or you notice an increase in conflict, use a richer medium like the phone instead of texting or sending e-mail, or use a web cam instead of the phone. If you're merely sharing routine, noncontroversial information, a lean medium (such as texting) should be fine.

In a few short lines, Rudyard Kipling captures the essence of what sociologists and anthropologists call ethnocentric thinking. Members of all societies tend to believe that "All nice people like Us, are We." They find comfort in the familiar and often denigrate or distrust others. Of course, with training or experience in other climes, they may learn to transcend their provincialism, placing themselves in others' shoes. Or, as Kipling put it,

> ... if you cross over the sea,
>
> Instead of over the way,
>
> You may end by (think of it!)
>
> Looking on We
>
> As only a sort of They.

In a real sense, a main lesson of intercultural communication is to begin to "cross over the sea," to learn to understand why other people think and act as they do and to be able to empathize with their perspectives.[83]

Marilyn had always been intrigued by Russia. Her dream was to travel the country by train, spending time in small villages as well as exploring the cultural riches of Moscow, Pyatigorsk, and St. Petersburg. Her first day in Russia was a disappointment, however. When she arrived in Moscow, she joined a tour touting the cultural traditions of Russia. When the tour bus stopped at Sparrow Hills, affording the visitors a breathtaking hilltop view of the Moscow skyline, she was perplexed and mildly shocked to see a woman dressed in an elegant wedding gown mounted on horseback and galloping through the parking lot. Men in suits were cheering her on as a crowd of tipsy revelers set off fireworks and danced wildly to a brass band. "What kind of people are these?" sniffed Marilyn.

"Oh," said the tour guide, "it is our custom to come here to celebrate immediately following the wedding ceremony."

"But in public, with such raucousness?" queried Marilyn.

"It is our tradition," said the guide.

"What a backward culture. They're nothing but a bunch of peasants!" pronounced Marilyn, who was used to more refined nuptial celebrations at a country club or an exclusive hotel.

For the rest of the tour, Marilyn judged every Russian behavior as inferior to that of Westerners. That first experience colored her perceptions, and her ethnocentric view served as a barrier to effective interpersonal communication with the Russian people she met.

Ethnocentrism stems from a conviction that our own cultural traditions and assumptions are superior to those of others. It is the opposite of an other-orientation that embraces and appreciates the elements that give another culture meaning. This kind of cultural snobbism is one of the fastest ways to create a barrier that inhibits rather than enhances communication.

Almost all cultural groups are ethnocentric to some degree.[84] Some even argue that it's not always bad to see one's own cultural group as superior; an ethnocentric tendency enhances group pride and patriotism and encourages cultural traditions.[85] A problem occurs, however, when a group views its own preferences as *always* the best way. Extreme ethnocentrism creates a barrier between the group and others.

ethnocentrism
Belief that your cultural traditions and assumptions are superior to those of others.

Colorful celebrations like this local festival in Bali can reinforce healthy ethnic pride. But if ethnic pride is taken to extremes, the resulting ethnocentrism may act as a barrier between groups.

BEING Other-ORIENTED

Most people are ethnocentric to some degree. But extreme ethnocentrism can be a major interpersonal communication barrier. What symptoms indicate when an ethnocentric mindset may be interfering with the quality of communication with another person? What kind of comments might signal that someone believes his or her cultural approaches are superior to those of another person?

What are specific strategies to avoid being ethnocentric? Consider these suggestions:

- *Be mindful*: You can't change what you aren't aware of. Honestly consider whether you harbor unhealthy ethnocentric views toward a cultural, co-cultural, or ethnic group.
- *Avoid stereotypes*: View people as individuals rather than as stereotypes or caricatures fueled by media or literature characterizations. People are not cartoon characters; they are multidimensional.
- *Separate the politics from the person*: The politics promoted by a given leader of a country are not necessarily representative of the people who live in that country. Whether you encounter a person from a country with unfriendly political views who lives in your community, or you visit a country with "questionable" political policies, separate the people you meet from the political views of the leaders of their countries.
- *Communicate interpersonally rather than impersonally*: When you interact with people often, seek to move beyond judgmental, impersonal communication to a more meaningful and authentic interpersonal relationship.

Different Communication Codes

You are on your first trip to Los Angeles. As you step off the bus and look around for Hollywood Boulevard, you realize you have gotten off at the wrong stop. You see what looks like an old-fashioned corner grocery store with "Bodega" painted on a red sign. So you walk in and ask the man behind the counter, "How do I get to Hollywood Boulevard, please?"

"No hablo inglés," says the man, smiling and shrugging his shoulders. But he points to a transit map pasted on the wall behind the counter.

Today, even when you travel within the United States, you are likely to encounter people who do not speak your language. Obviously, this kind of intercultural difference poses a formidable communication challenge. And even when you do speak the same language as someone else, he or she may come from a place where certain words and gestures have different meanings. As William Gudykunst wisely noted, "If we understand each others' languages, but not their cultures, we can make fluent fools of ourselves."[86] Research has found that your culture and ethnic background have a direct effect on the way you listen to others share information.[87] Ultimately, your ability to communicate effectively and appropriately depends on whether you can understand each other's verbal and nonverbal codes.

In the preceding example, although the man behind the counter did not understand your exact words, he noted the cut of your clothing, your backpack, and your anxiety, and he deduced that you were asking for directions. And you could understand what his gesture toward the transit map meant. Unfortunately, not every communication between speakers of two different languages is this successful.

Even when language is translated, meaning can be missed or mangled. Note the following examples of mistranslated advertisements:

- Colgate-Palmolive advertised its new toothpaste named "Cue" in France before the company realized that *Cue* also happened to be the name of a widely circulated pornographic book about oral sex.
- Pepsi-Cola's "Come Alive with Pepsi" campaign, when translated for the Taiwanese market, conveyed the unsettling news that "Pepsi brings your ancestors back from the grave."
- Parker Pen could not advertise its famous "Jotter" ballpoint pen in some languages because the translation sounded like "jockstrap" pen.
- One American airline operating in Brazil advertised that it had plush "rendezvous lounges" on its jets, unaware that in Portuguese (the language of Brazil), *rendezvous* implies a special room for making love.[88]

Stereotyping and Prejudice

All Europeans dress fashionably.

All Asians are good at math.

All Americans like to drive big cars.

These statements are stereotypes. They are all inaccurate. As we discussed in Chapter 3, to **stereotype** someone is to push him or her into an inflexible, all-encompassing category. Our tendency to simplify sensory stimuli can lead us to adopt stereotypes as we interpret and label the behavior of others.[89] As we also noted in Chapter 3, we often thin slice—make judgments about others in just seconds based on nonverbal cues. One study found that after viewing twenty seconds of silent videotape, subjects made stereotypical, biased racial judgments of others.[90] Stereotypes become a barrier to effective intercultural communication when we fail to consider the uniqueness of individuals, groups, or events. As we have already noted, when we observe people stereotyping others we in turn may give ourselves implicit permission to make stereotypical judgments of others.[91] In addition, research has found that we perpetuate stereotypes through interpersonal conversation. Just telling someone else about a stereotype we either hold or have observed reinforces the probability that the stereotype will persist. Researchers called it the "saying it is repeating" principle.[92] To reduce negative stereotypes, it is important to acknowledge the power of others to reinforce the existence of stereotypes. Anthropologists Kluckhohn and Murray suggest that every person is, in some respects, (1) like all other people, (2) like some other people, and (3) like no other people.[93] The challenge when meeting others is to sort out how they are alike and how they are unique.

Can stereotypes play any useful role in interpersonal communication? It may sometimes be appropriate to draw on stereotypes. If, for example, you are alone and lost in a large city at two o'clock in the morning and another car aggressively taps your rear bumper, it would be prudent to drive away as quickly as possible, rather than hop out of your car to make a new acquaintance. You would be wise to prejudge that the other driver might have some malicious intent. In most situations, however, **prejudice**—a judgment or opinion of someone formed on the basis of stereotypes or before you know all the facts—inhibits effective communication, especially if your labels are inaccurate or assume superiority on your part.[94]

Communication author and consultant Leslie Aguilar notes that regardless of whether we intend to perpetuate stereotypes and prejudice, we do so in seemingly innocent ways.[95] These ways may include telling jokes ("Have you heard the one about the minister and the rabbi?"); using labels (she's a real "blue hair" or he's "trailer trash") or rigid descriptions ("crotchety old man" or "bad woman driver"); making assumptions ("all men are insensitive" or "all women are physically weak"); or relying on "spokesperson syndrome" ("Don, what do Hispanic people think about this topic?").

stereotype

To place a person or group of persons into an inflexible, all-encompassing category.

prejudice

A judgment or opinion of someone, formed before you know all of the facts or the background of that person.

Certain prejudices are widespread. Although there are slightly more females than males in the world, one study found that even when a male and a female hold the same type of job, the male's job is considered more prestigious than the female's.[96] Today, gender and racial discrimination in hiring and promotion is illegal in the United States. But some people's opinions have not kept pace with the law.

Assuming Similarities

Just as it is inaccurate to assume that all people who belong to another social group or class are worlds apart from you, it is usually erroneous to assume that others act and think just as you do. Cultural differences *do* exist. Research and our own observations support the commonsense conclusion that people from different cultural and ethnic backgrounds do speak and behave differently.[97] Even if they appear to be like you, all people are not alike. Although this statement is not profound, it has profound implications. People often make the mistake of assuming that others value the same things they do, maintaining a self-focused perspective instead of an other-oriented one. As you read in Chapter 3, focusing on superficial factors such as appearance, clothing, and even a person's occupation can lead to false impressions. Instead, you must take the time to explore a person's background and cultural values before you can determine what you really have in common.

Assuming Differences

Although it may seem to contradict what we just discussed about assuming similarities, another barrier to intercultural communication is to automatically conclude that another person is different from you. It can be just as detrimental to communication to assume someone is different from you as it is to believe that others are similar to you. The fact is, human beings *do* share common experiences.

Acknowledging that humans have similarities as well as differences does not diminish the role of culture as a key element that influences communication. But it is important to recognize that despite cultural differences, we are all members of the human family. One research study found that just because we strongly identify with our own ethnic heritage does not mean we won't make and keep friends with different ethnical backgrounds. You don't have to abandon your own ethnic or cultural traditions to develop relationships with those who are different from you.[98] The words *communication* and *common* resemble one another. We communicate effectively and appropriately when we can connect to others based on what we hold in common. Identifying common cultural issues and similarities can also help us establish common ground with others.

How are we all alike? Cultural anthropologist Donald Brown has identified and compiled a list of hundreds of "surface" universals of behavior and language use. According to Brown, people in all cultures[99]

- have beliefs about death;
- divide labor on the basis of sex;
- experience envy, pain, jealousy, shame, and pride;
- have rules for etiquette;
- experience empathy;
- value some degree of collaboration or cooperation; and
- experience conflict and seek to manage or mediate conflict.

Of course, all cultures do not have the same beliefs about death, or divide labor according to sex in the same ways, but all cultures address these issues. Communication researcher David Kale believes that all humans seek to protect the dignity and worth of other people.[100] Thus, he suggests, all people can identify with the struggle to enhance their own dignity and worth, although different cultures

BEING Other-ORIENTED

We build bridges with others who are different from us when we can identify something we may have in common. Can you think of times when you've been communicating with someone who was quite different from you, but you sought to identify something you both had in common? What are some common human experiences that can create bridges as we seek to establish common ground with others?

express this in different ways. A second common value that Kale notes is the search for a world at peace.

Intercultural communication scholars Larry Samovar and Richard Porter suggest that people from all cultures seek physical, emotional, and psychological pleasure, and avoid personal harm.[101] They note that each culture and each person decides what is pleasurable or painful; nonetheless, Samovar and Porter argue, all people operate within this pleasure–pain continuum.

Linguist and scholar Steven Pinker is another advocate of common human values. Drawing on the work of anthropologists Richard Shweder and Alan Fiske, Pinker suggests that the following value themes are universally present in some form or degree in societies across the globe:[102]

- It is bad to harm others and good to help them.
- People have a sense of fairness; we should reciprocate favors, reward benefactors, and punish cheaters and those who do harm.
- People value loyalty to a group and sharing in a community or group.
- It is proper to defer to legitimate authority and to respect those with status and power.
- People should seek purity, cleanliness, and sanctity while shunning defilement and contamination.

What are the practical implications of trying to identify common human values or characteristics? Here's one implication: If you are speaking about an issue on which you and another person fundamentally differ, identifying a larger common value—such as the value of peace, prosperity, or the importance of family—can help you find a foothold so that the other person will at least listen to your ideas. It's useful, we believe, not just to categorize our differences but also to explore how human beings are similar to one another. Discovering how we are alike can provide a starting point for human understanding. Yes, we are all different, but we share things in common as well. Communication effectiveness is diminished when we assume we're all different from one another in *every* aspect, just as communication is affected negatively if we assume we're all alike.[103] We're more complicated than that.

Improving Intercultural Communication Competence

4.4 Identify and apply strategies for developing knowledge, motivation, and skills that can improve intercultural competence.

Eleanor Roosevelt once said, "We have to face the fact that either all of us are going to die together or we are going to live together, and if we are to live together we have to talk."[104] In essence, she was saying that to overcome differences, people need effective communication skills. It is not enough just to point to the barriers to effective intercultural communication and say, "Don't do that." Although identifying the causes of misunderstanding is a good first step to becoming interculturally competent, most people need specific strategies to help them overcome these barriers. In this book and in this chapter, we want to focus attention on the interpersonal communication strategies that can lead to intercultural communication competence.

Intercultural communication competence is the ability to adapt your behavior toward another person in ways that are appropriate to the other person's culture.[105] To be interculturally competent is more than merely being aware of what is appropriate or simply being sensitive to cultural differences. It is to behave in appropriate ways toward others. And to do so, you need to have knowledge about other cultures and the motivation to adapt or modify your behavior.

intercultural communication competence

Ability to adapt one's behavior toward another in ways that are appropriate to the other person's culture.

Although we've identified stages in the process of becoming interculturally competent, the question remains: How do you achieve intercultural communication competence? The remaining portion of this chapter presents specific strategies to help you bridge differences between yourself and people with other cultural perspectives.

You enhance your intercultural competence by doing what we introduced in Chapter 1: You become knowledgeable, motivated, and skilled.[106]

- *Develop Knowledge.* One of the barriers to effective intercultural communication is having different communication codes. Improving your knowledge of how others communicate can reduce the impact of this barrier.
- *Develop Motivation.* **Motivation** is an internal state of readiness to respond to something. A competent communicator wants to learn and improve. Developing strategies to appreciate others who are different from you may help you appreciate diverse cultural approaches to communication and relationships.
- *Develop Skill.* Developing **skill** in adapting to others focuses on specific behaviors that can help overcome barriers and cultural differences. As we discussed in Chapter 1, becoming other-oriented is critical to the process of relating to others.

motivation

Internal state of readiness to respond to something.

skill

Behavior that improves the effectiveness or quality of communication with others.

Communication and Emotion

Are Human Emotions Universal?

Do all humans experience and express emotions in the same way? The question of whether there are universal emotions or universal ways of expressing emotions has been studied and debated by scholars for decades.

One widely debated analysis, developed by psychologist Robert Plutchik and shown in Figure 4.1, suggests that there are eight primary human emotions: joy, acceptance, fear, surprise, sadness, disgust, anger, and anticipation.[107] Combinations of these eight primary emotions can produce eight secondary emotions. Although not all researchers agree that this is the definitive set of human emotions, a host of scholars argue that yes, there is a set of basic emotions that all humans experience.[108] They believe that through the biological process of evolution, all humans have a core set of emotional experiences. The debate about whether there are universal emotions boils down to whether you believe that nature (biology) or nurture (culture) determines common, core emotions. Those who think we are "wired" or programmed for common emotions believe that biology is the predominant influence in determining how we both interpret emotional expression and respond emotionally.

Researcher Paul Ekman has spent many years working with several colleagues to determine whether people from a wide variety of cultures interpret facial expressions of emotion in the same way. His conclusion: "Our evidence, and that of others, shows only that when people are experiencing strong emotions, are not making any attempt to mask their expressions, the expression will be the same regardless of age, race, culture, sex and education." That is a powerful finding.[109] Marc Pell and his colleagues have found evidence to support Ekman's conclusions: People from a variety of cultures appear to be able to accurately interpret emotions not just by looking at facial expressions but also by listening to vocal expressions.[110]

Other researchers have reached a different conclusion.[111] They have found that culture does play an important role in determining how people display and interpret facial expressions.[112] There is some evidence, for example, that people from collectivistic cultures are socialized not to express emotions that would disrupt harmony in the group. Specifically, people with collectivist values may work harder at regulating how they express emotions such as anger, contempt, and disgust—emotions that would hinder group peace.[113] And people from individualistic cultures may feel they have greater cultural license to express these emotions more freely. Although communication researcher Susan Kline and her colleagues found some similarities in the way people from Asian and American cultures express love in both romantic and friendship relationships, she also found some differences. Both cultures reported that caring, trust, respect, and honesty were important in maintaining a relationship.[114]

Why is it important to know whether emotional expression and interpretation are common to all humans or are learned, as other elements of culture are learned? If there are indeed universal human attributes common to *all* people, their existence provides powerful additional evidence for the theory of evolution. It also has implications for the development of a truly human theory of communication.

So are human emotions universal? Among experts, consensus is emerging that all humans have in common a biologically based tendency to express emotions, which explains why Ekman and others have found some cross-cultural similarities in the way facial expressions are interpreted. But although there may be a common basis for *expressing* emotions, certain cultural differences exist in how people *interpret* some emotions.

Figure 4.1 Robert Plutchik's Model of Emotions

SOURCE: From Robert Plutchik, *Emotion: A Psychoevolutionary Synthesis*, 1st ed., ©1979. Reprinted and electronically reproduced by permission of Pearson Education, Inc., Upper Saddle River, New Jersey.

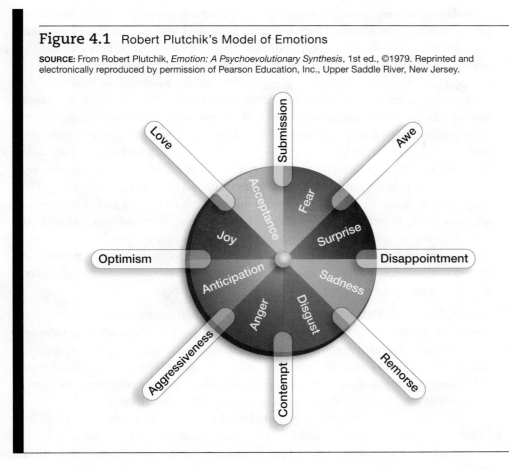

Develop Knowledge

Knowledge is power. To increase your knowledge of others who are different from you, actively seek information about others, ask questions and listen for the answers, and establish common ground.

SEEK INFORMATION   Seeking information about a culture or even about a specific communication situation enhances the quality of intercultural communication. Why? Because seeking information helps us manage the uncertainty and anxiety we may feel when we interact with people who are different from us.[115] Sometimes we feel uncomfortable in intercultural communication situations because we just don't know how to behave. We aren't sure what our role should be; we can't quite predict what will happen when we communicate with others because we're in a new or strange situation. Seeking new information can help counter inaccurate information and prejudice.

As we've noted, every person has a worldview based on cultural beliefs about the universe and key issues such as death, God, and the meaning of life.[116] These beliefs shape our thoughts, language, and behavior. Only through intercultural communication can we hope to understand how each individual views the world. As you speak to a person from another culture, think of yourself as a detective watching for implied, often unspoken messages that provide information about the values, norms, roles, and rules of that person's culture.

You can also prepare yourself by studying the culture. If you are going to another country, taking courses in the history, anthropology, art, or geography of that place can give you a head start on communicating with understanding. Learn not only from books and magazines, but also from individuals whenever possible.

Given the link between language and culture, the more you learn about another language, the more you will understand the traditions and customs of the culture.

Politicians have long known the value of using even a few words of their constituents' language. President Kennedy impressed and excited a crowd in Berlin by proclaiming, "Ich bin ein Berliner" ("I am a Berliner"). Even though his diction was less than perfect, he conveyed the message that he identified with his listeners.

You can also gain information about other cultures by spending time with people who are culturally and ethnically different from you.[117] According to the **contact hypothesis**, the more contact you have with people who are different from you, the more positive regard you will have for them, the less prejudice you will experience toward them, and the fewer stereotypes you will form about them. One study found that the more Facebook friends you have from other cultures or nations, the more likely you are to attract others from a culture or nation different than your own. This suggests that as we reach out and expand our network of friends and colleagues, we are more likely to attract others from a different culture.[118] In addition, research suggests that the more ethnically varied your friendships are, the less likely you are to define ethnicity by skin color alone.[119] So another way to gain information about others is to have a more culturally and ethnically diverse circle of friends; having diverse friends can also decrease your tendency to stereotype others.

ASK QUESTIONS AND LISTEN EFFECTIVELY. When you encounter a person from another background, asking questions and then pausing to listen is a simple technique for gathering information and also for confirming the accuracy of your expectations and assumptions. For example, some cultures, such as the Japanese, have clear expectations regarding gift giving. It is better to ask what these expectations are than to assume that your good old down-home manners will see you through.

When you ask questions, be prepared to share information about yourself, too. Otherwise, your partner may feel that you are interrogating him or her as a way to gain power and dominance rather than from a sincere desire to learn about cultural rules and norms.

Communication helps to reduce the uncertainty that is present in any relationship.[120] When you meet people, you will be uncertain about who they are and what they like and dislike. When you communicate with someone from another culture, the uncertainty level is particularly high. As you begin to interact, you exchange information that helps you develop greater understanding. If you continue to ask questions, eventually you will feel less uncertain about how the person is likely to behave.

You need to do more than just ask questions and share information about yourself to bridge differences in culture and background. It is equally important to listen to what others share. In the next chapter, we provide specific strategies for improving your listening skills.

CREATE A "THIRD CULTURE" Several researchers suggest that one way to enhance understanding when communicating over a period of time with someone from a different cultural background is to develop a **third culture**. This is created when communication partners join aspects of two separate cultures to create a third, "new" culture, which is more comprehensive and inclusive.[121] This "new," third culture fuses the values and expectations of the two "old" cultures. Some elements of the "old" cultures may be present in the "new" culture, but when cultural values conflict, a new way is developed. For example, if one spouse celebrates Hanukkah and the other Christmas, both traditions can be combined with common themes of gift giving; developing new creative, special foods (rather than the old cuisine); and celebrating with different kinds of music—say, jazz rather than classical or traditional songs. By using elements from the two cultural traditions of the past, a conscious effort is made to create a new nontraditional third culture.

contact hypothesis
The more contact you have with someone who is different from you, the more positive regard you will have for that person.

third culture
Common ground established when people from separate cultures create a third, "new," more comprehensive and inclusive culture.

Studying interpersonal communication helps us learn to bridge differences in age, gender, ethnicity, or ability that might act as barriers to effective communication.

How do you go about developing a third culture? In a word: talk. A third culture does not just happen all at once; it evolves from dialogue. The communicators construct a third culture *together*. After they realize that cultural differences may divide them, they may develop a third culture by making a conscious effort to develop common assumptions and perspectives for the relationship. Dialogue, negotiation, conversation, interaction, and a willingness to let go of old ways and experiment with new frameworks are the keys to developing a third culture as a basis for a new relationship.

Developing a third-culture mentality can reduce our tendency to approach cultural differences from an "us-versus-them" point of view. Rather than trying to eliminate communication barriers stemming from two different sets of experiences, adopting a third-culture framework creates a new understanding of the other on the part of both participants.[122] One study found that intercultural friendships develop based on both evident similarities and differences that make the conversation more interesting. Building on similarities as well as talking about differences to create a "third culture" can lead to enhanced friendship.[123]

Consider the example of Marsha, a businesswoman from Lincoln, Nebraska, and Tomiko, a businesswoman from Tokyo, Japan. In the context of their business relationship, it would be difficult for them to develop a comprehensive understanding of each other's cultural traditions. However, if they openly acknowledged the most significant differences and sought to create a third culture by identifying explicit rules and norms for their interaction, they might be able to develop a more comfortable relationship with each other. The cultural context includes all the elements of the culture (learned behaviors and rules, or "mental software") that affect the interaction. Do you come from a culture that takes a tea break each afternoon at 4 pm? Does your culture value hard work and achievement, or relaxation and enjoyment? Creating a third culture acknowledges the different cultural contexts and interactions participants have experienced and seeks to develop a new context for future interaction.

Develop Motivation: Strategies to Accept Others

Competent communicators want to learn and improve. They are motivated to enhance their ability to relate to others and to accept others as they are. A key to accepting others is to develop a positive attitude of tolerance and acceptance of those who are different from you. Three strategies can help you improve your acceptance and appreciation of others who differ from you: Tolerate ambiguity, become mindful, and avoid negative judgments of others.

TOLERATE AMBIGUITY   Communicating with someone from another culture produces uncertainty. It may take time and several exchanges to clarify a message. Be patient and try to expand your capacity to tolerate ambiguity if you are speaking to someone with a markedly different worldview.

When Ken and Rita visited Miami from Peoria, they asked their hotel concierge to direct them to a church of their faith, and they wound up at one with a predominantly Haitian congregation. They were not prepared for the exuberant chanting and verbal interchanges with the minister during the sermon. They weren't certain whether they should join in or simply sit quietly and observe. Ken whispered to Rita, "I'm not sure what to do. Let's just watch and see what is expected of us." In the end, they chose to sit and clap along with the chanting rather than to become actively involved in the worship. Rita felt uncomfortable and conspicuous, though, and had to fight the urge to bolt. But after the service, several members of the congregation came up to greet Ken and Rita, invited them to lunch, and expressed great happiness in their visit. "You know," said Rita later in the day, "I'm so grateful that we sat through our discomfort. We might never have met those terrific people. Now I understand why their worship is so noisy—they're just brimming with joy."

BEING Other-ORIENTED

Being motivated to establish positive relationships with others who are different from us is a key aspect of communicating in interculturally competent ways. What "self-talk" messages could you tell yourself (such as "I may feel uncomfortable right now, but I will keep listening to this person") to motivate you to increase your intercultural competence?

mindful
Being conscious of what you are doing, thinking, and sensing at any given moment.

BE MINDFUL "Our life is what our thoughts make it," said Marcus Aurelius in *Meditations*. As we noted in Chapter 3, to be mindful is to be consciously aware of what you are doing, thinking, and sensing. With regard to cultural differences, to be **mindful** is to consciously acknowledge that there is a connection between thoughts and deeds when you interact with a person from a background different from your own. William Gudykunst suggests that being mindful is one of the best ways to approach any new cultural encounter.[124] Research also suggests that being aware of one's cultural identity and the differences and similarities of others in the workplace can enhance the work climate.[125] Remember that there are and will be cultural differences, and try to keep them in your consciousness. Also try to consider the other individual's frame of reference, or worldview, and to use his or her cultural priorities and assumptions when you are communicating.[126] Adapt your behavior to minimize cultural noise and distortion.

You can become more mindful through self-talk, something we discussed in Chapter 2. Self-talk consists of messages you tell yourself to help you manage your emotions or discomfort with a certain situation. Imagine that you are working on a group project with several classmates. One classmate, Suji, was born in Iran. When interacting with you, he consistently stands about a foot away from you, whereas you are more comfortable with three or four feet between you. When Suji encroaches on your space, you could be mindful of the reason for this behavior by mentally noting, "Suji sure likes to get close to people when he talks to them. This may be how they do things in his culture." This self-talk message makes you consciously aware that there may be a difference in your interaction styles. If you still feel uncomfortable, instead of blurting out, "Hey, man, why so close?" you could express your own preferences with an "I" message: "Suji, I'd prefer a bit more space between us when we talk."

AVOID NEGATIVE JUDGMENTS

American tourist on her first visit to France:	Can you believe it? How repulsive! These people actually eat horse meat and think it's a delicacy.
Black teenager watching his White classmates dance:	Man, they don't know anything about good music! And those dances are so dumb. I don't call this a party.
Japanese businessperson visiting Argentina:	These people are never on time. No wonder they can never catch up to us.
German student, after watching a documentary about life in Japan:	No wonder they work so hard. They have dinky little houses. I'd work long hours too if I had to live like that.

The kind of ethnocentrism that underlies judgments like these is a communication barrier. It is also an underlying cause of suspicion and mistrust and, in extreme cases, a spark that ignites violence. Instead of making judgments about another culture, try simply to acknowledge differences and to view them as interesting challenges rather than as obstacles to be eradicated.

Develop Skill

To be skilled is to be capable of putting into action what you know and want to achieve. The skills underlying being interculturally competent are the abilities to be flexible, to be other-oriented, and to adapt your communication to others. Research suggests that having social skills—being other-oriented and communicating with others to provide social support when needed—can enhance the quality of interpersonal communication with people whose cultural background differs from your own.[127] We discuss these crucial skills as an introduction to the communication skills presented in the next four chapters.

DEVELOP CREATIVE FLEXIBILITY. When you encounter someone who comes from a very different background, remember Dorothy's famous line from *The Wizard of Oz* and remind yourself that you're "not in Kansas anymore." You can no longer rely on the assumptions of your own cultural heritage. Rather than relying on "scripts" you would use "back home in Kansas," it's important to be flexible and respond in creative and inventive ways. You may read guidebooks to prepare yourself for new cultural experiences, but you can only learn so much from books; you must be willing to learn as you communicate on the spot. Although in this chapter we've identified generalizations about different cultural groups, remember that these are only generalizations. Every individual is unique, so generalizations based on research will not always apply. For example, it would be inappropriate to automatically assume that someone from Japan will value collectivism instead of individual achievement. Many members of minority groups in the United States find it tiresome to correct these generalizations in their encounters with others.

It's important to be flexible in your responses to other cultures and people with different backgrounds. Traveling in other countries can hone your intercultural communication skills.

Relating to Diverse Others
Tao: A Universal Moral Code

Anthropologists and communication scholars who study intercultural communication expound the value of adapting to cultural differences in order to understand others better. But are there any universal values that are or have been embraced by all humans? To uncover such commonalities is to develop a truly human communication theory rather than a theory that applies to a specific cultural context.

C. S. Lewis, a British scholar, author, and educator who taught at both Oxford and Cambridge Universities, argued that there are universal ethical and moral principles that undergird all societies of civilized people, regardless of their religious beliefs, cultural background, or government structure. He suggested that the existence of Natural Laws, or what he called a *Tao*—a universal moral code—informs human ethical decisions. In his book *The Abolition of Man*, Lewis presented eight universal principles, or laws.[128] He did not claim that all societies have followed these laws—many of them have been clearly violated and continue

to be violated today—but he did suggest they provide a bedrock of values against which all societies may be measured. Here are his eight laws:

1. The Law of General Beneficence: Do not murder, be dishonest, or take from others what does not belong to us.
2. The Law of Special Beneficence: Value your family members.
3. Duties to Parents, Elders, and Ancestors: Especially hold your parents, those who are a generation older than you, and your ancestors with special honor and esteem.
4. Duties to Children and Posterity: We have a special obligation to respect the rights of the young and to value those who will come after us.
5. The Law of Justice: Honor the basic human rights of others; each person is of worth.
6. The Law of Good Faith and Veracity: Keep your promises, and do not lie.
7. The Law of Mercy: Be compassionate to those less fortunate than you are.

8. The Law of Magnanimity: Avoid unnecessary violence against other people.

To support his argument that these are universal values, Lewis offered quotations from several well-known sources, including religious, historical, and political writings, both contemporary and centuries old. Lewis implied that these eight laws may be viewed as a universal Bill of Rights, and that they constitute an underlying set of principles that either implicitly or explicitly guide all civilized society. Do you agree? Is it useful to search for underlying principles of humanness? Despite cultural differences, are there any underlying values or principles that should inform our interactions with others? Is there truly a universal human theory of communication? Or might it do more harm than good to suggest that universal principles underlie what it means to behave and communicate appropriately and effectively?

The skill of observing and responding with creative flexibility enhances your intercultural competence. It also calls on your ability to do a variety of things simultaneously. While you're listening to someone, you're also adapting your behavior to respond to the person's cultural expectations. Research further suggests that the amount of culture shock you experience when communicating with someone from a different culture decreases as you develop skills in interacting with people from that culture.[129]

How do you develop these skills? You'll need to pay close attention to the other person's nonverbal cues when you begin conversing (Is the person attentive? Does the person look interested? Confused?); then adjust your communication style and language as needed to put the person at ease. Listen and respond and, if necessary, create a new culture—a third culture—to forge a new way of interacting. You may, for example, prefer direct eye contact when you speak with another person, but someone from a different culture may prefer less direct eye contact. So you may need to modify the amount of eye contact you have with that person. As communication researchers Kathy Domenici and Stephen Littlejohn advocate, "Good intercultural communication requires a certain creativity, an ability to create new forms that bridge established cultural patterns."[130] Don't go on "automatic pilot" when interacting with anyone— but especially people from a different cultural context.

If you do make a culture-based mistake when communicating with someone from a different background, you can always apologize. Although not all cultures have the same rules for initiating and accepting an apology, offering a heartfelt "I'm sorry" is an other-oriented way of letting him or her know that you are aware of your error and you want to enhance your relationship.[131]

BECOME OTHER-ORIENTED Throughout the book, we have emphasized the importance of becoming other-oriented—focusing on others rather than yourself—as an important way to enhance your interpersonal competence.[132] We have also discussed the problems ethnocentrism can create when you attempt to communicate with others, especially with people whose culture differs from yours.

Although our focus in this discussion is on how to increase other-orientation in intercultural interactions, these principles apply to *all* interpersonal interactions. The major difference between intercultural interactions and those that occur within your own culture is primarily the obviousness of the differences between you and the other person.

To become other-oriented is to do two things: first, to take into account another person's thoughts and perspective, and second, to consider what the other person may be experiencing emotionally. These are skills we've emphasized before. The first skill is called social decentering. The second skill is empathy.

Social decentering is a *cognitive process* in which you take into account the other person's thoughts, values, background, and overall perspective. The greater the difference between you and another person, the more difficult it is to accomplish social decentering. As you meet someone from a different culture, ask yourself, "What might this person be thinking right now?" Of course, since you're not a mind reader, you won't be able to know definitively what someone is thinking. But you can think about what most people that you know might be thinking, or draw on your own experiences. Be sure to keep the other person's worldview and cultural values in mind as you make inferences about his or her cognitive perspective. After considering his or her cognitive point of view, consider what the person may be experiencing emotionally.

Empathy is an *emotional reaction* that is similar to the one being experienced by another person.[133] Empathy is about *emotions,* whereas social decentering is about cognitive processes. You develop empathy as you draw on your own experiences (what you might be feeling), your knowledge of other people in general, and what

---

BEING Other-ORIENTED

Being other-oriented does not mean becoming a "wishy-washy" person who only says or does what the other person wants. When you are other-oriented, you maintain your own sense of ethics and values while considering the needs and interests of others. Identify situations in which you have thought about what another person might want, yet have mindfully chosen to do something different. Do you think you can be other-oriented but not always do what another person wants you to do?

---

social decentering

Cognitive process in which we take into account another person's thoughts, feelings, values, background, and perspective.

---

empathy

Emotional reaction that is similar to the reaction being experienced by another person; empathizing is feeling what another person is feeling.

you know about the specific person you are interacting with. It's impossible to experience the emotions of another person with complete confidence and accuracy. But to be empathic is to do your best to put yourself in someone else's place emotionally and consider what that person is feeling. Being in touch emotionally is hard work, and some people are just naturally more empathic toward others.

Research has consistently found that your ability to be emotionally responsive can enhance your skill in communicating with others who are different from you. Specifically, if you can monitor and then appropriately adapt your emotional response to others, you are more likely to be perceived as socially skilled, a perception that will enhance interpersonal relationships with others. Yet if you tend to shut down and consistently suppress your emotional reactions to the extent that you are perceived to be difficult to figure out, other people may perceive you as less socially skilled.[134]

APPROPRIATELY ADAPT YOUR COMMUNICATION   The logical extension of being flexible and becoming other-oriented is to adapt your communication to enhance the quality and effectiveness of your interpersonal communication. To **adapt** means to adjust your behavior to accommodate others' differences and expectations. Appropriate adaptation occurs in the context of the relationship you have with the other person and what is happening in the communication environment. When we feel "in sync" with another person, it's because we are in a mutual adaptive rhythm with him or her. How we adapt what we say and how we say it is one of the key factors that determines how comfortable we feel with someone.[135]

Communication accommodation theory suggests that all people adapt their behavior to others to some extent. Those who adapt to others appropriately and sensitively are more likely to experience more positive communication.[136] Adapting to others doesn't mean you only tell others what they want to hear and do what others want you to do. Nor should you adapt your behavior only so that you can get your way; the goal is effective communication, not manipulation. Rather, you should be aware of what your communication partner is doing and saying, especially if there are cultural differences between you, so that your message is understood and you don't unwittingly offend the other person. Although it may seem like common sense, being sensitive and adapting behaviors to others are not as common as you might think.

Sometimes people adapt their behavior based on what they think someone will like. At other times, they adapt their communication after realizing they have done something wrong. When you modify your behavior in anticipation of an event, you **adapt predictively**. For example, you might decide to buy a friend flowers to soften the news about breaking a date because you know how much your friend likes flowers. When you modify your behavior after an event, you **adapt reactively**. For example, you might buy your friend flowers to apologize after a fight.

You often adapt your messages to enhance clarity. There are at least four reasons that explain why you might adapt your communication with another person.

- *Information:* You adapt your message in response to specific information that you already know about your partner, such as what he or she may like or dislike, or information that your partner has shared with you.
- *Perceived Behavior:* You adapt your communication in response to what you think the other person is thinking, what you see the person doing, and your observations of the person's emotional expressions and moods.
- *History:* You adapt your messages to others based on previous conversations, past shared experiences, and personal information they have shared with you.
- *Communication Context:* You adapt your message depending on where you are; you may whisper a brief comment to someone during a movie, yet shout to someone when attending a loud rock concert.

BEING Other-ORIENTED
At the heart of being other-oriented is adapting your behavior toward others in mindful and ethical ways. Review the adaptation strategies presented in Table 4.2. Identify other examples of various ways of adapting to others. Which strategies are the easiest for you to use, and which are the most challenging?

adapt
To adjust one's behavior in accord with what someone else does. We can adapt based on the individual, the relationship, or the situation.

communication accommodation theory
Theory that all people adapt their behaviors to others to some extent.

adapt predictively
To modify or change behavior in anticipation of an event.

adapt reactively
To modify or change behavior after an event.

Table 4.2 How Do We Adapt to Others?

Type of Adaptation	Examples
Adapting the Topic and Level of Intimacy of Your Conversation Choosing topics of conversation because of shared interests or things you have in common with your partner, including sharing information about yourself	• Talking about a class you both attend • Mentioning an article you read about a TV show your partner really likes • Telling someone about your depression because you believe he or she cares
Adapting How You Explain or Describe Something Providing additional information or detail because you recognize that your communication partner has certain gaps in his or her information	• Telling a story about Ike, whom your partner doesn't know, and explaining that Ike is your uncle • Describing Facebook to your grandparent, who doesn't use the Internet • Telling someone, "I know my behavior might seem a little erratic, but I'm under a lot of pressure at work right now and my parents are on my case"
Adapting by Withholding or Avoiding Information Not providing explanations of something your partner already knows; not providing information because you anticipate an undesired reaction from your partner; or not providing information because you fear how your partner might potentially use the information (such as sharing the information with other people)	• Not elaborating on the parts of an auto engine when describing a car problem because you know your partner is knowledgeable about cars • Not telling someone you saw his or her lover with someone else because he or she would be hurt • Not mentioning your interest in a mutual friend because you know the listener would blab about it to the mutual friend
Adapting Your Use of Examples, Comparisons, and Analogies Choosing messages you believe your partner will find relevant	• Describing a person your partner doesn't know by comparing the person to someone your partner does know • Explaining roller blading by comparing it to ice skating because your partner is an avid ice skater
Adapting Through Your Choice of Language Choosing or avoiding specific words because of the anticipated effect on your partner; consciously selecting words you believe your partner will understand; or using words that have a unique meaning to you and your partner	• Using formal address in response to status differences: "Thank you, Professor Smith" • Using slang when the relationship is perceived as informal • Using nicknames, inside jokes, or teasing comments with close friends

SOURCE: © Mark V. Redmond, "Interpersonal Content Adaptation In Everyday Interactions," paper presented at the annual meeting of the National Communication Association, Boston (2005).

In intercultural interactions, people frequently adapt their communication in response to the feedback or reactions they receive during a conversation. People from different cultures adapt differently.[137] An other-oriented communicator is constantly looking at and listening to the other person in order to appropriately adapt his or her communication behavior. Table 4.2 describes how we adapt our verbal messages to others and provides some examples.

People in conversations also adapt to nonverbal cues. For example, if you're talking to someone who speaks very loudly, you may raise the volume of your voice. Or if your communication partner likes to lean toward people when talking, you may respond by leaning towards him or her. We talk more about such nonverbal cues in Chapter 7.

Adaptation across intercultural contexts is usually more difficult than adaptation within your own culture. Imagine shaking hands with a stranger and having the stranger hold on to your hand as you continue to talk. In the United States, hand holding between strangers violates nonverbal norms. But in some cultures, maintaining physical contact while talking is expected. Pulling your hand away from this person would be rude. What may be mannerly in one culture is not always acceptable in another. Adapting to these cultural differences means developing that "third culture" that we talked about earlier in the chapter.

In an effective interpersonal relationship, your partner also orients himself or herself to you. A competent communicator has knowledge of others, is motivated to enhance the quality of communication, and possesses the skill of being other-oriented.

If you learn these skills and principles, will it really make a difference in your ability to relate to others? Evidence suggests that the answer is yes. A study by researcher Lori Carrell found that students who had been exposed to lessons in

Improving Your Communication Skills

Identifying and Adapting to Cultural Rules and Norms

What are the typical norms and rules that you expect when communicating with people in your own cultural and ethnic group in the following situations

Norms and rules regarding punctuality at meetings:

_____

_____

Norms and rules regarding greetings between good friends:

_____

_____

Norms and rules regarding giving and receiving gifts among friends:

_____

_____

Norms and rules regarding giving and receiving gifts among business associates:

_____

_____

Norms and rules regarding typical times for daily meals:

_____

_____

Norms and rules regarding appropriate use of someone's first name:

_____

_____

Share your answers with your classmates. Note the similarities and differences in your responses, both among people who share common cultural and ethnic backgrounds and those who have different cultural and ethnic backgrounds.

Which of the skills for enhancing intercultural competence discussed earlier in this chapter would help you adapt to different rules and expectations?

empathy—linked to a study of interpersonal and intercultural communication—improved their ability to empathize with others.[138] If you master these principles and skills, you will be rewarded with greater insight and ability to relate to others who are different from you.

Experienced travel writer Rick Steves echoes many of the skills and strategies we have presented in this chapter when encountering a culture different from your own. Some of his top tips for traveling abroad include the following:[139]

Be a cultural chameleon: When in Rome, do as the Romans do. Get in synch with your host culture. Consider trying the local food and beverages to experience the culture and cuisine.

Tune in to the local media: Watching, reading, or listening to local news reports or paying attention to local social media can give you additional insight about the culture.

Connect with people not just places: Do more than take pictures of iconic places; consider staying at a B&B (bed and breakfast) to get to know the locals or strike up a conversation with your waitperson in a restaurant.

Put yourself in the shoes of others: Empathize with others by learning about local customs, holidays, religious celebrations, and regional and national heroes. The heart of being other-oriented involves understanding the customs, traditions, heroes, and villains of a culture.

Accept rather than judge: When you meet someone from another culture whose values, behavior, or beliefs are different from your own, avoid assuming that his or her approach is inferior. Although you need not violate your own ethical standards, observe others rather than immediately condemning behavior that is different from your own.

Recap

How to Improve Your Intercultural Communication Competence

Develop Knowledge

Actively Seek Information	Learn about the worldview of someone from another culture
Listen and Ask Questions	Reduce uncertainty by asking for clarification and listening to the answer
Create a Third Culture	Create common ground by merging aspects of both cultural traditions to develop a common understanding

Develop Motivation

Tolerate Ambiguity	Take your time and expect some uncertainty
Be Mindful	Be conscious of cultural differences, rather than ignoring them
Avoid Negative Judgments	Resist thinking that your culture has all the answers

Develop Skill

Be Creatively Flexible	Learn as you interact and be willing to adjust your behavior as you learn
Become Other-Oriented	Put yourself in the other person's mental position (social decentering) and emotional mindset (empathizing)
Adapt Your Communication	Adjust your behavior to ethically accommodate others' differences and expectations

Applying an Other-Orientation

to Diversity: The Platinum Rule

Whether it's taste in music or food, greeting rituals, or a host of other culturally determined behaviors, the ultimate other-oriented behavior would be what communication researcher Milton Bennett calls **the Platinum Rule**: *Do to others as they themselves would like to be treated*.[140] Rather than treating people as *you* would like to be treated (the Golden Rule), interact with them the way you think *they* would like to be treated. According to Bennett, at its essence, empathy is "the imaginative, intellectual and emotional participation in another person's experience."[141] The goal, according to Bennett, is to attempt to think and feel what another person thinks and feels and to go beyond that by taking positive action toward others in response to your empathic feelings.

If you like hip-hop music but your friend prefers Mozart, taking her to a Mos Def concert may make you feel good about following the Golden Rule (that's how *you'd* like to be treated)—but the concert might be painful for her if she'd rather be listening to Mozart's Horn Quintet in E flat, K. 407. Apply the Platinum Rule and take her to a symphony performance instead.

But is the Platinum Rule realistic, or even possible? As you ponder the virtues and challenges of becoming other-oriented and adapting your communication behavior to enhance your intercultural communication competence, consider the following questions:

- What are some obstacles to applying the Platinum Rule, especially with people who are culturally different from you?
- Is the Platinum Rule always desirable? Would it be inappropriate to follow the Platinum Rule in some situations? Explain your answer.
- How can the Platinum Rule be useful when you are having a disagreement with another person?
- Think about a time when you applied the Platinum Rule. What was the effect on the person with whom you were communicating?

the Platinum Rule
Communicating or behaving toward another person as you assume he or she would like to be treated (as opposed to the Golden Rule, which is treat someone as you would like to be treated).

STUDY GUIDE
Review, Apply, and Assess

Understanding Diversity: Describing Our Differences

Objective 4.1   Describe five human differences that influence communication.

Key Terms

discrimination
sex
gender
race
ethnicity

Thinking Critically

What types of diversity do you find on your campus? In the workplace? In your community? Do you find that you communicate differently with people from different groups and cultures? Explain.

Assessing Your Skills

Which characteristics provide the best information on which to base your judgments of other people? Why? What would you need to know about another person to feel comfortable in making a prediction about him or her? How could you get that information?

Understanding Culture: Dimensions of Our Mental Software

Objective 4.2   Define culture and identify and describe the seven dimensions of culture.

Key Terms

culture
worldview
co-culture
enculturation
acculturation
cultural context
high-context culture
low-context culture
masculine culture
feminine culture

Thinking Critically

Name the co-cultures to which you belong. Would you describe your co-cultures as low or high context, masculine or feminine? Explain. What beliefs and norms characterize these co-cultures? What does your culture or co-culture value?

Assessing Your Skills

Based on the descriptions of cultural elements described earlier in this chapter, assess your own perspective on how you would assess your culture in terms of individualism (individualistic and collectivistic), context (high and low), gender (masculine and feminine), uncertainty (high and low), power (centralized and decentralized), and time (short-term and long-term).

Barriers to Effective Intercultural Communication

Objective 4.3   List and describe barriers that inhibit effective intercultural communication.

Key Terms

intercultural communication
culture shock
ethnocentrism
stereotype
prejudice

Thinking Critically

Jonna, an American, has just been accepted as an international exchange student in Germany. What potential cultural barriers may she face? How should she manage these potential barriers?

Assessing Your Skills

1.   Assessing Your Ethnocentrism

Communication researchers James Neuliep and James McCroskey developed the following measure of ethnocentrism. Answer the following questions honestly.

Directions: This instrument is composed of twenty-four statements concerning your feelings about your culture and other cultures. In the space provided to the left of each item, indicate the degree to which the statement applies to you by marking whether you (5) strongly agree, (4) agree, (3) are neutral, (2) disagree, or (1) strongly disagree with the statement. There are no right or wrong answers. Work quickly and record your first response.

_____ 1. Most other cultures are backward compared with my culture.

_____ 2. People in other cultures have a better lifestyle than we do in my culture.

_____ 3. Most people would be happier if they didn't live like people do in my culture.

_____ 4. My culture should be the role model for other cultures.

_____ 5. Lifestyles in other cultures are just as valid as those in my culture.

_____ 6. Other cultures should try to be more like my culture.

_____ 7. I'm not interested in the values and customs of other cultures.

_____ 8. It is not wise for other cultures to look up to my culture.

_____ 9. People in my culture could learn a lot from people in other cultures.

_____ 10. Most people from other cultures just don't know what's good for them.

_____ 11. People from my culture act strange and unusual when they go into other cultures.

_____ 12. I have little respect for the values and customs of other cultures.

_____ 13. Most people would be happier if they lived like people in my culture.

_____ 14. People in my culture have just about the best lifestyles of anywhere.

_____ 15. My culture is backward compared with most other cultures.

_____ 16. My culture is a poor role model for other cultures.

_____ 17. Lifestyles in other cultures are not as valid as those in my culture.

_____ 18. My culture should try to be more like other cultures.

_____ 19. I'm very interested in the values and customs of other cultures.

_____ 20. Most people in my culture just don't know what is good for them.

_____ 21. People in other cultures could learn a lot from people in my culture.

_____ 22. Other cultures are smart to look up to my culture.

_____ 23. I respect the values and customs of other cultures.

_____ 24. People from other cultures act strange and unusual when they come into my culture.

Scoring: To determine your ethnocentrism, _reverse_ your score for items 2, 3, 5, 8, 9, 11, 15, 16, 18, 19, 20, and 23. For these items, 5 = 1, 4 = 2, 3 = 3, 2 = 4, and 1 = 5. That is, if your original score was a 5, change it to a 1. If your original score was a 4, change it to a 2, and so forth. Once you have reversed your score for these twelve items, add up all twenty-four scores. This is your generalized ethnocentrism score. Scores greater than 80 indicate high ethnocentrism. Scores of 50 and below indicate low ethnocentrism.

SOURCE: J. W. Neuliep and J. C. McCroskey, "The Development of a U.S. and Generalized Ethnocentrism Scale," _Communication Research Reports_ 14 (1997): 393.

2. In small groups, identify examples from your own experiences of each barrier to effective intercultural communication discussed in the text. Use one of the examples as the basis for a script about two people from different cultures who are trying to communicate. Suggest how the skills and principles discussed in the chapter might have improved the communication between the characters in your script.

Improving Intercultural Communication Competence

Objective 4.4 **Identify and apply strategies for developing knowledge, motivation, and skills that can improve intercultural competence.**

Key Terms

intercultural communication competence	empathy
	adapt
motivation	communication
skill	accommodation theory
contact hypothesis	adapt predictively
third culture	adapt reactively
mindful	the Platinum Rule
social decentering	

Thinking Critically

Kosta is from Pyatigorsk, Russia, and has never been to the United States until arriving at your school to become a communication major. What communication strategies and behaviors could you enact to minimize intercultural communication challenges as you communicate with Kosta?

Assessing Your Skills

Based on the description of the skills and strategies for improving intercultural competence, rate yourself on the list of skills using a 1–10 scale with 1 = low and 10 = high. On those skills that you gave yourself the lowest rating, what could you do to enhance your skill?

_____ 1. I seek information about cultures that are unfamiliar to me.

_____ 2. I ask questions and listen effectively to people from other cultures.

_____ 3. I am skilled in creating a "third culture" when interacting with people from cultures different from my own.

_____ 4. I am able to tolerate ambiguity and uncertainty when interacting with someone from a different culture.

_____ 5. I am mindful of differences and similarities between me and someone from a different culture.

_____ 6. I avoid making negative judgments about people from different cultures.

_____ 7. I develop creative and flexible approaches to interacting with others from different cultures.

_____ 8. I am skillfully other-oriented when interacting with someone from a different culture.

_____ 9. I appropriately adapt my communication when interacting with someone from a culture different from my own.

Chapter 5
Listening and Responding Skills

"I never learned anything while I was talking."

Larry King

Learning Objectives

5.1 Define listening, and describe five elements of the listening process.

5.2 Identify characteristics of four listening styles.

5.3 List and describe barriers to effective listening.

5.4 Identify and use skills to enhance comprehension, empathy, and critical listening.

5.5 Identify and use skills to effectively and appropriately respond to others.

5.6 Identify and use skills to effectively and appropriately confirm others

Think about your best friend. What are some of the qualities you most admire in your friend? Many people would respond that one of the most valued qualities in a friend is his or her presence—supporting, comforting, and listening. As theologian Henri Nouwen eloquently put it:

> Listening is much more than allowing another to talk while waiting for a chance to respond. Listening is paying full attention to others and welcoming them into our very beings.... Listening is a form of spiritual hospitality by which you invite strangers to become friends, to get to know their inner selves more fully, and even dare to be silent with you.[1]

Simply stated, friends listen. They listen even if we sometimes say foolish things. Again, Nouwen describes it well: "True listeners...are free to receive, to welcome, to accept."[2] Among the essential skills of interpersonal communication, the skill of listening to others would be at or near the top of the list in terms of importance.[3] Skilled communicators appropriately respond to what we say. They confirm that they understand and care for us by providing both verbal and non-verbal feedback. There is also evidence that listening is the quintessential skill of an effective leader.[4]

Listening and responding skills are important for several reasons. Some researchers suggest that because listening is the first communication skill we learn (because we respond to sounds even while in our mother's womb), it's also the most important skill. Listening plays a key role in helping us learn to speak.[5]

Your skill as a listener has important implications for the relationships you establish. In interpersonal communication situations, the essence of being a good conversationalist is being a good listener. Rather than focusing only on what to say, a person skilled in the art of conversation listens and picks up on the interests and themes of others. One research study found that a key difference between couples who remained married and those who divorced was their ability to listen to each other.[6] Partners in enduring marriages report that being a good listener is essential to a satisfying marital relationship. Listening carefully can also earn you some tangible benefits. People who are perceived to be better listeners enjoy greater success in their jobs than do those who are perceived as poor listeners.[7] In addition, physicians, nurses, and other health professionals who are good listeners are perceived to be more competent and skilled.[8] Although engaging in social media does not involve the physiological act of hearing (unless we are using video and audio technology such as Skype), we increasingly use these platforms to meet our interpersonal-relational needs. For example, we still expect others to "listen" to our challenges and celebrations and to respond with appropriate, empathic responses.[9]

Another reason listening is important: You spend more time listening than participating in any other communication activity. In fact, you spend more time listening to others than doing almost anything else. Typical college students spend more than 80 percent of an average day communicating with other people, and as the pie chart in Figure 5.1 shows, of the total time they spend communicating, 55 percent is spent listening to others.[10] Ironically, most people's formal communication training focuses on writing, the activity to which they devote the least amount of communication time. Chances are that until now you have had no formal training in listening. In this chapter, we focus on this often neglected, yet crucial, skill for developing quality interpersonal relationships. Listening is the process by which people learn the most about others. In addition, we explore ways to respond appropriately to others.

Figure 5.1 What You Do with Your Communication Time

Listening Defined

5.1 **Define listening, and describe five elements of the listening process.**

"Hey, did you hear me? Where would you like to go for dinner tonight?" Shawn asks Pat. In fact, Pat probably did *hear* the question, but he may not have been *listening*. **Listening** is a complex process of selecting, attending to, creating meaning from, remembering, and responding to verbal and nonverbal messages.[11] When we listen, we hear words and try to make sense out of what we hear. The essence of being a good listener is being able to accurately interpret the messages expressed by others.[12]

Hearing is the physiological process of decoding sounds. You hear when sound vibrations reach your eardrum and cause the middle ear bones—the hammer, anvil, and stirrup—to move. Eventually, these sound vibrations are translated into electrical impulses that reach the brain. In order to listen to something, you must first select that sound from competing sounds. Then you must attend to it, understand it, and remember it. A fifth activity—responding—confirms that listening has occurred.[13]

listening

Process of selecting, attending to, creating meaning from, remembering, and responding to verbal and nonverbal messages.

hearing

Physiological process of decoding sounds.

Selecting

Selecting a sound is the process of choosing one sound as you sort through the various sounds competing for your attention. As you listen to someone in an interpersonal context, you focus on the words and nonverbal messages of your partner. Even now, as you are reading this book, there are undoubtedly countless noises within earshot. Stop reading for a moment and sort through the various sounds around you. Do you hear music? Is there noise from outside? How about the murmur of voices, the tick of a clock, the hum of a computer, the whoosh of an air conditioner or furnace? To listen, you must select which of these sounds will receive your attention.

selecting

Process of choosing one sound while sorting through various sounds competing for your attention.

Attending

Attending to a sound is the process of focusing on it after you have selected it. To attend to a sound is at the very heart of the listening process. The word *listen* stems from the Middle English term *listnen* which means "attention."[14] Attention can be fleeting. You may attend to the sound for a moment and then move on or return to other thoughts or other sounds, similar to how you might flip through channels on your TV before finally selecting a program, then stopping and attending to it. As we discussed in Chapter 3, your attention is sometimes selective. Either consciously or unconsciously, you are more likely to attend to those messages that meet your needs

attending

Process of focusing on a particular sound or message.

and are consistent with your attitudes or interests. Information that is novel or intense, or that somehow relates to you, may capture your attention. Finally, because listening is a transactional rather than a linear process (which means that you are both sending and receiving information *at the same time*), your listening skill is linked to your ability to attend to specific messages, especially during conversations when you're both talking and listening.[15]

Understanding

understanding

Process of assigning meaning to sounds.

remembering

Process of recalling information.

Whereas hearing is a physiological phenomenon, **understanding** is the process of assigning meaning to the sounds you select and to which you attend; to understand a message is to construct meaning from what you hear and see. There are several theories about how you assign meaning to words you hear, but there is no universally accepted notion of how this process works. One basic principle is that people understand best if they can relate what they are hearing to something they already know.

A second basic principle about how people understand others is this: The greater the similarity between individuals, the greater the likelihood of more accurate understanding. Individuals from different cultures who have substantially different religions, family lifestyles, values, and attitudes often have difficulty understanding each other, particularly in the early phases of a relationship.

A third principle is that you understand best what you also experience. Perhaps you have heard the Montessori school philosophy: "I hear, I forget; I see, I remember; I experience, I understand." Understanding happens when we derive meaning from the words we hear.

Healthy family relations result when parents and children are able to develop people-oriented listening styles.

Remembering

Remembering is the process of recalling information. Some researchers theorize that you store every detail you have ever heard or witnessed; your mind operates like a hard drive on a computer. But you cannot retrieve or remember all the information. Sometimes you were present at events, yet you have no recollection of what occurred.

Human brains have both short-term and long-term memory storage systems. Just as airports have only a few short-term parking spaces, but lots of spaces for long-term parking, brains can accommodate only a few things of fleeting significance, but acres of important information. Most of us forget hundreds of bits of insignificant information that pass through our brains each day.

The information stored in long-term memory includes events, conversations, and other data that are significant.

People tend to remember dramatic and vital information, as well as seemingly inconsequential details connected with such information.

Responding

Interpersonal communication is transactive; it involves both talking and responding. You are **responding** to people when you let them know you understand their messages. Responses can be nonverbal; direct eye contact and head nods let your partner know you're tuned in. Or you can respond verbally by asking questions to confirm the content of the message: "Are you saying you don't want us to spend as much time together as we once did?" or by making statements that reflect the feelings of the speaker: "So you are frustrated that you have to wait for someone to drive you where you want to go." We discuss responding skills in more detail later in the chapter.

responding

Process of confirming your understanding of a message.

Listening Styles

5.2 Identify characteristics of four listening styles.

Although we've described the typical elements in the listening process, not everyone has the same style or approach to listening. Your **listening style** is your preferred way of making sense out of the messages you hear. Some people, for example, prefer to focus on facts and analyze the information they hear. Others seem more interested in focusing on feelings and emotions.

What's your listening style? Knowing your style can help you adapt and adjust when listening to others. Listening researchers have found that people tend to listen using one or more of four listening styles: relational, analytic, critical, or task-oriented.[16]

listening style

Preferred way of making sense out of spoken messages.

Relational Listening Style

Relational listeners tend to prefer listening to people express their emotions and feelings. A person with a relational listening style searches for common interests and seeks to empathize with the feelings of others—she or he connects emotionally with the sentiments and passions others express.[17] Relational-oriented listeners are less apprehensive when communicating with others in small groups and interpersonal situations.[18]

Research shows that relational listeners have a greater tendency to be sympathetic to the person they are listening to.[19] A sympathetic listener is more likely to voice concern for the other person's welfare when that person is sharing personal information or news about a stressful situation. A sympathetic listener says things like "Oh, Pat, I'm so sorry to hear about your loss." Relational listeners may also be more empathic; they seem to have greater understanding of the thoughts and feelings of others.[20] An empathic listener may recognize another's feelings and respond, "You must feel so lonely and sad." One study found that jurors who are relational listeners (originally described as "people-oriented") are less likely to find the plaintiff at fault in a civil court trial, perhaps because of their tendency to empathize with others.[21] Research also suggests that people who strongly prefer the relational listening style are less anxious or apprehensive about listening, especially when listening to just one person.[22]

relational listeners

Those who prefer to focus on the emotions and feelings communicated verbally and nonverbally by others.

Analytical Listening Style

Analytical listeners focus on facts and tend to withhold judgment before reaching a specific conclusion. They would make good judges because they generally consider all sides of an issue before making a decision or reaching a conclusion. Analytical listeners tend to listen to an entire message before assessing the validity of the

analytical listeners

Those who withhold judgment, listen to all sides of an issue, and wait until they hear the facts before reaching a conclusion.

information they hear. To help analyze information, they take the perspective of the person to whom they are listening; this helps them suspend judgment. They also like information to be well organized so that they can clearly and easily analyze it. While listening to a rambling personal story, the analytical listener focuses on the facts and details rather than on the emotions being expressed. Analytical listeners prefer listening to rich message content and then finding ways of organizing or making sense out of the information.

Critical Listening Style

Critical listeners are good at evaluating information they hear. They are able to hone in on inconsistencies in what someone says. They are comfortable listening to detailed, complex information and focusing on the facts, yet they are especially adept in noting contradictions in the facts presented. Critical listeners are also likely to catch errors in the overall logic and reasoning that is being used to reach a conclusion.

Critical listeners tend to be a bit more skeptical than relational listeners about the information they hear. Researchers call this skepticism **second-guessing**—questioning the assumptions underlying a message.[23] It's called second-guessing because instead of assuming that what they hear is accurate or relevant, listeners make a second guess about the accuracy of the information they are listening to. Accuracy of information is especially important to critical listeners, because if they are going to use the information in some way, it should be valid.

Task-Oriented Listening Style

Task-oriented listeners are interested in focusing more on achieving a specific outcome or accomplishing a task than on focusing on the communication relationship when they listen to others. They emphasize completing a specific transaction, such as solving a problem, taking action, or making a purchase. Task-oriented listeners focus on verbs—what needs to be done. Consequently, they don't like to listen to rambling messages that lack a clear point. They appreciate efficient communicators who are sensitive to how much time is involved in delivering a message. They also like messages to be well organized so that they can focus on the outcomes. Task-oriented listeners want to do something with the information they hear; they want it to serve a purpose or function. They become impatient with information that doesn't seem to have a "bottom line."

Understanding Your Listening Style

How does knowing about listening styles benefit you? There are at least three reasons to give some thought to your listening style and the listening styles of others. First, knowing your own listening style can help you adapt and adjust to the listening situation. If, for example, you tend to be a relational-oriented listener and you're listening to a message that has little information about people but many technical details, be aware that you will have to work harder to stay tuned in to the message.

Second, it's important to understand that you probably have more than one style of listening. According to listening researchers Kitty Watson and Larry Barker, who have done extensive research about listening styles (although using different labels than the styles we've described), about 40 percent of all listeners have one primary listening style that they use most often, especially if they are under stress. Another 40 percent of listeners use more than one style—for example, they may prefer to listen to evaluate (critical listening style) and also want the information delivered in a short amount of time and focused on the task to be accomplished (task-oriented listening style). And about 20 percent of people do not have a listening style preference.

critical listeners
Those who prefer to listen for the facts and evidence to support key ideas and an underlying logic; they also listen for errors, inconsistencies, and discrepancies.

second-guessing
Questioning the ideas and assumptions underlying a message; assessing whether the message is true or false.

task-oriented listeners
Those who look at the overall structure of the message to see what action needs to be taken; they also like efficient, clear, and briefer messages.

BEING Other-ORIENTED
It's important to know your own preferred listening style, but it's also important to understand the listening style of your communication partner. How can you do this? Look for clues that help you identify your partner's listening style. Relational listeners want to hear stories and anecdotes about others. Analytical listeners will be interested in facts. Critical listeners will be more focused on errors, inconsistencies, and discrepancies when listening. Task-oriented listeners will be focused on verbs; they want to know what to do with the information they hear.

Recap

Listening Styles

Relational-oriented listening style	Listeners prefer to attend to feelings and emotions and to search for common areas of interest when listening to others.
Analytical-oriented listening style	Listeners prefer to withhold judgment, listen to all sides of an issue, and wait until they hear the facts before reaching a conclusion.
Critical listening style	Listeners are likely to listen for the facts and evidence to support key ideas and an underlying logic; they also listen for errors, inconsistencies, and discrepancies.
Task-oriented listening style	Listeners are focused on accomplishing something and look at the overall structure of the message to see what action needs to be taken; they also like efficient, clear, and brief messages.

Given that almost two-thirds of listeners have more than one style, it's likely the situation, time, listening goal, and place all impact the listening style or styles people adopt.[24] New research suggests that we adapt our listening style to fit our listening goal.[25] If, for example, you are listening to your boss provide key details about a complicated project, you are likely to adopt an analytical listening style. But when you receive a phone call from a friend who just wants to chat, you may adopt a relational listening style. We listen for many reasons and our approach or style of listening reflects those reasons.

Some research suggests that females are more likely to be relational listeners, whereas males have a tendency to assume one of the other listening styles.[26] Your listening style, however, may be less influenced by your sex than by the overall approach you take to interpreting and remembering the information you hear. Your cultural traditions may have a major influence on your particular listening style. People from a more individualistic, self-focused cultural perspective (such as people from the United States) tend to be more action-oriented listeners. Relational listeners, according to research, are more likely to have collectivistic values, are group-oriented, or were raised in a collaborative cultural tradition (such as some Asian cultures).[27]

Finally, it can be useful to be aware of the listening styles of others so you can communicate messages they are more likely to listen to. If you know your spouse is often an analytical listener, then communicate a message that is rich in information; that's what your spouse prefers. Tell the analytical-oriented listener, "Here are three things I have to tell you." Then say them. Of course, it may be difficult to determine someone's listening style, especially if you don't know the person very well. But it is both easier and worth the time to consider the listening styles of people you *do* know well (your family members, your coworkers, your boss). Knowing your own and others' listening styles can help you adapt your communication to enhance the accuracy of your own listening and the appropriateness of the way in which you communicate to others.

Listening Barriers

5.3   List and describe barriers to effective listening.

Although people spend much of their communication time listening, most don't listen as well as they should. Twenty-four hours after you hear a speech or class lecture, you have forgotten more than half of what was said. And it gets worse. In another twenty-four hours, you have forgotten half of what you remembered, so you really remember only a quarter of the lecture.

Interpersonal listening skills may be even worse. When you listen to a speech or lecture, you have a clearly defined listening role; one person talks, and you are expected to listen. But in interpersonal situations, you may have to alternate quickly between speaking and listening. Often you are thinking of what you want to say next, rather than listening. The possibility of receiving a text or phone call during a conversation can also be a distraction. Just the mere visible presence of a phone can reduce the quality of the conversation.[28]

One surprising study found that we sometimes listen better to strangers than to intimate friends or partners. Married couples in the study tended to interrupt each other more often and were generally less polite to each other than were strangers involved in a decision-making task.[29] Apparently, we take listening shortcuts when communicating with others in close relationships. As the Relating to Diverse Others feature suggests, the problem may be gender-related.

Inattentive listening is a bit like channel surfing when we watch TV. When we listen to others, we may tune in to the conversation for a moment, decide that the content is uninteresting, and then focus on a personal thought. These thoughts are barriers to communication, and they come in a variety of forms.

Are we more attentive listeners to TV? Apparently not. One research team phoned TV viewers as soon as the evening news program ended. On average, most people remembered only about 17 percent of what they heard. And even when researchers reminded viewers of some of the news coverage, most averaged no better than 25 percent recall.[30] Even though more highly educated viewers did a little better, the overall conclusion is not good: We often don't "catch" what we hear, even a few moments after hearing it. Let's explore several listening barriers that keep us from catching others' meaning.

Being Self-Absorbed

You're in your local grocery store during "rush hour." It appears that most of your community has also decided to forage for food at the same time. Shoppers clog the aisles and crowd the checkout stands. You find yourself becoming tense—not just because you are hungry, but because it seems like the grocery store is filled with

Relating to Diverse Others
Who Listens Better: Men or Women?

Research provides no clear-cut answer to the question "Who listens better, men or women?" There is evidence, however, that men and women may listen somewhat *differently*. The following general patterns have emerged from research, but are not necessarily applicable to all men and women:[31]

Men tend to listen to

- solve a problem.
- accomplish a task.
- look for a new structure in a message.
- focus on one element in a message.

Women tend to listen to

- search for relationships among pieces of information in the message.

- enhance a relationship.
- reinforce the existing structure in a message.
- understand multiple elements in a message.

These differences have been summarized with this statement: *Men listen to report while women listen to establish rapport.* Yet even this broad distinction between the ways men and women may process information is controversial. Communication researchers Stephanie Sargent and James Weaver suggest that pop psychology, which alleges dramatic "Mars" and "Venus" differences between the way men

and women listen, may simply be perpetuating stereotypes based on the way men and women think they are supposed to listen.[32] Additionally, although there may be some differences, the distinctions may not be based on a person's biological sex; they more likely reflect differences in gender (socially constructed, cultural, or co-cultural learned behavior).[33] As we have stressed, an other-oriented approach to interpersonal communication focuses on the individual needs or perspectives of the other person, rather than relying on stereotypes to make definitive judgments about another person.

self-absorbed people who are focused on getting *their* needs met and are oblivious to the needs of others.

Self-absorbed listeners focus on their needs rather than on yours; the message is about *them*, not *you*. During conversations with a self-absorbed communicator, you have difficulty sustaining the conversation about anything except your self-absorbed partner's ideas, experiences, and stories. This problem is also called **conversational narcissism**. To be narcissistic is to be in love with oneself, like the mythical Greek character Narcissus, who became enamored with his reflection in a pool of water.[34]

A related problem is **selective listening**: letting our pre-formed biases and expectations color what we hear, which is likely to result in missed meaning and a self-focused filtering of messages. When we selectively listen, we hear what we want or expect to hear, rather than what the speaker actually uttered.

The self-absorbed listener is actively involved in doing several things other than listening. He or she is much more likely to interrupt others in mid-sentence, while seeking ways to focus the attention on himself or herself. Rather than focusing on the speaker's message, the self-absorbed listener thinks about what he or she is going to say next. This focus on an internal message can keep a listener from selecting and attending to the other person's message. A good listener accepts the other person and is truly other-oriented rather than self-oriented.[35]

How do you short-circuit this listening problem in yourself? First, diagnose it. Note consciously when you find yourself drifting off, thinking about your agenda rather than concentrating on the speaker. Second, throttle up your powers of concentration when you find your internal messages are distracting you from listening well.

Unchecked Emotions

Words are powerful symbols that affect people's attitudes, behavior, and even blood pressure. Words arouse people emotionally, and your emotional state can affect how well you listen. **Emotional noise** occurs when emotional arousal interferes with communication effectiveness. If you grew up in a home in which R-rated language was never used, then four-letter words may be distracting to you. Words that insult your religious or ethnic heritage can be fighting words. Most people respond to certain trigger words like a bull to a waving cape; they want to charge in to correct the speaker or perhaps even do battle with him or her.

Sometimes, it is not specific words but rather concepts or ideas that cause an emotional eruption. Some talk-radio hosts and TV commentators try to boost their ratings by purposely using words that elicit passionate responses. Although listening to such shows can be interesting and entertaining, when your own emotions become aroused, you may lose your ability to focus on the message of another. Research suggests that being in a positive emotional state can actually make you a better listener because you are able to be more attentive and focused when you are in a good mood.[36]

If you are listening to someone who is emotionally distraught, you will be more likely to focus on the emotions than on the content of the message.[37] Communication author R. G. Owens advises that when you communicate with someone who is emotionally excited, you should remain calm and focused and try simply to communicate your interest in the other person.[38]

Your listening challenge is to avoid emotional sidetracks and keep your attention focused on what others are saying. When you find yourself distracted by emotional noise brought on by objectionable words or concepts, or by an emotional speaker, use self-talk (tell yourself to remain calm) to quiet the noise and steer back to the subject at hand.

conversational narcissism

A focus on personal agendas and self-absorption rather than on the needs and ideas of others.

selective listening

Letting pre-formed biases, prejudices, expectations, and stereotypes cause us to hear what we want to hear, instead of listening to what a speaker actually said.

BEING Other-ORIENTED

When someone "pushes your hot buttons" and you find yourself becoming emotionally upset, what can you do to calm yourself and remain centered? First, simply be aware that you are becoming emotionally upset. Then take action (such as focusing on your breathing) to lower the tension you are feeling. What are other strategies to help you remain calm when someone "pushes your buttons"?

emotional noise

Form of communication interference caused by emotional arousal.

Criticizing the Speaker

The late Mother Teresa once said, "If you judge people, you have no time to love them." Being critical of the speaker may distract a listener from focusing on the message. Ineffective listeners may quickly conclude that both the speaker and the topic are uninteresting. After mentally pronouncing the speaker boring, the bad listener smugly gives himself or herself permission to think about something else.

Do you remember seeing villains in movies about the Old West, waiting in the bushes, ready to jump out and ambush an unsuspecting passerby? Perhaps you know someone who is an **ambush listener**. This is a person who eagerly pounces on the speaker to argue, criticize, or find fault with what the speaker has said. Although the ambush listener may look as if she or he is listening, in reality this type of listener is just waiting to critique the speaker for a variety of reasons.

Superficial factors such as clothing, body size and shape, age, and other aspects of personal appearance all affect our interpretation of a message. Monitor your internal dialogue to make sure you are focusing on the message rather than judging the messenger. Good listeners say to themselves, "While it may be distracting, I am simply not going to let the appearance of this speaker keep my attention from the message."

ambush listener
Person who is overly critical and judgmental when listening to others.

Differing Speech Rate and Thought Rate

Your ability to think faster than people speak is another listening pitfall. The average person speaks at a rate of 125 words a minute. Some folks talk a bit faster, others more slowly. In contrast, you have the ability to process up to 600 or 800 words a minute. The difference between your mental ability to handle words and the speed at which they arrive at your cortical centers can cause trouble, allowing you time to daydream and to tune the speaker in and out while giving you the illusion that you are concentrating more attentively than you actually are.[39]

You can turn your listening speed into an advantage if you use the extra time to summarize what a speaker says. By periodically sprinkling in mental summaries during a conversation, you can dramatically increase your listening ability and make the speech-rate/thought-rate difference work to your advantage.

Information Overload

We live in an information-rich age. We are all constantly bombarded with sights and sounds, and experts suggest that the volume of information competing for our attention is likely to become even greater in the future. Information overload leads to fatigue that reduces our listening effectiveness. Smart phones, tablets, MP3 players, and other devices can interfere with conversations and distract us from listening to others. The very presence of these devices, even if we are not using them, has been found to affect the quality of communication with have with others.[40]

Be on the alert for interruptions from such sources when you talk with others. Don't assume that because you are ready to talk, the other person is ready to listen. If your message is particularly sensitive or important, you may want to ask your listening partner, "Is this a good time to talk?" Even if your partner says yes, look for eye contact and a responsive facial expression to make sure the positive response is genuine.

Information overload can prevent us from being able to communicate effectively with people around us.

External Noise

As you will recall, all the communication models in Chapter 1 include the element of noise—distractions that take your focus away from the message. Many households seem to be addicted to noise. Often, there is a TV on (sometimes more than one), a computer game beeping, and music emanating from another room. These and other sounds compete for your attention when you are listening to others.

Besides literal noise, there are other potential distractors. A headline about a lurid sex scandal may "shout" for your attention just when your son wants to talk with you about the science fiction story he's trying to write. A desire to listen to your recent download from Beck may drown out your spouse's overtures to have a heart-to-heart talk about your family's budget problems.

Distractions make it difficult to sustain attention to a message. You have a choice to make: listen through the competing distractions or modify the environment to reduce them. Turning off the music, stepping away from the computer, and establishing eye contact with the speaker can help minimize the noise barrier.

Listener Apprehension

Not only do some people become nervous and apprehensive about speaking to others, but some are also anxious about listening to others. **Listener apprehension** is the fear of misunderstanding, misinterpreting, or not being able to adjust psychologically to messages spoken by others.[41] Because some people are nervous or worried about missing the message, they *do* misunderstand the message; their fear and apprehension keep them from absorbing it.[42] If someone is speaking in a language that is not your primary language, you are more likely to experience apprehension than when listening to a message in your primary language.[43] And, not surprisingly, you listen more accurately when someone speaks in your primary language.[44] President Franklin Roosevelt's admonition that "The only thing we have to fear is fear itself" implies correctly that fear can become "noise" and keep people from listening to messages accurately. If you are one of those people who are nervous when listening, you may experience difficulty understanding all you hear.

If you're an apprehensive listener, you will have to work harder when you listen to others. When listening to a public speech, it may be acceptable to record it or to start taking notes; during interpersonal conversations, however, it's not appropriate or even always possible to have a recording device or paper and pencil to take notes. If you're on the phone, you can take notes when you listen to help remember the message content, but taping phone conversations without the other speaker's consent is not ethical. Whether you're face to face with the speaker or on the phone, you can try to mentally summarize the message as you're listening to it.

listener apprehension
The fear of misunderstanding, misinterpreting, or being unable to adjust to the spoken messages of others.

Recap

Listening Barriers

Listening Barrier	To Overcome the Barrier
Self-Absorption	Become conscious of the self-focus, and shift attention.
Unchecked Emotions	Use self-talk to manage emotions.
Criticism of the Speaker	Focus on the message, not the messenger.
Differing Speech and Thought Rate	Use the time difference between speech rate and thought rate to mentally summarize the message.
Information Overload	Realize when you or your partner is tired or distracted and not ready to listen.
External Noise	Take charge of the listening environment by eliminating distractions.
Listener Apprehension	Concentrate on the message as you mentally summarize what you hear.

Concentrating on the message by mentally summarizing what you hear can help take your mind off your anxiety and help you focus on the message.

Improving Your Listening Skills

5.4 **Identify and use skills to enhance comprehension, empathy, and critical listening.**

Many of the listening problems we have identified stem from focusing on one's self rather than on the messages of others. Dale Carnegie, in his classic book *How to Win Friends and Influence People,* offered this tip to enhance interpersonal relationships: "Focus first on being interested, not interesting."[45] In essence, he affirms the importance of being other-oriented when listening to others.

How to Improve Listening Comprehension Skills

You can become a more other-oriented listener by following three steps you probably first encountered in elementary school: (1) stop, (2) look, and (3) listen. Although these steps may sound simplistic and seem like common sense, they are not always common practice. But they can provide the necessary structure to help you refocus your mental energies and improve your ability to comprehend the messages of others. A considerable body of listening research supports these steps to improved listening. Let's consider each step separately.

STOP Stop what? What should you *not* do in order to be a better listener? You should not be attending to off-topic "self-talk."

Most interpersonal listening problems can be traced to a single source—ourselves. While listening to others, we also "talk" to ourselves. Our internal thoughts are like a play-by-play sportscast. We mentally comment on the words and sights we select and to which we attend. If we keep those mental comments focused on the message, they may be useful. But we often attend to our own internal dialogues instead of listening to others' messages. Then our listening effectiveness plummets.

Two researchers conducted a study to identify the specific behaviors that good listeners perform. What they discovered supports our admonition that to be a better listener, you should stop focusing on your own mental messages and be other-oriented. Specifically, you should take the following actions during what the researchers called the "pre-interaction phase" of listening:

- Put your own thoughts aside.
- Be there mentally as well as physically.
- Make a conscious, mindful effort to listen.
- Take adequate time to listen; don't rush the speaker; be patient.
- Be open-minded.[46]

It boils down to this: When you listen, you are either on-task or off-task. When you're on-task, you are concentrating on the message; when you're off-task, your mind may be a thousand miles away. What's important is to be mindful of what you are doing. You can increase your motivation to listen by reminding yourself why listening is important. And to enhance your listening skill, try sprinkling in a few on-task "self-talk" reminders of why the information you are listening to is important.[47]

Two other researchers studied how to enhance the performance of "professional listeners" who work in call centers where customers order products, make product suggestions, or lodge complaints.[48] They found that customers preferred listeners who were focused and communicated that they were devoting their full attention to the caller. Training listeners to avoid distractions, hone in on the essence of a caller's message, and stop and focus on what the callers were telling them, increased customers' confidence and satisfaction in the speaker–listener relationship. The researchers also concluded that the ability to stop and focus on the comments of others can be taught. People who learn how to stop mental distractions can improve their listening comprehension.

LOOK Nonverbal messages are powerful. As the primary ways we communicate feelings, emotions, and attitudes, they play a major role in the total communication process, particularly in the development of relationships. Facial expressions and vocal cues, as well as eye contact, posture, and use of gestures and movement, can dramatically color the meaning of a message. When the nonverbal message contradicts the verbal message, people almost always believe the nonverbal message. As you listen to others, it is vital to focus not only on the words, but also on the nonverbal messages.

Accurately interpreting nonverbal messages can help you "listen between the lines." By attending to your partner's unspoken message, you look for the **meta-message**—the message about the message. Metacommunication, as you learned in Chapter 1, is communication about communication. The nonverbal meta-message provides a source of information about the emotional and relational impact of what a speaker may be expressing with the verbal message. For example, a friend may not explicitly say that he or she is angry, upset, or irritated, but nonverbal cues let you know. The essence of the "look" step is to listen with your eyes as well as your ears.

Another reason to look at the other person is to establish eye contact, which signals that you are focusing your interest and attention on him or her. If your eyes are darting over your partner's head, looking for someone else, or peeking at your smart phone, your partner will rightly get the message that you're not really listening. Researcher Jinni Harrigan found that people telegraph desire to change roles from listener to speaker by increasing eye contact, using gestures such as a raised finger, and shifting posture.[49] So it is important to maintain eye contact and monitor your partner's nonverbal signals when you listen as well as when you speak.

The tricky part of the Look step is not to be distracted by nonverbal cues that may prevent you from interpreting the message correctly. A research team asked one group of college students to listen to a counselor, and another group to both watch and listen to the counselor.[50] The students then rated the counselor's effectiveness. Students who both saw and heard the counselor perceived him as *less* effective, because his distracting nonverbal behaviors affected their evaluations. Although it's important to look to discern the emotional meaning behind the words, don't let a speaker's delivery distract you from the content of the message.

LISTEN Effective listeners are active rather than passive. For example, during the normal course of actively listening to another person, effective listeners[51]

- just listen—they do not interrupt.[52]
- respond and provide appropriate verbal feedback ("yes, I see," "I understand") and nonverbal feedback (eye contact, nodding, appropriate facial expressions).
- appropriately contribute to the conversation.

Effective listeners are not only goal-oriented (listening for the point of the message) but are also people-oriented (listening to appropriately affirm the person). To maximize your listening effectiveness, we offer several more specific strategies and tips.

DETERMINE YOUR LISTENING GOAL You listen to other people for several reasons—to learn, to enjoy yourself, to evaluate, or to provide empathic support. With

meta-message
A message about a message; the message a person is expressing via nonverbal means (such as by facial expression, eye contact, and posture) about the message articulated with words.

Improving Your Communication Skills

How to Identify Both Major Ideas and Details to Enhance Listening

To become a skilled listener, you must know how to identify both the major ideas and details of a message. How do you do that?

- First, ask yourself, "What is the key idea? What does this person want or expect from me?" Or, "Is there one main idea or are there several ideas jumbled together?" Consider: Is your goal to *remember* the information, *take some action, empathize* with the speaker, or *just listen* to reflect and be a sounding board?

- Second, identify the overall emotional tone of the message. Is the speaker calm, angry, happy, peaceful, or upset? Assessing the emotion of the speaker can help you identify the speaker's purpose.

- Third, try to identify the overall organizational pattern. Is the speaker telling a story in chronological order? Is the message organized around general topics? Or is the speaker elaborating on the reasons why something is true or false? Perhaps there is no logical organization, in which case you'll have to find a way to organize the ideas in your own mind.

- Fourth, identify the specific details or essential pieces of information that help tell the story or establish the speaker's point. You can better chunk the message into manageable details if you know the overarching story or key idea.

- Finally, link the details you hear with what seems to be the speaker's purpose. Linking details with the major idea will both help you remember the details and confirm your understanding of the main point of the message.

Here's a chance to practice your skill in identifying and remembering bits of information, as well as the main meaning of a message.

Read each of the following statements. After you have read each statement, cover it with your hand or a piece of paper. First, list as many of the details as you can recall from the message. Second, summarize your understanding of the major idea or key point of the message. As a variation on this activity, rather than reading the statement, have someone read the statement to you, and then identify the details and major idea.

Statement 1: "I'm very confused. I reserved our conference room for 1 P.M. today for an important meeting. We all know that conference space is tight. I reserved the room last week with the administrative assistant. Now I learn that you plan to use the conference room at noon for a two-hour meeting. It's now 11 A.M. We need to solve this problem soon. I have no other option for holding my meeting. And if I don't hold my meeting today, the boss is going to be upset."

Statement 2: "Hello, Marcia? I'm calling on my cell phone. Where are you? I thought you were supposed to meet me at the circle drive forty-five minutes ago. You know I can't be late for my seminar this evening. What do you mean, you're waiting at the circle drive? I don't see you. No, I'm at Switzler Hall circle drive. You're where? No, that's not the circle drive I meant. I thought you'd know where I meant. Don't you ever listen? If you hurry, I can just make it to the seminar."

Statement 3: "Oh, Mary, I just don't know what to do. My daughter announced that when she turns eighteen next week she's going to shave her head, get a large tattoo, and put a ring in her nose and eyebrow. She said it's something she's always wanted to do and now she can do it without my permission. She's always been such a sweet, compliant girl, but she seems to have turned wild. I've tried talking with her. And her father isn't much help. He thinks it may look 'cool.' I just don't want her to look like a freak when she has her senior picture taken next month."

so many potential listening goals and options, it can be useful to consciously decide what your listening objective should be.

If you are listening to someone give you directions to the city park, then your mental summaries should focus on the details of when to turn left and how many streets past the courthouse you need to drive before you turn right. The details are crucial to achieving your objective. If, in contrast, your neighbor tells you about her father's triple bypass operation, then your goal is to empathize. It is probably not important to recall when her father checked into the hospital or any other details about his treatment. Your job is to listen patiently and to provide emotional support. Clarifying your listening objective in your own mind can help you use appropriate skills to maximize your listening effectiveness. Being aware that your style of listening should be influenced by your listening goal is a good thing. Consciously consider whether your listening style (relational, analytical, critical or task-oriented) matches your listening goal.[53]

TRANSFORM LISTENING BARRIERS INTO LISTENING GOALS If you can transform the listening barriers (that you read about earlier) into listening goals, you will be well on your way to improving your listening skill. Make it a goal not to focus on your personal agenda. Use self-talk to manage emotional noise. Do not criticize the speaker. Remind yourself before each conversation to create mental summaries capitalizing on the differences between your information processing rate and the speaker's verbal delivery rate.[54] And make it your business to choose a communication environment free of distraction from other incoming information or noise.

MENTALLY SUMMARIZE THE DETAILS OF THE MESSAGE This strategy may seem to contradict the earlier suggestion to avoid focusing only on facts; but if your goal is to recall information, it is important to grasp the details your partner provides. As we noted earlier, you can process words much more quickly than a person speaks. So, as you listen, periodically summarize the names, dates, and locations in the message. Organize the speaker's factual information into appropriate categories or try to place events in chronological order. Without a full understanding of the details, you will likely miss the speaker's major point.

MENTALLY WEAVE THESE SUMMARIES INTO A FOCUSED MAJOR POINT OR A SERIES OF MAJOR IDEAS Facts usually make the most sense when you can use them to help support an idea or major point. So, as you summarize, try to link the facts you have organized in your mind with key ideas and principles. Use facts to enhance your critical thinking as you analyze, synthesize, evaluate, and finally summarize the key points or ideas your listening partner is making.[55]

PRACTICE LISTENING TO CHALLENGING MATERIAL To improve or even maintain any skill, you need to practice it. Experts suggest that listening skills deteriorate if people do not practice what they know. Listening to difficult, challenging material can sharpen skills, so good listeners practice by listening to documentaries, debates, and other high-level material. One study found that as you gain experience listening on the job, you improve your listening skill. Being motivated to listen while you practice can also enhance your listening competence.[56]

How to Improve Empathic Listening Skills

Listening involves more than merely comprehending the words of others; it's also about understanding and experiencing the feelings and emotions expressed. As we noted in Chapter 4, at the core of being other-oriented is cultivating **empathy**—feeling what someone else is feeling.[57] When a friend has "one of those days," perhaps he or she seeks you out to talk about it. There may not be a specific problem to solve—perhaps it was just a day filled with miscommunication and squabbles with a partner

empathy
Emotional reaction that is similar to the reaction being experienced by another person; empathizing is feeling what another person is feeling.

Recap

How to Improve Listening Comprehension Skills

Step	Listening Skill	Action
Stop	Tune out distracting competing messages.	Become conscious of being distracted; use on-task self-talk to remain focused.
Look	Become aware of the speaker's nonverbal cues; monitor your own nonverbal cues to communicate your interest in the speaker.	Establish eye contact; avoid fidgeting or performing other tasks when someone is speaking to you; listen with your eyes.
Listen	Create meaning from your partner's verbal and nonverbal messages.	Mentally summarize details; link these details with main ideas.

#communicationandtechnology

Being "Listened to" by Our Facebook Friends

Listening to others is a way to show our support and express our affection toward them, especially if the other person is having a difficult time. When we have a difficult day or have had a disappointment, research suggests that we expect our friends to be there for us and support us.

There is evidence that we increasingly turn to Facebook and other social media to seek a "listening ear" when life gets tough.[58] Although we may have many close friends in whom we can confide, Facebook provides us with a broader audience of acquaintances as well as good, close friends who can listen to our concerns and life challenges. Research suggests

that if we are fearful of being judged by close friends or we feel at risk disclosing something personal that would invite a detailed response, we may turn to Facebook to seek support in the form of a quick "like"—enough for us to know that someone "hears" us and that we don't have to provide lengthy explanations.[59]

How do you enhance your empathic listening skills? First, think about what the other person may be thinking by socially decentering; second, focus on the feelings and emotions of your partner, truly empathizing with the other person.[60]

---

or coworkers. But the person wants a listener who focuses attention on him or her and cares about what he or she is saying. The friend is seeking someone who will empathize.

social decentering

Cognitive process in which we take into account another person's thoughts, feelings, values, background, and perspective.

IMAGINE WHAT YOUR PARTNER IS THINKING   We're not advocates of mindreading, yet people who are more skilled in empathizing with others make an effort to ponder what their partners may be thinking and experiencing when communicating with them. As noted in Chapter 4, **social decentering** is a *cognitive process* in which you take into account another person's thoughts, values, background, and perspectives as you interact with him or her. This process involves viewing the world from the other person's point of view. The greater the difference between you and your communication partner, the more difficult it is to accomplish social decentering.

There are three ways to socially decenter: (1) Develop an understanding of another person based on how you have responded when something similar has happened to you, (2) base your understanding on knowledge you have about the specific person, or (3) make generalizations about someone based on your understanding of how you think most people would feel or behave.[61]

Developing empathy requires more than simply understanding someone's situation. A person who is truly empathic "feels with" the other person—he or she experiences the emotions the other person is feeling.

Think About How You Would React   When you draw on your direct experience, you use your knowledge of what happened to you in the past to help you guess how someone else may feel. To the degree that the other person is similar to you, your reactions and those of the other person will be similar. For example, suppose you are talking to a friend who has just failed a midterm exam in an important course. You have also had this experience. Your own reaction was not to worry about the failed midterm because you had confidence you could still earn a passing grade in the course. You might use this self-understanding to predict your friend's reactions. To the degree that you are similar to your friend, your prediction will be accurate. But suppose your friend comes from a culture with high expectations for success. He might believe he has dishonored his family by his poor performance. In this situation, your understanding of your own reaction needs to be tempered by your awareness of how similar or dissimilar you and the other person are.

Reflect on What You Know About the Other Person   The second way to socially decenter is based on the specific knowledge you have of the person with whom you are interacting. Your memory of how your friend reacted to failing a midterm exam once before gives you a basis to more accurately predict his reaction this time. And even if you have not observed your friend's reaction to this particular situation, you can project how you think he feels based on what you know about his personality. As relationships become more intimate, you have more information to allow you to socially decenter with greater confidence.

Consider How Most People Would React   The third way to socially decenter is to apply your understanding of people in general, or of categories of people. Each of us develops personal theories about how people act. You might have a general theory to explain the behavior of men and another for that of women. You might have general theories about Mexicans, Japanese, Canadians, Slovenians, Texans, or Iowans. As you meet someone who falls into one of your categories, you draw on that concept to socially decenter. The more you can learn about a given culture, the stronger your general theories can be, and the more effectively you can use this method of socially decentering. The key, however, is to avoid developing inaccurate, inflexible stereotypes of others and basing your perceptions of others only on those generalizations. Making snap judgments based only on past associations may lead you to inaccurate conclusions. That's why it's so important to become other-oriented by being a good listener, learning all you can about the other person, and not just relying on generalizations.

IMAGINE WHAT YOUR PARTNER IS FEELING   As we've noted, empathy is an emotional reaction that is similar to the one being experienced by another person. In contrast to social decentering, which is a cognitive reaction, empathizing is feeling what the other person feels.

Listen Compassionately   Empathy is not a single skill but rather a collection of skills that help you predict how others will respond.[62] Diana Rehling suggests that **compassionate listening**—being open, nonjudgmental, and nondefensive—is a needed approach to listening to combat feelings of isolation, separation, and loneliness.[63] Listening with passion or acceptance takes empathic listening one step further because the listener is not only trying to experience the emotional response of others, but also accepting it, honoring it, and compassionately trying to confirm the worth of the other person. There is clear evidence that being empathic is linked to being a better listener.[64] Your ability to empathize with others is influenced by your personality and how you were raised, as well as by your listening habits and skill level. For example, boys whose fathers are affectionate and nurturing grow up with a greater capacity for empathy. There is also evidence that boys whose fathers are less affectionate toward them may have a tendency to compensate for this lack of close nurturing by expressing more affection toward their own sons.[65] So your capacity for empathy is both learned—based on your experiences, especially with your parents—and part of your nature.[66]

Your sensitivity and ability to empathize with others are based, according to some researchers, on your level of emotional intelligence. The Communication and Emotion feature in this chapter may give you some insight into your skill in connecting emotionally with others as well as understanding your own emotions.

But precisely how do you empathize with others? The essential empathy action steps are the same as those needed to be an effective listener: You stop, look, and listen. Although these steps may seem quite basic, they are nonetheless crucial to making emotional connections with others.

Listen Actively   Good listening, especially listening to empathize with another, is active, not passive. **Active listening** is the process of being physically and mentally

compassionate listening
Nonjudgmental, nondefensive, empathic listening to confirm the worth of another person.

active listening
The process of being physically and mentally engaged in the listening process and letting the listener know that you are engaged.

engaged in the listening process and letting the listener know that you are engaged. To listen passively is to sit with a blank stare or a frozen facial expression. A passive listener's thoughts and feelings could be anywhere, for all the speaker knows. Those who engage in active listening, in contrast, respond mentally, verbally, and nonverbally to a speaker's message and to what the speaker is doing. Responding to what others say and do serves several specific functions in empathizing with others.

Active listening confirms message understanding   Before you can empathize, you first have to accurately understand the message. If you burst out laughing as your friend tells you about losing his house in a flood, he'll know you either misunderstood or you weren't listening to him, or he'll think you are an insensitive oaf for not caring about his plight. Research confirms that if you are an active listener you will be a more accurate listener.[67]

Active listening confirms message affect   Your responses tell speakers how the message affects you. Monitoring your emotional reactions also gives you insight into your own emotional state. When you get tears in your eyes as you listen to your friend describe how lonely he has felt since his father died, he will know that you feel affected by his pain. You will sense an empathic connection with him and may also realize that you, too, are feeling down or emotional for other reasons. On the other hand, a genuine emotional reaction does not need to match the same intensity as the emotions the other person is experiencing. You may experience mild pity for your friend who has failed the midterm, in contrast to his stronger feeling of anguish and dishonor. An active listener is perceived as more socially attractive (well liked) than a passive listener.[68] One study found that when a teacher used active listening skills during a parent-teacher conference, the interaction was much more satisfying and effective, especially if the parent acted secure rather than anxious.[69]

Some emotional reactions are almost universal and cut across cultural boundaries. You may experience empathy when seeing photos or videos depicting emotion-arousing events occurring in other countries. Seeing a mother crying while holding her sick or dying child in a refugee camp might move you to tears and a sense of sadness or loss. Empathy can enhance interpersonal interactions by creating a bond between you and the other person: When you empathize, you are confirming, comforting, and supporting the other person. Empathy can also increase your understanding of others.

Being an active listener does not necessarily mean you will be an empathic listener. Researchers have found that they are two separate things.[70] Developing

Recap

How to Be an Empathic Listener

What to Do	How to Do It
Social decentering: A cognitive process of thinking about the other person's thoughts, values, background, and perspectives	• Think about how you would react in the given situation • Think about how the other person would react, based on what you know about his or her previous experiences and behavior • Think about how most people would react
Empathizing: An emotional reaction similar to the emotion being experienced by another person	• Stop focusing on your own thoughts and needs and imagine what the other person is feeling • Look for nonverbal cues that express emotion • Listen for the meaning of words and the meaning behind the words • Respond actively, not passively • Experience the emotion of the other person

empathy is different from sympathizing with others. When you offer **sympathy**, you tell someone you are sorry he or she feels what he or she is feeling: "I'm sorry your Uncle Joe died" or "I'm sorry to hear you failed your test." When you sympathize with others, you *acknowledge* their feelings. But when you empathize, you *experience* an emotional reaction similar to that of the other person; you, too, feel grief or sadness, elation or joy, excitement or apprehension—or whatever the other person is experiencing. Can people be taught to be more empathetic? Research suggests that the answer is a clear yes.[71] One goal of this book is to enhance your skill in being other-oriented—and empathy is at the heart of being other-oriented.[72]

Listening to empathize does not need to be the goal of *every* listening encounter you have; that would be tedious for both you and your listening partners. But when you do want to listen empathically, it's important to focus on your partner to

sympathy
Acknowledgment of someone else's feelings.

emotional intelligence
The ability to be aware of, understand, and manage one's own emotions and those of other people.

Communication and Emotion

What's Your Emotional Intelligence Level and Why Does It Matter?

You've undoubtedly heard about emotional intelligence, perhaps on TV or in the media. Researchers have found it is an important factor in how you relate to others.

What Is Emotional Intelligence?

Emotional intelligence (EI) is the ability to be empathic and aware of your own emotions as well as the emotions of others. Emotionally intelligent people are also able to manage their own emotions. It has been almost twenty-five years since Daniel Goleman's book *Emotional Intelligence: Why It Can Matter More than IQ* was published. That book, along with a *Time* magazine cover story about emotional intelligence (sometimes referred to as EQ, for "emotion quotient"), helped to popularize the concept.[73] But what does research about this concept tell us? Researchers Daisy Grewal and Peter Salovey have concluded that credible research does indeed support the popular and scientific interest in emotional intelligence.[74] Emotional intelligence has been linked to a variety of positive outcomes, including enhanced listening and leadership skills.[75]

Benefits of Emotional Intelligence

Today, researchers view emotional intelligence not as a single skill but as a set of several related skills.[76]

EI Helps You Accurately Perceive Messages

First, someone who is emotionally intelligent has the ability to accurately perceive the emotions of others by listening to people's voices and paying attention to facial expressions, posture, and other cues.

EI Helps You Think and Work More Effectively

Emotional intelligence can help you with other cognitive tasks. For example, if you know you are usually in a more productive, positive mood in the morning than in the evening, you will use the morning hours for tasks (such as writing) that require focused concentration.

EI Helps You Express Emotions

An emotionally intelligent person is able to express his or her own emotions—to use words accurately to describe feelings, moods, and emotions.

EI Helps You Manage Your Emotions

If you understand your own emotions, you have the ability to manage them, rather than letting them manage you, which is the fourth factor of emotional intelligence. If you're in a negative emotional state and you consciously decide to do something pleasant, such as take a walk, call a friend, or listen to music, you have taken a positive action to address your emotional state. There are also negative and destructive ways to manage your emotions, such as abusing alcohol or drugs. An emotionally intelligent person makes conscious choices to use constructive rather than destructive ways to manage emotions.

Furthermore, emotionally intelligent people can influence not only their own emotions, but also the emotions of others. A skilled public speaker, for example, knows how to use motivational appeals to persuade or motivate others. Of course, using one's emotional intelligence to manipulate others is unethical, just as it is unethical to use one's cognitive intelligence to be deceptive and trick others. Many thieves and con artists are quite emotionally intelligent, but they focus this intelligence on duping their victims. Emotional intelligence, like cognitive intelligence, is a gift that can be used for either good or bad purposes.

Research has documented that people who are emotionally intelligent are better listeners and are overall more socially skilled than people who are not emotionally intelligent.[77]

What's Your EQ?

Measuring emotional intelligence has been a topic of much debate and discussion among researchers who assess social skills. Some suggest that the concept is much too elusive and ill-defined to measure accurately. Yet several emotional intelligence measures have been created. One version that has received positive reviews from several researchers may be found at www.queendom.com.

Daniel Goleman summarizes the centrality of emotions in developing empathy by quoting Antoine de Saint-Exupéry: "It is with the heart that one sees rightly; what is essential is invisible to the eye."[78]

understand and experience the message from his or her perspective.[79] Psychologist and counselor Carl Rogers summarized the value of empathy when he said, "A high degree of empathy in a relationship is possibly the most potent factor in bringing about change and learning."[80] The short test to assess your empathy included at the end of this chapter can help you determine how effectively you empathize with others.

How to Improve Critical Listening Skills

After putting it off for several months, you've decided to buy a new smart phone. You find a bewildering number of factors to consider: Do you want a prepaid plan? A plan that includes unlimited text messaging? Do you want to check e-mail and surf the web? How many minutes of calling time do you need? You head to a store to see whether a salesperson can help you. The salesperson is friendly enough, but you become even more overwhelmed with the number of options to consider. As you try to make this decision, your listening goal is not to empathize with those who extol the virtues of smart phones. Nor do you need to take a multiple-choice test on the information they share. To sort through the information, you need to listen critically.

critical listening

Listening to evaluate and assess the quality, appropriateness, value, or importance of information.

Critical listening involves listening to evaluate the quality, appropriateness, value, or importance of the information you hear. *The goal of a critical listener is to use information to make a choice.* Whether you're selecting a new phone, deciding whom to vote for, choosing a potential date, or evaluating a new business plan, you will be faced with many opportunities to use your critical listening skills in interpersonal situations.

ASSESS INFORMATION QUALITY A critical listener does not necessarily offer negative comments but seeks to identify both good information and information that is flawed or less helpful. We call this process of evaluating and sorting **information triage**. *Triage* is a French term that usually describes the process used by emergency medical personnel to determine which of several patients is the most severely ill or injured and needs immediate medical attention. An effective critical listener is able to distinguish useful and accurate information and conclusions from information that is less useful, as well as conclusions that are inaccurate or invalid.

information triage

Process of evaluating information to sort good information from less useful or less valid information.

How do you develop the ability to perform information triage? Initially, listening critically involves the same strategies as listening to comprehend, which we discussed earlier. Before you evaluate information, it's vital that you first *understand* the information. Second, examine the logic or reasoning used in the message. And finally, be mindful of whether you are basing your evaluations on facts (something observed or verifiable) or inference (a conclusion based on partial information).

Effective critical listening skills are crucial in a business environment.

SEPARATE FACTS FROM INFERENCE Imagine that you are a detective investigating a death. You are given the following information: (1) Leo and Moshia are found lying together on the floor; (2) Leo and Moshia are both dead; (3) Leo and Moshia are surrounded by water and broken glass; (4) on the sofa near Leo and Moshia is a cat with its back arched, apparently ready to defend itself.

Given these sketchy details, do you, the detective assigned to the case, have any theories about the cause of Leo and Moshia's demise? Perhaps they slipped on the water, crashed into a table, broke a vase, and died (that would explain the water and broken glass). Or maybe their attacker recently left the scene, and the cat is still distressed by the commotion. Clearly, you could make several inferences (conclusions based on partial information) as to the probable cause of death. Oh yes, there is one detail we forgot to mention: Leo and Moshia are fish. Does that help?

People often spin grand explanations and hypotheses based on sketchy details. Making inferences, people may believe the "facts" clearly point to a specific conclusion. Determining the difference between a fact and an inference can help you more accurately use language to reach valid conclusions about what you see and experience.

What makes a fact a fact? Most students, when asked this question, respond by saying, "A fact is something that has been proven true." If that is the case, *how* has something been proven true? In a court of law, a **fact** is something that has been observed or witnessed. Anything else is speculation or inference.

> "Did you see my client in your house, taking your jewelry?" asks the defendant's clever attorney.
>
> "No," says the plaintiff.
>
> "Then you do not know for a fact that my client is a thief."
>
> "I guess not," the plaintiff admits.

Problems occur when we respond to something as if it were a fact (something observed), when in reality it is an **inference** (a conclusion based on speculation):

> "It's a fact that you will be poor all of your life."
>
> "It's a fact that you will fail this course."

Both of these statements, although they may very well be true, misuse the term *fact*. If you cannot recognize when you are making an inference instead of stating a fact, you may give your judgments more credibility than they deserve. Being sensitive to the differences between facts and inferences can improve both critical listening and responding skills.

fact
Something that has been directly observed to be true and thus has been proven to be true.

inference
Conclusion based on speculation.

Improving Your Responding Skills

5.5 **Identify and use skills to effectively and appropriately respond to others.**

We've offered several strategies for responding to others when your goal is to comprehend information, empathize with others, or evaluate messages. Regardless of your communication goal, the quality of your communication will be enhanced when you effectively and appropriately respond to others. Responding to what you hear is natural and normal. You don't need a textbook to tell you to respond. To be alive is to respond to stimuli that come your way. But there are some specific strategies and skills that can help you respond to others *skillfully*.

BEING Other-ORIENTED
A key to providing useful responses to another person is to think about the other person's needs rather than your own needs. Although it may feel liberating to express your own thoughts or feelings, consider whether your response is in the best interest of your communication partner. What strategies can you use to identify the needs of others?

How to Improve Accurate Responding Skills

Sometimes the best response is not a verbal one—it can be better to just keep listening. Your ability to ask appropriate questions and paraphrase what you hear can dramatically improve your understanding of a message. In addition, the timing of your responses, the usefulness of the information, the amount of detail, and the descriptiveness of your responses are important.

ASK APPROPRIATE QUESTIONS One of the first things to do after listening to someone share information is to ask appropriate questions to get additional details you may have missed and to make sure you understood the message.

Asking appropriate questions can help not only you but also the person sharing information with you. One research study by communication researchers Janet Bavelas, Linda Coates, and Trudy Johnson found that speakers did a better job of sharing a story if listeners asked appropriate questions and made appropriate responses to the story rather than offering no observation about what they heard.[81] The results suggest that an effective listener is really a "co-narrator," or an active participant in the communication process, rather than merely a passive listener. So when you ask appropriate questions and make appropriate comments, you can help your communication partner tell a story better. Asking appropriate and thoughtful questions also communicates that you were indeed listening and interested in what your partner had to say.

ACCURATELY PARAPHRASE   The only way to know whether you understand another person's message is to check your understanding of the facts and ideas by paraphrasing your understanding. Verbally reflecting what you understood the speaker to say can dramatically minimize misunderstanding. Respond with a statement such as

"Are you saying …"

"You seem to be describing …"

"So the point you are making seems to be …"

"Here is what I understand you to mean …"

"So here's what seems to have happened …"

Then summarize the events, details, or key points you think the speaker is trying to convey. Your summary need not be a word-for-word repetition of what the speaker has said, nor do you need to summarize the content of *each* phrase or minor detail. Rather, you will **paraphrase** to check the accuracy of your understanding. Here is an example:

Juan: This week I have so much extra work to do. I'm sorry if I haven't been able to help keep this place clean. I know it's my turn to do the dishes tonight, but I have to get back to work. Could you do the dishes tonight?

Brigid: So you want me to do the dishes tonight and for the rest of the week. Right?

Juan: Well, I'd like you to help with the dishes tonight. But I think I can handle it for the rest of the week.

Brigid: OK. So I'll do them tonight and you take over tomorrow.

Juan: Yes.

Does paraphrasing a speaker's message really enhance the overall quality and accuracy of communication? Several researchers have found considerable support for this assertion.[82] Listening researcher Harry Weger and his colleagues found that speakers perceived listeners who skillfully used paraphrasing as more "socially attractive" than were those who didn't use the paraphrasing skill.[83] The researchers also found that speakers liked skillful paraphrasers better even when the speakers didn't feel well understood or satisfied with the conversation. Another study found that when a listener paraphrases the content and feelings of a speaker, the speaker is more likely to trust and value the listener.[84]

Accurately and appropriately (which means not every message) paraphrasing not only increases message accuracy, but also enhances the quality of the relationship—you are more likely to be liked and trusted if you can accurately summarize the messages of others. Paraphrasing to check understanding is also a vital skill to use when you are trying to reconcile a difference of opinion. Chapter 8 shows you how to use it in that context.

paraphrase

Verbal summary of the key ideas of your partner's message that helps you check the accuracy of your understanding.

An effective listener uses questions and paraphrasing to make sure he or she understands what someone else has been saying.

PROVIDE WELL-TIMED RESPONSES Feedback is usually most effective when you offer it at the earliest opportunity, particularly if your objective is to teach someone a skill. For example, if you are teaching your friend how to make your famous egg rolls, you provide a step-by-step commentary as you watch your pupil. If he makes a mistake, you don't wait until the egg rolls are finished to tell him that he left out the cabbage. He needs immediate feedback to finish the rest of the sequence successfully.

Sometimes, however, if a person is already sensitive and upset about something, delaying feedback can be wise. Use your critical thinking skills to analyze when feedback will do the most good. Rather than automatically offering immediate correction, sometimes it may be best to use the just-in-time (JIT) approach and provide feedback just before the person might make another mistake. If, for example, your daughter typically rushes through math tests and fails to check her work, remind her right before her next test to double-check her answers, not immediately after the one she just failed. To provide feedback about a relationship, select a mutually agreeable place and time when both of you are rested and relaxed; avoid hurling feedback at someone "for his own good" immediately after he offends you.

PROVIDE USABLE INFORMATION Perhaps you've heard this advice: Never try to teach a pig to sing. It wastes your time. It doesn't sound pretty. And it annoys the pig. When you provide information to someone, be certain that it is useful and relevant. How can you make sure your partner can use the information you share? Try to understand your partner's mindset. Ask yourself, "If I were this person, how would I respond to this information? Is it information I can act on? Or is it information that may make matters worse?" Under the guise of providing effective feedback, you may be tempted to tell others your complete range of feelings and emotions. But selective feedback is best. In one study, married couples who practiced selective self-disclosure were more satisfied than couples who told each other everything they knew or were feeling.[85] Immersing your partner in information that is irrelevant or that may be damaging to the relationship may be cathartic, but it may not enhance the quality of your relationship or improve understanding.

When you are selecting meaningful information, also try to cut down on the volume of information. Don't overwhelm your listener with details that obscure the key point of your feedback. Hit only the high points that will benefit the listener. Be brief.

APPROPRIATELY ADAPT YOUR RESPONSES It's important to not only adapt the timing of your responses, but also the content of your message. According to **communication accommodation theory**, discussed in Chapter 4, we consciously and sometimes unconsciously adapt our messages to others. We adapt to make our message more efficient and effective; sometimes we also adapt our message length, style, word choice, and content to mirror the messages of others. For example, research suggests that when talking to a small child, you are likely to shorten your sentences, use simpler and more common words, and even raise the pitch of your voice.[86] Another study found that when responding to feedback from older speakers, listeners are more likely to simplify their speech.[87] We accommodate our feedback to enhance its impact.

Specifically, what are ways to adapt your responses to enhance message understanding and effectiveness? If you think someone doesn't understand what you are saying, stop talking and ask whether your message is clear. If not, speak more slowly and increase redundancy by repeating key ideas and summarizing the gist of your message. Increasing your volume, telling a story to clarify a point, and using shorter words and briefer messages are additional ways of adapting your feedback to ensure that your message is clear and well received.

communication accommodation theory
Theory that all people adapt their behavior to others to some extent.

How to Improve Empathic Responding Skills

For many people, to be listened to is to be loved, especially if you are being listened to empathically.[88] When your listening and responding goal is to empathize with another person, paraphrasing the content of what someone says and recognizing the emotion behind the words may be helpful. And your partner may be seeking more than understanding: He or she may be seeking social support. Your listening partner may want and need to know that you care about him or her. There are ways of responding that can enhance empathy and provide meaningful emotional support.

DON'T INTERRUPT   We noted earlier that one of the listening barriers people face is thinking about what they want to say next rather than just listening. And our own thoughts may lead us to blurt out a response, finish someone's sentence, or impose our own ideas on the speaker. Resist those temptations. Before you make your point, let the other person finish his or her point. You don't need to be a passive listener and endure a long, rambling, inarticulate verbal barrage from someone. But if interrupting others is your default listening response, you'll likely miss much of the meaning as well as disconfirm your partner. If you do need to stop someone from talking in order to make a point, do so mindfully rather than habitually and thoughtlessly.

PARAPHRASE EMOTIONS   The bottom line in empathic responding is to make certain that you accurately understand how the other person is feeling. You can paraphrase, beginning with such phrases as

"So you are feeling …"

"You must feel …"

"So now you feel …"

In the following example of empathic responding, the listener asks questions, paraphrases content, and summarizes feelings.

David:	I think I'm in over my head. My boss gave me a job to do, and I just don't know how to do it. I'm afraid I've bitten off more than I can chew.
Mike:	(Thinks how he would feel if he were given an important task at work but did not know how to complete the task, then asks for more information.) What job did she ask you to do?
David:	I'm supposed to do an inventory of all the items in the warehouse on the new computer system and have it finished by the end of the week. I don't have the foggiest notion of how to start. I've never even used that system.
Mike:	(Summarizes feelings.) So you feel panicked because you may not have enough time to learn the system *and* do the inventory.
David:	Well, I'm not only panicked; I'm afraid I may be fired.
Mike:	(Summarizes feelings.) So your fear that you might lose your job is getting in the way of just focusing on the task and seeing what you can get done. It's making you feel like you made a mistake in taking this job.
David:	That's exactly how I feel.

Note that toward the end of the dialogue, Mike tries a couple of times to summarize David's feelings accurately. Also note that Mike does a good job of listening and responding without giving advice. Just by being an active listener, you can help your partner clarify a problem.

Researcher John Gottman summarizes several specific ways to make listening active rather than passive:[89]

- Start by asking questions.
- Ask questions about the speaker's goals and visions of the future.
- Look for commonalities.
- Tune in with all your attention.
- Respond with an occasional brief nod or sound.
- From time to time, paraphrase what the speaker says.
- Maintain the right amount of eye contact.
- Let go of your own agenda.

We have discussed responding empathically and listening actively using a tidy step-by-step textbook approach. In practice, you may have to back up and clarify content, ask more questions, and rethink how you would feel before you attempt to summarize how someone else feels. Conversely, you may be able to summarize feelings *without* asking questions or paraphrasing content if the message is clear and it relates to a situation with which you are very familiar. Overusing paraphrasing can slow down a conversation and make the other person uncomfortable or irritated. But if you use it judiciously, paraphrasing can help both you and your partner keep focused on the issues and ideas at hand.

Reflecting content or feeling through paraphrasing can be especially useful in the following situations:

- Before you take an important action
- Before you argue or criticize
- When your partner has strong feelings or wants to talk over a problem
- When your partner is speaking "in code" or using unclear abbreviations
- When your partner wants to understand your feelings and thoughts
- When you are talking to yourself
- When you encounter new ideas[90]

Sometimes, however, you truly don't understand how another person really feels. At times like this, be cautious of telling others, "I know just how you feel." It may be more important simply to let others know that you care about them than to grill them about their feelings.

If you do decide to use paraphrasing skills, keep the following guidelines in mind:

- Use your own words.
- Don't go beyond the information communicated by the speaker.
- Be concise.
- Be specific.
- Be accurate.

Do *not* use paraphrasing skills if you aren't able to be open and accepting, if you do not trust the other person to find his or her own solution, if you are using these skills as a way of hiding yourself from another, or if you feel pressured, hassled, or tired. And as we have already discussed, overuse of paraphrasing can be distracting and unnatural.

Don't be discouraged if your initial attempts to use these skills seem awkward and uncomfortable. Any new skill takes time to learn and use well. The instructions and samples you have read should serve as guides, rather than as hard-and-fast prescriptions to follow during each conversation.

social support

Expression of empathy and concern for others that is communicated while listening to them and offering positive and encouraging words.

PROVIDE HELPFUL SOCIAL SUPPORT   There are times when it is clear that a communication partner is experiencing stress, pain, or a significant life problem. Just by listening and empathizing, you can help ease the pain and help the person manage the burden. Specifically, you provide **social support** when you offer positive, sincere, supportive messages, both verbal and nonverbal, when helping others deal with stress, anxiety, or uncertainty. Providing social support isn't the same as expressing pity for another person; it's providing a response that lets the other person know that he or she is both understood and valued. Nor does offering social support mean giving advice to solve the problem or take away the fear. Giving social support entails providing messages that help the person seek his or her own solution.

Most people don't need or want dramatic, over-the-top expressions of support when experiencing pain or loss. On the other hand, mild or timid expressions of support from others are not satisfying either. One study suggests that when we are experiencing stress, we prefer a mid-level amount of social support.[91] Genuine, sincere support that is not overly expressive is usually best. Research also suggests that females prefer a slightly higher level of comforting response than males.

An ability to listen empathically is important when you discern that someone needs social support. Although there are no magic words or phrases that will always ease someone's stress and anxiety, here's a summary of social support messages that seem to be appreciated by others:[92]

- Clearly express that you want to provide support. ("I would really like to help you.")
- Appropriately communicate that you have positive feelings for the other person; explicitly tell the other person that you are a friend, that you care about or love him or her. ("You mean a lot to me." "I really care about you.")
- Express your concern about the situation that the other person is in right now. ("I'm worried about you right now because I know you're feeling _____ [stressed, overwhelmed, sad, etc.].")
- Indicate that you are available to help, that you have time to support the person. ("I can be here for you when you need me.")
- Let the other person know how much you support her or him. ("I'm completely with you on this." "I'm here for you, and I'll always be here for you because I care about you.")
- Acknowledge that the other person is in a difficult situation. ("This must be very difficult for you.")
- Determine whether it is appropriate to paraphrase what the other person has told you about the issue or problem that is causing stress. ("So you became upset when she told you she didn't want to see you again?")
- Consider asking open-ended questions to see if the other person wants to talk. ("How are you doing now?")
- Let the other person know that you are listening and supporting him or her by providing conversational continuers such as "Yes, then what happened?" or "Oh, I see," or "Uh-huh."
- After expressing your compassion, empathy, and concern, just listen.

Some types of responses are less helpful when providing social support. Here are a few things *not* to do:

- Don't tell the other person that you know exactly how he or she feels.
- Don't criticize or negatively evaluate the other person; he or she needs support and validation, not judgmental comments.
- Don't tell the other person to stop feeling what he or she is feeling.
- Don't immediately offer advice. First, just listen.

- Don't tell the other person that "it's going to get better from here" or that "the worst is over."
- Don't tell the other person that there is really nothing to worry about or that "it's no big deal."
- Don't tell the other person that the problem can be solved easily. ("Oh, you can always find another girlfriend.")
- Don't blame the other person for the problem. ("Well, if you didn't always drive so fast, you wouldn't have had the accident.")
- Don't tell the other person that it is wrong to express feelings and emotions. ("Oh, you're just making yourself sick. Stop crying.")

Improving Your Confirmation Skills

5.6 Identify and use skills to effectively and appropriately confirm others.

Couple A:

Wife to husband:	"I just don't feel appreciated any more."
Husband to wife:	"Margaret, I'm so very sorry. I love you. You're the most important person in the world to me."

Couple B:

Wife to husband:	"I just don't feel appreciated any more."
Husband to wife:	"Well, what about my feelings? Don't my feelings count? You'll have to do what you have to do. What's for dinner?"

It doesn't take an expert in interpersonal communication to know that Couple B's relationship is not warm and confirming. Researchers have studied the specific kinds of responses people offer to others.[93] Some responses are confirming; other responses are disconfirming. A **confirming response** is an other-oriented statement that causes people to value themselves more; Wife A is likely to value herself more after her husband's confirming response. It is especially powerful to adapt your confirming responses to address the needs and expectations of the listener. One research team found that being "person centered," which is another way of saying other-oriented, was especially important when providing support to the listener.[94]

A **disconfirming response** is a statement that causes others to value themselves less. Wife B knows firsthand what it's like to have her feelings ignored and disconfirmed. Are you aware of whether your responses to others confirm them or disconfirm them? To help you be more aware of the kinds of responses you make to others, we'll review the results of studies that identify both confirming and disconfirming responses.[95]

confirming response
Statement that causes another person to value himself or herself more.

disconfirming response
Statement that causes another person to value himself or herself less.

How to Provide Confirming Responses

The adage "People judge us by our words and behavior rather than by our intent" summarizes the underlying principle of confirming responses. Those who receive your messages determine whether they have the effect you intended. Formulating confirming responses requires careful listening and attention to the other person. Does it really matter whether we confirm others? Marriage researcher John Gottman used video cameras and microphones to observe couples interacting in an apartment over an extended period of time. He found that a significant predictor of divorce was neglecting to confirm or affirm one's marriage partner during typical, everyday conversation—even though couples who were less likely to divorce spent only a few seconds more confirming their partner than couples who eventually did divorce. His research conclusion has powerful implications: Long-lasting relationships are characterized by supportive, confirming messages.[96] The everyday kinds of confirmation and support we offer need not be excessive—sincere moderate, heartfelt support is evaluated as the most positive and desirable kind.[97] Listening researcher John Shotter suggests that most people spend too much time speaking to make their point without truly listening to confirm "the other." Shotter suggests that we're sometimes too interested in our own monologue rather than in a confirming dialogue.[98] Shotter points to the work of Russian linguist Mikhail Bakhtin, who reminds us:

> Monologism, at its extreme, denies the existence outside itself of another consciousness with equal rights and equal responsibilities, another I with equal rights (thou). With a monologic approach (in its extreme pure form) another person remains wholly and merely an object of consciousness, and not another consciousness.[99]

The everyday kinds of confirmation and support we offer can change monologues into dialogues. We will describe several kinds of confirming responses that can create a climate of mutual, other-oriented support.

DIRECT ACKNOWLEDGMENT   When you respond directly to something another person says to you, you are acknowledging not only the statement, but also that the person is worth responding to.

Joan:	It certainly is a nice day for a canoe trip.
Mariko:	Yes, Joan, it's a great day to be outside.

AGREEMENT ABOUT JUDGMENTS   When you confirm someone's evaluation of something, you also affirm that person's sense of taste and judgment.

Nancy:	I think the steel guitar player's riff was fantastic.
Victor:	Yes, I think it was the best part of the performance.

SUPPORTIVE RESPONSE   When you express reassurance and understanding, you are confirming a person's right to his or her feelings.

Lionel:	I'm disappointed that I only scored 60 on my interpersonal communication test.
Sarah:	I'm sorry to see you so frustrated, Lionel. I know that test was important to you.

CLARIFYING RESPONSE   When you seek greater understanding of another person's message, you are confirming that he or she is worth your time and trouble. Clarifying responses also encourage the other person to talk in order to explore his or her feelings.

Larry:	I'm not feeling very good about my family situation these days.
Tyrone:	Is it tough with you and Margo working different shifts?

EXPRESSION OF POSITIVE FEELING   We feel confirmed or valued when someone else agrees with our expression of joy or excitement.

Lorraine:	I'm so excited! I was just promoted to associate professor.
Dorette:	Congratulations! I'm so proud of you! Heaven knows you deserve it.

COMPLIMENT When you tell people you like what they have done or said, what they are wearing, or how they look, you are confirming their sense of worth.

Jean-Christophe:	Did you get the invitation to my party?
Manny:	Yes! It looked so professional. I didn't know you could do calligraphy. You're a talented guy.

In each of these examples, note how the responder provides comments that confirm the worth or value of the other person. But keep in mind that confirming responses should be sincere. Offering false praise is manipulative, and your communication partner will probably sense your phoniness.

How to Avoid Disconfirming Responses

Some statements and responses can undermine another person's self-worth. Disconfirming others can lead to increased relational turbulence and hurt feelings.[100] We offer these categories so that you can avoid using them and also recognize them when someone uses them to chip away at your self-image and self-esteem.

IMPERVIOUS RESPONSE When a person fails to acknowledge your statement or attempt to communicate, even though you know he or she heard you, you may feel a sense of awkwardness or embarrassment.

Rosa:	I loved your speech, Harvey.
Harvey:	(No response, verbal or nonverbal.)

INTERRUPTING RESPONSE Interrupting another person is one of the most corrosive, disconfirming responses you can make.[101] Why is interrupting so irritating? Because when you interrupt someone, you are implying that what you have to say is more important than what the other person has to say. In effect, your behavior communicates that *you* are more important than the other person is. You may simply be enthusiastic or excited when the words tumble out of your mouth, interrupting your communication partner. Nonetheless, be especially mindful of not interrupting others. An interrupting response is a powerful disconfirming behavior, whether you are aware of its power or not.

Anna:	I just heard on the news that…
Sharon:	Oh yes. The stock market just went down 100 points.

IRRELEVANT RESPONSE An irrelevant response is one that has nothing at all to do with what you were saying. Chances are your partner is not listening to you at all.

Arnold:	First we're flying down to Rio, and then to Quito. I can hardly wait to …
Peter:	They're predicting a hard freeze tonight.

TANGENTIAL RESPONSE A tangential response is one that acknowledges you, but that is only minimally related to what you are talking about. Again, it indicates that the other person isn't really attending to your message.

Richard:	This new program will help us stay within our budget.
Samantha:	Yeah. I think I'll save some bucks and send this letter by regular mail.

IMPERSONAL RESPONSE A response that intellectualizes and uses the third person distances the other person from you and has the effect of trivializing what you say.

Diana:	Hey, Bill. I'd like to talk with you for a minute about getting your permission to take my vacation in July.
Bill:	One tends to become interested in taking a vacation about this time of year, doesn't one?

INCOHERENT RESPONSE   When a speaker mumbles, rambles, or makes some unintelligible effort to respond, you may end up wondering if what you said was of any value or use to the listener.

Paolo:	George, here's my suggestion for the merger deal with Techstar. Let's make them an offer of forty-eight dollars a share and see how they respond.
George:	Huh? Well…so…well…hmmm…I'm not sure.

INCONGRUOUS RESPONSE   When a verbal message is inconsistent with nonverbal behavior, people usually believe the nonverbal message, but they usually feel confused as well. An incongruous response is like a malfunctioning traffic light with red and green lights flashing simultaneously—you're just not sure whether the speaker wants you to go or stay.

Sue:	Honey, do you want me to go grocery shopping with you?
Steve:	(Shouting) OF COURSE I DO! WHY ARE YOU ASKING?

Although it may be impossible to eliminate all disconfirming responses from your repertoire, becoming aware of the power of your words and monitoring your conversation for offensive phrases may help you avoid unexpected and perhaps devastating consequences.

Applying an Other-Orientation
to Listening and Responding Skills

It's impossible to be other-oriented without listening and observing others. Listening to comprehend information, empathize, or critically evaluate what others say is the quintessential other-oriented skill. The following poem by an anonymous author, simply called "Listen," nicely summarizes the reason listening is such an important interpersonal skill.

Listen

When I ask you to listen to me and you start giving advice, you have not done what I asked.

When I ask you to listen to me and you begin to tell me why I shouldn't feel that way, you are trampling on my feelings.

When I ask you to listen to me and you feel you have to do something to solve my problems, you have failed me, strange as that may seem.

Listen! All I asked was that you listen. Not talk or do—just hear me.

Advice is cheap: 50 cents will get you both Dear Abby and Billy Graham in the same newspaper.

And I can do for myself; I'm not helpless. Maybe discouraged and faltering, but not helpless.

When you do something for me that I can and need to do for myself, you contribute to my fear and weakness.

But when you accept as a simple fact that I do feel what I feel, no matter how irrational, then I quit trying to convince you and can get about the business of understanding what's behind this irrational feeling.

And when that's clear, the answers are obvious and I don't need advice.

Irrational feelings make sense when we understand what's behind them.

Perhaps that's why prayer works, sometimes, for some people—because God is mute, and doesn't give advice or try to fix things,

God just listens and lets you work it out for yourself.

So, please listen and just hear me, and, if you want to talk, wait a minute for your turn, and I'll listen to you.

Anonymous

STUDY GUIDE
Review, Apply, and Assess

Listening Defined

Objective 5.1 Define listening, and describe five elements of the listening process

Key Terms

listening
hearing
selecting
attending

understanding
remembering
responding

Thinking Critically

Describe two recent communication exchanges in which you were an effective or ineffective listener. What factors contributed to your listening skill (or lack of skill)?

Assessing Your Skill

Over the next week, in your numerous communication exchanges with friends, family members, professors, and work colleagues, make an effort to listen carefully and effectively. Then, following each exchange, make a list of at least five items that you remember (things you discussed). Is there a difference in what you remember in each case? What factors contribute to your ability to listen, attend to, and remember details of each communication?

Listening Styles

Objective 5.2 Identify characteristics of four listening styles

Key Terms

listening style
relational listeners
analytical listeners

critical listeners
second-guessing
task-oriented listeners

Thinking Critically

Your friend Marq has a relational listening style, whereas you have both analytic and critical listening styles. What are some of the things you will need to do when you have a conversation with Marq?

Assessing Your Skill

Earlier in this chapter we identified four listening styles—relational, analytic, critical, and task-oriented. Based on the description in the text, identify your primary listening style or styles (you may have more than one). Next, consider three other people with whom you frequently communicate. How would you characterize their listening styles based on your interactions with them? Do some of these people use different styles at different times? What cues helped you to identify their styles? With which type of listeners do you find it easiest to communicate? Explain.

Listening Barriers

Objective 5.3 List and describe barriers to effective listening

Key Terms

conversational narcissism
selective listening
emotional noise

ambush listener
listener apprehension

Thinking Critically

In this age of communication technologies, what strategies can you use to reduce information overload and listen more effectively to others' messages?

Assessing Your Skill

Think about the many listening barriers you face every day. During class one day this week, keep track of the number of times your mind wandered from the lecture or you became distracted by something or someone in the room. What are some ways you might be able to overcome these listening barriers in the future?

Improving Your Listening Skills

Objective 5.4 Identify and use skills to enhance comprehension, empathy, and critical listening

Key Terms

meta-message
empathy
social decentering
compassionate listening
active listening
sympathy

emotional intelligence
critical listening
information triage
fact
inference

Thinking Critically

Miranda and Salvador often disagree about who should handle some of the child-rearing tasks in their home. What are some effective listening skills and strategies they can use in discussing these tasks and making sure they understand each other?

Assessing Your Skill

Test Your Empathy. Assess your skill in empathizing with others by rating yourself on each of the statements below using a scale ranging from 1 (low) to 10 (high).

_____ 1. People tell me that I am good at accurately describing how they are feeling.

_____ 2. I can accurately and effectively express my emotions and feelings to others.

_____ 3. I can accurately determine the meaning of other people's facial expressions.

_____ 4. I can usually accurately guess what other people are thinking.

_____ 5. I can usually accurately guess what other people are feeling.

_____ 6. When other people are talking, I usually focus on their message rather than what I am going to say next.

_____ 7. When people tell me how they are feeling emotionally it usually confirms what I thought they were feeling.

_____ 8. When other people feel sad or hurt I also feel sad or hurt along with them.

_____ 9. When listening to someone on the phone, I can sense his or her mood or what emotion he or she is experiencing.

_____ 10. When talking with someone I know, I effectively and accurately feel what he or she is feeling.

The closer your score reaches 100 the more empathic you are likely to be. As an additional application, ask one of your friends or family members to complete the scale about _you_. Then compare your own self-assessment score with the score generated by the person who assessed you.

Improving Your Responding Skills

Objective 5.5 Identify and use skills to effectively and appropriately respond to others

Key Terms

paraphrase   social support
communication
  accommodation theory

Thinking Critically

Your roommate (or partner or spouse) wants to tell you about his day. You are tired and really don't want to hear all the details. Should you fake attention so that you won't hurt his feelings, or simply tell him you are tired and would rather not hear the details right now?

Assessing Your Skills

Working in groups of three, ask person A to briefly identify a problem or conflict that he or she is having (or has had) with another person. Person B should use questioning, content paraphrase, and emotion paraphrasing skills to explore the problem. Person C should observe the discussion and evaluate person B's listening and responding skills, using the Observer Checklist. Work together and use the checklist to make a list of the

skills that person B used effectively. Explain how person B used these skills effectively. Why were these skills effective?

Observer Checklist

Nonverbal Skills

_____ Direct eye contact
_____ Open, relaxed body posture
_____ Uncrossed arms
_____ Uncrossed legs
_____ Appropriate hand gestures
_____ Reinforcing nods
_____ Responsive facial expression
_____ Appropriate tone of voice
_____ Appropriate volume

Verbal Skills

_____ Effective and appropriate questions
_____ Accurate paraphrase of content
_____ Accurate paraphrase of emotion
_____ Timely paraphrase
_____ Appropriate lead-in
_____ ("So," or "You seem to be saying")
_____ Didn't interrupt the speaker

Improving Your Confirmation Skills

Objective 5.6 Identify and use skills to effectively and appropriately confirm others

Key Terms

confirming response   disconfirming response

Thinking Critically

Your romantic partner says, "I'm not feeling very supported right now. My boss at work has dumped a lot of projects on me, and I'm also feeling overwhelmed with all of the work I have to do around our home." Based on the list of types of confirming statements found in this chapter, what could you say that provides a confirming response? What would you say that would likely disconfirm your partner?

Assessing Your Skills

Keep a journal for one day, being especially mindful of when you are consciously providing a confirming response to someone. Note the other person's verbal and nonverbal response to your confirming message. Also, be aware of whether you offered any disconfirming statements. What effect did disconfirming statements have on the nature of the interpersonal relationship?

Chapter 6
Verbal Communication Skills

"Words can destroy. What we call each other ultimately becomes what we think of each other, and it matters."

Jeanne J. Kirkpatrick

 ## Learning Objectives

CHAPTER OUTLINE

6.1 Describe how words create meaning.

How Words Work

6.2 Identify how words influence our perceptions, thoughts, actions, culture, and relationships.

The Power of Words

6.3 Identify and describe word barriers that lead to misunderstandings.

How to Manage Misunderstandings

6.4 Use words to provide support and comfort, and to avoid defensiveness.

How to Use Words of Support and Comfort

6.5 Use words to have a conversation with others.

How to Have a Conversation

6.6 Use words to offer an apology when appropriate.

How to Apologize

6.7 Use assertiveness skills appropriately and ethically.

How to Be Assertive

Words are powerful. Those who use them skillfully can exert great influence with just a few of them. Consider these notable achievements:

- Lincoln set the course for a nation in a 267-word speech: the Gettysburg Address.
- Shakespeare expressed the quintessence of the human condition in Hamlet's famous "To be, or not to be" soliloquy—363 words long.
- Two billion people accept a comprehensive moral code expressed in a mere 297 words: the Ten Commandments.

Words have great power in private life as well. In this chapter, we will examine ways to use them more effectively in interpersonal relationships. We'll investigate how to harness the power of words to affect emotions, thoughts, and actions, and we'll describe links between language and culture. We will also identify communication barriers that may keep you from using words effectively and note strategies and skills for managing those barriers. Finally, we will examine the role of speech in establishing supportive relationships with others.

According to one study, a person's ability to use words—more specifically, to participate in conversation with others—is one of the best predictors of communication competence.[1] Another study found that people who simply didn't talk much were perceived as being less interpersonally skilled than people who spent an appropriate amount of time engaged in conversation with others.[2] In addition, the quality of our verbal communication messages predicts how satisfied we are in our romantic relationships.[3] And it's not only through face-to-face conversations that verbal messages influence our relationships with others. Like many people, you probably relate to others via text, e-mail, Facebook, and other electronic means.[4] Being other-oriented online is just as important as when communicating face-to-face, maybe even more so because many online messages may exist for many years.[5] This chapter is designed to help you better understand the power of words and to use them with greater skill and confidence.

Throughout our discussion of the power of verbal messages, keep one important idea in mind: *You are not in charge of the meaning others derive from your messages.* That is, words don't have meaning; people create meaning.

How Words Work

6.1 Describe how words create meaning.

As you read the words on this page, how are you able to make sense out of these black marks? When you hear words spoken by others, how are you able to interpret those sounds? Although several theories attempt to explain how people learn language and ascribe meaning to both printed and uttered words, there is no single universally held view that neatly explains this mystery.

Words Are Symbols

symbol

Word, sound, or visual image that represents something else, such as a thought, concept, or object.

As we noted in Chapter 1, words are **symbols** that represent something else. Symbols evoke emotions. Seeing or hearing certain words can result in happiness or sadness. One study found that our moods can be charted just by examining the emotional messages embedded in our tweets (most of us are happiest on Sunday and least happy on Monday).[6]

A printed or spoken word triggers an image of an object, a sound, a concept, or an experience. Take the word *cat,* for instance. The word may conjure up in your mind's eye a hissing creature with bared claws and fangs. Or perhaps you envision a cherished pet curled up by a fireplace.

referent

The thing that a symbol represents.

thought

Mental process of creating an image, sound, concept, or experience triggered by a referent or symbol.

Developed by Charles Ogden and Ivor Richards, the classic model in Figure 6.1 explains the relationships between *referents, thought,* and *symbols.*[7] **Referents** are the things the symbols (words) represent. **Thought** is the mental process of creating an image, sound, concept, or experience triggered by the referent or the symbol. So the three elements—referents, thought, and symbols—are inextricably linked. Although

Figure 6.1 Triangle of Meaning

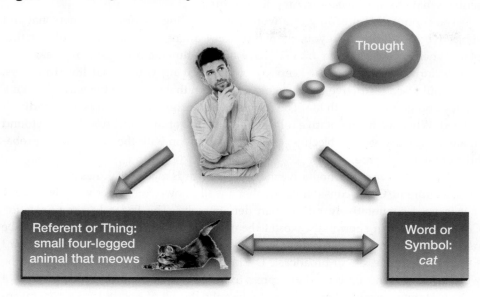

some scholars find this model too simplistic to explain how people link all words to meaning, it does illustrate the process of how we derive meaning from symbols through association.

The specific link between a word and the thing it symbolizes is not always clear. The meaning of a word is attributed by a person based on his or her experiences; meaning does not reside within the word itself. One slogan that summarizes this idea is: *Meanings are in people, not in things.* When your friend says, "Have you seen Matilda?" (meaning the Broadway show) and you say, "I don't know who she is" because you are thinking about a person you assume you should know, you are attributing a different meaning to the word *Matilda* than your friend. You are both using the same word, but thinking about different things. In Figure 6.2 the almost overlapping circles indicate that the meaning for a word is sometimes shared between you and another person. Yet at other times, what you mean by a word is completely misunderstood. For example, the area where the circles barely touch in Figure 6.2 suggests low or almost no shared meaning.

WORDS ARE DENOTATIVE AND CONNOTATIVE Language creates meaning on two levels: the denotative and the connotative. The **denotative meaning** of a word creates content: It is the word's restrictive or literal meaning. For example, here is one dictionary definition for the word *school:*

> An organization that provides instruction; an institution for the teaching of children; college, university.[8]

denotative meaning
Restrictive or literal definition of a word.

Figure 6.2 A Word Can Sometimes Mean Different Things for Different People Depending on Their Experiences

High shared meaning

Low shared meaning

This definition is the literal, or denotative, definition of the word *school;* it describes what the word means in American culture.

The **connotative meaning** of a word creates feelings. Words have personal and subjective associations. To you, the word *school* might mean a wonderful, exciting place where you meet your friends, have a good time, and occasionally take tests and perform other tasks that keep you from enjoying your social life. To others, *school* could be a restrictive, burdensome obligation that stands in the way of making money and getting on with life. The connotative meaning of a word is more individualized. Whereas the denotative (objective) meaning of the word *school* can be found in any dictionary, your subjective, personal association with the word would probably not be found there.

The denotative and connotative meanings of words made headlines in 2008, when the US Supreme Court considered whether a well-known four-letter word is obscene if it is used connotatively rather than denotatively.[9] The Federal Communication Commission doesn't permit the word to be used on public airways (although it can be used on cable TV or satellite radio). TV broadcasters were fined for allowing the word to be used in a live, on-air broadcast. The broadcasters fought back, arguing that the word is not obscene if it is used to express frustration or that things are a mess (one of its connotative meanings) rather than to describe the act of sex (its denotative meaning). The fact that the highest court in the country heard arguments to determine whether a word was obscene depending on its denotative and connotative meanings suggests that both the denotative and the connotative symbolic meanings of words are important.

connotative meaning

Personal and subjective association with a word.

Recap

Denotative and Connotative Meaning

Meaning	Definition	Examples
Denotative	Literal, restrictive definition of a word	Mother: the female person who gave birth to you
Connotative	Personal, subjective association with a word	Mother: the warm, caring woman who nurtured and loved you; or the cold, distant woman who always implied that you were not measuring up to her standards

WORDS ARE CONCRETE AND ABSTRACT Words can be placed along a continuum from concrete to abstract. People call a word *concrete* if they can experience its referent with one of their senses; if you can see, touch, smell, taste, or hear a word's referent, then the word is concrete. If you cannot do these things with the referent, then the word is abstract. You can visualize the continuum from concrete to abstract as a ladder. Language specialist S. I. Hayakawa first developed the concept of a ladder of abstraction in his classic book *Language in Thought and Action.*[10]

In Figure 6.3, the term at the bottom, *red Mercedes* C-230, is quite specific and concrete. You're likely to have a clear mental picture of a red Mercedes. In contrast, the word *transportation* is more abstract—it could mean anything from walking to jetting across the Atlantic. As you move up the ladder of abstraction, the terms become broader and more general. In general, the more concrete the language, the more likely it is that the precise meaning of a word will be communicated to a listener. There are times when being abstract is a good thing. Poetry, metaphors, and expressions couched in global, abstract terms may be the best way to express what's on your mind or in your heart. The goal is not to verbally hang out at the bottom of the ladder, but to be aware of how concrete or abstract you are and to be other-oriented: Think about how the words or phrases you use will be interpreted by others.

Figure 6.3 A Ladder of Abstraction

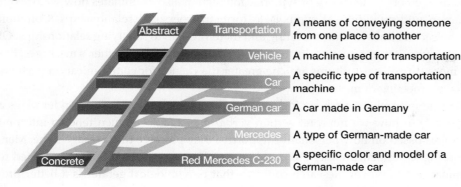

Many Words Are Arbitrary

American linguist (a person who studies the origin and nature of language) Charles Hockett suggested that words are, for the most part, arbitrary.[11] There's not always an obvious reason why many words represent what they refer to. The word *dog,* for example, does not look like a dog or sound like a dog. Yet there is a clear connection in your mind between your pet pooch and the symbol *dog.* The words we use have accepted general meanings, but there is not typically a logical connection between a word and what it represents. Yes, some words, such as *buzz, hum, snort,* and *giggle,* do recreate the sounds they represent. Words that, when pronounced, sound like the event or thing they are signifying are called onomatopoetic words. You probably learned about **onomatopoeia** in an English class. And many words can trace their origin to other languages.[12] Words can also be metaphorical. When referring to a table "leg," for example, we are using a metaphor to describe the table's vertical support. Yet other words have an arbitrary meaning. A linguistic group, such as all the people who speak English, has agreed that the word *tree,* for example, will represent the thing with bark, branches, and leaves growing in your yard or a nearby park. The arbitrary nature of most words means that there is no inherent meaning in a word. Therefore, unless we develop a common meaning for a word, misunderstanding and miscommunication may occur.

onomatopoeia
A word that imitates a sound associated with what is named; also, the use of such a word

Words Are Culture-Bound

As you learned in Chapter 4, culture consists of the rules, norms, and values of a group of people, which have been learned and shaped by successive generations. The meaning of a symbol such as a word can change from culture to culture. The meanings of words are shaped by our experiences. To a European, for example, a "Yankee" is someone from the United States; to a player on the Boston Red Sox, a "Yankee" is an opponent; and to someone from the American South, a "Yankee" is someone from the American North.

One way to measure how words reflect culture is to consider the new words added to dictionaries each year. Here are some new words that are finding their way into people's conversations:[13]

Bromance: A close nonsexual friendship between men

Hacktivist: A hacker who is an activist

Ridonkulous: Very ridiculous

The study of words and meaning is called *semantics.* One important semantic theory known as **symbolic interaction theory** suggests that a society is bound together by the common use of symbols. As discussed in Chapter 2, sociologists originally

symbolic interaction theory
Theory that people make sense of the world based on their interpretation of words or symbols used by others.

developed this theory as a way of making sense out of how societies and groups are linked together.[14] The theory of symbolic interaction also illuminates how we use our common understanding of symbols to form interpersonal relationships. Common symbols foster links in understanding and therefore lead to satisfying relationships. Of course, even within a given culture, people misunderstand each other's messages. But the more similar two cultures are, the greater the chance for communication partners to have a meeting of meanings.

Some researchers, such as linguist Deborah Tannen, suggest that gender plays a major role in how we interpret certain verbal messages.[15] Women tend to interpret messages based on how personally supportive they perceive the message to be. Men, according to Tannen, are more likely to interpret messages based on issues related to dominance and power. Research confirms that psychological gender is a better predictor than biological sex of the general framework we use to interpret messages.[16] Clearly, our life experiences help us interpret the words we hear.

The Power of Words

6.2 Identify how words influence our perceptions, thoughts, actions, culture, and relationships.

> Sticks and stones may break my bones,
> But words can never hurt me.

This old schoolyard chant may provide a ready retort for the desperate victim of name-calling, but it is hardly convincing. With more insight, the poet Robert Browning wrote, "Words break no bones; hearts though sometimes." And in his book *Science and Sanity*, mathematician and engineer Alfred Korzybski argued that the words we use (and misuse) have tremendous effects on our thoughts and actions.[17] Browning and Korzybski were right. As we said at the beginning of this chapter, words have power.

Words Create Perceptions

"To name is to call into existence—to call out of nothingness," wrote French philosopher Georges Gusdorff.[18] Words give you a tool to create how you perceive the world by naming and labeling what you experience. You undoubtedly learned in your elementary science class that Sir Isaac Newton discovered gravity. It would be more accurate to say that he *labeled* gravity rather than discovered it. His use of the word *gravity* gave us a cognitive category; we can now converse about the pull of the earth's forces that keeps us from flying into space. Words give us the symbolic vehicles to communicate our creations and discoveries to others.

You create your self-worth largely with self-talk and the labels you apply to yourself. Psychologist Albert Ellis believes that you also create your moods and emotional state with the words you use to label your feelings.[19] Although emotions may sometimes seem to wash over you like ocean waves, there is evidence that you have the ability to control your emotions through your ability to control what you think about, as well as the choice of words you use to describe your feelings. In Chapter 2, we talked about the appraisal theory of emotions, which suggests that we exert considerable control over our emotions based on how we frame what is happening to us.[20] If you get fired from a job, you might say that you feel angry and helpless, or you might declare that you feel liberated and excited. The first response might lead to depression, and the second to happiness. One fascinating study conducted over a thirty-five-year period found that people who described the world in pessimistic terms when they were younger were in poorer health during middle age than those who had been optimistic.[21] Your words and corresponding outlook have the power to affect your health. The concept of reframing, discussed in Chapter 2 as a way to improve self-concept, is based on the power of words to "call into existence" whatever we describe with them.

Words Influence Thoughts

If someone says, "Don't think about a pink elephant," it's hard *not* to think about a pink elephant, because just thinking about the words *pink elephant* more than likely triggers an image of a pink pachyderm. Words and thoughts are inextricably linked.

"We are what we think. All that we are arises with our thoughts. With our thoughts, we make the world."[22] These words, attributed to the Buddha, explain why it's important to consider how our words influence our thoughts, and in turn, us. Is it possible to think without using linguistic symbols (words or numbers)? Yes, we can certainly experience emotions without describing them in words and enjoy music without lyrics. Artists paint, dancers dance, and architects dream up new structures, all without words. Yet words transmit our dreams and emotions to others when we verbalize what we feel. Words have tremendous power to influence what we think about, just as our thinking influences the words we use. As Figure 6.4 illustrates, the process of hearing, seeing, or saying words influences different parts of the brain. How we use words literally changes our brain activity.

Because words have the power to influence our thoughts, the meaning of a word resides within us, rather than in the word itself. Words *symbolize* meaning, but the precise meaning of a word originates in the minds of both the sender and the receiver. The meaning of a word is not static; it evolves as a conversation evolves. Your meanings for words and phrases change as you gain additional experiences and have new thoughts about the words you use.[23]

Words Influence Actions

To paraphrase a well-known verse from the book of Proverbs in the Bible, "As a person thinks, so is he or she." Words not only have the power to create and influence your thoughts, they also influence your actions—because your thoughts, which are

Figure 6.4 Words Influence Brain Activity

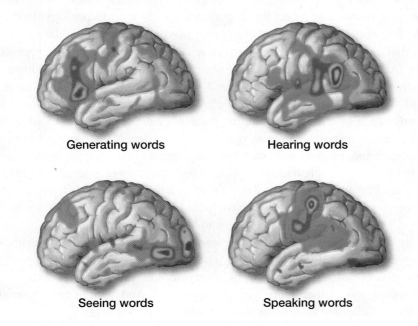

Generating words   Hearing words

Seeing words   Speaking words

Surfers have created their own special language as part of the culture they share.

linguistic determinism

Theory that describes how use of language determines or influences thoughts and perceptions.

linguistic relativity

Theory that each language includes some unique features that are not found in other languages.

Sapir–Whorf hypothesis

Based on the principles of linguistic determinism and linguistic relativity, the hypothesis that language shapes our thoughts and culture, and our culture and thoughts affect the language we use to describe our world.

worldview

Individual perceptions or perceptions by a culture or group of people about key beliefs and issues, such as death, God, and the meaning of life, which influence interaction with others.

influenced by words, affect how you behave. Advertisers have long known that slogans and catch phrases sell products. Political candidates also know that the words they use influence whether they will get your vote.

Research suggests that the way we use language can communicate the amount of power we have in a conversation.[24] We use language in ways that are both powerful and powerless. When we use powerless speech, we are less persuasive and exert less influence on the actions of others. Powerless speech is characterized by more frequent use of pauses, which may be filled with "umm," "ahhh," and "ehh." We also express our lack of power by using more hesitation and unnecessary verbal fillers like "you know" and "I mean." We communicate our low power when we hedge our conclusions by saying "I guess" and "sort of." Another way of communicating a lack of power is by tacking on a question at the end of a statement, such as "I'm right, aren't I?" or "This is what I think, OK?" So, the very way you speak can influence the thoughts and actions of others.[25]

Words Affect and Reflect Culture

In the early part of the twentieth century, anthropologists Edward Sapir and his student Benjamin Whorf worked simultaneously to refine a theory called **linguistic determinism**.[26] The essence of linguistic determinism is that language shapes the way we think. Our words also reflect our thoughts and culture. A related principle, called **linguistic relativity**, states that each language has unique elements embedded within it. Together these two principles form the underlying elements in the **Sapir–Whorf hypothesis**, which suggests that language shapes our culture and culture shapes our language. To support this theory, Benjamin Whorf studied the languages of several cultures, particularly that of Hopi Native Americans. He discovered that in Hopi, one word (*masa'ytaka*) is used for every creature that flies, except for birds. While this seems odd to an English speaker because the English language has many different words for flying creatures (and things such as airplanes, balloons, and rockets), for the Hopi, flying creatures (or objects) constitute a single category. Whorf saw this as support of his hypothesis that the words we use reflect our culture and our culture influences our words. Similarly, today's highly developed technological culture has given rise to many new words that reflect the importance we place on technology; terms such as *iPad, flash drive,* and *terabytes* weren't part of your grandparents' language. And the fact that a certain type of behavior is now labeled attention-deficit/hyperactivity disorder (ADHD) is an example of how words can create a reality in a culture. Your grandfather might argue that there weren't any ADHD kids in his day—some kids were just "rowdy."[27]

Words not only reflect your culture; there is evidence that they mold it. When Wendell Johnson, a speech therapist, noticed that very few Native Americans in a certain tribe stuttered, he also found that their language had no word for stuttering.[28] He concluded that few people had this affliction because it never entered their minds as a possibility. Perhaps you've heard that Eskimos have forty-nine different words for snow. Even though they really don't have quite that many, there is evidence they use more words for snow than someone native to Miami, Florida.[29]

These examples also show that the words people use affect their **worldview**—how they interpret what they experience. The words you select to describe your view of the world, including those you use in everyday interpersonal conversations with friends, reflect and further shape your perspective.[30] And you, in turn, help shape your culture's collective worldview through your use of language.

Words Make and Break Relationships

What you say and how you say it have a strong impact on how you relate to others. Relationships are the connections we make with others. As we noted in Chapter 1, to relate to another person is like dancing with him or her. When you dance with a partner, your moves and countermoves respond to the rhythm of the music and the moves your partner makes. In our interpersonal relationships with others, we "dance" as we relate to our communication partners with both language and nonverbal cues (something we'll discuss in more detail in the next chapter). A good conversation has a rhythm, created by both communicators as they listen and respond to each other. Even "small talk," our everyday, sometimes brief, responses and exchanges with others ("Nice weather we're having" or, simply, "Oh, that's nice"), is important in establishing how we feel about others.[31] Additionally, if we're feeling insecure in a relationship and we share that insecurity with our romantic partner, the mere expression of insecurity may increase feelings of uncertainty and concern about the relationship.[32] Expressing insecurities tends to perpetuate them.

Clues to Our Relationships Are Found in Our Word Choice

Interpersonal communication researcher Steve Duck suggests that we literally talk a relationship into being.[33] And what do we talk about? One research team simply looked at what satisfied couples talked about with each other during the course of a week. The team found that the most frequent topic was the couples themselves. They talked mostly about what they did during the day and how they were feeling, followed by general observations, and then responses to each other such as, "Yes, I see," and "Uh huh"—what researchers call *backchannel talk.* The researchers also found we're more likely to have conflicts with our partners on weekends. We're also more likely to use humor, talk about household tasks, and make general plans about the future on weekends.[34] Couples were least satisfied with their partners on Saturdays and Wednesdays; on Mondays they were most satisfied. What we talk about and the way we talk to people form the basis of how we relate to others.

It's through our verbal messages that we explicitly let others know we are interested in developing a relationship with them. One research team wanted to know the most effective ways to initiate a relationship by using "pick-up" lines.[35] Which "pick-up" line works best? The researchers studied strategies like being direct ("I'd like to meet you"), direct compliments ("What nice hair"), and humor ("It's hot enough to boil radishes"), as well as what they called "cute-flippant lines" and being introduced by a third party. The results: Being introduced by a third party and being direct were perceived as the most appropriate. A third-party introduction was also judged to be the most effective way to initiate a relationship. So what's the best research-based advice for connecting with someone? Be direct or have someone else introduce you.

Words influence relationships when we express our emotions and feelings during our conversations. Telling someone "I feel sad" or "I feel frustrated" has an obvious effect on a relationship with that person. Although emotions are primarily communicated via nonverbal messages (vocal cues and facial expressions), communication researcher Kristin Byron suggests that even our e-mail messages communicate considerable emotional content.[36] Another researcher found that couples participating in a four-minute speed dating session were three times more likely to date each other if they used more personal pronouns (*I, me, my*), articles (*the, a, an*), prepositions (*for, of, on*), conjunctions (*but, and*), and other short words. We process these kinds of words quickly and easily and they are also used in relationships in which we feel comfortable.[37] And it's not only romantic partners who use words to express affection. Our words also reveal the amount of affection we have towards family members. Did you ever wonder if grandma liked you best? One research duo found that grandparents express more verbal affection toward their biological grandchildren than their non-biological grandchildren, such as step grandchildren. We may think we are being equally positive in what we say to friends and family members, but our declarations of affection and the specific words we use tell the true story.[38]

Clues to Our Relationships Are Found in What We Don't Say

Some people never swear. The use of **profanity**, words that people consider obscene, rude, or insensitive, has an impact on our relationships with others. If you grew up in a home where family members never uttered profanities, you may not have developed a habit of using such words. Or, you may have made a conscious decision not to use profanity because of your religious or moral convictions. Yet profanity is prevalent in everyday conversations and the media. If you have heard the late comedian George Carlin's monologue "Seven Dirty Words You Can't Say on Television," then you have an idea of the words that form the bedrock of profane speech.

Whether or not a word can be considered profane is determined by context and culture. If you have British friends, then you know the word *bloody* is an obscene word synonymous with the "F word." Yet you may see nothing wrong with using the word *bloody* in your conversations. Dog breeders know that a female dog is a *bitch,* yet using that term to describe a female classmate would be considered profane.

Remember that the other person, not you, determines the effect of profanity on the relationship. Some people might be highly offended if you were to use one or more of George Carlin's seven "dirty" words in a conversation. Yet using profanity may signal your comfort with being yourself when you're with another person. Your use of profanity provides important information about your perception of the relationship you have with the other person.

Another clue to the nature of the relationship you have with someone is your use of euphemism. A **euphemism** is an expression that describes something vulgar or profane (or something people prefer not to talk about directly) but uses less explicit language. Earlier in this chapter, when we referred to "the F word" rather than spelling it out, we were using a euphemism. Not using euphemisms but more directly and explicitly describing your thoughts and feelings provides relational cues that you trust the other person to accept your blunt language. Politicians use euphemisms to soften the impact of an event. Rather than saying innocent people were killed, the spokesperson may say, "There was collateral damage." Noting your use of euphemisms and the use and frequency of euphemisms in others' speech can give you insights about the nature of your relationship with them.

Clues to Our Online Relationships Are Found in Our Tweets, Texts, and Posts

The words we use in our Facebook posts, tweets, texts, and other online messages provide important information about us in ways we may not be consciously aware of.[39] Because we usually want others to see us in a favorable way, we communicate more positive than negative messages about ourselves on Facebook.[40] Research has found that we don't like "downer" Facebook posts. Negative emotional expressions

Roz Chast/The New Yorker Collection/The Cartoon Bank.

profanity

Words considered obscene, blasphemous, irreverent, rude, or insensitive.

euphemism

A mild or indirect word that is substituted for one that describes something vulgar, profane, unpleasant, or embarrassing.

are viewed less favorably on Facebook than positive ones.[41] Yet there is evidence we also adapt to our Facebook audiences. One research team found that, perhaps aware that others don't like negative messages, we communicate fewer negative emotions in our status updates than we do in our person-to-person messages. This suggests when we are communicating online to many different audiences (family, friends, colleagues), we project a more positive self-presentation than with a private audience.[42]

We also tend to be highly verbally immediate online—which means we use more personal pronouns (*I*, *me*, and *my*), present tense verbs (*am, is, are*), conditional words (*could, should, would*), shorter words, and fewer articles (*a, an, the*) than we do in face-to-face conversations. Researchers suggest that using more verbally immediate language signals a more positive, close personal relationship with others online.[43] Yet another team of researchers found that when we perceive a relationship to be strong, we are more open and use more positive words and assurances. Even when we are jealous, we use more positive words and assurances, perhaps to hide our jealousy. But if we are jealous of someone, we also spend more time monitoring the relationship online.[44]

How to Manage Misunderstandings

6.3   **Identify and describe word barriers that lead to misunderstandings.**

A student pilot was on his first solo flight. When he called the tower for flight instructions, the air traffic controller asked, "Would you please give us your altitude and position?" The pilot replied, "I'm five feet ten inches, and I'm sitting up front." Like the student pilot, we often misunderstand others. According to theologian and educator Ruel Howe, a communication barrier is "something that keeps meaning from meeting."[45]

Words have the power to create monumental misunderstandings as well as deep connections.[46] How do you manage the inevitable misunderstandings that occur even between the best of friends? Read on.

Be Aware of Missed Meaning

If you are not aware of a misunderstanding, you won't be able to clarify your message. The problem may be obvious, but *how* to identify the missed meaning is less obvious. Meaning is fragile. And because meaning can be misunderstood, it's important to be aware of the potential for miscommunication.

One reason for misunderstanding is the problem of **bypassing**, which occurs when the same word or words mean different things to different people. You know what you mean when you exclaim "That's so gay!" You may intend the comment as a nonoffensive joke or a just-in-fun put down of someone; but others, especially someone who *is* gay, might not appreciate your "humor." As the expression goes, "I know that you believe you understand what you think I said, but I'm not sure you realize that what you heard is not what I meant."

The English language is imprecise. One researcher estimated that the 500 words used most often in daily conversations have more than 14,000 different dictionary definitions. And this number does not take into account personal connotations. So it is no wonder that bypassing is a common communication problem. Consider the unsubstantiated story about a young FBI employee who was put in charge of the supply department. In an effort to save money, he reduced the size of memo paper. One of the smaller sheets ended up on J. Edgar Hoover's desk. The director didn't like the small size and wrote on the narrow margin of the paper, "Watch the borders." For the next six weeks, it was extremely difficult to enter the United States from Canada or Mexico.

Pavlov's dog salivated when it heard the bell that it had learned to associate with food. Sometimes we respond to symbols the way Pavlov's dog did to the bell, forgetting that symbols (words) can have more than one meaning.

bypassing
Confusion caused by the fact that the same word can mean different things to different people.

How do you avoid bypassing and missing someone's meaning? Be aware of the potential problem. Use the listening and responding skills we talked about in the previous chapter to enhance communication accuracy. Ask questions if you're uncertain of the meaning. Listen and paraphrase your understanding of the message.

Be Clear

Alice Roosevelt Longworth writes about a merchant seaman who was being investigated under the McCarran Act. "Do you," asked the interrogator, "have any pornographic literature?"

"Pornographic literature!" the sailor burst out indignantly. "I don't even have a pornograph!"

At a ceremony in the Princeton University chapel, an older woman buttonholed an usher and commanded, "Be sure you get me a seat up front, young man. I understand they've always had trouble with the agnostics in the chapel!"

Each of these examples illustrates a **malapropism**, a confusion of one word or phrase for another that sounds similar to it. You have probably heard people confuse such word pairs as *construction* and *instruction,* or *subscription* and *prescription.* Although this confusion may at times be humorous, it may also result in failure to communicate clearly. There are many reasons for a lack of clarity. Using words out of context, using inappropriate grammar, or putting words in the wrong order creates murky meaning. Confusion when a message isn't clear is the inevitable result, as illustrated by these notes written to landlords:

- The toilet is blocked and we cannot bathe the children until it is cleared.
- Will you please send someone to mend our cracked sidewalk? Yesterday my wife tripped on it and is now pregnant.

These are funny examples, but in fact, incorrect or unclear language can launch a war or sink a ship. We give symbols meaning; we do not receive inherent meaning *from* symbols.

Besides avoiding malapropisms and being careful not to use the wrong words, how else can you speak with clarity? Consider these strategies to enhance message clarity:

- Think about what you mean before you speak. For many years, people who worked at the computer company IBM had a one-word sign on their desk: *Think.* This is good advice when clarity is the goal.
- When you speak, observe your listener's reactions. If you notice a grimace, frown, or quizzical look, it might mean that you're not making sense. Watching for feedback can help you assess whether you are being clear.
- Use appropriate examples; they need not be elaborate or highly detailed, but well-told examples can add clarity to your conversations.
- Ask the other person whether he or she can understand you or has questions.
- Consider the perspective and background of the person or persons to whom you are speaking. If you are other-oriented, you will assess how someone else will respond to your message and try to select those symbols that he or she is most likely to interpret as you intend.

Be Specific

For most communication, the object is to be as specific and concrete as possible. Vague language creates confusion and frustration. Consider this example:

Derrick:	Where's the aluminum foil?
Pam:	In the drawer.
Derrick:	What drawer?
Pam:	In the kitchen.

malapropism

Confusion of one word or phrase for another that sounds similar to it.

Derrick:	But where in the kitchen?
Pam:	By the fridge.
Derrick:	But which one? There are five drawers.
Pam:	Oh, the second one from the top.
Derrick:	Why didn't you say so in the first place?

But is it possible to be too specific? It is if you use a restricted code that has a meaning your listener does not know. A **restricted code** is a set of words that have a particular meaning to a subgroup or culture. If you send many text messages, you probably use a restricted code of *textisms*—brief abbreviations for common words, such as "c u" for "see you" or the ubiquitous "LOL" for "laughing out loud." To you, such restricted code is clear, but to someone who doesn't receive many text messages, these abbreviations can result in head-scratching confusion. In addition, researchers have wondered whether these textisms have spilled over into nontext writing such as letters or research papers. Initial research suggests that they have not. Although textisms may sometimes appear out of context, individuals generally adapt their writing style to the specific situation.[47]

We sometimes develop abbreviations or specialized terms to save time when we speak to others in our group. Musicians, for example, use special terms like "mash up" to mean mixing several songs together. Ham radio operators use codes known to other ham operators to communicate over the airwaves, such as "88," which means hugs and kisses. In both instances, this shorthand language would make little sense to an outsider. In fact, groups that rely on restricted codes may have greater cohesiveness because of this shared "secret" language, or **jargon**. Whatever your line of work, guard against lapsing into phrases that can only be interpreted by a few people.

Dot Mobile, a British cell phone service for students, used a restricted code to summarize classic literary phrases in a text-message format. Can you break the restricted code of the following phrases from classic literature?[48]

1. 2B?NTB? = ????
2. Ahors, m'kindom 4 Ahors
3. 2morrow &"&"
4. WenevaUFeelLykDissinNel,jstMembaDatADaOoubDaWrldHvntHd DaVantgstUvAd
5. IfURlyWnt2HrBoutit,Da1stFingUlProbWnt2NolsWhereIWsBorn&WotMyLousy ChldhdWsLyk&HwMyRentsWerOcupyd&AlB4TheyHdMe&ThtDaveCopafieldKi ndaCr"p,BtIDnFeelLykGolnintaltifUWannaNoDaTruf

Here are the answers:

1. "To be or not to be? That is the question." (William Shakespeare, *Hamlet*)
2. "A horse, a horse, my kingdom for a horse." (William Shakespeare, *Richard III*)
3. "Tomorrow and tomorrow and tomorrow." (William Shakespeare, *Macbeth*)
4. "Whenever you feel like criticizing anyone … just remember that all the people in this world haven't had the advantages that you've had." (F. Scott Fitzgerald, *The Great Gatsby*)
5. "If you really want to hear about it, the first thing you'll probably want to know is where I was born, and what my lousy childhood was like, and how my parents were occupied and all before they had me, and all that David Copperfield kind of crap, but I don't feel like going into it, if you want to know the truth." (J. D. Salinger, *The Catcher in the Rye*)

When people have known each other for a long time, they may also use restricted codes in their exchanges. Often, married couples communicate using short-hand speech that no outsider could ever interpret. To enhance the clarity of your messages with others, especially people who don't know you well, be as specific as you can to

restricted code
Set of words that have particular meaning to a person, group, or culture.

jargon
Another name for restricted code; specialized terms or abbreviations whose meanings are known only to members of a specific group.

reduce uncertainty. For example, rather than saying, "I may go to town today," one research team suggests you should be more specific and say, "There's a 50 percent chance I may go to town today."[49] Be precise to be clear.

allness

Tendency to use language to make unqualified, often untrue generalizations.

An additional challenge to clarity is the tendency to use language to make unqualified, often untrue generalizations called **allness** statements. Allness statements deny individual differences or variations. Statements such as "All women are poor drivers" and "People from the South love iced tea" are generalizations that imply the person making the pronouncement has examined all the information and has reached a definitive conclusion. Although the world would be much simpler if we *could* make such statements, reality rarely, if ever, provides evidence to support sweeping generalizations.

One way to avoid untrue generalizations is to remind yourself that your use and interpretation of a word are unique. Saying the words "to me" either to yourself or out loud before you offer an opinion or make a pronouncement can help communicate to others (and remind yourself) that your view is uniquely yours. Rather than announcing, "Curfews for teenagers are ridiculous," you could say, "To me, curfews for teenagers are ridiculous."

indexing

Avoiding generalizations by using statements that separate one situation, person, or example from another.

Indexing your comments and remarks is another way to avoid overgeneralizing allness statements. To index is to acknowledge that each individual, situation, or example is unique. Rather than declaring that all doctors act abruptly, you might say, "My child's pediatrician spends a lot of time with me, but my internist never answers my questions." This statement reminds you that not all doctors are the same.

Be Aware of Changes in Meaning

You change. Your world changes. An ancient Greek philosopher said it best: "You can never step in the same river twice." Yet we sometimes use words with an implicit assumption that our world doesn't change. Word meanings can change over time. A **static evaluation** is a statement that fails to recognize change; labels in particular have a tendency to freeze-frame our awareness. For example, Kirk, who was known as the class nerd in high school, is today a successful and polished business professional. So the old label no longer fits.

static evaluation

Pronouncement that does not take the possibility of change into consideration.

In addition, some people suffer from "hardening of the categories." Their worldview is so rigid that they can never change or expand their perspective. But the world is a technicolor moving target. Just about the time you think you have things neatly figured out and categorized, something moves. Your labels may not reflect the buzzing, booming, zipping process of change. It is important to acknowledge that perception is a process. Try to avoid attempting to nail things down permanently into all-inclusive categories.

BEING Other-ORIENTED

People change. You change. Yet our labels for and descriptions of others tend to freeze because the power of words affects our thoughts and perceptions. When interacting with others, how can you avoid the tendency to "step in the same river twice" and treat people as if they haven't changed?

General semanticists use the metaphorical expression "the map is not the territory" to illustrate the concept of static evaluation. Like a word, a map symbolizes or represents reality. Yet the road system is constantly changing. New roads get built and old ones close. If you used a 2010 map to find the fastest way to get from San Marcos, Texas, to Georgetown, Texas, you wouldn't know you could take the highway 130 Austin bypass; it didn't exist in 2010, but it does now. Similarly, if you use old labels and do not adjust your thinking to accommodate change, you will get lost semantically.

To avoid static evaluation, try dating your observations, and indicate to others the time period from which you are drawing your conclusion. For example, if your cousin comes to town for a visit, say, "When I last saw you, you loved to listen to Florence and the Machine." This allows for the possibility that your cousin's tastes may have changed during the last few years. Try to observe and acknowledge changes in others. If you are practicing what you know about becoming other-oriented, you are unlikely to erect this barrier.

Be Aware of Polarizing Either-Or Extremes

Polarization entails describing and evaluating what you observe in terms of extremes with an either-or perspective. Pronouncing something as either good or bad, old or new, beautiful or ugly, or brilliant or stupid misses the possibility that it's not that clear cut. General semanticists, people who study language and how it affects our behavior, remind us that the world is not black and white, but instead comes in a variety of colors, hues, and shades. If you describe things in polarizing extremes, leaving out the middle ground, then your language does not accurately reflect reality. And because of the power of words to create, you may believe your own pronouncements.

> "You either love me or don't love me," says Waylan.
> "You're either for me or against me," replies Meredith.

Both people are overstating the case, using language to polarize their perceptions of experience.

Family counselors who listen to family feuds find that the tendency to see things from an either-or point of view is a classic symptom of a troubled relationship. Placing the entire blame on your partner for a problem in your relationship is an example of polarizing. Few relational difficulties are exclusively one-sided.

polarization

Description and evaluation of what you observe in terms of extremes such as good or bad, old or new, beautiful or ugly.

Be Unbiased

Using words that reflect your biases toward other cultures or ethnic groups, the other gender, people with a different sexual orientation, or people who are different from you in some other way can create a barrier for your listeners. Because words, including the words used to describe people, have power to create and affect thoughts and behavior, they can also affect the quality of relationships with others. Although TV and radio shows and magazine articles may debate the merits of political correctness, there is no doubt that sexist or racially stereotypical language can offend others.

Hate speech is any word or phrase that is intended to offend and disrespect another person because of his or her race, ethnicity, cultural background, gender, age, sexual orientation, disability, social class, occupation, personal appearance, mental capacity, or any other personal aspect that could be perceived as demeaning. Some people use words to *intentionally* express their prejudice, bias, ignorance, or just plain meanness toward other people, hoping to hurt someone. Like sticks and stones hurled at others to intentionally inflict harm, hate speech is uttered with the explicit purpose of hurting someone. In the United States, the First Amendment to the Constitution provides for freedom of speech. But do people have the legal right to direct hurtful, venomous comments toward others, knowing that such comments will create mental anguish? Your college or university may have a speech code that prohibits hate speech, yet critics of such codes argue that it's impossible to prove the motivation or intent of someone who uses such language.

AVOID SEXIST LANGUAGE.   Sexist language is the use of words that reflect stereotypical attitudes or describe roles in exclusively male or female terms.

Words such as congress*man*, mail*man,* and *man*kind ignore the fact that women are part of the workforce and the human race. Contrast these with *member of Congress, letter carrier,* and *humankind,* which are gender-neutral and allow for the inclusion of both men and women. Or, rather than eliminating the word *man* from your vocabulary, try to use appropriate labels when you know the gender of the subject. A male police officer is a *policeman*; a female police officer is a *policewoman.* Rather than *salesperson,* you could say *salesman* or *saleswoman,* depending on the gender of the seller.

hate speech

Words or phrases intended to offend or show disrespect for someone's race, ethnicity, cultural background, gender, or some other aspect of that person's identity.

The term *policeman* fails to accurately describe the person shown here. A more inclusive term would be *police officer.*

Many of our social conventions also diminish or ignore the importance of women:

Sexist		Unbiased
I'd like you to meet Dr. and Mrs. John Chao.		I'd like you to meet Dr. Sue Ho and Dr. John Chao. They are husband and wife.
	Or,	I'd like you to meet John Chao and Sue Ho. They're both doctors at Mercy Hospital.
Let me introduce Mr. Tom Bertolone and his wife, Beverly.		Let me introduce Beverly and Tom Bertolone.

Additional evidence of the substantial progress and changed attitudes toward women in the professional arena is reflected by the terms used to describe workers now, compared with those used in the 1950s:

Terms Used Today	Terms Used in 1950s
Flight attendant	Stewardess
Firefighter	Fireman
Police officer	Policeman
Physician	Female doctor
Women at the office	Girls at work
Ms.	Miss/Mrs.
People/humans	Mankind

Consciously remembering to use nonsexist language will result in several benefits.[50] First, nonsexist language both reflects and reinforces nonsexist attitudes. Your attitudes are reflected in your speech, and your speech affects your attitudes. Monitoring your speech for sexist remarks can help you examine your attitudes about sexist assumptions you may hold. In addition, using nonsexist language will help you become more other-oriented. Monitoring your language for sexist remarks will reflect your sensitivity to others. Third, nonsexist language will make your speech more contemporary and unambiguous. By substituting the word *humankind* for *mankind*, for example, you communicate that you are including all people, not just men, in your observation or statement. And finally, your nonsexist language will empower others. By eliminating sexist bias from your speech, you will help confirm the value of all the individuals with whom you interact.

In addition to the debate over language that refers to gender, considerable discussion occurs about the way people talk about sexual orientation. The principle of being other-oriented suggests that you can be sensitive in the way you speak of someone's sexual orientation. Labeling someone a *fag, queer,* or *dyke* not only is offensive and hurtful to the person being labeled but also reflects a lack of sensitivity of the person doing the labeling. We're not suggesting that certain words be expunged from dictionaries or never uttered. But when describing others, be sensitive to how they wish to be addressed and discussed.

AVOID ETHNICALLY OR RACIALLY BIASED LANGUAGE   In addition to monitoring your language for sexual stereotypes, avoid racial and ethnic stereotypes. Using phrases such as "She's an Indian giver," or "He jewed him down on the price," or "He doesn't have a Chinaman's chance" demonstrates an insensitivity to members of other cultural groups. Monitor your speech so that you do not, even unintentionally, use phrases that depict a racial group or ethnic group in a negative, stereotypical fashion.

Is Supreme Court Justice Clarence Thomas Black or African American? According to a 2013 Gallup Poll, most Blacks or African Americans were divided over what they preferred to be called (17% said Black and 17% said African American), with most

BEING Other-ORIENTED

You don't determine whether a word or phrase is offensive—the person who's been called the name does. How can you assess whether terms, phrases, or labels you use may be offensive to someone?

Relating to Diverse Others

Do Men and Women Speak the Same Language?

John Gray's popular self-help book *Men Are from Mars, Women Are from Venus*[51] has been heralded by some as "the book that saved our relationship," yet some communication scholars have concluded that Gray overstated his case in claiming vast differences in the ways men and women speak to each other.[52] Men and women may sometimes have different assumptions about the function of talk in the development of relationships, but these differences are not so extensive that they cannot be bridged.

Julia Wood is a communication researcher who has criticized John Gray for oversimplifying the differences in how men and women talk to one another. She acknowledges that women tend to use language to establish and maintain relationships more than do men. In reviewing literature on women's speech, Wood found the following:[53]

- Women tend to seek to establish equality between themselves and others by using such phrases as "I know just how you feel" or "Yes, the same thing has happened to me."

- Women are more likely to show emotional support for others using statements such as "How wonderful" or "Oh, that sounds very frustrating."

- Women often spend time conducting conversational "maintenance work"—for example, trying to keep the conversation from lagging by asking open-ended questions that prompt a more detailed response.

- Women are more likely to be inclusive—to make sure everyone present is invited to talk.

- Women also have been found to be more tentative in the way they use language saying things like "*I thought* it was kind of boring" (rather than just saying "It was boring"). Tentativeness is also expressed by ending a phrase with a question—called a tag question—such as "That was a good class, *wasn't it*?"

- Women tend to spend more time composing e-mail messages to ensure that the message fits with social norms.[54]

- Women are more likely than men to pick up on relational cues in e-mail messages.

Language differences between men and women have been found to exist, both in person and online. One study found that when composing e-mail messages, women were perceived to express more interpersonal sensitivity and emotional warmth than were men.[55] When composing an e-mail, women also tend to adapt their language to the receiver of the message; compared to men, women wrote more personalized and polite e-mail messages to friends their own age and more formal e-mail messages to their professors.[56]

In contrast, men tend to use their verbal messages for "proving oneself and negotiating prestige."[57] Rather than talking about a relationship, men are more likely to engage in mutual activities to communicate friendship, such as going to a movie together or participating in sports. Wood's literature review suggests the following:[58]

- Men are less likely to present information that indicates their vulnerabilities. Men talk to establish their power, status, and worth.

- Men often talk to accomplish tasks rather than to express feelings—they are more instrumental in the way they use language. Men talk to seek information, share information, and solve problems.

- Men tend to use speech to sustain and even dominate a conversation; there is evidence that they interrupt others more than women do.

- Men are, according to research, more assertive and less tentative when talking with others.

- Men sometimes speak in more general, abstract ways and often are less concrete and specific when describing situations and events.

- Men tend to provide fewer responsive cues such as "I'm listening," "yes," "uh-hum," and "I'm with you."

Despite differences, researchers have also found much similarity, which is why many researchers and educators suggest that it's *not* helpful to compare and contrast the way men and women speak as if they were from separate planets. One research study suggests that it's not true that women talk more than men; both men and women use about the same number of words during a typical day of conversation.[59] Researcher Anthony Mulac has concluded that differences between men and women's speech are not significant enough to explain why conflicts may occur. Mulac found that readers could not accurately identify from written transcripts of conversations whether the speakers were men or women.[60]

Deborah Tannen suggests that differences between men and women are cultural.[61] Strategies for bridging cultural differences discussed in Chapter 4 can be useful in enhancing the quality of communication between men and women: Be mindful of different communication assumptions, tolerate some uncertainty and ambiguity in communication, ask questions, seek more information before reacting (or overreacting) to messages, be other-oriented, and adapt communication messages.

Recap

How to Manage Word Barriers

Problem	Example	What to Do
Bypassing: Confusion caused when the same word evokes different meanings for different people	W.C. might mean "wayside chapel" to a Swiss person and "water closet" (i.e., bathroom) to a British person.	• When speaking, provide specific examples. • When listening, ask questions to clarify the meaning.
Lack of clarity: Inappropriate or imprecise use of words	Sign in Acapulco hotel: "The manager has personally passed all the water served here."	• When speaking, use precise language whenever possible. Provide short, specific examples or indicate the probability of something happening: "There's a 40 percent chance I won't go shopping today." • When listening, paraphrase the message to ensure you understand it accurately.
Not being specific and using allness language: Tendency to lump things or people into all-encompassing categories	"All Texans drive pick-up trucks and hang rifles in their back windows."	• When speaking, say "to me" before you offer a generalization to indicate that the idea or perception is your own. Index a generalized statement by using phrases that separate one situation, person, or example from another. • When listening, ask the speaker whether he or she means to say that *all* situations or *every* person fits the generalization presented.
Static evaluation and not being aware of change: Labeling people, objects, or events without considering how things evolve	You still call your twenty-eight-year-old nephew a "juvenile delinquent" because he spray-painted your fence when he was eleven.	• When speaking, place your observation in a time frame: "I thought he was a difficult child when he was in elementary school." • When listening, ask the speaker whether the observation remains true today or if the same generalization applies now.
Either-Or Polarization: Use of either-or terms (good or bad, right or wrong)	"You're either for me or against me."	• When speaking, avoid using either-or terms and blaming something on a specific cause. • When listening, ask the speaker whether a statement really reflects an all-or-nothing, either-or proposition.
Biased language: Use of language that reflects gender, racial, ethnic, age, ability, or class bias	"His mom is a mailman."	• When speaking, be mindful of how insensitive language can hurt someone. Avoid using labels or derogatory terms. • When listening, try to keep your emotions in check when others use inappropriate words or derogatory phrases. You can't control what others do or say, only what *you* do and say and how *you* react. Consider appropriately but assertively communicating that a word, label, or phrase offends you.

responding "Does not matter." When asked about their preferred label, 70 percent of Latinos or Hispanics indicated it "does not matter"—although 19 percent leaned toward Hispanic.[62]

AVOID DEMEANING LANGUAGE   Language barriers are created not only when speakers use sexist or racially biased language, but also when they disparage a person's age, mental or physical ability, or social standing. Calling someone a "geezer," "retard," or "trailer trash" is disparaging.[63]

Discrimination based on age is a growing problem in the workplace. In some occupations, as a worker moves into his or her fifties, it may be difficult to change jobs or find work. Despite laws designed to guard against age discrimination, such discrimination clearly exists. As we have noted, the language that people use has power to affect attitudes and behavior. That's why using negative terms to describe the elderly can be a subtle—or sometimes not-so-subtle—way of expressing disrespect toward the older generation.

Similarly, the way someone describes people with disabilities can negatively affect how they may be perceived. A study by researcher John Seiter and his colleagues found that when people with a disability were called demeaning or disparaging names, they were perceived as less trustworthy, competent, persuasive, and sociable than when the same people were described in more positive or heroic terms.[64] At the end of their study, the authors note, "Communicators who want to be effective should avoid using derogatory language." Guard against calling attention to someone as a "cripple," "dim-witted," or "mental"; these terms are offensive. As communication researcher Dawn Braithwaite notes, one preferred term is "people with disabilities."[65]

Also monitor the way you talk about someone's social class. Although some societies and cultures make considerable distinctions among classes, it is nonetheless offensive today to use words that are intended to demean someone's social class. Terms such as "welfare recipient," "manual laborer," and "blue-collar worker" are often used derogatorily. Avoid labeling someone in a way that shows disrespect toward the person's social standing, education, or socioeconomic status.

How to Use Words of Support and Comfort

6.4 Use words to provide support and comfort, and to avoid defensiveness.

You can catch more flies with honey than vinegar. This commonsense conclusion is often used to describe the power of "sweet" over "sour" words in developing positive relationships with others. And no surprise, when it comes to developing and maintaining relationships, positive, supportive communication is preferred over negative messages. Being other-oriented by thoughtfully and specifically adapting comments to an individual is especially effective.[66] True dialogue requires establishing a climate of equality, listening with empathy, and trying to bring underlying assumptions into the open. An atmosphere of equality, empathy, and openness is more likely to prevail if you approach conversations as dialogues rather than debates to be won.[67]

Not just *how* you talk to others but also *what you talk about* can result in greater positive feelings. Talking about pleasant, supporting things can influence the nature of your relationship with others. Researchers have found, for example, that spouses who tell their partner about the most pleasant and positive events of their day have more positive feelings about the relationship.[68]

For more than three decades, Jack Gibb's observational research has been used as a framework for describing verbal behaviors that contribute to feeling either supported or defensive. His research, one of the most cited studies in communication textbooks in the past half century, is so popular because he's identified practical strategies for developing supportive relationships with others—dialogue rather than debate—through the way we talk to each other.[69] Gibb spent several years listening to and observing groups of people in meetings and conversations, noting that some exchanges seem to create a supportive climate, whereas others create a defensive one. Words and actions, he concluded, are tools we use to let someone know whether we support them. And an emotional response in one person is likely to trigger an emotional response in another.[70] Although some researchers have added more categories to Gibb's original six factors, we present his original conclusions here as a time-tested framework for describing how to use words in a supportive way.[71]

> **BEING Other-ORIENTED**
> There will be many times when you need to offer an opinion or react to something someone has said or done. What are effective ways of using the principles and skills presented in this chapter to be both honest and supportive of others?

Describe Your Feelings, Rather Than Evaluate Behavior

No one likes to be judged or evaluated. Criticizing and name-calling obviously can create relational problems, but so can attempts to diagnose others' problems or win their affection with insincere praise. In fact, any form of evaluation creates a climate of

A climate of defensiveness left unchecked can escalate into interpersonal conflict. Using descriptive "I" language rather than evaluative "you" language can help you manage tension and disagreement.

extended "I" language

Brief preface to a feedback statement, intended to communicate that you don't want your listener to take your message in an overly critical way.

defensiveness. As British statesman Winston Churchill declared, "I am always ready to learn, although I do not always like being taught." Not surprisingly, research has found that being positive and supportive are more characteristic of a satisfied and secure relationship than being dismissive and evaluative.[72] Correcting others, even when we are doing it "for their own good," can raise their hackles.

One way to avoid evaluating others is to eliminate the accusatory "you" from your language. Statements such as "You always come in late for supper" or "You never pick up the dirty clothes in your room" attack a person's sense of self-worth and usually result in a defensive reaction.

Instead, use the word "I" to describe your own feelings and thoughts about a situation or event:[73] "I find it hard to keep your supper warm when you're late," or "I don't enjoy the extra work of picking up your dirty clothes." When you describe your own feelings instead of berating the receiver of the message, you are, in essence, taking ownership of the problem. This approach leads to greater openness and trust because your listener is less likely to feel rejected or as if you were trying to control him or her. Also, when you express your emotions, make sure you choose the right words to communicate your feelings.

Although we've discussed the importance of using "I" messages, interpersonal communication researchers Amy Bippus and Stacy Young found that simply prefacing an emotionally charged piece of feedback with the word "I" instead of "you" doesn't always melt away relational tension.[74] These researchers had subjects in their study read hypothetical examples in which people used either "I" messages or "you" messages. The researchers found no significant difference in how people thought others would respond to the messages. In other words, an "I" message was not found to be better than a "you" message in all instances. (The fact that the subjects were reading a message rather than actually involved in their own conversation with a partner may have affected the results.) The researchers concluded that regardless of whether a message is prefaced with "I" or "you," people don't like hearing negative expressions of emotion directed toward them.

Sometimes simply using an "I" message may be too subtle to take the sting out of the negative message you want to express. You may need to add a longer justification when you provide negative, emotional information to another. We call this using **extended "I" language**, which is a brief preface to a feedback statement, intended to communicate that you don't want the person to think that you don't value or care about him or her even though you have a negative message to share. Saying something like, "I don't want you to misinterpret what I'm about to say, because I really do care about you," or "I don't think it's entirely your fault, but I'm feeling frustrated when I experience …" may have a better chance of enhancing communication than simply beginning a sentence with the word "I" instead of "You." Remember, *there are no magic words for enhancing communication.* However, strategies of being other-oriented do seem to enhance the quality of communication. The feature Developing Your Skills: Practice Using "I" Language and Extended "I" Language will help you practice expressing your feelings accurately and effectively.

Listening for the ways you use "I," "you," "me," and "we" can provide clues to the overall quality of the relationship. Research has found that couples who describe their relationship in terms of "we" rather than use the personal pronoun "I" are likely to be in a *less* distressed relationship.[75] Yet when studying couples' instant electronic messages, another research team found no evidence that satisfied couples used "we" more than "I."[76] Using "I" may reflect healthy self-disclosure, and it may also suggest that the couples are comfortably separate rather than tightly connected. Healthy separateness may reflect a freedom that they feel in the relationship. As is true in all communication, context and situation are important when analyzing the meaning of the use of "I," "me," and "we" to gain clues about the quality of a relationship.

Solve Problems Rather Than Control

Most of us don't like others' attempts to control us. Someone who presumes to tell us what's good for us, instead of helping us puzzle through issues and problems, is likely to engender defensiveness. Open-ended questions such as "What seems to be the problem?" or "How can we deal with the issue?" create a more supportive climate than critical comments, such as "Here's where you are wrong" or commands such as "Don't do that!"

Be Genuine Rather Than Manipulative

To be genuine means that you honestly seek to be yourself rather than someone you are not. It also means taking an honest interest in others, considering the uniqueness of each individual and situation, and avoiding generalizations or strategies focusing only on your own needs and desires. A manipulative person has hidden agendas; a genuine person discusses issues and problems openly and honestly.

Communication and Emotion

The Timing of Saying "I Love You": After You. No, After You.

Who is most likely to say "I love you" first in a romantic relationship—men or women? Research suggests that although most people *think* that women are more likely to confess love first, it is actually men who are more likely to be the first to utter those three little words.[77]

There are other gender differences in the way we communicate our love for our partner. One study analyzed the content of valentine cards sent to romantic partners. Women who sent cards to men were more likely to select cards that more explicitly expressed love and being together than men who sent cards to women.[78] Valentine-card-sending expressions of love are consistent with research that has found that women are more likely than men to express more vulnerable emotions such as being deeply in love.[79] In addition, women more readily reveal more personal details about themselves when expressing their love for their heterosexual partner.[80] Yet it is not always so clear cut which gender consistently expresses more personal and intimate details. Men, for

example, are more likely to disclose personal information than women in an *initial* conversation with a stranger. The reason? Researchers believe that expressing the personal information is a way of controlling the conversation.[81]

Does the meaning of "I love you" change if it's said before a couple has sex? Research suggests that the meaning of our declarations of love lies in the timing of the message. Sandra Metts found that if romantic partners explicitly express their love for one another before having sex, then there is a greater feeling of relational escalation after sex and fewer feelings of regret about having had sex. When one or both members of the couple don't explicitly say "I love you" before having sex, then there is more likely to be some regret about sexual intimacy. Of course, the words "I love you" are not magic words that reduce sexual regret if they are uttered; feelings need to accompany the words.

Men and women in heterosexual relationships appear to have different reactions to hearing "I love you" in terms of

whether it's heard before or after having sex. Research has found that men are more likely than women to have a positive reaction when they are told they are loved before sex. Yet after having sex, when men hear the words "I love you" from their lover, there is concern that those words may signal a more dramatic escalation of commitment than they may like. Before sex, "I love you" may mean sex is more likely to happen. After having sex, hearing those words may signal to a man what the researchers called "a desire for long-term commitment."[82]

This research implies that the meaning of telling your romantic partner that you love him or her is likely to be interpreted in relation to whether it's pre-sex or post-sex. As the "I love you" researchers Joshua Ackerman, Vladas Griskevicius, and Norman Li noted, "The words 'I love you' represent the essence of romantic devotion. Feelings of love are typically accompanied by countless forms of actual and symbolic commitment, from gift giving to sexual fidelity to 'Until death do us part.'"[83]

Improving Your Communication Skills

Practice Using "I" Language and Extended "I" Language

An essential skill in being supportive rather than causing defensiveness is describing what you want with "I" language or extended "I" language rather than "you" language. Rephrase the following "you" statements as "I" statements and extended "I" statements.

"You" Language	"I" Language	Extended "I" Language
You are messy when you cook.		
Your driving is terrible.		
You never listen to me.		
You just lie on the couch and never offer to help me.		
You always decide what we watch on TV.		

Carl Rogers, the founder of person-centered counseling, suggests that true understanding and dialogue occur when people adopt a genuine or honest positive regard for others.[84] If your goal is to look out only for your own interests, your language will reflect your self-focus. At the heart of being genuine is being other-oriented—being sincerely interested in those with whom you communicate. Although it's unrealistic to assume you will become best friends with everyone you meet, Rogers suggests that you can work to develop an unselfish interest, or what he called an unconditional positive regard for others. That's hard to do. But the effort will be rewarded with a more positive communication climate.

Empathize Rather Than Remain Detached

Empathy is one of the hallmarks of supportive relationships. As you learned earlier, empathy is the ability to understand the feelings of others and to predict the emotional responses they will have to different situations. Being empathic is the essence of being other-oriented. The opposite of empathy is neutrality. To be neutral is to be indifferent or apathetic toward another. Even when you express anger or irritation toward another, you are investing some energy in the relationship.

As you've been learning throughout this book, research suggests that being other-oriented is one of the most important things we can do to be empathic and supportive. When requesting something from someone, a subtle way to be other-oriented is to soften your language by saying "*May I* borrow the car?" rather than "*I want to* borrow the car." The first option is perceived as more polite and sensitive (although there were mixed results as to whether the softer language achieved the desired outcome).[85] Amy Bippus determined that most people want to receive messages of empathy and

BEING Other-ORIENTED

Developing empathy is a quintessential skill of being other-oriented. Yet, if you empathize and then feel smug or self-righteous about being empathic, your efforts to relate to another person may appear manipulative. How can you empathize with another person without focusing on yourself or appearing self-serving?

sensitivity first during times of stress, followed by other messages associated with problem solving, relating, refraining from general negativity, and offering a different perspective. Providing other-oriented messages resulted in positive interpersonal outcomes like a more upbeat mood, feelings of empowerment, and more focused, calmer thoughts.[86]

Be Flexible Rather Than Rigid

Most people don't like someone who always seems certain that he or she is right. A "you're wrong, I'm right" attitude creates a defensive climate. This does not mean that you should voice no opinions and go through life blithely agreeing to everything anyone says. And it doesn't mean that there is *never* one answer that is right and others that are wrong. But instead of making rigid pronouncements, you can use phrases such as "I may be wrong, but it seems to me …" or "Here's one way to look at this problem." This manner of speaking gives your opinions a softer edge that allows room for others to express a point of view.

Present Yourself as Equal Rather Than Superior

You can antagonize others by letting them know that you view yourself as better than they are. You may be gifted and intelligent, but it's not necessary to announce it. And although some people have the responsibility and authority to manage others, "pulling rank" does not usually produce a cooperative climate. With phrases such as "Let's work on this together" or "We each have a valid perspective," you can avoid erecting walls of resentment and suspicion.

Also, avoid using abstract language or professional jargon to impress others. Keep your messages short and clear, and use informal language. When you communicate with someone from another culture, you may need to use an **elaborated code** to get your message across. This means that your messages will have to be more explicit, but they should not be condescending. For example, two of this book's authors vividly remember trying to explain to a French exchange student what a fire ant was. First, we had to translate *ant* into French, and then we had to provide scientific, descriptive, and narrative evidence to help the student understand how these tiny biting insects terrorize people in the southern part of the United States.

Underlying the goal of creating a supportive rather than a defensive communication climate is the importance of providing social and emotional support when communicating with others. A basic principle of all healthy interpersonal relationships is the importance of communicating positive, supportive messages that impart liking or affection.[87] Several researchers have documented that providing verbal messages of comfort and support, not surprisingly, enhances the quality of a relationship.[88] As a relationship develops over time and the communication partners gain more credibility and influence, messages of comfort play an even more important role in maintaining the quality of the interpersonal relationship.[89] As you will learn in Chapter 7, we use not only words of comfort, but also nonverbal expressions of comfort.

Communication researchers have documented the power of humor in helping to turn a tense, potentially conflict-producing confrontation into a more supportive, positive conversation. Research by communication scholar Amy Bippus found that most people report using humor to provide comfort to others.[90] Humor is also perceived as a productive way to help a distressed person better cope with problems and stress.

elaborated code
Conversation that uses many words and various ways of describing an idea or concept to communicate its meaning.

Recap

Using Supportive Communication and Avoiding Defensive Communication

Supportive Communication Is ...	Defensive Communication Is ...
Descriptive: Use "I" language that describes your own feelings and ideas.	**Evaluative:** Avoid using "you" language that attacks the worth of another person.
Problem Oriented: Aim communication at solving problems and generating multiple options.	**Controlling:** Don't attempt to get others to do *only* what you want them to do in order to control outcomes.
Spontaneously Genuine: Be honest and authentic rather than fake and phony.	**Strategically Manipulative:** Avoid planning your conversation in advance to get what you want. Don't develop a script to manipulate the other person and accomplish your goal.
Empathic: Be emotionally involved in the conversation; attempt to understand what your partner thinks and feels.	**Neutrally Detached:** Avoid being emotionally indifferent or creating the impression that you don't care how another person is feeling.
Flexible: Be open to receiving new information; demonstrate flexibility in the positions you take.	**Certain and Rigid:** Don't take a dogmatic or rigid position on issues; be willing to listen to others.
Equal: Adopt a communication style based on mutual respect, and assume each person has a right to express ideas and share information.	**Superior:** Avoid assuming an attitude or mindset that your ideas are better than those of others.

How to Have a Conversation

6.5   Use words to have a conversation with others.

You noticed an interesting person when you walked in the room. You'd like to get better acquainted. How do you start a conversation and keep it going? Or, if you're talking with someone you'd rather avoid, how do you end a conversation? In this chapter devoted to words, we've presented textbook principles and practices about how words work, but how do words work in the real world? How do you start, maintain, and, when appropriate, end a simple conversation with someone?

conversation

The spontaneous, interactive exchange of messages with another person.

Conversation is the spontaneous, interactive exchange of messages with another person. The root meaning of the word *conversation* is to move together. Although you can certainly have a conversation with yourself (which we called intrapersonal communication in Chapter 1), conversation is typically with one person but may include several people. It's a natural process of visiting with another person or persons and discussing a range of topics from the mundane to the intimately personal.

Yet for all of its normalness and naturalness, a simple conversation with someone is made more difficult because of the cosmic array of distractions that technology offers. In her book, *Alone Together*, Sherry Turkle discusses the impact technology has on our lives and how it's getting harder to have face-to-face conversations with others. She observes, "In today's workplace, young people who have grown up fearing conversation show up on the job wearing earphones … Big ones. Like pilots. They turn their desks into cockpits." She adds, "Walking through a college library or the campus of a high-tech start-up, one sees the same thing: we are together, but each of us is in our own bubble, furiously connected to keyboards and tiny touch screens."[91] Given the potential distraction of technology, as well as a tendency to mind our own business coupled with a reluctance to talk to others, how do we start and maintain a simple conversation with others?

Starting a Conversation

The easiest way to start a natural conversation is to make a comment about something that is happening now, in the present moment. Although commenting about the weather may not be terribly creative, it's a safe way to discuss what's happening in the present. Remarking about the music that may be playing, or observing something about the room or location, are also standard opening lines.

If you are interested in more than conversation with another person, do clever pick-up lines work? One study found that women preferred a more direct, flattering conversational approach from men, such as "I noticed you when I was sitting across the room. I'm Arnie, what's your name?" rather than cute, clever comments ("If you were a tropical fruit, you'd be a Fine-apple" or "Do you have a map? I'm getting lost in your eyes").[92] By definition, a conversation is spontaneous, so having a pre-planned standard opening question may fall flat. Let the situation, time, location, and other person organically help you determine how to start a conversation, rather than using a canned pick-up line.

Sustaining a Conversation

What do you say after "hello"? The two most important skills involved in keeping the conversational ball rolling are: (1) asking good questions and (2) listening. Think of questions as mental can openers designed to open up the conversation. A good question should be other-oriented and give a person the opportunity to respond comfortably. After you ask your question and pause, just listen. As we noted in the last chapter, listening is about focusing on and adapting to the other person rather than yourself. Stopping your own mental chatter, looking at the other person, and then focusing on your partner's words are keys to good conversational listening. Then follow up with additional astute questions that directly relate to the other person. Research has found that conversation partners highly value being other-oriented and adapting messages to others, whether in person or online.[93]

Early on in the conversation, the focus is usually on small talk—nonthreatening information about what the other person does and where they live. If your conversational partner also has listening skills and asks questions, you will not have to do all of the conversational work. We noted in Chapter 2 that there is a normal, natural rhythm to what we self-disclose to others; the key in conversation is to listen and ask questions, but don't ask for too much information too soon.

Asking open-ended questions is the most effective way to keep a conversation rolling along. Open-ended questions can't be answered with a simple "yes" or "no," but call for a longer response. "Have you lived here long?" or "Where are you from?" are closed-ended questions. You're likely to get a one-word answer that quickly places the conversational ball back in your court. But asking, "What do you like best about living in Austin?" or "Why did you pick Texas State?" gives the person a chance to elaborate (or not). Sherry Turkle thinks that because of technology, we are accustomed to editing our messages or retouching our personal images. Part of the fun of conversation is to be natural and not worry about trying to be perfect. She notes, "Human relationships are rich; they're messy and demanding. We have learned the habit of cleaning them up with technology."[94]

As the conversation unfolds, focus on the other person and adapt to him or her. This doesn't mean you should withhold information from your conversational partner. Revealing information about yourself is a way to keep the conversation going, but you want to ensure that you are not monopolizing the conversation. In fact, one study found that by asking each other a series of thirty-six increasingly personal questions, two strangers were more likely to become friends or in some cases, romantic partners. Here is a sample of some of the questions asked:[95]

- What would constitute a "perfect" day for you?
- When did you last sing to yourself? To someone else?
- For what in life do you feel most grateful?
- What do you value most in a friendship?
- Is there something that you've dreamed of doing for a long time? Why haven't you done it?
- What roles do love and affection play in your life?
- Complete this sentence: "I wish I had someone with whom I could share …"

- What, if anything, is too serious to be joked about?
- When did you last cry in front of another person? By yourself?

We don't recommend asking predetermined or canned questions. Conversation should flow spontaneously from one topic to another. These questions merely illustrate the kinds of questions that got people to open up and, in some cases, develop a relationship. This study concluded by having the conversational partners silently look at each other for four minutes. No, we're not suggesting that technique as standard practice. But taking the time to focus on the other person and to communicate your interest in his or her verbal and nonverbal messages can enhance the art of conversation.

How do you graciously end a conversation? Sometimes it can be useful to reference an obligation after making a positive statement such as, "I've really enjoyed our conversation, but I have an appointment I need to get to." After noting your inaccessibility, express positive regard for the other person by offering thanks or letting him or her know you enjoyed the talk. ("I enjoyed getting to know more about your hometown of Grain Valley and I hope we can visit again soon.") Summarizing the key ideas you both mentioned is also a natural way to end a conversation. Saying, "So it sounds like you really enjoy your new job and I'm glad your family is doing well" summarizes the conversation in a positive way. Nonverbal messages called leave-taking cues can also signal that the conversation is concluding. Nodding, smiling, and leaning slightly forward are nonverbal ways of signaling your positive regard for another person as you end the conversation.[96]

How to Apologize

6.6   Use words to offer an apology when appropriate.

apology

Explicit admission of an error, along with a request for forgiveness.

In this chapter, we've talked about the power of words and how communication sometimes can create problems and bruise a relationship. There are times, if we're honest with ourselves, when we aren't as other-oriented as we should be, and we may say and do things that we shouldn't. We're human; we make mistakes. Words, however, not only inflict pain but also have power to repair relational damage.

One of the ways to mend a relational rift when we have made a mistake is to offer an **apology**—to explicitly admit that we made an error and to ask the person we offended to forgive us. An apology helps us save face and can repair relational stress. One research team found that people who received an apology felt less anger, were less likely to be aggressive, and had a better overall impression of the offender.[97] In addition, research has found that when we apologize to someone, the person we initially offended has greater empathy toward us and is less likely to avoid us or seek revenge.[98] An apology can calm a turbulent relationship.

Communication researchers Janet Meyer and Kyra Rothenberg found that the seriousness of the offense and the quality of the relationship we have with another person determine whether we are likely to apologize as well as the kind of apology we should offer.[99] Committing a serious blunder or error is more likely to result in an apology than committing a mild offense—especially if we believe we've hurt someone. We're also more likely to apologize to someone if we feel guilty or embarrassed by something we've said or done.[100] And the more intimate we are with someone, the more likely we are to apologize.[101]

What kinds of apologies are most effective? One of the most effective ways to apologize is simply to honestly and sincerely admit that you were wrong. It's not enough just to say, "I'm sorry I hurt you." A true apology acknowledges that the offending individual was wrong. Thus, it's better to say it explicitly: "I was wrong." Assuming responsibility for the error and offering to do something to repair the damage are specific kinds of behaviors that enhance the effectiveness of an apology. Researchers Cynthia McPherson Frantz and Courtney Bennigson found that it may not be best to

An apology can help you save face when you have made a relationship blunder and can relieve tension between you and another person.

apologize immediately after you make a mistake; their results indicated that it may be better to wait a short time before apologizing.[102] Your apology will be perceived as more sincere and heartfelt if the other person believes you truly understand how your mistake hurt him or her and that you want to repair the damage. An apology given too quickly may be perceived as insincere—the offended person may think that you're just trying to quickly dismiss the error. Being perceived as sincerely remorseful is one of the keys to an effective apology.

The words we use can hurt others. We can also use words to repair the damage we have done by offering an apology expressing that we were wrong (not simply sorry), we are sincerely remorseful, we want to do something to repair the damage, and we understand how much we may have hurt our communication partner. The book of Proverbs says, "Words fitly spoken are like apples of gold in pictures of silver." A well-worded apology can help restore luster to a relationship that may have become tarnished.

> **BEING Other-ORIENTED**
> Words can hurt and heal. Offering an apology when you are wrong is a way to restore a relationship and reconcile with another person. Yet sometimes you will express your regret and apologize for something you did or said but the other person will not accept your apology. What are appropriate ways of responding to someone if your apology has been rejected?

How to Be Assertive

6.7 Use assertiveness skills appropriately and ethically.

At times, you run across people who are verbally aggressive, obnoxious, or worse—they may try to coerce or intimidate you into doing things you'd rather not do. Should the other-oriented person politely accept obnoxious verbal assaults? No—being other-oriented doesn't mean you should ignore such boorish behavior. One research team found that you are more likely to let an overly aggressive comment slide by unanswered if you were raised in a family in which aggressive comments were more common.[103] But regardless of how you were raised, consider using your verbal skills to be appropriately assertive. To be **assertive** is to make requests, ask for information, stand up for your rights, and generally pursue your own best interests without denying your partner's rights.

assertive
Able to pursue one's own best interests without denying a partner's rights.

Each individual has rights. You have the right to refuse a request from someone, the right to express your feelings as long as you don't trample on the feelings of others, and the right to have your needs met if they don't infringe on the rights of others. Assertive people let their communication partners know when a message or behavior infringes on their rights.

Some people confuse the terms *assertive* and *aggressive*. Being **aggressive** means pursuing your interests by denying the rights of others. Being appropriately assertive is being other-oriented; aggressiveness is exclusively self-oriented. Aggressive people blame, judge, and evaluate to get what they want. We'll expand on our discussion of aggressive behavior when we discuss relationship challenges in Chapter 11. Aggressive communicators use communication tactics that contribute to defensiveness, including such intimidating nonverbal cues as steely stares, a bombastic voice, and flailing gestures. Assertive people can ask for what they want without judging or evaluating their partners.

aggressive
Expressing one's interests while denying the rights of others by blaming, judging, and evaluating other people.

Sometimes it's challenging to respond appropriately when another person (someone who has not taken a course in interpersonal communication) comes at you with an inappropriately aggressive, argumentative, or defensive message, especially if that message takes you by surprise. But you do not have to be passive when you are on the receiving end of such messages. You can develop skill in asserting yourself by practicing five key behaviors.[104]

Describe

Describe how you view the situation. To assert your position, you first need to describe how you view the situation. You need to be assertive because the other person has not been other-oriented. For example, Doug is growing increasingly frustrated with Maria's tardiness for weekly staff meetings. He approaches the problem by first describing his observation: "I have noticed that you are usually fifteen minutes late to

Improving Your Communication Skills

How to Express Your Emotions to Others

Communication is enhanced if you can clearly express with well-chosen words or phrases the emotions you are feeling. The following list gives you several options for expressing your feelings in positive, neutral, or negative terms. Categorizing these terms as positive, neutral, or negative doesn't mean you should only use positive or neutral terms and avoid negative terms. What's important is that you select a word that accurately helps you communicate your emotions to others.

Positive		Neutral	Negative	
calm	joyful	amazed	afraid	helpless
cheerful	loving	ambivalent	alone	horrible
comfortable	optimistic	apathetic	angry	humiliated
confident	passionate	bashful	annoyed	hysterical
content	peaceful	bored	bitter	intimidated
delighted	playful	detached	confused	listless
ecstatic	pleased	hurried	defeated	mad
elated	refreshed	lukewarm	defensive	mean
enthusiastic	romantic	numb	depressed	miserable
excited	sexy	possessive	devastated	paranoid
flattered	tender	sentimental	disappointed	rebellious
free	warm	vulnerable	disgusted	regretful
friendly	willing		disturbed	resentful
glad	wonderful		empty	restless
grateful			exhausted	sad
happy			fearful	shocked
high			frustrated	suspicious
hopeful			furious	terrified
interested			guilty	ugly

To practice expressing your emotions, imagine yourself in each of the following situations, and use some of the words listed here to write a response for each situation. Describe your response with either a single word or a short phrase, such as "I feel angry," or express your feelings in terms of what you'd like to do, such as "I'd be so embarrassed I would sink through the floor" or "I would feel like leaving and never coming back to this house."

- You have several thousand dollars in credit card debt, and you get fired from your job.

- Your best friend, with whom you spend a lot of time, is moving to another country.

- You have just learned that your adored aunt has died and left you a $35,000 inheritance.

- You have brought your two-year-old son to a worship service, but he talks and runs around and will not sit still. Other worshippers are looking at you with disapproval.

- You arrive at your vacation hotel, only to discover that they do not have a reservation for you, and you do not have your room confirmation number.

Another skill to help you accurately and appropriately express your emotions is to use a **word picture**, a short statement or story that dramatizes an emotion you have experienced.

Word pictures can be used to clarify how you feel, to offer praise or correction, and to create greater intimacy. A key goal of a word picture is to communicate your feelings and emotions. One effective type of word picture is a *simile*. A simile, as you may remember from English class, is a comparison that uses the word *like* or *as*. Jeff told his family, "I feel like a worn-out punching bag—I've been pounded time and time again, and now I feel torn and scuffed. I need a few minutes of peace and quiet." His visual image helped communicate how exhausted he really felt. The best word pictures use an image to which the listener can relate. To practice your skill, try to develop word pictures to express in a powerful and memorable way the feelings you might have in the following situations.

- You just learned that a cherished family pet has died.

- You want to tell your friends how happy you feel about receiving an A in a difficult course.

- You've asked your sister not to leave empty milk cartons in the refrigerator, but you discover another empty carton in the refrigerator.

- Your family is planning a vacation but didn't ask you to be involved in the planning.

our weekly staff meetings." A key to communicating your assertive message is to monitor your nonverbal message, especially your voice. Avoid sarcasm or excessive vocal intensity. Calmly yet confidently describe the problem.

Recap

Assertiveness versus Aggressiveness

Assertiveness ...	Aggressiveness ...
Expresses your interests without denying the rights of others.	Expresses your interests and denies the rights of others.
Is other-oriented.	Is self-oriented.
Describes what you want.	Evaluates the other person.
Discloses your needs using "I" messages.	Discloses your needs using "you" messages.

#communicationandtechnology

Relating to Others Online

In response to the statement "I feel addicted to Facebook," over one-third of more than 2,850 students who responded to a survey indicated that they "agreed" or "strongly agreed." One survey respondent wrote "Facebook, I hate you!" in acknowledgement of the pervasive power it had over her life.[105] On the positive side, research suggests that it's important for us to connect online[106] and our Facebook friends are just as important to us in providing emotional support as our realspace friends.[107]

Will using the written word in our texts and posts to relate to others change the very nature of interpersonal relationships? Linguist Naomi Baron suggests the following consequences of our increased reliance on the written word:

- Informality: We will write more informally as we write more.
- Language Use: We will become increasingly uncertain about how we use words, so we'll make up our own rules and not worry about precise language rules or usage in our informal text messages. About 25% of texters have very poor spelling.[108]

- Writing Influences Talking: The way we use electronically mediated communication (EMC) will influence how we communicate face to face. We'll use more abbreviations.

- Word Control: Because we can often see who's texting, calling, or e-mailing us, we'll decide when, where, and even if we will receive messages. We will have what Baron calls greater "volume control" about the number of EMC words that reach us.

- Written Culture: We will increasingly become a "written culture" because of the power and importance of texting, using instant messaging, and other ways of sharing written words.

- More Relationships in Less Depth: We'll know more people but also know less information about them. In an editorial in *The New York Times*, columnist Robert Wright noted, "Twenty years ago I rarely spoke by phone to more than five people in a day. Now I often send e-mail to dozens of people a day. I have so many friends! Um, can you remind me of their names?..."[109] We know more people more shallowly.

- Moment-to-Moment Contact: Because we can be in touch with others in real time with our cell phones, text messages, and a variety of other tools, we will be able to witness what others experience in real time.

- Deception: People who lie online tend to use more words than non-liars.[110] Liars also used more sensory-based words such as *seeing, touching,* and *smelling* than those telling the truth. Liars also used fewer self-oriented words (*I, me, my*) but more words about the other person (*you*).

Disclose

Disclose your feelings. After describing the situation from your perspective, let the other person know how you feel.[111] Disclosing your feelings will help to build empathy and avoid lengthy harangues about the other person's unjust treatment. "I feel disconfirmed when you don't take our weekly meetings seriously," continues Doug as he asserts his desire for Maria to be on time to the meeting. Note that Doug does not talk about how others are feeling ("Every member of our group is tired of your coming in late"); he describes how *he* feels.

Identify Effects

Identify the effects of the behavior. Next, you can identify the effects of the other person's behavior on you or others. "When you are late, it disrupts our meeting," says Doug.

word picture

Short statement or story that illustrates or describes an emotion; word pictures often use a simile (a comparison using the word like or as) to clarify the image.

Be Silent

Be silent and wait. After taking the first three steps, simply wait for a response. Some people find this step hard. Again, be sure to monitor your nonverbal cues. Make sure your facial expression does not contradict your verbal message. Delivering an assertive message with a broad grin might create a double bind for your listener, who may not be sure what the primary message is—the verbal one or the nonverbal one.

Paraphrase

Paraphrase content and feelings. After the other person responds, paraphrase both the content and the feelings of the message. Suppose Maria says, "Oh, I'm sorry. I didn't realize I was creating a problem. I have another meeting that usually goes overtime. It's difficult for me to arrive at the start of our meeting on time." Doug could respond, "So the key problem is a time conflict with another meeting. It must make you feel frustrated to try to do two things at once."

If the other person is evasive, unresponsive, or aggressive, you'll need to cycle through the steps again: Clearly describe what the other person is doing that is not acceptable; disclose how you feel; identify the effects; wait; then paraphrase and clarify as needed. A key goal of making an assertive response is to seek an empathic connection between you and your partner. Paraphrasing feelings is a way of ensuring that both parties connect.

If you tend to withdraw from conflict, how can you become assertive? Visualizing can help. Think of a past situation in which you wished you had been more assertive and then mentally replay the situation, imagining what you might have said. Also practice verbalizing assertive statements. When you are able to be appropriately assertive, consciously congratulate yourself for sticking up for your rights.

Recap

How to Assert Yourself

Step	Example
1. Describe.	"I see you haven't completed the report yet."
2. Disclose.	"I feel disrespected when work I ask you to do is not a priority for you."
3. Identify effects.	"Without that report, our team will not achieve our goal."
4. Wait.	Be silent, and wait for a response.
5. Use active listening skills:	
Question.	"Do you understand how I feel?"
Paraphrase content.	"So you were not aware the report was late."
Paraphrase feelings.	"Perhaps you feel embarrassed."

Applying an Other-Orientation

to Enhancing Your Verbal Skills

The key to shared understanding is a focus on the needs, goals, and mindset of your communication partner. Throughout this chapter, we have emphasized how to develop an other-oriented approach when communicating verbally. In focusing on others, keep the following principles in mind.

Meanings Are in People, Not in Words. Your communication partner creates meaning based on his or her own experiences. Don't assume that other people will always (or even usually) understand what you mean. Words are symbols and the potential for misunderstanding them is high. Meaning is fragile, so handle with care.

Words Have Power to Influence Others. Words have power to determine how people view the world. They also affect thoughts and behaviors. Be mindful of the potency of words for influencing how others react. Words can trigger wars and negotiate peace; they affect how others react to us.

Speak to Others as They Would Like to Be Spoken to. It's not enough to consider how you would react to words and phrases you use; you need to be tuned in to the kinds of messages another person might prefer. You may like "straight talk" and short messages that are to the point. Your communication partner may prefer a softer tone and a more positive, supportive message.

We're not suggesting that you should be a verbal chameleon and avoid asserting your own ideas and positions. We are suggesting that if you want to be heard and understood, thinking how others will interpret your message can enhance the communication process.

STUDY GUIDE
Review, Apply, and Assess

How Words Work

Objective 6.1   Describe how words create meaning.

Key Terms

symbol
referent
thought
denotative meaning

connotative meaning
onomatopoeia
symbolic interaction theory

Thinking Critically

Have you been in a situation in which someone used a familiar word but with a different meaning than you were accustomed to? How did you resolve the misunderstanding? Provide examples.

Assessing Your Skills

Make a list of ten to fifteen familiar, everyday words (such as *home, teacher,* or *communication*); write both their denotative and connotative meanings. Working in small groups, share your words with classmates and ask them to write down what the words mean to them. (Have them do the same with their own list of words.) Compare the connotative meanings. Are there differences in what a word means to different people? Is there a wide range of meanings? Can these differences be attributed to culture, gender, or differences in background and past experiences?

The Power of Words

Objective 6.2   Identify how words influence our perceptions, thoughts, actions, culture, and relationships.

Key Terms

linguistic determinism
linguistic relativity
Sapir–Whorf hypothesis

worldview
profanity
euphemism

Thinking Critically

Do you think the use of profanity in everyday life is increasing? Have new communication technologies, including texting, blogging, Skyping, instant messaging, tweeting, and the like, contributed to this increase? Do mass media contribute to the increase? Can you think of examples? Do you think the media have relaxed their standards for allowing profanity? Explain.

Assessing Your Skills

Collect print ads that feature catchy slogans or phrases. Make a list of other mass media ads (TV, radio, Internet, billboards, etc.) whose words or phrases grab your attention. Share the ads with your classmates and analyze as a group what makes the words or phrases powerful or memorable. Do the words influence your actions—for example, persuading you to do something or to buy a particular product? Explain.

How to Manage Misunderstandings

Objective 6.3   Identify and describe word barriers that lead to misunderstandings.

Key Terms

bypassing
malapropism
restricted code
jargon
allness

indexing
static evaluation
polarization
hate speech

Thinking Critically

Is it appropriate to correct someone when he or she uses sexist language or makes a stereotypical remark about someone's race, gender, or sexual orientation? What if that person is your boss or your teacher? Explain your answer.

Assessing Your Skills

1. Rephrase the following statements, using the skill of indexing:
   a. All politicians want power and control over others.
   b. All teachers are underpaid.
   c. All Texans like to brag about how great their state is.
2. In small groups, brainstorm lists of "restricted code" words and/or jargon, including "textspeak" (abbreviations used in IMing and texting). Come up with as many words as you can. Share the lists each group creates. Are the lists similar? Did classmates introduce you to words you hadn't heard before? Do the "restricted codes" seem to suggest a particular group or culture? What do people in these subgroups have in common—for example, age, gender, or ethnicity?

How to Use Words of Support

Objective 6.4   Use words to provide support and comfort, and to avoid defensiveness.

Key Terms

extended "I" language
elaborated code

Thinking Critically

Is it appropriate to mask your true feelings of anger and irritation with someone by using supportive statements or confirming statements when what you really want to do is tell the person off in no uncertain terms? Why or why not?

Assessing Your Skills

Participate in a role-play in which you are seeking to return an item to the store and you don't have a receipt. The "customer service" representative is not well trained and is illustrating several of the defensive communication behaviors described earlier in this chapter. Role-play trying to respond in supportive ways when the representative responds defensively.

How to Have a Conversation

Objective 6.5   Use words to have a conversation with others.

Key Terms

conversation

Thinking Critically

You have noticed Alex in your communication class and want to get to know him better. You think he is a communication major but you are not certain. You also see him talking with several people on the football team, so you think he may be interested in sports. What are questions you could ask Alex to start a conversation?

Assessing Your Skills

On a scale of 1 to 10 how would you rate your skills in each of the following stages of meeting and conversing with someone whom you don't know but would like to get to know better?

___Starting a conversation
___Sustaining a conversation
___Ending a conversation

If you rated yourself below "8" on these three phases of holding a conversation, how might you improve your skills? What are strategies you could use to be a better conversationalist?

How to Apologize

Objective 6.6   Use words to offer an apology when appropriate.

Key Terms

apology

Thinking Critically

Brent was late for dinner—again. He knew he should have called to tell his partner Cary that he was going to be late, but he didn't. What advice would you give Brent in developing an effective and appropriate apology?

Assessing Your Skills

Think of a situation in which you should have offered an apology but did not. Write an appropriate apology to that person that you now wish you had offered. How would the other person respond? Is it too late to offer an apology now?

How to Be Assertive

Objective 6.7   Use assertiveness skills appropriately and ethically.

Key Terms

assertive
aggressive
word picture

Thinking Critically

You've always had a difficult time expressing your feelings and you actively think, "I don't want to hurt someone's feelings by telling them what I really think." Your boss has suggested that you need to be more honest in expressing how you feel. What strategies or suggestions would help you be more assertive?

Assessing Your Skills

Working with a partner, describe a situation in which you could have been more assertive. Ask your partner to assume the role of the person toward whom you should have been more assertive. Now replay the situation, using the assertiveness skills described in the chapter. Ask your classmates to observe the role-play and provide feedback, using the following checklist. When you have finished asserting your point of view, reverse roles with your partner.

_____ Clearly describes the problem
_____ Effectively discloses how he or she felt
_____ Clearly describes the effects of the behavior
_____ Pauses or waits after describing the effects
_____ Uses effective questions to promote understanding
_____ Accurately paraphrases content
_____ Accurately paraphrases feelings
_____ Has good eye contact
_____ Leans forward while speaking
_____ Has an open body posture
_____ Has appropriate voice tone and quality

Chapter 7
Nonverbal Communication Skills

"What you are speaks so loudly that I cannot hear what you say."

Ralph Waldo Emerson

 ## Learning Objectives

7.1 Explain why nonverbal communication is an important area of study.

7.2 Identify and describe eight nonverbal communication codes.

7.3 Enhance your skill in interpreting nonverbal messages.

7.4 Enhance your skill in expressing nonverbal messages.

nonverbal communication

Behavior other than written or spoken language that creates meaning for someone.

You are being watched. Whether it's an officer of the Transportation Safety Administration carefully scrutinizing your facial expression when you go through airport security, or just a casual observer glancing your way as you walk around campus, people are watching you.[1] People watch you, and you watch other people. You can glean a vast amount of information about others from just their **nonverbal communication**, behavior other than written or spoken language that creates meaning.

Nonverbal communication also affects the quality of your interpersonal relationships. Interpreting others' unspoken messages and appropriately expressing your own feelings through nonverbal communication are key components of being other-oriented. To help you become more skilled at both expressing and interpreting nonverbal messages, we'll discuss why nonverbal communication is important in establishing interpersonal relationships. After we discuss several nonverbal communication codes, we'll offer tips that will help you more accurately interpret nonverbal communication.

Identifying the Importance of Nonverbal Communication

7.1   **Explain why nonverbal communication is an important area of study.**

Wherever You Go, There You Are is the title of a popular book about Zen meditation.[2] But the title could easily refer to nonverbal communication: Wherever you go, nonverbal communication is there. Nonverbal communication is an ever-present form of human expression. If you are alive, chances are that people are making inferences about you based on your nonverbal behavior. If you spend a lot of time on Facebook or text messaging, you may think nonverbal messages aren't really important as you make e-connections with others. But research has found that you provide many nonverbal messages in the Instagram photos and YouTube videos you post and other, more subtle nonverbal cues in the way you express yourself in your online and text messages.[3]

Are your people-watching guesses about others accurate? Sometimes yes, and sometimes no. This chapter is designed to help you increase your accuracy in evaluating the nonverbal messages of others. And just as you may inaccurately interpret others' nonverbal messages, so may other people misjudge your nonverbal cues. Because much of our nonverbal communication behavior is unconscious, most of us have only a limited awareness or understanding of it. Let's look at the multiple reasons nonverbal communication is so important in the total communication process.

Nonverbal Messages Are the Primary Way We Communicate Our Feelings and Attitudes

Nonverbal communication is a primary source of relationship cues. A person's tone of voice, eye contact, facial expressions, posture, movement, general appearance, use of personal space, manipulation of the communication environment, and a host of other nonverbal clues reveal how that person feels about others.

Psychologist Albert Mehrabian concluded that as little as 7 percent of the *emotional meaning* of a message is communicated through explicit verbal channels.[4] The most significant source of emotional communication is the face—according to Mehrabian's study, it channels as much as 55 percent of our meaning. Vocal cues such as volume, pitch, and intensity communicate another 38 percent of our emotional meaning. In all, we communicate approximately 93 percent of the emotional meaning of our messages nonverbally. Although these percentages do not apply to every communication situation, the results of Mehrabian's investigation do illustrate the potential power of nonverbal cues in communicating emotion.[5] Researchers are continuing to find new ways to measure the impact and power of nonverbal messages in the communication of emotions.[6]

ZITS © 2006 Zits Partnership. Dist. by King Features Syndicate.

Nonverbal Messages Are Usually More Believable Than Verbal Messages

"Honey, do you love me?" asks Pat.

"OF COURSE I LOVE YOU! HAVEN'T I ALWAYS TOLD YOU THAT I LOVE YOU? I LOVE YOU!" shouts Jill, keeping her eyes glued to her iPad.

Pat will probably not be totally reassured by Jill's pledge of affection. The contradiction between her spoken message of love and her nonverbal message of irritation and lack of interest will leave Pat wondering about Jill's true feelings.

Actions speak louder than words. This cliché became a cliché because nonverbal communication is more believable than verbal communication. Nonverbal messages are more difficult to fake. One research team concluded that people from the United States and Canada use the following cues, listed in order from most to least important, to help them discern when a person is lying.[7]

- Greater time lag in response to a question
- Reduced eye contact
- Increased shifts in posture
- Unfilled pauses
- Less smiling
- Slower speech
- Higher pitch in voice
- More deliberate pronunciation and articulation of words

Because it is difficult to manipulate an array of nonverbal cues, a skilled other-oriented observer can see when a person's true feelings leak out. Social psychologists Paul Ekman and Wallace Friesen have identified the face, hands, and feet as key sources of nonverbal cues. Are you aware of what your fingers and toes are doing as you read this book? Even if you become expert at masking and manipulating your face, you may first signal lack of interest or boredom with another person by finger wiggling or toe wagging. Or you may twiddle a pen or pencil. When you become emotionally aroused, the pupils of your eyes dilate, and you may blush, sweat, or change breathing patterns.[8] Lie detectors (polygraphs) rely on these unconscious clues. A polygraph measures a person's heart and breathing rate, as well as the electrical resistance of the skin (called *galvanic skin response*), to determine whether he or she is giving truthful verbal responses.

BEING Other-ORIENTED

Although it may be tempting to interpret someone's intentions from a single nonverbal behavior, be cautious of taking a single cue out of context. Can you think of a situation in which someone misinterpreted your nonverbal behavior? What can you do to increase the accuracy of your own observations?

Nonverbal Messages Work with Verbal Messages to Create Meaning

Although we rely heavily on nonverbal messages, especially to express and interpret emotions, they do not operate independently of spoken messages. Instead, verbal and nonverbal cues work together in two primary ways to help us make sense of others' messages: They help us manage the verbal message, and they augment the emotional meaning of what we say.

1. *Nonverbal cues help us manage verbal message.* Specifically, our nonverbal cues can substitute for verbal messages, as well as repeat, contradict, or regulate what we say. An extended thumb signals that a hitchhiker would like a ride. A circle formed by the thumb and index finger can either signal that everything is A-OK or convey an obscene message. When someone asks, "Which way did he go?" you can silently point to the back door. In these instances, you are substituting nonverbal cues for a verbal message.

   You can also use nonverbal cues to repeat or reinforce your words. "Where is the personnel department?" asks a job applicant.

   "Three flights up. Take the elevator," says the security guard, pointing to the elevator. The guard's pointing gesture repeats her verbal instruction and clarifies the message.

   We also use nonverbal cues to regulate our participation in verbal exchanges. In most informal conversations, it is not appropriate or necessary to signal your desire to speak by raising your hand. Yet somehow you are able to signal to others when you'd like to speak and when you'd rather not talk. How does this happen? You use eye contact, raised eyebrows, an open mouth, or perhaps a subtle, single raised index finger to signal that you would like to make a point. If your colleagues do not see these signals, especially the eye contact, they may think you are not interested in talking.[9]

2. *Nonverbal cues bolster the emotional meaning of verbal messages.* Our unspoken cues accent and complement verbal messages to increase or decrease the emotional impact of what we say. "Unless we vote to increase our tax base," bellows Mr. Coddlington, "we will not have enough classroom space to educate our children." While delivering his impassioned plea to the school board, Mr. Coddlington also loudly slaps the lectern to accent his message and reinforce its intensity. A scolding mother's wagging finger and an angry supervisor's raised voice are other nonverbal cues that augment verbal messages.

   Simultaneous and complementary verbal and nonverbal messages can also help to color the emotion we express or the attitude we convey. The length of a hug while you tell your son you are proud of him provides additional information about the intensity of your pride. The firmness of your handshake when you greet a job interviewer can confirm your verbal claim that you are eager for employment.

Nonverbal Messages Help People Respond and Adapt to Others

You sense that your best friend is upset. Even though she doesn't tell you she's angry, you sense her mood by observing her grimacing facial expression and lack of direct eye contact with you. To help lighten the mood, you tell a joke. Many times every day, you "read" the nonverbal cues of others, even before they utter a word, to gain a clue about what

Portrait artists pay close attention to nonverbal cues such as posture, facial expression, and gesture to capture their subjects' personalities. What do the nonverbal cues reveal about the woman in this Vincent van Gogh painting, *Portrait of Mme Ginoux (L'Arlésienne)*?

to say or how to react. Interpreting others' nonverbal messages helps us appropriately adapt our communication as we interact with them.

Interaction adaptation theory describes how people adapt to the communication behavior of others.[10] The theory suggests that we respond not only to what people say, but also to their nonverbal expressions to help us navigate through our interpersonal conversations each day.[11] If, for example, your friend leans forward to tell a story, you may lean forward to listen. Or if during a meeting you sit with folded arms, unconvinced of what you are hearing, you may look around the conference table and find others with similarly folded arms. As if we were part of an intricate dance, when we communicate, we relate to others by responding to their movements, eye contact, gestures, and other nonverbal cues.

Interactional synchrony is the process of mimicking or mirroring someone's communication behavior. Sometimes, we may find ourselves consciously gesturing in synch with someone's vocal pattern. At other times, you may not be aware that when your friend folds her arms while talking with you, you also fold your arms across your chest in a similar way. One researcher found that people evaluate such synchrony as positive; somewhat synchronized behavior (but not so synchronized that it feels as though someone is purposefully imitating you) communicates partners' mutual interest and positive regard.[12] Being nonverbally in synch with someone helps to establish rapport with another person—at least as long as it's not exaggerated or too overt.

interaction adaptation theory
Theory suggesting that people interact with others by adapting to their communication behaviors.

interactional synchrony
Mirroring of each other's nonverbal behavior by communication partners.

Nonverbal Messages Play a Major Role in Interpersonal Relationships

As you learned in Chapter 1, because of the ubiquitous nature of nonverbal communication, you cannot *not* communicate; psychologist Raymond Birdwhistell suggests that as much as 65 percent of the social, or relational, meaning in messages is based on nonverbal communication.[13] Of course, the meaning that others interpret from your behavior may not be the one you intended, and the inferences they draw based on nonverbal information may be right or wrong.

You learned in Chapter 3 that people begin making judgments about strangers just a fraction of a second after meeting them, based on nonverbal information. Within the first four minutes of interaction, you scope out the other person and draw conclusions about him or her.[14] Another research team found that you may decide whether a date is going to be pleasant or dull within the first thirty seconds of meeting, before he or she has had time to utter more than "Hello."[15] And just as we do in face-to-face relationships, we rely on nonverbal cues from photos posted on Facebook or Instagram to make inferences about others online. Research also suggests that people who share more photos on social networks such as Facebook are more likely to spend more time maintaining and developing relationships.[16] Nonverbal cues, whether online or offline, affect first impressions.

Nonverbal expressions of support also are important when providing comforting messages to others during times of stress and anxiety. Communication researchers Susanne Jones and Laura Guerrero found that being nonverbally expressive and supportive is important in helping people cope with stress.[17] Providing empathic, supportive facial expressions and vocal cues, hugs, and positive touch helps to reduce stress and enhance a person's overall well-being.

You've heard the directive, "Don't drink and drive." The results of one study suggest you could add, "Don't drink and date." You may not be at your nonverbal best when intoxicated. Researchers found that when under the influence of alcohol you are more likely to express agitation, anxiety, and negativity toward others.[18] In general, drinkers were less pro-relational and less positive during conversations. In addition, when intoxicated, you are likely to smile less and have less animated facial expressions.

BEING Other-ORIENTED
The most powerful way to let someone know you care may be to express your support nonverbally rather than verbally. Think of a close friend or a family member. What nonverbal behaviors would best communicate support and empathy to that person?

Nonverbal cues are important not only when people initiate relationships, but also as they maintain and develop mature relationships with others. In fact, the more intimate the relationship, the more people use and understand the nonverbal cues of their partners.

Long-married couples spend less time verbalizing their feelings and emotions to each other than they did when they were first dating; each learns how to interpret the other's subtle nonverbal cues.[19] The researchers who made that observation also found that the more satisfied a person was with his or her marriage, the more accurately he or she was able to interpret the nonverbal emotional expression of the partner.[20] The ability to *express* an emotion was not found to be related to the quality of the marriage, but the ability to accurately *interpret* an emotional expression was better in marriages that were more satisfying to the couple. In addition, a happily married spouse was less likely to assume that a negative emotional expression was specifically directed toward him or her. If your spouse is silent during dinner, you may know that her day was a tough one and you should give her a wide berth. And if, when you put on your new Kelly green pants, your husband grimaces as he asks, "New pants?" you may understand that he does not love them. In fact, all of us are more likely to use nonverbal cues to convey negative messages than to explicitly announce our dislike of something or someone. People also use nonverbal cues to signal changes in the level of satisfaction with a relationship.[21] When we want to cool things off, we may start using a less vibrant tone of voice and cut back on eye contact and physical contact with our partner.

turning point

Specific event or interaction associated with a positive or negative change in a relationship.

Researchers have found that nonverbal behaviors signal turning points in relationships. A **turning point** occurs when our relationship becomes closer or when the relationship may be cooling and less intimate because of something someone said or did. Harsh vocal cues, not surprisingly, were indicative of a negative judgment of what may be happening in the relationship. In contrast, increased touching predicted a more positive relational turning point. Increased eye contact also corresponded with a positive change in how a relationship was perceived.[22] As this research suggests: *You don't have to say it to say it.*

Understanding Nonverbal Communication Codes

7.2   Identify and describe eight nonverbal communication codes.

Here, we will look at the categories of nonverbal information that researchers have studied: movement and gestures, eye contact, facial expressions, vocal cues, use of space and territory, touch, and personal appearance. Although we will concentrate on the codes that fall within these categories in mainstream Western culture, we will also look at codes for other cultures and subcultures.

Body Movement and Posture

In 1774, when English explorer Captain James Cook arrived in the New Hebrides, he didn't speak the language of the natives. His only way of communicating was sign language. Through gestures, pointing, and hand waving, he established contact with the natives. People have used gestures to communicate since ancient times—especially to bridge cultural and language differences. The first recorded use of sign language to communicate is found in Xenophon's *The March Up Country,* in which he describes unspoken gestures used to help the Greeks cross Asia Minor around 400 BCE. Even when we do speak the same language as others, we use gestures to help us make our point.[23]

kinesics

Study of human movement and gesture.

Kinesics is the study of human movement and gesture. Francis Bacon once noted, "As the tongue speaketh to the ear, so the hand speaketh to the eye." People have long recognized that movement and gestures provide valuable information to others.

Various scholars and researchers have proposed paradigms for analyzing and coding these movements and gestures, just as grammarians have codified spoken or written language.[24]

One paradigm identifies four stages of "quasi-courtship behavior" that describes how you may signal your interest in someone.[25]

Stage One: *Courtship readiness.* When you are initially attracted to someone, you may suck in your stomach, tense your muscles, and stand up straight.

Stage Two: *Preening behaviors:* You actively enhance your appearance by combing your hair, applying makeup, straightening your tie, pulling up your socks, and double-checking your appearance in the mirror.

Stage Three: *Positional cues:* These behaviors involve using your posture and body orientation to ensure that you will be seen and noticed by others.

Stage Four: *Appeals to invitation:* Finally, more explicit efforts to express interest involve moving closer to someone, exposing skin, displaying an open body position (uncrossed arms and legs), and using direct eye contact to signal availability and interest.

One researcher found fifty-two specific gestures and nonverbal behaviors that women use to signal an interest in men. Among the top unspoken flirting cues were smiling, surveying a crowded room with the eyes, and moving closer to the person of interest.[26] Subjects in another study reported that both men and women were aware of using all of these specific techniques to promote an intimate relationship. We use these same nonverbal behaviors to express our interest in others even when we have no intention of developing a sexual relationship. People use these quasi-courtship behaviors to some extent in almost any situation in which they want to gain favorable attention from another. Albert Mehrabian identified the most common nonverbal cues used to communicate liking.[27] In a US population sample, these nonverbal cues included an open body and arm position, a forward lean, and a relaxed posture.

Another team of researchers focused on nonverbal behaviors that prompt people to label someone as warm and friendly, or cold and distant.[28] The team found that "warm" people face their communication partners directly, smile more, make more direct eye contact, fidget less, and generally make fewer unnecessary hand movements. "Cold" people make less eye contact, smile less, fidget more, and turn away from their partners.

Developing a paradigm to classify movement and gestures according to their function, Ekman and Friesen identified five categories: emblems, illustrators, affect displays, regulators, and adaptors.[29]

EMBLEMS **Emblems** are nonverbal cues that have specific, generally understood meanings in a given culture and may actually substitute for a word or phrase. When you are busy typing a report that is due tomorrow and your young son bounces in to ask for permission to buy a new computer game, you turn to him and hold up an open palm to indicate your desire for uninterrupted quiet. You want your children to stop talking in the library, so you put an index finger up to your pursed lips.

emblems

Nonverbal cues that have specific, generally understood meanings in a given culture and may substitute for a word or phrase.

ILLUSTRATORS **Illustrators** are nonverbal behaviors that either contradict, accent, or complement a verbal message. Slamming a book closed while announcing, "I don't want to read this anymore" or pounding a lectern while proclaiming, "This point is important!" are two examples of nonverbal behaviors that illustrate the verbal message. Typically, English speakers use nonverbal illustrators at the beginning of clauses or phrases.[30] TV newscasters, for example, sometimes either nod or turn a page to signal that they are moving to a new story or topic. You probably even use illustrators when you talk on the phone, although probably not as many as you use in face-to-face conversation.[31]

illustrators

Nonverbal behaviors that accompany a verbal message and either contradict, accent, or complement it.

AFFECT DISPLAYS Nonverbal movements and postures used to communicate emotion are called **affect displays**. As early as 1872, when Charles Darwin systematically

affect displays

Nonverbal behaviors that communicate emotions.

studied the expression of emotion in both humans and animals,[32] it was recognized that nonverbal cues are the primary ways to communicate emotion. Facial expressions, vocal cues, posture, and gestures convey the intensity of your emotions.[33] If you are happy, for example, your face will telegraph your joy to others. The intensity of your hand movements, the openness of your posture, and the speed with which you move will tell others *how* happy you are. Similarly, if you feel depressed, your face will probably reveal your sadness or dejection, while your slumped shoulders and lowered head will indicate the intensity of your despair. When you are feeling friendly, you use a soft tone of voice, an open smile, and a relaxed posture.[34] When you feel neutral about an issue, you signal it by putting little or no expression on your face or in your voice. When you feel hostile, you use a harsh voice, frown with your teeth showing, and keep your posture tense and rigid.

regulators

Nonverbal messages that help to control the interaction or flow of communication between two people.

REGULATORS   **Regulators** control the interaction or flow of communication between themselves and another person. When you are eager to respond to a message, you make eye contact, raise your eyebrows, open your mouth, raise an index finger, and lean forward slightly. In a classroom, you may raise your hand to overtly signal that you want to talk. When you do not want to be part of the conversation, you do the opposite: avert your eyes, close your mouth, cross your arms, and lean back in your seat or away from the verbal action in an attempt to stay out of the conversation.

adaptors

Nonverbal behaviors that satisfy a personal need and help a person adapt or respond to the immediate situation.

ADAPTORS   **Adaptors** are nonverbal behaviors that help you satisfy a personal need and adapt to the immediate situation. When you adjust your glasses, scratch a mosquito bite, or comb your hair, you use movement to help manage your personal needs and adapt to your surroundings—and you're communicating something about yourself to whoever may be present. Frequent self adaptors, such as touching your cheek, may signal increased nervousness or self consciousness.

Understanding these five categories of nonverbal behavior and being aware of how you use them can give you a new and more precise way to think about your own behavior. For example, it's good practice to be aware of whether your nonverbal behavior contradicts or supports what you say. Monitoring your use of illustrators can help you determine whether you are sending mixed signals to others. Be aware of your affect display. Knowing that your face and voice communicate emotion and that your posture and gestures indicate the intensity of your feelings can help you understand how others make inferences about your feelings and attitudes.

Since nonverbal cues are ambiguous, it may not be a good idea to rely on them solely to achieve a specific objective. But as you have seen, people are more likely to respond in predictable ways if you use behaviors they can recognize and interpret easily.

Recap

Categories of Movement and Gestures

Category	Definition	Example
Emblems	Behaviors that have specific, generally understood meaning within a given culture	Raising a hitchhiking thumb
Illustrators	Cues that accompany verbal messages and add meaning to the message	Pounding the lectern to emphasize a point
Affect displays	Expressions of emotion	Hugging someone to express love
Regulators	Cues that control and manage the flow of communication between two people	Looking at someone when you wish to speak
Adaptors	Behaviors that help you adapt to your environment	Scratching; combing your hair

Eye Contact

Your decision to look at someone or to avert your gaze has an enormous impact on your relationship with that person.[35] Researcher Adam Kendon has identified four functions of eye contact in interpersonal interactions.[36]

- **Cognitive function.** Eye contact provides clues to thinking patterns. For example, if your partner breaks eye contact after you ask him or her a question, you may conclude that he or she is probably thinking of something to say.
- **Monitoring function.** You look at others to observe and assess their behavior. You receive a major portion of information through your eyes. You look at others to determine whether they like what you are saying.
- **Regulatory function.** Eye contact regulates whom you are likely to talk with. When you look at someone, it's like you're inviting that person to speak to you. Looking away often means you don't want to communicate with that person. For example, when standing in a group at a crowded bakery, you fix your eyes on the clerk to signal, "My turn next. Please wait on me."
- **Expressive function.** Finally, the area around your eyes provides important information about the emotions you display. You may cry, blink, and widen or narrow your gaze to express your feelings, which is why the eyes have been called the "window to the soul."

When are you most likely to establish eye contact with another person? Researchers have found that you are likely to make eye contact if you like or love the other person, are listening rather than talking, are discussing pleasant topics, are an extrovert, have a big need to be liked, are trying to dominate the conversation, are interested in what your partner may say or do, or have nothing else especially interesting to look at.[37] Increased eye contact with a spouse is linked to increased satisfaction with the relationship.[38]

When people establish eye contact with others, it may seem like their gaze is constant. Yet research suggests that people actually spend the majority of their time looking somewhere other than the person's eyes. One research team found that people focus on something else, including their partner's mouth, 57 percent of the time.[39] It is not surprising, then, that facial expressions are another rich source of information in your communication with others.

Facial Expression

The city council of Palo Alto, California, may well have the distinction of being the first legislative body to try to regulate facial expression. They proposed a code of conduct banning facial expressions that show "disagreement or disgust."[40] The controversy generated by the proposal attests to the importance of facial expressions in the communication process. So, too, does our reliance on *emoticons* or *emojis* (🙄 😡 😂) to communicate facial expression via e-mail or text messages. The face is the primary exhibit gallery for emotional displays, even when you are not aware of your facial expression.

How readily we smile holds important information about how we relate to others. Do you smile when you're on the phone? Research has found that you smile less if a person approaches you when you are busy talking to someone else on the phone.[41] In this case, you are more focused on your phone partner than on the person in front of you. Smiling or lack of smiling can also reveal cues about sexual bias. One study found that men who have more hostile attitudes toward women smile less when interacting with women; men who had more benevolent and patronizing tendencies smiled more.[42] This doesn't mean you can make clear-cut assumptions about men's attitudes toward women based on whether men smile or not; smiling is just one of many cues that provide information about the nature of a relationship.

To interpret a partner's facial expressions accurately, you need to put your other-orientation skills to work, focusing on what the other person may be thinking or feeling. It helps if you know the person well, can see his or her whole face, have plenty of time to observe his or her facial expressions, and understand the situation that prompted the emotion.[43] There is also evidence that you can more accurately decode someone's facial and emotional expressions if he or she comes from the same racial or ethnic background as you do.[44] Generally speaking, the more characteristics you have in common with another person, the greater the chance that you will accurately interpret that person's facial expression. In addition to having a similar background, you also need to know the cues for "reading" facial expressions. One study found that based on someone's facial expression, people are able to make snap judgments about a person's sexual orientation with more than chance accuracy; however, researchers aren't sure what precisely allowed people to make that conclusion.[45]

Your face is versatile. According to Ekman and Friesen, it is capable of producing over 250,000 different expressions.[46] Research suggests that women have greater variety in their emotional expressions and spend more time smiling than men.[47] But all facial expressions can be grouped in six primary emotional categories; the following list describes the changes that occur on your face for each one.[48]

Surprise:	Wide-open eyes; raised and wrinkled brow; open mouth
Fear:	Open mouth; tense skin under the eyes; wrinkles in the center of the forehead
Disgust:	Raised or curled upper lip; wrinkled nose; raised cheeks; lowered brow; lowered upper eyelid
Anger:	Tensed lower eyelid; either pursed lips or open mouth; lowered and wrinkled brow; staring eyes
Happiness:	Smiling; mouth may be open or closed; raised cheeks; wrinkles around lower eyelids
Sadness:	Lip may tremble; corners of the lips turn downward; corners of the upper eyelid may be raised

BEING Other-ORIENTED

The face is the single most important source of information about a specific emotion someone may be expressing. Compare a situation in which you accurately decoded someone's emotion based on his or her facial expression and a situation in which your inference was inaccurate. Which factors increase the accuracy of your ability to interpret someone else's facial expressions?

How accurately do people interpret emotions expressed on the face? Several studies have attempted to measure subjects' skill in identifying emotional expressions of others.

Note the following research conclusions about facial expressions and people's interpretation of them:

- *You can control some facial expressions.* According to Ekman and Friesen, even though faces provide a great deal of information about emotions, people can learn how to control facial expressions—at least some of the time.[49]
- *Facial expressions are contagious.* One researcher who showed his subjects video clips of President Reagan giving speeches discovered that the subjects tended to smile when Reagan smiled and frown when Reagan appeared angry or threatening.[50]
- *Smiling is cross cultural.* There is evidence that the tendency to smile when others are smiling is a cross-cultural characteristic—responding and reacting to others' nonverbal expressions may be universal. Researchers have found, for example, that Japanese subjects were more likely to smile when they could see others smiling during interpersonal interactions.[51]
- *There may be a universal basis for interpreting facial expressions.* Researchers have found that people from different cultures can accurately interpret the spontaneous facial expressions of others. This lends support to the idea of a universal basis for the way humans express and interpret facial expression.[52]
- *Complex facial expressions are easier to interpret.* Research suggests that people are better able to judge the accuracy of facial expressions when the expressions are

more complex.[53] The distinctiveness of a facial expression with compound meanings may be what makes interpretation easier. It is also probable that people have more practice interpreting facial expressions with compound meanings than they do those that communicate a single emotion such as sadness or happiness.

Laughter is contagious.

- *It's likely you can spot a phony smile.* Despite the complexity of some facial expressions, we seem to be able to determine whether someone is really happy or merely offering a phony smile. One research team found that a genuine smile is more fleeting than a forced smile, which tends to last a bit too long.[54]

- *You express microexpressions.* The opposite of complex facial expressions are what Ekman calls "microexpressions," fleeting facial expressions that may last only .05 of a second. Most of Ekman's test groups, including policemen and judges, had difficulty detecting microexpressions. On the other hand, some Buddhists, whom Ekman calls "gymnasts of the mind," were surprisingly sensitive to microexpressions.[55]

Vocal Cues

Vocal cues communicate emotions and help us manage conversations. Even the lack of vocal cues communicates information.

We're able to make a variety of inferences about other people based on the pitch, rate, volume, and quality of their voices and on their skill in pronouncing words and articulating speech sounds. We make guesses about a person's personality, power, credibility, and sexuality based only on vocal cues. One group of speech and language researchers found subtle differences between gay and lesbian speakers' vocal cues compared to those of straight individuals.[56] Another research team found that people use stereotyped vocal cues to make inferences about a person's sexual orientation.[57] Although people tend to agree on which voices sound gay or straight, they are not always accurate. According to the research, gay males have a tendency to rate a voice as "gay sounding" more frequently than straight males. So is "gaydar" based only on vocal cues accurate? Not really: Although researchers have documented some recognizable differences between the vocal cues of gay and straight individuals, we're not always accurate in using the cues to determine a person's sexual orientation, unless the cues are stereotypically pronounced or exaggerated.

OUR VOCAL CUES COMMUNICATE EMOTIONS   Can you judge someone's mood just by listening to the tone of his or her voice? Most people can. According to a research study, people who work in call centers (otherwise known as the people who often interrupt your dinner) can accurately and immediately "read" their customers' disposition just from the tone of their voices.[58] Whether you are an infant or an adult, your voice is a major vehicle for communicating your emotions and a primary tool for communicating information about the nature of relationships between yourself and others.[59] As an adult, you use your voice to present one message on the surface (with words) and usually a more accurate expression of your feelings with your vocal quality. Say the following sentence out loud, as if you really mean it: "This looks great." Now say it sarcastically, as if you really don't think it looks great. Clearly, your vocal cues provide the real meaning.

Some vocal expressions of emotion are easier to identify than others. Expressions of joy and anger are obvious ones, whereas shame and love are the most difficult emotions to identify based on vocal cues alone.[60] People are also likely to confuse fear with nervousness, love with sadness, and pride with satisfaction.

Laughter is another vocal cue that you probably express every day; your laugh not only reflects your emotional state but, according to research, has a strong impact on the emotions of others. Laughter is contagious.[61] When you laugh, you are not only expressing your emotions but also increasing the likelihood that others will laugh with you.

Our Vocal Cues Provide Clues about Our Relationships

Is there a vocal language of love? One team of researchers concluded that it's primarily your voice that communicates your level of intimacy with others when expressing your ideas.[62] Another research study found that just by listening to vocal cues, people were able to determine whether a couple was romantically involved or merely friends. Our vocal cues provide important information about more than just our emotions, but also about the nature of our relationships with others.[63] The words you use may communicate explicit ideas and information, but it is your vocal cues that provide the primary relational cues, which truly indicate the degree of liking and trust that you feel toward others.

Your voice also provides information about your self-confidence and your knowledge of the subject matter in your messages. Most of us would conclude that a speaker who mumbles, speaks slowly, consistently mispronounces words, and uses "uhs" and "ums" is less credible and persuasive than one who speaks clearly, rapidly, and fluently.[64] Although mispronunciations and vocalized pauses ("ums" and "ahs") seem to have a negative effect on credibility, they do not seem to be a major impediment to changing people's attitudes. People may, for example, think that you are less knowledgeable if you stammer, but you may still be able to get your persuasive message across.

Not only "ums" and "ahs" but also a person's speaking rate can influence our perception of others. One team of researchers found that people from the United States evaluated speakers with a moderate to slightly faster speaking rate as more "socially attractive" than speakers who had a slow rate of speech.[65] American listeners also seem to prefer a speaking rate that is equal to or slightly faster than their own speaking rate.

VOCAL CUES HELP US MANAGE CONVERSATIONS In addition to providing information about emotions, self-confidence, and knowledge, vocal cues known as **backchannel cues** can serve a regulatory function in interpersonal situations, signaling when we want to talk and when we don't. When we are finished talking, we may lower the pitch of our final word. When we want to talk, we may start by interjecting sounds such as "I … I … I …" or "Ah … Ah … Ah …" to interrupt the speaker and grab the verbal ball. We may also use such cues as "Sure," "I understand," "Uh-huh," or "Okay" to signal that we understand the message of the other person and now we want to talk or end the conversation. These backchannel cues are particularly useful in telephone conversations when we have no other nonverbal cues to help us signal that we would like to get off the phone.

OUR USE OF SILENCE SPEAKS VOLUMES. Sometimes it is not what we say, or even how we say it, that communicates our feelings. Being silent may communicate volumes.[66] As one researcher commented "Silence is to speech as white paper is to this print…. The entire system of spoken language would fail without [people's] ability to both tolerate and create sign sequences of silence–sound–silence units."[67] Silence communicates not only when we're interacting with someone in a face-to-face situation but also when we're sending an e-mail message. Research has found that if we send a message and expect an immediate reply but don't receive one—there is "silence"—then our expectations are violated and we think less of the person we're waiting for.[68]

It is said that "silence is golden." But is it really? Would you be comfortable just sitting silently with a good friend? Sidney Baker's theory of silence suggests that the more at ease you are when you share a silence with a close friend, the more comfortable

backchannel cues

Vocal cues that signal your wish to speak or stop speaking.

Communication and Emotion

How to Accurately Interpret the Nonverbal Expression of Emotions

Are you skilled at accurately interpreting the emotions others are expressing? People who are more sensitive in interpreting emotions expressed nonverbally tend to be more popular and have a wider circle of friends, and are less likely to experience relationship anxiety. The following research conclusions may help you enhance both your ability and confidence in interpreting the emotional expressions of others.[69]

Facial Expression

- It is easier to interpret positive emotional expressions (happiness) than negative emotional expressions (sadness, anger, disgust).[70]

- You are more likely to confuse the expression of fear with surprise or anger because of the similar position of the eyes and especially the area around the brow.

- Because facial expressions can be grouped based on the dimensions of activity, intensity, and pleasantness, similar expressions are more likely to be confused. The more dramatically different the emotions being expressed are, the more likely you are to accurately identify these emotions based on facial expression alone.

Vocal Cues

- It's generally easier to interpret anger, sadness, happiness, and nervousness from vocal cues alone and harder to identify disgust, shame, fear, jealousy, love, satisfaction, and sympathy.[71]

- People sometimes have difficulty distinguishing love from sympathy, fear from sadness, and interest from happiness.[72]

- Knowing more about the context or reason for someone's nonverbal communication helps you interpret which emotion is being expressed by vocal cues.

General Principles of Interpreting Emotions

- Your interpretation of emotions is strongly influenced by your culture; although there is some common basis for expressing emotions, there are cultural variations in how emotions are interpreted.[73]

- You are more likely to accurately interpret emotions expressed by people who are from your own cultural or ethnic background.

- You are more likely to accurately interpret emotional expression in someone from a culture other than your own if the emotional expression is static (for example, a photograph of a facial expression) rather than dynamic (an in-person expression or a video of the expression).

- You are more likely to accurately interpret someone's emotional expression if it is genuine versus if it is fake.

- Your ability to interpret emotions improves as you get older, but your skill starts to decline as age begins to impact your ability to accurately see and hear others.[74]

- A person's facial expression and vocal cues communicate a specific emotional response; his or her posture and gestures communicate the *intensity* of the emotion expressed.

- In general, women are more likely than men to accurately interpret emotions in others.

- Research suggests that compared to men, women are typically more nonverbally expressive in social situations.[75]

- Your ability to accurately interpret emotions is a skill that does not appear to be related to race, education, or cognitive intelligence level.

- People who more accurately interpret the emotional expressions of others tend to work at people-oriented jobs more than people who do not have such skill.[76]

you are with just being together and enjoying each other's companionship. People need to talk until there is nothing left to say; by that point, the uncertainty has been managed. In most long-term relationships, partners may not feel a need to fill the air with sound. Just being together to enjoy each other's company may be most fulfilling. Baker calls such moments "positive silence."[77] Although we sometimes use "the silent treatment"—refusing to talk to someone—to communicate our irritation with a romantic partner, research has found that in committed relationships, couples are *less* likely to be silent as a signal of irritation.[78] Routinely avoiding problems by being silent (or what one researcher calls *stonewalling*) appears to be symptomatic of a stressed relationship.[79]

Space

Imagine that you are sitting alone in a booth at your local pizza parlor. As you sit munching your crispy, thin-crust pepperoni pizza, you are startled when a complete stranger sits down in your booth directly across from you. With several empty tables and booths in the restaurant, you feel very uncomfortable that this unknown individual has invaded "your" area.

Figure 7.1 Edward T. Hall's Four Zones of Space

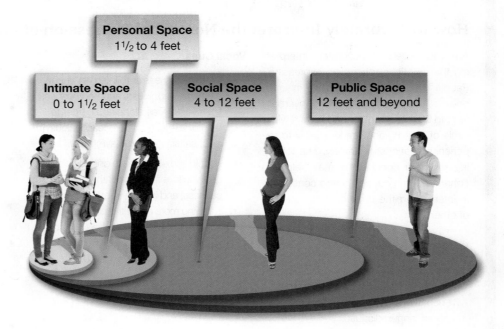

Normally, people do not think much about the rules of personal space, but in fact every culture has fairly rigid ways of regulating space in social interactions. Violations of these rules can be alarming and, as in the preceding scenario, even threatening. How close you are willing to get to others relates to how well you know them and to considerations of power and status.

One pioneer in helping people understand the silent language of personal space was Edward T. Hall. His study of **proxemics** investigated how close or how far away from people and things we arrange ourselves.[80] Hall identified four spatial zones that speakers in Western cultures sometimes define for themselves unconsciously, as shown in Figure 7.1.

- **Intimate space**. When you are between 0 and 1½ feet from someone, you are occupying intimate space. This is the zone in which the most intimate interpersonal communication occurs. It is open only to those with whom you are well acquainted, unless you are forced to stand in an elevator, a fast-food line, or some other crowded space. One research study found that when you are close enough to smell someone, you sometimes make inferences about the other person's personality, based on odor. No, it's not just about whether someone needs a shower, or should use less cologne. A person's natural odor was found to trigger perceptions of the other person's dominance and neuroticism.[81]
- **Personal space** Your personal space ranges from 1½ to 4 feet from a person. Most conversations with family and friends occur in this zone. If someone you don't know well invades this space on purpose, you may feel uncomfortable.
- **Social space**. Your social space ranges from 4 to 12 feet from a person. Most group interactions, as well as many professional relationships, take place in this zone. The interaction tends to be more formal than that in the first two zones.
- **Public space**. Your public space begins 12 feet from you. Interpersonal communication does not usually occur in this zone, and many public speakers and teachers position themselves even more than 12 feet from their audience.

Don't get the idea that these special zones described by Hall *always* occur precisely within the measurements that we've described. They don't. The specific space that you and others choose depends on several variables.[82] The more you like someone,

proxemics

Study of how close or far away from people and objects people position themselves.

intimate space

Zone of space most often used for very personal or intimate interactions, ranging from 0 to 1½ feet between individuals.

personal space

Zone of space most often used for conversations with family and friends, ranging from 1½ to 4 feet between individuals.

social space

Zone of space most often used for group interactions, ranging from 4 to 12 feet between individuals.

public space

Zone of space most often used by public speakers or anyone speaking to many people, ranging beyond 12 feet from the individual.

the closer you will stand to the person. We allow individuals with high status to have more space around them than we allow for people with lower status. Large people also usually have more space around them than smaller people do, and women stand closer to others than men do.[83] All of us tend to stand closer to others in a large room than we do in a small room. And our culture plays a significant role in determining how close to others we work or stand, as well as the power and status of individuals with whom we interact. People who live in **high-contact cultures**, which tend to be in warmer climates, will stand closer to others and may initiate touch more than people from **low-contact cultures**, which tend to be in cooler climates.[84]

In a group, who's in charge, who's important, and who talks to whom are reflected by the spatial arrangement people select. The more dominant group members tend to select seats at the head of a table, while shyer individuals often select a corner seat at a rectangular table.[85]

Territory

Territoriality is the study of how animals (including humans) use space and objects to communicate occupancy or ownership of space. Earlier, we gave the example of a stranger sitting down with you in a pizza parlor. In that case, you had assumed "ownership" of the booth in the pizza parlor and the accompanying "right" to determine who sat with you, because you and your pizza were occupying the booth. In addition to invading your personal space, the intrusive stranger broke the rules that govern territoriality.

People announce ownership of space with **territorial markers**—things that signify the area has been claimed—much as explorers once planted flags claiming uncharted land for their kings. When you are studying at a coffee shop, for example, and need to hop up to get a refill, you might leave behind a notebook or a pencil to "save" your spot. In rural areas, landowners post signs at the borders of their property to keep hunters off their territory. People use signs, locks, electronic security systems, and other devices to secure home and office territories.

You also use markers to indicate where your space stops and someone else's starts. "Good fences make good neighbors," wrote the poet Robert Frost. When someone sits too close, you may try to erect a physical barrier, such as a stack of books or a napkin holder, or you might use your body as a shield by turning away. If the intruder does not get the hint that "this land is my land," you may ultimately resort to words to announce that the space is occupied.

Touch

Standing elbow to elbow in a crowded elevator, you may find yourself in physical contact with total strangers. As you stiffen your body and avert your eyes, a baffling

high-contact cultures
Cultures in which people experience personal closeness and contact, often from warmer climates.

low-contact cultures
Cultures in which people experience less contact and personal closeness, often from cooler climates.

territoriality
Study of how animals and humans use space and objects to communicate occupancy or ownership of space.

territorial markers
Tangible objects that are used to signify that someone has claimed an area or space.

Recap

Edward T. Hall's Classification of Spatial Zones

	Distance from the Individual	Examples
Zone One	0 to 1½ feet	Communicating with our most intimate acquaintances
Zone Two	1½ feet to 4 feet	Conversing with good friends and family members
Zone Three	4 feet to 12 feet	Working with others in small groups and in professional situations
Zone Four	12 feet and beyond	Engaging in public speaking

sense of shame floods over you. If you are sitting at a conference table and you accidentally brush the toes of your shoes against your colleague's ankle, you may jerk away and even blush or apologize. Why do people react this way to unpremeditated touching? Normally, you touch to express intimacy. When intimacy is not your intended message, you instinctively react to modify the impression. Research confirms that increased touching usually means an escalation in both conversational and physical intimacy.[86] One study by communication researchers Graham Bodie and William Villaume confirmed that when we see a man and a woman holding hands, we conclude, not surprisingly, that they are affectionate with each other.[87] They also found that we make inferences about who has the most power or is most dominant in a relationship based on who controls hand-holding cues.

Countless studies have shown that intimate touching is vital to your personal development and well-being.[88] Infants and children need to be touched to confirm that they are valued and loved. Many hospitals invite volunteers in to hold and rock newborns whose mothers cannot do this themselves. Advocates of breastfeeding argue that the intimate touching it entails strengthens the bond between mother and child.[89]

The amount of touch you need, tolerate, receive, and initiate depends on many factors. The amount and kind of touching you receive in your family is one big influence. If your mom or dad greets you with hugs, caresses, and kisses, then you probably do this to others. If your family is less demonstrative, you may be restrained yourself. Studies by researcher Nancy Henley show that most of us are more likely to touch people when we are feeling friendly or happy, or under some of the following specific circumstances:[90]

- When we ask someone to do something for us
- When we share rather than ask for information
- When we try to persuade someone to do something
- When we are talking about intimate topics
- When we are in social settings that we choose to be in rather than in professional settings that are part of our job
- When we are thrilled and excited to share good news
- When we listen to a troubled or worried friend

Research has identified differences in the amount of touch men and women prefer to give and receive.[91] Men, according to researchers, generally have a more positive reaction to intimate touch than women.[92] Men are more likely than women to initiate touch in casual romantic heterosexual relationships, yet women are more likely than men to reach out and touch their spouses. As a general rule, men are more likely to initiate touch with a woman before they are married than after they are married. Nonverbal communication scholars Laura Guerrero and Peter Anderson found that people in long-term relationships touched each other *less* often than people who were in the earlier stages of dating and developing a relationship.[93] Quantity of touch is apparently more important when establishing a new relationship than in maintaining a marital or long-term relationship. North American men are more uncomfortable with being touched by other men than women are with being touched by other women. In addition to one's sex, personal preferences determine how much touch a person prefers to initiate or receive. Some people just don't like to be touched; they are what researchers call high-touch-avoidance individuals; to be touched by anyone simply makes them feel uncomfortable.

Appearance

In all interactions with others, appearance counts. American culture places a high value on how much you weigh, the style of your hair, and the clothes you wear; these things are particularly important in the early stages of relationship development. Attractive

Relating to Diverse Others
Cultural and Gender Differences in Interpreting Nonverbal Messages

	Culture Differences	Gender Differences
Gestures	Hand and body gestures with the most shared meaning among Africans, North Americans, and South Americans include pointing, shrugging, nodding the head, clapping, pointing the thumb down, waving hello, and beckoning. The "okay" gesture made by forming a circle with the thumb and finger has sexual connotations in some South American and Caribbean countries. In France, the "okay" sign means "worthless."	Overall, women appear to use fewer and less expansive gestures than men. Women are more likely, for example, to rest their hands on the arms of a chair while seated; men are more likely to gesture. Men and women position their legs differently: Women cross their legs at the knees or ankles, whereas men are more likely to sit with their legs apart. There is also evidence that women are more likely than men to adapt to the nonverbal interaction patterns of those with whom they are speaking.[94]
Eye Contact	There seems to be more eye contact between Arabs, South Americans, and Greeks than between people from other cultures. Some African Americans look at others less than Whites do when sending and receiving messages. One of the most universal expressions appears to be the eyebrow flash (the sudden raising of the eyebrows when meeting someone or interacting with others).	Women typically use a more prolonged gaze when speaking than men do. Women, however, are less likely to stare at someone; they break eye contact more frequently than men do. In general, women receive more eye contact from others than men do.[95]
Facial Expression	One research team found that some facial expressions such as those conveying happiness, sadness, anger, disgust, and surprise were the same in 68 to 92 percent of the cultures examined.[96] All humans probably share the same neurophysiological basis for expressing emotions, but they learn different rules for displaying and interpreting these expressions. For example, Japanese culture emphasizes "saving face" by not reinforcing the showing of negative emotions.	Research suggests that women smile more than men. It is also reported that women tend to be more emotionally expressive with their faces than men; this is perhaps related to the conclusion that women are more skilled at both displaying and interpreting facial expressions.
Space	Arabs, Latin Americans, and Southern Europeans generally stand closer to others than people do from Asia, India, Pakistan, and Northern Europe. Northern Europeans use the largest zone of personal space when interacting with others, followed by Asians, Caucasians (Central and Eastern Europeans), and those from Mediterranean countries. Hispanics use the smallest amount of personal space.[97]	Men tend to require more space around them than women do, and they are more likely to actively determine the amount of space around them. Women both approach and are approached more closely than men. And when conversing with others, women seem to prefer side-by-side interactions.
Touch	In high-contact cultures, people expect and value a higher degree of human touching when compared to people in other cultures. People from warmer climates tend to prefer closer distances and expect more touching behavior than people from cooler climates.[98] South Americans initiate and receive more touching behavior than North Americans do.[99]	Men are more likely than women to initiate touch at the beginning of relationships and to communicate power.[100] Women are touched more often than men. Men and women also attribute different meaning to touch; women are more likely than men to associate touch with warmth and expressiveness.

females have an easier time persuading others than do those who are perceived as less attractive. Whether seen on Facebook or visiting face-to-face, attractive people are perceived as more credible, happier, more popular, more sociable, and even more prosperous than less attractive people.[101] There is also evidence that if you believe that others think a person is attractive, you'll be more likely to evaluate that person as attractive as well.[102]

The shape and size of your body also affect how others perceive you. Heavier and rounder individuals are often perceived to be older, more old-fashioned, less good-looking, more talkative, and more good-natured than thin people, who are perceived to be more ambitious, more suspicious of others, more uptight and tense, more negative, and less talkative. Muscular and athletically fit folks are seen as better looking, taller, and more adventurous. These perceptions are, in fact, so common that they have become easily recognizable stereotypes on which casting directors for movies, TV shows, and plays rely in selecting actors and actresses.

Aside from keeping you warm and within the legal bounds of decency, your clothes also affect how others perceive you. The clothes you wear are a way of communicating to others how you want to be treated. One classic study found that a man who jaywalked while dressed in nice clothes attracted more fellow violators than he could when he was shabbily attired.[103] Although studies have attempted to identify a "power" look, and magazines are constantly giving prescriptions for ways to be attractive and stylish, there is no single formula for dressing for success.[104]

Skin color, another element of personal appearance, also influences perception. Research has confirmed the existence of bias and stereotypes based on skin color.[105] White Americans, for example, have been found to express bias against Black Americans.[106] And people's displays of nonverbal behavior sometimes reflect bias and prejudice.[107] Joshua Meadors and Carolyn Murray found that White subjects displayed a more "closed" posture when observing and describing Black suspects shown on a video than when watching White suspects. These research conclusions do not mean that everyone demonstrates bias and stereotypes based on skin color, but general trends have been observed and documented.[108]

#communicationandtechnology

Saying It Without Saying It Online

Metacommunication, as you recall from Chapter 1, is communication about communication; one channel of communication, such as nonverbal cues, provides information about another channel of communication, such as the words used. Even a lean communication medium such as instant messaging or e-mail offers subtle (and sometimes not-so-subtle) nonverbal cues that provide metamessages—information about the nature of your relationship with your communication partner. Regardless of whether you explicitly express your emotional meaning, you are "saying it" by the metamessage clues you include in your online text messages.

Emoticons and Emojis

One obvious way we express nonverbal messages that influence the meaning of our words is with the now-ubiquitous emoticons or emojis on our smartphones. Emoticons and emojis are used to express a range of emotions from happiness 😃 to surprise 😮, anger 😠 and even flirtatious winks. 😉 Even when used minimally, emoticons/emojis provide a shorthand way of expressing your feelings. Researchers have found that we use emoticons/emojis in text messages in places where we would pause or establish eye contact with others if we were talking face-to-face.[109]

One research team suggests that we use emoticons not just to express a specific emotion but also to get people's attention, be sarcastic, empathize with others, or communicate in an informal tone.[110] Another group of researchers concluded that we use emoticons/emojis to underscore humor and to soften a negative message with a smiley face.[111] Yet another study found cultural differences in the way we use emoticons: people from individualistic cultures (such as the United States) prefer vertical and eye-oriented emoticons like this:-o while people from collectivist cultures (such as Japan) use vertical and eye-oriented emoticons such as ^-^.[112]

Underlining and Italics

Just as gestures add emphasis to spoken words, underlining and *italicizing* words help the reader know what the writer wants to emphasize. Both underlining and italics take an additional second or two to add to your message; the extra effort of italicizing a word sends the message that you have thought about how you'd like to emphasize your idea.

Capitalization

Like the volume control on your TV or iPod, capitalization serves as a way to increase the volume of your message. When typed all in capital letters, the phrase "HEY, LET'S GET TO IT" communicates greater urgency than "Hey, let's get to it." Overuse of all capital letters would be like constantly raising your voice. So be careful to "shout" only when you need to add emphasis.

Message Length

If you send someone a chatty, fairly long e-mail message describing the details of your day, and you get a short and simple reply that says "Thanks," the unverbalized metamessage may be that your communication partner wasn't all that interested in you or your message. Reciprocation or nonreciprocation of message length provides metamessage cues about interest in your message.

Response Time

In addition to how long a return message is, you will likely make inferences about the other person's interest in hearing from you based on how quickly you get a response. The shorter the response time, the more likely you will be to conclude that the other person is interested in the conversation.

Media Choice

Canadian communication theorist Marshall McLuhan famously said, "The medium is the message." Your decision to send a text message, make a phone call, or schedule a time to connect via webcam provides information about the relationship. A richer medium (such as a webcam session, which allows you to see images and converse in real time when immediate feedback is possible) signals that the message you wish to convey is relatively important. *Flaming* is any type of antisocial or negative message or behavior exhibited online. There is evidence that you are more likely to flame when using a relatively lean medium such as text or e-mail than when using a webcam or interacting in person.[113]

Improving Your Skill in Interpreting Nonverbal Messages

7.3   Enhance your skill in interpreting nonverbal messages.

How do you make sense out of the postures, movements, gestures, eye contact, facial expressions, uses of space and territory, touch, and appearance of others? Everyone wants to know how to interpret these unspoken messages. One internationally known researcher, Peter Collett, uses the analogy that nonverbal cues are like **tells** in the game of poker. A poker tell is a nonverbal cue that gives away what we are thinking and feeling—whether we're smirking about holding a good set of cards or frowning because we don't have a winning hand.[114] How do you interpret these tells? Although there are limitations to decoding the meaning in nonverbal cues, here are several strategies to help you improve your ability to interpret nonverbal messages.

tells

Nonverbal cues, such as facial expressions, body postures, or eye behaviors, that give away what we are thinking and feeling.

Look for Dimensions of Meaning in Nonverbal Messages

Albert Mehrabian has found that people synthesize and interpret nonverbal cues along three primary dimensions: *immediacy, arousal,* and *dominance.*[115] These three dimensions provide a useful way to summarize how nonverbal cues may be interpreted.

OBSERVE IMMEDIACY CUES THAT COMMUNICATE LIKING   Sometimes we cannot put a finger on the precise reason we find a person likable or unlikable. Mehrabian believes that immediacy cues are a likely explanation. Immediacy cues are behaviors that communicate liking and engender feelings of pleasure. The principle underlying the communication of our feelings of **immediacy** is simple: We move toward persons and things we like, and we avoid or move away from those we dislike. Immediacy cues increase our sensory awareness of others. In addition to the use of space and territory, one of the most powerful cues is touch; others include a forward lean, increased eye contact, and an open body orientation. The meaning of these behaviors is usually implied rather than explicitly spelled out in words.

immediacy

Feelings of liking, pleasure, and closeness communicated by such nonverbal cues as increased eye contact, forward lean, touch, and open body orientation.

Not surprisingly, communication researcher Lois Hinkle found that spouses who reported high feelings of affection for their mates reported that their mates responded by expressing more immediacy cues toward them.[116] When someone expresses immediate or pleasant nonverbal messages toward us, we reciprocate by responding in a pleasant manner. Researchers Judee Burgoon and Beth Le Poire found that people adapt their nonverbal messages to others.[117] When people express immediacy or liking toward you, you are more likely to reciprocate and express a similar sentiment toward them. Immediacy is contagious. Yet another research study found that expressions of nonverbal immediacy, such as closer personal distance, touching, and a forward lean, on the part of someone trying to offer support and comfort helped reduce the other person's stress and tension.[118]

In brief, we use the following cues to communicate that we like someone:[119]

Proximity:	Close, forward lean
Body orientation:	Typically face-to-face, but could be side by side
Eye contact:	Mutual eye contact
Facial expression:	Smiling
Gestures:	Head nods, movement
Posture:	Open, arms oriented toward others
Touch:	Cultural- and context-appropriate touch
Voice:	Higher pitch, upward pitch

A person's surroundings can communicate her degree of power just as clearly as her clothing and behavior do.

arousal

Feelings of interest and excitement communicated by such nonverbal cues as vocal expression, facial expressions, and gestures.

dominance

Power, status, and control communicated by such nonverbal cues as a relaxed posture, greater personal space, and protected personal space.

OBSERVE AROUSAL CUES THAT COMMUNICATE RESPONSIVENESS
A person's face, voice, and movement are primary indicators of **arousal**. If we sense arousal cues, we conclude that another person is responsive to and interested in us. If the person acts passive or dull, we conclude that he or she is uninterested.

When you approach someone and ask whether he or she has a minute or two to talk, that person may signal interest with a change in facial expression and more animated vocal cues. People who are aroused and interested in you show animation in their face, voice, and gestures. A forward lean, a flash of the eyebrows, and a nod of the head are other cues that implicitly communicate arousal. Someone who says, "Sure, I have time to talk with you" in a monotone and with a flat, expressionless face is communicating the opposite. Think of arousal as an on-off switch. Sleeping is the ultimate switched-off state.

OBSERVE DOMINANCE CUES THAT COMMUNICATE POWER The third dimension of Mehrabian's framework for implicit cues communicates the balance of power in a relationship. **Dominance** cues communicate power, status, position, and importance.[120] Raising the head while looking someone in the eye is perceived as communicating greater dominance than lowering the head.[121] A person of high status tends to have a relaxed body posture when interacting with a person of lower status.[122] When you talk to a professor, he may lean back in his chair, put his feet on the desk, and fold his hands behind his head during the conversation. But unless your professor is a colleague or a friend, you will maintain a relatively formal posture during your interaction in his office.

Shaking hands is a centuries-old greeting or farewell ritual that communicates power or lack of it. Alan and Barbara Pease report that people in leadership positions are more likely to be the ones who initiate a handshake than are non-leaders.[123] The person who feels the most power in a relationship is more likely to shake hands with his or her palm facing down; a submissive handshake, explains nonverbal communication researcher Peter Collett, is offered with the palm facing up. Collett has meticulously analyzed handshakes of politicians and other leaders to reveal that the person who feels the most power literally takes the upper hand when shaking hands.[124]

Another dominance cue is the use of space. High-status individuals usually have more space around them; they have bigger offices and more "barriers" protecting them. A receptionist in an office is usually easily accessible, but to reach the president of the company, you may have to navigate through several corridors and past several administrative assistants who are "guarding" the door.

Are most people aware of the power cues they express or receive from others? Your ability to detect nonverbal expressions of power may relate to whether or not you think you are powerful. One research team found that subordinates were better at interpreting power cues from their supervisors than supervisors were at interpreting power cues from their subordinates.[125] This means that if you think you have less power in a relationship, you are more likely to be aware of the more dominant power of others' nonverbal cues. If you think you do have power, you may be less sensitive to any nonverbal expressions of power.

Other power cues that communicate dominance include use of furniture, clothing, and locations. You study with others at a table in the library; the college president has a large private desk. You may wear jeans and a T-shirt to class; the head of the university wears a business suit. Your dorm may be surrounded by other dorms; the president's residence may be a large house surrounded by a lush, landscaped garden in a prestigious neighborhood. People use space, territory, posture, and artifacts such as clothing and furniture to signal feelings of dominance or submissiveness in the presence of others.

BEING Other-ORIENTED

Feelings of immediacy (liking), arousal (interest), and dominance (power) are often communicated nonverbally rather than verbally. What behaviors do your friends, family, or colleagues use to communicate liking, interest, and power?

Recap

Dimensions for Interpreting Nonverbal Behavior

Dimension	Definition	Nonverbal Cues
Immediacy	Cues that communicate liking and pleasure	Eye contact, touch, forward lean, closeness to partner
Arousal	Cues that communicate active interest and emotional involvement	Eye contact, varied vocal cues, animated facial expressions, forward lean, movement
Dominance	Cues that communicate status and power	Protected space, relaxed posture, status symbols

Research confirms that we have certain expectations about how people who are perceived to have power will behave nonverbally.[126] People who are thought to have more power, for example, are thought to more freely express their anger and disgust than are people who have less power and status. British social psychologist Michael Argyle summarizes the nonverbal cues that communicate dominance:[127]

Use of space:	Height (on a platform or standing)
	Facing a group
	More space surrounding a person
Eye contact:	More when initially establishing dominance
	More when staring to establish power
	More when talking
Face:	Frown, no smile
Touch:	Initiating touch
Voice:	Loud, low pitch, greater pitch range
	Slow, more interruptions, more talk
	Slight hesitation before speaking
Gesture:	Pointing at the other or at his or her property
Posture:	Standing, hands on hips, expanded chest, more relaxed

Use Effective Strategies for Interpreting Nonverbal Messages

In addition to looking for general patterns or dimensions of nonverbal behavior, you can use several research-based strategies to increase your accuracy in interpreting nonverbal messages. These suggestions won't give you the ability to have 100 percent accuracy in decoding nonverbal cues, but they will help you enhance your "people watching" skill.

CONSIDER NONVERBAL CUES IN CONTEXT   Just as quoting someone out of context can change the meaning of a statement, trying to draw conclusions from an isolated snatch of behavior or a single cue can lead to misinterpretations. For example, beware of looking at someone's folded arms and concluding that he or she does not like you or is not interested in what you are saying. It could be that the air conditioner is set too low and the person is just trying to keep warm.

LOOK FOR CLUSTERS OF NONVERBAL CUES   Instead of focusing on a specific cue, look for corroborating cues that can lead you to a more accurate conclusion about the meaning of a behavior. Is the person making eye contact? Is he or she facing you? How far away is he or she standing from you? Always consider nonverbal behaviors in conjunction with other nonverbal cues, the environment, and the person's verbal message.

CONSIDER PAST EXPERIENCES WHEN INTERPRETING NONVERBAL CUES It may be that "familiarity breeds contempt," as the old saying goes, but familiarity with another person also increases your ability to interpret his or her nonverbal behavior. You may have learned, for example, that when your mother starts crying when you play the piano, it signals pride, not melancholy. Family members can probably interpret one another's nonverbal cues more accurately than outsiders can. But after knowing someone over a period of time, you begin to increase your sensitivity to certain glances, silences, movements, and vocal cues that might be overlooked or misunderstood by others.

COMPARE WHAT YOU EXPECT TO SEE WITH WHAT YOU ACTUALLY OBSERVE We often interpret messages based on how we *expect* people to behave in a specific situation. Comparing what you expect to see with what you actually see and hear can increase your observation skill.

expectancy violation theory
Theory that you interpret the messages of others based on how you expect others to behave.

One theory that helps explain how and why we interpret nonverbal messages the way we do is called **expectancy violation theory**. Developed by Judee Burgoon and several of her colleagues, this theory suggests that each of us interacts with others with certain preconceived expectations about their behavior.[128] Our expectations are based on our life experiences and our culture. The research conclusions we've summarized in this book about when eye contact is likely to occur, when we'll probably smile or frown, or how most people express immediacy, dominance, or arousal are based on the general expectations we have about how other people behave. For example, most Westerners expect that when meeting a business colleague for the first time, that person will smile, extend a hand, say, "Hello, I'm …," and then say his or her name. If, instead, the person clasps two hands together and bows demurely without uttering a word, this nonverbal behavior is not what we expect. This violation of our expectation would cause us to wonder what the "violator" might mean by bowing instead of offering to shake our hand. When our expectations are violated, we may feel uncomfortable.

But when people behave nonverbally in ways we may not expect, we adapt our behavior, especially if we are other-oriented and skilled in responding to other people.[129] If your new business colleague greets you with a bow rather than a handshake, it is appropriate to offer a bow in return, rather than trying to shake the person's hand. We're constantly making observations and comparing what we expect with what we experience, and then adapting our behavior based on what happens. By being aware of your expectations and comparing what you expect to see with what you actually observe, you can increase your skill at being mindful when interpreting nonverbal tells.

BE AWARE OF YOUR SKILL IN INTERPRETING NONVERBAL MESSAGES How can you assess your skill at interpreting nonverbal messages? Some people are simply better at interpreting nonverbal cues than others. By reflecting on your skill in accurately interpreting nonverbal cues, you can decide whether you need to increase your awareness of the unspoken messages of others.

BEING Other-ORIENTED
The ability to accurately interpret the nonverbal expressions of others is both a natural talent and a skill that can be enhanced. On a scale from 1 to 10, with 1 being low and 10 being high, how would you assess your own ability to accurately interpret the nonverbal messages of others?

Research offers some clues as to who is most likely to be skilled at accurately interpreting nonverbal messages.[130]

1. In general, women have been found to be more interpersonally sensitive than men, when interpersonal sensitivity was measured as the ability to accurately *recall* the nonverbal behavior of another person.[131]
2. People who are better at accurately expressing their feelings and emotions are also better able to interpret nonverbal expressions from others.
3. People who are skilled in interpreting one channel of information (for example, facial expression or vocal cues) are likely to be more accurate at interpreting nonverbal messages from other channels (such as posture or use of space).

Improving Your Communication Skills

Practicing Nonverbal Perception Checking

We have identified several strategies to improve your skill at interpreting the nonverbal messages of others, including being able to check your perceptions of others. Accurately perceiving others gets to the heart of becoming other-oriented.

Look at the following photographs. First, note the nonverbal behavior of the target person in the picture. Next, form a mental impression of what you think the person is thinking and feeling. Finally, compose a perception-checking question that the other person in the photo could ask to confirm the target person's thoughts and feelings.

Photo 1
A. Describe the student's nonverbal behavior.
B. What do you think the student is thinking and feeling?
C. What is a perception-checking question the teacher could ask her student?

Photo 2
A. Describe the customer's nonverbal behavior.
B. What do you think the customer is thinking and feeling?
C. What is a perception-checking question the salesman could ask the customer?

---

4. People with certain personality characteristics have been found to interpret nonverbal messages more accurately. For instance, people with high self-esteem who are expressive, extroverted, not shy, and nondogmatic typically do a better job of interpreting nonverbal messages than people who do not have these personality characteristics.
5. People who select people-oriented professions such as teaching, sales, and nursing often have more skill in interpreting nonverbal messages.

The ability to interpret nonverbal cues is *not* related to a person's race, amount of education, or intelligence. Even if you don't have a natural talent for interpreting nonverbal cues, with training and practice, you can enhance your sensitivity to and accuracy in interpreting them.

CHECK YOUR PERCEPTIONS WITH OTHERS   In Chapter 3, we discussed the key skill of **perception checking**. You can follow three steps to check your perception of someone's nonverbal behavior. First, observe the nonverbal cues, making a point to note such variables as eye contact, posture, use of gestures, facial expression, and tone of voice. Second, try to interpret what the individual is expressing through his or her nonverbal behavior. Finally, check your perception by asking him or her if it is accurate. Of course, you don't need to go through life constantly checking everyone's nonverbal cues. Overusing this skill would irritate most people. However, if you are uncertain about how someone feels and it is important to know, a perception check may be in order. Consider the following example.

perception checking

Asking someone whether your interpretation of his or her nonverbal behavior is accurate.

Deonna:	Mom, I wanted to let you know that Erik and I are going to have to miss the family reunion next weekend. Life has been so hectic lately that we and the kids haven't had much time together, so we're going to spend the weekend at home relaxing.
Muriel:	(Frowns, avoids eye contact, folds her arms, and uses a flat voice.) Oh, don't worry about it.
Deonna:	Well, you say not to worry about it, Mom, but it looks like you are upset. I know that look of yours. I also hear in your voice that you are not really pleased. Is it really OK, or are you a little miffed?
Muriel:	Well, yes, to be honest, Dad and I were really looking forward to getting all the kids together.
Deonna:	I'm sorry, Mom. We will make an effort to be at the next one. Thanks for sharing how you really feel.

Asking about a specific nonverbal cue will help you interpret your partner's behavior in future interactions as well. As noted earlier, evidence suggests that the longer couples are married, the more they rely on nonverbal behavior to communicate. One study claims that some couples spend less than eleven minutes a week in sustained conversation.[132] Even in marriages lasting fifty years, however, conversation is still occasionally required to clarify nonverbal responses.

BE AWARE THAT THE NONVERBAL EXPRESSION OF EMOTION IS CONTAGIOUS
Have you ever noticed that when you watch a funny movie, you are more likely to laugh out loud if other people around you are laughing? There's a reason this happens. Nonverbal emotional expressions are contagious. People often display the same emotions that a communication partner is displaying. **Emotional contagion theory** suggests that people tend to "catch" the emotions of others.[133] Interpersonal interactions with others can affect your nonverbal expression of emotions.[134] The ancient Roman orator Cicero knew this when he advised public speakers, "If you want your audience to experience joy, you must be a joyful speaker. Or, if you want to communicate fear, then you should express fear when you speak."

emotional contagion theory

Theory that emotional expression is contagious; people can "catch" emotions just by observing others' emotional expressions.

LOOK FOR CUES THAT MAY COMMUNICATE LYING   In a *60 Minutes* TV broadcast, baseball superstar Alex Rodriguez boldly claimed he had not taken steroids to enhance his athletic performance. Yet nonverbal communication expert Paul Ekman, after analyzing videotapes of the interview, found clear evidence that Rodriguez was not being truthful. Repeated shoulder shrugs, a tightened corner of his lip, and lengthwise stretching of his lips provided telltale signals that he was lying.[135]

Recap

How to Check Your Perceptions of Others' Nonverbal Cues

Steps	Consider...
1. Observe their nonverbal behavior	Are they frowning? Do they make eye contact? Are their arms crossed? How would you describe their tone of voice? What is their posture?
2. Form a mental impression of what you think they mean	Are they happy, sad, or angry? Is the nonverbal message contradicting the verbal message?
3. Ask questions to check whether your perception is accurate	"Are you upset? You look angry." "Your expression and your voice suggest you don't believe me. Do you think I'm lying?" "The look on your face tells me you really like it. Do you?"

Table 7.1 Who's Telling the Truth? Honest vs. Dishonest Communicators

Nonverbal Cue	Honest Communicators ...	Dishonest Communicators ...
Voice	Use fewer pauses when they talk. Speak fluently, smoothly. Speak at a normal rate.	Pause more; they are thinking about what "story" they want to give. Use more nonfluencies ("ah," "er," "um"). Speak a bit faster than normal.
Facial Expression	Smile genuinely and sincerely.	Display a plastered-on, phony smile. May smile a bit too long.
Gestures	Are less likely to play with objects as they speak. Use fewer gestures. Are not likely to shift body weight. Generally display less nervousness.	Are more likely to play with objects (for example, twiddle a pencil). Use more gestures and more self-adaptors like touching their face and body, and shrugging their shoulders. Are more likely to shift their posture. Display increased nervousness.
Eye Contact	Maintain normal eye contact—a steady, natural gaze. Have a normal eye-blink rate.	May look away or maintain less direct eye contact. Have an increased eye-blink rate, a sign of increased anxiety.

When it comes to using nonverbal cues to detect deception, you have to know what to look for. Research has found that when we can both see and hear a person, we have a tendency to believe the person is telling the truth—even when the person isn't being honest.[136] Perhaps we think we're pretty good at detecting deception if we can see the person, but that's not often the case.

Several researchers have been interested in identifying nonverbal cues that indicate deceit.[137] Remember not to place too much emphasis on a single cue. As we've just noted, you'll need to look for clusters of cues rather than pointing your finger when someone has less eye contact and saying, "Ah ha! Now I know you're a liar!" Table 7.1 summarizes research conclusions about nonverbal messages, comparing liars and those who are telling the truth.[138] Remember, these conclusions are general tendencies rather than definitive proof that someone is deceitful or truthful.

Researchers have found that when communicating on Facebook and in other electronically mediated settings, liars often (but not always) write more words, use more sensory references (seeing, touching, hearing), and use more other-oriented pronouns ("*You* should consider this ...") and fewer self-oriented pronouns ("Here's what I think ...").[139] So when you're trying to detect deceit in others, don't just rely on nonverbal cues. Consider the words as well.

It would be easier to detect deception if people had noses like Pinocchio's, which would grow whenever they told a lie. But in the real world, some of the best ways to detect whether someone is telling the truth are to (1) look for nonverbal clues, (2) listen to the content of what the person says, and (3) measure such physiological responses as heart rate, breathing, and other factors.[140] Although nonverbal cues (such as hand and finger movements, pauses, and increased use of illustrators) can be important in helping judges sort out truth-tellers from liars, ultimately it's better to listen to the message and monitor physiological responses (which, of course, may not always be practical).

Unless you have a portable lie detector to measure physiological responses such as heart rate, blood pressure, and breathing rate, the best approach may be to ask other people for corroborating information.[141] Or you can do your own investigation to ferret out whether someone is really telling the truth. Nonverbal cues may be important in giving us an *initial* hunch as to whether someone is telling the truth, but personal detective work may be the real way we ultimately confirm our hunches.

Be Aware of Limitations When Interpreting Nonverbal Messages

Even though we have made great claims for the value of studying nonverbal behaviors and identified suggestions for interpreting nonverbal communication, it is not always easy to decipher unspoken messages.[142] You have dictionaries to help interpret words, but there is no handy reference book to help you decode nonverbal cues. Although the term *body language* is often used in casual conversation, there is no universal or agreed-on interpretation for body movements or gestures. To help you with the decoding process, let's first look at some of the difficulties that hinder classification.

NONVERBAL MESSAGES ARE OFTEN AMBIGUOUS Most words carry a meaning that everyone who speaks the same language can recognize. But the meaning of nonverbal messages may be known only to the person displaying them. Perhaps even more importantly, that person may not intend for the behavior to have any meaning at all. And some people have difficulty expressing their emotions nonverbally. They may have a frozen facial expression or a monotone voice. Or they may be teasing you, but their deadpan expressions lead you to believe that their negative comments are heartfelt. Often, it is difficult to draw meaningful conclusions about another person's behavior, even if you know him or her quite well.

NONVERBAL MESSAGES ARE CONTINUOUS Words are discrete entities; they have a beginning and an end. You can circle the first word in this sentence and underline the last one. Nonverbal behaviors are not as easily dissected. Like the sweep of a second hand on a watch, many nonverbal behaviors are continuous. Some, such as a slap or a hand clap, have definite beginnings and endings. But more often than not, nonverbal behavior unfolds without clearly defined starting and stopping points. Gestures, facial expressions, and even eye contact can flow from one situation to the next with seamless ease. Researchers have difficulty studying nonverbal cues because of this continuous stream, so be aware that trying to categorize and interpret them will be challenging as well.

NONVERBAL CUES ARE MULTICHANNELED Like programs on a multichannel TV, nonverbal cues come at us simultaneously from a variety of sources. And just as you can really pay attention to only one program at a time on your multichannel television—although you can move among them very rapidly—so, too, can you actually attend to only one nonverbal cue at a time.[143] Social psychologist Michael Argyle suspects that negative nonverbal messages (frowns, grimaces, lack of eye contact) command attention before positive messages when the two compete.[144] Moreover, if the nonverbal message contradicts the verbal message, then you may have trouble interpreting either one correctly.[145]

Every culture has fairly rigid ways of regulating space in social interactions. People may consider violations of these implicit rules threatening.

NONVERBAL INTERPRETATION IS CULTURE-BASED There is some evidence that humans from every culture smile when they are happy and frown when they are unhappy.[146] We also all raise, or flash, our eyebrows when meeting or greeting others, and young children in many cultures wave to signal that they want their mothers, raise their arms to be picked up, and suck their thumbs for comfort.[147] These common behaviors suggest that there is some underlying basis for expressing emotion. Yet each culture may develop unique rules for displaying and interpreting these gestures and expressions. New research has found cultural differences not only when we interact face-to-face but also when using computer-generated avatars—"people" who exist only in virtual reality.[148]

For example, unless you grew up there, you might be startled when on a visit to New Orleans you stumble on a handkerchief-waving, dancing, exuberantly singing crowd and discover that it is an African American jazz funeral. What to the uninformed may seem like disrespect for the dead, others recognize as a joyous send-off to a better world.

Improving Your Skill in Expressing Nonverbal Messages

7.4   Enhance your skill in expressing nonverbal messages.

Although we've offered recommendations about how to accurately interpret nonverbal cues, you may wonder "What can I do to express my feelings accurately to others using nonverbal cues?" Consider the following tips.

Be Mindful of Your Nonverbal Behavior

Are you aware of your nonverbal behavior at this moment? What is your facial expression communicating to others? Are you twiddling a pen or pencil? Are your hands and feet jiggling as you read these words? Even if you may not be aware of feeling anxious or nervous, your nonverbal behaviors may send those messages unless you're mindful of what you are doing. Being aware of your nonverbal behavior is the first step in improving your skill in expressing your feelings to others. Most people "leak" nonverbal cues—we can't completely control all aspects of our nonverbal behavior, such as the size of the pupils in our eyes or our fleeting facial expressions. However, we can control many aspects of how we present ourselves to others. For example, now that you know the nonverbal behaviors that communicate liking, power, or interest, you can check to see if your behavior matches your intentions.

As we noted earlier, if your nonverbal message doesn't match your verbal message, it's your nonverbal message that will carry the most weight in terms of influencing the meaning of the message. If your communication goal is to express an emotion, nurture a relationship, or provide support and encouragement, check to ensure that your nonverbal message is expressing the sentiment that you convey verbally. You can undermine your verbalized message with an out-of-synch or contradictory nonverbal message. So be aware of what your nonverbal message may be communicating to others.

Observe Others' Reactions to Your Nonverbal Behavior

By being a keen observer of how other people respond to you, you can develop a greater understanding of how your behavior affects others. Be a detective on the lookout for clues about how your nonverbal behavior is creating meaning for others. For example, you may be in a good mood, but if others don't seem to be reacting positively to your positive feelings, take note of the reactions you're receiving. Are you doing something to trigger a negative reaction in others? Noting the amount and duration of eye contact you receive, the facial expressions of others with whom you interact, and even the openness of their body posture will provide clues to how other people are responding to your messages. Of course, their responses could be focused on something you've said rather than on your nonverbal behavior. So it's especially useful to monitor how people are reacting to you when you're listening and not speaking.

Ask Others About Your Nonverbal Behavior

It's good to have a close friend who can give you honest advice about the nonverbal impression you make on others. Just as you may ask a trusted confidant to give his or her reaction to what you're wearing, you can also ask people you trust for honest feedback about your nonverbal behavior. Consider asking whether your actions fit your words and whether the feeling and overall mood you have is what you're communicating nonverbally. Asking for others' perception of your nonverbal behavior—inviting perception checking—can help you evaluate your nonverbal behavior.

Applying an Other-Orientation
to Nonverbal Communication

Because nonverbal messages are more ambiguous than verbal messages, your interpretation of someone's nonverbal behavior may not always be accurate. One way to enhance your ability to interpret an individual's nonverbal communication is to be aware of that person's normal, baseline way of responding to others.

We noted, for example, that fidgeting fingers and tapping toes may be signs of inattention, frustration, or anxiety—but if you know that your communication partner *normally* fidgets or has a habit of tapping his fingers or wagging a pencil when listening, you have a baseline for interpreting the behavior. "Oh," you may think, "He does that all the time. So he's not nervous. It's just a habit." Knowing a person's normal, baseline nonverbal reactions will increase your accuracy in decoding his or her nonverbal messages.

Practice Your Nonverbal Behavior

If you've taken a public speaking class, your instructor has undoubtedly encouraged you to practice your speech so as to polish your delivery. Maybe you videotaped your speech or even practiced in front of a mirror to check your delivery. We're not suggesting that you rehearse "spontaneous" interpersonal conversations; that would cause you to sound stilted and artificial. But you can observe yourself on video to gain a sense of how others perceive you. If you think you need to polish your nonverbal social skills, you could consider practicing greeting others or expressing both positive and negative emotions. Again, you do not need to develop a script and memorize your message, but using a video camera or even a mirror to practice facial expressions and informal gestures and observe your posture can give you some insight into how to enhance your nonverbal persona. Over 100 years ago, elocution teachers used charts and other drills and practice techniques to help their students practice how to walk, move, and express themselves. We recommend that you approach practicing nonverbal behavior with a sense of play rather than as an assignment. Spending some time practicing and experimenting with how you express yourself nonverbally can increase your awareness of how others see you.

STUDY GUIDE
Review, Apply, and Assess

Identifying the Importance of Nonverbal Communication

Objective 7.1 Explain why nonverbal communication is an important area of study.

Key Terms

nonverbal communication
interaction adaptation theory
interactional synchrony
turning point

Thinking Critically

Consider a communication exchange you had recently. What nonverbal cues were present? What type of eye contact, body language, and facial expressions did you observe? Did you have difficulty interpreting the nonverbal cues of your communication partner(s)? Did the nonverbal cues communicate anything that was at odds with the spoken message? Explain.

Assessing Your Skills

Over the next week, do some serious people watching. Spend some time observing people in a public place, such as a café or coffee shop, on campus, at a bus stop, or at the mall. Make an ongoing list of nonverbal behaviors you observe. Do these behaviors support the verbal messages that you hear, such as greeting friends, asking for service, thanking someone, and the like? Do you observe gender and/or cultural differences in nonverbal behaviors? Make notes about your observations and discuss your findings with your classmates.

Understanding Nonverbal Communication Codes

Objective 7.2 Identify and describe eight nonverbal communication codes.

Key Terms

kinesics
emblems
illustrators
affect displays
regulators
adaptors
backchannel cues
proxemics

intimate space
personal space
social space
public space
high-contact cultures
low-contact cultures
territoriality
territorial markers

Thinking Critically

Consider some recent communication exchanges you had, either face-to-face or over the phone. How much information did you gather from your partner's vocal cues, including backchannel cues? Were you able to make inferences about your communication partner's mood and emotions just from the tone, pitch, rate, or quality of these vocal cues? Now compare these exchanges with some recent online communication you've had. Was it more difficult to make the same kinds of inferences about moods or emotions without vocal cues? Were there other ways in which emotions were communicated? Explain.

Assessing Your Skill

Go on a nonverbal communication scavenger hunt. Observe your family members, classmates, and friends to find one or more of the following sets of nonverbal communicators:

a. Examples of emblems, illustrators, affect displays, regulators, and adaptors
b. Examples of how people use the four zones of personal space
c. Examples of the cognitive, monitoring, regulatory, and expressive functions of eye contact
d. Examples of emotions expressed by facial expressions or vocal cues
e. Examples of how people use touch to communicate
f. Examples of clothing or accessories that reveal intentions or personality traits

Improving Your Skill in Interpreting Nonverbal Messages

Objective 7.3 Enhance your skill in interpreting nonverbal messages.

Key Terms

tells
immediacy
arousal
dominance

expectancy violation theory
perception checking
emotional contagion theory

Thinking Critically

What are some nonverbal strategies you could use during a job interview to appropriately express your interest in being hired for the position?

Assessing Your Skills

Evaluate your classroom based on the nonverbal messages this learning space communicates. Consider the following questions:

- What does the furniture arrangement communicate about the likelihood for interaction with others?
- Based on the room arrangement, what cues provide information about who has the most power and influence in this space?
- What do the colors of the classroom communicate? For example, are they contemporary or old-fashioned? Are they conducive to learning? Do they affect interpersonal communication?
- What does research about zones of personal space reveal about interpersonal communication in the room?
- On a scale from 1 to 10 (with 1 being low and 10 being high), how would you evaluate the overall attractiveness of the furniture and room décor (posters, photos, other art)? How does the attractiveness (or lack of attractiveness) of the space influence interpersonal communication? How does it enhance or detract from learning?
- What other aspects of the room have an effect on interpersonal communication and/or learning?

Use the questions in the above activity to evaluate another room where you spend a lot of time, such as your dorm room, the library, student center, or another place where you typically study when not in class. Describe how the room's arrangement and overall appearance influence interpersonal communication as well as learning and studying.

Improving Your Skill in Expressing Nonverbal Messages

Objective 7.4 Enhance your skill in expressing nonverbal messages.

Thinking Critically

1. Describe a situation in which you made eye contact with a stranger. Was it unpleasant or disturbing? Did the stranger's behavior communicate interest or liking? How did you react? Explain your observations in light of the principles about eye contact presented in the chapter.
2. What are some specific questions you could ask your close friends and family members that would help you better assess how your nonverbal mannerisms and expressions are being interpreted by them?

Assessing Your Skills

Record yourself as you participate in a role-play situation with another person. Perform one or more of the following situations:

- You're having a conversation with a professional colleague you just met for the first time.
- Try to sell a customer a smartphone or a computer. (Play the role of both the salesperson and the customer.)
- Participate in a performance appraisal interview in which your boss is expressing displeasure with your work behavior.
- You are listening to a friend, spouse, or partner tell a "story," but you believe he or she is lying to you.
- You are the friend, spouse, or partner telling a "story" that is not true.

Play back the video and observe your ability to express your nonverbal feelings and emotions. Consider these questions:

1. What nonverbal behaviors did you notice on the videotape that you were not aware of as you participated in the role-play?
2. What emotions and expressions did you perform effectively and appropriately?
3. What emotions and expressions were you not pleased with?
4. What did you learn about your skill in expressing nonverbal behaviors from observing your nonverbal expressions?
5. What nonverbal expression skills do you excel at?
6. Which nonverbal expression skills do you need to enhance?

Chapter 8
Conflict Management Skills

"Outside noisy, inside empty."

Chinese Proverb

∨ Learning Objectives

8.1 Define interpersonal conflict.

8.2 Identify commonly held myths about interpersonal conflict.

8.3 Compare and contrast three types of interpersonal conflict.

8.4 Describe the relationship between conflict and power.

8.5 Describe five conflict management styles.

8.6 Identify and use conflict management skills to help manage emotions, information, goals, and problems when attempting to resolve interpersonal differences.

Interpersonal conflict is a fact of life. Eventually, all relationships experience conflict. It's been estimated that people in stable, romantic relationships experience a conflict episode about twice a week.[1] You are more likely to have a quarrel with a romantic partner than with anyone else.[2] And the longer you know someone, the greater the likelihood that you'll experience conflict with that person, simply because you spend time together and know more about each other.[3] The key question of this chapter is "How can you best manage the inevitable conflict that occurs in your relationships with others?"

Conflict management is not a single skill, but a set of skills. But to manage conflict effectively involves more than learning simple techniques. The best route to success in resolving conflict effectively is acquiring knowledge about what conflict is, what makes it happen, and what we can do about it. With the ease of relating to others online or by phone or text, you need not meet in person to manage interpersonal conflict. But lean media such as text, e-mail, and instant messaging are not the best means of managing conflict, due to diminished nonverbal cues. This chapter provides principles and strategies to help you manage (not necessarily eliminate) the inevitable conflict that you experience in your relationships.

Conflict Defined

8.1 Define interpersonal conflict.

At the bedrock of all conflicts are differences—in goals, needs, and experiences. Unresolved and poorly managed interpersonal conflict is a significant predictor of an unsatisfactory interpersonal relationship. The opposite is also true: Partners in relationships in which conflict is effectively managed report being more satisfied with the relationship.[4] But precisely what is conflict? **Interpersonal conflict**, according to communication scholars William Wilmot and Joyce Hocker, includes four elements: It is (1) an expressed struggle (2) between at least two interdependent people (3) who perceive incompatible goals, scarce resources, or interference from others (4) and who are attempting to achieve specific goals.[5]

Conflict Elements

You probably don't need a textbook definition to determine whether you are experiencing conflict in a relationship. You know you're in conflict when your emotions become aroused, as evidenced by an increased heart rate, muscle tension, and a raised voice.[6] Conflict can occur whether the issue is about something personal or nonpersonal, or about something outside the relationship.[7] Yet looking at the elements of conflict can help you understand why conflict occurs and how to manage it.

AN EXPRESSED STRUGGLE You typically don't know that someone is upset with you until he or she expresses displeasure with a remark or by a nonverbal behavior such as a glare, a steely facial expression, or an emotion-laden tone of voice. The intensity of a conflict (as conveyed through the intensity of the emotion expressed) often correlates with the partners' perceptions of the importance of their unmet needs or goals. Sam Keltner developed the "struggle spectrum," shown in Figure 8.1, to describe conflicts ranging from mild differences to outright fights.[8] As conflict evolves in a relationship, it has the potential to escalate into physical abuse, especially in our most intimate

interpersonal conflict

An expressed struggle between at least two interdependent people who perceive incompatible goals, scarce resources, or interference in the achievement of their goals.

Figure 8.1 The Struggle Spectrum

Used by permission of the National Communication Association.

Mild Differences   Disagreement   Dispute   Campaign   Litigation   Fight

relationships. One research team estimated that 50–60 percent of US households have experienced at least minor forms of violence; there's evidence that in one out of every six romantic relationships, one partner has stalked the other.[9] Experts surmise that one reason violence is so prevalent in many relationships is that people don't have the skills to manage conflict.[10] They don't know how to effectively express their relational struggle.

BETWEEN AT LEAST TWO INTERDEPENDENT PEOPLE By **interdependent**, we mean that people are dependent on each other; what one person does or says affects the other.[11] If you were truly independent of someone, then what he or she did or said would have minimal effect on you. You are more likely to have conflict with people that you spend time with because you are connected to them in some way. Yes, you might have an emotional response to the anonymous driver who cuts you off in traffic, but the conflicts that weigh most heavily on us are those with people with whom we interact most frequently. And, as the old expression "it takes two to tango" suggests, it takes at least two people to have interpersonal conflict. You can certainly have intrapersonal conflict (conflict within yourself), but interpersonal conflict is between you and at least one other person.

Unresolved and poorly managed interpersonal conflict is a significant predictor of an unsatisfactory interpersonal relationship.

INCOMPATIBLE GOALS, SCARCE RESOURCES, AND INTERFERENCE Conflict often happens because two people want the same thing, but both can't have it, or what one person wants is the opposite of what the other wants. When resources (time, money, or something else) are scarce, tension is more likely.[12] Whether it's a battle between former spouses who both want custody of the children, or an argument over whether you spend the holidays with your parents or with your spouse's or partner's parents, conflict happens when goals are conflicting or incompatible, too little of something exists, or someone is blocking what you believe is rightfully yours.

ACHIEVING A GOAL People in conflict want something. As we noted, many conflicts occur because both people can't (or perceive that they can't) achieve their own goals. Understanding what the individuals in conflict want is an important step toward finding a way to manage the conflict. Most problems boil down to something you want more of or less of. Figuring out what you and the other person want more of or less of provides a starting point to getting to the end of conflict.

interdependent
Dependent on each other; one person's actions affect the other person.

Conflict Triggers

Now you know what conflict is, but what triggers it? A **conflict trigger** is a perceived cause of conflict. Note that we say, "*perceived* cause." When people communicate, especially during times of tension and conflict, perception becomes reality. What typically ticks people off? Here are some of the most common conflict triggers.

CRITICISM Receiving criticism is one of the most frequently mentioned conflict triggers. One study found that younger people were more likely to reject criticism from family elders (parents or grandparents) than from non-family elders.[13] Another study found that some husbands have a heightened sensitivity to what they perceive as criticism from women—not just their wives in particular, but women in general.[14] That is, some men have a bias for treating *any* comment from *any* female as negative. This sensitivity to criticism has been described as *empathic inaccuracy*. The greater their empathic inaccuracy, the more likely husbands were to respond to their wives with verbal aggression. Why does this phenomenon occur? Some men may have an insecure attachment style, a concept we discussed in Chapter 2. If a husband is insecure about his relationship with others, especially women, he may be more likely to lash out verbally when receiving negative comments from women. The research found that men who could better empathize with their spouses, and accurately infer that their

conflict trigger
A common perceived cause of interpersonal conflict.

spouses really did have specific and realistic points to make, reported having more satisfying and happier relationships.

FEELING ENTITLED   If we believe we're entitled to something—whether "something" is a good grade in a class, a new car, or a relationship with someone—and we're denied getting what we think is ours, then conflict is a likely result.

PERCEIVED LACK OF FAIRNESS   If we believe we have not been treated fairly or equitably, conflict is likely. "It's mine, not yours!" and "That's not fair!" are claims children make while playing with others in a sandbox; those same sentiments fuel conflict between adults, as well as international conflicts between nations.

MORE PERCEIVED COSTS THAN REWARDS   Another trigger for conflict escalation in a relationship occurs when one person feels that he or she is getting less out of the relationship than the other person.[15] Over time, if the perceived burdens are greater than the joy of being in a relationship, conflict ensues.

DIFFERENT PERSPECTIVES   Researcher Lawrence Kurdek found that regardless of whether couples are heterosexual, gay, or lesbian, several topics or issues serve as conflict triggers: (1) power (who's in charge), (2) social issues (such as politics and religion), (3) personal flaws (such as using drugs or alcohol, smoking, or being lazy), (4) distrust (concern about whether one person is telling the truth), (5) intimacy (differences about the frequency and timing of sex), and (6) personal distance (as evidenced by the amount of time each person commits to the relationship).[16] Couples argue about other things, such as money, but money conflicts are often really about power. These "big six" appear to be common conflict themes across a wide variety of relationships.

STRESS AND LACK OF REST   When you are not at your physical best—when you're tired, stressed, or overworked—it may be wise to steer clear of situations that are likely to trigger disagreement. Before you know it, what you thought was just a casual remark can quickly escalate into conflict. The beginning of a vacation—when you and your friend, partner, or spouse may be at the peak of fatigue—is a prime occasion for conflict. The end of a long work week may also be a time when it doesn't take much to turn a conversation into the Friday night fights. Not surprisingly, research has documented that being under the influence of alcohol or other substances that impair judgment increases the chances that conflict will erupt.[17]

DIALECTICAL TENSION   A **dialectical tension** stems from people's need or desire for two things at the same time.[18] This tension results in uncertainty and discomfort within the relationship. Here are two classic dialectical tensions experienced in many relationships.

- *Being separate and connected.*   You may have a desire to be both separate from other people and connected to them at the same time; we want our freedom, but we also want the comfort, predictability, and convenience of having someone who is a consistent part of our life. You may feel a personal dialectical tension because you want both things *at the same time*— to have your freedom *and* to be close to the other person.
- *Feelings of being open and closed.*   A second common dialectical tension is that we want and need various degrees of openness and closedness in our relationships. We want to share and disclose our thoughts and feelings, but we also want our privacy and secrecy.

Awareness of common conflict triggers allows you to spot them in your relationship before conflict escalates into intractable tension that is more challenging to manage.

Conflict as a Process

Conflict triggers may seem obvious when you read about them in a textbook, but in our lives they may be more difficult to identify. Cathy was reading her e-book,

---

BEING Other-ORIENTED

It's hard to be focused on others when you're under stress, tired, or worried about something. Have you noticed that you tend to experience more interpersonal conflict when either you or your communication partner are not at your best? What can you do to minimize conflict when you or others are fatigued or under stress?

---

dialectical tension

Tension arising from a person's need for two things at the same time.

Communication and Emotion

Do You Know What Your "Hot Buttons" Are?

Hot buttons are the things people say or do that trigger conflict. Specifically, they are behaviors that foster anger. Anger is an emotional response to fear. Stated another way, anger is an outward response to an inward feeling of fear. And fear is often about losing something or not getting something we believe is rightfully ours. Anger also occurs when we feel someone is keeping us from what we want and have a right to have, or someone is unjustly blaming or attacking us.

Although we have described specific behaviors that trigger conflict for many people, what pushes your hot buttons may not be the same thing that pushes someone else's. Do you know what your hot buttons are? "You don't know what you're talking about." "You sound just like your father." "You never listening to anything I say." Statements that begin with the word *you* are often hot buttons for people. *You* can sound like a horn honking at you in traffic, trying to urge you to move forward. You feel defensive and, with your hot button pushed, you reciprocate with anger and a few choice words. So again we ask, what are your hot buttons? Take a moment and list two or three of your hot buttons in the space below.

_____

_____

_____

_____

Next question: How long did it take for you to identify your hot buttons? If your unique hot buttons came to mind quickly, it's likely you've thought about what your hot buttons are before now. If it took you some time to think about specific things people say and do to push your buttons, then you may be more susceptible to having these buttons pushed. What do you do if someone pushes one of your buttons? Consider these suggestions:

- *Be aware that someone has pushed your hot button.* Hot buttons have more power over you if you are not aware of what they are. Taking time to reflect on what ticks you off is a first step to preventing an automatic response.

- *Breathe.* After you are aware that your button has been pushed, take a deep, calming breath or two. You do not need to dramatically heave a loud sigh. But just quietly calm yourself by taking several, unobtrusive breaths. You can do this whether you are on the phone or reading an e-mail or text message.

- *Take a moment.* If you are angry and afraid you might say or do something you'll regret, just be quiet and listen. Use self-talk to keep from loudly lashing back at your partner.

- *Remind yourself that you control your own emotions.* Although others may do and say things that can upset you, you are the only person who can control yourself and your response to others. Try to respond mindfully to others, rather than reacting emotionally to them.

- *Recognize that angry emotional outbursts rarely change someone's mind.* Exploding in an angry tirade may make you feel better for a moment by "getting it off your chest," but it usually does little to advance understanding and manage the issues at hand.

In all probability, the people who are close to you know what your buttons are and will sometimes purposely push them just to get a strong emotional response from you. There are certainly times to be assertive and express your feelings. But do so mindfully and not as an automatic response to someone who has pushed your buttons.

---

enjoying a second cup of coffee, and listening to her favorite music. All seemed peaceful. Suddenly, for no apparent reason, her partner Barb brusquely stormed into the room and shouted, "I can't stand it any more! We have to talk about who does what around here." Cathy was taken completely off guard. She had no idea her partner felt upset about the division of household chores. To her, this outburst seemed to come out of the blue; in reality, however, several events had triggered it.

Most relational disagreements have a source, a beginning, a middle, an end, and an aftermath.[19]

SOURCE: PRIOR CONDITIONS The first phase in the conflict process is the one that sets the stage for disagreement; it begins when you become aware of differences between you and another person. The differences may stem from role expectations, perceptions, goals, or resources. In the previous example, Barb perceived that she and Cathy played different roles in caring for the household.

In interpersonal relationships, *many* potential conflict triggers may be smoldering below the surface. It may take some time before they flare up into overt conflict.

Moreover, they may be compounded with other concerns, making them difficult to identify. It's likely that it's not just one conversation or issue that triggers conflict; multiple conflict "trip wires" may contribute to a conflict episode.[20]

BEGINNING: FRUSTRATION AWARENESS At this stage, at least one of you becomes aware that the differences in the relationship are increasingly problematic. You may begin to engage in self-talk, noting that something is wrong and creating frustration. Perhaps you realize that you won't be able to achieve an important goal or that someone else has the resources you need to achieve it. Or you may become aware of differences in perceptions. Barb knew that Cathy's family always spent their weekends relaxing. All the members of Barb's family, in contrast, pitched in on weekends to get household chores done for the week. Barb may have recognized that difference, even as her frustration level rose.

Becoming aware of differences in perception does not always lead to increased frustration. But when the differences interfere with something you want to accomplish, your frustration level rises. Barb wanted to get the house clean so that she could turn her attention to studying for a test she had the next day. Cathy's apparent indifference to helping Barb achieve that goal was a conflict trigger.

MIDDLE: ACTIVE CONFLICT When you bring your frustration to the attention of others, a conflict becomes an active *expressed struggle.*[21] If frustrations remain only as thoughts, the conflict is passive, not active. Active conflict does not necessarily mean that the differences are expressed with shouting or emotional intensity, although research suggests that if it is unmanaged, interpersonal conflict can escalate to interpersonal violence.[22] An expression of disagreement may be either verbal or nonverbal. Calmly asking someone to change an attitude or behavior to help you achieve your goal is a form of active conflict; so is kicking your brother under the table when he starts to reveal your secret to the rest of the family.

Communication, both intrapersonal and interpersonal, helps address issues that may lead to conflict. Cathy was not aware of the division of labor problem until Barb stormed into the room demanding a renegotiation. Barb had been aware of her frustration for some time, yet had not acted on it. Many experts advocate not waiting until your frustration level escalates to peak intensity before you approach someone with your conflict. Unexpressed frustration tends to erupt like soda in a can that has just been shaken. Being aware of potential conflict triggers can help you identify a conflict before it becomes active.

END: RESOLUTION When you begin to try to manage conflict, it has progressed to the resolution stage. Of course, not all conflicts can be neatly resolved. Couples who divorce, feuding business partners who dissolve their corporation, or former lovers who go their separate ways have all found solutions, even though they may not be amicable ones.

After Barb's outburst, she and Cathy were able to reach a workable compromise about the division of their household labor. Cathy agreed to clean the house every other week; Barb promised not to expect her to do it on weekends.

AFTERMATH: FOLLOW-UP As the late Yogi Berra once said, "It ain't over 'til it's over." After a conflict has been resolved, the follow-up stage involves dealing with hurt feelings or managing simmering grudges, and checking with the other person to confirm that the conflict has not retreated into the frustration awareness stage.[23] As we noted in Chapter 1, interpersonal relationships operate as transactive processes rather than as linear, step-by-step ones. Conflict does (mostly) progress in stages, but you may need to resolve the same conflict again unless you confirm your understanding of the issues with your partner.

The Friday after their discussion, Cathy proudly showed off a spotless apartment to Barb when she came home from class. Barb responded with a grin and a quick hug and privately resolved to get up early on Sunday morning so that she could go out to

Recap

Conflict as a Process

Prior Conditions	Frustration Awareness	Active Conflict	Resolution	Follow-Up
Differences exist in background, experience, culture, attitudes, beliefs, values, opinions, or preferences.	One individual becomes aware of differences. Thoughts and self-talk about the differences occur. The individual experiences frustration.	The conflict is expressed; this expression could range from a verbal communication of mild differences to physical violence.	One or more of the individuals involved seek to manage the conflict. Not all conflicts are managed successfully or resolved.	Individuals check to determine whether the conflict has been effectively and appropriately managed. They may need to revisit conflict management strategies.

get Cathy pastries before she awoke. This kind of mutual thoughtfulness exemplifies a successful follow-up in a conflict.

Understanding the stages of conflict can help you better manage the process. You'll also be in a better position to make the conflict a constructive rather than a destructive experience. Conflict is **constructive** if it helps provide new insights and establishes new patterns in a relationship. Airing differences can lead to a more satisfying relationship in the long run. David W. Johnson lists the following as benefits of conflict in interpersonal relationships. Interpersonal conflict…[24]

- focuses attention on problems that may have to be solved,
- clarifies what may need to be changed,
- focuses attention on what is important to you and your partner,
- clarifies who you are and what your values are,
- helps you learn more about your partner,
- keeps relationships interesting, and
- strengthens relationships by increasing your confidence that you can manage disagreements.

Conflict can also be **destructive**. The hallmark of destructive conflict is a lack of flexibility in responding to others.[25] Conflict can become destructive when people view their differences from a win–lose perspective, rather than looking for solutions that allow both individuals to gain. Conflict clearly has a dark side. Cyberbullying, hate crimes, stalking, aggressive verbal abuse, and physical abuse are some of the potential negative effects of escalating, unmanaged conflict. The Internet, smartphones, Skype, and YouTube make it easier to broadcast negative and destructive relational messages to more people at greater speed. A key purpose of this book, and specifically this chapter, is to identify sources of conflict *before* the relational turbulence becomes destructive. The principles, strategies, and skills we offer won't eliminate conflict, but they can help you manage it when it occurs in both face-to-face and electronically mediated relationships.

> **BEING Other-ORIENTED**
>
> When experiencing conflict with another person, identify some of the positive values or benefits of the conflict, and compare those with the costs or destructive nature of conflict. What could you do to increase the benefits and decrease the costs of conflict with others?

constructive conflict

Conflict that helps build new insights and establishes new patterns in a relationship.

destructive conflict

Conflict that dismantles rather than strengthens relationships.

Conflict Myths

8.2 Identify commonly held myths about interpersonal conflict.

Although not all conflict is destructive to relationships, many cultures have taboos against displaying conflict in public. Growing up, our families shape how we learn to express and manage conflict and they are also where we learn life lessons about relationships that remain with us.[26] According to one researcher, many of us were raised with four myths that contribute to our negative feelings about conflict.[27] In some American families, conflict is expressed openly and often. But even if your experience has been different, reading about these prevailing myths may help you understand your or your partner's emotional responses to conflict.

Myth 1: Conflict Is Always a Sign of a Poor Interpersonal Relationship

It is an oversimplification to assume that all conflict is rooted in underlying relational problems. Conflict is a normal part of any interpersonal relationship.[28] Although it is true that constant bickering and sniping can be symptomatic of deeper problems, disagreements do not necessarily signal that the relationship is on the rocks. In fact, overly polite, stilted conversation is more likely to signal a problem than periodic disagreements.[29] The free expression of honest disagreement is often a hallmark of healthy relationships. Assertively and honestly expressing ideas may mean that a person feels safe and comfortable enough with his or her partner to disagree.

Myth 2: Conflict Can Always Be Avoided

"If you can't say anything nice, don't say anything at all." Many of us were taught early in our lives that conflict is undesirable and that we should eliminate it from our conversations and relationships. Yet evidence suggests that conflict arises in virtually every relationship.[30] Because each of us has a unique perspective on our world, it would be extraordinary for us *always* to see eye to eye with another person. Although such conflicts may not be intense, many differences of opinion punctuate our relationships with people we care about.[31]

Research suggests that contentment in marriage relates not to the amount of conflict, but to the way in which partners manage it.[32] Conflict is also a normal and productive part of interaction in group deliberations.[33] It is a myth that conflict is inherently unproductive and something to be avoided. It happens, even in the best of relationships.

Myth 3: Conflict Always Occurs Because of Misunderstandings

"You just don't understand what my days are like. I need to go to sleep!" shouts Janice as she scoops up a pillow and blanket and stalks off to the living room. "Oh, yeah? Well, you don't understand what will happen if I don't get this budget in!" responds Ron, who is hunched over the desk in their bedroom. It is clear that Ron and Janice are having a conflict. They have identified the cause of their problem as a lack of understanding between them, but in reality they *do* understand each other. Ron knows that Janice wants to sleep; Janice knows he wants to stay up and work. Their problem is that they disagree about whose goal is more important. This disagreement, not lack of understanding, is the source of the conflict.

Myth 4: Conflict Can Always Be Resolved

Consultants, corporate training experts, and authors of self-help books often offer advice about how to resolve conflicts so that all will be well and harmony will prevail. Some people claim that with the application of a few skills and how-to techniques, conflicts can disappear like a stain from a shirt laundered with the right kind of detergent. This is simply not true. Not all differences can be resolved by listening harder or paraphrasing your partner's message. Some disagreements are so intense and perceptions so fixed that individuals may have to agree to disagree and live with it.

Conflict Types

8.3 **Compare and contrast three types of interpersonal conflict.**

At some time or another, many close relationships go through a conflict phase. "We're always fighting," complains a newlywed. But if she were to analyze these fights, she would discover important differences among them. According to communication researchers Gerald Miller and Mark Steinberg, most conflicts fit into one of three classic categories: (1) pseudoconflict—triggered by a lack of understanding; (2) simple conflict—stemming from different ideas, definitions, perceptions, or goals; and (3) ego conflict—which occurs when conflict gets personal.[34]

Pseudoconflict: Misunderstandings

Will:	Let's walk to the store.
Sean:	No, it's too far. Let's drive.
Will:	But the store is close.
Sean:	No, it's not.
Will:	Yes, it is. It's just off Market Street.
Sean:	Oh, you mean the convenience store.
Will:	Sure, that's exactly what I mean.
Sean:	Oh, no problem. I thought you meant the supermarket.

Pseudoconflict is simply a misunderstanding. Your partner may communicate confusion by facial expressions or other nonverbal behavior. Pseudoconflict can be resolved if partners ask for clarification, listen between the lines, and work to establish a supportive climate.

Pseudo means false or fake. **Pseudoconflict** occurs when we simply miss the meaning in a message. But unless we clear up the misunderstanding by asking for more information, a real conflict might ensue. Note that in this example, Will offers helpful information ("It's just off Market Street"), and Sean checks it with feedback ("Oh, you mean the convenience store").

How can you avoid pseudoconflict? A key strategy is to clarify the meaning of words and expressions that you don't understand. Keep the following strategies in mind to minimize misunderstandings before they occur:

- *Check your perceptions:* Ask for clarification of anything you don't understand; seek to determine whether your interpretation is the same as your partner's.
- *Listen between the lines:* Rather than voice a misunderstanding, people may express their uncertainty nonverbally. Look for puzzled or quizzical facial expressions from your partner. Or listen to his or her tone of voice to determine whether nonverbal behaviors are consistent with the verbal message.
- *Establish a supportive rather than a defensive climate for conversation:* Avoid evaluating, controlling, using manipulative strategies, being aloof, acting superior, or rigidly asserting that you're always right. These classic behaviors increase defensiveness and misunderstanding.

Simple Conflict: Different Stands on the Issues

Simple conflict stems from differences in ideas, definitions, perceptions, or goals. You want to go to Disney World for your vacation; your spouse wants to go to Washington, D.C. Your spouse wants to fly; you would rather take the train. You understand each other, but you disagree.

A key to unraveling a simple conflict is to keep the conversation focused on the issues at hand so that the expression of differences does not deteriorate into a battle focusing on personalities.

To keep simple conflict from escalating into personal attacks, consider the following strategies:

- *Clarify your and your partner's understanding* of the issues and your partner's understanding of the source of the disagreement.
- *Keep the discussion focused* on facts and the issue at hand, rather than drifting back to past battles and unrelated personal grievances.
- *Look for more than just the initial solutions* that you and your partner bring to the discussion; generate many options.

BEING Other-ORIENTED

Listening for the unspoken message is especially important when experiencing conflict with another person. What nonverbal cues can you look for to provide information about what the other person may be feeling or experiencing? How do you know whether you have made accurate inferences when "listening between the lines"?

---

pseudoconflict

Conflict triggered by a lack of understanding and miscommunication.

simple conflict

Conflict that stems from different ideas, definitions, perceptions, or goals.

Relating to Diverse Others

Gender and Conflict

Since conflict is often rooted in differences, it's not surprising that gender differences can influence how conflict is managed.

One difference that influences how we manage conflict is whether we have an overall feminine style or masculine style when managing conflict. A person with a *feminine style* focuses more on relationship issues, whereas someone with a *masculine style* typically focuses on tasks.[35] People with a feminine style often interact with others to achieve intimacy and closeness. In contrast, people with a masculine style often interact to get something done or to solve a problem. When pursuing a goal, people employing a masculine style tend to be more aggressive and assertive than those employing a feminine style.[36] The lists in this box summarize key differences that researchers have observed between feminine and masculine styles of responding to conflict. Note that individuals of either sex may employ some characteristics of both feminine and masculine gender styles.

Knowing your overall gender style and the style of the person with whom you are in conflict can help you respond and adapt to differing assumptions you may have about what the other person needs, wants, and expects.

Also, the overall attitude you have toward someone with a different gender style can influence how you manage conflict. One study found that men who expressed caring, positive, and protective attitudes toward women (in other words, had a more feminine style) were more likely to establish a warmer communication climate than men who focused on the task and were less relationally skilled.[38] As the saying goes, "You can catch more flies with honey than with vinegar."

Perceived Gender Differences in Responding to Conflict[37]

People with Feminine Styles ...	People with Masculine Styles ...
Are concerned with equity and caring; they connect with and feel responsible to others.	Are concerned with equality of rights and fairness; they adhere to abstract principles and rules.
Interact to achieve closeness and interdependence.	Interact to achieve specific goals; they seek autonomy and distance.
Attend to interpersonal dynamics to assess the relationship's health.	Are less aware of interpersonal dynamics but focus on the goal.
Encourage mutual involvement.	Protect self-interest.
Attribute crises to problems in the relationship.	Attribute crises to problems external to the relationship.
Are concerned with the impact of the relationship on personal identity.	Are neither self- nor relationship-centered.
Respond to conflict by often focusing mainly on the relationship.	Respond to conflict by often focusing on rules and being evasive until a unilateral decision is reached.

- *Don't try to tackle too many issues at once.* Perform "issue triage"—identify the important issues, and work on those.
- *Find the kernel of truth in what your partner is saying.* Find agreement where you can.
- *If tempers begin to flare and conflict is escalating, cool off.* Come back to the discussion when you and your partner are fresh.

Ego Conflict: Conflict Gets Personal

ego conflict

Conflict in which the original issue is ignored as partners attack each other's self-esteem.

Ego conflict occurs when the disagreement escalates, the conflict becomes personal, and a person's self-esteem is diminished. "You're a lousy driver!" "What a messy roommate you are!" "Must you always have music blaring?" Each of these accusations is a candidate for triggering ego conflict. After the first personal attack is launched, a counterattack is likely as each person in the conflict becomes more defensive about his or her position. Research has found that when you are under stress, you are more likely to be verbally aggressive toward someone.[39] It can take considerable time, skill, and patience to repair the damage caused by the things you said in a moment of anger and frustration.

If you find yourself involved in ego conflict, try to refrain from hurling a personal attack in response. Instead, take turns expressing your feelings and discussing the problem without interrupting each other. Then take time to cool off.[40] It is difficult to use effective listening skills when your emotions are at a high pitch. Marianne Mast and her colleagues found that when power differences exist between people, it's helpful to be more empathic—put yourself in the other person's position—to help establish

Recap

Types of Conflict

	Pseudoconflict	Simple Conflict	Ego Conflict
What It Is	Individuals misunderstand each other.	Individuals disagree over which action to pursue to achieve their goals.	Individuals feel personally attacked.
What to Do	Check your perceptions.	Clarify understanding.	Return to issues rather than personal attacks.
	Listen between the lines; look for nonverbal expressions of puzzlement.	Stay focused on facts and issues.	Talk about a problem to be solved rather than a fight to be won.
	Be supportive rather than defensive.	Generate many options rather than arguing over one or two options.	Write down rational arguments to support your position.
	Listen actively.	Find the kernel of truth in what your partner is saying; emphasize where you agree.	Use "I" messages rather than "you" messages.
			Avoid contemptuous verbal or nonverbal messages.

a positive, interpersonally sensitive communication climate.[41] Being other-oriented, especially during ego conflict, can help you manage the conflict more effectively.

Here are additional strategies to consider when conflict becomes personal:

- *Try to steer the ego conflict back to simple conflict:* Stay focused on issues ("Here's the problem") rather than personalities ("You're the problem").
- *Make the issue a problem to be solved rather than a battle to be won.*
- *Write down what you want to say:* It may help you to clarify your point, and you and your partner can develop your ideas without interruption. But by all means avoid putting angry personal attacks in writing. Make your written summary rational, logical, and brief rather than emotion-laden.
- *When things get personal, make a vow not to reciprocate:* Use "I" messages that we talked about in Chapter 5 ("I feel uncomfortable and threatened when we yell at each other.") rather than "you" messages ("You're such a little shyster. You never listen.") to express how you are feeling.
- *Avoid contempt:* To be contemptuous is to roll your eyes and sarcastically intone, "Oh, that's brilliant" to something your partner has said. Research has found that happy and satisfied couples rarely express contempt.[42] That doesn't mean there's no teasing, but caustic and corrosive contemptuous conversation is typically not present between people in a satisfying relationship.

Conflict and Power

8.4 **Describe the relationship between conflict and power.**

Often what we fight about is not what we're really fighting about. The topic of your argument may be anything from deciding which movie to see to something more significant, such as whether to have children. Yet underlying the surface issue may be a question about who has the power to make the decision. If, during an argument you or your partner says, "Who made you king?" or "What gives you the right to make this decision?" those comments indicate that underlying the conflict is an issue of power. Power and conflict go hand in hand, because people often use the sources of interpersonal power available to them to achieve their desired outcome when conflict occurs.

Interpersonal power is the degree to which a person is able to influence or control his or her relational partner. During a conflict, you may not even be aware of how you draw on the power that you have, or that the other person exerts power to influence you. Nonetheless, power issues are often the "back story" to the conflict.

interpersonal power

Degree to which a person is able to influence his or her partner.

Research has found gender differences in the way we use, interpret, and respond to power in our relationships.[43] Men's perception of whether they had power in a relationship was often not directly related to whether they were observed to dominate a conversation, nor did it correlate with what they actually did when talking with others. When women saw themselves as more powerful in a relationship, they sometimes surprisingly tended to view their partners as more dominant in the relationship. Perhaps when women perceived that their partner was dominant, they responded with increased power in response. Understanding principles of power and sources of power can give you greater insight into how you are using power to influence others to achieve your goals and how others are seeking to influence or control you, especially during conflict.

Power Principles

Most of us probably don't like to think that other people have power over us, but power is a fundamental element of all our personal relationships. Understanding the role of power in our relations with others can help explain and predict our thoughts, emotions, and behaviors, especially during relational conflict.

POWER EXISTS IN ALL RELATIONSHIPS   The definition of interpersonal communication presented in Chapter 1 suggests that *mutual influence* is an essential element any time you relate to others. When you talk, you are attempting to exert power over other people, if for no other purpose than to get them to listen to you. By definition, being in a relationship means letting someone have some influence on you *and* having influence on the other person.

POWER DERIVES FROM THE ABILITY TO MEET A PERSON'S NEEDS   If you can meet someone's needs, then you have power. The degree to which one person can satisfy another person's interpersonal needs (for inclusion, control, and affection) as well as other needs (for food, clothing, safety, sex, money) represents the amount of power that person has.

dependent relationship

Relationship in which one partner has a greater desire for the other to meet his or her needs.

In a **dependent relationship**, one person has a greater need for the partner to satisfy his or her needs; the power is out of balance and the person who depends on someone else to meet his or her needs has less power. One study of heterosexual romantic couples found that the partner with less emotional involvement in the relationship had more power, and this was generally the man.[44] The more we depend on one person to satisfy our needs, the more power that person has over us.

BOTH PEOPLE IN A RELATIONSHIP HAVE SOME POWER   Although sometimes one person in a relationship has more power (influence) than the other, each person has some degree of power. When you were a child, your parents clearly had more power than you did; during conflicts, especially when you were quite young, they used their power to resolve things in their favor. Now the power may be more balanced (or maybe not). When two people are satisfying each other's needs, they create an interdependent relationship; each person in the relationship has some amount of power over the other.

Underlying many interpersonal conflicts is the question of who has power to make decisions.

POWER IS CIRCUMSTANTIAL   Because our needs change, so does power. As you were growing up, you were very dependent on your parents and other adults. However, as you aged and developed skills, you no longer needed your parents to meet certain needs, and thus their power diminished. Depending on the circumstances, the power balance ebbs and flows in a relationship over time.

POWER IS NEGOTIATED   Partners often negotiate which individual will have decision-making responsibility over what issues. But people can disagree as to who has power to do what. If one partner wants the power to control the TV remote and the other person also wants to have channel-changing power, conflict and tension result, unless some negotiation occurs. "OK, you decide what we watch between 6:00 and 8:00 pm and I'll control the remote the next two hours" may be one couple's way of negotiating the power. With power negotiated, the conflict is managed—unless one of the individuals wants to revisit who is in charge of the remote. If the negotiation is about something more significant than who watches which TV program (such as sex, money, or children), the conflict can be more intense since more is at stake during the power negotiation.

Power Sources

Why does one person in a relationship have power over the other? Understanding the sources of power can help you analyze the power that you have and that others have over you. During conflict, being mindful of how people can influence you and how you may influence others can help you understand why some conflicts are managed as they are. John French and Bertram Raven developed a classic framework for identifying the sources of power.[45] The five sources of power they identified are legitimate (or position) power, referent power, expert power, reward power, and coercive power.

Legitimate power is based on respect for a position that a person holds. Teachers, parents, law officers, store managers, and company presidents all have power because of the position they hold relative to other people. When a police officer tells you to pull off to the side of the road, you respond to this enactment of power by obeying the officer's command.

Referent power comes from our attraction to another person or the charisma a person possesses. We let people we like influence us. We change our behavior to meet their demands or desires because we feel attracted to them.

Expert power is based on a person's knowledge and experience. We grant power to those who know more than we do or have some expertise we don't possess. You recognize, for example, that your teenage son knows more about computers than you do, so you let him try his hand at solving a computer glitch. Such expertise can include knowledge about how to manage a relationship effectively. We grant power to partners who have more experience in relationships.

Reward power is based on another person's ability to satisfy your needs. Some rewards, such as money and gifts, are tangible, but most rewards are more interpersonal in nature. Reward power is probably the most common form of power in interpersonal relationships. Withholding rewards (such as affection) is actually a form of punishment, or what is called *coercive power*.

Coercive power involves the use of sanctions or punishment to influence others. Sanctions include holding back or removing rewards. If you have a high need for physical affection, your partner might withhold that affection if you do not comply with a given request. Punishment involves imposing something on another person that he or she does not want.

Power to Persuade

When we have power, we may use it to manage conflict in order to achieve our goals and meet our needs using compliance-gaining strategies. **Compliance gaining** involves taking actions in interpersonal relationships to gain something from our partners—to get others to comply with our goals.

People's level of power affects which compliance-gaining strategies they employ. People with more power can be more efficient in gaining compliance by using simple, more direct (and sometimes inappropriate) strategies to accomplish their goals.[46] Those with less power need to carefully consider which strategies they can use that won't result in negative consequences. For example, telling your boss that you want Friday night off or you'll quit might result in a loss of a job. The appropriateness of

legitimate power
Power that is based on respect for a person's position.

referent power
Power that comes from our attraction to another person, or the charisma a person possesses.

expert power
Power based on a person's knowledge and experience.

reward power
Power based on a person's ability to satisfy our needs.

coercive power
Power based on the use of sanctions or punishments to influence others.

compliance gaining
Taking persuasive actions to get others to comply with our goals.

compliance gaining varies according to our goals. Research suggests that persuasive strategies involving either logic or emotion were viewed as more effective in face-to-face interactions than in computer-mediated ones.[47] Research has identified several compliance-gaining strategies we can use to negotiate power differences—some strategies are more personally affirming and others are more assertive or even aggressive.[48] Positive and affirming strategies include politely making requests, suggesting alternatives, summarizing areas of agreement, thanking the other person, making a promise, acknowledging similarities and differences, or assuring the other person that it will all be OK in the end. (Perhaps you've heard the phrase, "Everything will be OK in the end; if it's not OK, it's not the end.")

More assertive strategies of seeking compliance include accusing, arguing, blaming, challenging, complaining, criticizing, demanding, pleading, reprimanding, or issuing a warning. The specific strategy you select is based on a variety of factors including your goal and the goal of the other person.

Compliance-gaining strategies are responsive to the ongoing, transactive nature of interpersonal relationships.[49] We plot strategies that develop over a number of interactions and modify them in accordance with others' responses. For example, before you ask to borrow money from your friend, you might first do a few favors for her during the day. Then if your friend says no to your request for a loan, you might remind her that she owes you for all you've done for her. If she still says no, you might offer to help her over the weekend with her class project. The type of relationship you have established with the other person will affect your strategy selection.

Power Negotiation

If you realize you don't have as much power as you'd like, you may want to renegotiate the balance of power in a relationship. For example, in the first year of marriage, couples often argue about balancing job and family, financial problems (including who spends money and on what), the frequency of sexual relations, and the division of household tasks.[50] These problems involve issues of power, control, responsibility, and decision making that need to be negotiated.

Defining who has power can be a source of conflict in interpersonal relationships, potentially even bringing about the end of a relationship. When a partner abuses power, ending the relationship may be warranted. Ideally, partners negotiate a mutually acceptable and rewarding power relationship. To negotiate or renegotiate power in a relationship, consider both your needs and your partner's needs. Reflecting not just on your needs but also on the needs of the other person is an other-oriented strategy that can help you honestly and realistically start the negotiation process.

Conflict Management Styles

8.5 **Describe five conflict management styles.**

What's your typical approach to managing interpersonal conflict: fight or flight? Do you tackle conflict head-on or seek ways to remove yourself from it? Most of us do not have a single way of dealing with differences, but we do have a tendency to manage conflict by following patterns that we have used before, as well as considering the specific person with whom we are experiencing conflict.[51] For example, if your boss gives you an order, you respond differently from the way you do if your spouse gives you an order.

The conflict style we choose depends on several factors: our personality, our attachment style, the individuals with whom we are in conflict, the time and place of the confrontation, and other situational factors. Even the TV programs you watch can influence how you manage conflict. One study found that if a couple watches TV programs that include lots of conflict and bickering, the couple is slightly more likely to use more domineering strategies when managing conflict.[52]

Figure 8.2 Conflict Management Styles

The five conflict management styles in relation to concern for others and concern for self.

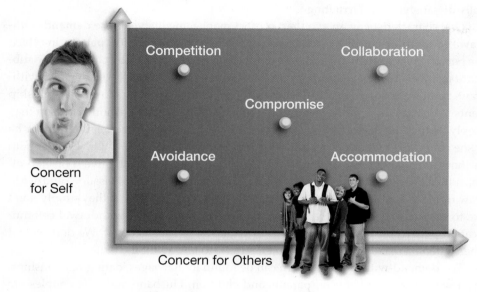

Virginia Satir, author of *Peoplemaking*, a book about family communication, suggests that we learn conflict response patterns early in life.[53] Ample research evidence supports Satir's conclusion.[54] How we manage conflict with others is related to how our family of origin dealt with conflict. One research team linked a person's attachment style (discussed in Chapter 2 as secure, anxious, or avoidant) to the style that person uses to manage conflict. People with a secure attachment style, for example, are less likely to avoid conflict and are generally less verbally aggressive during conflict.[55]

One of several classifications of **conflict management styles** is a five-style model based on the work of K. W. Thomas and R. H. Kilmann that includes two primary dimensions: concern for others and concern for self.[56] These two dimensions result in five conflict management styles, shown in Figure 8.2. The five styles are (1) avoidance, (2) accommodation, (3) competition, (4) compromise, and (5) collaboration.

conflict management styles
Consistent patterns or approaches people use to manage disagreements with others.

Avoidance

One approach to managing conflict is to back off and try to side-step the conflict. Typical responses from someone who uses this style are "I don't want to talk about it," "It's not my problem," "Don't bother me with that now," or "I'm not interested in that." The **avoidance** style might indicate that a person has low concern for others as well as for himself or herself. This is sometimes called the "lose–lose" approach to conflict. The person using the avoidance conflict style wishes the problem or conflict would go away by itself and appears uninterested in managing the conflict or in meeting the needs of the other person involved in the disagreement. People who avoid conflict may also just not like the hassle of dealing with a difficult, uncomfortable situation. Not dealing directly with conflict may also stem from being unassertive and unable to stand up for one's own rights. You may also want to avoid conflict with someone if you feel that the relationship is hopeless and not worth investing in.[57]

avoidance
Conflict management style that involves backing off and trying to side-step conflict.

Other times, people avoid conflict because they don't want to hurt the feelings of others. There may be times when avoiding a major blowup with someone is a wise strategy, but hoping the conflict will go away on its own is unlikely to be the best plan.

Evidence suggests that husbands are more likely to avoid confrontation as a way of managing conflict with their wives. One research team argues that males are likely to avoid conflict because of the way they process information, especially emotions.[58]

demand-withdrawal pattern of
conflict management

Pattern in which one person
makes a demand and the other
person avoids conflict by changing
the subject or walking away.

Husbands may implicitly reason that it's better to keep quiet and avoid conflict than to speak up and try to sort things out; for them, the dissonance that results from speaking up is not worth the effort. Women, on the other hand, find avoiding the issues especially dissatisfying and irritating.[59]

One characteristic of an avoidant conflict management style is the **demand-withdrawal pattern of conflict management**. This is a communication pattern in which one person makes a demand and the other person avoids conflict by changing the subject or just walking away—he or she withdraws from the conflict.[60] The demand-withdrawal pattern is speculated to occur because one of the partners in the relationship wants to change the relationship and the other person does not. Another reason may simply be that the person who withdraws may not care about the relationship, or he or she may care, but believes that more talking simply won't help.[61] Or, if one or both partners anticipate negative emotions (such as anger) and destructive, personal attacks, then they may think "What's the use of trying to solve this issue?" and withdraw from the conflict.[62] Yet another reason people withdraw is that they simply don't like to engage in conflict. Research has found that the demand-withdrawal communication pattern results in lower levels of relationship satisfaction.[63] We don't like it when a person makes demands and then refuses to talk about the issue.

The demand-withdrawal pattern can be found in marriages, dating relationships, and friendships, and between parents and children. Husband-and-wife couples are more likely to experience the demand-withdrawal pattern when they are talking about their relationship. Research on how parents and teenagers managed conflict found that the demand-withdrawal pattern was one of the *least* satisfying approaches to managing conflict.[64] Researchers have found that making repeated demands that aren't directly addressed, while also hurling put-downs at one another, results in a more distressed parent–teenager relationship. If you see that you're in a demand-withdrawal pattern of conflict, try to change the tone of the interaction so that it becomes a conversation rather than a shouting match or a standoff in which you both stop talking. Make it a goal to keep the conversation going rather than making a demand that results in the other person just walking away.

In some respects, avoiding conflict could be perceived as uncooperative. However, avoiding conflict has some advantages. Doing so provides time for each person to think about the issues, cool down, and ponder other approaches to dealing with the issues. If the conflict issue really is trivial, it may be advantageous not to throttle up the tension.

Avoiding conflict can also allow each person to save face. One of the ways people avoid conflict and try to de-escalate emotional tension is by being deliberately vague or ambiguous about what is causing the conflict. They provide general rather than specific feedback. Yet in certain situations people find a direct response more honest and competent than a vague one.[65] The trick is accurately reading a situation to know when to be vague and when to be specific.

Avoiding conflict also has several disadvantages. If you avoid the conflict, you may be sending a message that you really don't care about the other person's feelings; you're more concerned about your own needs. Avoiding the conflict may also make things worse. A simmering conflict may boil over if it's not tended to. And, of course, another disadvantage is that the issue remains unresolved. Like a lump in the throat, the conflict just sits there.

Accommodation

accommodation

Conflict management style that
involves giving in to the demands
of others.

To accommodate is to give in to the demands of others. People may sometimes adopt an **accommodation** style because they fear rejection if they rock the boat. Sometimes, people who accommodate don't seem to get angry or upset; they just do what others want them to do. But, in reality, they also accommodate to serve their own interests—to get people to like them. This conflict management style is sometimes called the "lose–win" approach. If you consistently accommodate, you sacrifice your own needs so that someone else can win the argument.

Using the accommodation style has several advantages. For one thing, it shows that you're reasonable and you want to help. If the issue is a minor or trivial one, you may gain some credibility by just letting it slide. Of course, if you are wrong or have made a mistake, accommodation is an appropriate response.

Like other conflict styles, accommodating has disadvantages. Throughout this book, we've stressed the importance of becoming other-oriented. But we've also noted that being other-oriented means considering the needs and position of the other person, without necessarily doing what the other person wants. A person may sometimes accommodate for self-protection rather than because he or she is genuinely interested in others. In the following exchange, note Luke's accommodation response to Martin:

> *Martin:*   Luke, I'm not in agreement with you on the QCN merger. I think the merger should be called off.
> *Luke:*   OK. Whatever you think is best. I just want you to feel good about your decision.

To accommodate can give the accommodator a false sense of security by producing a "pseudosolution"—one that doesn't really solve anything but just postpones the effort of seeking a solution to the problem. Also, if you consistently accommodate, you may diminish your power to the extent that others take advantage of you; the next time a conflict arises, the expectation may be that you'll give in and the other person will get his or her way again. In addition, if you accommodate too quickly, you short-circuit the possibility of finding a creative solution that is to everyone's liking.

Competition

"You're wrong!" shouts Ed. "Here's how to get our project in on time. We can't waste time in the library. We just have to write up what we have."

"But Ed," suggests Derrick, "the assignment calls for us to have three library sources."

"No. We don't have time. Just do it," Ed insists. Ed sees the issue as a competition that he must win.

Each of us has some need to control and also some need to be controlled by others. But people who have a **competition** conflict management style have a win–lose philosophy. They want to win at the expense of the other person, to claim victory over their opponents. They want to control others. They are typically not other-oriented; instead, they are focused on themselves.

People who compete often resort to blaming, or seeking a scapegoat, rather than assuming responsibility for a conflict. "I didn't do it," "Don't look at me," and "He made me do it" are typical blaming statements.

If these strategies do not work, people with a competitive style may try threats and warnings. *Threats* refer to actions that people can actually carry out.[66] Warnings are negative prophecies they cannot actually control. The boyfriend who says, "If you don't stop calling me names, I'm going to leave you," has issued a threat; he has the power to leave. If he were to say, "Don't call your parents names, or they'll write you out of their will," that would be a warning. In reality, he has no control over his partner's parents.

Obviously, threats are more powerful than warnings in changing behavior, and then only if the other person would genuinely find the threatened actions punishing or disruptive. If a parent threatens to ground a child, the child will take the threat seriously only if he or she knows the parent will carry it out.

Is it ever appropriate to compete with others? Yes, if you believe that your position is clearly the best approach and that anything short of achieving your goal would be

competition
Conflict management style that stresses winning a conflict at the expense of the other person involved.

harmful to you and to others.[67] In an election, someone will win and someone will lose. At the conclusion of a judicial trial, someone typically wins and someone loses. But even hard-fought elections and controversial trials have rules designed to maintain fairness for all involved in the conflict or decision. During often-emotional periods of competition, those involved nonetheless need to maintain an ethical concern for others.

Compromise

compromise

Conflict management style that attempts to find the middle ground in a conflict.

To compromise is to attempt to find a middle ground—a solution that somewhat meets the needs of all concerned. The word *somewhat* is important. Often, when people compromise, no one gets precisely what he or she wants; each has to give up a bit of what he or she had hoped to get. When trying to craft a compromise, you're really expecting to lose something and win something simultaneously; you also expect your partner to lose and win. That's why the **compromise** style is called "a lose/win–lose/win" approach to conflict. As shown in Figure 8.2, when you compromise, you have some concern for others as well as some concern for yourself. Research has found that college students are more likely to try a compromise conflict management style first than any other style.[68]

Compromise has some advantages. It can be a good thing if a quick resolution to the conflict is needed. And it reinforces the notion that all parties involved share in equal power. Compromise can also be useful if what is needed is a temporary solution. And it has the advantage of helping everyone save face, because everyone wins at least something.

But if compromising results in each person giving in but no person feeling pleased with the compromise, then a more collaborative approach to managing the conflict may be appropriate.

Collaboration

BEING Other-ORIENTED

Collaboration would be impossible if you failed to consider the thoughts and feelings of the other person. What are ways to identify the interests you have in common with the person with whom you are in conflict? How can you determine where your goal overlaps with the other person's goal?

collaboration

Conflict management style that uses other-oriented strategies to achieve a positive solution for all involved.

flaming

Sending an overly negative online message that personally attacks another person.

disinhibition effect

The loss of inhibitions when interacting with someone online that leads to the tendency to escalate conflict.

To collaborate is to have a high concern for both yourself and others. People who use a **collaboration** style of conflict management are more likely to view conflict as a set of problems to be solved rather than a game in which one person wins and another loses.

The collaboration conflict style is best used when

- all sides of the conflict need fresh, new ideas;
- enhanced commitment to a solution is important because all are involved in shaping the outcome;
- it's important to establish rapport and a positive relational climate;
- emotional feelings are intense, and all involved in the conflict need to be listened to; or
- it's important to affirm the value of the interpersonal relationship.

It may sound as though collaboration is always the best approach to managing conflict. However, at times, its disadvantages may outweigh the advantages.[69] One of the biggest disadvantages is the time, skill, patience, and energy required to manage conflict collaboratively. If a solution is needed quickly, other approaches such as compromise may be best.

So, which style of managing conflict is best? The short answer to this question is "It depends." It depends on the outcome you seek, the amount of time you have, the quality of the relationship you have with the other people involved, your own personality and approach to managing conflict, and the amount of perceived power you and others have.[73] Each style has advantages and disadvantages; no style has an inherent advantage all of the time. The competent, other-oriented communicator consciously decides whether to compete, avoid, compromise, accommodate, or collaborate. Research suggests that most people find the following *least* effective: (1) no clear resolution, (2) a poorly managed process, or (3) the avoidance of issues one or both

#communicationandtechnology
Conflict Happens

Conflict happens not only during our face-to-face interactions but online as well. In fact, conflict may be even more likely to occur when we communicate online.

Managing Conflict Online
Reduced Nonverbal Cues

Because we may miss some of the subtle relational cues that exist in face-to-face situations, pseudoconflict in cyberspace can escalate from a mere misunderstanding to substantive differences (simple conflict). And if those differences become personal (ego conflict), the conflict is much more difficult to unravel.

Haste

Sometimes in our haste and informality, we tap out a message that is perfectly clear to us, but not to the recipient. Missed meaning because of a too-cryptic message often occurs online.

Flaming

Flaming occurs when someone sends an overly negative message that personally attacks someone else.[70] The flamer can further intensify the negative message by "shouting" the message in ALL CAPITAL LETTERS. People are more likely to use flaming language online than when talking in person.

The Disinhibition Effect

The tendency to escalate conflict online is called the **disinhibition effect**. Without another person physically present, and with emotional tension rising, people tend to lash out—they lose some of their inhibitions; hence the term disinhibition effect.

Strategies for Managing Conflict Online

What should you do when you find yourself in an online conflict? Some of the same strategies you would use when interacting in person can be useful, but you can consider other specific options in cyberspace.

Avoid Counterflaming; Take Time to Cool Off

Because of the disinhibition effect, your first impulse may be to respond immediately with a reciprocal flaming message. Don't. It may be cathartic to lash out in response to an unfair criticism or hurtful comment, but escalating the conflict makes it more difficult to manage.

Move to a Richer Medium

If it's possible, talk to your communication partner in person; if that's not possible, reach for the phone to talk in real time rather than asynchronously.

Make Sure You Understand the Issues Before Responding

Before you write or say anything further, reread the previous messages. Rather than looking for ways to justify your actions or feelings, read the messages as if you were looking at the information for the first time.

Paraphrase

Paraphrase first to yourself, and then to the other person what you understand your partner to be communicating. Then give the other person a chance to agree or disagree with your paraphrase. Don't make demands or requests. Turn the conversation into one about clarification rather than about what you both want.

Increase Redundancy

Repeat key points and summarize what you'd like to have happen during the conflict to ensure you are being "listened to." Slow the process down, especially when emotions may be running high; rather than piling on more details, make sure your essential points are clear.[71]

Use Caution When Trying to Lighten the Tone

In face-to-face contexts, humor can help break the tension. But when you're with someone physically, you can more accurately read your partner's nonverbal behavior to know when a joke is helping to reduce the tension and when it's not. Online, with limited nonverbal cues, what you think might reduce tension could escalate it.

Self Reflect

Take a "time out" to analyze your emotional reactions. Why are you getting upset and angry? Understanding why you've become upset can help you understand how to begin managing the conflict.

Put Yourself in the Other Person's Position

Use the other-oriented skill of decentering by asking yourself, "What was the other person thinking when he or she wrote that message?" Research suggests that we are more likely to think about ourselves rather than the other person during online conflict.[72] After considering the other person's thought process, empathize by asking yourself "What was the other person feeling?"

Conflict occurs both in person and online. Understanding that conflict may occur and rapidly escalate because of the disinhibition effect, and then implementing some of the suggestions presented here, may help you cool a heated conflict and return your interaction to "room temperature."

partners still want to discuss.[74] *No single conflict management style "works" in all situations.* We do, however, strongly suggest that when time and other factors permit, a collaborative (win–win) conflict management style is worth exploring.[75] The conflict management skills presented in the final section of this chapter are anchored in a collaborative approach to managing conflict.

If both people involved in a conflict have a secure attachment style (as discussed in Chapter 2, meaning they were raised in a "secure" family that fostered trust, love, and support), then they are likely to use a collaboration or compromise style as opposed to a competing or avoiding style during conflict. If one person is "secure" and the other "insecure" in terms of attachment style, mutual avoidance and withdrawal from untangling the issues are more likely. Researchers have also found that, overall, gay and lesbian couples used more mutual avoidance and withholding communication during conflict than did heterosexual couples.[76] Communication researcher Mitchell Hammer suggests that people from highly individualistic cultures (such as the predominant US culture) prefer a conflict management style that is more direct in addressing conflict-producing issues.[77] People in collectivistic cultures—those that emphasize group and team interests over individual interests—typically prefer a more indirect approach to addressing conflict. Hammer also suggests that our cultural preferences for expressing or restraining our emotions have an important influence on our preferred conflict management style.[78] People from cultures that emphasize less explicit expression of emotions (Asian cultures, for example) will find intense emotional expressions of anger and frustration distracting and unproductive in managing conflict. Your culture strongly influences the degree to which you are direct or indirect when you communicate with others during conflict. Your culture also influences how emotionally expressive or restrained you are when you experience interpersonal conflict.

Recap

Conflict Management Styles

	The person who uses this style ...
Avoidance	Withdraws from conflict; tries to side-step confrontation; finds conflict uncomfortable. A lose–lose approach to conflict.
Accommodation	Easily gives in to the demands of others; typically wants to be liked by others. A lose–win approach to conflict.
Competition	Dominates the discussion and wants to accomplish the goal even at the expense of others. A win–lose approach to conflict.
Compromise	Seeks the middle ground; will give up something to get something. A lose/win–lose/win approach to conflict.
Collaboration	Views conflict as a problem to be solved; negotiates to achieve a positive solution for all involved. A win–win approach to conflict.

Conflict Management Skills

8.6   Identify and use conflict management skills to help manage emotions, information, goals, and problems when attempting to resolve interpersonal differences.

For many people, at the heart of enhancing the quality of interpersonal relationships is learning how to effectively manage conflict.[79] Managing conflict, especially emotion-charged ego conflict, is not easy. The more stress and anxiety you feel at any given time, the more likely you are to experience conflict in your relationships with others. When you are under stress or feeling lonely, it's more likely that conflict will become personal and degenerate into ego conflict.[80] And the opposite is also true: When you're rested and relaxed, you're less likely to experience conflict. But even while relaxed and with a fully developed set of skills, don't expect to avoid conflict. Conflict happens. The following skills can help you generate options that promote understanding and provide a framework for collaboration.[81]

"Cool! My new cell phone allows me to see your angry face as well as hear your angry voice."

© 2015 Michael Maslin

Manage Your Emotions

For weeks, you have been working on a brochure with a tight deadline. You turned it over to the production department with instructions two weeks ago. Today, you call to check on its progress, and you discover that it is still sitting on the production coordinator's desk. You feel your anger begin to build. You're tempted to march into the production coordinator's office and scream at her, or to shout at her supervisor.

Try to avoid taking action when you are in such a state. You may regret what you say, and you will probably escalate the conflict.

Often, the first sign that we are in a conflict situation is a feeling of anger, frustration, fear, or even sadness, which sweeps over us like an ocean wave.[82] If we feel powerless to control our own emotions, we will have difficulty taking a logical or rational approach to managing the conflict. Expressing our feelings in an emotional outburst may make us feel better for the moment, but it may close the door to logical, rational negotiation.

When we are emotionally charged, we experience physical changes as well. One researcher found that

> … our adrenaline flows faster and our strength increases by about 20 percent. The liver, pumping sugar into the bloodstream, demands more oxygen from the heart and lungs. The veins become enlarged and the cortical centers where thinking takes place do not perform nearly as well…. The blood supply to the problem-solving part of the brain is severely decreased because, under stress, a greater portion of blood is diverted to the body's extremities.[83]

Such changes fuel our fight–flight responses. If we choose to stay, verbal or physical violence may erupt; if we flee from the conflict, we cannot resolve it. Until we can tone down (not eliminate) our emotions, we will find it difficult to apply other skills. Let's look at some specific strategies that you can draw on when an intense emotional response to conflict clouds your judgment and decision-making skills.[84]

BE AWARE THAT YOU ARE BECOMING ANGRY AND EMOTIONALLY VOLATILE
One characteristic of people who "lose it" is that they let their emotions get the best of them. Before they know it, they are saying and doing things they later regret. Unbridled and uncensored emotional outbursts rarely enhance the quality of an interpersonal relationship. An emotional purge may make you feel better, but your partner is likely to reciprocate, which will only escalate the conflict spiral.

Before that happens, become aware of what is happening to you. As we described earlier, your body will start to react to your emotions with an increased heart rate. Be sensitive to what is happening to you physically.

SEEK TO UNDERSTAND WHY YOU ARE ANGRY AND EMOTIONAL Understanding what's behind your anger can help you manage it. Realize that it is normal and natural to be angry. It's a feeling everyone experiences. You need not feel guilty about it. Anger is often expressed as a defense when you feel violated or when you are fearful of losing something that is important to you. The conflict triggers presented earlier in this chapter can help you identify the source of your anger. Think about the last time you became very angry. Often, you experience a sense of righteous indignation when you are angry. You are being denied something you feel you should have.

MAKE A CONSCIOUS DECISION ABOUT WHETHER TO EXPRESS YOUR ANGER
Rather than just letting anger and frustration build and erupt out of control, make a conscious choice about whether you should express your frustration and irritation. We're not denying that valid reasons for anger and frustration may exist, or suggesting that you should not express your feelings. Sometimes, forcefully expressing your irritation or anger is the only way to let someone know how important an issue is to you. As these lines from William Blake illustrate, sometimes the wisest strategy is to be honest with others and express how you feel.

> I was angry with my friend:
>
> I told my wrath, my wrath did end.
>
> I was angry with my foe:
>
> I told it not, my wrath did grow.

If you do decide to express your anger, don't lose control. Be direct and descriptive. The guidelines for listening and responding provided in Chapter 5 can serve you well. Keep your anger focused on issues rather than personalities.

SELECT A MUTUALLY ACCEPTABLE TIME AND PLACE TO DISCUSS A CONFLICT
If you are upset, or even tired, you risk becoming involved in an emotion-charged shouting match. If you ambush someone with an angry attack, don't expect him or her to be in a receptive frame of mind. Instead, give yourself time to cool off before you try to resolve a conflict. In the case of the lapsed deadline mentioned earlier, you could call both the production coordinator and her boss and schedule an appointment to meet with them later in the day. By that time, you could gain control of your feelings and also think the issue through. Of course, issues sometimes need to be discussed on the spot; you may not have the luxury of waiting. But whenever practical, make sure the other person is ready to receive you and your message. You may have heard the conventional wisdom "Never go to bed angry with your partner or spouse." Research suggests that the better application might be "Don't fight before bed." Couples who had experienced an "expressed struggle" conflict (more than just a mild difference of opinion) were less likely to sleep.[85]

PLAN YOUR MESSAGE If you are approaching someone to discuss a disagreement, take care to organize your message. Consider rehearsing what you will say. Identify your goal, and determine what outcome you would like; do not barge in and pour out your emotions.

BREATHE One of the simplest yet most effective ways to avoid overheating is to breathe. As you become aware that your emotions are starting to erupt, take a slow, deep breath. Then breathe again. This can help calm you and manage the physiological changes that adrenaline creates. Deep breathing—the prime strategy women use to manage the pain of childbirth—can be a powerful way to restore calmness to your spirit. Focusing on your breathing is also one of the primary methods of meditation. We're not suggesting that you hyperventilate. But taking deep, slow breaths that not only fill your upper lungs but move your diaphragm—the muscle that moves as your lungs expand and contract—is an active strategy to help you regain rational control.

MONITOR NONVERBAL MESSAGES As you learned in Chapter 7, your actions play a key role in establishing the emotional climate in any relationship. Monitoring

---

BEING Other-ORIENTED

Identifying mutually agreeable approaches to managing a conflict is also a way to manage emotions. What other strategies have worked for you in managing your emotions during conflict?

BEING Other-ORIENTED

Saving face is giving the other person a way to maintain his or her dignity, even if his or her initial ideas and proposals are not accepted in the final resolution of a conflict. What strategies have you used to help others save face and maintain their personal dignity during conflict?

your nonverbal messages can help to de-escalate an emotion-charged situation. Speaking calmly, using direct eye contact, and maintaining a calm, nonthreatening facial expression will signal that you wish to collaborate rather than control. Your nonverbal message should also support your verbal response. If you say you are listening to someone, but you continue to watch TV or work on a report, you are communicating a lack of interest in the speaker and the message.

AVOID PERSONAL ATTACKS, NAME CALLING, AND EMOTIONAL OVERSTATEMENT Using threats and derogatory names can turn a simple conflict into an ego conflict. When people feel attacked, they respond by protecting themselves. Research has found that when husbands and wives feel disconfirmed during conflict because of name calling or because their partner has made nasty comments, relational satisfaction significantly decreases.[86] It's not surprising that people don't like to be called names. Although you may feel hurt and angry, try to avoid exaggerating your emotions and hurling negative, personal comments at your partner.[87] If you say you are irritated or annoyed rather than furious, you can still communicate your emotions, but you take the harsh sting out of your description. We're not advocating that you be dishonest about how you are feeling; just don't overstate your emotions for dramatic effect. It may make you feel better, but it may make matters worse.[88]

Also avoid the bad habit of **gunny-sacking**. This occurs when you dredge up old problems and issues from the past, like pulling them out of an old bag or gunny sack, to use against your partner. Keep your focus on the issues at hand, not on old hurts. Gunny-sacking usually succeeds only in increasing tension, escalating emotions, and reducing listening effectiveness.

TAKE TIME TO ESTABLISH RAPPORT Evidence suggests that you'll be more successful in managing conflict if you don't immediately dive in and attempt to sort out the issues with your partner.[89] Taking time to establish a positive emotional climate can pay big dividends; this is especially important if you're not well acquainted with the person you're having the conflict with. One study compared how effectively conflict was managed in two different groups.[90] In one group, the conflict negotiators spent time face to face, "schmoozing" and getting to know one another, before trying to negotiate a solution to a conflict. In the other group, the negotiators exchanged information via e-mail but did not meet face to face. The negotiators who spent time establishing a positive relationship in person were more successful in managing the conflict to everyone's satisfaction.

Even if you know the other person well, take some time to build rapport. Chatting about such seemingly innocuous topics as the weather or local events can help break the ice and provide a basis for a more positive conversational climate. A positive emotional climate is especially important when trying to sort through vexing, conflict-producing issues. Research has found that taking time to listen and thoughtfully respond to others during conflict goes a long way toward creating a positive climate that is more likely to enhance rather than detract from the accuracy of communication.[91]

Another way to establish rapport is to consider using appropriate humor to lighten the mood. One study found that using humor effectively during a period of emotionally infused conflict can help take the sting out of discussions of difficult topics.[92] But we offer this important caution: Be certain that what *you* think is funny will be perceived by *your partner* as humorous. Trying to make a joke out of something that your partner does not find funny can backfire. It's especially important to be other-oriented when using humor to defuse tense moments. Several researchers also note how important it is to help the other person in the conflict save face—not to leave the conversation feeling demoralized and humiliated.

USE SELF-TALK Kosta was chairing the committee meeting when Monique accused him of falsifying the attendance numbers at the last fine arts festival. Instead

gunny-sacking
Dredging up old problems and issues from the past to use against your partner.

of lashing back at Monique, he paused, took a slow, deep breath, and thought, "I'm tired. If I snarl back, all we will do is escalate this issue out of proportion. I'll talk with Monique later, after we have both cooled down." Perhaps you think that talking to yourself is an eccentricity. Nothing could be further from the truth. As you saw in Chapter 2, thoughts are directly linked to feelings,[93] and the messages we tell ourselves play a major role in how we feel and respond to others. Ask yourself whether an emotional tirade and an escalating conflict will produce the results you want. When Eleanor Roosevelt noted, "No one can make you feel inferior without your consent," she was acknowledging the power of self-talk to affect your emotional response to what others say and do.

As you read the discussion about managing emotions, you may wonder if it's ever useful or productive to express negative emotions, especially anger, overtly when negotiating an issue. One research study found that expressing your anger and frustration might be a productive conflict management strategy if you are negotiating with someone who simply offers no useful alternatives.[94] By expressing your irritation, you may motivate the other person to come up with better alternatives. In most cases, escalating emotional tension decreases the likelihood that the conflict will be managed smoothly and effectively. But sometimes, being honest in expressing your bubbling frustration may nudge things along in a productive way, especially if no good alternatives exist.

Manage Information

Because uncertainty, misinformation, and misunderstanding are often byproducts of conflict and disagreement, skills that promote mutual understanding are an important component of cooperative conflict management. Based on the listening and responding skills discussed in Chapter 5, the following specific suggestions can help you reduce uncertainty and enhance the quality of communication during conflict.

CLEARLY DESCRIBE THE CONFLICT-PRODUCING EVENTS Instead of just blurting out your complaints in random order, think of delivering a brief, well-organized mini-speech. Offer your perspective on what created the conflict, sequencing the events like a well-organized story. Describe the events dispassionately so that the other person shares your understanding of the problem.

When Marsha almost had a car accident, she came home and told her husband, "Last week, you said you would get the brakes fixed on the car. On Monday, when you still hadn't taken the car in, you said you would do it on Wednesday. Now it's Friday, and the brakes are in even worse shape. I had a close call this afternoon when the car almost wouldn't stop. We've got to get those brakes fixed before anyone drives that car again."

TAKE TURNS TALKING It's simple, yet powerful. Research has found that consciously taking turns when discussing a conflict increases the likelihood that the conflict will be managed effectively.[95] Although this strategy will not guarantee that the disagreement will be resolved, it does help establish a climate of mutual concern. When taking turns, it's also important to listen and remain calm when the other person is speaking.

"OWN" YOUR STATEMENTS BY USING DESCRIPTIVE "I" LANGUAGE "I feel upset when you post the week's volunteer schedule without first consulting with me," reveals Katrina. Her statement is an example of **"I" language**, which expresses how a speaker is feeling. The use of the word *I* conveys a willingness to "own" one's feelings and the statements made about them.

And sometimes, to make sure your communication partner doesn't miss the subtlety of your owning your feelings by using an "I" message, it may be useful to extend your "I" message[96] by saying, for example, "I really don't want you to take this the

"I" language

Statements that use the word *I* to express how a speaker is feeling.

wrong way. I really care about you. But I want you to know that when you take food from my plate, I feel uncomfortable. My sister sometimes did that when I was a kid, and I didn't like it."

One final tip about using "I" messages: Monitor your **"but" messages**. What's a *"but"* message? It's a statement that makes it seem as though whatever you've said prior to the word *but* is not truly the way you feel. Here's an example: "I love you. I really love you. But I feel really frustrated when you leave your clothes lying on every chair." A *"but"* message diminishes the positive sentiment you expressed with your "I" language. We're not suggesting that you never say *but*, only that you realize how the word may create noise for the listener; it may make your entire statement seem untrue.

USE EFFECTIVE LISTENING SKILLS   Managing information is a two-way process. Whether you are describing a conflict situation to someone, or that individual is bringing a conflict to your attention, good listening skills will be invaluable.

Give your full attention to the speaker and make a conscious point of tuning out your internal messages. Sometimes, the best thing to do after describing the conflict-producing events is simply to wait for a response. If you don't stop talking and give the other person a chance to respond, he or she will feel frustrated, the emotional pitch will go up a notch, and it will become more difficult to reach an understanding.

Finally, remember to not only focus on the facts or details, but also analyze them so you can understand the major point the speaker is making. Try to use your understanding of the details to interpret the speaker's major ideas. Remember to stay other-oriented and to "seek to understand rather than to be understood."[97]

CHECK YOUR UNDERSTANDING OF WHAT OTHERS SAY AND DO   Respond clearly and appropriately. Your and your conflict partner's responses will confirm that you have understood each other. Checking perceptions is vital when emotions run high.

If you are genuinely unsure about facts, issues, or major ideas addressed during a conflict, ask questions to help you sort through them instead of barging ahead with solutions. Then summarize your understanding of the information; do not parrot the speaker's words or paraphrase every statement, but check key points to ensure that you have understood the message. Note how Ted adeptly paraphrases to check his understanding:

Maggie: I don't like the conclusion you've written for the conference report. It doesn't mention anything about the ideas suggested at the symposium. I think you have also misinterpreted the CEO's key message.

Ted: So if I understand you, Maggie, you're saying the report missed some key information and may also include an inaccurate summary of the CEO's speech.

Maggie: Yes, Ted. Those are my concerns.

BE EMPATHIC   Understand others not only with your head, but also with your heart. To truly understand another person, you need to do more than catch the meaning of his or her words; you need to put yourself in the person's place emotionally. Ask yourself these questions: What emotions is the other person feeling? Why is he or she experiencing these emotions? Throughout this book, we have stressed the importance of becoming other-oriented. It's especially important to be other-oriented when you disagree with another person.[98] Trying to understand what's behind your partner's emotions may give you the insight you need to reframe the conflict from your partner's point of view. And with this other-oriented perspective, you may see new possibilities for managing the conflict.

"but" messages
Statements using the word *but* that may communicate that whatever you've said prior to *but* is not really true.

BEING Other-ORIENTED

Being empathic, which is a core skill, allows you to be other-oriented. When you're involved in conflict with another person, what are the factors that hinder your ability to empathize with the other person? What actions and thoughts will enhance your skill in empathizing with another person?

Manage Goals

As you've seen, conflict is goal-driven. Both individuals involved in an interpersonal conflict want something. And for some reason, be it competition, scarce resources, or lack of understanding, goals appear to be in conflict. To manage conflict, you must seek an accurate understanding of these goals and identify where they overlap.

Communication researchers Sandra Lakey and Daniel Canary found clear support for the importance of being sensitive to and aware of your communication partner's goals when trying to manage conflict.[99] People who were focused on the other person's goals were perceived as much more competent than people who weren't aware of what the other person wanted to accomplish. Another study found that stating the goal of developing a positive outcome for the other person, especially in a romantic relationship, makes you more likely to enhance the conflict management process.[100] Let's look at some specific strategies to help manage conflict by being aware of the other person's goals.

IDENTIFY YOUR GOAL AND YOUR PARTNER'S GOAL   After you describe, listen, and respond, your next task should be to identify what you would like to have happen. What is your goal? Most goal statements can be phrased in terms of wants or desires. Consider the following examples:

Problem	Goals
Your boss wants you to work overtime; you need to pick up your son from day care.	You want to leave work on time; your boss wants the work completed ASAP.
Your spouse wants to sleep with the window open; you like a warm room and sleep better with the window closed.	You want a good night's rest; your spouse wants a good night's rest.

Often in conflicts you will face balancing your goal against the goal of maintaining the relationship you have with your partner. Eventually, you may decide that the latter goal is more important than the substantive conflict issue.

Next, it is useful to identify your partner's goal. In order to manage conflict, you need to know what the other person wants. Use effective listening and responding skills to determine what each of you wants and to verbalize your goals. Obviously, if you both keep your goals hidden, it will be difficult to manage the conflict.

IDENTIFY WHERE YOUR GOALS AND YOUR PARTNER'S GOALS OVERLAP   The authors of the best-selling book *Getting to Yes*, Roger Fisher and William Ury, stress the importance of focusing on shared interests when seeking to manage differences.[101] Armed with an understanding of what you want and what your partner wants, you can then determine whether the goals overlap. In the conflict over whether the window should be open or closed, the goal of both parties is the same: Each wants a good night's sleep. Framing the problem as "How can we achieve our mutual goal?" rather than arguing over whether the window should be up or down moves the discussion to a more productive level. If you focus on shared interests (common goals) and develop objective, rather than subjective, criteria for the solution, hope exists for finding a resolution that will satisfy both parties.

Manage the Problem

If you can structure conflicts as problems to be solved, rather than as battles to be won or lost, you are well on your way to finding strategies to manage the issues that confront you and your partner. Of course, as we have stressed, not all conflicts can be resolved. However, approaching the core of a conflict as a problem to be managed can provide a constructive way of seeking resolution. Structuring a conflict as a problem also helps to manage emotions, and it keeps the conversation focused on issues (simple conflict) rather than personalities (ego conflict). How do you do that? We recommend

Improving Your Communication Skills

Dealing with Prickly People

Some people just seem to rub us the wrong way. They generate both friction and heat when we're trying to negotiate with them. In his popular book *Getting Past No*, William Ury suggests we try to change face-to-face confrontation into side-by-side problem solving.[102] Here are Ury's tips for managing conflict with difficult people, based on his review of negotiation literature.[103]

- *Go to the Balcony.* "Going to the balcony" is a metaphor for taking a time out. Take a moment to excuse yourself to cool off when someone pushes your buttons. Staying on the "main stage" to keep banging out a solution may be counterproductive.

- *Step to the Side.* Rather than continuing to debate and refute every argument, step to the side by just asking questions and listening. Change the dynamic of the relationship from a confrontation to a conversation.

- *Change the Frame.* Reframe by trying to see more than an either-or way of managing the conflict. Try to see it from a third, fourth, or fifth point of view. Change your overall perspective for viewing the conflict by not being you: Consider how someone else may view the issue.

- *Build a Golden Bridge.* To "build a golden bridge" is a metaphor for identifying ways to help the other person say yes by saving face. Find an alternative that allows the other person his or her dignity by using objective standards to find a solution.

- *Make It Hard to Say No.* Use information to educate rather than pummel the other person. As Ury puts it, bring people to their senses, not their knees. Help the other person understand the consequences of what he or she supports and the benefits of your alternatives.

Consider a conflict that you had with a prickly person that did not have a satisfying conclusion. How could you have implemented one or more of the five suggestions we've summarized from Ury's research? If it were possible to have a "do over" with this difficult person, what would you do differently? Use the following worksheet to help you identify alternatives for dealing with the prickly person in the situation you have in mind.

Go to the Balcony. At what point in the conflict could you have suggested a cooling-off period?

_____

_____

Step to the Side. Instead of adding new ideas and arguments, when and how could you have stepped to the side to listen and paraphrase?

_____

_____

Change the Frame. How could you have changed the frame of the conflict? What would have been a different way of looking at the issue that created the conflict?

_____

_____

Build a Golden Bridge. What could you have done or said that would have helped the other person save face?

_____

_____

Make It Hard to Say No. What could you have said or done that would have helped the other person see the benefits of what you were proposing?

_____

_____

three sets of skills: (1) use principled negotiation strategies, (2) use a problem-solving structure, and (3) develop a solution that helps each person save face.

USE PRINCIPLED NEGOTIATION STRATEGIES To use principled negotiation strategies is to use a *collaborative*, win–win framework, even as you acknowledge a problem. Approaching conflict as a problem to be solved requires other-oriented strategies based on the following principles offered by Harvard researchers Roger Fisher and William Ury.[104]

Separate the People from the Problem Leave personal grievances out of the discussion, describing problems without making judgmental or evaluative statements about personalities. But what do you do if the other person continues to be emotionally upset and makes the disagreement personal? Consider the following behaviors.[105]

1. Acknowledge the person's feelings.
2. Determine what specific behavior is causing the intense feelings.
3. Assess the intensity and importance of the issue.
4. Invite the other person to join you in working toward solutions.
5. Make a positive relational statement.

It's vital to be able to manage your emotions when you find yourself in an interpersonal conflict.

Focus on Shared Interests.   Ask questions such as "What do we both want? What do we both value? Where are we already agreeing?" to emphasize common interests, values, and goals. If the discussions seem to be getting off track and conflict seems to be escalating, return to areas of mutual agreement.

Generate Many Options to Solve the Problem.   You are more likely to reach a mutually acceptable solution if you identify many possible options rather than debate only one or two. Collaborators conduct research to find options, talk with other people for ideas, and use brainstorming techniques to generate alternative solutions.

Base Decisions on Objective Criteria.   Try to establish standards for an acceptable solution to a problem; these standards may involve cost, timing, and other factors. Suppose, for example, that you and your neighbor are discussing possible ways to stop another neighbor's dog from barking throughout the night. You decide on these criteria: The solution must not harm the dog; it must be easy for the owner to implement; the owner must agree to it; it should not cost more than fifty dollars; and it must keep the dog from disturbing the sleep of others. Your neighbor says, "Maybe the dog can sleep in the owner's garage at night." This solution meets all but one of your criteria, so you call the owner, who agrees to put the dog in the garage by 10 pm. Now everyone wins because the solution meets a sound, well-considered set of objective criteria.

USE A PROBLEM-SOLVING STRUCTURE.   To pursue a proven method for problem solving, you can apply all of the skills described so far. The method is straightforward: Define the problem, analyze the problem's causes and effects, determine the goals you and your partner seek, generate many possible options, and then select the option that best achieves both your goals and those of your partner. Most problems boil down to something you or your conflict partner want more or less of. [106] Rationally define and analyze what the issues are. Then try to understand the issues and goals from the other person's point of view. [107] Another way to structure the conversation is to write down the pros and the cons of each option creating conflict, and then talk about them together.

face

A person's positive perception of himself or herself in interactions with others.

Making efforts to structure a conflict as a problem to be solved through mutual effort can keep the conversation focused on issues, so that the conflict does not escalate.

DEVELOP A SOLUTION THAT HELPS EACH PERSON SAVE FACE.   The concept of **face**, first introduced in Chapter 2, refers to the positive self-image or self-respect that you and your partner seek to maintain. [108] The goal of managing conflict is not just to solve a problem, but to help work through relational issues with your partner, especially if your partner thinks he or she has "lost" the conflict. When seeking a solution to relationship problems, try to find ways for your partner to "win" while you also achieve your goal. Help your partner save face. Lingering feelings of guilt, shame, and anger can interfere with helping others to save face. [109] Communication researcher Stella Ting-Toomey and her colleagues have conducted studies that emphasize the importance of face saving or maintaining a positive image, especially in collectivist cultures such as those in Asia, where maintaining face is especially important. [110]

How do you help someone save face and avoid embarrassment? Sometimes you can offer genuine forgiveness. Or you can offer explanations that help reframe the differences, perhaps suggesting that it was really just a misunderstanding that led to the disagreement. [111] Such face-restoring comments can help mend bruised egos. Finding ways to be gracious or allow your partner to save face is an important other-oriented approach to dealing with people. After a family feud between a mother and her teenage daughter, Mom might say, "You're right, I should not get so upset. I'm sorry I lost my temper. You're a great daughter." Admitting that you're wrong and offering an affirming, positive expression of support can begin to help heal a rift and help the other person save face.[112] One research study found that it is often more difficult for parents to get over past hurts and relational bruises than adolescent children.[113] Until past hurts heal it's difficult to completely manage the conflict.

If you are the wronged person in the conflict and the person who instigated the conflict has apologized, then you have a choice to make: Do you forgive the person who offended you? The most common form of forgiveness is indirect forgiveness,[114] which occurs when a person does not explicitly tell someone that he or she is forgiven, but the resumption of normal relationships and communication patterns leads the other person to "understand" he or she is forgiven. You are more likely to indirectly forgive a friend than someone you are dating; dating couples report more conditional forgiveness ("I forgive you *if* you stop doing X"). If you forgive someone conditionally, it's more likely that the negative feelings of the conflict will linger longer. Directly forgiving someone without conditions is the most effective way to get the issue resolved for both of you.

Even though we have presented these conflict management steps as prescriptive suggestions, it is important to remember that *conflict is rarely a linear, step-by-step sequence of events.* These skills are designed to serve as a general framework for collaboratively managing differences. But if your partner does not want to collaborate, your job will be more challenging.

In reality, you don't simply manage your emotions and then move neatly on to develop greater understanding with another person. Sorting out your goals and your partner's goals is not something you do once and then put behind you. Time and patience are required to balance your immediate goal with the goal of maintaining a relationship with your partner. In fact, as you try to manage a conflict, you will more than likely bounce

Applying an Other-Orientation
to Conflict Management

To manage differences with others, consider the conflict-producing issue or issues from the other person's point of view. We don't claim that an other-orientation will resolve all conflicts. As we noted earlier, it's a myth that all conflict can be resolved. But being other-oriented is an important element in managing differences and disagreements. The following five strategies drawn not only from this chapter but from the previous skill-development chapters distill the essence of being other-oriented.

- **Stop:** Socially decenter by taking into account the other person's thoughts, feelings, values, culture, and perspective. Stop making arguments and concentrate on your partner's points. How is your partner "making sense" out of what has happened to him or her?

- **Look:** Monitor your partner's emotions by observing his or her nonverbal messages. Look for emotional cues in your partner's face; observe posture and gestures to gauge the intensity of the feelings being expressed.

- **Listen:** Listen both for the details and for the main points; also listen for tone of voice. Focus on the overall story your partner is telling.

- **Imagine:** Imagine how you would feel if you were in your partner's place. Based on your knowledge of the person you're in conflict with, as well as of people in general, imagine the conflict from his or her point of view.

- **Question:** If you need more information about what a partner has experienced or more clarification about something you don't understand, gently ask appropriate questions.

- **Paraphrase:** To confirm your understanding of your partner's point of view, briefly summarize the essence of what you think your partner is thinking or feeling.

No checklist of skills will magically melt tensions resulting from long-standing or entrenched conflicts. But honestly trying to understand both a person's position and the emotion behind it is a good first step in developing understanding—a prerequisite to managing differences.

forward and backward from one step to another. The framework we've described gives you an overarching perspective for understanding and actively managing disagreements, but the nature of interpersonal relationships means that you and your partner will respond—sometimes in unpredictable ways—to a variety of cues (psychological, sociological, physical) when communicating. Think of the skills you have learned as options to consider, rather than as hard-and-fast rules to follow in every situation.

STUDY GUIDE
Review, Apply, and Assess

Conflict Defined

Objective 8.1   Define interpersonal conflict.

Key Terms

interpersonal conflict
interdependent
conflict trigger
dialectical tension
constructive conflict
destructive conflict

Thinking Critically

Think of a recent communication exchange with a friend, spouse, or coworker that began as a seemingly casual conversation but escalated into a conflict. Can you identify a reason for this, such as one or both of you feeling tired, stressed, or anxious? Is there anything you could have done to avoid the conflict? What cues might each of you have looked for to understand the other's mood?

Assessing Your Skills

Based on the discussion of conflict presented earlier in this chapter, think of a recent conflict you had with someone or a conflict that is still ongoing. To help you better understand and manage the process, answer the following questions:

Prior Conditions Stage

• What were the prior conditions that led to the conflict?

Frustration Awareness Stage

• When did you become aware that you were frustrated and that your needs weren't being met or that there was an issue to resolve and the person was upset?

Active Conflict Stage

• What caused the conflict to move from frustration to active conflict?

Resolution Stage

• What conflict management skills did you use (or are you and the other person using) to manage emotions, information, goals, or the problem?

Follow-Up Stage

• Has the conflict been truly managed and resolved, or not? What leads you to that conclusion?

Conflict Myths

Objective 8.2   Identify commonly held myths about interpersonal conflict.

Thinking Critically

How might accepting one or more of the conflict myths as true have an effect on your interpersonal relationships?

Assessing Your Skills

Of the four myths listed in the chapter, rank them in order from most important to least important. A ranking of 1 means that buying into the myth would have the most serious consequences for a relationship. A ranking of 4 means the myth would have the least impact on a relationship. Share your rankings with your classmates and discuss them.

Conflict Types

Objective 8.3   Compare and contrast three types of interpersonal conflict.

Key Terms

pseudoconflict
simple conflict
ego conflict

Thinking Critically

Pat and Chris have noticed an increase in the amount of conflict they are having in their romantic relationship. What are questions they could ask themselves to assess the type of conflict they may be experiencing?

Assessing Your Skills

Think of three different conflicts you have had with another person. Assess what type of conflict each one was.

1. How effectively did you manage the conflict?
2. What strategies listed earlier in this chapter did you use to manage the conflict?
3. Are there strategies you could have used but didn't choose that would have helped you manage the conflict more effectively?

Conflict and Power

Objective 8.4   Describe the relationship between conflict and power.

Key Terms

interpersonal power	expert power
dependent relationship	reward power
legitimate power	coercive power
referent power	compliance gaining

Thinking Critically

Examine several recent interpersonal conflicts for unresolved power issues. (For example, consider conflicts that have focused on managing money, household tasks, or intimacy.) What role did power play in the conflict? What type of power is it? Does one of you have more power over the other? How might you renegotiate that power imbalance?

Assessing Your Skills

Statements about Conflict: Read each statement once, and on a separate piece of paper, indicate whether you agree (A) or disagree (D) with each statement. Take five or six minutes to do this.

1. Most people find an argument interesting and exciting.
2. In most conflicts, someone must win and someone must lose. That's the way conflict is.
3. The best way to handle a conflict is simply to let everyone cool off.
4. Most people get upset at a person who disagrees with them.
5. If people spend enough time together, they will find something to disagree about and will eventually become upset with each other.
6. Conflicts can be solved if people just take the time to listen to one another.
7. If you disagree with someone, it is usually better to keep quiet than to express your personal opinion.
8. To compromise is to take the easy way out of conflict.
9. Some people produce more conflict and tension than others. These people should be restricted from working with others.

After you have indicated whether you agree or disagree with the statements, ask a good friend, roommate, family member, or romantic partner to read each statement and indicate whether he or she agrees or disagrees. Compare answers and discuss the results. Use this activity as a way of identifying underlying assumptions you and the other person have about conflict. You could also do this activity in a small group. After comparing responses with others, the entire group could seek to develop a consensus about each statement. If conflict occurs about a specific statement, use the principles of conflict management that are presented in the chapter to assist you in managing the disagreement.

Conflict Management Styles

Objective 8.5   Describe five conflict management styles.

Key Terms

conflict management styles	competition
avoidance	compromise
demand-withdrawal pattern	collaboration
of conflict management	flaming
accommodation	disinhibition effect

Thinking Critically

Have you experienced the disinhibition effect when communicating with others online? Was this in response to a blatantly negative message? Or was it your perception that you were being attacked? What was the result? How did you respond? What strategies could you have employed to avoid a conflict?

Assessing Your Skills

Over the next week or so, keep a list of every conflict you observe or are involved in.

1. Make a note of what the conflict was about, whether there were underlying power issues (that you could detect), whether the conflict was resolved satisfactorily for both parties, and, if so, which strategies and skills were employed.
2. Could you identify a specific conflict management style that was used?
3. If the conflict involved you, did you use the style you typically use? Why or why not? Discuss your findings with your classmates.

Conflict Management Skills

Objective 8.6   Identify and use conflict management skills to help manage emotions, information, goals, and problems when attempting to resolve interpersonal differences.

Key Terms

gunny-sacking	"but" messages
"I" language	face

Thinking Critically

How can you develop your skill in managing conflict without making it seem like you are using manipulative techniques to get your way?

Assessing Your Skills

1. Which of the skills sets (manage emotions, manage information, manage goals, manage the problem) are easier for you to use? Which are more challenging for you to implement?

2. On a scale of 1 to 10 rate yourself on each of the conflict management skills listed earlier in this chapter. 1 = low and 10 = high. What strategies could you use to increase your skill level on those items that received your lowest rating?

Chapter 9

Understanding Interpersonal Relationships

"You can hardly make a friend in a year, but you can lose one in an hour."

Chinese Proverb

⌄ Learning Objectives

9.1 Define interpersonal relationships and identify two ways to distinguish among them.

9.2 Identify and differentiate between short-term initial attraction and long-term maintenance attraction.

9.3 Identify and describe the stages of relational escalation and de-escalation.

9.4 Describe the main components of the three theories that explain relational development.

CHAPTER OUTLINE

Interpersonal Relationships Defined

Genesis of Interpersonal Relationships: Attraction

Stages of Interpersonal Relationship Development

Theories of Interpersonal Relationship Development

Jan:	Hi, aren't you in my communication course?
Sung Li:	Oh, yeah, I've seen you across the room.
Jan:	What do you think about the course so far?
Sung Li:	It's okay, but I feel a little intimidated by some of the class activities.
Jan:	I know what you mean. It gets kind of scary to talk about yourself in front of everyone else.
Sung Li:	Yeah. Plus some of the stuff you hear. I was paired up with this one student the other day who started talking about being arrested last year on a drug charge. It made me feel uncomfortable.
Jan:	Really? I bet I know who that is. I don't think you have to worry about it.
Sung Li:	Don't mention that I said anything.
Jan:	It's okay. I know that guy, and he just likes to act big.
Sung Li:	Would you mind if I texted you sometime?
Jan:	No, that'd be nice. Here's my cell number.

This interaction between Jan and Sung Li illustrates the reciprocal nature of interpersonal communication and interpersonal relationships. The character and quality of interpersonal communication are affected, in turn, by the nature of the interpersonal relationship. The conversation begins with a casual acknowledgment but quickly proceeds to a higher level of intimacy. Sung Li confides in Jan and Jan engages in some of the communication skills covered in earlier chapters—being an other-oriented listener, offering confirmation, and providing support. These responses encourage Sung Li to confide even more. In this brief encounter, Jan and Sung Li have laid the groundwork for transforming their casual acquaintanceship into an intimate interpersonal relationship. The first eight chapters of this book covered skills that contribute to managing your interpersonal relationships. Now we turn to examining the nature of those relationships and how those skills can be applied to developing, maintaining, and terminating them. This chapter examines the nature of interpersonal relationships such as Jan and Sung Li's, as well as the stages experienced in the escalation and de-escalation of interpersonal relationships.

Interpersonal Relationships Defined

9.1 **Define interpersonal relationships and identify two ways to distinguish among them.**

relationship

Connection established when one person communicates with another.

interpersonal relationship

Perception shared by two people of an ongoing interdependent connection that results in the development of relational expectations and varies in interpersonal intimacy.

In Chapter 1, we defined a **relationship** as a connection you establish when you communicate with another person. So every time you engage in interpersonal communication, you are in a relationship; but it is only through ongoing, recurring interactions that you develop interpersonal relationships. An **interpersonal relationship** is a perception shared by two people of an ongoing interdependent connection that results in the development of relational expectations and varies in interpersonal intimacy. Let's first consider the four elements that constitute this definition: shared perception, ongoing interdependent connection, relational expectations, and interpersonal intimacy. We'll then consider the impact of circumstance, choice, and power in defining the nature of interpersonal relationships.

Shared Perception

To be in an interpersonal relationship, both individuals must share a perception that they have an ongoing relationship. Sometimes, only one person believes a relationship exists—stalking is an extreme example of such a belief. Even when each partner recognizes that he or she has a relationship with the other, the partners do not necessarily think of the relationship in the same way. Discrepancies in the perceptions of the relationship can be a source of interpersonal conflict, requiring heart-to-heart talks about each person's wants and relational expectations. Generally, the greater the similarity in partners' perceptions of their relationship, the stronger their relationship will be.

Ongoing Interdependent Connection

An ongoing interpersonal relationship is dynamic—constantly changing and evolving at times through stages that differ in levels of trust, self-disclosure, and intimacy. Each interaction adds to the cumulative history of the relationship, and this history affects subsequent interactions. The *Harry Potter* books and films provide good examples of this ongoing nature of relationships. The relationships among the three main characters—Harry, Hermione, and Ron—evolve and change as the young wizards share experiences and learn more about one another.

In an intimate, trusting relationship, we can feel safe in telling our deepest secrets to another person.

As you learned in Chapter 8, being *interdependent* means that people are dependent on each other; one person's actions affect the other person. Interdependence creates a relational system or transactional process in which both partners affect each other simultaneously. As a result, a change in one partner directly impacts the relationship and the other partner. For example, you've probably had friends who are moody at times (or maybe you're the moody one), and when they are, it affects you and how you talk to them. Thus, being interdependent means partners influence and constrain one another in that they must coordinate and integrate their life tasks, personal preferences and personalities, relationship goals, and feelings of trust and commitment.[1] As part of the definition of interpersonal relationships, interdependence *involves each partner relying fairly equally on the other to meet needs.* Such interdependence provides motivation to sustain an ongoing connection: Both partners want to continue to get together because their needs are being satisfied.

Relational Expectations

As you continue to interact and develop your relationships, you also form relational expectations. Any time you interact with someone, you bring a set of pre-formed expectations based on your socialization and experiences; but as you develop an interpersonal relationship, you and your partner establish expectations specific to that relationship that continually evolve. For example, you might have a friend with whom you primarily play video games; thus, you know what your time together will be like, how you'll talk, what you'll talk about, and so on.

Sometimes, expectations are violated, which can create turmoil in the relationship (this problem is discussed further in Chapter 10). Such violations of expectations create uncertainty, and uncertainty creates stress. For example, if you're used to getting daily text messages from a friend and you suddenly start getting messages only once or twice a week, it creates relational uncertainty and stress. According to uncertainty reduction theory (as discussed in Chapter 3), we seek to reduce the stress and uncertainty in relationships. The presence of expectations helps reduce uncertainty—we know what to expect in a given relationship. Interpersonal communication scholars Denise Solomon and Leanne Knobloch hypothesize that in more intimate relationships, people exhibit direct information-seeking behavior to reduce uncertainties, whereas those in less intimate relationships exhibit indirect behaviors. In other words, when something unexpected happens in an intimate relationship,

interpersonal intimacy

Degree to which relational partners mutually accept and confirm each other's sense of self.

like a friend failing to return a call, we'll probably use direct information-seeking to reduce our uncertainty, perhaps texting or calling later to ask what happened.[2] In a less intimate relationship like a casual friendship, we're likely to use an indirect approach, such as waiting until we meet the person again to comment about not getting a call.

Interpersonal Intimacy

Interpersonal intimacy is the degree to which relational partners mutually confirm, value, and accept each other's sense of self. As self-disclosure and closeness increase, each partner becomes more and more dependent upon the other as the source for this confirmation. We are also able to relax more and be ourselves. In the most intimate relationships, our partners know our strengths and weaknesses but still accept us; we don't have to hide our flaws or fear rejection. Our most intimate relationships enhance our self-esteem and confidence while helping us learn about ourselves. The more intimate the relationship, the more we depend on the other for acceptance and confirmation of our self-image.[3] British sociologist Derek Layder writes, "Mutual attention to partner's needs for self-esteem, security, confidence, self-value, and so on is the heart and soul of good quality intimacy."[4]

> ### BEING Other-ORIENTED
> The healthiest relationships are those in which both partners have an agreed-on and clear understanding of the relationship. Think about some of your closest relationships. How close do you think those partners would say their relationship with you is? In what ways do they communicate the level of intimacy and feelings they have about the relationship? What nonverbal cues do they send? Are they clear or ambiguous? What have your partners said to let you know their assessment of the relationship?

Think about the range of interpersonal relationships you have. You should be able to classify them according to their level of interpersonal intimacy (level of self-disclosure and confirmation of your self). Use Figure 9.1 to see where your relationships fall according to their relative intimacy. Even casual relationships can provide some confirmation; we look for others to implicitly (and sometimes explicitly) tell us that they like who we are.

We communicate our sense of intimacy to others both directly, through our words, and indirectly, through our actions. We might tell another person how we feel about him or her and how much we value the relationship. On the other hand, we might communicate intimacy indirectly by disclosing personal information to convey our trust, or through nonverbal cues such as physical proximity, eye contact, tone of voice, touch, and the amount of time we spend with the other person.[5] The choice to become intimate distinguishes some relationships from others that exist only because of circumstance.

relationship of circumstance

Interpersonal relationship that exists because of life circumstances (who your family members are, where you work or study, and so on).

relationship of choice

Interpersonal relationship you choose to initiate, maintain, and, perhaps, terminate.

Circumstance or Choice

Relationships of circumstance form simply because our lives overlap with others' in some way. Relationships with families of origin, teachers, classmates, and coworkers fall into this category. In contrast, relationships that we seek out and intentionally develop are **relationships of choice**. These relationships might include relationships with friends, romantic partners, spouses, and counselors. Of course, these categories are not mutually exclusive. Relationships of circumstance can also be relationships of choice: Your brother, sister, or work colleague can also be your best friend.

Figure 9.1 Continuum of Interpersonal Intimacy and Friendship

Non-Intimate   Highly Intimate

Stranger ⟷ Acquaintance ⟷ Casual Friend ⟷ Friend ⟷ Close Friend ⟷ Best Friend/Spouse

We act and communicate differently in the two types of relationships because the stakes are different. The effect of the same behavior on different relationships can be dramatic. If we act in foolish or inappropriate ways, a friend might end our relationship. If we act the same way within the confines of our family, our relatives may not like us much, but we will still remain family.

In some sense, all relationships begin by circumstance; through circumstance, we become aware of another person. What we learn as a result of circumstance serves as the basis for our interpersonal attraction toward the other person and any decision to pursue a relationship of choice. Part of that movement from circumstance to choice involves negotiating how decision making and power will be managed within the relationship.

Power

Relationships can also be defined according to the way partners share power or decision-making responsibilities—the relative power role that each partner plays. Relationships require merging needs and styles, negotiating how decisions are made that affect both partners, and managing inevitable interpersonal conflicts. How power is distributed affects relational satisfaction.[6] As discussed in Chapter 8, conflicts often involve negotiating power. Failure to agree on roles can lead to instability, and attempts to change an agreed-on definition of roles can meet resistance. Nonetheless, decision-making and power-sharing roles are continually tweaked. Think about how each of the following descriptions of power sharing applies to your relationships with friends, family, and coworkers and to the conflicts that arise in these relationships.

COMPLEMENTARY RELATIONSHIPS   In a **complementary relationship**, one partner usually dominates or makes most of the decisions. Maybe one person likes to talk, and the other likes to listen; one person likes to decide what movies to watch, and the other will watch anything. People in complementary relationships experience relatively few decision-making conflicts, because one partner readily defers to the other. As a child, your relationship with your parents was probably complementary—they made the decisions. But, as you grew older, attempts to break free of the complementary style might have been a source of conflict.

competitive symmetrical relationship
Relationship in which power is divided unevenly, with one partner dominating and the other submitting.

COMPETITIVE AND SUBMISSIVE SYMMETRICAL RELATIONSHIPS   In a **symmetrical relationship**, both partners behave toward power in the same way, either both wanting power or both avoiding it.[7] A **competitive symmetrical relationship** exists when both people vie for power and control of decision making. For example, each partner wants to play a different video game, and neither one wants to give in to the other. Equality of power is likely to result in more overt attempts at control than take place when one partner has more power than the other.[8] Effective management of decision making requires strong conflict management skills. When neither partner wants to take control or make decisions, a **submissive symmetrical relationship** is created. Because neither partner feels comfortable imposing his or her will on the other, both partners may flounder, unable to make a decision or to act. Perhaps both people want to play a video game, but neither wants to declare which video game the other should have to play.

symmetrical relationship
Relationship in which both partners behave toward power in the same way, either both wanting power or both avoiding it.

competitive symmetrical relationship
Relationship in which both people vie for power and control of decision making.

submissive symmetrical relationship
Relationship in which neither partner wants to take control or make decisions.

PARALLEL RELATIONSHIPS   In reflecting on your current relationships, you might find that few seem to fit the descriptions of complementary or symmetrical relationships. Instead, most of your relationships are probably **parallel relationships** involving a shifting back and forth of the power between the partners, depending on the situation. You might defer the video game selection to your friend Riley who knows about every video game on the planet. On the other hand, Riley defers to you about deciding where to order pizza. Establishing this arrangement with Riley might have involved initial conflict until you both felt comfortable with your roles. Parallel relationships often involve continual negotiation of who has decision-making power over which issues, particularly as the relationship moves from one stage to another.

parallel relationship
Relationship in which power shifts back and forth between the partners, depending on the situation.

Genesis of Interpersonal Relationships: Attraction

9.2   **Identify and differentiate between short-term initial attraction and long-term maintenance attraction.**

interpersonal attraction

Degree to which you want to form or maintain an interpersonal relationship.

short-term initial attraction

Degree to which you sense a potential for developing an interpersonal relationship.

long-term maintenance attraction

Degree of liking or positive feelings that motivate us to maintain or escalate a relationship.

Attraction acts as the genesis or beginning of interpersonal relationships. **Interpersonal attraction** is the degree to which you want to (1) form or (2) maintain an interpersonal relationship.

You are constantly evaluating individuals you encounter to determine the potential for developing an interpersonal relationship; this is **short-term initial attraction**. For example, you might find one of your classmates (a relationship of circumstance) physically attractive but never move to introduce yourself. You decide, for whatever reason, that there is not much potential for a relationship, and therefore you do not act on your attraction. On the other hand, as you walk out of the class, you might strike up a conversation with another classmate about an upcoming concert by one of your favorite bands, which happens to be this classmate's favorite as well. This commonality leads to initial attraction and a decision to go together.

Over time, you discover other areas of compatibility and attraction that serve as the foundation for a long-term friendship with your concert-going classmate. **Long-term maintenance attraction** is the level of liking or positive feelings that motivate us to maintain or escalate a relationship. Through interpersonal communication, self-disclosure, and continued interactions, we learn information about others that either fosters or diminishes our long-term maintenance attraction to them.

Both types of attraction involve assessing and acting on the potential value of a relationship. We try to determine how promising, viable, and rewarding the relationship might be, and we continue to make such assessments throughout the course of the relationship. According to communication scholar Michael Sunnafrank's theory of *predicted outcome value theory* (POV) (also discussed in Chapter 3), we assess the potential for any given relationship to meet our need for self-image confirmation and weigh that assessment against the potential costs.[9] Such assessment is readily apparent in speed dating venues where participants have a short time to determine the desire for future interaction.[10] We are attracted to others with whom a relationship may yield a high outcome value (the rewards exceeding the costs).

Over time, our assessments may change. In the movie *50 First Dates*, Henry (Adam Sandler) has a pleasant first encounter with Lucy (Drew Barrymore). The two are attracted to each other, each predicting a positive outcome in terms of a potential relationship that meets their social needs. Henry approaches their second encounter expecting continued positive outcomes; however, Lucy's memory problem leaves her without any relational expectations. As Henry's attraction continues to grow, Lucy's inability to sustain a positive assessment of the relationship potential produces a series of comical events. Not until he devises a way for her to sustain a sense of the value of the relationship can love triumph.

Like these film characters, most of us begin predicting outcome values in initial interactions and continually modify our predictions as we learn more about the other person. We pursue attractions beyond the initial interaction stage if we think they can yield positive outcomes, and generally avoid or terminate relationships for which we predict negative outcomes.[11]

COMMUNICATION AND ATTRACTION   Of particular interest is the interdependence of attraction and interpersonal communication. Short-term initial attraction acts as the impetus to communicate interpersonally—it prompts us to interact with others. The resulting interpersonal communication provides additional information that might contribute to long-term maintenance attraction. When participants in a recent study were assigned to chat online from one to eight times with someone they didn't know, the reported attraction was greatest among those participants who chatted the most.[12] While attraction increases our likelihood of actually talking to another person, what occurs during these interactions really determines whether we remain attracted to the person.[13] Common among the sources of attraction discussed below is that they either lead to increased communication and thus attraction (e.g., proximity) or they develop as a result of communication (e.g., finding commonalities).

Sources of Initial Attraction

You enter a room filled with people you don't know and proceed to the area where beverages are being served. As you look around the room, to whom are you attracted? Whom do you approach? Two sources of attraction in such situations are proximity and physical appearance.

Interpersonal attraction leads us to form or maintain our personal relationships.

PROXIMITY   You are more likely to form relationships with classmates sitting on either side of you than with those seated at the opposite end of the room. This is partly because physical **proximity** increases communication opportunities. We are more likely to talk, and therefore feel attracted, to neighbors who live next door than to those who live down the block. Any circumstance that increases the possibilities for interacting is also likely to increase attraction.

proximity

Physical nearness to another that promotes communication and thus attraction.

PHYSICAL APPEARANCE   If you entered a room where everyone was of a different age, culture, or race than you except for one person ten feet away, whom would you approach for conversation? Physical similarity to another person creates an attraction because we assume the other person will have values and interests similar to ours. We use **physical appearance**, the nonverbal cues that you observe about another person, to make predictions about who is most likely to reciprocate our overtures for conversation—that is, who is most likely to have something in common with us. Appearance acts as a filter to reduce relationship possibilities.[14]

physical appearance

Nonverbal cues that allow us to assess relationship potential.

Physical appearance has an impact online as well. Researchers created male and female Facebook profiles that included limited information and either an attractive photo, an unattractive photo, or no photo.[15] Although males' desire to initiate friendship with an attractive female was significantly greater than the females' desire to initiate friendship with an attractive male, both male and female participants reported more desire to initiate a friendship with the individuals in the attractive photos than with those in the unattractive ones. No such sex difference was found for the profiles without a photo.

You have probably found that even if you initially see a person as physically attractive, or if you and the other person are of a similar age, culture, or race, you won't continue a relationship if you don't have much else in common. However, positive social interactions and increased liking of another appear to increase how physically attractive that person appears to others.[16] In other words, the more you like someone, the more physically attractive you are likely to find her or him.

Sexual attraction also influences interest in forming relationships. At the most basic level, people might seek partners for physical affection and gratification of sexual needs.[17] This is probably why in short-term sexual relationships, physical appearance tends to be more important than in long-term romantic relationships.[18] However, in the process of meeting sexual needs, people may develop other forms of attraction leading them to form long-term relationships.

In cross-sex romantic relationships, the evolutionary theory of mate selection suggests that men and women use physical appearance to determine the adequacy of potential mates. This theory is based on biological principles related to hormones, body

We are attracted to people on the basis of similarity—we like people whose interests, personalities, values, and backgrounds are similar to ours.

competence

The quality of being skilled, intelligent, charismatic, and credible.

shapes, health, and reproductive value. Women are judged attractive based on their fertility, receptiveness, and prospects for motherhood; and men, by their ability to protect and provide resources to raise children.[19]

Sources of Both Initial and Long-Term Attraction

While proximity and physical appearance are more important factors in initial attraction than in maintenance attraction,[20] other factors lead us both to initiate relationships and to continue developing them. These factors have some impact when we first meet someone and that impact increases as we gather more information about the person.

COMPETENCE   Most of us are attracted to individuals we perceive as **competent**—those seen as skilled, intelligent, charismatic, and credible. Intelligence is a more important predictor of initial attraction in eventual romantic relationships than in friendships.[21] Charismatic people attract us with their charm and demeanor. We find people credible if they display a blend of enthusiasm, trustworthiness, competence, and power.

SELF-DISCLOSURE   Self-disclosure has a positive impact on liking between strangers and an even greater impact in more developed relationships.[22] As relationships progress from initiation to intimacy, self-disclosure increases attraction. In one study of newly acquainted men and women who interacted for eight minutes, participants perceived self-disclosure as communicating openness and interest.[23] Another study found that expressiveness and openness were among the most desirable qualities in a partner, regardless of the type of relationship.[24] In addition, our attraction to another person increases our tendency to self-disclose.[25] However, the imbalance created when one person discloses while the other just listens can result in the discloser feeling less liking, enjoyment, and closeness than the listener.[26] In developing your relationships try to balance the level of self-disclosure between you and the other person. Don't disclose too much, too soon, or share anything too intimate or too negative until the relationship has reached an appropriate level of trust and intimacy.

reciprocation of liking

Liking those who like us.

RECIPROCATION OF LIKING   **Reciprocation of liking** means that we like those who like us. One way to get other people to reciprocate liking, particularly in romantic relationships, is to show that we like them.[27] In a study in which participants were instructed to display liking, the frequency of their smiles, intensity of gaze, proximity during a conversation, forward leaning, and variations in vocal pitch correlated with their partners' reports of social attraction.[28] Displaying attraction toward another person seems to have the greatest impact if it is perceived by the other person as being uniquely directed toward him or her, rather than as a general, indiscriminate display of interest in everyone (not being very choosy).[29] In another study, pairs of male and female college students interacting for the first time underestimated the amount of attraction that their partners felt after a brief get-acquainted conversation.[30] Perhaps we protect ourselves—"save face"—by assuming the other person doesn't like us much; it is probably less embarrassing to find out someone likes us more than we thought than to find out we've overestimated the person's attraction to us.

similarity

Having comparable personalities, values, upbringing, personal experiences, attitudes, and interests.

SIMILARITIES   In general, we are attracted to people on the basis of **similarity**—we like people whose personalities, values, upbringing, personal experiences, attitudes, and interests are similar to ours. We seek them out through shared activities. For example, you may join a campus environmental group because of your interests in the environment. Within the group, you would be especially attracted to those who share the same attitudes on other issues or who enjoy some of the other activities that you do. Similarly, joining a Facebook group or connecting on LinkedIn because of a shared interest could lead to online friendships. Similarity of interests and leisure activities appears to be more important in same-sex friendships than in opposite-sex relationships.[31] Similarity as a basis for attraction is at the heart of some online dating sites such as eHarmony.com, which uses 436 questions to identify and match partners; unfortunately, compatibility is not just a matter of matching questionnaires.

In the initial stages of a relationship, we try to create a positive and attractive image. We reveal those aspects of ourselves that we believe we have in common with the other person, and the other person does the same.[32] We save our revelations about important attitudes and issues for a later stage in the relational development process.[33] Attitude similarity is more likely to be a source of long-term maintenance attraction than of short-term initial attraction.

Results of a study by communication scholars Leslie Baxter and Lee West indicate that the main reason for placing a positive value on similarity is that it facilitates communication.[34] Similarities give people something in common to talk about, making interactions comfortable and communication effective. Similarities are also viewed as positive because they represent sources of shared fun and pleasure as well as a basis for social and emotional support.

Susan Sprecher, who has studied relationships for over thirty years, confirmed previous research on getting-acquainted interactions in a study that showed *perceived* similarity has a greater impact on liking than *actual* similarity.[35] Similarly, a study done at speed-dating sessions found that a general perception of similarity was more related to romantic attraction than actual similarity or the perception of specific similar qualities.[36] Sprecher also found that liking in an initial interaction increased perceived similarity more than similarity increased liking.[37] This could lead you to discover that someone you initially liked really wasn't as similar to you as you first thought.

DIFFERENCES AND COMPLEMENTARY NEEDS "Vive la différence!" "Opposites attract." "Variety is the spice of life." Such phrases reflect a positive attitude toward differences. One reason we are drawn to people who are different from us is that we learn and grow by such exposure.[38] Although differences can lead to points of conflict and hamper our ability to effectively communicate,[39] people who are different from us also expose us to new ideas, activities, and perspectives and prompt self-assessment.

Recap

Genesis of Interpersonal Relationships: Attraction

Interpersonal Attraction	Degree to which you want to form or maintain an interpersonal relationship
Short-Term Initial Attraction	Degree to which you sense a potential for developing a relationship
Long-Term Maintenance Attraction	Level of liking or positive feelings motivating you to maintain or escalate a relationship
Predicted Outcome Value (POV)	Potential for a relationship to confirm your self-image compared to its potential costs
Sources of Initial Attraction	
Proximity	Physical nearness to someone that promotes communication and thus attraction
Physical Appearance	Nonverbal cues that allow you to assess relationship potential (POV)
Sources of Initial and Long-Term Attraction	
Competence	A synthesis of skills, intelligence, charisma, and credibility that in and of itself evokes attraction
Self-Disclosure	Conveys openness and interest, which increase attraction
Reciprocation of Liking	Attraction toward a person who seems attracted to you
Similarities	Comparable personalities, values, upbringing, experiences, attitudes, and interests
Differences and Complementary Needs	Appreciation of diversity; matching needs

complementary needs

Needs that match; each partner contributes something to the relationship that the other partner needs.

People in a relationship have **complementary needs** when each partner contributes something to the relationship that the other partner wants or needs. Perhaps you are witty and have a great sense of humor, which is appealing to Pat because Pat likes to laugh. Pat is good at planning and doing exciting things on the weekends while you tend to sit around unable to decide what to do. A relationship might develop between you and Pat because you complement each other's needs.

Short-term initial attraction gets relationships started, but the process of changing to long-term maintenance attraction involves working through a series of stages, each reflecting changes in attraction, self-disclosure, and intimacy. The remainder of this chapter focuses on the nature of those stages and on theories that explain how and why interpersonal attraction and intimacy increase and decrease.

Stages of Interpersonal Relationship Development

9.3   Identify and describe the stages of relational escalation and de-escalation.

relational development

Movement of a relationship from one stage to another, either toward or away from greater intimacy.

Although researchers use different terms and different numbers of stages, all agree that **relational development** proceeds in discernible stages, escalating as we become closer and de-escalating as the relationship deteriorates. The relational elevator in Figure 9.2 serves as a metaphor for this process. Interpersonal communication is the tool we use to move the relationship from stage to stage (floor to floor), and the stage (floor) we are in affects our interpersonal communication. These stages apply to all interpersonal relationships, although they are generally more obvious in romantic relationships, in which people are more deliberate about becoming closer.

Relational Escalation

relational escalation

Movement of a relationship toward intimacy through five stages: preinteraction awareness, acquaintance, exploration, intensification, and intimacy.

Relational escalation is the movement of a relationship toward greater intimacy. Each stage is accompanied by specific communication patterns, significant events, and relational expectations. As individuals move toward intimacy, they discuss topics and display nonverbal behaviors that do not appear in the earlier stages of a relationship. Even our use of Facebook changes as the relationship escalates. When first getting to

Figure 9.2 Model of Relational Development

Types of Relationships	Escalation Stages	De-Escalation Stages
Best Friend/ Lover/ Spouse	Intimacy	Turmoil or Stagnation
Close Friend	Intensification	Deintensification
Friend	Exploration	Individualization
Acquaintance	Acquaintance	Separation
Stranger	Preinteraction Awareness	Post-Separation Effects

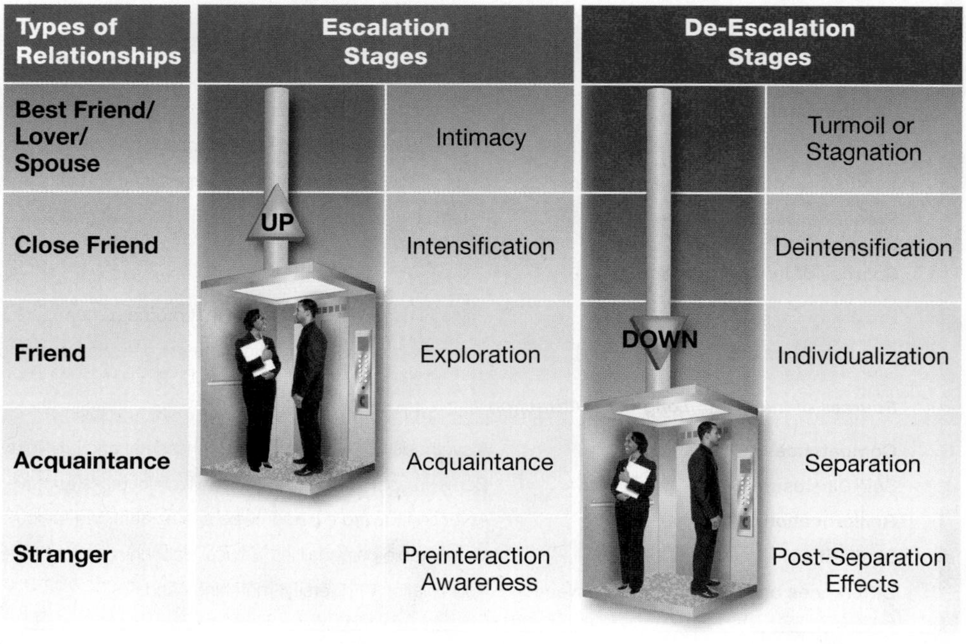

know someone we might use a passive strategy for getting information (for example, looking at pictures and scrolling through a person's timeline), but as the relationship nears intimacy, we use a more active strategy by making Facebook friend requests of a partner's family and friends.[40]

PREINTERACTION AWARENESS   As you can see in the model in Figure 9.2, the first floor is the *preinteraction awareness stage*. At this stage, you gain information about others by observing them or talking with others about them without having any direct interactions, a passive strategy by which you form initial impressions.[41] Through these passive strategies, you form initial impressions. You might never move beyond the preinteraction awareness stage if those impressions are not favorable or the circumstances aren't right. During this stage, one person might signal his or her openness to being approached by the other, but these cues, such as smiling or making eye contact, can be misread.[42] Such misreadings might result in failure at the next stage.

ACQUAINTANCE   A positive impression in the preinteraction awareness stage might motivate you to interact, or you might choose to interact with someone on the spur of the moment without preinteraction awareness. In either case, the very first interaction begins the *acquaintance stage,* in which you stick to safe and superficial topics of conversation and present a "public self" to the other person. Conversations emphasize sociability.[43]

The acquaintance stage has two sub-stages: introductions and casual banter. In the **introductions** sub-stage, which usually comes first, we tell each other our names and share basic demographic information—where we're from, what we do, and so on. In this sub-stage, the interaction typically is routine—partners usually spend the first four minutes asking each other various standard questions.[44] Once we have finished the introduction sub-stage, our future interactions don't require us to introduce ourselves again (unless, of course, you've forgotten the other person's name).

The second sub-stage is **casual banter**, which might occur before or without the introduction sub-stage and involves talking about impersonal topics with little or no self-disclosure. These conversations center on the weather, current events, common experiences (what happened in class today or how the company picnic went), or specific impersonal tasks involving the two partners. Many relationships remain in the acquaintance stage, such as those with "neighbors" (for example, others in your apartment building or those seated next to you in class), coworkers, or clients.[45] Subsequent interactions with an acquaintance continue as casual banter.

EXPLORATION   If you and your partner decide to go to the next floor, *exploration,* you will begin to share more in-depth information about yourselves. During this stage, communication becomes easier, and a large amount of low-risk disclosure occurs about your interests and hobbies, where you grew up, and what your families are like. But a social distance is maintained with limited physical contact and the amount of time you spend together is also limited. This stage can begin as part of your first interaction after moving quickly through the acquaintance stage.

INTENSIFICATION   If you proceed to the *intensification stage,* you will start to depend on each other for self-confirmation and engage in more risky self-disclosure. You will spend more time together, increase the variety of activities you share, adopt a more personal physical distance, engage in more physical contact, and personalize your language. For example, couples in escalating relationships were found to use more personal idioms (words or gestures with special meaning to the couple such as nicknames or special ways of expressing affection) than those in de-escalating relationships.[46] You might discuss the nature of the relationship, perhaps deciding to become roommates or to date exclusively. You describe each other as "girlfriend," "boyfriend," "my BFF," or "best buddy." In romantic relationships, couples might decide to become "Facebook Official" (FBO) by changing their status to "in a relationship" and perhaps even adding their partner's name. This process of becoming FBO sometimes involves joking around and discussion before making the relationship public on social networks.[47]

introductions

Sub-stage of the acquaintance stage of relationship development, in which interaction is routine and basic information is shared.

casual banter

Sub-stage of the acquaintance stage of relationship development, in which impersonal topics are discussed but very limited personal information is shared.

Improving Your Communication Skills

Graphing Your Relationship Changes

Think of an interpersonal relationship that you have had for at least a year. On the graph, plot the development of that relationship from stage to stage, indicating the relative amount of time you spent in each stage. You can also indicate any movement back to a previous stage.

If possible, have your relational partner create a similar graph, and compare your perceptions of how the relationship has developed. What differences are there and why?

You also might want to compare your graph with those of classmates to see how different relationships develop. What can you tell from the graphs about the nature of their relationships?

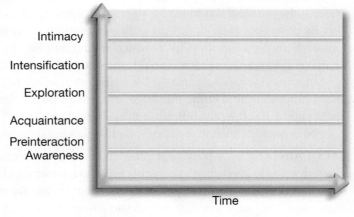

INTIMACY You have probably had a friend or romantic partner with whom you could talk about anything and everything and share intimate disclosures. If so, you probably were in the *intimacy stage*. In this stage, partners confirm and accept each other's sense of self, and their communication is highly personalized and synchronized. Partners further develop their own language code (idioms and inside jokes), use fewer words to communicate, rely more on nonverbal cues, increase physical contact, and decrease physical distance during conversations.[48] They define and discuss their roles and their relationship. Of course, reaching this stage takes time—time to build trust, time to share personal information, time to observe each other in various situations, and time to build commitment and an emotional bond. In romantic relationships, this commitment may be formalized through marriage.

Relational De-Escalation

relational de-escalation

Movement of a relationship away from intimacy through five stages: turmoil or stagnation, deintensification, individualization, separation, and post-separation.

post-intimacy relationship

Formerly intimate relationship that is maintained at a less intimate stage.

Relational de-escalation is the movement that occurs when a relationship decreases in intimacy or comes to an end. The process of ending a relationship is not as simple as going down the same elevator you came up on; it is not a mere reversal of the relationship formation process. Relational de-escalation might involve only moving back down one or two stages. When we maintain a relationship that had once been in the intimate stage, we create a **post-intimacy relationship**—changing an intimate romantic relationship to a friendship.

TURMOIL OR STAGNATION The first stage of relational de-escalation is *turmoil* or *stagnation.* Turmoil involves an increase in coercive conflict (use of negative tactics and unequal outcomes),[49] as one or both partners tend to find more faults in the other. The goals and definition of the relationship lose clarity, mutual acceptance declines, the communication climate becomes tense, and exchanges are difficult. Stagnation occurs when the relationship loses its vitality and the partners become complacent, experiencing *relational boredom*. Communication and physical contact between the partners decrease; they spend less time together, but do not necessarily fight. Partners in a stagnating relationship tend to go through the motions of an intimate relationship without the commitment; they simply follow their established relational routines. According to research, relational boredom encompasses a lack of fun, excitement, and spark, as well as feelings of being sick and tired of the partner. As such, boredom represents a "destructive relationship challenge."[50]

DEINTENSIFICATION If turmoil or stagnation continues, individuals might reach a threshold where they move to the *deintensification stage,* decreasing their interactions; increasing their physical, emotional, and psychological distance; and decreasing their dependence on the other for self-confirmation. They might discuss redefining their relationship, question its future, and assess each partner's level of satisfaction or dissatisfaction.

INDIVIDUALIZATION On the next floor down, the *individualization stage,* the partners tend to define their lives more as individuals and less in terms of their relationship. Neither views the other as "best friend" or "boyfriend/girlfriend" anymore. Interactions are limited. The perspective changes from "we" and "us" to "you" and "me," and property is defined in terms of "mine" or "yours" rather than "ours." Both partners turn to others for confirmation of their self-concepts.

SEPARATION In the *separation stage,* individuals make an intentional decision to eliminate or minimize further interpersonal interaction. At this stage, friends, resources, and property are divided between the partners. Despite separating, individuals still cope with feelings of commitment. One study of post-dissolution romantic relationships found four specific patterns of commitment change after a breakup: a *linear process,* in which commitment stayed the same—creating a flat horizontal line; a *relational decline* (the most common), in which commitment continued to decline over time; *upward relational progression,* in which commitment actually increased (perhaps re-escalating the relationship); and *turbulent relational progression*, in which the commitment increased and decreased several times.[51]

Circumstances such as attending the same classes, working in the same office, or sharing the same circle of friends and activities might lead to continued contact with an "ex." Partners' personal knowledge about each other often makes such interactions uncomfortable, and they return to awkward casual banter. Over time, each partner knows less about who the other person has become, and the acquaintance stage is re-established. For example, even after spending just a few years away from your high school friends, you might have difficulty interacting with them because your knowledge of one another is out of date—you're back to being acquaintances.

POST-SEPARATION EFFECTS Although interaction may cease altogether, the effect of the relationship is not over. Like something from science fiction, once you get on the elevator you can never get off—any relationship you begin will always be a part of you. The bottom floor on the down elevator, where you remain, is the *post-separation stage.* This floor represents the lasting effects the relationship has on you and, therefore, on your other interactions and relationships. Noted relationship scholar Steve Duck calls this final stage of terminating relationships "grave-dressing," in which we try to put a positive spin on the death of our relationship.[52] We create a public statement for people who ask why we broke up and also come to grips with losing the relationship. Sometimes, our sense of self gets battered during the final stages of a relationship, and we have to work hard to regain a healthy sense of self.

Principles Underlying Relational Stages

The relational elevator provides a number of additional metaphors reflecting key qualities and principles associated with relational development. Figure 9.3 shows the path a relationship might take; the letters correspond to the various principles covered next:

1. **You can choose to remain in a given relational stage** (to stay on a given floor). We might reach a given floor and never get back on the elevator, electing instead to stay at a particular stage of relational development (Periods B and E). Such a decision is based on finding the stage where we are most comfortable in the relationship. In order to stay at a given stage we engage in relational maintenance strategies—behaviors that maintain the same level of closeness and attraction. Specific maintenance strategies are presented in Chapter 11.

2. **Speed of progressing through the stages varies** (some elevator rides are faster than others). The amount of time you spend sharing information with someone can be concentrated in a few days or extended over a few years; thus, the length of the

BEING Other-ORIENTED
Relationships involve continual negotiation of the movement toward or away from intimacy. One partner often moves toward or away from intimacy before the other catches up. Not knowing what stage your partner is in creates discontent and conflict. Think about a relationship you have that has recently become closer. Who sees the relationship as closer, you or your partner? Does your partner also recognize this difference? How do you think your partner feels about it?

Figure 9.3 Sample Relational Development Graph

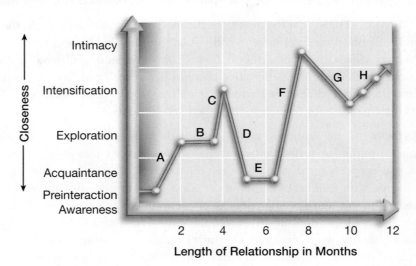

elevator ride from stage to stage and the time it takes to reach the top vary. Periods C and F show rapid increases in closeness while period H shows a slower increase. Generally, in reaching intimacy, all the escalating stages are experienced but sometimes so swiftly it's hard to distinguish them. On the other hand, an express down elevator can bypass all the normal stages of de-escalation for a quick exit.

3. **Changes in relationships are signaled** (elevator lights indicate when you reach a floor). **Turning points** (the blue dots on the graph) are specific events or interactions that signal positive or negative changes in a relationship.[53] A first date might signal a move from the acquaintance to the exploration stage. Movement to intensification might be signaled by having sex for the first time. Saying "I love you" for the first time might signal intimacy. Or the day you move all of your stuff out of the apartment might signal separation. Turning points occur within each stage, as well as between stages (Period H). A **causal turning point** is an event that directly affects the relationship, such as when a significant lie from a friend causes you to end the relationship. Because the event *caused* a change in the relationship, it is a causal turning point. On the other hand, a **reflective turning point** signals a change that has occurred in the definition of the relationship. Receiving and accepting an invitation to visit a friend's family for the first time does not cause a change in the relationship, but it *reflects* a change in how you and your friend perceive the relationship. Turning points can help clarify relational expectations by stimulating relationship talk—discussion about the nature of the relationship.[54]

turning point

Specific event or interaction associated with a positive or negative change in a relationship.

causal turning point

Event that brings about a change in a relationship.

reflective turning point

Event that signals a change in the way a relationship is defined.

4. **Change occurs within each stage** (while visiting a floor). Each stage spans a range of behaviors and changes that occur before moving on to the next stage. Lots of relational qualities increase within a given stage—trust grows, closeness increases, and commitment develops. For example, the exploration stage begins with sharing information that is identified as common to both of you, but as the stage progresses you develop greater trust and the breadth of disclosures increases.

5. **Change occurs between stages** (while you move between floors). While you spend most of your time on a given floor, you also spend some time between floors as you transition from one stage to another. During these transitional periods, your relationship has qualities of both stages, slowly increasing the characteristics of the next stage until the elevator stops and the doors open to the new stage.

6. **Movement through the stages can be forward, backward, or on-again/off-again** (the elevator can go up or down). We often ride the elevator up a floor or two, then drop down for a while, and then go back up again (Periods F, G, H). Sometimes the relationship ends but gets restarted, sometimes repeatedly, creating an on-again/off-again relationship (Periods D, E, F). On-again/off-again relationships can be caused by one dominant partner's change of mind or by external factors such as life changes (summer break, graduating, or moving).[55] While some relationships proceed in a linear escalating manner, they more often go through periods of becoming more and less close[56]—feeling more like a roller coaster ride than a tram ride up a mountain.

7. **Relational development involves negotiating change** (both parties must agree on which button to push). Movement to another stage involves implicitly or explicitly negotiating the definition of the relationship, the roles, and the expectations. If you want to take the elevator to the next floor but your partner doesn't, you either stay on the floor your partner desires or engage in strategies to convince your partner to push the button to go up. In other words, when only one partner desires to redefine the relationship, that partner must gain compliance or agreement from the other.[57] If you are unsuccessful in moving the relationship toward intimacy, you might decide to end the relationship altogether.

Theories of Interpersonal Relationship Development

9.4 **Describe the main components of the three theories that explain relational development.**

Think about some of your closer relationships. How did you move from being acquaintances to being close friends? Steve Duck suggests we go through a process of **filtering**, in which we reduce the number of partners at each stage of relational development by applying selection criteria that a potential close friend must meet.[58] We filter out partners as we move from one stage to another, assessing the relationships and deciding how we want to proceed—escalate, maintain, or de-escalate. Three theories explain how such decision making occurs: social exchange theory, relational dialectics theory, and social penetration theory (self-disclosure).

filtering
Process of reducing the number of partners at each stage of relational development by applying selection criteria.

Social Exchange Theory

You've probably been in a difficult relationship in which you have asked yourself, "Is this relationship really worth it?" You wonder whether the rewards you gain from the relationship are worth the trouble or expense (costs) necessary to sustain it. **Social exchange theory** asserts that we base relational decisions on getting the greatest amount of reward with the least amount of cost.[59] Relational rewards include friendship and love, fun and laughter, money or favors, support and assistance, and confirmation of

social exchange theory
Theory that claims people make relationship decisions by assessing and comparing the costs and rewards.

our value. Costs include loss of time, loss of freedom, financial loss, denigration of our self-esteem, and even psychological or physical abuse.

Rewards and costs affect our decisions to escalate, maintain, or terminate a relationship. For example, couples in one study who ended their romantic relationships maintained friendships when they continued to provide each other with rewards or resources (love, status, services, information, goods, or money).[60] Those for whom there were costs or barriers (lack of support for the friendship by family and friends, involvement in new romances, or where neglect was used to end the relationship) had lower-quality friendships. Deciding to remain in a relationship is a complex process that involves couples evaluating their current relationship, the outlook for their relationship, what they've accumulated in their relationship, and what they think they deserve.[61] A significant question regarding this theory is the degree to which we are as rational and deliberative as the theory suggests.[62] Consider whether you keep a running tally of the costs and rewards associated with your relationships, as described below.

immediate rewards and costs

Rewards and costs that are associated with a relationship at the present moment.

forecasted rewards and costs

Rewards and costs that an individual assumes will occur, based on projection and prediction.

IMMEDIATE AND FORECASTED REWARDS AND COSTS **Immediate rewards and costs** occur in a relationship in the present moment. Think about a couple of your relationships and consider how much you currently put into and get out of each. **Forecasted rewards and costs** are based on projection or prediction (predicted outcome value/POV). When you meet someone, you forecast whether a relationship with this person would be rewarding. You also use forecasting to decide whether to remain in existing relationships during troubled times (when costs escalate or rewards deteriorate). You can tolerate the increased costs associated with a roommate who's intolerable to live with during finals week because you know once finals are done, those costs will be gone and the relationship will be rewarding again.

cumulative rewards and costs

Total rewards and costs accrued during a relationship.

CUMULATIVE REWARDS AND COSTS **Cumulative rewards and costs** represent the total rewards and costs accrued over the duration of the relationship. One reason people remain in relationships during periods of low immediate rewards has to do with cumulative rewards and costs. Relationships represent investments. And the more we have invested, the more likely we are to hold on to that investment. An investment that has been profitable in the past is not immediately dropped when its profits decrease—we hang on for a while before deciding to divest ourselves. If, over a year, you developed a friendship that included a lot of great times and those great times stopped, you'd probably hang on to the friendship for a while but eventually let it fade away.

expected rewards and costs

Expectation of how much reward we should get from a given relationship in comparison to its costs.

When a couple commits to a relationship, both partners must find a new balance between autonomy and connection.

EXPECTED REWARDS AND COSTS **Expected rewards and costs** represent the expectations and ideals implicit in people's relational templates. We have mental models for relationships such as the ideal friend, the ideal lover, and the ideal coworker, against which we measure the costs and rewards associated with the actual relationships. We might abandon a relationship if it doesn't match or have the potential to match our ideal. If that ideal is unrealistic, we may experience continual dissatisfaction with actual relationships. For example, some parents avoid arguing in front of their children, creating an expectation in their children that marriage does not have any conflict costs. As adults, the children might evaluate their own marriages as unsuccessful when they experience unexpected conflict costs. If you find that you are continually unable to find relationships that measure up to your ideals, you may need to reassess your expected rewards and costs.

COMPARISON TO ALTERNATIVES We also compare the rewards and costs of our current relationships to the forecasted rewards and costs of other potential relationships. Perhaps you decided to end a romantic relationship that fell below your expected rewards or exceeded expected costs because there was an alternative relationship you believed could exceed your expected rewards. Social exchange theory explains your decision. Communication researchers Gerald Miller and Malcolm Parks observed that we move quickly to terminate relationships that fall below our expectations when we have opportunities to develop new relationships with the potential to exceed those expectations.[63]

Relational Dialectics Theory

As illustrated in Figure 9.3, relationships move in an erratic, non-linear cycle between becoming closer and backing off. Relational dialectics explain why relationships develop in this manner. **Relational dialectics theory** views relationship development as the management of the tensions that pull us in two directions at the same time. For example, more than half the respondents in one study described a friendship that moved toward closeness, then deteriorated, then became close again, with each change signaled by a turning point.[64] According to relational dialectics theory, each change occurred in conjunction with managing dialectical tensions.

relational dialectics theory
Theory that views relational development as the management of tensions that are pulling us in two directions at the same time (connection–autonomy; predictability–novelty; openness–closedness).

IDENTIFYING DIALECTICAL TENSIONS Relationship researcher Leslie Baxter identified three dialectical tensions that have been widely researched.[65]

- **Connection versus Autonomy.** We have both a desire to connect and be interdependent with others and a desire to remain autonomous and independent. We want to be loved, but we love our independence. In one study of married couples, the desire to be both connected and autonomous was the most frequently occurring dialectical tension.[66]

- **Predictability versus Novelty (Certainty versus Uncertainty).** Knowing what to expect and being able to predict the circumstances around us helps reduce the tension that occurs from uncertainty. Yet we get bored by constant repetition and routine and therefore are attracted to novelty and the unexpected. Relationships that fall into routines may be comfortable, but they suffer from a need for freshness.

- **Openness versus Closedness.** One ideal we seem to want to achieve in relationships is the ability to be totally open with our partners. We wish to disclose information to others and to have those we are attracted to disclose to us. However, we also value our privacy and feel a desire to hold back information. This tension was identified in the study of married couples mentioned earlier as the most important of the three tensions, although it did not occur as often as the other two.[67]

USING DIALECTICAL TENSIONS TO EXPLAIN RELATIONAL MOVEMENT According to relational dialectics, each tension is present in every relationship, but the impact of each one changes as a relationship progresses. Movement in relationships can be seen as a shift that occurs because of more pull from one of the two forces in tension. For example, when you begin developing a new friendship, you have to decide how much freedom to do your own thing (autonomy) you are willing to give up in order to spend time with this other person (connection). Notice the similarity to social exchange theory, in that you weigh costs (giving up autonomy) against rewards (becoming connected).

Forces of autonomy and connection can be found even in close relationships.[68] Generally, such tension between autonomy and connection diminishes as we become more intimate; however, engagements have been called off at the last minute when the pull toward autonomy was stronger than connection. Although long-married couples have usually settled the issue of interdependence versus independence, relational dialectics asserts (and research supports) that tension from these forces remains. One study of married couples found that dialectical tensions existed both at the individual level (for example, with the wife or the husband trying to decide whether to be open or closed) and at the relational level (partners differing in terms of desires for autonomy, openness, or novelty).[69]

Tensions are an inherent part of being in a relationship. Movement in relationships is seen to occur because some element of tension has been resolved or overcome.[70] At the intensification stage of a romantic relationship, you experience a desire to be closer, yet you have autonomy. You can decide to become closer, which moves the relationship toward intimacy, or you can decide to be more autonomous, de-escalating the relationship. Decisions regarding each dialectical tension produce corresponding changes in the relationship. Even Facebook can be a source of dialectical tensions. College student focus groups identified problems with maintaining their privacy and autonomy when they posted information about their relationships that became accessible to their entire social network.[71] Deciding to change a status from "in a relationship" to "it's complicated" creates an inherent tension between openness and closedness.

COPING WITH DIALECTICAL TENSIONS (PRAXIS)   You find yourself excited yet very uncomfortable in a new romantic relationship where your partner wants you to give up your free time on the weekends so you can be together. You have several options for managing this connection versus autonomy tension.[72]

You might give up your free time and ignore your feelings (denial), or wallow and flounder in uncertainty about what to do (disorientation). Neither of these strategies is particularly healthy because the tension (pull toward autonomy) continues to eat at you. You need strategies that give you some control and let you cope with the tension.

You could become more involved but agree that every other Saturday you get to hang out with your friends (cyclic alternation), or negotiate for occasional solo weekend activities like a fishing or shopping trip (segmentation). These strategies allow for connection while protecting a certain degree of autonomy.

You might find some balance that includes both connection and autonomy, such as letting your partner join you on your fishing or shopping trips with the understanding that your partner gives you space and doesn't take control (moderation).

Finally, you and your partner might reach an understanding that you will become closer, yet still appreciate that you are separate individuals and have your own lives outside the relationship (recalibration). Rather than a perceived threat to connection, autonomy becomes part of accepting each other more completely (reframing). Being

#communicationandtechnology
Do Cell Phones Threaten Your Autonomy?

In 2011, eighteen- to twenty-four-year-olds who owned a cell phone sent and received an average of more than 109 text messages per day and eighteen- to twenty-nine-year-olds averaged 17.1 calls a day.[73] In 2013, 97 percent of eighteen- to twenty-nine-year-olds used their cell phones for texting, 73 percent for e-mailing, and 40 percent for video chats.[74] The picture these statistics paint is that college-age people are very connected. That connection could be a direct dialectical tension to autonomy.

In a study at an East Coast college, 61 percent of participants in romantic relationships reported arguing over cell phone use. Those respondents who reported high autonomy–connection tension were more likely than low-tension respondents to have conflicts about not calling or texting enough, engaging in calls or texts with members of the opposite sex, and not answering the phone or texts.[75] On one hand, some students wanted more connection and contact with their partners than they were receiving and felt tension from not being able to contact their partners or their partners failing to contact them. On the other hand, for those who wanted more autonomy,

a partner's excessive calling and texting caused tension, creating an expectation that the partner be constantly available for contact. The strategy used by half of those experiencing conflict was either to accept or reject the partner's position—for example, agree to call more—or to end the relationship.

Consider your own experiences with cell phone use. Have your friends or romantic partners irritated you with too many calls, too few calls, or some other phone call behavior? Have others requested changes in your cell phone use?

in relationships means you are in a constant state of dialectical tension; thus, you must develop and apply various coping strategies if the relationships are to succeed.

Self-Disclosure and Social Penetration Theory

You probably recall from Chapter 2 that *self-disclosure* occurs when we purposefully provide information to others about ourselves that they would not learn if we did not tell them. Your Facebook page reflects a form of self-disclosure, allowing anyone who "friends you" access to personal information. As relationships develop, we might use electronically mediated communication to self-disclose further.[76] In this chapter, self-disclosure is presented as an important part of the process of developing relationships. In fact, it is so important that social psychologists Irwin Altman and Dalmas Taylor built a theory based on it.[77] The main premise of their **social penetration theory** is that the movement toward intimacy is connected to increased breadth and depth of self-disclosing, as reflected in their model (Figure 9.4).

UNDERSTANDING THE SOCIAL PENETRATION MODEL   The **social penetration model** starts with a circle that represents all the potential information about yourself that you could disclose to someone (see Figure 9.4, circle A). This circle is divided into many pieces like a pie, with each piece representing a particular aspect of your "self," like hobbies, religious beliefs, family, school, political interests, and fears. These many pieces represent the **breadth** of information available about you.

The concentric circles in the pie represent the depth of information you could disclose. By **depth**, we mean how personal or intimate the information is; telling your friend about your fear of elevators is more intimate than telling someone that your favorite ice cream is vanilla. In this way, social penetration is like an onion, where

social penetration theory

Theory of relational development that posits that increases in intimacy are connected to increases in self-disclosure.

social penetration model

A model of the self that reflects both the breadth and the depth of information that can potentially be disclosed.

breadth

The various pieces of self, like hobbies, beliefs, family, school, and fears, that can be potentially disclosed.

depth

How personal or intimate the information is that might be disclosed.

Figure 9.4 Social Penetration Model

A

Your "self" with all its various dimensions. The wedges represent the breadth of your "self," and the rings represent depth.

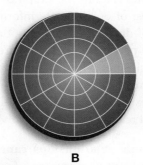

B

A limited relationship in which one dimension of your "self" has been disclosed to another person.

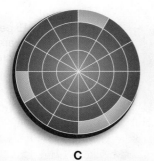

C

A relationship with greater breadth than B but with no intimacy.

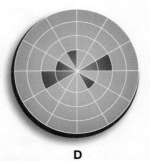

D

A highly intimate, close relationship in which there has been extensive breadth and depth of disclosure.

each layer of the onion is peeled away as you move toward the onion core. The center circle represents this core, the most personal information. Each of your relationships involves social penetration, or the extent to which others learn intimate information (depth) as well as the number of different pieces of information they learn (breadth). The shading on circle B shows a relationship with one aspect revealed but with a high degree of penetration/depth. Can you think of a relationship that you have that fits this pattern—someone that knows a lot about only one aspect of your life, for example a coworker, classmate, or doctor? In circle C, more pieces of the pie are shaded, but the information is all fairly safe, superficial information about you, such as where you went to school, your hometown, or your major. These would be the kind of disclosures associated with a new friendship. Circle D represents almost complete social penetration, the kind achieved in an intimate, well-developed relationship in which a large amount of self-disclosure has occurred.

ENHANCING INTIMACY BY SELF-DISCLOSING OVER TIME   As social penetration theory asserts, it is through the process of revealing information that it becomes possible for relationships to become more intimate. In an intimate friendship, we become aware of things about our friends that few people, if any, know. Simply disclosing information about yourself is no guarantee that your relationship will become intimate (with *intimate* here referring to both greater depth and greater breadth of self-disclosure).[78] As we mutually self-disclose, we often discover incompatibilities or even negative information, which may lead to relational de-escalation.

Typically, a large *amount* of low-risk self-disclosure takes place in the early stages of relational development, and that amount decreases as the relationship becomes more and more intimate (Figure 9.5, Graph A). There is only so much information to share about ourselves, so the amount of disclosure slows down as the relationship continues, assuming the partners have remained open. While the amount decreases, the *intimacy* (depth) of our disclosures, which are limited initially, increases as the relationship escalates (Figure 9.5, Graph B)—but that too eventually decreases after we have shared most of our intimate information. However, the pattern of the amount and intimacy of disclosure is often not as neat as the two graphs indicate. Relationships experience periods of marked increases and decreases in the amount and intimacy of self-disclosure, reflecting some change in the relationship. Even long-term relationships can experience dramatic increases and decreases in disclosure; for example, first-time expectant parents are likely to disclose their intimate fears and expectations about child rearing (as shown on the graph).

Interpersonal relationships cannot achieve intimacy without self-disclosure. Without true self-disclosure, we form only superficial relationships. You can confirm

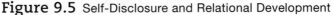

Figure 9.5 Self-Disclosure and Relational Development

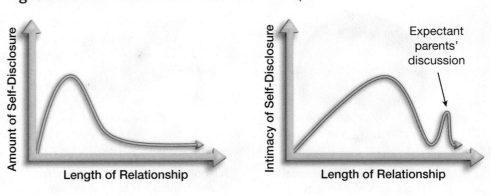

another person's self-concept, and have your self-concept confirmed, only if both you and your partner have revealed yourselves to each other—you have both self-disclosed.

CHARACTERISTICS OF SELF-DISCLOSURE People come to know us and, we hope, to like us as we reveal who we are within the normal course of conversations.[79] But as you probably know, there's a lot more to self-disclosing than just opening your soul to someone. Let's examine some of the factors that connect self-disclosure to our interpersonal interactions and relationships.

1. Self-disclosing is moderated by rules and boundaries. **Communication privacy management theory (CPM)** suggests that we each have individual rules or boundaries about how much private information we share and with whom we share that information.[80] Our cultural background, our need to connect to others, and the amount of risk involved in sharing information (whether the information would embarrass us or others) are factors that determine how much and how quickly we share information about our personal lives.[81] Our disclosures can be accompanied by implicit privacy rules (e.g., not revealing things said during an intimate conversation), explicit privacy rules (e.g., "This is just between you and me"), or no rules.[82] These rules affect both the disclosure and the recipient. The more ownership a person sharing the disclosure feels toward the information, the more both explicit and implicit rules are in play.[83] What information has a friend recently told you that you know should not be shared with anyone else? Are you guided by implicit or explicit rules?

2. Self-Disclosure Usually Occurs in Small Increments. We typically don't share all that we know about ourselves with people when we first meet. We usually reveal information about ourselves a little bit at a time, rather than delivering our autobiography all at once. CPM and social penetration theories both reflect how we control the amount of self-disclosure we share relative to other factors such as the stage of the relationship and the culture. Do you reveal information at a greater depth sooner than you should? If you do, others may be uncomfortable with your openness. Appropriate self-disclosure needs to fit the occasion, the relationship, and the expectations of the individuals involved.

3. Self-Disclosure Moves from Less Personal to More Personal Information. As the social penetration model (Figure 9.4) illustrates, we can describe the depth of our self-disclosure by the intimacy level of the information we share. John Powell, author of *Why Am I Afraid to Tell You Who I Am?*, describes five levels of information we disclose as we progress toward intimacy.[84]

communication privacy management theory
Theory that suggests we each manage our own degree of privacy by means of personal boundaries and rules for sharing information.

Relating to Diverse Others
Cultural Differences in Self-Disclosure

People's cultural backgrounds affect both the kinds of things they reveal to others and the level of intimacy of that information. Intercultural communication scholar William Gudykunst found that North Americans are more likely than the Japanese to reveal more personal and intimate information about themselves to people whom they consider close friends.[85] Self-disclosure researcher Mie Kito had the same findings; Japanese students disclosed less about themselves than did students from North America.[86] Both Japanese and American students disclosed more about themselves in romantic relationships than with their friends. Americans were more likely than the Japanese to talk about their sex lives, dating patterns, and love interests and to reveal their emotions. A researcher investigating Korean communication patterns found that North Americans tended to disclose more than Koreans about their marital status, sexual morality, and use of birth control.[87] But Koreans were more likely than Americans to talk about issues related to education and family rules.

As you interact with diverse others, try to develop sensitivity to how cultural differences affect what is considered appropriate to disclose and thus avoid creating an uncomfortable or embarrassing situation.

Our relationships develop as we disclose more and more pieces of our selves.

dyadic effect

The reciprocal nature of self-disclosure: "You disclose to me, and I'll disclose to you."

Level 5: *Cliché communication.* In acknowledging the presence of another person with standard phrases such as "Hello" or the more contemporary "What's up?" we signal the desire to initiate a relationship, even if it is a brief, superficial one.

Level 4: *Facts and biographical information.* After using cliché phrases and responses to establish contact, we typically reveal nonthreatening information, such as our names, hometowns, or majors.

Level 3: *Attitudes and personal ideas.* After noting our name and other basic information, we might begin talking about more personal information, such as our attitudes about work or school, our likes and dislikes, and noncontroversial topics.

Level 2: *Personal feelings.* After we've developed rapport and trust with someone, we share more intimate fears, secrets, and attitudes.

Level 1: *Peak or gut level communication.* Powell calls this the ultimate level of self-disclosure, which is seldom reached because of the risk involved in being so revealing. Powell says we might not even reach this level of intimacy with our life partners, parents, or children.

4. Self-Disclosure Is Reciprocal. In mainstream US culture, a **dyadic effect** occurs when one person's sharing of information about himself or herself prompts disclosure of similar information by the other person, particularly in the initial stages of relationships. When we introduce ourselves and mention where we are from, we expect the other person to do likewise. Such reciprocation demonstrates trust and tends to increase liking.[88] This effect might be one reason strangers appear to tolerate but not necessarily to reciprocate even highly intimate information.[89] The dyadic effect might be even stronger in your online exchanges. In a recent experiment, participants in a computer-mediated communication (CMC) exchange reciprocated intimate disclosures more than participants in a similar face-to-face (FtF) exchange.[90] CMC disclosures were perceived as more intimate and thus CMC participants reciprocated with more intimate disclosures than did the FtF participants.

We sometimes employ the dyadic effect as a strategy to gain information about others—we want to know about someone's family, so we tell that person about our family first. If we don't see a relationship as having the potential to become more intimate, we are less likely to reciprocate.[91]

In closer relationships, we might not reciprocate during a given interaction, but we expect reciprocation over the course of the relationship. A friend having difficulties in school might share those difficulties with you without expecting reciprocal self-disclosure; however, at some other time, you might share similar intimate information.[92]

5. Self-Disclosure Involves Risk and Requires Trust. Although self-disclosure is a building block for establishing intimacy with others, it can be risky. Facebook continues to grapple with issues of information privacy and the risks associated with posting personal information. Once you self-disclose to someone, that person could share the information with others, even though you might have established explicit privacy rules. Or, if you disclose your weaknesses and fears, you might scare someone away. We take this risk when we feel we can trust the person not to share our information with others nor reject us. According to British social psychologists Michael Argyle, Monica Henderson, and Adrian Furnham, one of the most fundamental expectations people have of their friends is that they will not reveal confidences.[93]

But should we keep secrets about ourselves from others? Sometimes, sharing secrets can have a positive impact. Interpersonal communication researchers Anita

BEING Other-ORIENTED
You probably have a good sense of what information you are comfortable disclosing to any given individual. But do you have a good sense of what other people are comfortable disclosing to you? Consider some of your casual and close relationships; are those partners more or less comfortable with disclosing personal information than you are? To what degree do these differences affect you, your partners, and the relationships?

Improving Your Communication Skills

Self-Disclosure as a Dance

Think of self-disclosure as a dance during which you and your partner react to each other's moves. If one is slow in disclosing, the other should follow that lead. The following are some self-disclosure dance suggestions for you to practice.

Enhancing Your Moves

Be Other-Oriented

Think about something you are considering disclosing to someone. What do you know about the other person and how he or she might react? Consider that the other person might perceive your self-disclosure as a reflection of your trust and how close you see the relationship. Are you comfortable with that perception? Likewise, consider how the other person's self-disclosures convey trust in you and his or her perception of the relationship. Be aware that what *you* perceive as intimate and what it says about the relationship is likely to be different than the other person's perception.

Monitor Nonverbal Cues

Just as you focus on a dance partner's body movement, you need to monitor a relational partner's nonverbal feedback to your disclosures. Can you recall a time when you disclosed information that appeared to make another person uncomfortable? Watch for such nonverbal cues as avoiding eye contact or unexpected facial expressions that show a person's level of comfort with what's being disclosed. The amount you disclose and the depth of your disclosures need to be appropriate to the relational context.

Adapt to the Other's Moves

Whether you're leading or following the dance, you adjust your moves to those of your partner. In a relationship, your level of disclosure should match that of your partner, but only if you are comfortable doing so. If your partner discloses information you feel is too personal, don't feel compelled to reciprocate. Ideally, your partner will sense your discomfort and adjust his or her moves to you. The two of you are creating a dance that reflects the comfort levels of both.

Promoting Your Partner's Moves

Be Trustworthy

People dance with people they trust; people open up to those they trust. Do other people see you as someone who can be trusted? What kind of signals do you send about your trustworthiness? Some trust develops over time as information is shared and kept confidential. However, showing sincere interest and caring during a conversation will also build some trust. Telling your partner that you recognize the difficulty and importance of what he or she is saying, as well as expressing appreciation for his or her trust in you, shows empathy and can increase your trustworthiness.

Provide Social Support and Confirming Responses

Your dance partners want you to be there for them if they slip and to make them feel good about dancing. How do you typically react when a person shares delicate, embarrassing, or intimate information? Are you receptive, critical, indifferent, or noticeably uncomfortable? When people self-disclose negative information about themselves, they are often seeking social support and confirmation of their value. To be evaluative or judgmental of such a disclosure would be a great misstep. Apply good interpersonal listening skills, paraphrase what you've heard, and, when appropriate, don't say anything—just be there for the other person.

Vangelisti, John Caughlin, and Lindsay Timmerman found that we would be *more* likely to share a family secret if [94]

- during an intimate conversation with another person, we found out that this person had a similar problem or we thought revealing the secret would help the other person;
- we thought the secret would eventually come to light, even if we didn't reveal it;
- there was some urgency or importance in revealing the secret such that continuing to conceal the secret would create more problems than revealing it;
- we thought the family member would not mind if the secret were told; the family member would still accept us; or
- the topic came up in conversation, and it seemed normal and natural to reveal the secret.

You might worry after reading this list that your family members might tell things they know about you that you'd rather they did not reveal. Don't worry (too much). If sharing the secret with others would hurt its owner, then there is less likelihood that the secret will be shared.[95] And there are some secrets that people would never disclose. Are there secrets in your family that you would never reveal?

warranting

Looking for clues to validate or invalidate an online claim.

Sometimes we wonder whether we should believe what another person has shared, especially when we are dealing with online disclosures, in which deception can be hard to identify. Looking for clues to validate or invalidate an online claim is called **warranting**.[96] We are more inclined to trust what we can observe for ourselves (pictures and posted comments by others) than believe what we are told by the online source (profile information). Warranting information, like pictures, is seen as information the poster cannot manipulate.[97]

6. Self-Disclosure Reflects Perceptions About the Nature of Your Relationships. What you reveal about yourself to others and what others reveal to you about themselves provide important information about how each of you perceives the quality, intimacy, and nature of your relationships. If you find your partner unwilling to disclose, that partner might be implicitly conveying to you a lack of interest in escalating the relationship. On the other hand, when a friend reveals her GPA of 2.8 out of 4.0, which is very embarrassing to her, she is taking a risk, conveying trust, and letting you know that you are important to her.

However, interpreting the level of intimacy based on what a person discloses is challenging; what is risky and intimate to one person might not be perceived that way by another. Suppose GPAs are no big deal to you, and you tell your friend's GPA to others. Your failure to see her GPA as highly sensitive means you have also failed to recognize the trust she felt in you.

Recap

Theories of Interpersonal Relationship Development

Theory	Definition	Application
Social Exchange Theory	People make relational decisions based on getting the greatest amount of reward with the least amount of cost.	You break up a long-distance relationship because the expense (driving time, cell phone bills) seems greater than what is gained from the relationship (fun, support).
Relational Dialectics Theory	Relational development involves the management of tensions that are pulling each other in two directions at the same time.	The time you spend with your new romantic partner is taking time away from your other friends. You must decide how to deal with your desire to be in the romantic relationship and still maintain your friendships.
Social Penetration Theory	Movement toward intimacy is connected to the breadth and depth of self-disclosure.	Your casual relationship with a roommate centers primarily on rent, shared bills, and housecleaning. One night your roommate shares the news that his parents are getting a divorce. You listen empathically as he shares his thoughts and feelings, sharing similar information when appropriate. From that point on, your relationship becomes closer and more intimate.

Applying an Other-Orientation

to Understanding Interpersonal Relationships

This chapter focused on the movement of relationships toward and away from intimacy; on relational costs and rewards, dialectical tensions, and self-disclosure; and on attraction. These relational elements were discussed primarily from your perspective—the rewards you may perceive, the tensions you experience, and your attraction to others. But reflecting from time to time on these elements from your relational partners' points of view can enhance your relationships. Why not start right now? Take a moment to identify: (1) a close relationship with a specific friend and (2) a new relationship that is becoming closer.

Identify the stage each relationship is in and how far along it is in that stage. What cues does each partner provide to indicate how far the relationship has escalated or de-escalated? How does your perception compare to where each of your partners sees the relationship? How sure are you of your assessment of each partner's perspective? How can you increase your certainty?

Using a scale from 0 to 100, how rewarding would you say each relationship is? How costly? Consider whether your two partners see the relationship as more or less rewarding than you do. Does each see the relationship as more costly or less costly than you do?

How comfortable are you with the current balance between connection and autonomy in each relationship? How comfortable is each partner?

What percentage (from 0 percent to 100 percent) of your "self" have you disclosed to each partner? How much do you think your partners would say they have revealed about themselves to you? What differences do you think your partners perceive between what you've revealed and what they have revealed?

What was the source of your initial attraction to each partner? What was the basis of each person's attraction to you?

What is your long-term maintenance attraction to each person based on? What continues their attraction toward you?

Rarely do two people view their relationship in exactly the same way. What impact have any of the differences you've identified had on the relationships? On each person's satisfaction? If you didn't find any significant discrepancies between your views and your partners' views, you might be missing some information. Look for additional cues that might help you more completely understand your partners' perspectives, or consider sharing your views with them while seeking theirs.

STUDY GUIDE

Review, Apply, and Assess

Interpersonal Relationships Defined

Objective 9.1   Define interpersonal relationships and identify two ways to distinguish among them.

Key Terms

relationship
interpersonal relationship
interpersonal intimacy
relationship of circumstance
relationship of choice
complementary relationship

symmetrical relationship
competitive symmetrical relationship
submissive symmetrical relationship
parallel relationship

Thinking Critically

Identify qualities beyond those cited in the text's definition of an interpersonal relationship that vary among your relationships. Why do you suppose those weren't included in the text's definition?

Assessing Your Skills

Create two columns on a piece of paper. In the first column, write the names of three individuals with whom you have different relationships (for example, a parent, best same-sex friend, coworker). Using a scale of 1 (low) to 5 (high), indicate the degree to which each person likes to be in control and make decisions when you're together. In the second column, indicate the degree to which you like to be in control and make decisions when you're with each person. How do these differences and similarities affect your relationships? How effective do you think you could be in changing the power if you wanted?

Genesis of Interpersonal Relationships: Attraction

Objective 9.2   Identify and differentiate between short-term initial attraction and long-term maintenance attraction.

Key Terms

interpersonal attraction
short-term initial attraction
long-term maintenance attraction
proximity

physical appearance
competence
reciprocation of liking
similarity
complementary needs

Thinking Critically

Which source of attraction is probably the most important for sustaining a long-term relationship? Why? Which is least important? Why?

Assessing Your Skill

What is it that attracts you to other people? Why are other people attracted to you? Make a list of the first names of your closest friends. Using the sources of attraction in the text, identify which sources explain your attraction to the people on your list. Which source of attraction appears the most often and which sources most strongly affect you? Which source has the least amount of impact? What would each friend say was the reason he or she is attracted to you?

Stages of Interpersonal Relationship Development

Objective 9.3   Identify and describe the stages of relational escalation and de-escalation.

Key Terms

relational development
relational escalation
introductions
casual banter
relational de-escalation

post-intimacy relationship
turning point
causal turning point
reflective turning point

Thinking Critically

Think about three relationships you have that have remained in the exploration or intensification stage. What has prevented the relationships from escalating to the next stage? Why have you sustained the relationships?

Assessing Your Skill

Some people are good at initiating relationships, some are good at moving a relationship to intimacy, but few are good at terminating them. Consider each of the escalating and de-escalating stages and identify the stages in which you are most competent in moving a relationship. What skills do you have that help you achieve each of those stages? Among the de-escalating stages, what interpersonal skills do you have that could help you move a relationship to a given stage? How would those skills help?

Theories of Interpersonal Relationship Development

Objective 9.4 **Describe the main components of the three theories that explain relational development.**

Key Terms

filtering	cumulative rewards and costs
social exchange theory	expected rewards and costs
immediate rewards and costs	relational dialectics theory
forecasted rewards and costs	social penetration theory

social penetration model	management theory
breadth	dyadic effect
depth	warranting
communication privacy	

Thinking Critically

Explain (a) how social exchange theory relates to dialectical theory, (b) how social exchange theory relates to social penetration theory, and (c) how dialectical theory relates to social penetration theory and to self-disclosure.

Assessing Your Skills

Make a list of ten pieces of information about yourself that vary in their level of intimacy or risk (its depth). Put (+) next to those you know are appropriate to disclose to a fellow student you have just met. Put (–) next to those you know are inappropriate and (?) next to those you are unsure about. Under what circumstances might the pieces of information you marked with (–) or (?) be appropriate to disclose? Put a (✓) by those pieces of information that you are comfortable actually sharing with that fellow student and an (x) by those you are not. If you have information that is appropriate to disclose, but you are uncomfortable doing so, what can you do to become more comfortable sharing that information? How have your initial interactions been affected by (a) your disclosing information that might be viewed as inappropriate and (b) *not* disclosing appropriate information?

Chapter 10
Managing Relationship Challenges

"Love begins with a smile, grows with a kiss, and ends with a teardrop."

Anonymous

Learning Objectives

10.1 Identify and explain the challenges that individuals involved in interpersonal relationships must navigate to be successful.

10.2 Describe the issues that constitute the dark side of interpersonal communication and those that constitute the dark side of interpersonal relationships.

10.3 Explain the process of relational de-escalation and termination, including strategies for terminating and recovering.

Charise:	I heard you went to the new Fast and Furious movie last night.
Simon:	Yeah, it was pretty good.
Charise:	I thought we agreed to go see it together?
Simon:	Oh, sorry. I forgot; besides, you were busy anyway.
Charise:	Don't lie. You didn't forget—you just didn't want to go with me.
Simon:	Hey, wait a minute. It's no big deal. It was just a movie.
Charise:	Who'd you go with?
Simon:	A gang of us from work went.
Charise:	Who?
Simon:	Just some people from work.
Charise:	You're a liar! I heard it was just you and some girl.

Throughout this book you have read about various factors that can impede effective interpersonal communication: language misunderstandings, biased perceptions, misinterpretation of nonverbal cues, weak listening skills, destructive conflict styles, and inappropriate self-disclosures. All of these factors can also negatively affect interpersonal relationships.

The above exchange between Charise and Simon reflects another set of issues that are covered in this chapter. Simon has obviously broken a promise he made to Charise about seeing a movie together, which places a strain on the relationship. Simon compounds the problem by being deceptive, but Charise calls him on it. Unlike the specific conflicts that you read about in Chapter 8, the challenges covered in this chapter reflect larger, more systemic relational issues. Interpersonal communication also has a dark side, in that it can be used in ways that are detrimental to others. These include being deceitful, as Simon is, and saying things that hurt other people's feelings, as Charise does. Such relationship challenges and the darker aspects of interpersonal communication can contribute to relational de-escalation and termination.

Relationship and Communication Challenges

10.1 Identify and explain the challenges that individuals involved in interpersonal relationships must navigate to be successful.

The movement toward an intimate relationship doesn't always go smoothly. Chapter 9 described some general expectations about how relationships develop, and you have your own additional set of expectations about relationships. When our partners fail to meet these expectations (a failure event or transgression), we face the challenge of managing our way through those unmet expectations. Other challenges we face in relationships include delivering bad news or addressing grief, maintaining relationships over long distances, and sustaining relationships that face social bias. Successfully managing each of these challenges requires strong resolve and commitment by the relationship partners.

Violating Expectations

Just as relational expectations are part of the definition of relationships, violations of those expectations are an unavoidable part of relationship development.

UNDERSTANDING RELATIONAL EXPECTATIONS AND VIOLATIONS Relationship expectations can be classified according to their social origins, their relationship origins, and their severity.

Socially Based Expectations You have expectations for what it means to be a best friend, for how you should be treated by a romantic partner or spouse, for how an opposite-sex friend behaves toward you, and so on. Violations of these socially based expectations arouse uncertainty and produce emotional reactions such as hurt and anger.[1] You might assess a relationship in light of your expectations and decide to de-escalate or terminate it if it fails to meet your expectations. Or you might change your expectations so that a given event is no longer a violation. For example, if you held the expectation that friends lend other friends money, but your friends kept turning down your loan requests, you might stop seeing money lending as a quality of friendship. Finally, you might decide to discuss the violation of the expectation with the other person, in an attempt to persuade him or her to change, thereby improving your relational satisfaction and the health of the relationship.

Relationship-Specific Expectations   You and your partners also develop sets of implicit and explicit expectations and understandings specific to your relationship. *Implicit understandings* represent an unspoken compact between partners about the relationship and each other; *explicit understandings* are stated compacts and agreements. Violations of both types of understandings arouse uncertainty and evoke various responses. For example, you share some very personal information with someone you regard as trustworthy (an implicit understanding), and the information becomes known to all your other friends. Your roommate agrees to clean up the apartment over the weekend (an explicit understanding) and then fails to do so. Your boyfriend or girlfriend is seen on a date (either an implicit or an explicit understanding) with your best friend. Each of these violations represents a **failure event or transgression**—an incident marked by the breaking of a relational understanding or agreement. Effective management of a failure event or transgression can clarify expectations (for example, make an implicit expectation explicit) as well as clarify the relationship.

failure event or transgression
An incident marked by the breaking or violating of a relational understanding or agreement.

Severity   Failure events and transgressions can be thought of as occurring along a continuum of severity, with those that are least severe often being ignored altogether. At the more severe end of the continuum would be unfaithfulness in dating relationships, which might include spending time with another person, breaking a promise, flirting, betraying a trust or confidence, keeping secrets from the partner, or failing to return affection.[2] The most severe violations can have a traumatic impact on a relationship. For example, because a defining characteristic of intimate romantic relationships is often sexual fidelity, cheating on one's partner is considered a severe moral transgression and often leads to the termination of the relationship.[3] The timing of the behavior impacts its interpretation; for example, offering too much affection at the wrong time or not enough affection at another time can be a failure event.

We don't all assess the severity of a violation in the same way; we might see flirting as a minor failure event while our partner views it as severe. And regardless of how severe we feel the transgression is, we still might not end the relationship if we believe our partner is the only person who can really meet our relational needs—a phenomenon known as *perceived partner uniqueness*.[4] Severity and feelings of hurt also appear to be reduced when the violating partner has been providing high amounts of affectionate communication (verbal and nonverbal messages of love, support, and fondness).[5] You can strengthen your relationships by being other-centered. Discuss your expectations and violations with your partner to improve your understanding of how he or she perceives these violations.

RESPONDING WITH DISCUSSION   The process of addressing failure events often follows the reproach-account pattern, in which both partners must make a number of decisions. The first decision is whether a failure event has actually occurred. Does this transgression violate an inherent social expectation? If not, had both parties agreed to a specific rule or expectation? Did both parties understand the rule? Was the rule appropriate, applicable, and accepted?

After answering these questions, both parties must decide whether to discuss the failure.[6] If we don't care that much about either the relationship or the issue, we might opt to ignore the failure, deciding it is not worth the effort. The decision to complain to or reproach a partner should be motivated by a desire to clarify relational expectations or to avoid the failure event in the future by modifying the partner's behaviors.[7]

A recent study examined responses to violations of expectations about personal information, such as betraying confidences or passing along private information.[8] While respondents reported anger and hurt, relational improvement was more likely to occur when people responded by explaining feelings and talking about the violation rather than venting, yelling, cursing, and confronting partners.

reproach

Message that a failure event has occurred.

A **reproach** is a message that indicates an expectation has been violated, pointing out a failure event. Reproaches are usually direct statements, but they can also be conveyed indirectly through hints or nonverbal messages. For example, if you are upset that a close friend forgot your birthday, you might act cold and distant or speak harshly. In Chapter 6, you learned how your word choice can evoke defensiveness in your listeners. The wording of your reproach can range from *mitigating* (mild) to *aggravating* (threatening and severe). For example, if your friend forgets to return a book she borrowed, you might offer a mitigating reproach such as "Hey, Sally, I was wondering if you were done with that book I loaned you?" On the other hand, "Remind me to never loan you a book again, Sally; you are obviously irresponsible" is an aggravating reproach that is likely to evoke a defensive retort (account) from Sally.

account

Response to a reproach.

The response to a reproach is called an **account**. In the preceding example, the nature of your reproach affects the kind of account Sally is likely to provide.[9] Had she realized her failure, she might have provided an account preemptively before you reproached her. Relationship scholar Frank Fincham postulated that self-initiated accounts are more likely to evoke a favorable reaction from a partner than are accounts given in response to reproaches.[10] Apologizing as you arrive late at a friend's house for dinner is more likely to appease the irritated friend than acting as if you've done nothing wrong or apologizing only *after* being reproached. Accounts typically take one of five forms:

- *Apologies* include admission that the failure event occurred, acceptance of responsibility, and expression of regret. Example: "I'm really sorry I'm late. I won't make any excuses. I just hope you can forgive me."

- *Excuses* include admission that the failure event occurred, coupled with a contention that nothing could have been done to prevent the failure; it was due to unforeseen circumstances. Example: "I'm really sorry I'm late. The traffic was really heavy coming over, so it took longer than I planned."

- *Justifications* involve accepting responsibility for the event but redefining the event as not a failure. Example: "I know I'm late, but as I was leaving, my roommate came in all upset about a friend's death. I couldn't leave. I stayed a while to talk and provide comfort."

- *Denials* are statements that the failure event never took place. Example: "I'm not late. I never said exactly what time I'd be here."

- *Absence of an account,* or *silence,* involves ignoring a reproach or refusing to address it. Example: After arriving late and being reproached with, "You're late," you respond, "Well, are you ready or not? Let's go."

In developing your account, honestly and objectively consider how much you are to blame. Adopt an other-oriented perspective by considering the reproacher's objectives, desires, and feelings so that you can understand his or her reason for reproaching you. Regardless of the legitimacy of the reproach, the person's feelings and reactions are real, and you must determine the most appropriate response. Sometimes simply admitting your failure and making a genuine effort to correct it is the best account.

Once they receive an account, reproachers must decide whether or not to accept it and consider the issue resolved. When accounts are rejected, account givers often offer another account. However, rejection of accounts can escalate the failure event into an interpersonal conflict. Conflict management requires the skills and strategies discussed in Chapter 8.

RESPONDING WITH FORGIVENESS   In one study, respondents defined forgiveness of a failure event or interpersonal transgression as accepting the event, moving on,

BEING Other-ORIENTED

Failure to understand another person's relational expectations can be a source of conflict and can undermine relational development. Think about how decisions are made in one of your relationships. What are *your* expectations for your role in making decisions; what are *your* expectations for your partner's role? What are your *partner's* expectations for his or her decision-making role and for your decision-making role? To what degree are differences in these expectations the source of failure events or transgressions?

coming to terms, getting over it, letting go of negative feelings and grudges, and continuing the relationship.[11] These respondents reported forgiving others because of the importance of the relationship or for personal health and happiness.[12] In essence, we forgive others when it is in our own best interest to do so. Empathizing with the transgressor and the transgression increases our understanding of our partner and creates a connection that relates to increased forgiving.[13] Studies have found that we are more likely to forgive those who make sincere apologies, are remorseful, admit and accept responsibility for their violation, and/or make restitution.[14] The woman's comment in the cartoon below emphasizes the need for remorse—the transgressor must feel bad. To forgive, we must believe the apology. Intimate relationships rarely survive interpersonal transgressions that are not forgiven. Sometimes we might say, "I accept your apology" but not really mean it and continue to suffer ongoing negative affect (hurt, anger, sadness). Forgiveness researcher Andy Merolla found that the best outcomes occur when "forgiveness is internally genuine and externally direct"—we actually need to feel forgiving and explicitly grant forgiveness.[15] Communication scholars Vincent Waldron and Douglas Kelley suggest taking these seven steps to achieve forgiveness in a relationship:[16]

"I don't want your apology -- I want you to be sorry."

Barbara Smaller/The New Yorker Collection/The Cartoon Bank

1. *Confront the transgression:* The failure event and hurt must be acknowledged by both partners.

2. *Manage emotion:* Emotions must be acknowledged, expressed, and accepted by both partners.

3. *Engage in sense making:* Both partners need to understand and empathize. Ideally, the wounded partner feels what the transgressor felt and understands the reasons for the transgression.

4. *Seek forgiveness:* The transgressor requests forgiveness, offers an apology, expresses regret, and acknowledges the other's hurt. We tend to seek forgiveness relative to how much guilt we feel, which is affected by our sense of responsibility, the severity of the transgression, and our continued thinking about it.[17]

5. *Grant forgiveness:* Forgiveness can be immediate or conditional. To manage the wounded partner's anguish, granting forgiveness can be viewed as a gift or a show of mercy.

6. *Negotiate values and rules:* Both partners need to clarify, negotiate, and renew commitment to relevant relational rules and morals.

7. *Transition, monitor, maintain, or renegotiate:* Time is needed to re-establish trust while readjusting to the pre-transgression state. Partners should continue to review and renegotiate rules as needed.

Each step addresses an important part of the forgiveness process, and some can be further broken down. For example, one study identified five forgiveness-granting strategies: *nonverbal display* (not directly saying that the other is forgiven, but acting in ways that show he or she is, such as showing affection or resuming interactions); *conditional* (expressing forgiveness but with stipulations—"You're forgiven as long as you …"); *minimizing* (shrugging off the offense as not very serious); *discussion* (acknowledging and talking about the failure event, sharing perspectives); and *explicit* (a straight declaration of forgiveness, often in combination with the other strategies).[18]

Whether forgiveness is achieved ultimately depends on a number of factors such as personality (including the ability to empathize), the quality of the relationship, the nature and severity of the transgression, sincere acknowledgment of responsibility, and the

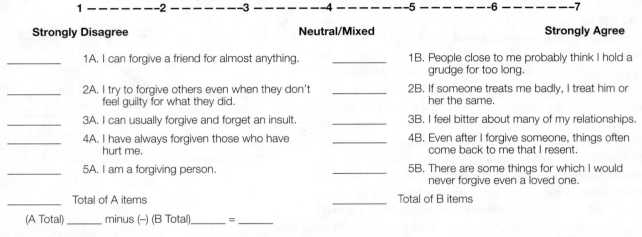

Improving Your Communication Skills

Trait Forgiveness

How forgiving are you? Some people, by their very personality, tend to be more forgiving than others; they have trait forgiveness. The following scale was developed to assess these forgiving personalities. Be honest and objective in assessing your own behaviors. Indicate the degree to which you agree or disagree with each of the statements, using the following scale:

1 — — — — — —2 — — — — — —3 — — — — — —4 — — — — —5 — — — — —6 — — — — —7

Strongly Disagree   **Neutral/Mixed**   **Strongly Agree**

_____ 1A. I can forgive a friend for almost anything.

_____ 2A. I try to forgive others even when they don't feel guilty for what they did.

_____ 3A. I can usually forgive and forget an insult.

_____ 4A. I have always forgiven those who have hurt me.

_____ 5A. I am a forgiving person.

_____ Total of A items

_____ 1B. People close to me probably think I hold a grudge for too long.

_____ 2B. If someone treats me badly, I treat him or her the same.

_____ 3B. I feel bitter about many of my relationships.

_____ 4B. Even after I forgive someone, things often come back to me that I resent.

_____ 5B. There are some things for which I would never forgive even a loved one.

_____ Total of B items

(A Total) _____ minus (–) (B Total)_____ = _____

The possible totals on this scale range from +30 to –30, with 0 being the midpoint. The more positive your total, the more likely you are to be a forgiving person. Examine your lower scores for the A items. Which ones could be improved? Examine your higher scores for the B items. What could you do to change those?

SOURCE: J. W. Berry, E. Worthington, L. O'Connor, L. Parrott, and N. Wade, "Forgiveness, Vengeful Rumination and Affective Traits," *Journal of Personality* 73 (2005): 183–225.

perceived intentionality and selfishness of the transgressor.[19] Forgiveness is also affected by the history of transgressions in the relationship. We're less likely to forgive our partner if he or she repeats the same transgression; but if our partner forgave our transgression, we are more likely to later forgive our partner for a similar transgression.[20] Deciding to forgive is also affected by the responses provided by our confidants (friends, family, or others). Third parties can provide needed emotional support and validate our view of the issue.[21] Forgiving is more likely when these third parties help us gain a new perspective on the transgression, provide practical advice, and encourage us to forgive our partner.[22] When our confidants help us vent anger, encourage confronting our partner, and/or paint our partner as a bad person, we are less inclined to forgive.[23]

RESPONDING WITH RETALIATION   Failure events might be met with retaliation instead of a reproach. Retaliation involves an attempt to hurt the partner in response to the hurt she or he has caused—to "even the score."[24] For example, an act of infidelity can motivate a partner to even the score by also being unfaithful.[25] We might want our partner to feel the same degree of hurt that we felt, thus creating a sense of equity and balance. Or we might retaliate to convey how hurt we are, to regain some power, and to discourage future transgressions.[26] In one study, motivation to retaliate was higher for those with fewer relational investments and when the transgression was seen as intentional.[27] Retaliation behaviors can include aggressive communication (yelling, accusing, and sarcasm), active distancing (giving the partner the silent treatment or withholding affection), manipulation attempts (evoking the transgressor's jealousy or guilt, or testing his or her loyalty), contacting a rival, and violence.[28]

EXAMINING A MODEL OF FORGIVENESS RESPONSES   Relationship researchers Laura Guerrero and Guy Bachman created a model (see Figure 10.1) of the possible responses to transgressions, based on the severity of the transgression and the quality of the relationship. Each of the four quadrants reflects a possible response to the

Figure 10.1 Forgiveness Responses to Transgressions[29]

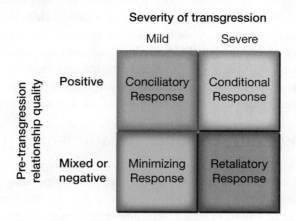

Severity of transgression

	Mild	Severe
Positive	Conciliatory Response	Conditional Response
Mixed or negative	Minimizing Response	Retaliatory Response

Pre-transgression relationship quality

conditions, with a focus on the rewards and costs associated with that quadrant. The model helps to explain why a severe offense in an unsatisfying relationship is likely to evoke retaliation, whereas a severe offense in a valued relationship is likely to evoke a conditional response, granting forgiveness on a trial basis. A positive relationship might compensate for a mild infraction and produce a conciliatory response to hasten the return to the rewarding relationship. Finally, a mild transgression in a mixed or negative relationship is likely to be discarded as "no big deal," thus minimizing the offense. Whether that relationship will continue probably depends on whether the victim has alternative relationships available.[30]

Challenging Communication: Addressing Grief and Delivering Bad News

One situation that most of us find particularly challenging is talking with someone who has recently lost a loved one. What should you say to someone dealing with a recent death? How should you act? In this book, we've already covered a number of skills and strategies that you can employ. Socially decenter and think about how you'd like to be treated if you were in the same situation. Apply strong confirming listening skills, provide support, and engage in comforting communication. In a study, adolescents who had experienced the loss of a significant relationship through death evaluated various support statements.[31] The highest rated statements were those in which the speaker offered to be there for the other, expressed a willingness to listen, and shared his or her care and concern. Sometimes the best choice may be giving someone a hug and just being there without saying anything. Several factors affect the supportive statement you should offer, including the closeness of the relationship and the amount of time that has passed since the death. You might be surprised to learn that expressing humor, smiling, and laughing can be more beneficial than trying to repress these feelings when talking about the loss.[32] Being able to laugh together over a shared memory can help in coping with the other emotions being experienced.

Another communication challenge is having to deliver bad news, which usually creates stress for both the messenger and recipient. Bad news is information that is unknown but relevant to the recipient and that the messenger believes will have negative repercussions.[33] Communicating that your roommate's boyfriend is cheating on her, that you have damaged your parents' car, and that you have decided to break up with your romantic partner are all examples of bad news. Understandably, people tend to be reluctant to share bad news and therefore experience the MUM effect (i.e., keeping **M**um about **U**ndesirable **M**essages).[34] We might be motivated by a desire to protect ourselves (not telling your parents about their damaged car) or to protect the other (not telling your roommate about her boyfriend's infidelity). In a study of doctors delivering bad news to patients, researchers identified four strategies from patient accounts: direct (honest, straightforward message), indirect (little to no disclosure or use of implication), comforting (messages designed to alleviate negative emotions), and empowerment (providing choice and control to the recipient).[35] Satisfaction for each strategy depended upon the content of the message and the manner in which it was presented, as well as its appropriateness to the situation and its patient-centeredness. To create the most effective message, be other-oriented in considering ways to deliver the information that protect the receiver's face and feelings, as well as your own. Strong empathic listening skills will help you respond to questions, address emotions, and provide comfort and support.

Maintaining Long-Distance Relationships (LDRs)

The mobility of today's population means that we are often moving away or being separated for a time from people with whom we have formed interpersonal relationships. We tend to think of long-distance relationships primarily as dating relationships. However, you probably have or will have long-distance relationships with your parents, spouse, children, siblings, and other family members; with friends; and even with coworkers or clients. While we are likely to turn to our geographically close (GC) best friends for social support more often than our long-distance (LD) friends, if we feel we really need to, we turn to LD best friends just as much, particularly for their emotional support.[36] Long-distance romantic relationships affect your feelings, thoughts, and behaviors: You feel sadness, separation, sexual desire, and loss. You think about the future with your partner, wonder what your partner is doing, and reminisce. You want to communicate with and touch your partner, talk about your partner with others (maybe even annoyingly so), and look at your partner's picture.[37] You will likely depend on electronically mediated communication (EMC), such as text messages, Twitter, Facebook, Snapchats, and video chats to create a sense of social or relational presence over long distances.[38] Wives with deployed husbands reported strong use of EMC to help them cope with distance, even using the Internet and web cameras to house hunt, shop, and play games together.[39]

THE NATURE OF THE SEPARATION   Each long-distance relationship requires specific maintenance strategies in order to be successfully managed.[40] Long-distance relationships vary in terms of expected length of separation, length of time between face-to-face visits, the actual distance between the partners, and whether separation was by choice or circumstance. While temporary separation requires some adjustment and management by the partners, permanent physical separation produces different expectations, interactions, and relational management strategies. Being deployed is separation by circumstance, while deciding to move to a new area after graduation is separation by choice and may raise questions about relational commitment.

Partners in long-distance relationships must use specific maintenance strategies if the relationship is to be successful.

EFFECTS OF TIME BETWEEN VISITS   How often partners are able to get together face-to-face also affects the impact of the physical distance. One study suggests that people who are in long-distance romantic relationships but are able to get together at least once a week can maintain relationships similar to those between people who are geographically close.[41]

Sometimes partners are relatively close geographically but limited in how often they can get together. The infrequency of face-to-face interactions can have an artificially positive effect on the partners because they are on their good behavior when they get together.[42] This good behavior is probably one reason partners in romantic long-distance relationships report as much satisfaction and closeness as those who are geographically close.[43] Another reason for this reported satisfaction is that it is apparently easier to maintain an idealized image of a romantic relationship when you don't spend as much time with your partner.[44] Communication researchers Laura Stafford and James Reske found that couples in long-distance premarital relationships had less communication but surprisingly greater satisfaction and higher expectation for the likelihood of marriage than those in *proximal*, or geographically close, relationships.[45] Less communication means you avoid learning information that might challenge the idealized image you've created. Military wives with deployed husbands confront a dialectical tension of maintaining open communication or restricting what they share.[46] Discussing day-to-day events and not sheltering the partner from information can be seen as a way to maintain closeness. On the other hand, restricting disclosures to positive news might reduce a partner's burden and concerns.

COSTS AND REWARDS   In Chapter 9, social exchange theory (analysis of costs and rewards) was used to explain our decision to escalate or de-escalate a relationship. Social exchange theory also offers a way to analyze the survival of long-distance relationships.[47] Distance adds costs to maintaining a relationship: the actual monetary costs (gasoline, airline tickets, and food); the time spent commuting; and the disruption of normal routines, leaving less time available for other activities. These costs are weighed against the relational rewards. Obviously, if you are looking for a relationship that meets physical needs, a permanent long-distance relationship might prove unsatisfactory. If you need only a confidant, a long-distance arrangement might be acceptable.[48] You might sustain your commitment to a relationship in which you view the costs as a long-term investment.[49] Some relationships continue for a lifetime with little face-to-face time because the rewards of interacting far exceed any costs.

TENSIONS CREATED BY LDRS   Tensions sometimes arise when one person is trying to maintain both the long-distance relationship and proximal relationships (those in close proximity).[50] For example, the autonomy that a long-distance relationship affords provides more time for proximal relationships with others. Visits by a long-distance partner can put strains on other relationships if the visiting partner and other people don't get along or compete for time.[51] Long-distance couples also create tensions when they try so hard not to waste their time together that they over-plan activities, discussion topics, and even sex.[52]

Minimizing idealization and maintaining communication are probably the most important factors in sustaining strong relationships, even over long distances. The more open and honest you can keep the communication and the more mundane time you can spend together, the more similar your long-distance relationships will be to proximal ones.

Relationships That Challenge Social Norms

Cultures base norms for appropriate and inappropriate relationships on social values, biases, and prejudices. Among the types of relationships often discouraged are those between people of different races, religions, or ethnicities. In addition, many societies have social mores against romantic relationships between individuals who differ significantly in age or who are of the same sex. Those who choose such relationships face social pressure to terminate them or risk being ostracized. Fortunately, norms change, and in the United States, the number of relational restrictions have decreased in the last thirty years. Nonetheless, developing these types of relationships still presents challenges.

Partners in intercultural relationships face the challenge of communicating and interacting effectively, as discussed in Chapter 4. They might also confront bias against the relationship.[53] Movies such as *Guess Who*, *Save the Last Dance*, *Crazy/Beautiful*, *Remember the Titans*, *Jungle Fever*, and *Snow Falling on Cedars* explore both the communication challenges and the negative social reactions often experienced by partners in intercultural and interracial relationships. Such relationships may be viewed as a threat to the norms of a given culture, race, ethnic group, or religious group. The more different the interloper is perceived to be, the greater are the perceived threat and negative reactions.[54] For example, Catholics might feel more hostility toward a Jewish–Catholic couple than toward a Lutheran–Catholic one. Those outside the relationship have difficulty understanding the attraction between the partners and might minimize it as simply motivated by the appeal of "forbidden fruit."[55] In contrast, those in the relationship often see their differences as an opportunity to learn both about others

BEING Other-ORIENTED

Long-distance relationships add an extra obstacle to your ability to be other-oriented. The lack of face-to-face nonverbal cues limits the information you might otherwise receive to help you better understand your partner's perspective. For example, how aware are you of how your current long-distance partners (family, friends, or romantic partners) feel about how often you communicate and how often you get together? What problems can be attributed to the challenge of being other-oriented in long-distance relationships?

Improving Your Communication Skills
Friends with a Difference

Think of someone you know, or imagine yourself in a friendship with someone, from each of the following groups: (a) someone at least ten years older than you; (b) someone from a country where people speak a different language than you; (c) someone with a different sexual orientation; (d) someone of a different race; (e) someone of a different religion.

1. With which of these people is communication easiest? Why?

2. With which of these people is communication hardest? Why?
3. How do your family and friends react to this relationship? Why?
4. How have your differences affected your interpersonal communication in each friendship?
5. How does this friendship compare to friendships with those who are similar to you?

and about themselves; they focus on the similarities in their values and personal characteristics rather than on differences.[56]

The importance of discussing and supporting each other's ethnic, racial, or religious identity was underscored in a study of interracial and interethnic romantic relationships between college students. Compared to same-culture and same-faith relationships, intercultural and interfaith relationships experienced more conflict related to differences.[57] But the more each partner was open to and supportive of his or her partner's culture or faith, the less relational distress they experienced.[58] Finding similarities in culture and values is one way to offset conflicts associated with differences.[59] Culture differences appear to be more challenging to manage than faith differences; intercultural romantic relationships were more likely to end than same-culture relationships, while no such difference was found between interfaith and same-faith relationships.[60]

Romantic gay and lesbian relationships are increasingly accepted in US culture, with most states now accepting same-sex marriage. Nonetheless, efforts continue to prohibit such marriages, reflecting the social hostility gay and lesbian couples still face. Despite these social pressures, gay and lesbian couples engage in the same kinds of relational maintenance activities as heterosexual couples.[61]

What about relationships between heterosexuals and homosexuals? Such relationships can be healthy and supportive, as exemplified in such TV shows as *Grey's Anatomy*, *Glee*, and *Modern Family*. An individual's sexual orientation shouldn't be a factor in whether you form a friendship, any more than a person's race, ethnicity, or age should be—but it sometimes is. One study found that heterosexual respondents reported that even if they had a lot in common with someone identified as homosexual, they were more inclined to forgo a friendship with that person and restrict themselves to relationships with other heterosexuals.[62] This tendency was significantly stronger for the male respondents than for the females. Fortunately, as with many prejudices, actually interacting with homosexuals has a positive influence on the attitudes of heterosexuals toward them.[63] Regardless of your own sexual orientation, take time to consider your attitudes toward and openness to forming relationships with all people, no matter how they differ from you.

The Dark Side of Interpersonal Communication and Relationships

10.2 Describe the issues that constitute the dark side of interpersonal communication and those that constitute the dark side of interpersonal relationships.

Communication scholars William Cupach and Brian Spitzberg first introduced the phrase "dark side" to reflect interpersonal communication used in damaging, unethical ways.[64] Throughout the text, we have focused primarily on how interpersonal communication can be used for developing fulfilling relationships, for managing conflict cooperatively, for improving relationships, and for helping you meet your interpersonal needs. However, interpersonal communication can also be used to deceive and hurt people. Regrettably, the dark side of interpersonal communication and relationships is more prevalent than you might think; for example, studies focusing on deception have found that it is pervasive in interpersonal interactions.[65] The dark side of relationships includes obsessive relational intrusion, stalking, jealousy, and relational violence.

Deception

Creating a deceptive Facebook profile might not be as serious as deceiving your parents about what websites you visit.

You wake up to discover you've overslept, but because an absence would hurt your grade, you come to class late and tell the instructor that you had car trouble. Your roommate is going on a date wearing an outfit that you think is nice—but not on her. When asked what you think, you say, "I've always liked that outfit," omitting the fact that you don't think it suits her. You're involved in an intimate relationship but find you no longer have strong feelings toward your partner. Your partner asks, "Do you still love me?" and you answer, "Yes." You are developing a close physical relationship with someone but choose not to disclose the extent of your previous sexual relationships. In an attempt to appear "hip," you list several rock bands as favorites on your Facebook page, even though they're not.

Each of these scenarios represents a situation marked by deception, but the impact and seriousness of the deceptions differ. One way to assess the seriousness is to ask yourself, "What would happen if the other person discovered my deception?" Your instructor and your roommate might be upset, but deceiving them would probably not have the same impact as falsely declaring your love or not disclosing your prior sexual activity to a partner. Communication scholar Mark Knapp classifies lies as *low stake* and *high stake*.[66] The size of the stake represents how much might be gained by the deception and how much might be lost if the lie were detected. The lie to the instructor, the roommate, and one's Facebook friends are low stake lies, while not revealing previous sexual activity might be considered a high stake lie.

Deception occurs both in what we say (our words) and what we do (nonverbal behaviors)—obviously we can "tell" a lie, but we can also act in deceitful ways. Participants in a study on romantic relationships kept detailed journals on their use of deceptive affective messages (DAM). DAMs are instances in which people express feelings they don't really have—for example, hugging a partner when feeling distant or telling a partner that they weren't feeling jealous when they really were. Participants averaged over three DAMs a week, of which about half were verbal and half nonverbal.[67] Think about the times in the past week when you said something or acted in a way contrary to how you really were feeling. What were your reasons?

Interpersonal deception theory, as developed by Judee Burgoon and David Buller, is an explanation of deception and detection as processes affected by the interplay between the deceiver and the detector during interpersonal interactions.[68] According to this theory, individuals intentionally and strategically manipulate information to achieve some goal, while others listen and evaluate the truthfulness of that information. In other words, one person tries to get away with a lie, and the other person decides whether or not to believe it. To avoid being caught, deceivers implement deception strategies and monitor listeners' responses. Listeners might accept the deception without pause, express skepticism, or blatantly challenge the deception. Each listener reaction lets the deceiver know his or her next course of action.

Think about the last time you tried to deceive someone and he or she questioned whether you were telling the truth. How did you respond? Perhaps you acted indignant, restated your claim more forcefully, added more convincing evidence, or came clean and admitted your lie. Deception, the detection of deception, and the deceiver's response to

interpersonal deception theory
An explanation of deception and detection as processes affected by the transactional nature of interpersonal interactions.

detection are all factors in interpersonal deception theory. Interestingly, in close relationships, we might be better at detecting deception in online messages than when face-to-face; we can focus more on the actual content and not be distracted by nonverbal cues. In addition, we can check against previous messages for inconsistencies, we have more time to examine the messages, and the deceiver is less able to detect and counteract suspicion.[69]

deception by omission (concealment)

Intentionally holding back some of the information another person has requested or that you are expected to share.

DECEPTION BY OMISSION (CONCEALMENT) Deception by omission (concealment) involves intentionally holding back some of the information another person has requested or that you are expected to share. For example, your parents ask where you were last night, and you reply that you went to the movies. While that is true, you don't tell your parents that you also went to a party at a friend's house afterward. You have not "lied," but if your intention is to avoid their response to your partying, then your omission is deceptive.

We can also leave out information to mislead a listener. Telling your roommate, "I've always liked that outfit" is intended to create the impression that you think the outfit is attractive on her. If your roommate complains later that you didn't warn her that she looked bad in the outfit, you might innocently say, "I never said it looked good on you." Despite this claim, your roommate probably knows your intention was to deceive. These types of omissions are sometimes called "half-truths," because the statements themselves are truthful, but they are not the complete truth.

Deception by omission can undermine decision making. For example, not disclosing sexual history can prevent one's partner from making informed decisions about the level of risk he or she might be encountering.[70] Although omitting information usually is not considered as grievous as falsifying information,[71] when the omitted information is important, omission is just as deceptive as falsifying.[72]

deception by commission (lying)

Deliberate presentation of false information.

DECEPTION BY COMMISSION (LYING) Deception by commission is the deliberate presentation of false information[73]—lying. Among the types of deception by commission are white lies, exaggeration or embellishment, and bald-faced lies.

white lies

Deceptions by commission involving only a slight degree of falsification that has a minimal consequence.

White lies typically involve only a slight degree of falsification that has a minimal consequence. Calling these deceptions "white lies" seems to make us feel a little less guilty. If you list a band on Facebook as a favorite when it isn't, that's generally a white lie.

exaggeration

Deception by commission involving "stretching the truth" or embellishing the facts.

Sometimes we use exaggeration—"stretching the truth" or embellishing the facts. Telling someone you were at the library for a couple of hours when it was only twenty minutes is an exaggeration. Most of us have stories that we've told over and over that continue to become more embellished as we tell them.

bald-faced lies

Deceptions by commission involving outright falsification of information intended to deceive the listener.

Bald-faced lies are outright falsifications of information intended to deceive the listener. A study using diary reports from students in romantic relationships found lies to be the most used type of deception.[74] Bald-faced lies impact the behavior of those who hear them more than do white lies or exaggeration. When such deception is detected, the emotional impact is related to the importance of the relationship, the importance of the information, and the importance of honesty to the people involved.[75] The potential negative impacts explain why we are less likely to lie to our best friends than we are to strangers.[76] The MTV show *Catfish* spotlights the impact that such bald-faced deception can have on those pursuing romantic relationships on the Internet. On the show, people create entirely false profiles and use them to build real online romantic relationships. But when their targets discover the deception, they often terminate these relationships. The show explores the reasons people engage in such deceptions, which may fall into any of the five categories listed below.

REASONS FOR DECEPTION While people can be deceptive for a variety of reasons,[77] these reasons can be divided into two general categories: altruistic and self-serving. Altruism, the desire to protect and avoid hurting someone, is a common reason for lying to a close friend (for example, not telling your roommate her outfit is unbecoming). Self-serving deceptions are motivated by personal gain or the desire to avoid undesirable consequences; deceiving your boss about why you were late might be an attempt to avoid a negative consequence. Lies to strangers and acquaintances are more likely to be for personal gain or exploitation, whereas relatively more of our lies to friends are altruistic or other-centered.[78] In addition to distinguishing lies as altruistic or self-serving, we might categorize them according to a number of additional, more specific reasons for deception.

1. *To gain resources.* Deception might help you acquire material resources, such as money or property. It might help you achieve intangible goals, such as fostering a relationship or bolstering your self-esteem. For example, if you're interested in someone who works out a lot, you might tell him or her that you work out every day too (but you really don't).

2. *To avoid harm or loss of resources.* Deception may be used to prevent another person's negative reaction or to protect your resources. If an angry friend suspected you had broken her computer, you might lie if you feared she would damage something of yours in retaliation or demand that you pay for a new computer.

3. *To protect one's self-image/save face.* You might use deception when something threatens your positive face (how you want others to see you). For instance, if you were late for an appointment, but you want to be viewed as punctual, you might exaggerate about how bad the traffic was.

4. *For entertainment.* Teasing can be a form of deception when we say things that aren't true. While a group of friends is hanging out, they all might laugh when one friend tells another, "That girl is really checking you out"—and after he looks, declares, "Not!" The reason for this deception is to laugh at the other person's reaction.

5. *To protect another person's resources, self-image/face, or safety.* When we believe information might be harmful to another person, we might lie to avoid hurting the other person's feelings.[79] This reason ranked first in the study discussed earlier on DAMs. Participants indicated that they wanted to improve their partner's mood or didn't want to hurt their partner's feelings.[80] However, we might deceive ourselves by thinking that we're being altruistic when we're really being self-serving.

EFFECTS OF DECEPTION While at times it seems acceptable because of the benefits it provides, deception, as well as the discovery or detection of deception, can also result in harm. Here are some of the more obvious ways deception can be harmful:

1. *Incorrect decision making or actions.* Decision making based on false information might result in the wrong course of action.

2. *Harm to relationships.* While undetected deception can indirectly harm a relationship, detected deception can cause direct and immediate harm to a relationship and might even lead to its termination.

3. *Loss of trust.* Once deception has been detected, it may be hard for partners to regain the fundamental element of trust.[81] Repeated deception and detection may result in one person assuming that anything the other person says is a lie.

4. *Harm to innocent bystanders.* Lies often have a ripple effect, whereby other people (innocent bystanders) are harmed. For example, having a friend lie on your behalf could result in damage to your friend's reputation.

5. *Additional harms.* Other negative consequences of deception include punishment, embarrassment, a guilty conscience, and a damaged reputation.[82]

The closer the relationship, the more effective people become at recognizing their partners' deceptions.[83] But because they also know what cues their partners are suspicious of, they become better equipped to adapt and avoid detection of their deception.[84]

While being totally honest all the time is appealing, honesty can be hurtful. To be successful in relationships, one must effectively weigh the potential hurtfulness of an honest message against the harms of deception and act accordingly.

BEING Other-ORIENTED

Most of us react pretty negatively to the discovery that a friend has deceived us. Deception is seen as a violation of honesty and trust—fundamental qualities associated with friendship. But why would a friend lie to you or deceive you? Consider the most recent time you found out you had been deceived. What possible motives might your friend have had? What factors might have influenced your friend's decision (for example, your reaction to the truth, the effect of the truth on the relationship, or potential harm to the friend)?

What we say and how we say it can hurt other people's feelings, especially those of family members or romantic partners.

Communication That Hurts Feelings

When people discover that they have been deceived, they usually feel betrayed, foolish, angry, and/or hurt. But deception is only one way in which we hurt people's feelings. As we discussed earlier, truth can hurt, too. One of the more powerful aspects of language is that it can cause emotional pain. We can be hurt by insults; criticism; or teasing about our personality, intelligence, abilities, ethnicity, relationships, or sexual behavior.[85] When we receive a hurtful message, we usually try to determine the speaker's intention, which affects how hurt we feel.[86] Sometimes an unintentionally hurtful comment can be alleviated with a heartfelt apology such as, "I'm sorry, I didn't mean it like it sounded." In some instances, speakers can minimize the impact by claiming they were "just kidding."

Interpersonal researchers Stacy Young and Amy Bippus found that as the perceived intentionality of hurtful messages increased, so did the reported emotional pain.[87] In addition, they determined that, in general, humorously phrased hurtful messages were found to be less hurtful than comments phrased without humor. However, humorous messages were found to hurt more than nonhumorous messages when they were about abilities or intelligence, de-escalating the relationship, or a person's hopes or plans. Apparently, for some issues, like our abilities or dreams, kidding is more hurtful than straightforward comments.

One study of college students in romantic relationships found that close to 88 percent reported being the recipient of a hurtful tease (a hurtful message or criticism followed by a smile, a laugh, or "just kidding"), with women reporting being teased more than men; however, they all felt there was some degree of truth in the remarks.[88] Teasing was seen as a way to disguise the truth.

Sometimes we say something that is true when we didn't mean to say it—we just blurt it out. Blurting is defined as "speech that is spontaneous, unedited, and negative in its repercussions."[89] Most of us have said things we wish we could take back—we've just "blurted" out something without considering that it might hurt the other person's feelings. We often blurt because of frustration, anger, or a lack of motivation to consider the potential negative impact of a message.[90]

Our reactions to hurtful messages can be verbal or nonverbal and emotional—for example, displaying anger after being criticized.[91] Research by Anita Vangelisti and Linda Crumley identified three general categories of verbal reactions to messages that hurt.[92]

active verbal responses

Reactive statements made in response to a hurtful message.

acquiescent responses

Crying, conceding, or apologizing in response to a hurtful message.

invulnerable responses

Ignoring, laughing, or being silent in response to a hurtful message.

1. **Active verbal responses.** This category includes reactive statements made by the hurt person, such as counterattacks, self-defense statements, sarcastic comments, and demands for explanations.
2. **Acquiescent responses.** The second category includes crying, conceding, or apologizing.
3. **Invulnerable responses.** This category includes those responses that attempt to show that the message did not hurt—for example, ignoring the message, laughing, or being silent.

Among their other findings on hurtful messages, Vangelisti and Crumley found that people are more hurt by messages from family members than from nonfamily members and that romantic relationships are more damaged by hurtful messages than either family or nonromantic, nonfamily relationships.[93] In romantic relationships, honest but hurtful messages about the relationship were found to be more hurtful than messages about a person's personality, appearance, or behaviors.[94] Such relationally oriented messages tended to threaten receivers' face, probably because such statements implied the potential loss of the relationship.[95] The way the message is conveyed also affects its impact, with harsh, abrasive messages creating greater hurt.[96] The quality of the relationship at the time of the message also affects people's perceptions of a hurtful message.

The more tumultuous the relationship, the greater the hurtfulness and the more likely people are to view such messages as intentionally hurtful.[97]

Hurting someone's feelings by what we say is probably unavoidable in interpersonal relationships; even our text messages can sometimes hurt someone's feelings.[98] But how we respond to and manage the impact of such messages affects the level of relational satisfaction and happiness. When you are the recipient of a hurtful message let the speaker know that your feelings are hurt. Since the speaker might not even realize that the message was hurtful, you might ask him or her to clarify the reason for making it. A strong other-orientation is needed to monitor the impact of your messages on other people. Generally, understanding your partner can help you to anticipate what messages might be hurtful and to select the best strategies for presenting unavoidable hurtful messages.

Jealousy

If you have ever wished you drove a car as nice or received grades as high as one of your classmates, then you have experienced envy. **Envy** is a discontented feeling that arises from a desire for something someone else has. But if you have been upset because one of your good friends spent more and more time with coworkers instead of hanging out with you, or because your boyfriend or girlfriend showed interest in another person, then you have experienced jealousy. **Jealousy** is a reaction to the threat of losing a valued relationship[99]—the future of the relationship is in doubt and the partner's loyalty is questioned.[100]

Jealousy manifests itself in your thoughts, feelings, and behaviors. **Cognitive jealousy** includes thoughts about the loss of your partner, reflections on decreases in your partner's time with you, and analyses of behaviors or occurrences deemed suspicious. **Emotional or affective jealousy** includes feelings of anger, hurt, distrust, worry, or concern aroused by the threat of losing the relationship. **Behavioral jealousy** represents actions taken to monitor or alter a partner's jealousy-evoking activity, such as watching your partner obsessively at social gatherings; telling a partner to stop flirting; or secretly checking a partner's texts, e-mails, or Facebook posts.

We usually think of jealousy occurring because a partner is attracted to someone else, but it can also result from other factors that jeopardize the relationship—a partner turning to others for advice; loss of influence over a partner to someone else; or a partner's spending more time on hobbies, school, or work.[101] Jealousy presents a paradox: On the one hand, it represents a strong display of interest and love, but on the other hand, it represents paranoia and a lack of trust.[102] Sometimes people are flattered by another's jealousy and even seek to evoke it to confirm the value of a relationship. At other times, jealousy is seen as a statement of possessiveness and restriction.[103] Interestingly, the two partners in a relationship usually have contrasting emotional reactions to the jealousy. For the person feeling jealous, the potential loss of the relationship creates fear, anger, and sadness.[104] The person's partner might have negative feelings like guilt, fear, distress, irritation, and uncertainty about his or her own feelings and behaviors; positive feelings like interest or determination; or behavioral reactions like aggressiveness and attacking.[105]

USING JEALOUSY AS A TACTIC   You can probably think of several TV shows or movies in which one character tries to make some other character jealous. The reasons for evoking jealousy include relational rewards (to test the strength of the relationship, to bolster one's self-esteem, or to improve the relationship) and relational revenge (to teach the partner a lesson or to punish the partner).[106]

Among the tactics people use to make another person jealous are *distancing* (being too busy to get together, excluding the other from plans, or ignoring the other person); *flirtation façade* (leaving fake phone numbers or pictures of oneself with others, or expressing attraction to another); and *relational alternatives* (letting your partner know you are thinking about other relationships or talking about past relationships).[107]

Jealousy is a feeling that arises when we fear a relationship is in doubt, and the feeling can lead to jealous behavior.

envy
A feeling of discontent arising from a desire for something someone else has.

jealousy
Reaction to the threat of losing a valued relationship.

cognitive jealousy
Thoughts about the loss of a partner, reflections on decreases in time spent with the partner, and analyses of behaviors or occurrences deemed suspicious.

emotional or affective jealousy
Feelings of anger, hurt, distrust, worry, or concern aroused by the threat of losing a relationship.

behavioral jealousy
Actions taken to monitor or alter a partner's jealousy-evoking activity.

Using jealousy to improve a relationship is risky. If your partner discovers that you intentionally evoked his or her jealousy, your partner may view your behavior as deceptive and manipulative, and respond defensively (as discussed in Chapter 6).

MANAGING JEALOUSY   Concern about the possible loss of a relationship or a significant change in relationship status is neither inappropriate nor unusual. The belief that a friend is spending more time on some other interest implicitly disconfirms us—the implication being that the object of the friend's attention is more important than we are. Jealousy reflects uncertainty about our value and the relationship.

Jealousy expert Laura Guerrero researched four forms of jealous communication: destructive (trying to control or hurt the partner with threatening or hurtful messages), constructive (explaining feelings or seeking to sustain the relationship), avoidant (being silent or claiming no jealousy), and rival-focused (such as spying or contacting the rival).[108] Guerrero found that the use of destructive communication in response to jealousy, rather than jealousy itself, affects the level of relational satisfaction.

Expressing jealousy can arouse uncertainty in a partner, particularly when the jealousy is expressed indirectly through crying or acting hurt or depressed.[109] Directly discussing the situation with a partner and asking for an explanation tends to evoke a more positive response than spying or seeking information from a third party.[110] Sensitivity and responsiveness to both partners' commitment to the relationship can help avoid or minimize jealousy.

Unwanted Attention

When a person we are attracted to shuns our interest, or when a partner is no longer attracted to us, most of us move on. Unfortunately, some individuals do not give up when another person fails to reciprocate their attraction, has no interest in a relationship, or desires to terminate a relationship. These individuals might engage in obsessive behaviors, trying to form or to continue a relationship. In some instances, such pursuit is simply annoying, but at its extreme, it arouses well-founded fears for personal safety.

obsessive relational intrusion (ORI)

Repeated invasion of a person's privacy by a stranger or acquaintance who desires or assumes a close relationship.

OBSESSIVE RELATIONAL INTRUSION (ORI)   Communication scholars William Cupach and Brian Spitzberg use the term **obsessive relational intrusion (ORI)** to describe situations in which a stranger or acquaintance who desires or assumes a close relationship with another person repeatedly invades the other person's privacy.[111] In other words, an individual wants a relationship with someone else who is not interested in him or her. Sometimes former partners try to maintain the relationship to the point of being very intrusive in your life. Unlike stalking, ORI is usually annoying and frustrating but not threatening.[112]

Obsessive relational intrusion is marked by such behaviors as unregulated self-disclosing; trying to get the other person to disclose; offering unwanted gifts, notes, calls, and other expressions of affection; arranging coincidental meetings; and expressing a desire for physical contact.[113] Only a fine line exists between trying to hang on to or pursue a relationship and becoming obsessive. The repeated and sustained display of these behaviors after rejection makes it ORI. Relationships are often indirectly or implicitly negotiated, increasing the likelihood that one partner will misunderstand the other's intentions and interest. For instance, the ambiguity of nonverbal messages means that smiling because you're in a good mood could be interpreted by a stranger as an invitation, leading to an unwanted attempt to start a conversation. Confusion about relational goals and definitions might lead to intrusion into your privacy when a partner thinks the relationship is more intimate than you do. Clarify such confusions by clearly discussing your relational goals, interests, desires, and the nature of the relationship, and find out your partner's perspective as well.

stalking

Repeated, unwelcome intrusions that create concern for personal safety and fear in the target.

STALKING   **Stalking** involves repeated, unwelcome intrusions that create concern for personal safety and fear in the target.[114] Unwanted phone calls, letters, e-mails, texts, and tweets are ways stalkers instill fear; they also post on Facebook and even engage in face-to-face conversations. Stalking can be thought of as an extreme form of ORI, although sometimes it is motivated by revenge and not the pursuit of a relationship.[115] One survey found that 30 percent of the time the victim reported having been in an intimate relationship with the stalker, and another 45 percent knew the stalker in some other capacity.[116] A survey of students at one university found that 42.5 percent of the female respondents and 35.7 percent of the males reported experiencing at least one behavioral indicator of stalking.[117] The lack of social and relational skills in young adults and the close proximity and sharing of space that occurs on campuses are possible causes of college stalking.[118]

A person who feels stalked experiences concern for her or his personal safety and fear of unwelcome intrusions.

Unfortunately, no absolutely safe and effective way exists to halt ORI and stalking, but based on advice from other scholars and professionals, Spitzberg and Cupach offer three recommendations for responding to ORI and stalking:[119]

1. *Harden the target.* "Hardening the target" involves making it harder for someone to contact you or invade your space. For example, get an unlisted phone number, rent a mailbox, change locks, eliminate access and information on Facebook, and/ or install a security system.

2. *Keep others apprised.* You should apprise family, friends, coworkers, employers, school officials, and law enforcement officers of your situation. Also, consider informing people in other places you frequent (such as a gym, restaurant, or bar). Let everyone know you don't want contact with the person and provide photos of the person if possible.

3. *Avoidance.* After telling the intruder or stalker to leave you alone, avoid any further contact. Don't answer calls, don't respond to e-mails or texts, ignore and turn away from any approaches the person might make—don't interact. Your actions should support your insistence that the relationship is over.

Relational Violence

Relational violence can occur in any relationship—with a spouse, a dating partner, children, family members, friends, or coworkers. Unlike acts of violence against unknown individuals, relational violence occurs within the context of an ongoing relationship and is sometimes a defining characteristic or dynamic of the relationship.[120] *Intimate partner violence* is violence that is specifically directed toward a current or former spouse or partner.[121]

Sadly, relational violence is a form of communication—the dark side of communication. Acts of relational violence communicate anger, frustration, lack of control, and disregard for a partner and the relationship, while instilling fear and engendering retaliation, counterattacks, and subversion. The results of a study of males participating in a domestic violence program found that compared to nonviolent males, violent males engaged in more name-calling, criticizing, blaming, swearing, ridiculing, and mutual verbal aggression with their partners.[122] Patterns of negative communication, ineffective conflict management and problem-solving skills, and lack of good argumentation skills all appear to contribute to an individual's propensity for relational violence.

Stalking, obsessive relational intrusion, and jealousy can all be precursors to violent behavior in relationships. However **relational violence** extends beyond these behaviors to refer to the full range of destructive behaviors aimed at other people, including aggressiveness; threats; violent acts; and verbal, psychological, and physical abuse. At the extreme, relational violence involves forceful acts against another person. But punching your fist through a plaster wall in rage during an argument

relational violence
Range of destructive behaviors aimed at other people, including aggressiveness, threats, violent acts, and verbal, psychological, or physical abuse.

#communicationandtechnology

Cyberstalking, Cyberbullying, and Partner Surveillance

Electronically mediated communication (EMC) allows us to quickly and easily stay in touch with our friends, colleagues, family members, and other people we love. But in addition to the benefits we've noted, EMC messages can have a dark side. If personal or private information about you becomes known to others, it can be used to embarrass you or create significant negative financial consequences. More than 40 percent of respondents on one college campus survey reported cyberstalking.[123] Not only is cyberstalking prevalent, it is also targeted to specific groups. Women were cyberstalked more than men (46 percent vs. 32 percent), non-Whites more than Whites (48 percent vs. 40 percent), and non-heterosexuals more than heterosexuals (56 percent vs. 40 percent).

News reports linking the deaths of students to cyberbullying reflects the potential power and abuse of EMC. Cyberbullying has been defined as "the deliberate and repeated misuse of communication technology by an individual or group to threaten or harm others."[124] In a survey of incoming college freshman, nearly 35 percent of males and 35 percent of females reported cyberbullying someone their senior year in high school.[125] Cyberbullying extends into college and seems to be increasing, with both students and faculty becoming victims.[126] Posting spiteful messages on RateMyProfessor, making fun of someone on Facebook, or teasing someone on Twitter are forms of cyberbullying that you might have inadvertently committed. Avoidance strategies (ignoring the problem and not seeking help) were associated with low self-esteem, depression, and anxiety, while approach strategies (addressing the problem and seeking social support) related only to anxiety.[127] It's important for the person being bullied to restore his or her self-esteem and address any issues of depression or anxiety.[128]

While people worry about the NSA scanning their every Internet post, it's more likely that someone you know, like a current or previous romantic partner, is doing the monitoring. The obvious place for partner surveillance is on Facebook, where it's easy to keep track of messages posted by others, look at pictures, and peruse lists of friends. Unlike stalking, partner surveillance occurs within an ongoing relationship. Surprisingly, one study found that neither a previous infidelity nor long-distance had an impact on differences in online surveillance, but those who use social networks as part of their daily routine and those confident in their Internet skills were more apt to engage in partner surveillance.[129] Rather than being an issue in a relationship, the tendency to surveil seems to be more personality based and might even be considered normal in today's world of readily accessible online information. How do you feel about someone constantly checking out your posts?

EMC does allow users some protection of privacy. Fifty-eight percent of social network users report setting their main profile to private, with women being more private (67 percent) than men (48 percent).[130] Younger users and women are more active than their counterparts in unfriending others, deleting comments, and untagging photos—thus increasing their control of privacy.[131] However, 48 percent of all users indicate difficulty in managing privacy controls. And people to whom we give access can still engage in surveillance, ranging from checking in on us to obsessively monitoring our Facebook page, online postings, pictures, and so on.[132] In addition to invading our privacy, such surveillance can arouse jealousy and conflict in a romantic partner who is upset by the messages or photos posted on your page.

Regardless of the type of problems you might encounter from others on the Internet, following some general rules can help you protect your privacy:

- Avoid providing or posting personal information on websites or social networking sites, or limit what you do post.

- Just as you are careful about sharing your phone number, you should be careful about sharing your e-mail address (although both are often available through an assortment of directories if a person knows your name).

- If you are faced with EMC harassment, provide a clear and assertive statement that you do *not* want to be contacted, and keep copies of any messages you receive.

- Since many harassing and cyberbullying behaviors are illegal, it is also appropriate to report the incidents to college and law enforcement officials.

is certainly a violent act. It instills fear, and the violence it represents can escalate. Sociologist Michael Johnson separates partner violence into three types:[133]

1. *Intimate terrorism:* Using violence to control or dominate
2. *Violent resistance:* Meeting attempts at control with a violent response
3. *Situational couple violence:* Responding with violence to a specific relational conflict or tension

Males are responsible for almost all intimate terrorism, and females for violent resistance. Both men and women engage in situational couple violence, which is probably the most frequently occurring form of relational violence.[134] The presence of intimate terrorism will most likely lead to the abused partner leaving the relationship, whereas incidents of situational couple violence are usually not so severe as to end the relationship.[135] Brian Spitzberg, one of the major researchers of the dark side of communication and relationships, extensively studies intimate partner violence. He observes that intimate violence is not really about power or gender, but rather reflects a process of face-threat (such as failure events and weak accounts), negative emotional arousal, conflict, emotional intensification, attack, and self-protection, building to frustration with irresolvable conflicts and provoking further aggressive communication and acts of violence.[136] Such a model places a premium on effective interpersonal communication and sensitivity to facework.

Avoiding relational violence is a strong reason for improving interpersonal communication skills. Relational violence is never acceptable, nor is it the fault of the victim; do not accept relational violence as a condition of your relationships. If you find yourself either the victim or the perpetrator of relational violence, you should seek professional help. An online search will direct you to numerous support agencies.

Recap

The Dark Side of Interpersonal Communication and Relationships

Deception	Using communication to deceive through false or misleading information.
Deception by Omission	Holding back information so as to leave an incorrect impression with a listener.
Deception by Commission	Deliberately presenting false information in such forms as white lies, exaggeration, or bald-faced lies.
Communication That Hurts Feelings	Causing pain to others either intentionally or unintentionally, by such means as offering unwelcome or negative information or criticizing traits or abilities.
Obsessive Relational Intrusion	Repeatedly invading a person's privacy out of a desire for or assumption of a close relationship with the other person.
Stalking	Making repeated, unwelcome intrusions that create concern for personal safety and fear in the target.
Jealousy	Reacting to the threat of losing a valued relationship.
Relational Violence	Engaging in a range of destructive behaviors aimed at other people, including aggressiveness; threats; violent acts; and verbal, psychological, and physical abuse.

Relationship De-Escalation and Termination

10.3 Explain the process of relational de-escalation and termination, including strategies for terminating and recovering.

The inability to effectively manage relational challenges and/or the dark side of interpersonal communication can contribute to the de-escalation or even termination of a relationship. When you pick up signals of relational problems, you have four choices: wait to see what happens, redefine the relationship (such as, change from dating to friends), repair and/or rejuvenate the relationship, or end the relationship.

Signs of Relationship Problems

Part of effective relationship management is sensitivity to cues that signal relational problems or change. Women usually sense trouble in a relationship earlier than men—but what exactly do they sense? Because each stage in a relationship has unique communication qualities, specific verbal and nonverbal cues can tip us off when a relationship begins to de-escalate. Here are a few signs that might signal relationship problems:[137]

Less touching or physical contact	Interactions are more impersonal
Less vocal expressiveness	Separation of possessions
Less smiling	Less time talking on any given topic
Interactions don't flow as easily	Less use of present tense
Increased physical distance	More passive language
Less eye contact	Fewer references to the future
Increase in time between interactions	More qualifiers ("maybe")
Less sexual activity	More conflict
Fewer intimate terms	Decreases in evaluative statements
Decreases in time together	Less personal language
	Less self-disclosure

John Gottman, who studies married couples, identified four categories of communication behavior that indicate increasing problems in a marriage.[138]

1. *Criticisms:* Being critical of or attacking the partner's personality
2. *Contempt:* Engaging in insults and psychological abuse
3. *Defensive behaviors:* Denying responsibility by making excuses, whining, and counter-complaining
4. *Stonewalling:* Withdrawing, not responding to each other, and minimally engaging in the relationship

Relating to Diverse Others

Women's and Men's Responses to Relationship Challenges

Women and men differ in their management of relational challenges. Women tend to be stronger monitors of their relationships, so they often detect trouble before their male partners. In a study of married couples' initiation of relationship discussions, wives reported a higher likelihood of initiating discussions than the husbands reported.[139] And both partners underestimated their spouse's self-reports of initiating relationship discussions, which might reflect a need for increased other-centeredness. Relationship discussions might be spurred by failure events or transgressions by a partner, which appear to affect men and women differently. Females in romantic relationships reported more intense hurt than males reported when their partners transgressed.[140] Men forgave the women more readily than the women forgave the men, but the more intense hurt women felt might have made them less inclined to forgive.

Women's sensitivity to the health of the relationship may be one factor that makes them more likely to initiate the termination of a relationship.[141] However, men who want out of a relationship might engage in behaviors that women find totally unacceptable, thus prompting the women to be the ones that actually end the relationship. For example, when men avoided interaction by stonewalling and responding defensively to complaints, the couples were more likely to divorce.[142] Men also report greater likelihood of being unfaithful than women.[143] However, men were more effective than women in forestalling a breakup by increasing their relational commitment.[144]

Rejection in a romantic relationship has greater costs for a woman than for a man, with women experiencing greater fear and insecurity over the loss of their partners' protection.[145]

In one study of divorce, men tended to see the later part of the process as more difficult, whereas women said the period before they made the decision to divorce was more difficult. In addition, two-thirds of the women were likely to discuss marital problems with their children, as compared to only one-fourth of the men. Men were twice as likely to say that no one helped them cope with the worst part of the process.[146] To what degree have you noticed such differences in your own relational experiences?

These behaviors undermine effective communication between couples and can lead to the end of the relationship. Among the four, stonewalling is the single strongest predictor of divorce. If all four signs are consistently present, there is a 94 percent chance the couple will eventually divorce.[147] Most couples experience some of these behaviors, but happy couples develop effective communication patterns to overcome them. To what degree do you think these problems and predictions are applicable to dating relationships?

Repair and Rejuvenation

Underlying the success of any repair effort is the degree to which both partners want to keep the relationship going. The nature of the problem, the stage of the relationship, motivation, and an assortment of relational qualities all affect the success of repair efforts. Among the relationship qualities that can reduce the likelihood of dissolution are a positive perception of our partner, commitment, dependence, love, closeness, trust, self-disclosure, investment, satisfaction, relational adjustment, and support from friends and family.[148] No single quick solution to relational problems exists because so many factors influence each problem. You need to focus on the specific concerns, needs, and issues that underlie the problem; then adapt specific strategies to resolve it. Depending upon the level of intimacy and commitment, a couple might want to consider professional counseling.

Partners may experience one of three types of relationship termination: fading away, in which the partners drift slowly apart; sudden death, in which separation is immediate; or incrementalism, in which conflicts gradually build until the couple reaches the breaking point.

Another response to signs of relationship disintegration is to rejuvenate the relationship—to put new life back in it. Explicit efforts to rejuvenate a relationship include serious relational talks, reconnecting after a separation (reconciliation), accepting or forgiving a partner's transgression, and getting outside help.[149] The ability to rejuvenate a relationship depends on the degree to which partners recognize the reasons for relational decay and the level of their interest in rejuvenating the relationship. When only one partner wishes to rejuvenate the relationship, the first task becomes convincing the uninterested partner of the value of doing so. If the loss of relational energy is linked to the presence or absence of specific behaviors or activities, then commitment to changing those behaviors is one avenue for re-energizing the relationship.

In general, rejuvenation is usually conducted through implicit moves rather than direct discussion.[150] In other words, we change or engage in behaviors hoping our partner recognizes our efforts, feels more positive about the relationship, and/or reciprocates the change. Think about times when you have made a change or put forth extra effort for friends or family members to help reduce relational tension—spending more time with someone, doing the dishes without being asked, or baking your friend some cookies. However, you might feel slighted (lose face) if the other fails to appreciate your efforts, which might make the situation worse.

The Decision to End a Relationship

If you do choose to change the level of intimacy in a relationship, consider your goals. Do you want to continue the relationship at a less intimate level, or terminate it altogether? Do you care enough about the other person to want to preserve his or her self-esteem? Are you aware of the costs of ending the relationship? No single correct or best way exists for ending a relationship, nor is ending relationships a skill set that you would necessarily want to become really good at. But you *can* increase the effective management of relational termination by using decentering, being empathic, and adapting to your partner.

Terminating or de-escalating a relationship is not inherently bad. Not all relationships are meant to endure. For example, how likely would you be to continue a relationship after discovering that your partner is a deceitful person? Ending a relationship can be a healthy move if the relationship is harmful, if we no longer feel valued, or if it no longer satisfies our interpersonal needs. Also, ending a relationship can open the door to new ones. De-escalating a relationship also can be healthier if such de-escalation reduces relational costs and/or improves benefits. Once a deception has been uncovered, relationships are more likely to be terminated when the offender can be avoided and there is lack of overall communication.[151]

Breaking up an intimate relationship is hard because of the degree to which you become dependent on the other person to confirm your sense of self. The most satisfying breakups are those that confirm both partners' worth rather than degrade it. "I just can't be what you want me to be"; "I'll always love you, but …"; or "You're a very special person, but I need other things in life" are all examples of statements intended to protect the other person's self-esteem. The loss of intimacy, companionship, and validation of our value can be offset by our relationships with friends and family. Social networks provide support and comfort to help us manage this loss. While friends and family might be quick with the advice, the greatest help they provide is in confirming that we are worthwhile as people.

The process of ending a relationship is considerably different when only one party wants out of the relationship than it is when both parties agree to the breakup.[152] In **bilateral dissolutions**, both parties are predisposed to ending the relationship; they simply need to sort out details such as agreeing on timing, dividing possessions, and defining conditions for contact after the breakup. In a **unilateral dissolution**, when one party wants the relationship to continue, the person who wants to end the relationship often tries to persuade his or her partner to break up. Sometimes, however, people simply walk out of a relationship. If a friend stops calling or visiting, should you just assume the relationship is over and leave it alone, or should you call and ask what's up? People lose contact for a myriad of reasons. Sometimes it is beneficial to ask someone directly whether he or she is breaking off the relationship, although such direct requests place your self-esteem and face on the line. How should you react if your friend confirms a desire to end the relationship? If possible, try to have a focused discussion on what has contributed to his or her decision. You might get information you need to repair the relationship. Or you might gain insights that will help you in future relationships.

How Relationships End

A declining relationship usually follows one of several paths.

FADING AWAY Sometimes a relationship loses energy slowly, like a dying battery. Instead of a single event causing the breakup, the relationship ends by **fading away**—the two partners just drift further and further apart. They spend less time together, let more time go by between interactions, and reduce and finally stop self-disclosing. How many of your relationships can you recall that have simply faded away?

SUDDEN DEATH Some relationships end in sudden death.[153] As the name suggests, **sudden death** is the abrupt and unplanned ending of a relationship. One partner might unexpectedly move away or even die; more frequently, however, a single precipitating event such as infidelity, breaking a confidence, or a major conflict precipitates the breakup. Sudden death is like taking an express elevator from the top floor to ground level. Such an end is difficult because we are not prepared for it and we have not had a chance to reach closure—to say goodbye.

INCREMENTALISM In between fading away and sudden death lies incrementalism. **Incrementalism** is the systematic progression through each of the de-escalation stages

---

bilateral dissolution

Ending of a relationship by mutual agreement of both parties.

unilateral dissolution

Ending of a relationship by one partner, even though the other partner wants it to continue.

fading away

Ending a relationship by slowly drifting apart.

sudden death

Abrupt and unplanned ending of a relationship.

incrementalism

Systematic progression of a relationship through each of the de-escalation stages.

presented in Chapter 9. At each stage, the relationship reaches a threshold, at which point the relationship moves down another level. Turmoil or stagnation in an intimate relationship leads one or both partners to evaluate the relationship, and if they determine that they have reached a certain threshold of intolerance (that is, the costs exceed the rewards), the relationship moves to deintensification. Then, if and when another threshold is reached, the relationship de-escalates to individualization, and finally to separation.

Reasons for De-Escalating and Terminating

When a relationship comes to an end, we often ask ourselves, "What happened? Why did the relationship end?"[154] We engage in this "postmortem" regardless of who initiated the breakup. If your partner initiated the breakup and did not provide adequate explanations, you are left to wonder what happened. Without knowing what you have done to cause the breakup, you could continue behaving in ways that undermine your next relationship.

Researcher Michael Cody had students assess what caused their intimate heterosexual relationships to break up.[155] "Faults" were cited as the number-one cause. These were personality traits or behaviors in one partner that the other partner disliked. The number-two cause, "unwillingness to compromise," represents a variety of failings on the part of one or both partners, including failure to put enough effort into the relationship, a decrease in effort, or failure to make concessions for the good of the relationship. The final cause, "feeling constrained," reflects one partner's desire to be free of the commitments and constraints of a relationship—in essence, feeling greater pull toward autonomy than connectedness.

Lack of "emotional access" or love was cited by both male and female students in another study as more likely to end a committed relationship than a lack of "sexual access."[156] Loss of interest in the other person, desire for independence, and conflicting attitudes about issues affecting the relationship can also contribute to the breakup of nonromantic relationships, while these issues, in addition to sexual conduct, marriage, and infidelity, affect romantic relationships.

Friendships differ from romantic relationships in many ways, including the reasons for relational disintegration. When one researcher asked individuals to identify why their same-sex friendships ended, first on the list was physical separation.[157] Second was new friends replacing old friends as circumstances changed. Third was growing to dislike a characteristic of the friend's behavior or personality. And finally, dating activity or romantic relationships interfered with and contributed to the decay of a friendship.

Relating to Diverse Others
Empathy and Sexual Orientation

I once volunteered as a crisis phone counselor in a large metropolitan area. We were trained to use effective counseling skills, such as empathy, in relating to the callers' crises.

One night, a call came in from a very distressed and depressed man about his breakup with his same-sex partner, with whom he had had a long-term intimate relationship. At first I was uncomfortable dealing with the situation. Despite extensive training and role-playing, I wondered how I, as a heterosexual male, could empathize with or relate to this caller. However, I continued to ask questions about how he felt, what he saw as his needs, and his perception of the problems. The more we talked, the more empathic I became, because I realized that his description was very familiar. I had been divorced some four years earlier, and this caller's descriptions of his feelings matched the feelings I experienced during that time. Talking with him about some of the feelings I had experienced seemed to help him understand his own situation.

I came to understand that though the sex of our partners was different, the overriding issue was the loss of an intimate relationship. I grew a little wiser that night.

—Mark V. Redmond

Just as behavioral rules exist for making and maintaining friends, other behaviors, if pursued, will almost certainly cost you a friendship. In the tradition of *Late Show with David Letterman*, here's a top-ten list in order of increasing offensiveness:[158]

10. Nagging your friend

9. Not showing emotional support

8. Not being tolerant of your friend's other friends

7. Not standing up for your friend in his or her absence

6. Not showing positive regard for your friend

5. Criticizing your friend in public

4. Not trusting or confiding in your friend

3. Not volunteering help in time of need

2. Discussing with others what your friend said in confidence

1. Acting jealous or being critical of your relationship

It should come as no surprise that casual friendships are more likely to end than those between close or intimate friends. Close friendships are better able to withstand change, uncertainty, and separation.

The Relational Dissolution Process

In Chapter 9, we presented our model of the relational de-escalation stages. Another model, developed by relationship scholar Steve Duck, emphasizes the phases or processes tied to relational dissolution decision making and related social interactions.[159] We have adapted his approach to explain the overall relational dissolution process.

INTRAPSYCHIC PHASE   As Figure 10.2 shows, we reach a point at which our level of relational dissatisfaction (threshold) becomes so strong that we enter an **intrapsychic phase** where we privately evaluate the relationship and our partner. Social exchange theory suggests that we would assess the relational costs and rewards at this time, potentially deciding to terminate a relationship that is no longer "profitable."[160] As discussed in Chapter 9, we might delay terminating a relationship if we predict that the relationship will become profitable again, or offset the immediate costs by drawing on the cumulative rewards until they are exhausted.

From time to time we all become frustrated with a relationship, sometimes reaching a threshold that leads us to evaluate the relationship seriously—to enter the intrapsychic phase. After reflection, we might decide to remain in the relationship without proceeding further. However, during this time, our thoughts and feelings might be "leaked" by what we say and how we behave. For example, emotional displays of hostility, anxiety, stress, or guilt might trigger questions or confrontation from our partner. After evaluating our relationship in the intrapsychic phase, we might pass another threshold where we feel compelled to move to the next phase: either the confidant phase or the dyadic phase.

CONFIDANT PHASE   Research indicates that we sometimes turn to friends, family, or counselors for support when a relationship is not measuring up to expectations.[161] In the **confidant phase** we discuss and evaluate the relationship, our concerns, and options with someone other than our partner (friends, family, or counselors). These confidants might act as mediators, encouraging reconciliation and suggesting ways to repair the relationship. Or they might reinforce a decision to separate.

Discussing terminating a relationship with a confidant can occur either before or after having such a conversation with our partner. We might not even discuss our concerns with our partner if the conversation with our confidant reduces our negative appraisal or produces strategies to improve our satisfaction.

DYADIC PHASE   The **dyadic phase** involves a discussion with our partner about relationship concerns and thoughts about terminating the relationship. This phase can involve a shared evaluation of the relationship and termination, or a more unilateral

---

intrapsychic phase

First phase in relationship termination, when an individual engages in an internal evaluation of the partner.

confidant phase

Discussion and evaluation of a relationship, our concerns, and options with someone other than our partner (friends, family, or counselors).

dyadic phase

A phase in relationship termination, when the individual discusses termination with the partner.

Figure 10.2 Relational Dissolution Processes

SOURCE: Based on S. Duck, "A Typography of Relationship Disengagement and Dissolution," from *Personal Relationships, 4: Dissolving Relationships* (London: Academic Press, 1982): 16.

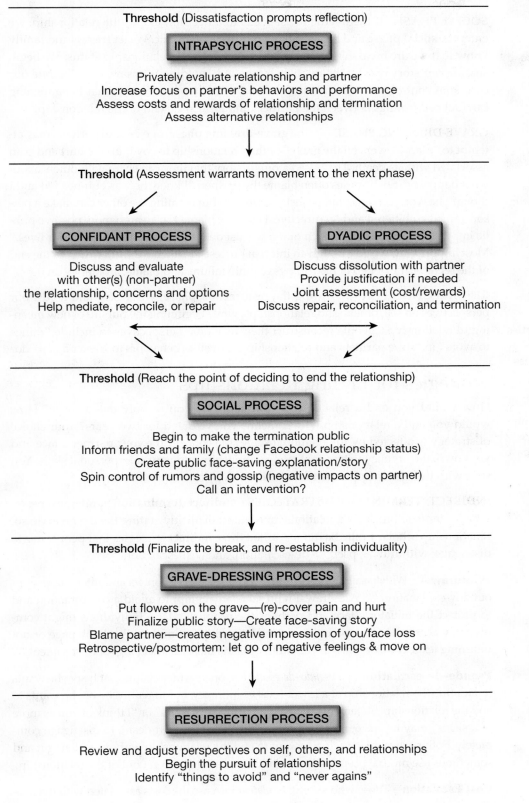

RELATIONAL DISSOLUTION PROCESSES

Threshold (Dissatisfaction prompts reflection)

INTRAPSYCHIC PROCESS

Privately evaluate relationship and partner
Increase focus on partner's behaviors and performance
Assess costs and rewards of relationship and termination
Assess alternative relationships

Threshold (Assessment warrants movement to the next phase)

CONFIDANT PROCESS

Discuss and evaluate
with other(s) (non-partner)
the relationship, concerns and options
Help mediate, reconcile, or repair

DYADIC PROCESS

Discuss dissolution with partner
Provide justification if needed
Joint assessment (cost/rewards)
Discuss repair, reconciliation, and termination

Threshold (Reach the point of deciding to end the relationship)

SOCIAL PROCESS

Begin to make the termination public
Inform friends and family (change Facebook relationship status)
Create public face-saving explanation/story
Spin control of rumors and gossip (negative impacts on partner)
Call an intervention?

Threshold (Finalize the break, and re-establish individuality)

GRAVE-DRESSING PROCESS

Put flowers on the grave—(re)-cover pain and hurt
Finalize public story—Create face-saving story
Blame partner—creates negative impression of you/face loss
Retrospective/postmortem: let go of negative feelings & move on

RESURRECTION PROCESS

Review and adjust perspectives on self, others, and relationships
Begin the pursuit of relationships
Identify "things to avoid" and "never agains"

BEING Other-ORIENTED

Being other-oriented might cause you to refrain from ending a relationship because you know the pain it will cause your partner. But an other-orientation can also lead to face-saving approaches. What do you know about any of your former partners that might have helped end those relationships more positively? Being other-oriented when someone ends a relationship with you can be difficult. Consider a time someone ended a relationship with you. To what degree could you appreciate his or her perspective and feelings at the time? What about now? To what degree did your partner use his or her understanding of you to dissolve the relationship in a positive manner?

social phase

A phase in relationship termination, in which members of the social network around both parties are informed of and become involved in the termination process.

grave-dressing phase

The phase in relationship termination, when the partners generate public explanations and move past the relationship.

resurrection phase

Review and adjustment of our perspectives on self, others, and relationships while beginning the pursuit of new meaningful relationships.

indirect termination strategies

Attempts to break up a relationship without explicitly stating the desire to do so.

declaration of our intent to end the relationship. If our partner feels challenged and intimidated by our desire to end the relationship, we might have to justify our thoughts and feelings while enduring criticism from our partner. The discussion can also lead to a joint decision to repair the relationship, perhaps seeking outside help (both partners participating in a joint confidant phase).

SOCIAL PHASE   If the dyadic phase leads to a decision to end the relationship, we enter the **social phase** and begin making our decision public. We let friends and family know that we are breaking up; we change our Facebook relationship status. We begin sharing our story of why the relationship ended, molding it to save face. Despite our own spin control, rumors and stories about what happened and what is happening can fuel bad feelings between the partners and hasten the end of the relationship.

GRAVE-DRESSING PHASE   In the **grave-dressing phase**, one or both partners may attempt to "place flowers on the grave" of their relationship to cover up the hurt and pain associated with its death. They need a public story that they can share with others about what happened. Such stories often blame the partner: "I knew he was bull-headed and I thought he would change, but he just got worse." But blaming the other can make a person appear embittered and unattractive. Diffusing blame can create a more positive public impression: "We still love each other; we just decided we needed more in our lives." Most importantly, we go through an internal process in which we work to accept the end of the relationship, let go of the feelings of guilt, failure, and blame, and move on.

RESURRECTION PHASE   During the **resurrection phase**, we review and adjust our perspectives on self, others, and relationships, while beginning the pursuit of new meaningful relationships. People reconstruct their relational perspectives to include "things to avoid" in future partners and relationships, as well as behaviors to "never again" do.

Strategies for Ending Relationships

How would you end a relationship with someone you've only dated twice? How would you end a relationship with someone you've dated for two years? Your choice of strategy is affected by the relational stage, the concern for your partner's face and your own, the urgency to terminate the relationship, and your interpersonal skills. You start with two general options: an indirect strategy or a direct strategy.

INDIRECT TERMINATION STRATEGIES   **Indirect termination strategies** represent attempts to break up a relationship without explicitly stating the desire to do so. Relationship scholar Leslie Baxter identified three indirect strategies that people use to disengage: withdrawal, pseudo–de-escalation, and cost escalation.

Withdrawal   *Withdrawal* involves reducing the amount of contact and interaction without any explanation.[162] Withdrawal represents an attempt to avoid a confrontation and to protect the initiator's face and perhaps the recipient's face. Individuals might communicate withdrawal by removing "in a relationship" from their Facebook page or not returning texts, calls, or e-mails. This strategy is the most dissatisfying for the recipient.[163]

Pseudo–de-escalation   In *pseudo–de-escalation*, one partner claims that he or she wants to redefine the relationship at a lower level of intimacy, but in reality, he or she wants to end the relationship. Statements such as "Let's just be friends" or "I think of you as more of a sister" may be sincere, or they may reflect an unspoken desire to disengage completely. Both parties might actually want to end the relationship without realizing it and sometimes use mutual pseudo–de-escalation as a strategy to get out of the relationship.

Cost Escalation   Those who use *cost escalation* increase the costs associated with the relationship in order to encourage the other person to terminate it. A dissatisfied partner may ask for an inordinate amount of the other person's time, pick fights, criticize the other person, or violate relational rules. Men appear to use this strategy more often than women do.

DIRECT TERMINATION STRATEGIES **Direct termination strategies** involve explicit statements of a desire to break up a relationship. Baxter identified four direct strategies that people use to terminate relationships: negative identity management, justification, de-escalation, and positive tone.[164]

direct termination strategies
Explicit statements of a desire to break up a relationship.

Negative Identity Management *Negative identity management* is a direct statement of the desire to terminate the relationship. It does not take into account the other's feelings, and it may even include criticisms. How much face threat do you see in these examples? "I want out of our relationship." "I just can't stand to be around you anymore." "I can't believe I ever wanted to be around someone like you."

Justification *Justification* is a clear statement of the desire to end the relationship, accompanied by an honest explanation of the reasons. Justifications may be honest but still hurtful: "I've found someone else who makes me happy and I want to spend more time with him" and "I feel as if I've grown a great deal and need more than this relationship provides." A person who uses justification does not fault the other person, and he or she makes some attempt to protect both parties' sense of self. Recipients of breakup messages rated this the best choice for communicating desire to end the relationship.[165]

De-escalation *De-escalation* is an honest statement of a desire to redefine the relationship at a lower level of intimacy or to move toward ending the relationship. One partner might ask for a trial separation so that both people can explore other opportunities and gain a clearer understanding of their needs:[166] "Neither of us seems to be too happy with the relationship right now, so I think we should cool it for a while and see what happens."

Positive Tone *Positive tone* can seem almost contradictory; the initiator affirms the other's positive qualities and worth, while declaring an end to the relationship in spite of such positive qualities. Which of the following would least hurt your feelings? "I love you; but it's just not working out." "I really don't want to hurt your feelings, but I'm afraid it's over." "You really are a wonderful person. I know you'll find someone."

Recovery Strategies

Our identities are often tied to our relationships, and the more intimate the relationship, the more our identity is likely to be threatened when a relationship ends. Letting go of a close relationship is not easy, and the grief and pain can be debilitating. Maintaining positive self-esteem and moving on to new relationships requires a successful recovery

Recap
Strategies for Ending Relationships

	Term	Explanation
How Relationships End	Fading away	Dissolving slowly as intimacy declines.
	Sudden death	Ending abruptly, usually in response to some precipitating event.
	Incrementalism	Progressing systematically through each of the de-escalation stages.
Indirect Termination Strategies	Withdrawal	Reducing the amount of contact, without any explanation.
	Pseudo–de-escalation	Claiming a desire for less intimacy, when you really want out.
	Cost escalation	Increasing relational costs to encourage the other to end the relationship.
Direct Termination Strategies	Negative identity management	Directly stating a desire to end the relationship, without concern for the other person's feelings.
	Justification	Directly stating a desire to end the relationship, with an explanation of the reasons.
	De-escalation	Directly stating a desire to lower the level of intimacy or move toward termination.
	Positive tone	Directly stating a desire to end the relationship, while affirming the other person's value.

from the dissolution. Keep in mind that you may experience an initial intensity bias, whereby you predict more distress than you actually experience at the end of a romantic relationship.[167] In other words, you might not feel as bad as you expected.

Relationship researcher Ann Weber created a list of strategies to help address the grief and loss of nonmarital breakups.[168] The following strategies are adapted from her list:

1. *Express your emotions.* You need to vent your feelings—if not to your "ex," then to a sympathetic listener—in a journal or in some other forum. (There are even websites where you can share your story.)

2. *Figure out what happened.* Understanding what occurred in the relationship is one way to get a handle on your current emotions. You need to accept the reasons for the breakup and work toward acceptance.

3. *Realize, don't idealize.* We sometimes view the end of a relationship as the death of a dream. In order to deal with a loss more realistically, Weber suggests mentally reviewing your partner's flaws.

4. *Prepare to feel better.* You might be surprised to find yourself feeling relief and joy. Finding the humor and irony in the breakup can help you cope with the grief.

Communication and Emotion

Assessing Your Emotional Responses to Relationship Challenges

We experience certain emotions when we first confront a situation; other emotions emerge as we address the issue; and still other emotions appear after the challenge has passed. This chapter could be subtitled "Experiencing Negative Emotions," because most of the issues discussed involve such negative emotions as anger, fear, sadness, jealousy, resentment, humiliation, uncertainty, disappointment, and heartbreak.

However, positive feelings can arise when we successfully navigate relational challenges. Having a partner sincerely apologize for a failure event, deception, or a hurtful message can make us feel better and perhaps even increase affection for

the partner. We might even feel relief and a sense of freedom when a negative relationship finally comes to an end.

Read the list below of various topics covered in this chapter. Think of a particular time when you experienced each, and identify the positive and negative emotions that you experienced both initially and subsequently.

Then consider the following questions.

Questions to Consider

- Which situations produced the strongest negative emotional responses?
- What about the situations caused these negative responses?

- How did you manage the negative emotional reactions?
- What could you do in the future to lessen or shorten the negative reactions?
- Which situations resulted in positive emotional responses?
- During which, if any, of the relational challenges did you discuss your emotional reactions with your partner? With a confidant?
- What impact did the discussion have on the relationships? On you? On your partner? On the confidant?

Relational Challenge	Initial Emotional Reactions	Subsequent Emotional Reactions
1. A violation of a relational expectation, a failure event, or a transgression on the part of a close friend		
2. Prolonged physical separation from a close friend or family member		
3. Negative reactions from others to a relationship of yours that was outside social norms		
4. Discovery that a friend deceived you by omission (not telling you something important)		
5. Finding out that a romantic partner lied to you		
6. Receiving a hurtful message from a boss or teacher		
7. Being the target of obsessive relational intrusion, stalking, cyberbullying, or relational violence		
8. Being the target of jealousy on the part of a friend, coworker, or romantic partner		
9. Apparent de-escalation of a friendship		
10. A romantic partner informing you that he or she wants to end the relationship		

5. *Expect to heal.*   Some of the hardest words to accept from others are "It will get better." Although we may not want to believe it, we do recover.

6. *Talk to others.*   Isolation is usually not a very healthy way to handle grief. Friends expect to provide comfort by listening to you discuss your feelings. Don't be afraid to be direct in explaining to friends what you want or need from them; they can't read your mind.

7. *Get some perspective.*   This strategy involves a little bit of wallowing in your misery. Reading stories, seeing movies, or listening to songs about other people's experiences in breaking up can help you put your own situation into perspective.

8. *Be ready for further punishment, or maybe reward.*   Weber suggests that once you've gone through the above strategies, it's time to explore potential relationships. Learn from your past experiences, hang on to pleasant memories, and move forward.

The ending of a relationship that has meant a great deal to you is one of the more difficult experiences you will face in your social life. The more intimate and involved the relationship is, the more heartbreaking the end will be. But as the advice above suggests, life continues after the breakup of a relationship, and it is important to go through a recovery cycle that includes accepting the breakup, accepting the pain, realizing that you still have value and worth, and then moving on. Of course, all of this is easy to say and much more difficult to accomplish—which is one reason you should not isolate yourself but, instead, lean on other interpersonal relationships and family members to help you cope. Regrettably, relationships do end. But just as you develop skills in initiating relationships, you can develop the ability to cope effectively with their termination and, with reflection, experience personal growth.

Applying an Other-Orientation

to Relationship Challenges

Most of the challenges discussed in this chapter can be managed more effectively if you apply an other-orientation, whether you are the perpetrator or the victim. You can use other-orientation to mediate your relationship challenges in several ways.

Avoiding or Minimizing Relational Challenges. An other-orientation might lead you to not engage in a behavior that could result in some harm or stress for your partner. Consider a recent failure event or interpersonal transgression that you committed. If you had considered your partner's feelings and response beforehand, would you still have committed the violation? Such preemptive other-orientation can lead us to alter what we say or do—or avoid saying or doing it at all—thus avoiding hurtful messages or deception.

Selecting Appropriate Repair Strategies. Perhaps you have considered your partner's reaction, but engaged in a failure event anyway. Intentionality makes it more difficult to achieve forgiveness or ameliorate hurt feelings. Nonetheless, by socially decentering, you anticipate your partner's thoughts and feelings about your transgression, helping you plan an appropriate repair strategy. For example, you are better able to choose between offering a simple apology or making significant reparations to restore the relationship.

Appreciating Your Partner's Reactions to Challenges. By social decentering you can better understand your partner's reactions to relationship challenges. For example, suppose your girlfriend or boyfriend returns after a semester studying abroad

and acts distant and even belligerent to you after you introduce the new friends you've made. Your other-orientation would help you appreciate how your partner is affected by the change from a long-distance relationship back to a proximal one and understand why your partner feels jealous of your new friendships.

Managing Relational Termination. Being other-oriented can make de-escalating or terminating a relationship more difficult, because of an increased sensitivity to what your partner might feel about your decision. You might avoid or delay ending the relationship because you know how it will hurt the other person. On the other hand, maintaining a relationship when you no longer care about someone in the same way is a form of deception. The challenge is to use your understanding of the other to develop an approach that minimizes the hurt and best protects your partner's face, such as developing a direct, positive-tone strategy.

Forgiving. As the recipient of a partner's interpersonal transgression, deception, hurtful message, or decision to de-escalate or terminate the relationship, you might find that an other-orientation can contribute to healing and even to forgiving your partner. Suppose you know your partner's need to be independent is greater than his or her desire for an intimate relationship. If so, it should be easier to come to terms with the end of the relationship than if you failed to recognize this need. Forgiving does not mean ignoring what occurred or excusing your partner. But your own mental health generally is improved by forgiving.

STUDY GUIDE
Review, Apply, and Assess

Relationship and Communication Challenges

Objective 10.1 Identify and explain the challenges that individuals involved in interpersonal relationships must navigate to be successful.

Key Terms

failure event or transgression
reproach
account

Thinking Critically

James was supposed to help clean up the apartment on Saturday, but he was gone all day. His roommate reproached him when he returned. Create three accounts that James could provide that differ in terms of how likely they are to make the situation worse.

Assessing Your Skills

Think about an existing situation in your life where someone has upset you or not met your expectations, and you have not forgiven him or her. What impact is not forgiving the person having on you? What's in the way of your forgiving the person? What can you do to reach forgiveness?

The Dark Side of Interpersonal Communication and Relationships

Objective 10.2 Describe the issues that constitute the dark side of interpersonal communication and those that constitute the dark side of interpersonal relationships.

Key Terms

interpersonal deception theory
deception by omission
  (concealment)
deception by commission (lying)
white lies
exaggeration
bald-faced lies
active verbal responses
acquiescent responses
invulnerable responses

envy
jealousy
cognitive jealousy
emotional or affective jealousy
behavioral jealousy
obsessive relational intrusion
  (ORI)
stalking
relational violence

Thinking Critically

Ethics: You suspect a male friend is engaging in obsessive relational intrusion toward his former girlfriend. What obligation do you have to act on this? What would you do? What if your friend was a woman obsessively intruding on a former boyfriend?

Assessing Your Skills

How honest are you? Decide if each statement is true or false in describing your behaviors.

1. When my friends go out on dates, I won't tell them if I think their clothes are unbecoming.
2. If I were on a first date with someone with bad breath and was asked if his or her breadth smelled, I'd just say something like, "It seems fine to me."
3. If I were late for a class because I overslept, I would probably make up some other excuse.
4. If a boss asked me where a report was that I was supposed to have finished, I'd tell her it would be done very soon, even when I knew it would take a lot longer.

A strict policy of being honest can be difficult. To what degree did you have any reservations about your answer? Why? How reflective are you in considering when to be honest and when to deceive?

Relationship De-Escalation and Termination

Objective 10.3 Explain the process of relational de-escalation and termination, including strategies for terminating and recovering.

Key Terms

bilateral dissolution
unilateral dissolution
fading away
sudden death
incrementalism
intrapsychic phase
confidant phase

dyadic phase
social phase
grave-dressing phase
resurrection phase
indirect termination strategies
direct termination strategies

Thinking Critically

1. Think of a romantic relationship that you've had that you chose to end. How well does the model of the relationship dissolution process fit what happened to you? What happened that is not reflected in this model?

2. Ethics: Under what circumstances is it ethical for someone to use sudden death or withdrawal as a strategy for ending an intimate relationship? Under what circumstances would this behavior be unethical?

Assessing Your Skills

Identify two relationships that you ended and two relationships that the other person ended. In each case, try to determine which of the indirect or direct strategies were used. What differences were there in how the relationships ended? What effects do you think the choice of strategy had on you and your partner? What strategies did you use to recover from the breakup? Which was the most helpful? Least helpful? What other strategies for recovery have you used that helped?

Chapter 11
Interpersonal Relationships: Friendship and Romance

"A friend is one who knows us, but loves us anyway."

Fr. Jerome Cummings

Learning Objectives

11.1 Understand the nature of friendships across our lifespan, same-sex friendships, and cross-sex (opposite-sex) friendships.

11.2 Explain how love, commitment, and physical affection define romantic relationships, and describe how such relationships are developed through dating.

11.3 Describe the strategies used to initiate, escalate, and maintain relationships.

CHAPTER OUTLINE

Friendship

Romantic Relationships

Interpersonal Relationship Strategies

Chris and Lee have been friends since fourth grade. They hung out together throughout high school, sharing secrets, playing in the high school band together, and often staying at each other's homes. In college, they roomed together and continued to depend on each other for support and companionship. During their junior year, Chris began to develop a significant romantic relationship with Jan. Chris often sought Lee's advice as the romantic relationship developed. Chris, Lee, and Jan often hung out together, and Lee became good friends with Jan. After graduation, Chris and Jan got married, with Lee providing support and assistance to both.

This scenario provides a very brief introduction to several types of relationships—same-sex best friendships, romantic relationships, and opposite-sex friendships. Underlying the scenario are some subtle but significant questions: Why did Chris feel the need to develop a romantic relationship? Why wasn't the relationship with Lee sufficient to meet Chris's needs for companionship and love? What needs are met by romantic relationships that aren't satisfied through friendship?

Both friendship and romance are relationships of choice; for the most part, we can opt out of them whenever we want. When we begin each relationship, we don't know how intimate it will become—although, as mentioned in Chapter 9, we probably try to predict the likelihood of an intimate and satisfying relationship. Both friendships and romantic relationships can lead to intimate, loving, and lasting relationships.

friendship-based intimacy

A type of intimacy based on feelings of warmth, understanding, and emotional connection.

passion-based intimacy

A type of intimacy based on romantic and sexual feelings.

Intimacy comes in two forms: **friendship-based intimacy**, based on feelings of warmth, understanding, and emotional connection, and **passion-based intimacy**, based on romantic and sexual feelings.[1] Friendship and romance differ in that friendships develop solely from friendship-based intimacy, whereas romantic relationships involve both friendship-based and passion-based intimacy. Chris's relationship with Lee evolved from friendship-based intimacy, whereas the relationship between Chris and Jan reflected both types of intimacy.

Another obvious difference between friendship and romance is that romance includes sexual expectations and, ultimately, the prospect of creating a family. Romantic loving relationships are typified by a high degree of intimacy, attachment, and sexual activity and/or attraction.[2] Historically, marriage has been considered the most intimate relationship between a man and a woman, rooted in the goal of procreation and forming a family.[3] Today, for most, marriage is no longer exclusively rooted in childbearing, nor is it restricted to being between a man and a woman, as gay and lesbian couples also unite in marriage. Both friendships and romantic relationships significantly contribute to mental and physical well-being throughout our lives. This chapter discusses the qualities of each type of relationship; their similarities and differences; the role each plays in our lives; and the skills needed to initiate, escalate, and maintain them.

Friendship

11.1 Understand the nature of friendships across our lifespan, same-sex friendships, and cross-sex (opposite-sex) friendships.

friendship

A relationship of choice that exists over time between people who share a common history.

Friendship is a relationship of choice that exists over time between people who share a common history.[4] A friend is someone we like and who likes us. We trust our friends. We share good and bad times with them. We want to be with them, and we make time for that purpose.

Friendship can be examined in terms of the qualities that distinguish it from other relationships, the values it provides us, and the principles that guide it.

1. *Qualities of friendship.* The following qualities of friendship represent the findings of multiple studies:[5]

   - Self-disclosure/freedom to express intimate information
   - Openness/honesty/authenticity

- Compatibility/similarity
- Ego-reinforcement/self-concept support
- Acceptance of one's individuality
- Respect
- Helping behavior
- Positive evaluation
- Trust
- Concern and empathy

Your own expectations of a friendship probably include some of the items from this list, as well as additional qualities. How well a given person meets these expectations affects your satisfaction with the friendship and its sustainment. In one study, women were more critical than men in their reactions to vignettes that describe a friend failing to meet expectations, such as canceling plans or sharing secrets.[6]

In adolescence we develop cliques and friendship networks.

Friendship develops naturally into an interdependent relationship that is different from other interpersonal relationships; friends have no external constraints that keep them together, such as a job, school, or family, even though we often make friends with people in these situations.

2. *Values of friendship.* Besides helping us enjoy a healthy life, friends provide valuable support in other ways:

- Help us cope with stress and take care of physical needs, and even contribute to the development of our personality.
- Significantly contribute to our social support networks, providing assistance in times of crisis.[7]
- Provide material help when needed, such as feeding our cat while we are away or picking us up if we're stranded by car trouble.
- Help shape our attitudes and beliefs.
- Help us cope with uncertainty and have a profound influence on our behavior, especially during periods of change in our lives, such as adolescence and retirement.[8]
- Help us manage the mundane; we seek out friends just to talk, to share a meal, or to enjoy their company.
- Bolster our self-esteem, provide encouragement, and tell us that we are decent and likable. Being accepted by friends counteracts the nicks and bruises that our self-worth suffers in the course of daily living.

3. *Common principles of friendship:*

- We usually form friendships with our equals, and other types of relationships with people of different ages or social backgrounds.[9]
- We tend to expect equality and equity in our friendships, in contrast to what we accept from our family relationships, with both friends providing similar amounts of emotional and material support and neither one becoming overly indebted.[10]
- Typically, people have up to five close friends, fifteen other friends, twenty or more members in a social network (which could include family members), and many more people who are simply acquaintances.[11]
- In all our social interactions, we are happiest when we are in the company of our friends. Perhaps the ancient Roman orator Cicero said it best: *A friend multiplies our joys and divides our sorrows.*

Making Friends

How do you go about making friends? The first requirement is to interact with new people. Fortunately, you are surrounded with opportunities. You can meet people at school or work, people living near you, people with whom you share activities, and people in your existing friends' social networks (mutual acquaintances). An important rule of making friends is to be yourself. Being yourself increases the likelihood of finding real commonalities with someone. In college you share a number of commonalities with those around you—interest in getting an education, in bettering yourself, and in pursuing a career. One study has found five factors that affect the development of college friendships. These factors provide a good checklist of how to go about making friends:[12]

1. Similarity of attitudes (Look for and present things you and others feel the same about.)
2. An expectation that the other person will like us (Show confidence in your likeability.)
3. Reciprocating self-disclosures (Share personal information in keeping with the other's disclosures.)
4. Proximity (Find opportunities to be near others, and use them as opportunities to talk.)
5. Accessibility or availability (Convey your ability to spend time together.)

Friendships at Different Stages in Life

Our need for intimacy changes throughout our lives and affects the nature of our closest friendships. For example, psychologist Howard Markman and his colleagues found that self-disclosure did not seem to change in depth or amount from young adulthood through age ninety-one.[13] However, as friends grew older, they engaged in more negative self-disclosure. Apparently, as we age, we are more willing to tell our friends less positive things about ourselves. Another change that occurs as we age is the development of a more complex view of friendship. Young adults tend to lump "best friends" together, while older adults differentiate among best friends from their youth, best friends from work, best friends to do activities with, and so on.[14] Figure 11.1 highlights some of the key qualities discussed in the subsequent sections addressing friendships throughout our lives.

Figure 11.1 Key Qualities Associated with Friendships Throughout the Lifetime

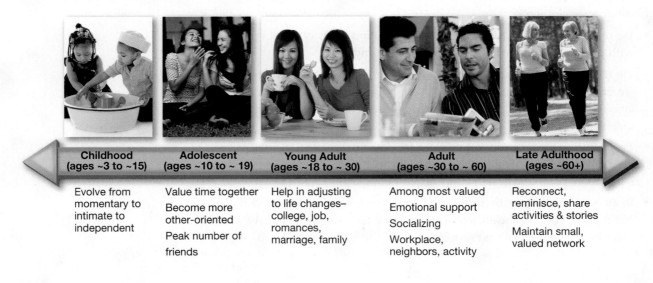

Childhood (ages ~3 to ~15)	Adolescent (ages ~10 to ~19)	Young Adult (ages ~18 to ~30)	Adult (ages ~30 to ~60)	Late Adulthood (ages ~60+)
Evolve from momentary to intimate to independent	Value time together Become more other-oriented Peak number of friends	Help in adjusting to life changes– college, job, romances, marriage, family	Among most valued Emotional support Socializing Workplace, neighbors, activity	Reconnect, reminisce, share activities & stories Maintain small, valued network

Relationship scholars W. J. Dickens and Daniel Perlman examined the differences among friendships at four stages in life: childhood, adolescence, adulthood, and old age.[15] Current research suggests an additional delineation called "young adulthood"—the period between adolescence and adulthood.

CHILDHOOD FRIENDSHIPS   At about the age of two, when we start to talk, we begin parallel play with others. As toddlers, we perceive our playmates as people who can help meet our needs. Our first friendships are usually superficial and self-centered. Childhood friendships can be categorized into five sometimes overlapping stages.[16]

- *Momentary Playmates Stage* **(ages 3–7):**   We interact with those who are nearest, most accessible.
- *One-Way Assistance Stage* **(ages 4–9):**   We still view friendships from a "take" perspective, as instruments to help meet our needs, rather than from a "give" or "give-and-take" perspective.
- *Fair-Weather Friend Stage* **(ages 6–12):**   Friendships are characterized by more give-and-take, more cooperation. The relationship is likely to end if problems and conflicts develop.
- *Mutual Intimacy Stage* **(ages 9–15):**   We develop close friendships, but become possessive of these friendships and experience jealousy.
- *Independence Stage* **(ages 12–adulthood):**   While our interdependence leads to increased intimacy and sharing, we also tolerate friends making friends with others (independence).

ADOLESCENT FRIENDSHIPS   Beginning with the onset of puberty at around age twelve, we move away from relationships with parents and other adults and toward greater intimacy with our peers. During adolescence, peer relationships significantly influence our identity and social skills.[17] We explore values, negotiate new relationships with family members, discover romantic and sexual opportunities, become more other-oriented, and seek increased intimacy. Adolescents consider spending time with friends their most enjoyable activity.[18] Adolescents place value on personality (character, trustworthiness, similarity) and interpersonal qualities (companionship, acceptance, intimacy) in both same-sex and cross-sex friendships.[19] The number of friendships usually peaks in late adolescence and early adulthood, before we select a mate.[20]

YOUNG ADULT FRIENDSHIPS   Young adult friendships, those occurring in our late teens through our early thirties, are linked to a succession of significant changes in our lifestyles and goals, such as going to college, getting a job, pursuing serious romantic relationships, getting married, buying a house, and starting a family.

Those who go directly into the workforce after high school have different friendship experiences than those who leave home to continue their education. Those who opt out of college seek to sustain their high school–based friendships while developing new friendships at their workplace.

For college students who maintain their best friendships from high school, either because they commute or because they attend the same college as their high school friends, the likelihood of forming new best friends in college is reduced.[21] Close high school friendships help new college students manage the stress and successfully adjust to college, but further adjustment requires the development of new friendships during the first year at college.[22] Although larger universities seem to offer possibilities for more diverse friendships, similarities between friends is actually greater at larger universities than at smaller ones because the larger number of students also means a higher likelihood of finding more similar friends.[23]

For those who move away to attend college, high school relationships often de-escalate because of changing interests and the time and energy needed to maintain the friendships. The loss of these relationships, changes in family interactions, and the challenge of forming new relationships may often result in feelings of loneliness;

however, new friendships are usually developed that are regarded as even more satisfying than previous ones.[24] Students interviewed in one study reported that Facebook allowed them to stay connected with friends from home and reduced feelings of homesickness, while also affording them the opportunity to quickly connect with new friends at their college.[25] But the continued connection with old friends made it difficult for them to leave their past and develop their college identity. Students also grappled with the dialectic tension of openness and closedness in deciding what information to post on Facebook, since it would be read by both old and new friends, thereby raising concerns for how both might perceive them.

Young adults particularly value friends who reciprocate their caring, trust, commitment, self-disclosure, helpfulness, and support, and who also have strong character.[26] These friendships help young adults learn and hone the skills needed for developing successful romantic relationships, and provide confidants for discussing romantic experiences.

ADULT FRIENDSHIPS While the exact age ranges that define friendships are debatable, we consider adult friendships as those beginning in our thirties and continuing into our sixties—in essence, those relationships during the prime of our work and family lives.[27] Some young adult friendships continue as adult friendships, with friends experiencing similar life events such as marriage, careers, and children that act as a foundation for mutual empathy and support, as well as the focus of conversations.

Adult friendships are among our most valued relationships, providing emotional support, partners for activities, and socializing opportunities.[28] In addition to continued friendships from young adulthood, friendships emerge with coworkers, neighbors, relatives, and co-members of community organizations. Since these often start as relationships of circumstance, they may be temporary and fade away as circumstances change, such as moving away or taking a new job. The importance of the marital relationship may cause friendships to become secondary, and the likelihood of cross-sex friendships diminishes. Although the number of friends married people have declines over the course of their lives,[29] romantic relationships and marriage introduce partners to each other's social networks, affording additional opportunities for new friends. Marriage can also lead to friendships with brothers- or sisters-in-law or other family members. And you and your spouse may become friends with other couples. Unfortunately, single friends can get left out as couples gravitate to other couples.

LATE ADULTHOOD FRIENDSHIPS Compared to younger adults, older adults report greater relational satisfaction and less relational conflict, have a more positive perspective on conflicts that occur, express more positive messages to each other, and are more forgiving of each other.[30] During retirement, when people have more time for socializing, friendships become increasingly important, but older adults are less likely to form new friendships. They tend to maintain a small, highly valued network of long-established friends, perhaps because older adults focus on maintaining rewarding relationships while dropping those that are problematic.[31] Some friendships are rekindled as the elderly act on their longings to reconnect with close friends with whom they have lost contact.[32] Late adulthood friendships keep individuals socially integrated as they reminisce, share stories, or engage in activities; in addition, their shared experiences add to their ability to be caring and supportive.[33] Friendships often provide richer interactions than those older adults experience with their own family members, although family relationships remain an important part of their lives.

Same-Sex Friendships

An ongoing debate surrounds how men and women approach friendship, particularly their same-sex friendships. One claim is that women define their female friendships by intimacy, whereas men define their male friendships in terms of activities. In one study, men reported having more "best" friends than women; however, women spent more hours talking with their "best" friends than men did, but the time spent talking to "close" friends was similar for both men and women.[34] Men also reported engaging in more physical activities in groups, whereas women spent more time discussing social relationship and school issues. Nonetheless, men do value their close friendships with other men, and women do develop friendships with other women on the basis of their mutual activity.

EXPECTATIONS   What are your expectations for relationships with same-sex friends? The answer to this question was the focus of a study by personal relationship scholar Beverley Fehr, who examined *prototypes* (our expectations about relationships). Both men and women reported that self-disclosure, emotional support, loyalty, and trust contributed the most to a sense of intimacy in their same-sex friendships.[35] However, women rated all of these behaviors as more likely to produce intimacy than did men, and as more important to friendship satisfaction. Women also appeared to have a stronger need or desire for intimacy in same-sex friendships than did men.[36]

FUNCTIONS   Close same-sex relationships serve similar functions for both men and women. Both value intimacy, trust, interpersonal sensitivity, emotional expressiveness, and authenticity in their same-sex friendships.[37] Both men and women also value engaging in activities, conversing, having fun, and relaxing with their same-sex friends.[38]

Overall, men's and women's same-sex friendships appear to differ not in the qualities they possess, but in the degree to which they possess these qualities. Compared to men, women see their same-sex friendships as more satisfying, more enjoyable, and more intimate or close. Women's same-sex friendships also involve more talk about talking (metacommunication), and are more person-centered and expressive.[39] Females in same-sex friendships have more physical affection for each other and compliment each other more, whereas men are more openly competitive.[40] While very close male friends are not extremely interpersonally competitive, one study did find that same-sex male friends are more competitive than either same-sex female friends or cross-sex friends.[41] Men acted less interpersonally competitive in their friendships with women, but women's competitiveness increased in their friendships with males. For all friendships, being more competitive related to less friendship satisfaction.

As with all such generalizations, the conclusions of these studies don't fit every relationship. We all have individual friendship preferences and expectations that we use to judge the value of each of our female and male friendships.

Cross-Sex Friendships

Perhaps as you grew up, you had close friends of the opposite sex. Adolescents often develop opposite-sex, or *cross-sex*, friendships that are not romantic.[42] However, the development of male–female friendships between heterosexual adults is sometimes a challenge because of underlying sexual attraction. In the movie *When Harry Met Sally*, Harry proclaims that "… men and women can't be friends. The sex part always gets in the way." Fortunately, research and your own experiences might indicate that Harry wasn't totally correct. We can develop cross-sex adult friendships with minimal sexual attraction, or redefine romantic relationships as friendships.

Adult cross-sex relationships are facilitated by opportunities for men and women to interact nonromantically—in college, at work, and in leisure activities.[43] In one study, partners in cross-sex friendships reported less everyday talk (like gossiping, complaining, and small talk) in their face-to-face and telephone conversations than those in same-sex friendships, but no difference was found in their online conversations.[44] The researchers speculate that cross-sex online conversations might reduce sexual tension.

Heidi Reeder, a communication researcher, conducted two studies on cross-sex relationships: one in which she interviewed twenty pairs of cross-sex friends and the other in which 231 students completed questionnaires.[45] Both studies found that romantic attraction and physical/sexual attraction diminished as the relationship progressed over time, while friendship attraction increased. In another study men reported a stronger desire for touch in low-intimacy relationships than when intimacy was higher.[46] One explanation is that men viewed touch in low-intimacy relationships as less likely to be confused with movement toward a romantic relationship.[47] While sexual attraction might indeed be an issue within cross-sex relationships, it is reduced when there is a commitment to develop and maintain the relationship as friends.

Not all cross-sex friendships are devoid of sex. Friendship, romantic relationships, and sex have been found to connect in several ways.[48] People in relationships labeled *friends with benefits (FWB)* have both sexual and nonsexual interactions but value their friendship above all; such relationships contrast with relationships that are primarily sexual and in which the couple are only minimally friends. FWB relationships are sometimes intentionally or unintentionally used as stepping stones to romantic relationships, both successfully and unsuccessfully. What happens when the sexual activity ends? A survey of 308 post-FWB participants found that 81.5 percent remained friends, with 31.5 percent feeling less close, 35.4 percent feeling the same closeness as before, and 14.6 percent feeling closer.[49]

Reasons for engaging in FWB relationships include the avoidance of relational commitment, a desire to engage in sex with a friend, a perception that such relationships are simpler and less problematic than romantic ones, a desire to feel closer to the friend, and a general desire to have an FWB experience.[50] Reasons for not engaging in FWB relationships include concern with complicating or jeopardizing the friendship, belief in limiting sex to romantic relationships, and moral convictions.[51] Participants in one study reported discussing and establishing specific relational maintenance rules, with the most frequent being emotional rules (not falling in love or being jealous) and communication rules (guidelines about honesty, what topics are okay to talk about, and phone calling).[52] But participants in another study reported engaging in FWB relationships without discussing their expectations or setting ground rules.[53] Such avoidance can add stress to the relationship and even lead to the end of the friendship.

Cross-sex friendships can help you better understand the opposite sex. On the basis of interviews with 300 men and women about their cross-sex friendships, psychotherapist and author Lillian Rubin found that the men reported feeling a higher level of intimacy and friendship than their female counterparts (some women were surprised to find out they were even considered friends).[54] Men seemed to gain more from their friendships with women than women did from men. Men valued their friendships with women for providing more nurturance and intimacy than their male friendships. Although women did not feel their male friendships were as intimate or rewarding as their female friendships, women did enjoy the masculine interaction style, the fun activities, and learning about the male perspective.

In interacting with people of either sex, focus on working toward a mutual understanding and acceptance of your expectations for your friendship. Great value exists in forming relationships with individuals who are different from you; not only can you learn about other people, but you can also gain a better sense of yourself. Learning how another person's age, race, ethnicity, or sex affects his or her values, thoughts, and behaviors can increase your awareness of how those factors have influenced your own personal development.

Diverse Friendships

Most of our friendships are with people who are fairly similar to us. Similarity makes it easier to communicate effectively and to reach mutual understanding. The more we differ from other people, the greater the challenges that must be overcome to maintain a relationship, as discussed in Chapter 4. However, both friendships and romantic relationships

---

BEING Other-ORIENTED

Same-sex and cross-sex friends share commonalities but also have distinct qualities. Think about your best same-sex friend and your best cross-sex friend. What qualities do they have in common? What qualities do they have that differ? To what degree are the differences related to general sex role differences? How do those differences affect your attitudes and interactions with each friend?

do develop between people who differ in culture, age, and race. Part of the success of these relationships depends on whether the difference is more superficial than profound.

INTERGENERATIONAL FRIENDSHIPS The impact of a ten-year age difference between you and another person is likely to be minimal if you both have the same interests and similar values. However, someone forty years older might have an outlook on life very different from yours. Usually, the older people become, the less impact age differences have on them.[55] A fifteen-year-old's interaction with a thirty-year-old represents a very different kind of relationship than that of a thirty-year-old and a forty-five-year-old.

How many close friendships do you have with anyone significantly older or younger? Because developing and sustaining such relationships often require special effort, we are more likely to have casual intergenerational friendships. One study compared close friendships between peers of similar age with those of friends who were at least ten years different in age.[56] The sample included participants who ranged from eighteen to seventy-six. Close relationships with peers, as compared to relationships with those of a different age, were seen as providing more companionship, satisfaction, intimacy, and nurturance, and as being more likely to continue in the future.

Friends who choose to establish relationships outside of a culture's norms face challenges and social pressures.

INTERCULTURAL AND INTERRACIAL FRIENDSHIPS The qualities and expectations associated with being a friend differ among cultures, ethnic groups, and racial groups. You might engage in behavior that you think is appropriate in your friendship with a person from another culture, only to find that you have offended your friend by violating his or her culturally based expectations. In fact, one study that examined the qualities associated with friendship in various ethnic groups in the United States found that "Latinos emphasized relational support; Asian Americans emphasized a caring, positive exchange of ideas; African Americans emphasized respect and acceptance; and Anglo Americans emphasized recognizing the needs of the individual."[57] Realize, of course, that such generalities may not be valid for a particular member of an ethnic group. However, the study also found that in developing interethnic relationships, individuals seemed unaware of cultural or ethnic differences; rather, they developed a unique relationship defined by their own relational rules rather than by cultural rules.[58] Such uniqueness is similar to the notion of developing a third culture, as discussed in Chapter 4. True respect for and deep understanding of a partner's culture develops as the relationship becomes very close, at which point cultural violations are viewed less negatively and may even be joked about.[59]

As in the development of most relationships, factors such as proximity and communication affect attraction in intercultural friendships. However, four factors have been identified that specifically affect the development of intercultural friendships.[60]

1. *Cultural similarities* exist across cultures, creating common ground that nurtures the development of friendship—for example, sharing the same passion for soccer as someone from Brazil or a love of anime with someone from Japan.

2. *Cultural differences* can actually heighten interest in the other person and prompt initial conversations. You might seek more information from someone from another culture about how their nonverbal communication code differs from yours, or about the holidays they observe and how they celebrate them.

3. *Prior intercultural experiences* help reduce uncertainty about developing friendships with people from other cultures and serve as the foundation for new friendships. Of course, this factor can be somewhat unilateral, in that you might have experience with the other person's culture, but not vice versa.

Improving Your Communication Skills
Understanding Your Relational Expectations

Canadian researcher Beverly Fehr found that people hold certain expectations (*prototypes*) for the kinds of interactions that lead to a sense of intimacy in friendships. People use these expected interaction patterns as a standard that helps them first determine the level of intimacy in a relationship and then evaluate that intimacy.

Changes in the number and intensity of your prototype interaction patterns let you know whether you are moving toward or away from intimate friendships. How aware are you of your expectations? Do you have the same expectations for all relationships, or do they differ depending on the type of relationship?

The statements listed later in this section reflect the top *prototypes* found in Fehr's study. Think about your general expectations for each of the listed relationships. Put 2 on the line if the interaction pattern strongly reflects your explanation of what **should** occur in each relationship, 1 if it somewhat reflects your expectation, and 0 if it doesn't apply.

- Examine each of the four types of relationship, and note which patterns you marked with a 2. How do these expectations compare to what you actually experience in these relationships? How has meeting or failing to meet your strongest expectations affected the level of intimacy in each relationship?

- Overall, for which patterns did you mark zeros across the four types of relationship? How do your low expectations affect your relationships with people who perceive these expectations as important?

- For each type of relationship, do you expect any patterns of interaction that are not listed?

- How do the rating totals relate to your level of satisfaction and closeness in each of the relationships listed?

- How do differences in your rating totals reflect and explain differences in your relationships?

SOURCE: Based on Beverly Fehr, "Intimacy Expectations in Same-Sex Friendships: A Prototype Interaction-Pattern Model," *Journal of Personality and Social Psychology* 86 (2004): 265–84.

	Close Same-Sex Friend	Close Cross-Sex Friend	Close Romantic Partner	Mother or Father
If I need to talk, this person will listen.	_____	_____	_____	_____
If I am in trouble, this person will help me.	_____	_____	_____	_____
If I need this person, he or she will be there for me.	_____	_____	_____	_____
If someone is insulting me or saying negative things behind my back, this person will stick up for me.	_____	_____	_____	_____
If I need food, clothing, or a place to stay, this person will provide it.	_____	_____	_____	_____
No matter who I am or what I do, this person will accept me.	_____	_____	_____	_____
If we have a fight or an argument, we will work it out.	_____	_____	_____	_____
Even if I feel as though no one cares, I know this person does.	_____	_____	_____	_____
If this person upsets me, I am able to let him or her know.	_____	_____	_____	_____
If something good happens to me, this person will be happy for me.	_____	_____	_____	_____
If I set a goal, this person will support and encourage me.	_____	_____	_____	_____
If I am lonely, this person will provide companionship.	_____	_____	_____	_____
Totals:	_____	_____	_____	_____

4. *Targeted socializing* occurs as partners move from acquaintanceship to friendship, socializing within the specific cultural or intercultural context of one of the partners, such as an American student attending a Chinese New Year's party with a Chinese classmate.

Opportunities to socialize also affect the development of interracial friendships. An analysis of a large national survey found that the formation of interracial friendships in the United States is associated with participation in nonreligious civic groups, socializing with coworkers, social status, shared neighborhoods, and the diversity of the community.[61] Many of these factors led to Blacks, Hispanics, and Asians being more likely than Whites to have an interracial friend. However, Whites who lived in communities with more diversity were more likely to have interracial friends. Blacks,

Hispanics, and Asians were more likely to report having White friends when they belonged to nonreligious civic groups and/or socialized with coworkers. For immigrants who must bridge both cultural and racial differences, language skills and citizenship affect their ability to join groups and socialize with coworkers, thus affecting their development of interracial or interethnic friendships.

While intercultural and interracial friendships share similarities, a unique issue confronting interracial friendships is the fact that usually both people are from the same culture. Thus, they assume that they share the same cultural values, identity, and experiences, and fail to appreciate the impact of race on their perspectives.

Communication scholar William Rawlins identifies prerequisites for the formation of friendships between Blacks and Whites.[62] He begins with the premise that White people have difficulty seeing themselves from a racial perspective, whereas Black people have both a racial identity and feelings of being marginalized and demeaned by Whites.[63] According to Rawlins, friends of different races need to recognize that racism is a reality that affects our relationships; we are all potentially racist, and racism can appear in many different forms.[64] For example, thinking you're doing a favor for someone of another race by being his or her friend might reflect an inherent belief in your superiority.

Finally, friends of different races need to guard against either overaccommodating or overassimilating—each person needs to retain his or her own racial identity while appreciating that of the other.[65] Rather than changing to gain acceptance, interracial friends need to accept race as a part of each other's identity.

Romantic Relationships

11.2 Explain how love, commitment, and physical affection define romantic relationships, and describe how such relationships are developed through dating.

The closest relationship you ever develop with another human being will probably be a romantic one, perhaps a marriage. However, even without being married, 47 percent of students surveyed in one study indicated their closest relationships were with romantic partners.[66] This closeness is reflected in many behaviors; for example, romantic couples are more likely than friends to talk about what attracted them to each other, to celebrate anniversaries, and to mark other milestones in formal ways, such as with a card or a special dinner.

At the most rudimentary level, romantic relationships are about mating and creating a family. Your immediate reaction might be to exclaim that this was the last thing on your mind during your high school and college romances. Nonetheless, the complex process of seeking a mate begins with fairly innocuous interactions such as hanging out and talking. One of your authors conducted a survey about the differences among male–female relationships labeled as friends, hanging out, talking, casual dating, dating, boyfriend/girlfriend, and romantic.[67] Each participant rated a relationship on the basis of what he or she expected from or associated with the relationship. Results indicated three general relational categories: nonromantic (friends), pre-romantic, and romantic (see Figure 11.2). The relationships in each category had similar qualities, activities, and types of information shared. Negative information (personal or family problems, doubts and fears, and negative emotions) and intimate information (religious background, secrets about past, and sex/sexual concern) were seen as significantly more appropriate to discuss in relationships labeled as boyfriend/girlfriend and romantic. Cross-sex friendships had some similarities with pre-romantic and romantic relationships, but were also unique in their own way. For example, discussing potential romantic partners was more appropriate between

Figure 11.2 Continuum of Male-Female Relationships

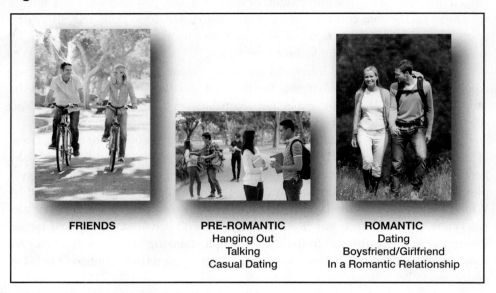

FRIENDS

PRE-ROMANTIC
Hanging Out
Talking
Casual Dating

ROMANTIC
Dating
Boyfriend/Girlfriend
In a Romantic Relationship

friends than in the other kinds of relationships. Discussing other potential partners with your romantic or pre-romantic partner is likely to undermine the relationship. Respondents were also asked how appropriate it was to use different forms of communication. Across all relationships, e-mail and posting on Facebook were not seen as particularly appropriate ways to interact. Phone calls and texting were seen as more appropriate, and exchanging Snapchats and face-to-face conversations were viewed as most appropriate. These forms of interaction seem to parallel increasing levels of personalness and intimacy, with e-mail being impersonal and face-to-face conversations being very personal.

Engaged and *married* are additional labels we use to signify particular types of romantic relationships. Regardless of the label, movement toward intimacy in romantic relationships involves increasing commitment, love, self-disclosure, and physical expression of intimacy, as well as a growing expectation for exclusivity (fidelity).

Both cross-sex and same-sex couples may have romantic relationships, with gay and lesbian romantic relationships sharing many of the qualities of heterosexual relationships. More specifically, research examining same-sex and cross sex romantic relationships report the following similarities:

> Same-sex couples show similar communication and conflict resolution skills as heterosexual couples; similar degrees of interpersonal empathy; similar appraisals of intimacy, autonomy, equality, and mutual trust; similar day-to-day cognitive and behavioral strategies for maintaining their relationships; similar struggles over equity, housework, and fairness; and even similar strategies for deciding to parent and cope with the birth of a new child.[68]

Same-sex couples often face social mores, restrictive laws, and condemning attitudes, which can create an additional pressure for couples to manage. Comparing married heterosexual couples and married homosexual couples is difficult, since in many US states, marriage has only recently become available to same-sex couples. Nonetheless, one study found that committed gay and lesbian couples displayed patterns similar to those of married heterosexual couples in terms of change in satisfaction over a five-year period.[69] However, same-sex couples were more likely than opposite-sex married couples to end their relationships within those five years, perhaps because of social pressures or lack of social acceptance. Changes in social attitudes and the legal right to marry are likely to reduce those pressures.

Qualities of Romantic Relationships

In the chapter's opening scenario, Chris's development of a romantic relationship with Jan was linked to both friendship-based and passion-based intimacy—it was a relationship that included those qualities most typical of romantic relationships: love, commitment, and physical affection and sex.

LOVE   One pair of researchers suggests that love differs from friendship "in the identity of interest that the partners share. Love exists to the extent that the outcomes enjoyed or suffered by each are enjoyed or suffered by both."[70] Love involves an increase in a sense of "we-ness," of passionate solidarity and identification with the other. Love has also been conceptualized as an individual's having the goal of preserving and promoting the well-being of a person who is valued.[71]

Zick Rubin, a lawyer and social psychologist, attempted to identify differences between love and friendship by developing two scales—one to measure love and the other to measure liking.[72] He found that people describe love relationships as more passionate and intimate than friendships, but interestingly, people like their romantic partners only slightly more than they like their friends. Women make greater distinctions between love and liking than do men.

The **triangular theory of love**, developed by psychologist Robert Sternberg, identifies three dimensions that can be used to describe variations in loving relationships: intimacy, commitment, and passion.[73] In this model (Figure 11.3), *intimacy* includes such attributes as trust, caring, honesty, supportiveness, understanding, and openness. The second dimension, *commitment*, includes loyalty, devotion, putting the other first, and needing each other. The final dimension, *passion*, includes excitement, and sexual interest and activity. Passion is defined as "A state of intense longing for union with another."[74] These three dimensions relate to relationship satisfaction,[75] with passion identified as the most important dimension for developing romantic relationships.[76]

These dimensions also provide a useful way of thinking about how love manifests itself in relationships. According to the triangular theory of love, the presence and strength of each of these dimensions vary from relationship to relationship, with each combination defining a style of love. For example, relationships strong in intimacy and commitment but weak in passion are identified as *companionate love,* and relationships strong only in passion constitute *infatuation.* One study found that friends with benefits reported moderate intimacy, low passion, and low commitment, with greater regard for *liking love* over sexual contact.[77] Relationships change as each dimension ebbs and flows.

We can also experience **compassionate love** in which our feelings, thoughts, and behaviors reflect our caring, concern, support, and understanding of another

triangular theory of love
Theory that suggests that all loving relationships can be described according to three dimensions: intimacy, commitment, and passion.

compassionate love
Feelings, cognitions, and behaviors that are focused on caring, concern, tenderness, and an orientation toward supporting, helping, and understanding the other.

Figure 11.3 Sternberg's Triangular Theory of Love

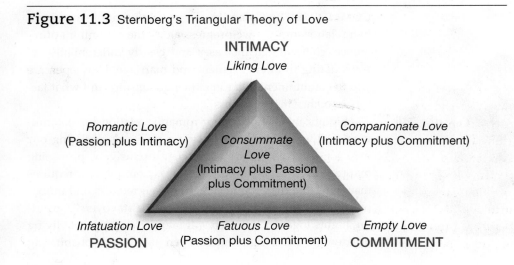

person.[78] While women generally display compassionate love more than men, men and women are similar in feeling compassionate love for their romantic partners.[79] Both giving and receiving compassionate love positively relate to feelings of relational satisfaction and commitment.[80] And when relationships end, compassionate love has been related to the use of openness and positive tone strategies. This is probably because we try to avoid harming the partner for whom we feel compassionate love.[81]

Sociologist John Alan Lee created a similar scheme that defined six types of love found in both romantic and nonromantic relationships: eros, ludus, storge, mania, pragma, and agape.[82] These types of love can also reflect a person's particular style of love. Which of these types or styles best reflects your general approach to love in a romantic relationship?

Eros is sexual love based on the pursuit of beauty and pleasure. The physical need for sex brings many couples together. Erotic lovers crave sexual intimacy and passionately seek sexual activity to satisfy their need. Eros includes feelings of being meant for each other and seeing the partner as beautiful or handsome.

Ludus describes love as a game, something to pass the time. Ludic lovers are not seeking long-term relationships; rather, they seek immediate gratification and their partners' affection. Early dating relationships are often of the ludic type. For example, going on a date to a junior high dance is a casual pleasure, not a prelude to a lifelong commitment. Ludus lasts as long as the partners have fun and find the relationship mutually satisfying.

Storge is the sort of love found in most friendships and in relationships with siblings and other family members. Sexual consummation is not a factor in this sort of love, although sexual attraction may be present. A storgic relationship usually develops over a long period of time, and it is solid and more resistant to change than erotic love. Trust, caring, and compassion are high; selfishness is low.

Mania describes a love relationship that swings wildly between extreme highs and lows. A manic lover is obsessed with the relationship, which can foster jealousy. Each of the lovers may have an insatiable need for attention, often fueled by low self-esteem.

Pragma is the root word for *pragmatic*, meaning practical. This kind of relationship works because the partners' individual requirements, personalities, backgrounds, likes, and dislikes are compatible. Pragma partners approach love logically, assess each other in terms of the right fit, and value direct communication.

Agape love is based on a spiritual ideal of love. It involves the giving of oneself and expecting nothing in return. This kind of "pure" love may characterize the relationship between a parent and a child, or the relationship between a spiritual leader and his or her followers.

COMMITMENT Commitment is our intention to remain in a relationship. As we progress along the continuum of romance, commitment increases and clearly differentiates serious dating from engagement and marriage. How open are you to commitment in a romantic relationship, and what factors influence that openness?

Significant changes in our romantic relationship commitments are marked by such turning points as declaring our love for someone, pledging to date exclusively, proposing marriage, and saying wedding vows. Commitment requires managing the dialectic tension of connectedness and autonomy and explains why couples engage in "stayovers" (spending nights together but each still maintaining separate living quarters) as a turning point between dating and cohabitating

eros

Sexual, erotic love based on the pursuit of physical beauty and pleasure.

ludus

Game-playing love based on the enjoyment of another.

storge

Solid love found in friendships and family, based on trust and caring.

mania

Obsessive love driven by mutual needs.

pragma

Practical love based on mutual benefits.

agape

Selfless love based on the giving of yourself for others.

commitment

Our intention to remain in a relationship.

According to one view, passionate love is one component of romantic love, and it usually declines as the relationship evolves.

or marriage.[83] A study of married and romantically involved couples found that the level of commitment was related to six sets of behaviors:[84]

1. Being supportive and encouraging (e.g., listening and being courteous)
2. Reassuring our partner of our feelings (e.g., expressing love and confirming the importance of the relationship)
3. Offering tangible reminders (e.g., giving gifts and assistance)
4. Creating a relationship future (e.g., doing things together and making plans together)
5. Behaving with integrity (e.g., being honest, being faithful, and keeping promises)
6. Working on the relationship (e.g., talking out problems and expressing trust)

Women, more than men, showed commitment by being supportive, creating a relationship future, and behaving with integrity; men showed commitment by offering tangible reminders (gifts and assistance) more than women. Partners' feelings and expressions of commitment appear to be interdependent and cyclical. For example, a display of commitment by one partner tends to lead to increased feelings and displays of commitment by the other.[85] How do you convey commitment and how does it impact your partner's commitment?

Commitment can also be demonstrated when partners post on Facebook that they are in a relationship. Facebook official (FBO) represents a public announcement of the relationship that confirms the commitment and also lets others know about the relationship. FBO can be a source of tension when only one partner lists "in a relationship" or when a person feels pressured to post FBO by her or his partner. It's healthier if partners talk about becoming FBO and both agree to this level of commitment.

Besides becoming FBO, we have other specific expectations about our romantic relationships, depending on the relationship's progress. In general, we expect partners in committed relationships to be faithful, to respect us, to help maintain our face when the relationship is troubled, and to help us through hard times.[86] This list of expectations almost sounds like wedding vows, which are in essence a statement of our commitment to our partner. As we grow up, our families convey messages to us about what commitment means in a relationship.[87] We also learn about commitment indirectly; for example, having divorced parents was found to relate to having a less positive attitude about marriage among college students, which in turn related to a weaker sense of commitment in dating relationships.[88]

PHYSICAL AFFECTION AND SEX **Physical affection** is the use of touch to convey love and caring for another person. Physical affection, in and of itself, is not unique to romantic relationships. It is also a part of our interactions with friends and family—hugs, kisses, and snuggling, for example. However, affection through touch is a significant component of and expectation in romantic relationships, and changes as our romantic relationship changes. As discussed in Chapter 7, more affectionate touching occurs in the earlier part of a romantic relationship. As intimacy is achieved, the need to continue displaying physical affection appears to decline.[89]

Physical affection depends on both the physical (actual behavior) and the emotional (affection). In a study that measured the verbal and nonverbal expression of affection, commitment was found to serve as the foundation for affection and satisfaction: The stronger a person's commitment, the more affection he or she expressed, and the more affection that was expressed, the more relationally satisfied the partner was.[90] However, we sometimes intentionally withhold affection even when we would like to be affectionate. Some reasons for withholding affection include concern for how our partner will perceive us (too clingy), inappropriate circumstances (discomfort with public displays of affection), negative feelings, concerns about rejection, external/internal factors (busy or tired), punishment, contrary relational expectations, teasing, and relational de-escalation.[91]

physical affection
The use of touch to convey emotional feelings of love and caring for another person.

BEING Other-ORIENTED

Not understanding a romantic partner can negatively impact the relationship. Recall what you knew about a former romantic partner during the peak of your relationship. How would your partner describe the relationship in terms of the three dimensions of the triangular theory of love? How do you think your partner believed you would have described the relationship? What really was your description? To what degree did these differences in understanding affect the relationship? Discuss with your classmates the challenge of understanding a partner's perception of the relationship in terms of the three dimensions.

The ultimate goal of many romantic relationships is creating a family with children; sex is obviously the way to accomplish this goal. However, humans frequently engage in sexual intercourse with no intent to produce children, which makes the role of sex in romantic relationships complex and perplexing. Besides a desire to procreate, sex can be motivated by a desire to show that the partner is valued, to nurture the partner, to show or feel power, to release stress, to feel valued by the partner, or simply to experience pleasure.[92] Motivation to engage in sex has been linked to people's attachment styles (discussed in Chapter 2), with attachment anxiety related to engaging in sex to please a partner and express love.[93] The stronger a person's attachment avoidance, the less sex occurs as an expression of love, or a show of intimacy, or to please the partner, and the more it's done to avoid angering the partner.[94]

Traditionally, sexual activity and intercourse were reserved for marriage, as they still are for some. However, romantic relationships today most often involve and are even defined by sexual activity, and sex occurs even outside the bounds of romantic relationships. Research shows that relationship satisfaction in intimate relationships (married and dating couples) positively correlates with sexual satisfaction, but this correlation might be because another variable (such as good communication) is responsible for both relationship and sexual satisfaction.[95] Indeed, higher levels of relational uncertainty experienced by husbands and wives relates to more indirect communication about sex, which then relates to lower sexual satisfaction.[96] Uncertainty about a relationship hampers and inhibits effective communication and thus impacts sexual satisfaction. These results highlight the importance of developing effective communication as a tool to reduce relational uncertainties.

Talking to your partner about sex, self-disclosing, and discussing previous sexual activity all affect sexual and relational satisfaction. One study of romantically involved college students found that the level of sexual communication related to the level of relational satisfaction, particularly for males.[97] However, over time, that relationship diminished for males, while it increased for females. That is, for women there was a stronger correlation between relational satisfaction and sexual communication in relationships lasting more than one year than in those less than one year long. Talking about sexual intentions and desires was found to increase sexual satisfaction, relational satisfaction, and intimacy.[98] People appear most comfortable self-disclosing sexual information in relationships that are positive, that already have a high level of self-disclosure on nonsexual topics, and where sexual disclosure is reciprocated.[99]

Besides providing personal sexual information, communication also serves to manage sexual activity. Rather than talking about likes, dislikes, or fantasies when interviewed, married people focused on explaining the process they used to manage sexual activity.[100] They revealed the use of verbal or nonverbal, and explicit or implicit *priming messages* to determine a spouse's interest in sexual activity. Responses to priming messages fell into three categories: in-synch messages such as reciprocating affection or directly agreeing; token acceptance involving compliance to demonstrate commitment without strong sexual desire; and out-of-synch messages used to convey that sexual interest was not shared at that time. The creation of these sexual scripts can reduce relational uncertainty, increase comfort with sexual activity, and improve relational satisfaction.[101]

Explicit communication surrounding the first time a couple has sex creates a more accurate shared perception and reduces uncertainty about both sexual and relational expectations.[102] Explicit communication is also considered a safe-sex practice. But you might find open discussion about your sexual history and expectations threatening. In some instances, such disclosures might even damage a relationship. One study found that 32 percent of students reported withholding information about their previous sexual activity from at least one partner, and 17 percent withheld it from all their partners; in addition, 25 percent misrepresented their sexual histories.[103] Such deceptions ultimately impair relational development and intimacy.

In exclusive romantic relationships, especially marriage, infidelity is a form of deception that similarly puts a partner at risk. Agreeing to an exclusive sexual relationship might be more about committing to an intimate, romantic relationship than about limiting sexual partners; infidelity thus threatens the very essence of the relationship. As you develop your own romantic relationships, strive to be as direct and explicit as you can in discussing your expectations for all aspects of the relationship, including sex.

From Friendship to Romance

Many romantic relationships begin as friendships. Establishing friendship-based intimacy first is an effective way to determine, with less risk and commitment, the potential for a more passion-based relationship. The primary focus in a friendship is on compatibility, attraction, and other qualities of friendship. So if no romantic relationship develops from an existing friendship, the intimacy lost is less than if it were a romantic relationship that failed to escalate or ended.

To move from friendship to romance involves adding passion-based intimacy to the existing friendship-based intimacy. This transition to a romantic relationship is accompanied by causal and/or reflective turning points, such as significant and intimate self-disclosure, a shared interaction that is seen as a "first date," or the occurrence of sex.[104] Such turning points might precipitate relationship talk: discussing roles and expectations, assessing the costs and rewards (benefits and risks), figuring out how to manage dialectical tensions (particularly the balance between autonomy and connectedness), and managing the relationship within each partner's social networks.

Expending extra effort at sustaining the relationship; increasing talk, interactions, and activities; offering support; engaging in positive behaviors; flirting; and talking about the relationship are ways we signal interest in moving to a romantic relationship.[105] We use such indirect methods because directly stating a desire for a romantic relationship can be face-threatening to both parties, and even constitute a failure event if it violates an agreement to remain platonic. The dilemma is further complicated by the fact that expressing such a desire might cause the loss of the friendship, while not expressing the desire might mean a missed opportunity for romance.[106] In such a situation, we might be better served by using *secret tests* to reduce uncertainty about our partner's feelings and to indirectly signal our interest.[107]

A **secret test** is a behavior strategically chosen to indirectly determine a partner's feelings, such as flirting to gauge his or her response. Other secret tests include making indirect suggestions (hinting or joking about becoming romantic); separation tests (decreasing or eliminating time together to see if we are missed, or not contacting our partner to see whether he or she will initiate contact); endurance tests (increasing demands on or costs to our partner to see whether he or she is willing to "pay" the price to sustain the relationship); and triangle tests (disclosing potential romantic relationships to test for jealousy, or determining our partner's interest in others to test his or her fidelity to us).[108] Each secret test is intended to determine our partner's interest in and commitment to the relationship, or openness to becoming romantic, while protecting our face and the relationship.

secret test

Behavior designed to indirectly determine a partner's feelings.

Dating

So when is a social interaction with someone considered just hanging out, and when is it a date? When you label an interaction with someone "a date," you are usually signaling an openness to a romantic relationship with the other person and a desire to change the expectations and roles. "Dating" tends to be the term for any ongoing romantic relationship that precedes "being engaged." Technology has become a factor in the dating process, with one study finding the following progression of steps leading to a date: Meet face to face, check out the other's Facebook page and make a friend request, request a phone number, begin texting and suggest hanging out in a group setting, post and engage in messaging on Facebook, and finally call or go on a

We can learn the skills that can help us reduce the interpersonal tensions that most of us feel at the start of a relationship.

date.[109] And if dating goes well, the relationship can become Facebook Official.

So what is a date? Maybe you've never been on one. Regardless of how you initiated and developed romantic relationships in high school and college, dates and dating play a significant role in the development of romantic relationships outside of school.

DATE GOALS   Given the limited number of dates college students experience, it is understandable that they would have different goals for and expectations of a date than would other single adults. Both groups see dates as activity-focused events involving couples sharing information to reduce uncertainty.[110] However, college students see dates as more social, more public, and more about attraction.[111] In contrast, single adults see dates as providing immediate enjoyment, potentially leading to a future relationship, being initiated by one person, and involving someone paying for an activity.[112] Sociologist Kathleen Bogle's interviews with recent college graduates found that they had abandoned hooking up for dating, which for many was the first time they actually had been on a date.[113] If you are among those who have not been on a formal date, then understanding dating dynamics and your partner's expectations should help reduce your uncertainties and anxiety.

REQUESTS FOR A DATE   Moving from being friends to going on a date involves different issues and concerns than does requesting a date with an acquaintance. Students in one study were asked to imagine asking out a classmate who might not even know their name.[114] The students reported they would feel anxiety, fear, and discomfort, but also excitement, a sense of pride in taking a risk, and a positive feeling for finally making the attempt. They hoped the other person would feel flattered and maybe good or great, but also saw the possibility for uncertainty, surprise, awkwardness (maybe even creepiness), or discomfort. Among the general concerns students expressed were the possibility of rejection, discovery that the other was already involved, uncertainty about what the person was really like, lack of reciprocal interest, and awkwardness in future class periods. Students also expressed concerns about their own physical attractiveness, as well as about appearing too pushy, too desperate, a "psycho," a fool or stupid, or a loser. These are probably the same concerns anyone would feel about asking out any acquaintance.

To actually ask someone for a date probably requires feeling that the risk is worth the potential loss of face, that the predicted outcome value of the relationship is high, and that your request will likely be accepted. Secret tests to reduce some uncertainty about the other person's interest in a date might include finding out what your mutual friends know about him or her, using affinity-seeking strategies (such as showing up at activities or parties you know the other person will be attending), or simply getting better acquainted before seeking a date. Our friends and family also affect whom we decide to date. An experimental study using a virtual dating game found that participants rated prospects higher when friends allegedly supported their choice more than when parents allegedly supported it. But disapproval of the choice by the friend or parent did not create a corresponding lower rating.[115] In essence, approval of a prospective date by our social network boosts the appeal of the date, but we tend to ignore disapproval.

DATES AND NONVERBAL CONFUSION   The indirect manner in which we often communicate, particularly when dating, causes misperceptions and awkwardness. Fear of rejection often holds us back from asking someone out. However, we fail to realize that person might not ask us out for the same reason—fear of rejection. Instead, we assume the person doesn't have interest in us,[116] an assumption based on potential misinterpretation of nonverbal cues. Another problem is that when women confirm their attraction and affection toward their dates with smiles and other positive nonverbal affiliative cues, men may read these behaviors as cues of sexual interest.[117]

To avoid such confusions, re-examine the suggestions for improving nonverbal sensitivity discussed in Chapter 7, while applying them to the dating context. Although when we begin to date, social norms discourage mutual discussion of thoughts and feelings about the new relationship, direct but tactful expression of interest, expectations, and goals by both parties can contribute to clarity and understanding.

DATE EXPECTATIONS How a date proceeds depends on your relationship with the other person prior to the date, the event that is the focus of the date (a concert, a movie, a party), the cost of the date, and who initiated the date. Nonetheless, one study found that respondents shared many of the same expectations for a first date.[118] These expectations, reflecting traditional gender roles, included men picking up the women and taking them home, as well as paying for the date, even if the women initiated the date.

In addition to engaging in the agreed-on activity (going to a movie, for coffee, to a party), a significant expectation is that dating partners will talk. Talk is an important component of a date because both partners understand the need to begin self-disclosing and gaining information about each other to reduce uncertainty. Following these cultural scripts or expectations while enacting socially defined sex roles may help reduce your anxiety as you get to know your date.[119]

As the date winds down, partners expect that there will be some discussion of future plans to call or text each other, an expression of interest in getting together again, and perhaps some discussion of another date. Neither partner wants to be put in a position of having to reject the other or be rejected after making a direct request, so in order to save each person's face, plans for the future are often rather vague. Following up a date with a text message within twenty-four hours seems to be a growing expectation among college students. Such a text might confirm that you had a good time and express your desire to get together again.

Relating to Diverse Others
Female and Male Dating Roles

According to custom in the United States, men are expected to take the initiative in asking women out. While certain taboos or negative impressions have been associated with women initiating dates, more women seem to be taking on this role.

Communication scholars Paul Mongeau, Jerold Hale, Kristin Johnson, and Jacqueline Hillis examined male-initiated versus female-initiated date requests. For one part of their study, they created four written scenarios describing a male asking a female out, a male or a female initiating the date request after hints from the other, and a female asking a male out. More than 400 student participants evaluated the females and males in these scenarios.

In comparison to the woman who waited for the man to ask her out, the woman who directly asked the man out was seen as more active, flexible, truthful, and extroverted; more of a feminist; more socially liberal; and less physically attractive (although no pictures were provided). Female students perceived the female initiator as more likeable and tactful than did the males.

What is your view of a woman who asks a man out for a first date? To what degree does your view differ if the woman asks the man to (a) go to a movie, (b) come over to her apartment for dinner, or (c) go to a party with her?

(Male students should answer these questions):

> Has a woman ever asked you out on a first date?
> How was your attitude toward her affected by her request?

(Female students should answer these questions):

> Have you ever asked a man out for a first date?
> How do you think the man's attitude toward you was affected by your request?
> If you haven't initiated a date with a man, how do you think a man would react if you did?

Survey five or six of your male and female friends and collect their answers to the above questions. How similar are their responses? To what degree do males and females agree or disagree?

SOURCE: P. A. Mongeau, J. L. Hale, K. L. Johnson, and J. D. Hillis. "Who's Wooing Whom? An Investigation of Female Initiated Dating," in P. J. Kalbleisch, Ed., *Interpersonal Communication: Evolving Interpersonal Relationships* (Hillsdale, NJ: Erlbaum, 1993), 51–68.

HOOKING UP AS AN ALTERNATIVE TO DATES If you are a typical college student between the ages of eighteen and twenty-one, then most of your experiences with the opposite sex have probably occurred in group interactions and as "hooking up." Sociologist Kathleen Bogle writes that hooking up has essentially replaced dating on college campuses.[120] Although the term *hooking up* has lots of meanings, generally students use it to describe a nonromantic, short-term physical encounter. Hooking up is like being friends with benefits, but without the friendship requirement. The level of physical intimacy ranges from kissing to sexual intercourse, and the interaction is generally without attachment, although some students, particularly women, report hoping for more.[121] Bogle found that most hookups were not one-night stands or "randoms" with strangers, but rather encounters between friends or classmates, often preceded by the consumption of alcohol. Although it happens infrequently, hookups *can* lead to romantic relationships, particularly if the hookup produced a positive emotional experience for both partners, there was some small talk and talk of future interactions, and both had similar motivations.[122]

Unrequited Romantic Interest (URI)

unrequited romantic interest
Feelings created when one partner desires a more intimate, romantic relationship than the other partner would like.

Unrequited romantic interest (URI) occurs when one partner desires a more intimate, romantic relationship than the other partner would like. Examples of URI include when an acquaintance's desire for friendship or romance is rejected, a cross-sex friend's desire to move toward romance is rebuffed, or when a romantic partner's desire for greater intimacy is not reciprocated.

One study of college students found that unrequited romantic interest between friends was fairly common, leading to feelings of awkwardness and embarrassment. When students expressed their romantic interest, over half the relationships actually ended because both partners felt embarrassed or awkward, the rejected partner felt hurt, and the other partner felt pressured to act differently.[123] In friendships that persevered, both partners worked toward maintaining the friendship; the friendship was solid, long-established, open, and honest; and the partner who wanted more accepted that the feelings were not mutual. The results of this study suggest what you might do to preserve a friendship if your expression of romantic interest is not reciprocated:[124]

1. Affirm the importance of the friendship to you and continue to work on it.
2. Tell your partner you accept his or her position and then drop the issue.
3. To reduce embarrassment and awkwardness, try to go back to old relational patterns.
4. Avoid pressuring your partner to feel more than he or she does: Don't flirt with him or her, accept his or her interest in others, and give up on developing a romantic relationship.
5. Don't complain about the difference in feelings.
6. Don't suggest that maybe the relationship can be romantic sometime in the future.
7. Don't tell other friends about what happened.

On the other hand, how should you handle someone else's overtures to you if you don't feel the same way? People in this position tend to use either (1) indirect strategies—being rude or ambiguous or avoiding the other person; (2) a direct strategy without justification—simply stating a lack of reciprocal feelings; (3) a direct strategy of blaming themselves while stating lack of mutual interest ("I'm just not ready for a romantic relationship right now"); or (4) a direct strategy of blaming external factors while indicating a lack of interest ("I'm involved with someone else").[125] Which of those strategies would you want your partner to use? Which have you used or would you most likely use?

A study in which college students recalled times they expressed interest in developing a romantic relationship found that the results differed depending on whether the relationship was initially a friendship or was a romantic relationship that one person wished to deepen.[126] The indirect strategy was found to be the least desirable

#communicationandtechnology

Friendship, Romance, and the Internet

Electronically mediated communication (EMC) provides avenues for initiating, maintaining, and ending both friendships and romantic relationships. Social networking sites in particular provide opportunities for greatly expanding your network to include new people with whom you connect through listings of mutual friends. In a 2014 survey of adult Internet users, 71 percent used Facebook, 28 percent LinkedIn, 28 percent Pinterest, 26 percent Instagram, and 23 percent Twitter.[127] As of 2014, 91 percent of eighteen- to twenty-nine-year-olds had social networking on their smartphones.[128] In a 2013 survey of eighteen- to twenty-nine-year-olds, for those in serious relationships, 41 percent felt closer as a result of conversations online or texting, and 23 percent of those struggling with an argument resolved it through EMC. On the negative side, 42 percent reported a partner being distracted by his or her cell phone when they were together, and 18 percent had arguments about the amount of time a partner spent online.[129]

Your Facebook profile provides information (some of which you might not even realize you are revealing) that affects others' impressions of you and that might either enhance or detract from a friendship. You might recall the study discussed in Chapter 3 that found that with everything else constant, a person whose profile included 302 friends was rated as more socially attractive than people reporting 102, 502, 702, or 902 friends.[130] Those with 102 friends (who were perhaps seen as too aloof) and those with 902 friends (who were perhaps regarded as too indiscriminate) were the least attractive. Those with 502 friends were seen as the most extroverted, and those with 102 or 302 friends were seen as the least.

In face-to-face (FtF) interactions, you control and tailor what you disclose, withholding information from those you are less interested in. Your online profile also involves self-disclosing, and you choose what to include or exclude—relationship status, attitudes, beliefs, interests, names of clubs or organizations you belong to, your online group memberships, pictures, video clips, and quiz results, among other information. Your ability to deliberate, edit, and filter your messages in EMC interactions gives you greater control of information than when you are face to face.[131] However, unlike your tailored, FtF disclosures, the information in your online profile is not restricted. Your wall and your posts are visible to anyone you accept as a friend. And those people can cut and paste any of that information and circulate it freely to others. In addition, Facebook itself analyzes your information. For example, Facebook data found that on Valentine's Day 49 percent more relationships were listed as new than as broken off. The day after Valentine's Day resulted in a 22 percent increase, Christmas Eve 28 percent, and Christmas Day 34 percent.[132]

Can you form intimate romantic relationships strictly through the Internet? Factors that work against such a relationship include the absence of information gained from social interaction; having so many potential partners, which reduces our willingness to commit to one; and idealized and unrealistic expectations created by extensive EMC before meeting FtF.[133] However, assuming an open and honest exchange of information, individuals can learn enough through EMC to establish intimacy. Almost everyone knows of someone who has gotten married to a person he or she met through the Internet. Online dating services have grown in popularity perhaps because they provide easy access to a large pool of potential partners and a means of judging initial compatibility before meeting FtF. Creating an appealing profile often leads online daters to present inaccurate information and photos. In one study, 81 percent of online daters lied about their weight (the most frequent deception), age, or height but just enough to enhance their attractiveness.[134]

Friends can also act as go-betweens in facilitating matches, suggesting an e-mail exchange or instant messaging that allows individuals to share information and engage in casual banter before moving to the exploration stage of the relationship. Online networks such as Facebook can also allow people to initiate romantic relationships.

Satisfaction with online romantic relationships is affected by such factors as trust, intimacy (perceived closeness), and communication satisfaction (measured by enjoyment of conversations, perceived ease of conversations, interest, and ability to say what one wants).[135] You can easily see why communication satisfaction is a key element, since such EMC-based romantic relationships are so dependent on effective and satisfying communication in the absence of shared activities or direct observation of behaviors.[136] The more times online romantic couples communicate during the week, the more they appear to experience communication satisfaction, trust, intimacy, commitment, similarity, and ability to predict their partners' behaviors.[137] Couples in relationships primarily or exclusively maintained on the Internet report using openness (self-disclosing, providing and seeking advice, and talking about the relationship) and positivity (being cheerful and making the interactions pleasant) to maintain their relationships.[138]

strategy for rejecting a friend's attempt to escalate the relationship, since it was seen as inappropriate. Similarly, blaming external factors was found to be undesirable for rejecting a romantic partner's attempt to escalate the relationship, perhaps because people don't expect a romantic partner to be evasive.

Interestingly, students accepted rejection of their attempts to escalate friendships better than rejection of their attempts to escalate romantic relationships. We probably have expectations that romantic relationships will escalate as part of the relational development process, so rejection of escalation is unexpected and disappointing.

Regardless of whether you are the one whose effort to escalate a relationship is rejected or the one rejecting another's request, you both need to assess the type of relationship you are willing to accept and decide whether such a relationship is possible, knowing that one of you feels more romantically inclined than the other.

Interpersonal Relationship Strategies

11.3 Describe the strategies used to initiate, escalate, and maintain relationships.

So far, this chapter has focused on the nature of friendship and romantic relationships. Now the focus shifts to discussing specific strategies for starting, escalating, and maintaining those relationships. The strategies described are not fail-safe, and the lists provided are not complete—they are intended primarily to stimulate consideration of your own thoughts and behaviors as you develop new relationships. Some strategies are better suited for developing friendships and others for romance, but the foundations for both are similar.

When you meet someone you initially like, how do you go about fostering a friendship or a romance? Once you have established a relationship, how do you ensure that it remains healthy and at the level of intimacy with which you are most comfortable? We'll provide strategies you can use to address these questions. First, we'll discuss strategies used primarily to initiate interaction. Then, we'll cover strategies used in both initiating and escalating relationships. Finally, we'll focus on strategies used in either maintaining a relationship or increasing intimacy in an established relationship.

Strategies Used Primarily to Initiate a Relationship

Two paths for beginning a relationship were presented in the model of relational development in Chapter 9. One begins with interacting with a complete stranger for the very first time, and the other begins with observing and forming an initial impression of the other person before interacting (pre-interaction awareness). We'll present strategies you can employ on either path.

OBSERVE AND ACT ON APPROACHABILITY CUES Subway riders around the world learn to avoid eye contact because it is a signal of approachability. But if you want to approach someone or be approached, establishing eye contact is a good start. Besides making eye contact, you can signal approachability by turning toward another person, smiling, being animated, saying hello, using an open body posture, winking, and waving. Conversely, the absence of these cues generally conveys a desire to be left alone.

IDENTIFY AND USE CONVERSATION STARTERS By being observant, you can identify a certain amount of "free" information that you can use as a starting point for a conversation. If someone is walking a dog of the same breed as your childhood pet, you can open a conversation by commenting on some peculiarity of the breed. If someone is carrying a book from a class you took last semester, you might ask how the course is going. Logos on T-shirts, tags or stickers on backpacks, or even tattoos can be conversation starters. No perfect line exists for beginning a conversation, so directness is probably your best bet.[139]

FOLLOW INITIATION NORMS   Many of the initial interactions in a relationship are almost ritualistic, or at least scripted. In the United States, when two strangers meet, they typically follow the same general pattern of conversation:[140] greetings; introductions; and discussion of initial topics such as the weather, hometown, majors, education, or occupations; followed by discussion of general topics such as sports, TV, movies, or family. If the conversation goes well, they might discuss getting together and exchange contact information, and then end with typical pleasantries, closing the conversation, and saying goodbye. As you follow the script, take advantage of opportunities to expand and develop the conversation in safe ways. Listen for details about the person's background and interests that you can inquire about, and share information about your own interests.

Following a script provides some comfort and security because it reduces the uncertainties associated with meeting a stranger; deviating from the script might increase uncertainty and become a turnoff. For example, you might be leery of continuing an interaction with a stranger who follows "Hi. How's it going?" with "Don't you agree that television is becoming the vast wasteland of American intellect, draining the very life blood of our youth?"

"I just said how are you - I didn't think you'd get on the bus to tell me."

Geoff McNeill/CartoonStock.com

ASK QUESTIONS   The very act of asking questions can enhance your partner's attraction to you.[141] Asking questions shows your interest in the other person and promotes reciprocity of liking, allowing you to gain information, reduce uncertainty, and improve your ability to adapt to your partner.

Ask open-ended questions that invite elaboration and discussion, and learn to ask meaningful follow-up or probing questions without appearing to interrogate the other person. Starting with impersonal, specific questions, often about the circumstance or surroundings, encourages a response by reducing a person's reluctance to answer (for example, while standing in a movie line, you might ask "Have you heard any reviews of this movie?"). After the initial question, advance the conversation by asking open-ended and encompassing questions related to his or her answer ("What did the reviewers have to say?").

Short responses without any reciprocal questions may be a signal that the person you're talking to is not particularly interested in interacting. If so, you're probably better off not pursuing the interaction any further. Usually, however, the other person will also ask you questions. Be open and provide information about yourself that is relevant to the questions.

Strategies Used to Initiate and/or Escalate Relationships

"No kidding! I love chocolate-covered strawberries, too." "It's nice to be able to talk to someone else who's a fan of *Modern Family*." Statements like these emphasize commonalities and are used to encourage a listener to like the speaker (*affinity seeking*). We sometimes make these types of statements when we are first getting to know someone, but we also use such statements when trying to escalate a relationship. Trying to increase someone's attraction to us is just one strategy that is common to both the initiation and the escalation of interpersonal relationships.

COMMUNICATE AND CULTIVATE ATTRACTION   Communicating your attraction to someone increases the likelihood that your partner will reciprocate, thus cultivating his or her attraction to you. You can also communicate liking through indirect strategies such as nonverbal immediacy. For instance, you might sit closer to

BEING Other-ORIENTED

A lack of specific knowledge about a new acquaintance means that being other-oriented involves drawing on your own thoughts, feelings, and perspective to understand the other person, and/or drawing on your understanding of people in general. Which of the affinity-seeking strategies listed in Table 11.1 would raise your attraction to another person the most? Which do you believe would raise the attraction of other people in general the most? Which information are you most comfortable disclosing? Which information do you think most people in general are comfortable disclosing? What do you want to learn initially to reduce your uncertainties? What do you think most people want to learn?

affinity-seeking strategies

Strategies we use to increase others' liking us.

someone, make more eye contact, increase your touching, lean forward, and smile more. Or you might use such direct verbal strategies as more informal and personal language, the person's first name, and increased use of "you and I" and "we." Simply spending time talking is another way to show interest and commitment. You display and cultivate interest by asking questions and probing for details, listening responsively, and referring to previously shared information. All these behaviors confirm that you value the other person and what he or she is saying, which can be very rewarding. These behaviors also serve as part of *strategic self-presentation* by which you present yourself as a desirable partner.[142] A more subtle approach would be to offer a compliment, such as praise for a particular trait or ability, outfit, hairstyle, or the way the person handled an irritating customer. Table 11.1 lists other ways you might try to encourage another person to like you more through the use of **affinity-seeking strategies**.[143] Displaying nonverbal immediacy cues and verbally confirming the other person not only communicate your attraction but also increase the probability that he or she will like you.

BE OPEN AND SELF-DISCLOSE APPROPRIATELY Your self-disclosure helps your partner make informed decisions about initiating or escalating a relationship with you (predicted outcome value). Even if you have enough information about your partner and want to escalate the relationship, your partner might not know enough about you. Chapter 9 discussed the need for mutual self-disclosure to form a truly intimate relationship. A partner's openness to self-disclose has been identified as the most important factor contributing to the development and sustainment of relationships.[144]

TABLE 11.1 Affinity-Seeking Strategies

	Strategies	Examples
1. Control	Present yourself as in control, independent, free-thinking; show that you have the ability to reward the other person.	• "I'm planning on going to grad school, and after that I'm going to Japan to teach English." • "You can borrow my notes for the class you missed if you'd like."
2. Visibility	Look and dress attractively; present yourself as an interesting, energetic, and enthusiastic person; increase your visibility to the other person.	• "Wow, that was a great show about Chinese acrobats. I'm a gymnast too. You should come watch our next meet."
3. Mutual Trust	Present yourself as honest and reliable; display trustworthy behaviors; self-disclose to show that you trust the other person.	• "I don't usually talk to people about this, but I'm adopted and have always hoped I could find my birth parents."
4. Politeness	Follow appropriate conversational rules; let the other person assume control of the interaction.	• "I'm sorry I interrupted. I thought you were done. Please, go on." • "No, you're not boring me at all; it's very interesting. What happened next?"
5. Concern and Caring	Show interest in and ask questions about the other person; listen; show support and be sensitive; help the other person accomplish something or feel good about himself or herself.	• "How is your mother doing after her operation?" • "I'd like to help out at the benefit you're chairing this weekend."
6. Other-Involvement	Put a positive spin on activities you share; draw the other person into your activities; display nonverbal immediacy and involvement with the other person.	• "This is a great party. I'm glad you came." • "A group of us are going to get a midnight snack; how about coming along?"
7. Self-Involvement	Try to arrange for encounters and interactions; engage in behaviors that encourage the other person to form a closer relationship.	• "Oh, hi! I was hoping I'd run into you here." • "It would really be fun to go camping together this summer; I have this favorite place."
8. Commonalities	Point out similarities between yourself and the other person; try to establish equality (balanced power); present yourself as comfortable and at ease around the other person.	• "I've got that computer game, too. Don't you love the robots?" • "Let's work on the project together. We're a great team." • "I really enjoy talking with you. It's nice to find someone with so much in common."

SOURCE: Adapted from R. A. Bell and J. A. Daly, "The Affinity Seeking Function of Communication," *Communication Monographs* 51 (1984): 91–115.

The depth of self-disclosure needs to be appropriate to the intimacy level of the relationship, and the timing of disclosures requires sensitivity from both partners. On the other hand, restricting self-disclosure is one way to control the development of a relationship. For example, you can reduce how much you are self-disclosing if you feel a relationship is moving too fast.

GATHER INFORMATION TO REDUCE UNCERTAINTY   We all feel uneasy and uncertain when faced with the unknown, the unexpected, or the unpredictable. According to **uncertainty reduction theory**, we want control and predictability in our lives; therefore we are driven to gain information to reduce that uncertainty.[145] Generally, gaining information about a partner increases our ability to predict his or her thoughts and behaviors—we know what to expect, thus reducing the inherent stress. We are particularly motivated to gain information early in a relationship, when uncertainty is the greatest and we are trying to evaluate the relationship potential—its predicted outcome value.[146]

uncertainty reduction theory
Theory that claims people seek information in order to reduce uncertainty, thus achieving control and predictability.

Technology can play a role in reducing our uncertainties; for example, we use Facebook to learn about people. Participants in one study reported less relational uncertainty with more frequent and longer voice calls, but text messaging had no relationship to reducing uncertainty.[147] In another study on romantic relationships among college students, uncertainty about a partner's feelings or the definition of the relationship related to increased monitoring of the partner's Facebook page.[148] But researchers observed that the public nature of Facebook appeared to restrict the use of relational maintenance strategies that involved expressing assurance or feelings toward the partner.

Sometimes we experience uncertainty about the very nature and definition of our relationships and our partners' regard for us. Such uncertainty can hamper the development, escalation, and maintenance of those relationships. What does your new friend think about the relationship? How intimate a relationship does your boyfriend or girlfriend want? Why hasn't your best friend called you in the last two weeks? The most obvious approach to addressing these questions would be simply to ask the other person; however, we risk "losing face" when using such direct strategies. At times, uncertainty is preferable to certainty—for example, uncertainty about your romantic partner's desire to end the relationship can be preferable to finding out for sure. Relationship researchers Leanne Knobloch and Jennifer Theiss found that uncertainty about relationships was associated with less talk about the relationship. On the other hand, engaging in relationship talk one week was followed by less relational uncertainty the next.[149] Despite learning that your partner is considering ending your relationship, you should think about engaging in talk to reduce uncertainties and strengthen the relationship. In general, the less relational uncertainty you have, the greater the relationship satisfaction.[150]

LISTEN ACTIVELY AND RESPOND EFFECTIVELY   As you learned in Chapter 5, listening is critical to effective interpersonal communication and relationships. Listening clues you in to people's needs, wants, and values. It enables you to respond to people in appropriate ways and demonstrates your ongoing interest in them. In all relationships, no matter how intimate, it is always important to stop, look, and listen—to put down the newspaper or turn off your iPod when your friend begins talking to you. You particularly need to engage in empathic listening and effective responding, as discussed in Chapter 5. Your confirming responses increase your partner's sense of self-worth and communicate the value you place on him or her and the relationship.

SOCIALLY DECENTER AND ADOPT AN OTHER-ORIENTED PERSPECTIVE
Social decentering helps you better understand your partner, and that understanding allows you to choose effective strategies for accomplishing your communication goals, adapting to your partner's current behavior, and anticipating his or her

relationship-specific social decentering

Other-oriented skills based on the knowledge and understanding gained in a specific intimate relationship.

responses. For example, social decentering can help you decide when to disclose information about your previous romantic relationships to the person you've just begun to date.

Even individuals weak in general social decentering skills can develop **relationship-specific social decentering**—decentering skills based on the knowledge and understanding they gained about a specific relational partner. Studies conducted by one of your authors found that the more intimate the relationship, the higher the respondents' relationship-specific social decentering scores were, and the higher the relational satisfaction reported by both partners was.[151] Underlying our intimate relationships is the expectation that our partner understands and treats us in a manner that reflects that understanding. In another study on reactions to beliefs that romantic partners should understand about each other ("mind reading"), respondents became upset when their partners failed to recognize the emotional impact of the partners' behaviors on the respondents.[152] For example, after getting angry with your partner for not doing the dishes as agreed, you are likely to get even more upset if you find that your partner didn't realize she or he had made you angry. Repeated failure to display relationship-specific social decentering behavior is likely to contribute to relational dissatisfaction. As you develop intimate relationships, your interactions with your partners should reflect your understanding and appreciation of their thoughts, feelings, and needs. You might convey such understanding by expressing agreement that reflects shared understanding with your partner, being attentive and nonverbally involved, and providing positive affirmation (showing consideration, kindness, and respect).[153]

Strategies Used to Escalate and/or Maintain Relationships

To escalate or maintain a relationship requires time, effort, and a commitment to the relationship. One research study found that time spent playing video games was related to less relational maintenance, which can result in deterioration of the relationship.[154] However, low relational satisfaction might lead to seeking escape in video game playing and less relational maintenance. If you want to escalate or maintain a relationship, be careful about how much time you devote to playing video games and instead work to develop and apply these skills and strategies.

EXPRESS EMOTIONS Expressing emotions is a particular form of self-disclosure—sometimes the most intimate kind—which is why trust and commitment usually must be established before certain feelings can be shared. You might be uncomfortable expressing your feelings, but in order for a relationship to fully develop, you will need to share them. The more intimate the relationship, the higher the expectation and need for sharing feelings. You might show your love for someone by your behaviors, but your partner might need you to actually declare your love; the words "I love you" are powerful and enduring.

Many of the emotions you share are not related to your partner, such as your sadness over the death of a family member or fears about what you'll do after graduation. Other feelings relate to your partner—feelings of attraction, love, anger, or disappointment. Most of us are comfortable sharing positive emotions, such as happiness and joy, but are more reserved about sharing negative emotions, such as fear or disappointment, because we worry that we might appear weak or vulnerable. In a study of 46 committed, romantic couples, the participants reported that the number-one communication problem was partners' withholding the expression of negative feelings ("When she gets upset, she stops talking" or "He just silently pouts").[155] We generally want to know how our intimate partners are feeling, even if those feelings are negative.

However, a constant barrage of negative expressions can also alienate a partner. Not surprisingly, research has found that marital satisfaction rises with the number of positive feelings the partners disclose, not with the number of negative ones.[156] Happy couples tend to display their positive emotional state in their smiles, laughs, and affectionate behavior; distressed couples display agitation, anger, and coldness.[157] Sharing positive experiences with attentive partners boosts the positive effects of those experiences and results in greater happiness and feelings of satisfaction with life.[158] You, your partner, and your relationship benefit when each of you shares good news and the other revels in a partner's good fortune. Make an effort to share *both* your positive and negative feelings, keeping in mind the need to present an overall positive disposition.

PROVIDE COMFORT AND SOCIAL SUPPORT   The ability to provide comfort, social support, and ego support is a quality associated with being a best friend.[159] We expect to be able to turn to our friends to help us through emotionally trying events. Offering social support and comfort not only directly benefits the partner but also confirms the value of the relationship and the partner. Communication scholar Brant Burleson found that being other-oriented was a key factor in being able to offer effective comforting messages. Other-oriented comforting messages confirm and accept the other person's feelings, help him or her express and examine those feelings, and help put the feelings into a broader context.[160] One research study found three outcomes of comforting messages: (1) they put the distressed person in a more positive mood, (2) they empower the person to better manage the issues, and (3) they help reduce brooding (rumination) about the problems.[161]

Providing social and emotional support can be challenging. Sometimes our attempts even make the situation worse and/or negatively affect the other person's self-esteem.[162] For example, providing support might undermine the other person's self-esteem and autonomy, create undue focus on stressors, increase stress by creating a sense of indebtedness ("Now I owe you"), or be perceived as criticism or interference.[163] Displaying empathy to a distressed friend by sharing your similar experiences can provide some insight, but it also risks disconfirming your friend because you have changed the discussion to focus on you and your life. Use social decentering to consider what you'd like to hear if you were in the other person's situation, while adapting to differences between you and the other person. What is comforting to one person can be threatening to another.

One pair of researchers, Ruth Ann Clark and Jesse Delia, studied how people wanted to be treated by their friends in six different distressing situations.[164] Clark and Delia found that people did not have a strong desire to talk about the situations. When people were distressed, they wanted to be the ones to decide whether to bring up the issue. And they wanted their friends to keep attempts at comforting short. Sometimes the best support involves saying nothing at all, but simply being with the other person or providing a hug.

Another study identified three comforting behaviors that also help maintain a distressed person's face: (1) encouraging the partner to express and discuss feelings, (2) recognizing and praising the efforts already being made by the partner to cope with the problem, and (3) being pleasant and respecting the partner's autonomy to make decisions—not taking over control.[165] Think about how you might integrate these behaviors into your own comforting support.

A friend or romantic partner who is chronically insecure (high attachment anxiety or low self-esteem) can benefit from ego support. Sensitivity and vigilance are needed to monitor such chronically insecure individuals and provide timely support.[166] Exaggerated affection can also lead them

Well-adjusted couples display support and affection for each other through positive nonverbal cues.

to feel more valued.[167] However, providing such support requires a commitment that we sometimes don't feel, as well as a willingness to be deceptive (exaggerating feelings) that we can't sustain and that can result in ending the relationship.[168] Providing support and comfort to others requires skill and is a testament to your commitment to them. Being able to both revel in your partner's positive news and provide support during the bad times would be the ideal, but doing both is challenging. Fortunately, the ability to do one well appears to offset weakness in the other since either demonstrates your interest and commitment in your partner.[169] Showing your partner that you feel excited by his or her good news can offset your weaker responses to his or her problems.

COMMUNICATE AND ENGAGE IN RELATIONSHIP TALK   The very act of interacting with someone helps maintain the relationship by confirming the value of the person and the relationship. For example, on Facebook, we expect our closest friends to actively post on our wall, comment on our photos, and chat with us online and in person.[170] A study found that decreased talking on the phone and e-mailing between friends before and after one moved away related to decreased closeness, increased calling related to increased closeness, and sustained or increased e-mailing maintained closeness.[171]

relationship talk

Talk about the nature, quality, direction, or definition of a relationship.

Relationship talk is conversation about the nature, quality, direction, or definition of a relationship. For example, "I'm happy with how close we've become. How are you feeling about the relationship?" or "Since I'm about to graduate, it doesn't make too much sense for me to get very involved right now." Although relationship talk is generally considered inappropriate in the early stages of a relationship, as relationships move toward greater intimacy, the amount of direct relationship talk increases as does the expectation for such talk. Willingness to talk about the relationship is one way to implicitly signal your level of interest and commitment. One study of cross-sex friendships found that those in which both partners had an interest in becoming romantic included more relational talk than those in which the friends wished to maintain a platonic relationship.[172] In more intimate relationships, you are likely to discuss the future of the relationship, how to manage the relationship during summer break, or what will happen to the relationship after graduation. In more intimate relationships, relationship talk at this stage also helps the partners resolve differences in their perceptions of the relationship that might be contributing to conflict and dissatisfaction. Although it can be difficult, expressing your concerns about whether you want the relationship to escalate or de-escalate might be unavoidable. Unwillingness to engage in relationship talk in an intimate relationship can send a negative message that ultimately drives a partner away.

Relational talk appears to be viewed differently by men and women. Men tend to view talk as an instrumental way to fix problems. While women might share this view, they also see relationship talk as part of the routine for maintaining the relationship.[173]

In a recent study, college students in romantic relationships evaluated the degree to which they engaged in "relationship work" when talking with their partners or best friends.[174] Relationship work includes how often partners discuss relationship problems and concerns related to how well they communicate, how they make decisions, financial concerns, getting along with each other's families, and how they spend their free time together. Engaging in relationship talk with a partner was directly related to higher levels of happiness, commitment, and love. Talking about relationship concerns with a best friend and not the romantic partner related to less happiness, commitment, and love. For males, talking to both a best friend and their romantic partner related most strongly to happiness, commitment, and love. Relationship talk with our romantic partners shows commitment and a willingness to address issues, and ultimately strengthens the relationship.

BE TOLERANT AND TACTFUL   The most satisfying relationships are those in which partners learn to accept each other and refrain from continually disagreeing, criticizing, pointing out flaws or failures, and making negative comments to each other. One study found that well-adjusted couples focus their complaints on specific behaviors, whereas maladjusted couples complain about each other's personal characteristics.[175] Another study found that when people want their partner to make a specific change, being forthright and direct produces the desired change over time, particularly when the partner responds in a positive and tactful manner.[176] Partners expect honesty and directness, but also tact—which involves requesting a change while respecting the other person's face and feelings.

Well-adjusted couples are kinder, more positive, and have more humor in their interactions. They tend to agree with each other's complaints: "You're right, honey, I wasn't listening—let me turn the TV off so I won't be distracted," whereas partners in maladjusted relationships launch counter-complaints: "I *was* listening!—you just chatter on and on about the same garbage!" In addition, happy couples demonstrate more affection through positive nonverbal cues, display more supportive behaviors, and make more attempts to avoid conflict than unhappy couples do.[177] Maintaining relationships requires tolerance and tact. You must learn to accept your partner for who he or she is, put up with some things you dislike, and tactfully manage necessary changes.

MANAGE CONFLICT COOPERATIVELY   Conflicts are inevitable in interpersonal relationships. As relationships develop, individuals share more personal information and spend more time together, so the likelihood for conflict increases. The key to successful relational development and maintenance is not to avoid conflict, but rather to manage it effectively. As we discussed in Chapter 8, a collaborative management style can actually transform conflict into an experience that strengthens a relationship. It can clarify the definition of a relationship, increase the exchange of information, and create a collaborative atmosphere for problem solving. Constructive conflicts in good-quality relationships can produce benefits; destructive conflicts in poor-quality relationships can be detrimental.[178]

Recap

Interpersonal Relationship Strategies

Strategies Used Primarily to Initiate a Relationship

- Observe and act on approachability cues
- Ask questions
- Identify and use conversation starters
- Don't expect too much from the initial interaction
- Follow initiation norms

Strategies Used to Initiate and/or Escalate Relationships

- Communicate and cultivate attraction
- Listen actively and respond effectively
- Be open and self-disclose appropriately
- Socially decenter and adopt an other-oriented perspective
- Gather information to reduce uncertainty

Strategies Used to Escalate and/or Maintain Relationships

- Express emotions
- Be tolerant and tactful
- Provide comfort and social support
- Manage conflict cooperatively
- Communicate and engage in relationship talk

Applying an Other-Orientation

to Friends and Romantic Partners

As you develop friendships and romantic relationships, you continue to gain more information about your partners—about their beliefs, values, attitudes, needs, interests, desires, fears, and hopes. This accumulation of knowledge provides the foundation for a better understanding and ability to predict your partners' behaviors and reactions (relationship-specific social decentering), and it also creates the expectation that you will anticipate and adapt to the person's behaviors and needs. From a partner's perspective, it is a failure event when you don't incorporate your accumulated knowledge and understanding of your partner into your actions. For example, forgetting that your friend dislikes horror movies when you choose one for your weekly Friday night movie is likely to evoke a comment such as "But you know I hate horror movies; I can't believe you picked it anyway." Imagine the impact on a relationship of frequently committing such failure events. Your partner might interpret your failure to be other-oriented and to adapt as a lack of caring and concern for his or her needs and desires, or as a move toward withdrawing from the relationship.

On the other hand, increasing knowledge about your friends and romantic partners improves your ability to adapt to their behavior and to anticipate responses. Knowledge of your closest same-sex friend and closest cross-sex friend should lead you to unique interpretations of their behaviors and to adaptation of your behavior, particularly in your selection of relevant communication strategies. Such empowerment does not necessarily mean greater relational satisfaction. For example, understanding that your romantic partner's discomfort with physical affection is a result of his or her upbringing won't necessarily offset your own desire for physical affection.

The most significant challenge to being other-oriented in our friendships and romances is overcoming egocentric biases or distorted perceptions of our friends and lovers. In essence, we make errors in our mind reading of others. The perceptual barriers identified in Chapter 3 undermine your ability to gain the accurate information needed to be other-oriented.

Another error occurs when you assume similarities between yourself and your partner that don't really exist. Assuming similarity leads to projecting your feelings, motivations, and needs on your partner, which leads to errors when relevant differences are unaccounted for. On the other hand, when you and your partner are indeed similar, then such projecting can provide accurate understanding.

A final barrier to effective other-orientation occurs when your perspective and your feelings are so strong that they prevent you from accurately recognizing your partner's perspective and feelings.[179] For example, after discovering that your partner has cheated on you, the weight of your emotional pain can prevent you from understanding your romantic partner's perspective. You might not even be motivated to try. Ultimately, the application of any other-orientation to your friendships and romantic relationships requires a motivation to do so.

STUDY GUIDE
Review, Apply, and Assess

Friendship

Objective 11.1 Understand the nature of friendships across our lifespan, same-sex friendships, and cross-sex (opposite-sex) friendships.

Key Terms

friendship-based intimacy
passion-based intimacy
friendship

Thinking Critically

What qualities are most important to you in a friend? Why?

Assessing Your Skills

Identify three friends: a close same-sex friend of a similar age as you; a close cross-sex friend of a similar age; and an interracial, intercultural, or intergenerational friend.

What values to you do these relationships share? What values are unique to each friendship? Which friendship is the easiest to manage? Why? Which is the most difficult? Why?

Romantic Relationships

Objective 11.2 Explain how love, commitment, and physical affection define romantic relationships, and describe how such relationships are developed through dating.

Key Terms

triangular theory of love	pragma
compassionate love	agape
eros	commitment
ludus	physical affection
storge	secret test
mania	unrequited romantic interest

Thinking Critically

Write a short answer to the question "What is love?" within the context of a romantic relationship. Why is defining love so difficult? How well do you think you know what love is? Why is love so important to humans?

Assessing Your Skills

Evaluate two of your romantic relationships, regardless of their level of intimacy, using the triangular theory of love. For a previous relationship, evaluate the relationship at its closest and most satisfying time. Assign a score of 1 (low) to 10 (high) for each of the three dimensions: commitment, intimacy, and passion. How do the two relationships compare? How did the differences in the dimensions affect the communication and behaviors? How easy or difficult was it for you to rate each dimension? Why?

Interpersonal Relationship Strategies

Objective 11.3 **Describe the strategies used to initiate, escalate, and maintain relationships.**

Key Terms

affinity-seeking strategies
uncertainty reduction theory

relationship-specific social decentering
relationship talk

Thinking Critically

Of all the interpersonal relationship strategies, which three are the most important? Why? Which three are the least important? Why?

Assessing Your Skills

Describe two conversations you began with strangers that you think were successful. What made them successful? What was the outcome? Describe two conversations with strangers that you think were unsuccessful. What made them unsuccessful? Compare your responses to those of your classmates. To what degree are your answers similar or different? What did they do well that you could try? What did you learn to avoid?

Chapter 12
Interpersonal Relationships: Family and Workplace

"Family isn't about whose blood you have. It's about who you care about. And that's why I feel like you guys are more than just friends. You're my family. Except for Cartman."

Kyle, South Park

CHAPTER OUTLINE	Learning Objectives
Family Relationships	**12.1** Identify and describe the types of families, the models used to describe family interactions, the ways to improve family communication, and the types of relationships among married couples and siblings.
Workplace Relationships	**12.2** Describe the values and functions of workplace friendships, the unique values and challenges associated with romantic relationships in the workplace, and the types of formal relationships and communication in the workplace.

Think about the progression of relationships that you experience in your life: It starts with family and ends with family. In between, there's school for a few years and then work for quite a few more. You are born into a family—your first relationships are with your mother, father, siblings, grandparents, aunts and uncles, and cousins. And the longest-lasting relationships that you experience are with your siblings—longer than those with your parents or spouse. Outside the family, you form other important relationships—friendships and romantic relationships. Your workplace becomes one of the major contexts where such relationships develop. This chapter focuses on family and workplace relationships.

Whereas marriage is a relationship of choice, families create relationships of circumstance. But the friendships you develop with some family members represent a change to relationships of choice. Similarly, workplace relationships with a boss, coworkers, or clients begin as relationships of circumstance but can also become relationships of choice if they develop into friendships or romantic relationships. In such instances, balancing professional responsibilities with interpersonal interests requires sensitivity and skill.

Family Relationships

12.1 **Identify and describe the types of families, the models used to describe family interactions, the ways to improve family communication, and the types of relationships among married couples and siblings.**

Families have changed since your parents and grandparents were children. At one time, almost two-thirds of American families consisted of a working father, a stay-at-home mother, and at least two biological children. Today, according to the U.S. Bureau of the Census, only about 10 percent of all American families fit that description. A number of factors have dramatically altered the nature of American families: divorce, single-parent families, mothers with careers outside the home, the longer wait to start families, the move from an agrarian to an industrial society, and increased mobility. Communication within the family has changed too. The way family members interact with one another has been altered by a variety of social influences, including electronically mediated communication.

Like many other entities covered in this book, families are dynamic and changing. As the members of a family get older, roles and relationships change. In addition, families add members and lose others. As new children are born, or as a member moves out of the home, the dynamics of the family change. Ultimately, what is true of a family at one moment in time may not hold true later. You have experienced change in your own family as you have become older and gone from being very dependent on your parents to becoming more independent. As you get older, you may discover that your relationship with your parents continues to change, perhaps to the point where you may end up providing care for them. As you consider your family experiences and the prospect of starting your own family, apply the principles we discuss in this chapter and remember above all to monitor your family relationships, recognize changes, and adapt accordingly.

Family Defined

Because families are basic to human existence, you may think no formal definition of a *family* is needed—but in fact, controversy clouds what constitutes a family. Which of these constitute a "family" in your mind: a single mother and her child; two brothers sharing an apartment; two gay men living together and sharing a bank account; a lesbian couple raising two children; or a husband and wife who have separated now that their children are grown?

Traditional definitions of a family focused on the roles of husbands, wives, and children who all live together under one roof. According to a 1949 definition, a family consists of "adults of both sexes, at least two of whom maintain a socially approved sexual relationship, and one or more children, of one's own or adopted, of the sexually cohabiting adults."[1]

By 1982, a family was more broadly defined as "a social group having specified roles and statuses (e.g., husband, wife, father, mother, son, daughter) with ties of blood, marriage, or adoption who usually share a common residence and cooperate economically."[2] Because our goal in this section is for you to understand that many relationships might be regarded as family, we have chosen to define a **family** even more broadly *as a self-defined unit made up of any number of persons who live or have lived in relationship with one another over time in a common living space, and who are usually, but not always, united by marriage and kinship*. The notion of "self-defined" is probably the most significant aspect of this definition. Two people who cohabit might think of themselves as close friends, but having a child together might cause them to redefine themselves as a family. As the chapter opening line from *South Park* attests, the perception of any relationship as a family lies within the hearts and minds of the individuals. We might also have friends about whom we declare "He's like a father to me" or "She's like a sister." Such a declaration is a statement of loyalty and commitment.[3] Maybe as you grew up, you spent so much time at a friend's house that you were considered "one of the family."

But not everyone accepts such a broad definition of *family*. When workers from nontraditional families (gay, lesbian, transgender, childfree, and single) were asked about their treatment in the workplace, respondents reported that they sometimes felt invisible and excluded because conversations focused on "traditional families" (husband, wife, and children). At other times, they felt hypervisible when receiving excessive attention and questioning. They also reported feeling pressured to put the needs of those in traditional families above their own, and/or they failed to receive the same kind of support offered to members of more traditional families (for example, family leave time).[4] In another study, mothers in lesbian-headed families reported facing a variety of reactions ranging from rebuke and rejection to being nosy. They also experienced social hurdles like school forms with labels like "mother" and "father" instead of parents.[5] Their advice to couples for coping with such hurdles included being yourself (be a model for others), managing emotions (avoid confrontation and defensiveness), surrounding the family with supportive people, and focusing on the kids. Such advice is probably valuable to any family facing social challenges.

Family Types

Family members' roles, relationships, and communication are impacted by the type of family to which they belong. Even within each major family type, variations exist. For example, a family consisting of a single mother raising two sons will have different dynamics than one composed of a single father raising two daughters. If you are familiar with the television series *Modern Family*, see if you can determine in which of the following categories each of the show's three families fits.

NATURAL OR NUCLEAR FAMILY   A **natural or nuclear family** consists of a mother, a father, and their biological children. Changes in culture, values, economics, and other factors have rendered this once most traditional family type no longer typical. Today, such a family is sometimes called an *idealized natural family*.

EXTENDED FAMILY   An **extended family** includes additional relatives—aunts, uncles, cousins, or grandparents—as part of the family unit. Some extended families also include individuals who are not related by marriage or kinship but are treated like family.

family

A self-defined unit made up of any number of persons who live or have lived in relationship with one another over time in a common living space and who are usually, but not always, united by marriage and kinship.

natural or nuclear family

A mother, father, and their biological children.

extended family

Relatives such as aunts, uncles, cousins, or grandparents and/or unrelated persons who are part of a family unit.

BLENDED FAMILY   The increasingly common **blended family** consists of two adults and one or more children who come together as a result of divorce, separation, death, or adoption. The children are the offspring of other biological parents or of just one of the adults raising them. Blended families are constituted from many possible relationships. For example, in a blended family with children from two previous relationships (for example, *The Brady Bunch* or the movie *Blended*), a multitude of relationship combinations are possible between the biological parent, stepparent, stepchildren, biological siblings, stepsiblings, half-siblings, noncustodial biological parent, and noncustodial stepparent. Given so many relationships, communication becomes an especially significant factor in the development and maintenance of a healthy blended family. Although communication relates strongly to satisfaction in blended families, it is unclear whether more communication leads to greater satisfaction or whether greater satisfaction leads to more communication. Nonetheless, one study found that the more stepparents and stepchildren engaged in everyday talk, the more satisfied both felt about their relationships.[6] At the same time, more everyday talk between a biological parent and his or her children increased the children's relational satisfaction, but not that of the parent. The biological parent's everyday talk with the stepparent related to greater satisfaction for the stepparent, but not for the biological parent. Another study found that stepfamilies that function well not only engage in everyday talk but also spend time together having fun and developing a sense of unity and shared purpose. They also have clear rules and boundaries within and across families, engage in family problem solving, and promote a positive image of the noncustodial parent.[7]

Families with adopted children might struggle with creating a unified sense of family, particularly if the adopted children look physically different from other family members. Families adopting children from different ethnic or racial groups may experience a dialectical tension between creating a family identity and honoring the children's biological heritage. Should a family in Iowa raising a child from China raise the child with a sense of Chinese culture?

Factors that create variation among adoptive families include the age at which the child was adopted, the presence of the parents' biological children or other adopted children, and the history or background of the adopted child. One factor that affects a sense of family is the degree to which the adoption is kept secret.[8] The social stigma once attached to adoption has greatly diminished. Rather than having one "big talk" in which a child is told he or she is adopted, parents are encouraged to engage in an ongoing dialogue that includes the sharing of narratives or stories about how the child came to be placed for adoption and how the parents came to adopt the child.[9]

Sometimes adoptive parents have very little information to share with the child, and other times parents might feel the background story would hurt the child's sense of self-worth. But the lack of a story can create a sense of loss for the child.[10] Results of one study of adult adoptees found that about one-third of those interviewed felt no sense of loss or uncertainty surrounding their adoption. Almost all had adoptive parents who were open about the adoption and who conveyed love and closeness.[11] Interestingly, the adoptees accepted the stories they were told even when those stories didn't seem true. They were viewed as simply part of the family stories.

SINGLE-PARENT FAMILY   Divorce, unmarried parenthood, separation, desertion, and death create the **single-parent family**, a family with one parent and at least one child, which represents 34 percent of the families in the United States today. The different causes of single parenthood directly affect the nature of the parent–child relationship.

Children of divorced parents who share joint custody still have ongoing relationships with both parents. However, the nature of those relationships is affected by each parent's level of involvement in the children's lives, the degree to which one parent attempts to block or undermine the other parent's relationship with the children, and

blended family
Two adults and their children. Because of divorce, separation, death, or adoption, the children are the offspring of other biological parents or of just one of the adults raising them.

single-parent family
One parent raising one or more children.

Extended families involve unique relationships and communication patterns.

how the children support or resist the continuation of a given relationship.[12] Many such children must navigate between two households, essentially living in two single-parent families until one or both parents remarry. This navigation is affected by the relationship between the divorced parents, which can be one of three types: (1) conflicted co-parenting (frequent conflicts, poor conflict management, and failure to emotionally disengage); (2) parallel co-parenting (low conflict, low communication, and emotional disengagement); or (3) cooperative co-parenting (good communication, coordination, and some flexibility in planning).[13] The mother is often made the custodial parent, and the resulting restricted visitation schedule often leaves children frequently wanting more contact with their fathers.[14] Children often have an interest in equal timesharing, and those who actually have such arrangements report less sense of loss and less focus on the divorce than those in sole custody.[15]

In 2013, more than four out of ten children in the United States were born to unmarried women.[16] Understanding the dynamics of such families is confounded by socioeconomic issues. One study found that almost 80 percent of unmarried mothers found employment the year after the birth, and many women received some support from the child's father as well as from family, friends, and the government.[17] Despite such support, unmarried women typically have less income and more challenges in dealing with childcare than other mothers. Unmarried working mothers have less time for their children and depend on them for more household contributions, including childcare for younger siblings. All of these factors affect the nature of the mother–child relationship as well as relationships among siblings. Families of unmarried mothers are faced with overcoming numerous socioeconomic obstacles as they strive to adopt the communication patterns typical of functioning two-parent families as discussed in the next section.

family of origin
Family in which a person is raised.

FAMILY OF ORIGIN The **family of origin** overlaps the other types of families, since it refers to the family in which you were raised, no matter what type it is. You may have been reared in more than one family of origin because of divorce and remarriage. It is in your family of origin that you learned the rules and skills of interpersonal communication and developed your basic assumptions about relationships. Variations in families of origin are reflected in the two models discussed in the next section.

voluntary (fictive) kin
Individuals considered family regardless of their legal or blood connection.

VOLUNTARY (FICTIVE) KIN The types of families just discussed primarily reflect legal or blood relations, but our definition includes **voluntary kin**, individuals considered family regardless of their legal or blood connection. One study found four such relationships.[18]

Substitute voluntary kin fill in for other family members who have died or are out of the picture. Perhaps a neighbor was like a mom to you after your own mother passed away.

Supplemental voluntary kin occur in parallel to existing family relationships, often meeting a void or deficit with an actual family member. A friend may be like a brother or sister, closer to you than your own biological siblings.

Convenience voluntary kin arise because the context makes them easily accessible. For example, workplace members may be considered family, but this type of family is dissolved when members leave.

Extended family voluntary kin are relationships with extended family members that are closer than might typically occur. Examples include cousins who are like siblings, or aunts and uncles who are like second parents. Extended family voluntary kin occur when families engage in highly integrated activities—living next door, sharing meals, or vacationing together. The relationships among voluntary kin are similar to other family relationships, but the dynamics are likely to differ since they are relationships of choice.

Figure 12.1 Sources of Family Difficulties

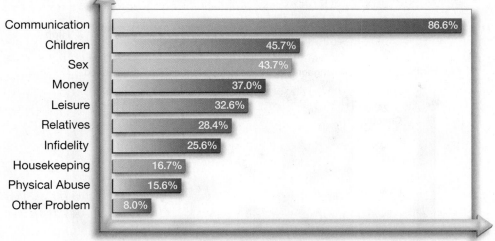

Percentage of Couples in Counseling Reporting Problem

Category	Percentage
Communication	86.6%
Children	45.7%
Sex	43.7%
Money	37.0%
Leisure	32.6%
Relatives	28.4%
Infidelity	25.6%
Housekeeping	16.7%
Physical Abuse	15.6%
Other Problem	8.0%

Two Models of Family Interaction

Communication within a family plays a major role in determining the quality of family life and the development of children.[19] As shown in Figure 12.1, one research team found that over 86 percent of the families who reported family difficulty and stress said that communication was the key source of the problem.[20] Psychologist Howard Markman found that the more positively premarital couples rated their communication with their partners, the more satisfied they were with their marriage relationships more than five years later.[21] Two models provide additional insight into the dynamics of family interaction.

CIRCUMPLEX MODEL   The **circumplex model of family interaction**, illustrated in Figure 12.2, was developed to explain functional and dysfunctional family systems.[22] The model's three basic dimensions are adaptability, cohesion, and communication. Complete the Developing Your Skills exercise about family systems to find out how these dimensions apply to your family.

1. *Adaptability.*   **Adaptability**, which ranges from chaotic to rigid, is the family's ability to modify and respond to changes in its own power structure and roles. For some families, tradition, stability, and historical perspective are important to maintaining a sense of comfort and well-being. Other families that are less tradition-bound are better able to adapt to new circumstances.

2. *Cohesion.*   The term **cohesion** refers to the emotional bonding and feelings of togetherness that families experience. Family cohesion ranges from excessively tight, or enmeshed, to disengaged. Because family systems are dynamic, families usually move back and forth along the continuum from disengaged to enmeshed.

3. *Communication.*   The third key element in the model—and the most critical one—is communication. It is not specifically labeled in Figure 12.2 because *everything* in the model is influenced by communication. Communication determines how cohesive and adaptable families can be. Communication keeps the family operating as a system. Through communication, families can adapt and change (or not), and maintain either enmeshed or disengaged relationships or something in between. The nature of communication in a family directly impacts the development of family members' interpersonal communication skills. For example, one study found that the abilities to self-disclose, to offer emotional support, and to manage conflicts among friends and romantic partners were related to being raised in a

circumplex model of family interaction

Model of the relationships among family adaptability, cohesion, and communication.

adaptability

A family's ability to modify and respond to changes in the family's power structure and roles.

cohesion

Emotional bonding and feelings of togetherness that families experience.

Figure 12.2 A Circumplex Model of Family Interaction

SOURCE: Data from David H. L. Olson, Candyce S. Russell, and Douglas H. Sprenkle (Eds.), *Circumplex Model: Systemic Assessment and Treatment of Families* (New York: Haworth Press, 1989). Used by permission.

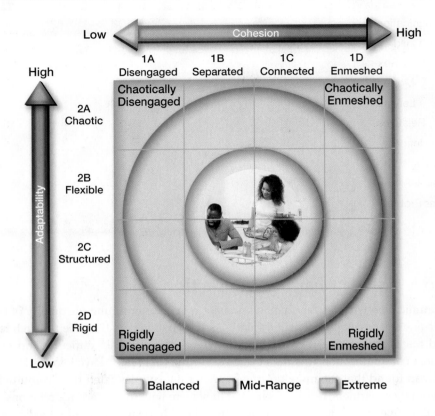

family that supports learning about a diverse world and sharing opinions without fear of condemnation (a family on the higher side of flexibility and cohesion).[23] Distinguished family therapist Virginia Satir thinks good family communication is so important that she calls it "the largest single factor determining the kinds of relationships [we make] with others."[24]

The circumplex model helps explain relationships among family cohesiveness, adaptability, and communication at different stages of family development. The intersection of the two dimensions creates labels that are often attached to the family types, such as *chaotically disengaged* for a family that has no rules or structure and no cohesion, or *structurally connected* for a family that has a number of rules but is still flexible while feeling close to each other but with some independence. At the center of the circle are four family types that balance moderate amounts of cohesion and adaptability. In general, families with these balanced levels of cohesion and adaptability usually have better communication skills and function better across the entire family life cycle than do those at the extremes. Balanced families can often adapt better to changing circumstances and manage stressful periods, such as the children's adolescence. Read the *Improving Communication Skills* box to identify what your family system might be.

Research suggests that *there is no single best way to be a family*. At some stages of family life, the ideal of the balanced family may not apply. Older couples, for example, seem to operate more effectively with more rigid structure and a lower level of cohesiveness. Families with younger children seem to function well with high levels of both cohesion and adaptability. Only one thing is constant as we go through family life: Effective communication skills play an important role in helping families change their levels of cohesiveness or adaptability. These skills include active listening, problem solving, empathy, and being supportive. Dysfunctional families—those that are unable to adapt or

Improving Your Communication Skills

Identifying Your Family System

Choose the statement from each set of four that best describes the typical behavior in your family.

Level of Cohesion

1A. My family is not especially close. We are all pretty independent of one another. None of us have any real strong feelings of attachment to the family, and once the kids move out, there's not much drive to stay connected with the family.

1B. My family experiences some closeness and some interdependence, but not much—we each do our own thing. The family usually gets together just for special occasions.

1C. My family is connected to one another, but we also have our independence. We get together at times besides just the holidays. We feel loyal to the family, and we are pretty close to one another.

1D. My family is very close-knit and tight. We need and depend a lot on one another. We are always doing things together. Family members would do anything for one another.

Level of Adaptability

2A. We observe few rules about how to behave at the dinner table. My parents don't have a particular role at dinner. Family members come and go as they see fit.

2B. We have a few rules for dinner table behavior. My mom and dad are about equal in terms of who says what the kids should do, but the kids get a lot of say in what happens and how things are done. Both parents play a similar role.

2C. In my family, usually one parent makes most of the decisions, and the other parent goes along with them. The kids get to have some input about what happens. We usually get together for dinner and have a set of rules to follow.

2D. Only one parent in my family makes the decisions, and the other parent follows along. We have many rules for how the kids should behave and family roles are well defined—who clears the dishes, who disciplines the children, etc.

Look at the circumplex model in Figure 12.2, and determine where the statement you chose from the first set fits along the Cohesion continuum; then locate your choice from the second set on the Adaptability continuum. Draw a vertical line down from the point you marked on the Cohesion continuum and then draw a horizontal line to the right from the point you marked on the Adaptability continuum. Where the lines intersect should give you a rough idea of what your family might be like in terms of its cohesion and adaptability. What communication behaviors might be expected in a family with these levels of cohesion and adaptability? Does your family exhibit these behaviors?

alter their levels of cohesion—invariably display poor communication skills. Family members blame others for problems, criticize one another, and listen poorly.

FAMILY COMMUNICATION PATTERNS MODEL   The **family communication patterns model**, as developed by family communication scholars Mary Ann Fitzpatrick, L. David Ritchie, and Ascan Koerner, is based on the idea that communication in families can be described in terms of two dimensions: *the level of conversation*, which is the degree to which family members are encouraged to discuss any topic; and the *level of conformity*, which is the degree to which the family emphasizes embracing the same values, attitudes, and beliefs.[25]

Families with a strong conversation orientation engage in frequent discussions, all family members share their thoughts and feelings, and they all share in decision making. Families strong on conformity seek homogeneity, harmony, avoidance of conflict, and obedience to elders. Families range from strong to weak in their conversation and conformity orientations, as shown in the two-dimensional model in Figure 12.3. The intersection of the two dimensions produces four types of families, each with its own unique communication pattern. As you read about each type, think about which one best describes your family's communication pattern.

Consensual Families   Families with a high orientation toward both conversation and conformity are **consensual families**. Children are encouraged to talk but are expected to accept their parents' explanations and values as the parents make the decisions.[26] In essence, children must give in to whatever their parents say, which undoubtedly creates stress for the children. As a matter of fact, a lot of negative feelings are expressed in consensual families, and such families rely heavily on external social support.[27]

family communication patterns model

A model of family communication based on two dimensions: conversation and conformity.

consensual families

Families with a high orientation toward both conversation and conformity.

Figure 12.3 Model of Family Communication Patterns

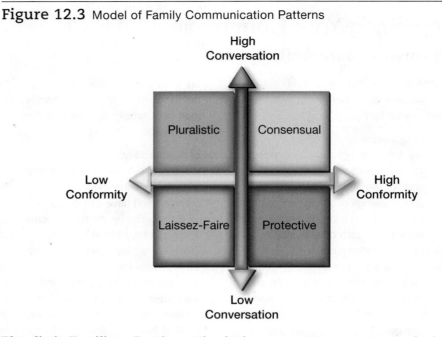

pluralistic families

Families with a high orientation toward conversation but a low orientation toward conformity.

protective families

Families with a low orientation toward conversation but a high orientation toward conformity.

laissez-faire families

Families with a low orientation toward both conversation and conformity.

Pluralistic Families   Families with a high conversation orientation and a low conformity orientation are **pluralistic families**. They have very open, unrestrained conversations; they emphasize talking without a concern for conforming.[28] Parents do not try to control their children's thinking, but they do expect quality arguments and support. Family members do not express many negative feelings, and hostility levels are low, probably because family members are free to discuss conflicts and are not pressured to conform.[29] Pluralistic families have the most positive family relationships among the four family types.

Protective Families   Families with a low conversation orientation and a high orientation toward conformity are **protective families**. They emphasize obedience and the parents' authority in decision making without discussions or explanations.[30] Because harmony, agreement, and conformity are the goals, conflict is discouraged, and without conflict experience, family members are actually ill-equipped to manage conflict outside the family. The lack of conflict-management skills leads members of protective families to experience higher levels of hostile feelings, more venting of those feelings, and short emotional outbursts.[31]

Laissez-Faire Families   Finally, families with a low orientation toward both conversation and conformity are **laissez-faire families**. They tend to have few interactions on only a small number of topics. Parents support individual decision making but do not take much interest in the decisions. This pattern eventually undermines the children's confidence in their own decision-making abilities.[32] With little reason for hostility and little investment in relationships, conflicts are infrequent, as is venting of negative feelings—children feel disassociated from the family.[33]

The communication pattern in a family directly impacts both the well-being of family members and the development of interpersonal communication skills. One group of reviewers who analyzed research on family communication patterns discovered that the conversation orientation related more to psychosocial factors (self-esteem, mental and physical health, closeness, and relational satisfaction) than did the conformity orientation.[34] In essence, open communication appears to be one of the most significant and positive communication dynamics a family can adopt; it enhances critical thinking, flexibility, and adaptability.[35] Coming from a family with a strong conversation orientation relates to strong relationship maintenance skills, which in turn create more closeness in friendships.[36] Conformity, on the other hand, appears to reduce the flexibility and spontaneity underlying effective relationship maintenance skills.[37] A study of college students found those from conversation-oriented families tended toward lower verbal aggressiveness trait scores, while those from conformity-oriented families tended toward higher verbally aggressive trait scores.[38] Research suggests that conversation-oriented families engage in constructive conflict management and healthy argument, which reduces the likelihood of developing a verbally aggressive style. On the other hand, the failure to develop information-processing skills in conformity-oriented families undermines healthy argumentation skills.

The family communication patterns model is not a complete picture of complex family dynamics, but it does provide a foundation for an understanding of healthy family communication patterns.

Strategies for Improving Family Communication

In terms of the circumplex model and the family communication patterns model, how would you classify this family? What cues support your classification?

Wouldn't it be fantastic if you could learn special techniques guaranteed to enrich your family life? Although no sure-fire prescriptions can transform your family system into one that a TV sitcom family would envy, we can pass on some skills and principles that researchers have either observed in healthy families or applied successfully to improve dysfunctional ones.

In his study, John Caughlin identified ten factors that were associated with families that had good communication.[39] Those factors, in order of impact, are the following:

1. Openness
2. Maintenance of structural stability
3. Expression of affection
4. Emotional/instrumental support
5. Mind reading (knowing what others are thinking and feeling)
6. Politeness
7. Discipline (clear rules and consequences)
8. Humor/sarcasm
9. Regular routine interaction
10. Avoidance of personal and hurtful topics

After reviewing several research studies, family communication scholars Kathleen Galvin and Bernard Brommel identified the following eight qualities exhibited by functional families: [40]

1. Interactions are patterned and understood.
2. Compassion prevails over cruelty.
3. Problems are addressed to the person who created them—other family members are not scapegoated.
4. Families exercise self-restraint.
5. Boundaries about safe territories and roles are clear.
6. Life includes joy and humor.
7. Misperceptions are minimal.
8. Positive interactions outweigh negative ones.

Which of the qualities identified by Caughlin, Galvin, and Brommel are present in your family? Which qualities do you think your family could use more of? The following sections explore some of the specific skills and strategies you can use to improve your family communication.

TAKE TIME TO TALK Healthy families talk.[41] The quantity of communication depends on family members' needs, expectations, personalities, careers, and activities. Joking around and talking about the day's events are specific forms of communication

---

BEING Other-ORIENTED

Mind reading is identified as a factor that contributes to good communication in a family. The ability of family members to know what other members are thinking and feeling means they can more effectively adapt. How well do members of your family read each other's minds? How does this ability, or the lack of it, affect your overall family communication? What is needed to improve this ability in your family?

linked to higher family satisfaction.[42] But talking also extends to issues that help the family adapt to change and maintain a sense of cohesiveness.

Often, because of the crush of everyday responsibilities and tasks, family members may lapse into talking only about the task-oriented, mundane aspects of making life work: housekeeping, grocery shopping, running errands, and other uninspiring topics. Healthy families communicate about much more: their relationships, their feelings, and others' feelings. They make time to converse, no matter how busy they are. Talking about relationships relates directly to family satisfaction.[43] Family members display an other-orientation in these conversations, instead of focusing on themselves. In addition, they enjoy one another and don't take themselves too seriously.[44] If you haven't done so recently, talk with your family members about how they really are and about how things are going for you.

LISTEN ACTIVELY, CLARIFY MEANINGS, AND RESPOND APPROPRIATELY Because talking about relationships is important in healthy families, it is not surprising that effective other-centered listening is also important. In Chapter 5, we presented fundamental skills for listening and responding to messages. Family members will communicate with greater accuracy if they learn to stop, look, and listen:

- *Stop*: Minimize mental and outside distractions; don't try to carry on important conversations while watching TV, playing video games, or listening to your MP3 player.

- *Look*: Constantly monitor the rich meaning in nonverbal messages. Remember that the face and voice are prime sources for revealing emotional meaning and that body posture and gestures provide clues about the intensity of an emotion.

- *Listen*: Focus on both details and major ideas. Asking appropriate follow-up questions and reflecting content and feelings are other vital skills for clarifying the meaning of messages. And remember the importance of checking your perceptions of the meaning of nonverbal messages.

Most of us have had to bring up difficult topics with our families, such as money problems, access to birth control, failing grades, or moving out of the house. Initiating such discussions can be extremely difficult due to fear of the family's reaction and conflict. But in one study over 75 percent of respondents reported that discussing a difficult topic actually strengthened the family relationship by increasing trust, understanding, and openness.[45] Part of the reason for the positive outcome was because a family member responded in a more positive manner than expected (such as showing support and understanding). Try to provide confirming and supportive responses to your family members whether in everyday interactions or when dealing with difficult topics or problems.

SUPPORT AND ENCOURAGE ONE ANOTHER Virginia Satir suggested that many, if not most, sources of dysfunction in families are related to feelings of low self-worth.[46] Through communication, people can let others know that they support and value them. Healthy families take time to nurture one another, express confirming messages, and take a genuine interest in each person's unique contributions to the family. Researchers have found that supportive messages—those that offer praise, approval, help, and affection—can lead to higher self-esteem in children, more conformity to the wishes of the parent, higher moral standards, and less aggressive and antisocial behavior.[47] How can you let your family members know you value and support them?

USE PRODUCTIVE STRATEGIES FOR MANAGING CONFLICT, STRESS, AND CHANGE A family's inability to manage conflict and stress may contribute to family violence. Chapter 10 discusses relational violence, which is the extreme result of what can happen when people fail to resolve conflicts in a collaborative manner. Committed partners must learn to manage conflict in constructive ways and to deal with their conflicts with their children similarly.

John Gottman developed a set of suggestions for handling conflict between couples, some of which apply equally well to parent–child and sibling conflicts.[48] Many of his suggestions reflect recommendations made in Chapter 8 on managing conflict. For example, Gottman suggests picking your battles carefully, scheduling the discussion, employing a structure (build an agenda, persuade and argue, resolve), and moderating your emotions. In dealing with your partner, acknowledge his or her viewpoint before presenting your own, trust your partner, communicate nondefensively, and provide comfort and positive reinforcement. Conflict might be tempered by enhancing the romance and finding enjoyment in the relationship. Gottman further suggests taking stock of the relationship and knowing when to seek help or to end the relationship.

No list of dos and don'ts will help you manage all differences in family relationships. The suggestions offered here provide only a starting point; you will need to adapt these skills and suggestions to the context of your unique family system. But remember that research consistently affirms good listening skills and empathy as strong predictors of family satisfaction.

Specific Family Relationships

Most of you will choose a life partner and/or get married at some point in your life, and many of you will become parents. Most of you had a relationship with your parents or other adults that greatly influenced your development through childhood. And many of you grew up with at least one sibling. These affiliations represent the most common family relationships.

COMMITTED PARTNERS   What drives people to form a lifelong commitment to a partner? Many people seek such a commitment as a precursor to having children and forming a nuclear family. And marriage represents the ultimate intimate, romantic relationship to which we vow lifelong commitment. Formal recognition and cultural approval of a relationship through the ritual of marriage adds both meaning and challenges to the relationship. Gaining public and legal recognition is one reason some gay and lesbian committed partners seek the right to marry.

Marriage has significant benefits. On average, married people live longer than unmarried ones, for a variety of reasons. One reason is that marriage has generally been linked to psychological well-being. A recent study found that spouses in marriages that weren't completely satisfying still enjoyed some psychological well-being if they had positive relationships with other family members and a best friend.[49] Nevertheless, those positive relationships were not enough to overcome the negative impact of a poor-quality marriage, demonstrating that although friends contribute to our daily well-being, marriage maintains our overall well-being.[50]

When two people enter into marriage, the nature of their relationship depends on a variety of factors, such as how they distribute power and make decisions (symmetric, complementary, or parallel) and what roles each partner assumes. Both heterosexual

Recap

How to Improve Family Relationships

Take time to talk.
- Be other-oriented in your focus.
- Don't take yourself too seriously.

Listen actively and clarify the meaning of messages.
- Stop, look, and listen.
- Check your interpretation of messages.

Support and encourage one another.
- Use confirming messages.
- Be selective in disclosing your feelings.

Use productive strategies for managing conflict, stress, and change.
- Pick your battles carefully and schedule discussion.
- Acknowledge your partner's viewpoint.

and homosexual partners can be classified according to how they communicate with each other.[51] Researcher Mary Anne Fitzpatrick identified four types of married couples found in American society: traditional, independent, separate, and mixed.[52]

traditional couples

Married partners who are interdependent and who exhibit a lot of sharing and companionship.

Traditional Couple According to Fitzpatrick, **traditional couples** are interdependent, exhibit a lot of sharing and companionship, follow a daily routine, are not assertive, have conflicts, emphasize stability over spontaneity, and follow traditional community customs (such as the wife taking the husband's last name).

independent couples

Married partners who exhibit sharing and companionship and are psychologically interdependent but allow each other individual space.

Independent Couple **Independent couples** share and exhibit companionship but allow each other individual space; they believe the relationship should not limit their individual freedoms. They are psychologically interdependent but have a hard time matching schedules, and they also engage in conflict.

separate couples

Married partners who support the notion of marriage and family but stress the individual over the couple.

Separate Couple Couples that support traditional marriage and family values but stress their individuality and autonomy over their relationship as a couple are labeled **separate couples**. They have low interdependence and avoid conflict. They display less companionship and sharing than the other couple types, but they still try to keep a daily routine.

mixed couples

Married couples in which the two partners each adopt a different perspective (traditional, independent, separate) on the marriage.

Mixed Couple In each of the preceding three types of married couples, both the wife and the husband share the same perspective about the nature of their relationship. But when the husband and the wife have divergent perspectives on their roles, they are a **mixed couple** (the fourth type). Mixed couples include the following combinations:

- One partner is independent and the other is traditional.
- One partner is separate and the other is traditional.
- One partner is independent and the other is separate.

If you're thinking that the separate style sounds appealing, you should know that research shows traditional couples are the most satisfied, whereas separate couples are the least.[53] One explanation for this is that traditional partners are the most likely to meet each other's relational expectations.[54]

You might be wondering what it takes to ensure a happy marriage. Generally, research has done a better job of explaining what will lead to the failure of a marriage than what will ensure its success. Chapter 10 lists the four communication markers identified by marriage researcher John Gottman as highly predictive of divorce: criticism, contempt, defensive behaviors, and stonewalling. But the absence of these behaviors does not ensure happiness. What is known is that the behaviors Gottman identified—poor communication in general and the inability to manage conflict constructively—are likely to lead to dissatisfaction, dysfunction, and/or relational termination. But marital satisfaction can be enhanced. The ability to forgive and the use of nonverbal forgiveness strategies such as hugging without saying anything after a transgression have been found

Many gays and lesbians seek public and legal recognition of their relationships in the form of marriage.

to relate to higher marital satisfaction.[55] But with more severe transgressions, there is greater dissatisfaction and it takes longer to reach forgiveness.

If you are good at communicating and managing conflict, will you have a happy marriage? Not necessarily. Communicating does not guarantee increased happiness; you might not like what you hear. Good communication just means openly sharing more information—information that has the potential to have a positive or negative effect, depending on what you learn. Hearing your spouse's constant complaints about family members, financial issues, personal distress, doubts about the marriage, or desires to engage in activities you dislike might reduce your relational satisfaction. Nonetheless, the negative impact of *not* communicating seems potentially much greater than the negative impact of communicating. Partners should strive to establish effective communication and use that communication to honestly share and explore each other's expectations.

PARENTS AND CHILDREN   A great deal of study has explored the nature of the interaction between parents and their children. Most studies have focused on identifying the most effective ways for parents to communicate with their children or on describing the nature of parent–child interactions. For example, in one study, college students who perceived their mothers as being attentive and friendly reported higher communication and relationship satisfaction. That relationship satisfaction, in turn, contributed to the college students initiating more communication with their mothers.[56] Some studies have examined the impact of a parent's communication on the development of the child's communication skills as an adult. Your parents have affected your interpersonal communication development in three ways: by interacting with you, by providing instruction about communication rules and principles, and by engaging in communication that you observed.

Wise parents use support and encouragement rather than coercion as a primary strategy for shaping their children's behavior. The challenge is to find a middle ground that tempers support with appropriate control.

1. *Children Learn Through Interaction.*   The way your parents interacted with you affects your behavior and attitude, although the effect is not always straightforward. One study found a correlation between mothers' self-reports of aggressive communication styles and the styles of their college-aged children, but did not find such a relationship between fathers' communication styles and those of their children.[57] Another study found that seventh-graders' views on openness in sharing thoughts and feelings were similar to the views of their mothers, while their views on conformity and authority were similar to those of their fathers. By the eleventh grade, however, children's views on openness matched those of their fathers, whereas their views on conformity matched those of their mothers.[58] Students' views on sex and alcohol use were not found to correlate with their parents' attitudes, but the more the family openly communicated about sex and alcohol, the more likely students were to engage in safe behavior.[59]

2. *Children Learn Through Instruction.*   Your parents also affected your communication development by providing you with specific instructions. They overtly conveyed such communication rules as not to interrupt others, to be polite, and to maintain eye contact when talking. Parents also teach us about friendships and romantic relationships; for example, imparting memorable messages such as the importance of valuing oneself and the qualities of a good relationship.[60] Values can also be conveyed in messages received from parents. One study found that memorable messages received from fathers while the child participated in sports included not giving up, acting like a good sport, being part of a team, and being loyal.[61] Participants reported greater satisfaction in their current relationships with their fathers if they had received encouragement for exerting more effort (trying your best) and having fun than did those participants whose fathers emphasized messages about physical skills/techniques and performance (winning). What messages did your parents express to you that relate to your values, friendships, and romantic relationships?

   Another study examined how parents instill gender roles (being feminine or masculine) in their children.[62] Both male and female respondents reported that their mothers were more likely to emphasize being soft-spoken, sympathetic, compassionate, and cheerful (typically considered feminine communication qualities). Fathers were more likely to emphasize to their sons the qualities of being self-reliant, dominant, aggressive, competitive, and ambitious (typically masculine qualities). Mothers emphasized the masculine traits equally to sons and daughters.

3. *Children Learn Through Observation.*   Your communication behaviors are also affected by observing your parents' interactions—notably, their approaches to handling conflict. Observing destructive and hostile conflicts between parents can lead children to adopt similar styles in marriage. Similarly, your observations of how your parents interacted with friends, coworkers, and strangers all served as potential models for your own communication behaviors.

Parents who engage in ego conflicts, gunny-sacking, and other destructive conflict behaviors can either instill those styles in their children or implant a fear of conflict, leading children to avoid or accommodate. Parents who avoid conflict or hide conflict interactions from their children might be teaching their children to repress conflict issues or creating an expectation of a conflict-free marriage. On the other hand, children who observe their parents managing conflicts constructively are more prosocial—considerate, empathic, cooperative, and sharing.[63] In addition to conflict skills, children's sense of well-being is affected by observing aggressive behavior and weak conflict management. In one study, the prevalence of demand-withdraw patterns of conflict between parents affected the self-reported mental well-being of their college-aged children.[64] Demand-withdraw patterns

#communicationandtechnology

Networked Families

Although engagement with the Internet, video games, and smartphones might reduce the face-to-face time that families spend together, electronically mediated communication (EMC) can also enhance and supplement family communication, particularly when family members are away from the home.

Impact on Married or Partnered Adults[65]

- 72 percent reported that the Internet had no real impact on their relationship, 17 percent reported a minor impact, and 7 percent reported a major impact. Among those impacted, 74 percent reported a positive impact, 20 percent reported a mostly negative impact, and 4 percent said it had both a good and bad impact.

- You don't have to be far away to text. Twenty-five percent of respondents said they texted their partners even when they were home together at the time. Online exchanges and texting led 21 percent of the respondents to feel closer to their spouse/partner. And 9 percent reported that they were able to resolve a conflict online or through texting when they were struggling to resolve it in person.

- In terms of negative impacts, 25 percent felt their partner was distracted by the cell phone when they were together, 8 percent reported an argument about how much time they were online, and 4 percent got upset by something their partner was doing online.

Family Communication and EMC

Motivated by a desire to protect their children, parents may give them cell phones to monitor and be alerted about the children's whereabouts. Concern over the content of children's Internet and cell phone use, including such issues as sexting, has also led parents to "friend" their children on Facebook and to examine their texts, cell phone use, bills, and Internet usage. Parents might also impose restrictions by blocking content. Because such actions could reflect a lack of trust and respect for privacy, these actions might also generate potential conflict and reduce family cohesiveness.[66]

A study of phone calls and texting between thirteen- to eighteen-year-olds and their parents found that children called and texted their mothers more often than their fathers.[67] Talking in person was the most frequent form of interaction followed by calling, texting, and e-mailing. Adolescents talked on the phone to their fathers one to two days a week and texted them every few weeks. Adolescents from higher conversation-oriented families were more likely to e-mail their parents than those from lower conversation-oriented families. Those in lower conformity families were more likely to e-mail their mothers than those from high-conformity families. Compared to texting, e-mail affords children and parents more opportunities to expand on and discuss ideas and thus seems more likely to occur in conversation-oriented rather than conformity families.

In one study, college students reported more phone calls and texts with their mothers than their fathers. These phone calls and texts were viewed as an important way to communicate with their mothers, but not as much so with their fathers.[68] Overall relationship satisfaction with parents related to how satisfied students felt about their cell phone communications with their parents. Since on average these students had cell phones since they were thirteen, the researchers observed that students were able to develop rules for cell phone use with their parents. Students' perceptions of rules included that they and their mothers be available and respond immediately to calls/texts but with restrictions about what time of the day they called and/or texted. These rules related to greater relational satisfaction with mothers but not with fathers.

If you're away at college, EMC is probably a major way you connect with your family. Perhaps you've allowed your parents to friend you on Facebook, providing them with a snapshot of your college life. As a new grandparent, this author particularly appreciates getting to see pictures and videos of his grandchildren posted on Facebook. On the other hand, you might not want your parents to be aware of some things you or your friends have posted on Facebook. What role does EMC play in your family relationships? How often do you e-mail, text, or call your parents? Your siblings? Other relatives? How often do they contact you?

also led to less supportive co-parenting and more antagonistic co-parenting (conflicting or criticizing each other's parenting), which in turn negatively impacted students' mental well-being.

Since interpersonal relationships are transactional, the combination of both parents' communication styles affects children's mental well-being and communication development. Take a moment to consider how each of your parents or other significant relatives has had an impact on your communication behavior. To what degree have they shaped your response to interpersonal conflict? How have they affected your ability to express caring, love, warmth, and affection? What impact have they had on your listening skills, respect for others, and openness?

Some of your communication behaviors might not match those of your parents because you developed them as reactions to your parents' patterns. For example, your dislike for your parents' aggressiveness might lead you to be passive. Other qualities might not be learned at all, because they are communibiological—passed down genetically. Nonetheless, if you become a parent, realize that your children's communication skill development is impacted by the way you communicate with them and by the models you present in your interactions with others. Recognize and use each teachable moment as an opportunity to develop your children's interpersonal communication skills.[69]

SIBLINGS Although relationships with brothers and sisters tend to be the most enduring relationships in our lives, generalizing about communication between siblings is difficult, because sex, age, number of siblings, and even parenting styles influence the nature of these relationships. For example, a warm, consistent, and non-punitive parenting style contributes to warmer and closer sibling relationships.[70]

Among the reasons for maintaining sibling relationships are preserving a sense of family, providing support, and pursuing similar interests.[71] Overall, however, we are motivated to communicate with siblings because of feelings of intimacy—a desire to sustain the relationship, to keep in touch, to show caring and concern, and to encourage.[72] Communication among siblings between the ages of eighteen and thirty-four differs from communication during later years because younger siblings are more motivated to do something together, to get something from one another, to escape from doing something else, to accomplish things together, to get information, or simply to continue a routine or habit.[73] Besides changes in motives, additional changes occur as siblings move through three stages of sibling relationships: childhood and adolescence, early and middle adulthood, and late adulthood and old age.[74]

Childhood and Adolescence During childhood and adolescence, siblings provide companionship, emotional support, surrogate caretaking, and protection and assistance (even forming coalitions against parents).[75] Children's first playmates are often their brothers and sisters. Through interactions with siblings, children gain valuable psychosocial skills that translate into how they interact with friends and peers. When a large age difference exists between siblings, the older children may play nurturing roles and learn parenting skills. In divorced families, the older sibling might be particularly nurturing, although the younger children may tend to resent the older siblings' control.[76]

Family communication researcher Patricia Noller notes that warm sibling relationships help us maintain positive self-evaluations. Siblings provide emotional support and advice. One study found that high school and college students were more likely to turn to their siblings than their parents to discuss such things as their dating experiences and life problems.[77] In addition, these students preferred talking to a same-sex sibling about sexual matters, rather than talking to any other family member, because they felt less fear of evoking disappointment or disapproval from a sibling than from a parent.[78]

Communication and Emotion

Emotions at Home

We probably express and experience *more* emotions within the context of our families than in any other interpersonal situation. In the majority of families, the feeling and expression of love—between committed partners, between parents and children, between siblings—is pervasive. Some emotions are present at birth, but the process of interpreting and managing those emotions is learned.[79]

Our initial emotional socialization comes from observations of our parents' emotional behavior, from direct instruction from our parents ("You should be happy about that" or "Don't be afraid of the dark"), from subtly conveyed parental expectations about our emotional behaviors, and from reinforcement of our emotional behavior by our parents (giving us a piece of candy if we stop crying or reciprocating our hug).[80] Although the types of families and related family communication patterns vary in terms of openness toward emotional expression and the likelihood of positive or negative emotional expressions, in general, boys in the United States are often taught to be emotionally guarded, whereas girls are expected to give and receive emotional support.[81]

The ability to manage negative emotions in marriage impacts a couple's satisfaction. The results of a longitudinal study of marital couples who were observed discussing a topic of continuing conflict in their marriage found that the wives' ability to reduce their negative emotional feelings and behaviors strongly related to current and future marital satisfaction.[82] The faster wives regulated their negative responses, the sooner they were able to engage in constructive communication. The researchers surmised that women are generally seen as the emotional center of the marriage and more adept at regulating negative emotions in conflict. When couples avoid becoming centered on negative emotions and restore emotional equilibrium they are in a better position to understand each other's position and manage the conflict.

Take a minute to think about your own experiences with emotions in your family. Identify a time when you experienced and expressed a positive emotion. How did others respond to you when you expressed yourself? Now identify a time when you experienced and expressed a negative emotion. How did others respond? Finally, think about emotions you experienced that you did not express explicitly. What inhibited your expression? What did you think would happen if you expressed emotion? How adept were those around you at picking up cues about your emotional state? How adept were you at responding effectively to emotions expressed by your family members?

Children without siblings may be at a disadvantage as a result of missing the opportunity to practice and develop certain interpersonal skills. One study of first- through sixth-graders found that only children were not any different from those with siblings in terms of the number or quality of friends; however, only children were less well liked, more aggressive, and more often victimized by their peers.[83] The researchers suggested that these problems reflect only children's difficulty in managing interpersonal conflict.

But having siblings is not without its drawbacks. Differential treatment of children by parents is likely to undermine warm, supportive sibling relationships.[84] During childhood, sibling rivalry often occurs as children vie for their parents' love or compete with one another. This rivalry can last throughout the siblings' lifetime. Nonetheless, if today you have effective conflict management skills, perhaps they were nurtured as you were forced to work through sibling squabbles in your childhood.

Early and Middle Adulthood   A number of significant changes occur in sibling relationships as they leave home and begin their adult lives. You probably have experienced or are experiencing some of those changes already. Without day-to-day contact, communication and other interactions tend to decrease. The continuation and intimacy of the sibling relationship become more a question of choice than circumstance. You decide how much contact and interaction you want with your siblings. Closeness at this stage is affected by how close you were in the earlier stage, by commonalities, and by life events, such as having to care for aging parents, experiencing a divorce, or grieving a family member's death.[85] Family reunions and visits occur during this stage. Perhaps you can recall from your childhood when your parents were at this stage with their siblings—getting together, everyone bringing their kids, storytelling and reminiscing; for you, these opportunities meant developing relationships with your aunts, uncles, and cousins.

BEING Other-ORIENTED

Despite being raised under the same roof, siblings differ due to a variety of factors ranging from communibiology to birth order. If you have siblings, what experiences have they had that differ from yours (being born first or last, having to move when they were in high school)? How have those experiences affected them? How are their values and beliefs similar to or different from yours? Why?

During early and middle adulthood, you and your siblings are likely to provide one another with strong emotional support (caring and assistance) rather than help with specific tasks, with sisters giving more emotional support than brothers.[86] Receiving emotional support from siblings increases the relational satisfaction of the recipient.[87] However, support tends to be directed to those perceived to need it the most, such as siblings who are single, divorced, or widowed. In contrast, decreasing amounts of support are provided as siblings get married and have children.[88]

Late Adulthood   As you grow older and move into retirement, family relationships, including those with siblings, become increasingly important. Even with infrequent interactions over the course of a lifetime, siblings share a special bond. Communication among siblings increases during this stage.[89] Although important family events (weddings, christenings, funerals) still bring siblings together, factors such as poor health, limited income or mobility, and distance can reduce visits. An important function of sibling relationships in late adulthood is reminiscing and validating memories—activities that are linked to higher self-esteem, less depression, and higher morale.[90] But before they can engage in reminiscing, siblings might need to resolve any long-standing issues, such as rivalries. For example, they might have to address feelings of envy over one sibling's preferential treatment from the parents. During this stage of our lives, we are often faced with the death of a spouse, death of another family member, or personal health challenges. Thus, another function of these sibling relationships is to provide psychological support during times of crisis.[91] Depending on who else (spouses, children, or friends) is around to provide instrumental support (cooking, cleaning, nursing), siblings might pitch in to help one another. For example, a brother might take care of his widowed sister's house if she has no children; or a sister might cook meals for her brother.

Close sibling relationships can enhance your lifelong emotional, psychological, and physical well-being. Maintaining close sibling relationships is no different than maintaining other intimate relationships—you need to communicate, be open, be supportive, and adapt. If you are not as close to a sibling as you would like to be, examine any issues that might be hampering that relationship, and consider which communication skills and strategies you might use to address these issues. Take advantage of today's technology. Become Facebook friends and post comments on each other's pages. Send texts, tweets, Snapchats, and utilize video chatting. Positive sibling relationships provide a lifetime of rewards. Although your sibling relationships exist because of circumstance, having a sibling as a friend is a rewarding choice that requires the same commitment and effort as other friendships.

One feature you probably recognize about your own family relationships is how they have changed and continue to change. Your current relationships with your parents and siblings are considerably different than when you were a pre-adolescent. Your relationship with your spouse will also change over the course of your marriage, as will your relationships with your own children. Your sensitivity to changes and ability to adapt to them are critical to maintaining family relationships.

Improving Your Communication Skills

Other-Orientation at Home and Work

Throughout this book we have advocated taking an other-oriented approach to interpersonal communication. But taking an other-oriented perspective or being empathic might sometimes mean you are ignoring your own needs, values, or priorities. Look at the following situations and consider how being other-oriented might be counterproductive or lead to poor decisions. How can you be other-oriented and still make good decisions in each situation?

- You receive a call from the middle-school principal, who tells you that your seventh-grade son is being

suspended for two days for fighting with another student. Because you are other-oriented, you understand the following about your son: He is very self-conscious about being overweight, and the other kids make fun of him for it. He has been struggling with his studies because he has a hard time concentrating and reading. He has low self-esteem and does not feel that other kids like him. What would you say to your son about his suspension? What actions would you take? How would being other-oriented affect your decisions?

- You are a manager and one of your subordinates is increasingly arriving late to work, missing deadlines and appointments, and turning in poor work. Taking an other-oriented approach, you remind yourself that this employee is facing a divorce, has a child who was recently arrested, and is suffering from panic attacks. What would you say to the employee? What actions would you take toward the employee? How would being other-oriented affect your decisions?

Workplace Relationships

12.2 Describe the values and functions of workplace friendships, the unique values and challenges associated with romantic relationships in the workplace, and the types of formal relationships and communication in the workplace.

Organizations look for employees who can relate effectively to other people—bosses, subordinates, peers, and clients. All the skills you have been studying throughout this book can improve your effectiveness in organizational relationships.

After you graduate, the workplace becomes a major source for developing interpersonal relationships. You may socialize with various coworkers, sometimes hanging out together after work, and even forming friendships with some. However, personal relationships at work can affect job-related decisions and cause conflict. For example, as a manager, you might become friends with some of your subordinates, but if the work performance of one of those subordinates falls below a satisfactory level, the friendship could interfere with your ability to address that problem. However, although many companies at one time had policies prohibiting socializing among employees, such policies created strong dissatisfaction and discontent. Organizational policies that nurture relationships among employees build camaraderie and a supportive work atmosphere.

Workplace Friendships

The TV show *The Office* frequently focused on the ebb and flow of friendships in the workplace. As the show often illustrated, workplace friendships can develop with anyone in an organization, although friendship is most likely between coworkers who are at the same status level. However, friendships also develop between supervisors and subordinates, between employees and clients, and between members of totally different departments within an organization.

Friendships at work are like any other relationships in terms of their dimensions and development. Organizational communication scholar Patricia Sias and her colleagues identified three distinct transitions based on extensive interviews: from acquaintance to friend, from friend to close friend, and from close friend to "almost best" friend.[92] Interestingly, respondents were hesitant to refer to a coworker as a "best" friend, opting instead for "best friend at work" or "very close." The initial development of workplace friendships occurred for a variety of reasons, such as proximity, sharing tasks, sharing a similar life event, or perceiving similar interests.[93] As the relationships developed, the changes identified in this study were similar to those typically found in any developing friendship—easier and more flexible communication, increased self-disclosing, more frequent interactions, more socializing, and increased discussion of both work problems and nonwork topics.[94]

Workplace friendships can develop with anyone in the organization.

The adoption of communication technology in the workplace is having an impact on workplace friendships—proximity is no longer a limiting factor. In a 2012 survey, Dr. Sias and her colleagues found that personality, similarity, and shared tasks were the most important factors (in that order) contributing to friendship development while proximity was the least important.[95] But the more time workers spent telecommuting, the more shared tasks became the foundation for initiating relationships. Face-to-face interactions were still seen as the most important way of communicating followed by phone calls, e-mail, and texting. In contrast, the least important ways of communicating for on-site employees were teleconferencing, social networking, instant messaging, and sharing paper documents. Obviously, the more time spent telecommuting, the less opportunity for face-to-face interactions, which is probably why teleconferencing was the most important communication method for people working off-site. While technology allows increased independence from the workplace, it's important not to forgo the opportunity to develop and maintain coworker friendships.

WORKPLACE FRIENDSHIPS AND CONTEXT Workplace friendships might be limited to a particular context: a shared lunch hour or a project assignment. One of your authors once worked the night shift at a hospital, a schedule that limited opportunities for evening activities with friends outside of the hospital. Sometimes a group of night-shift workers from several departments would go out for breakfast together, which led to the development of "breakfast friendships."

Unlike other friendships, workplace friendships often involve people who differ in age or status.[96] For example, you may find yourself becoming friends with a supervisor or subordinate who is considerably older or younger than you. Sometimes this friendship begins within the context of a mentorship, in which the veteran employee either formally or informally provides advice and support to a new hire.

Having a cross-sex friend may be more likely in a work situation than it would be outside of work, where such relationships might be expected to become romantic or might threaten existing intimate relationships. In one study, men felt that socializing outside the workplace was more important to their friendships with male coworkers than to friendships with female coworkers.[97] In addition, as their workplace relationships became more intimate, same-sex friends continued and expanded their relationships outside the workplace while cross-sex relationships continued to be defined specifically as "workplace friendships."

VALUES AND FUNCTIONS OF WORKPLACE FRIENDSHIPS Besides the typical benefits associated with friendships, workplace friendships help individuals with their organizational lives, and also help the organization. Workplace friendships provide the following values and functions:

1. *Information exchange*: One of the primary functions of workplace friendships is information exchange.[98] Information within an organization flows more openly between friends. You are more likely to share critical and even private news you hear because of friendship and trust. Your friendship network alerts you to important news such as reorganizations, job openings, cutbacks, or reviews.

2. *Social support*: Workplace friends are in a position to help you manage the stress and challenges unique to your job, such as a hostile boss, cutbacks in hours, or overtime

Interpersonal communication skills help in interactions with coworkers. Developing satisfying interpersonal relationships in an organization is often a rewarding part of a job.

work. These friends provide empathy, insight, comfort, support, and advice because they understand the dynamics and demands of the company and of your position.[99]

3. *Organizational support*: Workplace friends are allies and advocates who will help you address organizational challenges or conflicts. A boss who is also your friend will probably argue harder for your promotion than one who is indifferent. Friends also can form alliances and become a team to challenge unjust or questionable organizational policies.

4. *Newcomer assimilation*: The tension that comes from a new job can be greatly reduced if you are able to form friendships with those with whom you work. Friendship formation helps you adjust socially and integrate into a new organization. Being accepted into an existing social network within an organization can be challenging because others do not have the same needs as you. So, as a newcomer to an organization, you are likely to form friendships with other new hires.

5. *Improved performance*: Workplace friends can help ensure you do a better job. Besides giving you important information, friends provide objective advice and feedback, help you make decisions, provide resources, and lend a hand when needed. Friendships also provide "social capital," the benefit you accrue because of who you know.[100] For example, in a meeting with coworkers, your friendship with the boss provides extra "capital" as you argue for adoption of your ideas.

6. *Retention*: Once you are settled into your job, friendship increases the likelihood that you will stay in it. One study of workers at a fast food restaurant found that the number of friends was more significant in employee retention than the depth of those friendships.[101] Perhaps you've had jobs that you didn't particularly like but kept because you enjoyed the camaraderie and friendships.

7. *Organizational change*: The trust and sense of identity that develop from friendship networks can help the distribution and adoption of organizational changes.[102] We are more amenable to changes that our friends support and help us understand. For example, you might resist management's introduction of a new computer system and software, but if your friends like the plan, you'll probably be more accepting of the change.

8. *Organizational enhancement*: The preceding seven functions and values of workplace friendships combine to enhance the overall quality and efficiency of an organization by increasing information exchange and improving employee satisfaction, thus reducing turnover.

DETERIORATION AND TERMINATION OF WORKPLACE FRIENDSHIPS Like any friendship, workplace friendships can deteriorate and end. However, unlike other friendships, workplace friendships continue as relationships of circumstance with coworkers, superiors, or subordinates. Some reasons for the deterioration of workplace friendships are personality issues, interference of personal life with work, problems balancing friendship and workplace roles, promotion of one person to a position of authority over the other, and betrayal of trust.[103] However, just as with any friendship, we might seek to preserve a workplace friendship by presenting a good mood, striking up informal conversations, offering help, or openly discussing the relationship.[104]

How do you go about ending workplace friendships? Chapter 10 discussed both direct and indirect strategies for ending relationships that also apply to workplace friendships. Other indirect strategies specific to the workplace include keeping all conversations focused on work topics; nonverbally distancing yourself from the other (through the use of a condescending tone or disapproving facial expressions); escalating the cost of maintaining the friendship by being more independent or making more demands (although this strategy might have a negative impact on the continuing work

BEING Other-ORIENTED

The same workplace friendship can have different values for each partner. These differences can be the source of conflict and even harassment. What values or functions have you sought in a recent workplace friendship? What would your friend say you wanted out of the friendship? What values or functions did your friend see in the relationship? If you've had a workplace friendship end, what would your former friend say were the reasons it ended?

relationship); and avoiding socializing outside the workplace.[105] When all else fails, some of our students have reported quitting their jobs to end a workplace relationship. The ability to redefine a friendship as only a work-based relationship requires strong relationship management skills to minimize the stress and the potential resentment of a coworker or a subordinate.

Workplace Romances

The workplace provides an opportune arena for the development of romantic relationships because of the convenience and exposure to a pool of potential partners. Various surveys have found that 40 to 80 percent of respondents have dated a coworker.[106] Many people find their future spouses in the workplace. A 2014 national survey for Careerbuilder.com found that 31 percent of workers surveyed had married a person they dated at work. Some companies even hire married couples because they see a value in having both partners working for the same company. On the other hand, some companies have policies prohibiting dating among coworkers—but how can a policy prevent people from becoming attracted to each other?

In the workplace, you interact with people in a safe and defined context that affords the opportunity to learn about others and share information about yourself. Trust evolves, similarities are discovered, attraction develops, and the interactions increase in intimacy. The same principles and factors discussed in the last chapter on romantic relationships apply to workplace romances. The processes of self-disclosing and moving toward intimacy, physical affection and sex, and even marriage are also a part of workplace romances.

REASONS FOR AND VALUES OF WORKPLACE ROMANCE Several factors inherent in the workplace foster attraction and relational development.[107] The proximity afforded by work spaces such as offices or cubicles increases the likelihood of personal interactions. Meetings and other collaborative tasks require you to interact with others. And incidental interactions can occur in such shared space as a coffee room, cafeteria, lobby, or elevator. All of these circumstances provide the opportunity for initiating relationships. In fact, many of these circumstances lead to repeated interactions, which increase the opportunity for sharing information. In a 2014 survey sponsored by Careerbuilders.com, 12 percent of respondents cited running into each other outside of work as initiating the romance, 11 percent cited working late at the office, 12 percent cited meeting at happy hour, 11 percent cited meeting at lunch, and 10 percent cited working late at night.[108]

The values and functions associated with friendships also apply to romantic relationships. For example, in TV shows such as *Grey's Anatomy*, *The Office*, or *The Good Wife*, workplace romantic partners are often seen sharing organizational, professional, and personal information; providing emotional comfort and understanding; pitching in and helping on a given task; or acting as advocates. These shows also illustrate how workplace romances can energize the partners as well as their work associates, as they all share the joy and excitement of the relationship, which bolsters workplace morale. On the downside, such romances can also be the source of jealousy.[109] Unlike friendships, workplace romances offer the additional prospect of becoming intimate, loving relationships and leading to marriage.

THE CHALLENGES OF WORKPLACE ROMANCES In general, dating in the workplace is not particularly problematic when those involved work in different units of the company or when they have no job-related power issues to deal with. But dating among members of the same unit can be a problem if it interferes with the ability of the couple to perform their jobs. In addition, coworkers are sometimes uncomfortable around romantic partners and may worry about inappropriate sharing of information, unequal work distribution, or other potential problems.

A survey of coworkers in several insurance companies found that 14 percent felt uncomfortable about colleagues being romantic partners and 18 percent felt romantic partners were less productive.[110] These low percentages might be because of the level of professionalism displayed by those in the romance. However, dating colleagues appears to be more acceptable than dating bosses. Workers viewed colleagues who dated superiors as driven more by job motives than by love; they also were seen as more likely to receive unfair advantages and be less trustworthy. Workers were also less inclined to confide in these colleagues than those who dated peers or subordinates.[111]

Dating coworkers still carries a stigma, with women in workplace romances being perceived more negatively than men, suffering more negative consequences, and being berated for taking a romance too seriously.[112] Participants in one study perceived women who dated a superior as less caring and trustworthy than women dating a peer, while this effect was not found for men.[113]

MANAGEMENT'S RESPONSE TO WORKPLACE ROMANCES Managers are responsible for maintaining a safe and efficient workplace. Generally, it is inappropriate for a manager to intercede in the personal lives of employees; however, if those personal lives interfere with the workplace climate or performance, then a manager has a responsibility to intercede. For example, managers should know their companies' policies for dating between coworkers and apply them consistently. Not only do managers need to ensure that their units are unaffected by ongoing workplace romances, but the aftermath of dissolved relationships might also require intercession. Breakups can be the source of ill feelings and can undermine former romantic partners' working relationships, as well as their relationships with their coworkers. Managers should also be prepared to provide conflict mediation if needed.

GUIDELINES FOR WORKPLACE ROMANCES Communication in the workplace is expected to be professional, with employees' interactions reflecting their roles. Employees who date need to keep their romantic relationship from interfering with their professional roles and be prepared to manage the possible fallout over their romance from fellow employees.

Dialectical tension may exist regarding whether to reveal or conceal a relationship, but unless company policies explicitly prohibit dating coworkers, you generally don't have to keep the relationship secret. Some companies actually have policies requiring that romantic relationships be revealed and even have partners sign "love contracts" indicating the relationship is consensual, thus limiting the company's liabilities. Human resource experts Cindy Schaefer and Thomas Tudor offer the following guidelines for those involved in workplace romances:[114]

1. Be professional in workplace interactions with your partner, be discreet, and avoid public displays of affection.

2. Don't take long lunches or extended breaks together.

3. Avoid romances with clients or suppliers; they pose a potential conflict of interest.

4. It is acceptable to ask a coworker for a date if the employer's policies allow it, but do not persist if you are rejected. Persistence may develop into harassing behavior. Harassment is strictly prohibited.

5. Be careful about sending personal messages on company communication systems because they might be monitored.

6. Do not call in sick on the same day. Coworkers will suspect you are not really ill and resent the perceived deceit, which can damage your reputation.

7. If you are employed by an international firm, be familiar with cultural differences in dating and acceptable behavior between males and females.

Relating to Diverse Others

Male–Female Communication in the Workplace

Male–Female Communication Characteristics

Here are some general variations in the way men and women communicate.

- Men focus on power, rank, and status. Women focus on relationships.

- Men talk to give information or report. Women talk to collect information or gain rapport.

- Men talk about things (such as business, sports, and food). Women talk about people and relationships.

- Men focus on facts, reason, and logic. Women focus on feelings, senses, and meaning.

- Men thrive on competing and achieving. Women thrive on harmony and relating.

- Men "know" by analyzing and figuring things out. Women "know" by intuiting.

- Men are more assertive. Women are more cooperative.

- Men tend to be focused, specific, and logical. Women are holistic and organic.

- Men are at ease with order, rules, and structure. Women are comfortable with fluidity.

- Men immediately want to get working on a project. Women tend to ask lots of questions before beginning a project.

- Men want to think. Women want to feel.

Strategies for Bridging the Gender Communication Gap

- **Information issues.** According to Sandra Beckwith, author of the book *Why Can't a Man Be More Like a Woman?*, "Women gather information by asking questions, but men view question-asking as a sign of weakness." Now we know why men won't ask for directions! Men need to understand this information-gathering process and listen to the questions. Women must be sure men have adequate information, because if they don't understand, they may not ask for help.

- **Managing metaphors.** Women frequently use stories or illustrations about home or relationships. Men tend to rely on metaphors about sports or war. This sets the stage for miscommunication. Women often do not follow the touchdown analogies, while men would have trouble following home decorating stories. We should avoid simply gender-reversing descriptions to communicate. Instead, consider using gender-neutral images (weather, nature, movies, etc.).

- **Power struggles.** Women tend to be more cooperative, focusing on relationships. However men tend to be more assertive and focus on rank and status in an organization. Women see men as being too focused on power, while men see women as weak. In this case, each gender can learn from the other. Men can focus more on a collaborative approach. Women need to be more assertive.

- **Getting to the point.** Women like to tell and hear stories, including methods of coping with distress and finding solutions. It's their way of connecting and building the relationships. Men don't want to hear stories, they just want to get to the point. They don't care about the route, just the destination. The problem is that each gender becomes impatient. Women push for details while men look for the big-picture message. Each gender can benefit from the other's communication style. Men need to explain their thinking and not simply jump to conclusions. Women need to get to the point in a speedier manner.

- **Facts and feelings.** Women are generally more comfortable talking about their feelings. Men prefer to focus on the facts and skip the feelings. This can result in significant communication problems. Every type of communication has both an intellectual and an emotional element. It is important for both genders to see these two parts at play. A man can increase the feeling quotient by making this type of statement: "I know this project has been very stressful for you. Let's talk about ways to manage the difficulties we're facing." A woman can dim the emotional intensity by saying: "I think we need to discuss the major issues blocking the implementation of the new plan."

SOURCE: Excerpted from "Men & Women Communicating in the Workplace: Effective Strategies to Smooth Out Gender Differences," by Edward Leigh. Reprinted from the "Joy on the Job Newsletter," a complimentary electronic newsletter featuring informative and entertaining tips for creating positive workplaces. Subscribe at www.EdwardLeigh.com and receive the complimentary special report, "25 Ways to Create a Positive Workplace."

Formal Relationships and Communication Directions in the Workplace

So far you have read about the formation of informal interpersonal relationships in organizations, but the organizational structure also creates a set of specific, formal communication expectations. The reasons a manager talks to an employee differ from the reasons an employee seeks out a manager.

Recap

Workplace Relationships

Workplace Friendships:	Workplace Romances:
• The workplace can be a significant source of friendships.	• The workplace provides opportunities for learning about others, becoming attracted, and increasing intimacy.
• Workplace friendships develop like other friendships but are often context specific.	• Workplace romances develop for similar reasons and values as friendships, but greater intimacy, love, and potential for marriage exist.
• Workplace friendships provide special values and functions, such as being a source of information and social support.	• Some challenges of workplace romances include potential interference with job performance and negative effects on coworkers.
• As with other friendships, workplace friendships can deteriorate and terminate, but work-related interaction must continue.	• Managers must enforce policies that insure a safe and efficient workplace.
	• Guidelines for workplace romances include being professional with each other at the workplace and not persisting if rejected.

The following sections describe the four directions in which communication flows within an organization: upward (from subordinate to supervisor), downward (from supervisor to subordinate), horizontally (from peer to peer), and outward (from members of an organization to clients or vendors). These formal channels of communication coexist with the informal, personal channels discussed earlier, sometimes enhancing them and sometimes interfering with them. A boss who is friends with an employee might be reluctant to reprimand or evaluate the employee, thus failing to perform one of the formal functions expected of a supervisor. The quality of formal relationships and communication directly affects the efficiency and effectiveness of an organization.

UPWARD COMMUNICATION: TALKING WITH YOUR BOSS "Please place your suggestions in the suggestion box," announces the boss. The suggestion box is the symbol for **upward communication** from subordinates to superiors. Today's organizations recognize that good communication improves the quality of goods and services, with many organizations encouraging communication from lower levels to higher levels. However, effective upward communication is still far from the norm. Many employees fear that candid comments will not be well received. Others may wonder, "Why bother?" If managers offer no incentive for sharing information up the line, it is unlikely that their subordinates will make the effort.

In 1952, organizational researcher Donald Pelz discovered an effect that was subsequently named for him; the **Pelz effect** describes the phenomenon that subordinates are more satisfied in their jobs when they feel their immediate supervisor has influence on decisions made at higher levels.[115] Subsequent research by organizational communication scholar Fred Jablin found that when subordinates perceived their supervisors as supportive, the Pelz effect was particularly strong in creating a sense of openness and satisfaction.[116] Having a supportive and influential superior enhances communication because employees are more open to sharing information.

If little upward communication occurs, the organization may be in a precarious situation. Those lower down in the organization are often the ones who contact the customer, make the product, or develop and deliver the product or service; they hear feedback about the product's virtues and problems. If supervisors remain unaware of these problems, productivity or quality may suffer. In addition, if employees have no opportunities to share problems and complaints with their boss, their frustration can be detrimental to the organization.

Upward communication helps managers deal quickly with problems and gather suggestions for improving processes and procedures. One pair of researchers suggests that subordinates can "manage up" by being sensitive

upward communication

Communication that flows from subordinates to superiors.

Pelz effect

Subordinates feel more satisfied in their jobs the more their supervisors are able to influence higher-level decisions.

Workplace satisfaction is related to the quality of the communication between the boss and employees.

to the needs of supervisors.[117] By being other-oriented toward your boss, you can use your knowledge of your boss's goals, strengths, weaknesses, and preferred working style, to establish a more meaningful relationship that will benefit both of you.

If you are a manager, encourage your subordinates to share both good news and bad. Be visible and cultivate trust by developing a system that elicits feedback and comments. Use a suggestion box (paper or electronic), informal discussions, or more formal meetings and presentations. Formal meetings with structured

#communicationandtechnology
Networked Workers

Electronically mediated communication (EMC) has changed the way people perform their jobs, which influences both their effectiveness and their lives. A 2014 survey of workers by the Pew Internet & American Life Project yielded the following data concerning the impact of technology on the workplace:*

- For 78 percent of the office-based workers surveyed, e-mail was very important for doing their job. Survey results also indicated that 68 percent of respondents said the Internet was very important to their jobs, followed by landlines (37%), cell/smart phones (22%), and social networking (7%).

- For those who frequently work remotely, 51 percent felt the Internet expanded the number of people outside their company with whom they communicated, 39 percent felt the Internet gave them more work-hour flexibility, and 35 percent felt the Internet increased the amount of time they spent working.

- For those with office-based jobs, 59 percent felt the Internet expanded the number of people outside their company with whom they communicated, 51 percent felt the Internet gave them more work-hour flexibility, and 47 percent felt the Internet increased the amount of time they spent working.

- Of those using the Internet, 46 percent reported it has made them more productive, 46 percent reported no affect, and 7 percent reported being less productive.

- Forty-six percent of the workers surveyed reported that their employers blocked access to certain websites and 46 percent reported having employer rules about what can be said or posted online. This is an increase from 2006 when only 20 percent of employers had such restrictions.

As the above statistics indicate, widespread access to EMC has led companies to be more aggressive in developing policies and monitoring use and abuse—from requiring access to your Facebook page when you apply for a job, to restricting cell phone camera use. E-mails, Internet use, and company cell phone messages may be monitored, raising questions of privacy, protection, and even productivity in the workplace. A study in Australia found that a degree of brief but frequent "workplace Internet leisure browsing" was actually associated with increased productivity, although excess use reduced productivity.[119]

Technology provides many people with the opportunity to work from home. However, mediated communication produces a paradox for teleworkers—it provides autonomy but also allows for excessive interruptions. One study found that EMC interruptions caused stress, but did not impact workers' organizational identification (feelings of attachment, identity, and belonging related to the organization).[120] Stress for both office-based and teleworkers related to interruptions caused by face-to-face communication and e-mail, but only among teleworkers was stress related to instant messaging and teleconferencing. The researchers observed that office-based workers appeared to go overboard in trying to keep teleworkers in the loop. It was suggested that teleworkers set boundaries or schedule quiet times when they can work without interruption.

What expectations do companies have for employees' use of EMC? As a supervisor, how would you feel about employees using their computers to surf the Internet for fun, send personal e-mails, shop online, or log on to Facebook? Should you call, text, or e-mail your coworker or boss with a work question? How often would you feel compelled to e-mail or videoconference with teleworkers? The rules governing appropriate use of technology are often vague or nonexistent. When you begin a new job, find out the formal and informal rules governing EMC use.

*SOURCE: Kristen Purcell, Lee Rainie. Pew Research Center, December 2014. "Technology's Impact on Workers" Available at: http://www.pewInternet.org/2014/12/30/technologys-impact-on-workers

agendas appear more conducive to problem solving and negotiation than informal meetings, which seem less focused and task oriented.[118] Making time for these exchanges will pay off in the long run.

Open communication between managers and employees does raise the risk of emotional confrontations. However, most organizations have an unwritten rule that employees will control and restrain expressions of anger toward supervisors or subordinates. Indeed, 560 respondents to a recent survey reported a low level of outward expression of anger; somewhat surprisingly, though, lower-status employees were more likely to express anger to higher-status employees than vice versa.[121] Despite the stereotype of women being more emotional, lower-status males were more likely to express anger than lower-status females; however, no significant difference was found between men and women at higher status levels.[122] These results suggest that lower-status males are slow to conform to the organizational rules that govern expression of anger in the workplace. Your career success is affected by your understanding of and your willingness to adapt to the organizational communication expectations and rules that affect your communication, both upward and downward.

DOWNWARD COMMUNICATION: TALKING WITH YOUR SUBORDINATES The owner of the local movie theater tells the manager that she plans to change the theater format to specialize in international and independent films. During a weekly meeting, the manager tells the shift supervisors of the impending change. Your supervisor then tells you and the rest of the crew working Friday nights about the new format. This sequence of interactions represents **downward communication**, the flow of information from those higher up in an organization to those of lower rank. It can happen via memo, phone call, newsletter, poster, e-mail, or, of course, face-to-face communication. Most downward communication consists of

- instructions about how to do a job;
- rationales for doing things;
- statements about organizational policies and procedures;
- feedback about job performance; and
- information that helps develop the mission or vision of the organization.[123]

Leader-member exchange (LMX) theory recognizes that supervisors develop different types of relationships with different subordinates, and seeks to explain those differences and their impact on subordinates' satisfaction and productivity. LMX theory recognizes that, like relationships outside of work, relationships between supervisors and subordinates vary in type and quality. For example, *supervisory relationships* are formal and task oriented and *leadership relationships* are less formal and characterized by free-flowing information.[124] Another taxonomy distinguishes among strangers, acquaintances, and partners:

- As strangers, supervisors and subordinates stay within their roles and task responsibilities.
- As acquaintances, their relationship becomes more personal.
- As partners (the *maturity* level), the strongest level, their relationship is characterized by mutual trust, respect, and support—evolving to leadership relationships.[125]

Employees in one study were given a hypothetical situation and asked to describe how their supervisor would communicate with them in that situation.[126] Those who described more person-centered communication (PCC) by their bosses also reported stronger leader–member relationships and higher job satisfaction. Besides higher job satisfaction, strong PCC and LMX relationships improve employee commitment, autonomy, and negotiation latitude, and benefit supervisors and organizations by reducing turnover and increasing productivity.[127] The amount and quality of the information a manager provides to subordinates also determine the quality of the relationship between them and the attitude of the employees. Information that is timely, useful, and accurate results in better relationships and fosters more satisfaction and commitment to the organization among employees.[128]

downward communication
Communication that flows from superiors to subordinates.

leader-member exchange (LMX) theory
Theory that supervisors develop different types of relationships with different subordinates and that seeks to explain those differences.

In Chapter 7 you read about nonverbal behaviors such as smiling, eye contact, and proximity that communicate liking and approachability (immediacy). Subordinates who perceived these behaviors had a more positive impression of their supervisors and in turn reported being more motivated, satisfied, and empowered, as well as feeling less job burnout.[129] As a manager, good interpersonal communication skills will be an asset to you, not only making your job easier but, according to one study, in contributing to opportunities for promotion.[130]

What is the best way to communicate with employees—in writing or face to face? It depends on the situation. Often it is best to communicate orally, with a written follow-up. If you need immediate employee action, face-to-face communication followed by a written reminder is the most effective; sending only a written memo is the least effective.[131] On the other hand, if you are communicating about long-term actions, a written message is the most effective. Certain situations, such as reprimanding an employee or settling a dispute, are best handled in face-to-face interactions rather than through the use of any written messages.[132] The best managers take care to develop and send ethical, other-oriented messages. Then they follow up to ensure that the receiver understood the message and that it achieved its intended effect. Managers need to be especially other-oriented when they are sharing sensitive information or broaching personal topics.

HORIZONTAL COMMUNICATION: TALKING WITH YOUR COLLEAGUES You poke your head into your coworker's office and say, "Did you hear about the possible

Relating to Diverse Others
Intercultural Bargaining and Deal-Making

Whether you travel to another country to do business or work in the United States with someone from another country, you should seek information about that other culture to enhance your interactions.

In Japan

Silence is acceptable during a meeting. Because of face issues, if asked something directly, the Japanese will rarely say "No" but will rather say something like "I will consider this" or even "Yes" to avoid threatening your face. Given Japanese collectivistic values, you should offer compliments to the group or company rather than to an individual. Senior members of firms are expected to negotiate; having junior members conduct negotiations would be insulting. Talking with your hands (making lots of gestures) is considered distracting. Avoid touching or public displays of emotion.

In France

The approach to business is generally formal and conservative, and you will need to dress with style. Informality at a meeting might be seen as disrespectful—if you're a man, leave your jacket on. Although the French might be late for meetings, they expect you to be on time. As people examine all the possibilities of any proposal you make, they will raise many objections; this is just the French way of doing business. Relationships are important, so networking is beneficial. Employers have family-like relationships with employees. Employees have strict job descriptions to which they adhere.

In Saudi Arabia

You should learn and use the Arabic greeting "Salaam." Use appropriate titles to show respect. After shaking your hand, a man might place his left hand on your right shoulder, lightly kiss you on both cheeks, and hold your hand for a prolonged time. A Saudi might offer to shake a woman's hand, but that is all; women should adapt to their hosts. Business hierarchy is important. If you are meeting with someone higher up, that person may interrupt your meeting to focus on other things that need attention. Meetings might be scheduled around or interrupted for prayers. Eye contact is common, but people tend not to make eye contact with superiors. Gift giving is customary, but be sensitive to Muslim laws and customs—for example, do not give liquor, pig products, or pictures of women as gifts. Men accept gifts from men; women from women. A woman should not offer a gift on her own behalf to a man; it must be on behalf of another male.

In Mexico

Men usually exchange one quick, firm handshake pump upon meeting; those who have known each other for a long time might embrace with a strong hug. Women might kiss each other on the cheek. Using some Spanish, as well as using "Señor" or "Señorita," or the person's title along with his or her last name, shows respect. Wait to be introduced by a third party; women will be introduced first, then the highest-ranking or eldest men. Meetings do not begin on time, but be sure to arrive promptly nonetheless; being an hour late for social events is typical. Business attire tends to be more European: conservative yet stylish and highlighted by accessories. An easygoing and friendly manner is common. Family and friendship are highly valued. You need to establish friendship and mutual trust before you can work on business concerns.

SOURCE: Adapted primarily from Dan Blacharski, *The Savvy Business Traveler's Guide to Customs and Practices in Other Countries: The Dos and Don'ts to Impress Your Hosts and Make the Sale* (Ocala, FL: Atlantic Publishing Group, 2008).

horizontal communication

Communication among colleagues or coworkers at the same level within an organization.

merger between Byteware and Datamass?" Or while you toss pizza dough at the Pizza Palace, one of your fellow workers asks how much pepperoni to put on a Super Duper Supreme. Both situations illustrate horizontal communication. **Horizontal communication** refers to communication among coworkers at the same level within an organization. In larger organizations, you may talk with other workers in different departments or divisions who perform similar jobs at a similar level—that, too, is horizontal communication. Most often horizontal communication is used to

- coordinate job tasks;
- share plans and information;
- solve problems;
- make sure you understand procedures;
- manage conflict; or
- get emotional support on the job.[133]

Information and gossip travel through a workplace by way of "the grapevine" and sometimes errors creep into workplace information spread this way. Although grapevine errors can cause problems, most organizations continue to encourage horizontal coworker communication because it enhances teamwork and allows the work group to develop a certain degree of independence. Some organizations even try to formalize horizontal communication by forming *quality circles,* or groups of employees who meet together on a regular basis. These groups usually talk about such issues as how to improve the quality of services or products, reduce mistakes, lower costs, improve safety, or develop better ways of working together.

outward communication

Communication that flows to those outside an organization (such as customers).

OUTWARD COMMUNICATION: TALKING WITH YOUR CUSTOMERS   One of the most important factors for success in service-oriented companies is building positive relationships with customers and clients. This pursuit has been formalized by organizations as "relationship marketing." Company members are taught many of the lessons contained in this book about building relationships. Successful organizations are other-oriented; they focus on the needs of those they serve through **outward communication**. They train their staff to develop more empathy, better listening skills, and more awareness of nonverbal messages from customers.

The Dark Side of Workplace Communication

While the challenges and dark side of interpersonal communication discussed in Chapter 10 apply to relationships within organizations, other forms of communication within the workplace also have negative consequences. These include sexual harassment, hostile work environments, workplace bullying, backstabbing, and hesitancy to share bad news (MUM effect).

quid pro quo harassment

Implied or explicit promise of reward in exchange for sexual favors or threat of retaliation if sexual favors are withheld, given to an employee by a coworker or a superior. The Latin phrase quid pro quo roughly means "You do something for me and I'll do something for you."

The most significant problems in workplace romances occur when a relationship is between a boss and his or her employee. The employee might feel coerced into the romantic relationship, which constitutes sexual harassment. Even if the superior does not threaten or show favoritism to the subordinate, the subordinate might believe that rejecting the superior's advances would be professionally detrimental. This type of sexual harassment is usually referred to as **quid pro quo harassment**. *Quid pro quo* is a Latin phrase that basically means "You do something for me and I'll do something for you." A supervisor who says or implies "If you want this promotion, you should have sex with me" is obviously using his or her power as a boss to gain sexual favors in exchange for something the employee wants. To avoid these situations, organizations often develop extensive sexual harassment policies. You should learn the policies of any organization where you are employed and assert your rights if you find yourself being sexually harassed.

hostile environment

Type of harassment (often with a sexual component) in which an employee's rights are threatened through offensive working conditions or behavior on the part of other workers.

Besides needing to address issues of harassment, supervisors also have a responsibility to eliminate another dark side of interpersonal communication: the hostile environment. An employee in a **hostile environment** feels that his or her rights are being violated because of working conditions or offensive behavior on the part of other workers. Hostile environments often have a sexual component, but can also emerge from issues of race, ethnicity, sexual orientation, or general bullying—such as telling lewd or obscene stories or jokes about members of the opposite sex, using degrading terms to describe coworkers, or posting cartoons that degrade a person because of race or sexual orientation.

A supervisor who either creates or fails to change work situations that are threatening to a subordinate is a party to that hostile environment. Jokes are not innocent and pictures are not "all in fun" if they make an employee feel degraded. Supervisors must adopt an other-oriented approach with respect to this issue, as it is the receiver, not the sender, of the message who determines whether the behavior is hostile. Defendants have won court cases by proving that a supervisor tolerated a hostile work environment, even if the supervisor did not directly participate in the offensive behavior. As a supervisor, do not wait for a problem to occur; take a proactive approach. You can schedule seminars on how to avoid engaging in offensive behavior and what actions to take if workers become victims of sexual harassment, a hostile environment, or workplace bullying. You're probably well aware of the problem of bullying in schools, but bullying also occurs in the workplace. Workplace bullying is defined as repeated verbal and/or nonverbal acts aimed at a worker for the purpose of humiliation and harm.[134] A 2014 national survey found that 27 percent of respondents reported abusive conduct that can be considered bullying including threats, intimidation, humiliation, sabotage of work, or verbal abuse resulting in 61 percent of them leaving their jobs or being terminated.[135] The effects of bullying range from lower self-esteem and anxiety to alcohol abuse and post-traumatic stress disorder, as well as indirect effects on coworkers and family.[136]

You might find yourself the target of or witness to bullying, or you might be the supervisor responsible for addressing this issue. When describing the bullying, most targets tell stories that are chaotic, fragmented, and unfinished.[137] Their narratives reflect feelings of isolation and loss. In addition, targets often have coworkers who minimize their experiences. An appropriate response to bullying requires efforts from the target, coworkers, and the organization. In particular, confirmation from coworkers strengthens the formal complaint against a bully, reduces any blame directed at the target, and makes it harder for organizations to ignore.[138]

Backstabbing can be thought of as a type of bullying that involves acts of aggression such as spreading rumors, gossiping, or telling lies that cause someone personal or professional harm. If you ever complained about a coworker or boss to other workers, you've engaged in a form of backstabbing. You might also have been the victim of a coworker talking about you behind your back. If so, how did that make you feel? A survey asking graduate students about their work experience identified five active backstabbing categories. In order of frequency these categories included talking behind someone's back, sabotaging someone, lying, stealing credit, blaming, and falsely accusing someone. They also identified three passive categories including an organization's broken promise (no promised time off), a coworker's broken promise, or withheld or concealed information.[139] Reasons for backstabbing included the perpetrator seeking self-advancement, a power struggle, a character flaw, insecurity, envy, and revenge. So how do you manage backstabbing? Responses identified in the study included interactive strategies such as confronting the coworker and discussing with or complaining to the boss or other people in the organization. As a result of bullying, sometimes the victim left the job or sought legal action. In other cases, the perpetrator was fired, suspended, or transferred. Some respondents reported simply ignoring the backstabbing or avoiding or withdrawing from any further contact with the coworker. In this book, particularly the conflict chapter, you've already learned some of the best skills and strategies for managing backstabbing. Use social decentering to consider what may be going on in the other person's life as you prepare to discuss the issue. If appropriate, apply collaborative and constructive conflict strategies in your discussions with the backstabber. You might need to involve administrators, even going above your own boss' head if necessary. Finally, having a strong support system that includes other coworkers will help regardless of how you choose to respond.

To what degree do employees have an ethical responsibility to share negative information? In Chapter 10 we presented the notion of the MUM (keeping Mum about Undesirable Messages) effect whereby a person is hesitant to share bad news or negative information. Within organizations, the MUM effect can have serious ramifications not only for the effectiveness of the organization but also the morale of its members. One factor contributing to bullying and backstabbing is the hesitancy of workers to speak up. You might find yourself hesitant to tell your boss that you believe one of your coworkers is being harassed. The negative consequences whistleblowers often endure certainly don't encourage employees to speak out. One study found that subordinates were less direct when giving their bosses negative information than were coworkers to other coworkers or bosses to employees. Even then, bosses and coworkers were still indirect when communicating.[140] The study also suggests that it is important for managers to pick up on their employees' use of indirect language that hints at underlying problems in order to offset the MUM effect.

Recognizing the dangers inherent in the dark side of organizational communication is the first step to being prepared to confront them. The skills and strategies discussed throughout this text provide suggestions for managing their detrimental impact. Underlying whatever action you take should be a sense of morality and ethics reflected in all your interpersonal interactions. Being other centered provides a guide and fundamental philosophy that will serve you well in all your interactions.

Applying an Other-Orientation
to Family and Workplace Relationships

Family Relationships:

Your parents probably will like this part of the text if the other-orientation exercise described below results in your increased appreciation of them. For you, the benefit is a better understanding of arguably the most influential family members in your life: your parents.

Effective other-orientation requires a consideration of your parents' backgrounds: their treatment as children by their parents, siblings, and other relatives; their educational and work experiences; and finally, the community and historical era in which they were raised. Imagine that you are writing a biography of your parents. Ask them about their upbringing, their childhood experiences, their education, their friends, their challenges—doing so, of course, while using your best listening skills. To gain a more complete perspective on your parents, talk to your uncles, aunts, grandparents, parent's friends, or older siblings. Socially decenter by putting yourself in their situation, imagining what it would have been like to grow up as they did, to work and raise a family. The goal of such reflections is to understand your parents' behaviors and the choices they have made in creating a family and raising you.

Workplace Relationships:

Applying an other-orientation to your understanding of coworkers, managers, subordinates, and clients can enhance your workplace effectiveness by improving your relationships and success in achieving your goals. One of our colleagues used to announce to his large lecture classes that the key to succeeding in his class was to figure out what he wanted and to give it to him—a pretty simple application of an other-orientation. Similarly, by figuring out what your boss, employees, or clients want, you are in a better position to adapt. Unlike the lecture situation, you do have options about how to respond in the workplace. For example, knowing that an employee is having difficulty at home with his family doesn't mean you simply give the person lots of time off, since you also have a responsibility to the company to ensure that various jobs get done. In some ways, this is a situation in which being empathetic can make a manager's decision making more difficult.

In business negotiation simulations with MBA students, those who thought about the interests and goals of their counterparts (perspective-taking) gained more benefits for themselves and their counterparts in contrast to those who were concerned with the others' feelings (empathy), or those who negotiated without considering either.[141] Empathy was less effective and sometimes even detrimental to gaining benefits for the negotiators. However, since empathy creates the greatest satisfaction for the other person, the positive relationship it builds could be beneficial in future interactions.[142] These findings suggest that considering the other person's perspective can help you develop creative solutions that take into account both your goals and the goals of your partners (a principle of collaborative conflict management). Given that many of your organizational relationships will be long-term, showing empathy can help establish trust and satisfaction for others; however, perspective-taking is also needed to help ensure that both parties benefit.

STUDY GUIDE
Review, Apply, and Assess

Family Relationships

Objective 12.1   Identify and describe the types of families, the models used to describe family interactions, the ways to improve family communication, and the types of relationships among married couples and siblings.

Key Terms

family
natural or nuclear family
extended family
blended family
single-parent family
family of origin
voluntary (fictive) kin
circumplex model of family
   interaction
adaptability
cohesion

family communication patterns
   model
consensual families
pluralistic families
protective families
laissez-faire families
traditional couples
independent couples
separate couples
mixed couples

Thinking Critically

Family communication changes throughout the life of the family. For example, a married couple has a certain communication style that changes with the arrival of a first child and subsequent children. How might changes over the lifetime of a typical family cause it to evolve from one type of family to another in each of the two models of family communication?

Assessing Your Skills

What are your attitudes about families? Indicate whether you agree or disagree with the following statements. Talk to other class members and find out which items you agree and disagree on. Try to find reasons for differences of opinion. Decide together how you might reword statements to make ones on which you'd both agree.

_____1. Most family members know how to communicate effectively; they just don't take the time to practice what they know.

_____2. Family conflict is harmful to family harmony, and conflict should be avoided as much as possible.

_____3. Most family conflict occurs because we don't understand the other family member; we fail to communicate effectively.

_____4. Families function best with one leader.

_____5. Ineffective communication is the single most important cause of family conflict, divorce, and family tension.

_____6. In a family, nonverbal communication (facial expressions, eye contact, tone of voice, posture, and so on) is more important than verbal communication; what you do is more important than what you say.

_____7. It is sometimes necessary to ignore the feelings of others in order to reach a family decision.

_____8. Generally speaking, technology and changing cultural values are deteriorating the quality of family today.

_____9. There is one best approach or set of rules and principles that will ensure an effectively functioning family.

Workplace Relationships

Objective 12.2   Describe the values and functions of workplace friendships, the unique values and challenges associated with romantic relationships in the workplace, and the types of formal relationships and communication in the workplace.

Key Terms

upward communication
Pelz effect
downward communication
leader-member exchange
   (LMX) theory

horizontal communication
outward communication
quid pro quo harassment
hostile environment

Thinking Critically

In what ways are workplace friendships different from friendships outside the workplace? In what ways are they similar? Which kind of relationship is more challenging to maintain? Why?

Assessing Your Skills

Make a list of the values and functions of a workplace friendship that are most important to you. To what degree have you been successful in fulfilling these values and functions at your current or previous job? For those that were not met, to what degree has that been the result of your failure, your partner's failure, or the organization/context?

Notes

Chapter 1

1. M. K. Laliker and P. J. Lannutti, "Remapping the Topography of Couples' Daily Interactions: Electronic Messages," *Communication Research Reports* 31.3 (2014): 262–71.

2. M. Broussard, "Dating Stats You Should Know: Numbers about Love that Make a Difference," www.match.com/magazine/article/4671. Accessed February 15, 2015.

3. For a discussion of the role of communication and intentionality, see J. B. Bavelas, "Forum: Can One Not Communicate? Behaving and Communicating: A Reply to Motley," *Western Journal of Speech Communication* 54 (Fall 1990): 593–602.

4. E. T. Klemmer and F. W. Snyder, "Measurement of Time Spent Communicating," *Journal of Communication* 20 (June 1972): 142; also see L. Barker, K. Gladney, R. Edwards, F. Holley, and C. Gaines, "An Investigation of Proportional Time Spent in Various Communication Activities of College Students," *Journal of Applied Communication Research* 8 (1981): 101–9; R. Emanuel, J. Adams, K. Baker, E. K. Daufin, C. Ellington, E. Fitts, J. Himsel, L. Holladay, and D. Okeowo, "How College Students Spend Their Time Communicating," *International Journal of Listening* 22 (2008): 12–28.

5. A. Smith, "How Americans Use Text Messaging," *Pew Research Center* (September 19, 2011): 1–7.

6. E. E. Graham and C. K. Shue, "Reflections on the Past, Directions for the Future: A Template for the Study and Instruction of Interpersonal Communication," *Communication Research Reports* 17 (Fall 2000): 337–48.

7. C. Hsing, S. H. Konrath, and E. H. O'Brien, "Changes in Dispositional Empathy in American College Students Over Time: A Meta-Analysis," *Personality and Social Psychology Review* (2010).

8. F. E. X. Dance and C. Larson, *Speech Communication: Concepts and Behavior* (New York: Holt, Rinehart and Winston, 1972).

9. Dance and Larson, *Speech Communication*.

10. J. T. Masterson, S. A. Beebe, and N. H. Watson, *Invitation to Effective Speech Communication* (Glenview, IL: Scott, Foresman, 1989).

11. L. M. Webb and M. E. Thompson-Hayes, "Do Popular Collegiate Textbooks in Interpersonal Communication Reflect a Common Theory Base? A Telling Content Analysis," *Communication Education* 51 (April 2002): 210–24.

12. W. Carl and S. Duck, "How to Do Things with Relationships … and How Relationships Do Things with Us," *Communication Yearbook* 28 (2004): 1–28; J. Manning,

"A Constitutive Approach to Interpersonal Communication Studies," *Communication Studies* 65 (2014): 432–40.

13. A. Ramirez, Jr. and K. Broneck, "'IM me': Instant Messaging as Relational Maintenance and Everyday Communication," *Journal of Social and Personal Relationships* 26, no. 2–3 (2009): 291–314; also see E. J. Finkel, P. W. Eastwick, B. R. Karney, H. T. Reis, and S. Sprecher, "Online Dating: A Critical Analysis from the Perspective of Psychological Science," *Psychological Science in the Public Interest* 20 (2012): 1–66; K. Baek, M. Coddington, A. E. Holton, and C. Yaschur, "Seeking and Sharing: Motivations for Linking on Twitter," *Communication Research Reports* 31.1 (2014): 33–40.

14. A. K. Przybylski and N. Weinstein, "Can You Connect with Me Now? How the Presence of Mobile Communication Technology Influences Face-to-Face Conversation Quality," *Journal of Social and Personal Relationships* 30.3 (2012): 237–46.

15. M. Buber, *I and Thou* (New York: Scribners, 1958); also see M. Buber, *Between Man and Man* (New York: Macmillan, 1965). For a detailed discussion of perspectives on interpersonal communication and relationship development, see G. H. Stamp, "A Qualitatively Constructed Interpersonal Communication Model: A Grounded Theory Analysis," *Human Communication Research* 25 (June 1999): 531–47; J. P. Dillard, D. H. Solomon, and M. T. Palmer, "Structuring the Concept of Relational Communication," *Communication Monographs* 66 (March 1999): 49–65.

16. Buber, *I and Thou*.

17. Buber, *I and Thou*.

18. K. Domenici and S. W. Littlejohn, *Facework: Bridging Theory and Practice* (Thousand Oaks, CA: Sage 2006), 91.

19. For a summary of research and documentation of these research conclusions see P. M. Valkenburg and J. Peter, "The Effects of Instant Messaging on the Quality of Adolescents' Existing Friendships: A Longitudinal Study," *Journal of Communication* 59 (2009): 79–97.

20. For a discussion of the past and projections for the future of interpersonal research see: A. Kunkel and J. Rosenburg, "Interpersonal Communication's Past, Present, and Bright Future," *Communication Studies* 65.4 (2014): 426–28; A. M. Ledbetter, "The Past and Future of Technology in Interpersonal Communication Theory and Research," *Communication Studies* 65.4 (2014): 456–59; D. O. Braithwaite, "'Opening the Door': The History and Future of Qualitative Scholarship in Interpersonal Communication," *Communication Studies* 65.4 (2014): 441–45.

21. V. Satir, *Peoplemaking* (Palo Alto, CA: Science and Behavior Books, 1972); J. B.

Miller and P. A. deWinstanley, "The Role of Interpersonal Competence in Memory for Conversation," *Personality and Social Psychology Bulletin* 28 (January 2002): 78–89.

22. K. E. Davis and M. Todd, "Assessing Friendship: Prototypes, Paradigm Cases, and Relationship Description," in *Understanding Personal Relationships,* edited by S. W. Duck and D. Perlman (London: Sage, 1985); B. Wellman, "From Social Support to Social Network," in *Social Support, Theory, Research and Applications,* edited by I. G. Sarason and B. R. Sarason (Dordrecht, Netherlands: Nijhoff, 1985); R. Hopper, M. L. Knapp, and L. Scott, "Couples' Personal Idioms: Exploring Intimate Talk," *Journal of Communication* 31 (1981): 23–33; S. Pendell, "Affection in Interpersonal Relationships: Not Just 'A Fond or Tender Feeling,'" in *Communication Yearbook* 26, edited by W. B. Gudykunst (Mahwah, NJ: Erlbaum, 2002): 71–115.

23. M. Argyle and M. Hendershot, *The Anatomy of Relationships* (London: Penguin Books, 1985), 14.

24. R. E. Riggio, "Assessment of Basic Social Skills," *Journal of Personality and Social Psychology* 51, no. 3 (1986): 649–60.

25. J. Fox, D. C. Makstaller, and K. M. Warber, "The Role of Facebook in Romantic Relationship Development: An Exploration of Knapp's Relational Stage Model," *Journal of Social and Personal Relationships* 30.6 (2013): 771–94.

26. See J. L. Winsor, D. B. Curtis, and R. D. Stephens, "National Preferences in Business and Communication Education: A Survey Update," *Journal of the Association for Communication Administration* 3 (September 1997), 174; *The Wall Street Journal,* September 9, 2002: 1A.

27. K. Martell and S. Carroll, "Stress the Functional Skills When Hiring Top Managers," *HRMagazine* 39 (1994): 85–7; E. Tanyel, M. Mitchell, and H. G. McAlum, "The Skill Set for Success of New Business School Graduates: Do Prospective Employers and University Faculty Agree?" *Journal of Education for Business* 75 (1999): 33–7; W. J. Wardrope, "Department Chairs' Perceptions of the Importance of Business Communication Skills," *Business Communication Quarterly* 65 (2002): 60–72; G. E. Hynes, "Improving Employees' Interpersonal Communication Competencies: A Qualitative Study," *Business Communication Quarterly* 75.4 (2012): 466–75.

28. M. Argyle, *The Psychology of Happiness* (London: Routledge, 1987).

29. J. J. Lynch, *The Broken Heart: The Medical Consequences of Loneliness* (New York: Basic Books, 1977).

30. R. Korbin and G. Hendershot, "Do Family Ties Reduce Mortality: Evidence from the United States 1968," *Journal of Marriage and the Family* 39(1977): 737–45.

31. D. P. Phillips, "Deathday and Birthday: An Unexpected Connection," in *Statistics: A Guide to the Unknown,* edited by J. M. Tanur (San Francisco: Holden Day, 1972).

32. Argyle, *The Psychology of Happiness.*

33. B. L. Fredrickson and M. F. Losada, "Positive Affect and the Complex Dynamics of Human Flourishing," *American Psychologist* (October 2005): 678–86.

34. For a comprehensive overview of the history of the study of interpersonal communication, see M. L. Knapp, J. A. Daly, K. F. Albada, and G. R. Miller, "Background and Current Trends in the Study of Interpersonal Communication," in *Handbook of Interpersonal Communication,* edited by M. L. Knapp and J. A. Daly (Thousand Oaks, CA: Sage, 2002), 3–20.

35. V. Goel, "Facebook Tinkers with Users' Emotions in News Feed Experiment, Stirring Outcry," *The New York Times* (June 29, 2014): 1–3.

36. Among the first scholars to identify a link between the sender of a message and message context was Kurt Lewin in K. Lewin, *A Dynamic Theory of Personality* (New York: McGraw-Hill, 1935); Carl and Duck, "How to Do Things with Relationships."

37. I. Reed, "The World Is Here," in *Writin' Is Fightin'* (New York: Atheneum, 1988).

38. See V. E. Cronen, W. B. Pearce, and L. M. Harris, "The Coordinated Management of Meaning: A Theory of Communication," in *Human Communication Theory: Comparative Essays,* edited by F. E. X. Dance (New York: Harper & Row, 1982), 61–89.

39. C. R. Berger and J. J. Bradac, *Language and Social Knowledge: Uncertainty in Interpersonal Relations* (London: Arnold, 1982); C. R. Berger and R. J. Calabrese, "Some Explorations in Initial Interaction and Beyond: Toward a Developmental Theory of Interpersonal Communication," *Human Communication Research* 1 (1975): 99–112.

40. See D. Barnlund, *Interpersonal Communication: Survey and Studies* (Boston: Houghton Mifflin, 1968).

41. O. Wiio, *Wiio's Laws—and Some Others* (Espoo, Finland: WelinGoos, 1978).

42. S. B. Shimanoff, *Communication Rules: The Theory and Research* (Beverly Hills: Sage, 1980).

43. M. Argyle, M. Hendershot, and A. Furnham "The Rules of Social Relationships," *British Journal of Social Psychology* 24 (1985): 125–39.

44. P. Watzlawick, J. Bevelas, and D. Jackson, *The Pragmatics of Human Communication* (New York: Norton, 1967).

45. Sherry Turkle, TED Talk, March 2012, on.ted.com/Turkle. Accessed April 5, 2012.

46. M. Kohring and P. Vorderer, "Permanently Online: A Challenge for Media and Communication Research," *International Journal of Communication* 7 (2013): 188–96; Laliker and Lannutti,

"Remapping the Topography of Couples' Daily Interactions."

47. Przybylski and Weinstein, and "Can You Connect with Me Now?"

48. For an excellent review of theories of mediated communication and their applications to interpersonal communication see J. B. Walther, "Theories of Computer-Mediated Communication and Interpersonal Relations," in *The Sage Handbook of Interpersonal Communication,* edited by M. L. Knapp and J. A. Daly, (Los Angeles: Sage, 2011): 443–79.

49. L. C. Tidwell and J. B. Walther, "Computer-Mediated Communication Effects on Disclosure, Impressions, and Interpersonal Evaluations: Getting to Know One Another a Bit at a Time," *Human Communication* 28 (July 2002): 317–48.

50. B. Parkinson, A. H. Fischer, and A. S. R. Manstead, *Emotion in Social Relations: Cultural, Group, and Interpersonal Processes* (New York: Psychology Press, 2004).

51. W. Gerrod Parrott, "The Nature of Emotion," in M. B. Brewer and M. Hewston, *Emotion and Motivation* (Oxford, England: Blackwell Publishing, 2004), 6.

52. M. S. Clark, J. Fitness, and I. Brissette, "Understanding People's Perceptions of Relationships Is Crucial to Understanding Their Emotional Lives," in M. B. Brewer and M. Hewston, *Emotion and Motivation* (Oxford, England: Blackwell Publishing, 2004), 21–46.

53. D. Matsumoto, J. LeRoux, C. Wilson-Cohn, J. Raroque, K. Kooken, P. Ekman, N. Yrizarry, S. Loewinger, H. Uchida, A. Yee, L. Amo, and A. Goh, "A New Test to Measure Emotion Recognition Ability: Matsumoto and Ekman's Japanese and Caucasian Brief Affect Recognition Test (JACBART)," *Journal of Nonverbal Behavior* 24 (Fall 2000): 179–209; F. Trompenaars and C. Hampden-Turner, *Riding the Waves of Culture* (New York: McGraw Hill, 1988); M. R. Hammer, "The Intercultural Conflict Style Inventory: A Conceptual Framework and Measure of Intercultural Conflict Resolution Approaches," *International Journal of Intercultural Relations* 29 (2005): 675–95.

54. P. Ekman and W. Friesen, "Constants Across Cultures in the Face and Emotion," *Journal of Personality and Social Psychology* 12 (1971): 124–29.

55. For an excellent review of emotional contagion, see E. Hatfield, J. T. Cacioppo, and R. L. Rapson, *Emotional Contagion* (New York: Cambridge University Press, 1994).

56. N. Michaeli, "Interpersonal Competence Among Users of Computer-Mediated Communication," (Alliant International University, Los Angeles, California, 2013).

57. G. Brandle, R. San-Roman, and C. Zapatero, "Interpersonal Communication in the Web 2.0. The Relations of Young People with Strangers," *Revista Latina de Comunicacion Socal* 68 (2013): 436–56.

58. J. B. Walther, B. Van Der Heide, S. T. Tong, C. T. Carr, and C. K. Atkin, "Effects of Interpersonal Goals on Inadvertent

Intrapersonal Influence in Computer-Mediated Communication," *Human Communication* 36 (2010): 323–47.

59. S. J. Lee, "Online Communication and Adolescent Social Ties: Who Benefits More From Internet Use?" *Journal of Computer-Mediated Communication* 14 (2009): 509–31. Also see C. L. Kujath, "Facebook and MySpace: Complement or Substitute for Face-to-Face Interaction?" *Cyberpsychology, Behavior, and Social Networking* 14, no. 1–2 (2011): 75–8.

60. J. B. Walther, "Computer-Mediated Communication: Impersonal, Interpersonal, and Hyperpersonal Interaction," *Communication Research* 23 (1996): 3–43; J. B. Walther, C. L. Slovacek, and L. C. Tidwell, "Is a Picture Worth a Thousand Words? Photographic Images in Long-Term and Short-Term Computer-Mediated Communication," *Communication Research* 28 (2001): 105–34.

61. Tidwell and Walther, "Computer-Mediated Communication Effects on Disclosure, Impressions, and Interpersonal Evaluations."

62. R. Kraut, S. Kiesler, B. Boneva, J. Cummings, V. Helgeson, and A. Crawford, "Internet Paradox Revisited," *Journal of Social Issues* 58 (2002): 49–74; P. E. N. Howard, L. Raine, and S. Jones, "Days and Nights on the Internet: The Impact of a Diffusing Technology," *American Behavioral Scientist* 45 (2001): 383–404.

63. September 2005 Daily Tracking Survey/Online Dating Extension, Pew Internet & American Life Project, http://www.pewinternet.org/files/old-media/Files/Questionnaire/Old/Online_Dating_Questions.pdf.

64. L. Kelly, J. A. Keaton, M. Hazel, and J. A. Williams, "Effects of Reticence, Affect for Communication Channels, and Self-Perceived Competence on Usage of Instant Messaging," *Communication Research Reports* 27, no. 2 (April–June 2010): 131–42.

65. N. S. Baron, *Always On: Language in an Online and Mobile World* (New York: Oxford University Press, 2008), 24; also see D. Crystal, *txtng: The gr8 db8* (Oxford: Oxford University Press, 2008).

66. Y. Amichai-Hamburger, *The Social Net: Human Behavior in Cyberspace* (Oxford, England: Oxford University Press, 2005), v.

67. E. Bakke, "A Model and Measure of Mobile Communication Competence," *Human Communication* 36 (2010): 348–71.

68. D. Knox, V. Daniels, L. Sturdivant, and M. E. Zusman, "College Student Use of the Internet for Mate Selection," *College Student Journal* 35 (March 2001): 158.

69. For additional information about mediated communication and deception see C. Nass and C. Yen, *The Man Who Lied to His Laptop: What Machines Teach Us About Human Relationships* (New York: Penguin Group, 2010).

70. K. M. Cornetto, "Suspicion in Cyberspace: Deception and Detection in the Context of Internet Relay Chat Rooms," paper presented at the annual meeting of

the National Communication Association, Chicago (November 1999).

71. J. B. Walther and J. K. Burgoon, "Relational Communication in Computer-Mediated Interaction," *Human Communication Research* 19 (1992): 50–88.

72. Cornetto, "Suspicion in Cyberspace."

73. D. Rodriguez and M. Wise, "Detecting Deceptive Communication Through Computer-Mediated Technology: Applying Interpersonal Deception Theory to Texting Behavior," *Communication Research Reports* 30.4 (2013): 342–46.

74. S. Rosenbloom, "Love, Lies and What They Learned," *The New York Times*, November 13, 2011: ST1 and 8.

75. C. L. Toma as cited by S. Rosenbloom, "Love, Lies and What They Learned," *The New York Times*, November 13, 2011: STI and 8.

76. R. R. Provine, R. J. Spencer, and D. L. Mandell, "Emotional Expression Online: Emoticons Punctuate Website Text Message," *Journal of Language and Social Psychology* 26 (2007): 299–307.

77. J. P. Walther, B. Van Der Heide, S.-Y. Kim, D. Westerman, and S. T. Tong, "The Role of Friends' Appearance and Behavior on Evaluations of Individuals on Facebook: Are We Known by the Company We Keep?" *Human Communication Research* 34 (2008): 28–49; also see Baron, *Always On*, 64–70; N. Chesley, "Blurring Boundaries? Linking Technology Use, Spillover, Individual Distress, and Family Satisfaction," *Journal of Marriage and Family* 67 (December 2005): 1237–48; D. K.-S. Chan and G. H.-L. Cheng, "A Comparison of Offline and Online Friendship Qualities at Different Stages of Relationship Development," *Journal of Social and Personal Relationships* 21 (2004): 305–20; Provine, Spencer, and Mandell, "Emotional Expression Online."

78. J. Suler, "E-Mail Communication and Relationships," in *The Psychology of Cyberspace*, http://truecenterpublishing.com/psycyber/emailrel.html (August 1998).

79. I. Sproull and S. Kiesler, "Reducing Social Context Cues: Electronic Mail in Organizational Communication," *Management Science* 32 (1986): 1492–513.

80. L. K. Trevino, R. L. Draft, and R. H. Lengel, "Understanding Managers' Media Choices: A Symbolic Interactionist Perspective," in *Organizations and Communication Technology*, edited by J. Fulk and C. Steinfield (Newbury Park, CA: Sage, 1990), 71–4.

81. Tidwell and Walther, "Computer-Mediated Communication Effects on Disclosure, Impressions, and Interpersonal Evaluations."

82. Walther and Burgoon, "Relational Communication in Computer-Mediated Interaction."

83. W. S. Sanders, "Uncertainty Reduction and Information-Seeking Strategies on Facebook," paper presented to the National Communication Association, San Diego, CA (November 2008).

84. Tidwell and Walther, "Computer-Mediated Communication Effects on Disclosure, Impressions, and Interpersonal Evaluations."

85. J. B. Walther and L. Tidwell, "When Is Mediated Communication Not Interpersonal?" in K. Galvin and P. Cooper, *Making Connections* (Los Angeles, CA: Roxbury Press, 1996).

86. Baron, *Always On*, 27.

87. Pew Research Center, Internet User Demographics for January 2014, http://www.pewinternet.org/data-trend/internet-use/latest-stats. Accessed February 15, 2015.

88. E. Protalinski, "Facebook Passes 1.23 Billion Monthly Active Users, 945 Million Mobile Users, and 757 Million Daily Users," http://thenextweb.com/facebook/2014/01/29/facebook-passes-1-23-billion-monthly-active-users-945-million-mobile-users-757-million-daily-users. Accessed February 15, 2015.

89. S. Turkle, "Stop Googling. Let's Talk" Sunday Review: The New York Times, Sunday, September 27, 2015, p. 1.

90. Adapted from Crystal, *txtng: The gr8 db8*.

91. See J. C. McCroskey and M. J. Beatty, "The Communibiological Perspective: Implications for Communication in Instruction," *Communication Education* 49 (January 2000): 1–6; M. J. Beatty and M. J. McCroskey, "Theory, Scientific Evidence, and the Communibiological Paradigm: Reflections on Misguided Criticism," *Communication Education* 49 (January 2000): 36–44. Also see J. C. McCroskey, J. A. Daly, M. M. Martin, and M. J. Beatty (eds.), *Communication and Personality: Trait Perspectives* (Cresskill, NJ: Hampton Press, 1998); and M. J. Beatty, A. D. Heisel, A. E. Hall, T. R. Levine, and B. H. La France, "What Can We Learn from the Study of Twins about Genetic and Environmental Influences on Interpersonal Affiliation, Aggressiveness, and Social Anxiety? A Meta-Analytic Study," *Communication Monographs* 69 (March 2002): 1–18.

92. S. R. Wilson and C. M. Sabee, "Explicating Communicative Competence as a Theoretical Term," in *Handbook of Communication and Social Interaction Skills*, edited by J. O. Greene and B. R. Burleson (Mahwah, NJ: Erlbaum, 2003), 3–50.

93. M. J. Collier, "Researching Cultural Identity: Reconciling Interpretive and Post-colonial Approaches," in *Communication and Identity Across Cultures*, edited by D. Tanno and A. Gonzalez (Thousand Oaks, CA: Sage, 1998), 142. Also see S. DeTurk, "Intercultural Empathy: Myth, Competency, or Possibility for Alliance Building?" *Communication Education* 50 (October 2001): 374–84.

94. G. A. Hullman, "Interpersonal Communication Motives and Message Design Logic: Exploring Their Interaction on Perceptions of Competence," *Communication Monographs* 71 (2004): 208–25.

95. E. P. Almeida, "A Disclosure Analysis of Student Perceptions of Their Communication Competence," *Communication Education* 53, no. 4 (2004): 38–64.

96. Miller and deWinstanley, "The Role of Interpersonal Competence in Memory for Conversation."

97. L. Carrell and S. C. Wilmington, "A Comparison of Self-Report and Performance Data in Assessing Speaking and Listening Competence," *Communication Reports* 9, no. 2 (1996): 185–91.

98. For an excellent review of the history, development, and importance of interpersonal skills see B. H. Spizberg and W. R. Cupach, "Interpersonal Skills," in *The Sage Handbook of Interpersonal Communication*, M. L. Knapp and J. A. Daly (eds.), (Los Angeles: Sage, 2011): 481–524.

99. J. Hakansson and H. Montgomery, "Empathy as an Interpersonal Phenomenon," *Journal of Social and Personal Relationships* 20 (2003): 267–84; Y. Nakatani, "The Effects of Awareness-Raising Training on Oral Communication Strategy Use," *The Modern Language Journal* 89 (2005): 76–91.

100. For additional information about the importance of self-preservation and evolution, *see* R. Dawkins, *The Selfish Gene* (Oxford: Oxford University Press, 1976).

101. K. J. K. Asada, E. Lee, T. R Levine, and M. H. Ferrara, "Narcissism and Empathy as Predictors of Obsessive Relational Intrusion," *Communication Research Reports* 21 (2004): 379–90.

102. J. M. Twenge, *Generation Me: Why Today's Young Americans Are More Confident, Assertive, Entitled—and More Miserable Than Ever Before* (New York: Free Press, 2006) 69.

103. Twenge, *Generation Me*.

104. J. Bryner, "Brain Scans Show How Teens Are More 'Me-First' Than Adults," *Live Science Managing Editor*, January 26, 2011. http://www.livescience.com/11647-brain-scans-show-teens-adults.html.

105. M. V. Redmond, "Adaptation in Everyday Interactions," paper presented at the annual meeting of the National Communication Association (November 1997).

106. M. Argyle is widely acknowledged as the first scholar to suggest a systematic approach to applying learning theory to the development of social skills, including interpersonal communication skills. See M. Argyle, *The Psychology of Interpersonal Behavior* (London: Penguin, 1983).

Chapter 2

1. K. Horney, *Neurosis and Human Growth* (New York: Norton, 1950), 17.

2. Our definition is based on a discussion of mindfulness in K. Domenici and S. W. Littlejohn, *Facework: Bridging Theory and Practice* (Thousand Oaks, CA: Sage, 2008), 158.

3. R. A. Baron and D. Byrne, *Social Psychology* (Boston: Allyn & Bacon, 2003).

4. E. Goffman, *The Presentation of Self in Everyday Life* (Garden City, NY: Doubleday, Anchor Books, 1959). Also see E. Goffman, *Frame Analysis: An Essay on the Organization*

of Experience (Cambridge, MA: Harvard University Press, 1974).

5. Goffman, *Frame Analysis*, 508.

6. W. James, *The Principles of Psychology* (New York: Holt, 1890).

7. E. K. Kim, "What Would You Change About Your Body: Watch How Differently Kids and Adults Answer." Today Parents. www.today.com/parents/what-would-you-change-about-your-body-kids-adults-reply-1D80265960. Accessed February 24, 2015.

8. Adapted from W. Ham, *Man's Living Religions* (Independence, MO: Herald Publishing House, 1966), 39–40.

9. C. H. Cooley, *Human Nature and the Social Order* (New York: Scribner's, 1902).

10. G. H. Mead, *Mind, Self, and Society* (Chicago: University of Chicago Press, 1934).

11. H. S. Sullivan, *The Interpersonal Theory of Psychiatry* (New York: Norton, 1953).

12. See M. D. S. Ainsworth, M. C. Blehar, E. Waters, and S. Wall, *The Patterns of Attachment: A Psychological Study of the Strange Situation* (Hillsdale, NJ: Erlbaum, 1978); J. Bowlby, *Attachment and Loss: Volume 1* (London: Hogarth Press, 1969); C. Hazan and P. R. Shaver, "Romantic Love Conceptualized as an Attachment Process," *Journal of Personality and Social Psychology* 52 (1987): 511–24; K. Bartholomew, "Avoidance of Intimacy: An Attachment Perspective," *Journal of Social and Personal Relationships* 7 (1990): 147–78; A. J. Z. Henderson, K. Bartholomew, J. S. Trinke, and M. J. Kwong, "When Loving Means Hurting: An Exploration of Attachment and Intimacy Abuse in a Community Sample," *Journal of Family Violence* 20 (2005): 219–30.

13. P. R. Shaver and M. Mikulincer, "New Directions in Attachment Theory and Research," *Journal of Social and Personal Relationships* 27, no. 2 (2010): 163–72; J. A. Simpson and W. S. Rhodes, "Attachment and Relationships: Milestones and Future Directions," *Journal of Social and Personal Relationships* 27, no. 2 (2010): 173–80; L. M. Diamond and C. P. Fagundes, "Psychobiological Research on Attachment," *Journal of Social and Personal Relationships* 27, no. 2 (2010): 218–25.

14. R. Lento, K. S. Rosen, and S. Snapp, "Why Do They Hook Up? Attachment Style and Motives of College Students," *Personal Relationships* 21 (2014): 468–81.

15. Ainsworth, Blehar, Waters, and Wall, *The Patterns of Attachment*; Bowlby, *Attachment and Loss*.

16. J. He, N. Li and T. Li, "Adult Attachment and Incidental Memory for Emotional Words," *Interpersona: A Journal on Relationships, Society & Culture* 4 (December 2010): 1–20; C. Hesse and S. L. Trask, "Trait Affection and Adult Attachment Styles: Analyzing Relationships and Group Differences," *Communication Research Reports* 31.1 (2014): 53–61; S. Bolkan and A. K. Goodboy, "Attachment and the Use of Negative Relational Maintenance Behaviors in Romantic Relationships," *Communication Research Reports* 28.4 (2011): 327–36.

17. R. D. Welch and M. E. Houser, "Extending the Four-Category Model of Adult Attachment: An Interpersonal Model of Friendship Attachment," *Journal of Social and Personal Relationships* 27, no. 3 (2010): 351–66.

18. M. C. Pistole, A. Roberts, and M. L. Chapman, "Attachment, Relationship Maintenance, and Stress in Long-Distance and Geographically Close Romantic Relationships," *Journal of Social and Personal Relationships* 27, no. 4 (2010): 535–52.

19. O. Mayseless, "Attachment and the Leader-Follower Relationship," *Journal of Social and Personal Relationships* 27, no. 2 (2010): 271–80.

20. K. D. Mickelson, R. Kessler, and P. R. Shaver, "Adult Attachment in a Nationally Representative Sample," *Journal of Personality and Social Psychology* 73 (1997): 1092–1106.

21. G. Sadikaj, D. S. Moskowitz, and D. C. Zuroff, "Attachment-Related Affective Dynamics: Differential Reactivity to Others' Interpersonal Behavior," *Journal of Personality and Social Psychology* 100, no. 5 (2011): 905–17; J. E. Lydon and M. J. McClure, "Anxiety Doesn't Become You: How Attachment Anxiety Compromises Relational Opportunities," *Journal of Personality and Social Psychology* 106 (2014): 89–111.

22. K. Benjanyan, G. D. Castro, R. A. Lee, and T. C. Marshall, "Attachment Styles as Predictors of sFacebook-Related Jealousy and Surveillance in Romantic Relationships," *Personal Relationships* 20 (2013): 1–22.

23. Mickelson, Kessler, and Shaver, "Adult Attachment in a Nationally Representative Sample."

24. Lento, Rosen, and Snapp, "Why Do They Hook Up?"

25. B. Jin and J. F. Pena, "Mobile Communication in Romantic Relationships: Mobile Phone Use, Relational Uncertainty, Love, Commitment, and Attachment Styles," *Communication Reports* 23, no. 1 (January–June 2010): 39–51.

26. H. Zhang, "Self-Improvement as a Response to Interpersonal Regulation in Close Relationships: The Role of Attachment Styles," *The Journal of Social Psychology* 152.6 (2012): 697–712.

27. Mickelson, Kessler, and Shaver, "Adult Attachment in a Nationally Representative Sample."

28. L. A. Beck, C. J. DeBuse, P. R. Pietromonaco, S. I. Powers, and A. G. Sayer, "Spouses' Attachment Pairings Predict Neuroendocrine, Behavioral, and Psychological Responses to Marital Conflict," *Journal of Personality and Social Psychology* 105 (2013): 388–424.

29. J. T. Masterson, *Speech Communication in Traditional and Contemporary Marriages* (doctoral dissertation, University of Denver, 1977). Also see S. A. Beebe and J. T. Masterson, *Family Talk: Interpersonal Communication in the Family* (New York: Random House, 1986), 91–100.

30. I. Siles, "Web Technologies of the Self: The Arising of the 'Blogger' Identity," *Journal of Computer-Mediated Communication* 17 (2012): 408–21.

31. B. Marcus, F. Machilek, and A. Schutz, "Personality in Cyberspace: Personal Web Sites as Media for Personality Expressions and Impressions," *Journal of Personality and Social Psychology* 90, no. 6 (2006): 1014–31; J. B. Walther, B. Van Der Heide, S. Y. Kim, D. Westerman, and S. T. Tong, "The Role of Friends' Appearance and Behavior on Evaluations of Individuals on Facebook: Are We Known by the Company We Keep?" *Human Communication Research* 34 (2008): 28–49.

32. L. C. Tidwell and J. B. Walther, "Computer-Mediated Communication Effects on Disclosure, Impressions, and Interpersonal Evaluations: Getting to Know One Another a Bit at a Time," *Human Communication Research* 28 (July 2002): 317–48.

33. S. S. Ho and D. M. McLeod, "Social-Psychological Influences on Opinion Expression in Face-to-Face and Computer-Mediated Communication," *Communication Research* 35 (2008): 190–207.

34. A. M. Ledbetter, "Measuring Online Communication Attitude: Instrument Development and Validation," *Communication Monographs* (2009): 463–86. Also see A. M. Ledbetter, J. P Mazer, J. M. DeGroot, K. R. Meyer, Y. Mao, and B. Swafford, "Attitudes Toward Online Social Connection and Self-Disclosure as Predictors of Facebook Communication and Relational Closeness," *Communication Research* 38, no. 1 (2011): 27–53.

35. B. Cornwell and D. C. Lundgren, "Love on the Internet: Involvement and Misrepresentation in Romantic Relationships in Cyberspace vs. Realspace," *Computers in Human Behavior* 17 (2001): 197–211.

36. D. Knox, V. Daniels, L. Sturdivant, and M. E. Zusman, "College Student Use of the Internet for Mate Selection," *College Student Journal* 35 (March 2001): 158.

37. N. B. Ellison, R. Gray, C. Lampe, and J. Vitak, "Cultivating Social Resources on Social Network Sites: Facebook Relationship Maintenance Behaviors and Their Role in Social Capital Processes," *Journal of Computer-Mediated Communication* 19 (2014): 855–70.

38. M. K. Matsuba, "Searching for Self and Relationships Online," *CyberPsychology & Behavior* 3 (2006): 275–84.

39. D. Atkin, D. Hunt, and A. Krishnan, "The Influence of Computer-Mediated Communication Apprehension on Motives for Facebook Use," *Journal of Broadcasting & Electronic Media* 56.2 (2012): 187–202.

40. R. L. Duran, L. Kelly, and B. C. McKinney, "Narcissism or Openness?: College Students' Use of Facebook and Twitter," *Communication Research Reports* 29 (2012): 108–18.

41. D. G. Ancona, "Groups in Organizations: Extending Laboratory Models,"

in *Annual Review of Personality and Social Psychology: Group and Intergroup Processes*, edited by C. Hendrick (Beverly Hills, CA: Sage, 1987), 207–31. Also see D. G. Ancona and D. E. Caldwell, "Beyond Task and Maintenance: Defining External Functions in Groups," *Group and Organizational Studies* 13 (1988): 468–94.

42. S. L. Bern, "The Measurement of Psychological Androgyny," *Journal of Consulting and Clinical Psychology* 42 (1974): 155–62.

43. L. A. Lefton, *Psychology* (Boston: Allyn & Bacon, 2000).

44. For research supporting the Big Five Personality Traits see: R. R. McCrae and P. T. Costa, "Validation of the Five-Factor Model of Personality Across Instruments and Observers," *Journal of Personality and Social Psychology* 52 (1987): 81–90; S. V. Paunonen and M. S. Ashton, "Big Five Factors and Facets and the Prediction of Behavior," *Journal of Personality & Social Psychology* 81 (2001): 524–39; H. E. Cattell, "The Original Big Five: A Historical Perspective," *European Review of Applied Psychology* (1996): 5–14.

45. N. Egbert and J. Rosenberg, "Online Impression Management: Personality Traits and Concerns for Secondary Goals as Predictors of Self-Presentation Tactics on Facebook," *Journal of Computer-Mediated Communication* 17 (2011): 1–18.

46. J. C. McCroskey and M. J. Beatty, "The Communibiological Perspective: Implications for Communication Instruction," *Communication Education* 49 (January 2000): 1–28.

47. See J. Ayres and T. S. Hopf, "The Long-Term Effect of Visualization in the Classroom: A Brief Research Report," *Communication Education* 39 (1990): 75–78; and J. Ayres and T. S. Hopf, "Visualization: A Means of Reducing Speech Anxiety," *Communication Education* 34 (1985): 7–24.

48. C. M. Condit, "Culture and Biology in Human Communication: Toward a Multi-Causal Model," *Communication Education* 49 (January 2000): 7–24. Also see K. Floyd, A. C. Mikkelson, and C. Hesse, *The Biology of Human Communication* (Mason, OH: Cengage Learning), 2008. For a contrasting view of the importance of biology in shaping our behavior, see S. Begley, "When DNA Is Not Destiny," *Newsweek* (December 1, 2008): 14.

49. A. Bandura, *Social Learning Theory* (Englewood Cliffs, NJ: Prentice-Hall, 1977).

50. P. Zimbardo, *Shyness: What It Is, What to Do About It* (Reading, MA: Addison-Wesley, 1977).

51. S. Booth-Butterfield, "Instructional Interventions for Situational Anxiety and Avoidance," *Communication Education* 37 (1988): 214–23.

52. J. C. McCroskey and V. P. Richmond, *Fundamentals of Human Communication: An Interpersonal Perspective* (Prospect Heights, IL: Waveland Press, 1996).

53. Booth-Butterfield, "Instructional Interventions."

54. Zimbardo, *Shyness.*

55. W. Gerrod Parrott, "The Nature of Emotion," in *Emotion and Motivation*, edited by M. B. Brewer and M. Hewston (Oxford, England: Blackwell Publishing, 2004), 6. Also see R. A. Baron, B. Earhard, and M. Ozier, *Psychology* (Toronto: Pearson Education, 2001).

56. See W. James, "What Is an Emotion?" *Mind* 9 (1884): 188–205. Also see B. Parkinson, A. H. Fischer, and A. S. R. Manstead, *Emotion in Social Relations: Cultural, Group, and Interpersonal Processes* (New York: Psychology Press, 2004).

57. S. Schacter and J. E. Singer, "Cognitive, Social, and Physiological Determinants of Emotional States," *Psychological Review* 69 (1962): 379–99.

58. E. Sahlstein and M. Allen, "Sex Differences in Self-Esteem: A Meta-Analytic Assessment," in *Interpersonal Communication Research: Advances Through Meta-Analysis*, edited by M. Allen, R. W. Preiss, B. M. Gayle, and N. A. Burrell (Mahwah, NJ: Erlbaum, 2002), 59–72; K. Dindia, "Self-Disclosure Research: Knowledge Through Meta-Analysis," in *Interpersonal Communication Research: Advances Through Meta-Analysis*, edited by M. Allen, R. W. Preiss, B. M. Gayle, and N. A. Burrell (Mahwah, NJ: Erlbaum, 2002), 169–85; G. V. Caprara and P. Steca, "Self-Efficacy Beliefs as Determinants of Prosocial Behavior Conducive to Life Satisfaction Across Ages," *Journal of Social and Clinical Psychology* 24 (2005): 191–217.

59. S. M. Pottebaum, T. Z. Keith, and S. W. Ehly, "Is There a Causal Relation Between Self-Concept and Academic Achievement?" *Journal of Educational Research* 79, no. 3 (January/February 1986): 140–44.

60. R. F. Baumeister, J. D. Campbell, J. I. Krueger, and K. D. Vohs, "Does High Self-Esteem Cause Better Performance, Interpersonal Success, Happiness, or Healthier Lifestyles?" *Psychological Science in the Public Interest* 4, no. 1 (May 2003): 1–44. Also see S. Lyubomirsky, C. Tkach, and M. R. Dimatteo, "What Are the Differences Between Happiness and Self-Esteem?" *Social Indicators Research* 78 (2006): 363–404.

61. For a discussion of self-efficacy see A. Bandura "Self-Efficacy: Toward a Unifying Theory of Behavior Change," *Psychological Review* 84, no. 2 (1977): 191–215; A. Bandura and N. E. Adams, "Analysis of Self-Efficacy Theory of Behavioral Change," *Cognitive Therapy and Research* 1, no. 4 (1977): 287–310.

62. P. Mahatanankoon and P. O'Sullivan, "Attitude Toward Mobile Text Messaging: An Expectancy-Based Perspective," *Journal of Computer-Mediated Communication* 13 (2008): 973–92.

63. L. E. Park and J. Crocker, "Contingencies of Self-Worth and Responses to Negative Interpersonal Feedback," *Self and Identity* 7 (2008): 184–203.

64. N. Fay, A. C. Page, and C. Serfaty, "Listeners Influence Speakers' Perceived Communication Effectiveness," *Journal of Experimental Social Psychology* 46 (2010): 689–92.

65. E. Berne, *Games People Play* (New York: Grove Press, 1964).

66. A. Holman and J. Stephenson-Abetz, "Home Is Where the Heart Is: Facebook and the Negotiation of 'Old' and 'New' During the Transition to College," *Western Journal of Communication* 76 (2012): 175–193.

67. S. Ting Toomey, J. G. Oetzel, and K. YeeJung, "Self-Construal Types and Conflict Management Styles," *Communication Reports* 14 (Summer 2001): 87–104.

68. W. R. Cupach and S. Metts, *Facework* (Thousand Oaks, CA: Sage, 1994).

69. For a comprehensive discussion of the history of facework, see Domenici and Littlejohn, *Facework.*

70. Goffman, *The Presentation of Self in Everyday Life.*

71. L. A. Withers and J. C. Sherblom, "Embarrassment: The Communication of an Awkward Actor Anticipating a Negative Evaluation," *Human Communication* 11 (2008): 237–54.

72. D. Estrada, C. Fleuriet, and M. L. Houser, "The Cyber Factor: An Analysis of Relational Maintenance Through the Use of Computer-Mediated Communication," *Communication Research Reports* 29 (2012): 34–43.

73. Domenici and Littlejohn, *Facework.*

74. Domenici and Littlejohn, *Facework.*

75. P. Brown and S. C. Levinson, *Politeness: Some Universals in Language Use* (Cambridge, England: Cambridge University Press, 1987).

76. Domenici and Littlejohn, *Facework.*

77. Barbra Streisand as told to Oprah Winfrey, September 23, 2009. www.oprah.com/oprahshow/Barbra-Streisands-Stage-Fright-Video. Accessed August 29, 2012.

78. Jane Pauley, *Your Life Calling: Reimagining the Rest of Your Life.* (New York: Simon & Schuster), 65–6.

79. J. L. S. Borton, L. J. Markowitz, and J. Dieterich, "Effects of Suppressing Negative Self-Referent Thoughts on Mood and Self-Esteem," *Journal of Social and Clinical Psychology* 24 (2005): 172–90.

80. D. B. Feldman and C. R. Snyder, "Hope and the Meaningful Life: Theoretical and Empirical Associations Between Goal-Directed Thinking and Life Meaning," *Journal of Social and Clinical Psychology* 24 (2005): J401–21.

81. Ayres and Hopf, "The Long-Term Effect of Visualization in the Classroom."

82. J. W. Younger, R. L. Piferi, R. L. Jobe, and K. A. Lawler, "Dimensions of Forgiveness: The Views of Laypersons," *Journal of Social and Personal Relationships* 21 (2004): 837–55.

83. K. Weber, A. Johnson, and M. Corrigan, "Communicating Emotional Support and Its Relationship to Feelings of Being Understood, Trust, and Self-Disclosure," *Communication Research Reports* 21 (2004): 316–23.

84. A. J. Holmstrom, "What Helps—and What Doesn't—When Self-Esteem is Threatened?: Retrospective Reports of

Esteem Support," *Communication Studies* 63 (2012): 77–98.

85. A. Gustafson and R. S. Tokunaga, "Seeking Interpersonal Information over the Internet: An Application of the Theory of Motivated Information Management to Internet Use," *Journal of Social and Personal Relationships* 31.8 (2014): 1019–39.

86. F. E. X. Dance and C. Larson, *The Functions of Human Communication* (New York: Holt, Rinehart and Winston, 1976), 141.

87. Mead, *Mind, Self, and Society.*

88. P. A. Siegel, J. Scillitoe, and R. Parks-Yancy, "Reducing the Tendency to Self-Handicap: The Effect of Self-Affirmation," *Journal of Experimental Social Psychology* 41, no. 6 (2005): 589–97.

89. Caprara and Steca, "Self-Efficacy Beliefs as Determinants of Prosocial Behavior."

90. H. Brody, *The Placebo Response: How You Can Release Your Body's Inner Pharmacy for Better Health* (New York: HarperCollins, 2000). Also see H. Brody, "Tapping the Power of the Placebo," *Newsweek* (August 14, 2000): 68.

91. A. A. Milne, "Pooh Does a Good Deed," in *Pooh Sleepytime Stories* (New York: Golden Press, 1979), 44.

92. *Looking Out/Looking In,* edited by R. B. Adler and N. Towne (Fort Worth, TX: Harcourt Brace Jovanovich, 1993). Also see C. R. Berger, "Self Conception and Social Information Processing," in *Personality and Interpersonal Communication,* edited by J. C. McCroskey and J. A. Daly (1986): 275–303.

93. A. A. Milne, "Owl Finds a Home," in *Pooh Sleepytime Stories* (New York: Golden Press, 1979), 28.

94. D. E. Harnachek, *Encounters with the Self* (New York: Holt, Rinehart and Winston, 1982); Berger, "Self-Conception."

95. W. C. Schutz, *FIRO: A Three-Dimensional Theory of Interpersonal Behavior* (New York: Holt, Rinehart and Winston, 1958).

96. J. S. Aubrey and L. Rill, "Investigating Relations Between Facebook Use and Social Capital Among College Undergraduates," *Communication Quarterly* 61 (2013): 479–96.

97. K. Floyd, "Relational and Health Correlates of Affection Deprivation," *Western Journal of Communication* 78 (September 2014): 383–403.

98. V. J. Derlega, B. A. Winstead, A. Mathews, and A. L. Braitman, "Why Does Someone Reveal Highly Personal Information? Attributions For and Against Self-Disclosure in Close Relationships," *Communication Research Reports* 25, no. 2 (May 2008): 115–30.

99. Dindia, "Self-Disclosure Research."

100. J. P. Forgas, "Affective Influence on Self-Disclosure: Mood Effects on the Intimacy and Reciprocity of Disclosing Personal Information," *Journal of Personality and Social Psychology* 100, no. 3 (2011): 449–61.

101. B. J. Bond, "He Posted, She Posted: Gender Differences in Self-Disclosure on Social Network Sites," *Rocky Mountain Communication Review* 6, no. 2 (October 2009): 29–37.

102. Bond, "He Posted, She Posted," 29.

103. M. K. Everett and E. E. Hollenbaugh, "The Effects of Anonymity on Self-Disclosure in Blogs: An Application of the Online Disinhibition Effect," *Journal of Computer-Mediated Communication* 18 (2013): 283–302.

104. J. Luft, *Group Process: An Introduction to Group Dynamics* (Palo Alto, CA: Mayfield, 1970).

105. C. G. Jung, *Psychological Types* (Princeton, NJ: Princeton University Press, 1976).

106. For a review of applied social style research, see R. Bolton and D. G. Bolton, *People Styles at Work: Making Bad Relationships Good and Good Relationships Better* (New York: AMACOM, 1996). For an excellent review of communication and social style research literature, see W. B. Snavely and J. D. McNeill, "Communicator Style and Social Style: Testing a Theoretical Interface," *Journal of Leadership and Organizational Studies* 14, no. 3 (February 2008): 219–32.

107. Snavely and McNeill, "Communicator Style and Social Style," 220.

108. Snavely and McNeill, "Communicator Style and Social Style," 219.

109. Bolton and Bolton, *People Styles at Work,* 82.

110. Bolton and Bolton, *People Styles at Work,* 83.

Chapter 3

1. P. R. Hinton, *The Psychology of Interpersonal Perception* (New York: Routledge, 1993).

2. M. Gladwell, *Blink: The Power of Thinking Without Thinking* (New York: Little, Brown and Company, 2005).

3. O. Kang and D. L. Rubin, "Reverse Linguistic Stereotyping: Measuring the Effect of Listener Expectations on Speech Evaluations," *Journal of Language and Social Psychology* 28, no. 4 (2009): 441–546.

4. P. Watzlawick, J. Bevelas, and D. Jackson, *The Pragmatics of Human Communication* (New York: Norton, 1967).

5. A. L. Sillars, "Attribution and Communication: Are People Naive Scientists or Just Naive?" in *Social Cognition and Communication,* edited by M. E. Roloff and C. R. Berger (Beverly Hills, CA: Sage, 1982), 73–106.

6. Watzlawick et al., *The Pragmatics of Human Communication.*

7. F. R. D. Carpentier, C. T. Northup, and M. S. Parrott, "When First Comes Love (or Lust): How Romantic and Sexual Cues Bias First Impressions in Online Social Networking," *The Journal of Social Psychology* 154 (2014): 423–40.

8. S. Bruner and R. Tagiuri, "The Perception of People," in *Handbook of Social Psychology,* edited by G. Lindzey (Cambridge, MA: Addison-Wesley, 1954).

9. G. A. Kelly, *The Psychology of Personal Constructs* (New York: Norton, 1995).

10. C. R. Berger and J. J. Bradac, *Language and Social Knowledge* (Baltimore: Edward Arnold, 1982).

11. S. Utz, "Show Me Your Friends and I Will Tell You What Type of Person You Are: How One's Profile, Number of Friends, and Type of Friends Influence Impression Formation on Social Networking Sites," *Journal of Computer-Mediated Communication* 15 (2010): 314–35.

12. S. D. Gosling, D. Gaddis, and S. Vazier, "Personality Impressions Based on Facebook Profiles," in *Proceedings of the International Conference on Weblogs and Social Media* (Boulder, CO, March 26–28, 2007).

13. S. T. Tong, B. Van Der Heide, L. Langwell, and J. B. Walther, "Too Much of a Good Thing? The Relationship Between Number of Friends and Interpersonal Impressions on Facebook," *Journal of Computer-Mediated Communication* 13 (2008): 531–49.

14. S. Graham, "More Than Friends: Popularity on Facebook and its Role in Impression Formation," *Journal of Computer-Mediated Communication* 19 (2014): 358–72.

15. S. Asch, "Forming Impressions of Personality," *Journal of Abnormal and Social Psychology* 41 (1946): 258–90.

16. M. Sunnafrank, "Predicted Outcome Value During Initial Interactions: A Reformulation of Uncertainty Reduction Theory," *Human Communication Research* 13 (1986): 3–33; M. Sunnafrank, "Predicted Outcome Value in Initial Conversations," *Communication Research Reports* 5 (1988): 169–72; M. Sunnafrank and A. Ramirez, "At First Sight: Persistent Relational Effects of Get-Acquainted Conversations," *Journal of Social and Personal Relationships* 21 (2004): 361–79.

17. S. M. Horan, M. M. Martin, N. Smith, M. Schoo, M. Eidsness, and A. Johnson, "Can We Talk? How Learning of an Invisible Illness Impacts Forecasted Relational Outcomes," *Communication Studies* 60, no. 1 (January-March 2009): 66–81.

18. D. M. Wegner and R. R Vallacher, *Implicit Psychology: An Introduction to Social Cognition* (New York: Oxford University Press, 1977).

19. A. L. Sillars, "Attributions and Communication in Roommate Conflicts," *Communication Monographs* 47 (1980): 180–200.

20. J. H. Yoo, "The Power of Sharing Negative Information in a Dyadic Context," *Communication Reports* 22, no. 1 (January-June 2009): 29–40.

21. R. F. Baumeister, E. Bratslavsky, C. Finkenauer, and K. D. Vohs. "Bad is Stronger Than Good," *Review of General Psychology,* 5, no. 4 (2001): 323–70.

22. D. A. Infante and A. S. Rancer, "Argumentativeness and Verbal Aggressiveness: A Review of Recent Theory and Research," in *Communication Yearbook* 19, edited by B. R. Burleson (Thousand Oaks, CA: Sage, 1996), 319–52.

23. D. Hample, "The Life Space of Personalized Conflicts," in *Communication Yearbook* 23, edited by M. E. Roloff (Thousand Oaks, CA: Sage, 1999), 171–208.

24. F. Heider, *The Psychology of Interpersonal Relations* (New York: Wiley, 1958). Also see E. E. Jones and K. E. Davis, "From Acts to Dispositions: The Attribution Process in Person Perception," in *Advances in Experimental Social Psychology* 2, edited by L. Berkowitz (New York: Academic Press, 1965).

25. G. A. Kelly, *The Psychology of Personal Constructs* (New York: Norton, 1955).

26. D. F. Henson and K. C. Dybvig-Pawelko, "The Effects of Loneliness on Relational Maintenance Behaviors: An Attributional Perspective," *Communication Research Reports* 21 (2004): 411–19.

27. A. L. Vangelisti and S. L. Young, "When Words Hurt: The Effects of Perceived Intentionality on Interpersonal Relationships," *Journal of Social and Personal Relationships* 17 (2000): 393–424.

28. G. W. F. Hegel, *Phenomenology of Mind* (Germany: Wurzburg & Bamburg, 1807).

29. R. M. Kowalski, S. Walker, R. Wilkinson, A. Queen, and B. Sharpe, "Lying, Cheating, Complaining, and Other Aversive Interpersonal Behaviors: A Narrative Examination of the Darker Side of Relationships," *Journal of Social and Personal Relationships* 20 (2003): 472–90.

30. P. Cateora and J. Hess, *International Marketing* (Homewood, IL: Irwin, 1979), 89; as discussed by L. A. Samovar and R. E. Porter, *Communication Between Cultures* (Belmont, CA: Wadsworth, 2001), 52.

31. F. T. McAndrew, A. Akande, R. Bridgstock, L. Mealey, S. C. Gordon, J. E. Scheib, B. E. Akande-Adetoun, F. Odewale, A. Morakinyo, P. Nyahete, and G. Mubvakure, "A Multicultural Study of Stereotyping in English-Speaking Countries," *The Journal of Social Psychology* 140 (2000): 487–502.

32. See G. W. Allport, *The Nature of Prejudice* (Reading, MA: Addison-Wesley, 1979); P. C. Hughes and J. R. Baldwin, "Communication and Stereotypical Impressions," *The Howard Journal of Communications* 13 (2002): 113–28.

33. D. G. Embrick, C. S. Walther, and C. M. Wickens, "Working Class Masculinity: Keeping Gay Men and Lesbians Out of the Workplace," *Sex Roles* 56 (2007): 757–66; Hughes and Baldwin, "Communication and Stereotypical Impressions"; T. Mottet, "The Role of Sexual Orientation in Predicting Outcome Value and Anticipated Communication Behaviors," *Communication Quarterly* 43 (Summer 2000): 223–39.

34. Embrick, Walther, and Wickens, "Working Class Masculinity;" Hughes and Baldwin, "Communication and Stereotypical Impressions."

35. M. M. Duguid and M. C. Thomas-Hunt, "Condoning Stereotyping?: How Awareness of Stereotyping Prevalence Impacts Expression of Stereotypes," *Journal of Applied Psychology* (October 2014).

36. A. Lyons and Y. Kashima, "How Are Stereotypes Maintained Through Communication? The Influence of Stereotype Sharedness," *Journal of Personality and Social Psychology* 85, no. 6 (2003): 989–1005.

37. E. E. Jones and R. Nisbett, "The Actor and the Observer: Divergent Perceptions of the Causes of Behavior," in *Attribution: Perceiving the Causes of Behavior,* edited by E. E. Jones, D. Kanouse, H. Kelley, R. Nisbett, S. Valins, and B. Weiner, (Morristown, NJ: General Learning Press, 1972), 79–94; D. E. Kanouse and L. R. Hanson, Jr., "Negativity in Evaluations," in Jones et al., *Attribution,* 47–62.

38. R. Nisbett and L. Ross, *Human Inference: Strategies and Shortcomings of Social Judgment* (Englewood Cliffs, NJ: Prentice Hall, 1980).

39. See E.-J. Lee, "Effects of Gendered Language on Gender Stereotyping in Computer-Mediated Communication: The Moderating Role of Depersonalization and Gender-Role Orientation," *Human Communication Research* 33 (2007): 515–35.

40. N. Epley and J. Kruger, "When What You Type Isn't What They Read: The Perseverance of Stereotypes and Expectancies over Email," *Journal of Experimental Social Psychology* 41 (2005): 414–22.

41. E.-J. Lee, "Effects of the Influence Agent's Sex and Self-Confidence on Informational Influence in Computer-Mediated Communication: Quantitative vs. Verbal Presentation," *Communication Research* 32 (2005): 29–58.

42. J. B. Walther, B. Van Der Heide, S. Y. Kim, D. Westerman, and S. T. Tong, "The Role of Friends' Appearance and Behavior on Evaluations of Individuals on Facebook: Are We Known by the Company We Keep?" *Human Communication Research* 34 (2008): 28–49

43. Walther, Van Der Heide, Kim, Westerman, and Tong, "The Role of Friends' Appearance and Behavior on Evaluations of Individuals on Facebook."

44. E. M. Boucher, J. T. Hancock, and P. J. Dunham, "Interpersonal Sensitivity in Computer-Mediated and Face-to-Face Conversations," *Media Psychology* 11 (2008): 235–58.

45. F. F. Jordan-Jackson and K. A. Davis, "Men Talk: An Exploratory Study of Communication Patterns and Communication Apprehension of Black and White Males," *The Journal of Men's Studies* 13 (2005): 347–67.

46. A. G. Greenwald, D. E. McGhee, and J. L. K. Schwartz, "Measuring Individual Differences in Implicit Cognition: The Implicit Association Test," *Journal of Personality and Social Psychology* 74, no. 6 (1998): 1464–80; A. H. Eagly, M. G. Makhijani, R. D. Ashmore, and L. C. Longo, "What Is Beautiful Is Good, But ... A Meta-Analytic Review of Research of the Physical Attractiveness Stereotype," *Psychological Bulletin* 110, no. 1 (1991): 109–28.

47. Nisbett and Ross, *Human Inference.*

48. Asch, "Forming Impressions of Personality."

49. K. Floyd, "Attributions for Nonverbal Expressions of Liking and Disliking: The Extended Self-Serving Bias," *Western Journal of Communication* 64 (Fall 2000): 388.

50. S. LaBelle and M. M. Martin, "Attribution Theory in the College Classroom: Examining the Relationship of Student Attributions and Instructional Dissent," *Communication Research Reports* 31.1 (January–March 2014): 110–16.

51. N. Epley, T. Gilovich, and K. Savitsky, "Empathy Neglect: Reconciling the Spotlight Effect and the Correspondence Bias," *Journal of Personality and Social Psychology* 83, no. 2 (2002): 300–12.

52. E. Goffman, *The Presentation of Self in Everyday Life* (New York: Doubleday, 1959).

53. P. Brown and S. C. Levinson, *Politeness: Some Universals in Language Use* (Cambridge, England: Cambridge University Press, 1987).

54. G. W. Lewandowsky Jr., B. A. Mattingly, and A. Pedreiro, "Under Pressure: The Effects of Stress on Positive and Negative Relationship Behaviors," *The Journal of Social Psychology* 154 (2014): 463–73.

55. J. Gasiorek, "'I Was Impolite to Her Because That's How She Was to Me': Perceptions of Motive and Young Adults' Communicative Responses to Underaccommodation," *Western Journal of Communication* 77.5 (October–December 2013): 604–24.

56. M. V. Redmond, "The Functions of Empathy (Decentering) in Human Relations," *Human Relations* 42, no. 4 (1993): 593–606.

Chapter 4

1. J. Kantor, "Nation's Many Faces in Extended First Family," *The New York Times,* (January 21, 2009): AI.

2. W. B. Gudykunst and Y. Y. Kim, *Communicating with Strangers: An Approach to Intercultural Communication* (New York: McGraw-Hill, Inc. 1997). Also see W. B. Gudykunst, "Similarities and Differences in Perceptions of Initial Intracultural and Intercultural Encounters," *Southern Speech Communication Journal* 49 (1983): 49–65; W. B. Gudykunst, "Theorizing in Intercultural Communication: An Introduction," in *Intercultural Communication Theory: Current Perspectives,* edited by W. B. Gudykunst (Beverly Hills, CA: Sage, 1983), 13–20; W. B. Gudykunst, "A Model of Uncertainty Reduction in Intercultural Encounters," *Journal of Language and Social Psychology* 4 (1985): 79–97; W. B. Gudykunst, E. Chua, and A. Gray, "Cultural Dissimilarities and Uncertainty Reduction Processes," in *Communication Yearbook 10,* edited by M. L. McLaughlin (Beverly Hills, CA: Sage, 1987), 456–69; W. B. Gudykunst and T. Nishida, "Individual and Cultural Influences on Uncertainty Reduction," *Communication Monographs* 51 (1984): 23–36; W. B. Gudykunst, S.-M. Yang, and T. Nishida, "Cultural Differences in Self-Consciousness and Self-Monitoring," *Communication Monographs* 14 (1987): 7–14; J. R. Baldwin and S. K. Hunt, "Information-Seeking Behavior in Intercultural and Intergroup

Communication," *Human Communication Research* 8 (April 2002): 272–86.

3. Gudykunst and Kim, *Communicating with Strangers*, 20.

4. D. Matsumoto and L. Juang, *Culture and Psychology* (Belmont, CA: Wadsworth/ Thomson, 2004), 80–1.

5. M. E. Ryan, "Another Way to Teach Migrant Students," *Los Angeles Times* (March 31, 1991): B20, as cited by M. W. Lustig and J. Koester, *Intercultural Competence: Interpersonal Communication Across Cultures* (Boston: Allyn & Bacon, 2009), 11.

6. Lustig and Koester, *Intercultural Competence*, 8.

7. G. Chen and W. J. Starosta, "A Review of the Concept of Intercultural Sensitivity," *Human Communication* 1 (1997): 7.

8. Lustig and Koester, *Intercultural Competence*, 10; L. Lucic, "Use of Evaluative Devices by Youth for Sense-Making of Culturally Diverse Interpersonal Interactions," *International Journal of Intercultural Relations* 37 (2013): 434–49.

9. B. Larmer, V. Chambers, A. Figueroa, P. Wingert, and J. Weingarten, "Latino America," *Newsweek,* July 12, 1999, 51.

10. U.S. Bureau of the Census, *Statistical Abstract of the United States: 1996*, 116th ed. (Washington, DC: 1996), as cited by Lustig and Koester, *Intercultural Competence*, 8.

11. Los Angeles Almanac, www.laalmanac.com/population/po55.htm. Accessed May 26, 2008.

12. Yankelovich, Inc. 2003, "Beyond the Boomers: Millennials and Generation X," http://resources.ketchum.com/weblboomers.pdf. Accessed May 26, 2008.

13. "One Nation, One Language?" *U.S. News & World Report* (September 25, 1995):40, as cited by Lustig and Koester, *Intercultural Competence*, 10.

14. S. Roberts, *Who We Are Now: The Changing Face of America in the Twenty-First Century* (New York: Henry Holt, 2004), 122.

15. Roberts, *Who We Are Now*, 126.

16. W. Wang, "The Rise of Intermarriage" Pew Research Center: Social & Geographic Trends, February, 2012 www.pewsocialtrends.org/2012/02/16/the-rise-of-intermarriage/. Accessed February 15, 2015.

17. R. Bernstein, press release, Public Information Office, U.S. Census Bureau, www.census.gov/Press-Release/www/releases/archives/population/010048.html.

18. We acknowledge and appreciate the contributions in this section of D. Ivy, from her work in D. K. Ivy and P. Backlund, *GenderSpeak: Personal Effectiveness in Gender Communication* (Boston: Allyn & Bacon, 2009); S. A. Beebe, S. J. Beebe, and D. K. Ivy, *Communication: Principles for a Lifetime* (Boston: Allyn & Bacon, 2010); W. Wood and A. H. Eagly, "A Cross-Cultural Analysis of the Behavior of Women and Men: Implications for the Origins of Sex Differences," *Psychological Bulletin* 128, no. 5 (2002): 699–727.

19. J. Gray, *Men Are from Mars, Women Are from Venus* (New York: HarperCollins, 1992).

20. J. T. Wood, "A Critical Response to John Gray's Mars and Venus Portrayals of Men and Women," *The Southern Communication Journal* 67 (2002): 201–11.

21. E. Hatfield, R. L Rapson, and Y. L. Le, "Ethnic and Gender Differences in Emotional Ideology, Experience, and Expression," *Interpersona* 3, no. 1 (2009): 31–54.

22. R. Edwards and M. A. Hamilton, "You Need to Understand My Gender Role: An Empirical Test of Tannen's Model of Gender and Communication," *Sex Roles* 50, no. 718 (2004): 491–504.

23. D. Tannen, *You Just Don't Understand* (New York: William Morrow, 1990).

24. L. J. Dixon, "Gendered Space: The Digital Divide between Male and Female Users in Internet Public Access Sites," *Journal of Computer-Mediated Communication* 19 (2014): 991–1009.

25. K. Barry, D. Biagini, C. Hart, L. Jack, S. Mackey-Kallis, J. Rose, and L. Shyles, "Face It: The Impact of Gender on Social Media Images," *Communication Quarterly* 60 (2012): 588–607.

26. J. A. Hall, N. Park, H. Song, and M. J. Cody, "Strategic Misrepresentation in Online Dating: The Effects of Gender, Self-Monitoring, and Personality Traits," *Journal of Social and Personal Relationships* 27, no. 1 (2010): 117–35.

27. Tannen, *You Just Don't Understand*.

28. S. Sprecher and M. Toro-Morn, "A Study of Men and Women from Different Sides of Earth to Determine if Men Are from Mars and Women Are from Venus in Their Beliefs About Love and Romantic Relationships," *Sex Roles* 46, no. 5/6 (March 2002): 131–47.

29. P. Gibson, "Gay Male and Lesbian Youth Suicide," *Report of the Secretary's Task Force on Youth Suicide,* edited by M. R. Feinleib (Washington, DC: U.S. Department of Health and Human Services, January 1989).

30. T. Mottet, "The Role of Sexual Orientation in Predicting Outcome Value and Anticipated Communication Behaviors," *Communication Quarterly* 43 (Summer 2000): 223–39.

31. G. M. Herek, "Heterosexuals' Attitudes Toward Lesbian and Gay Men: Correlates and Gender Differences," *The Journal of Sex Research* 25 (1988): 451–77.

32. G. M. Herek, "Heterosexuals' Attitudes Toward Lesbian and Gay Men"; M. S. Weinberg and C. J. Williams, *Male Homosexuals: Their Problems and Adaptations* (New York: The Free Press, 1974); T. Mottet, "The Role of Sexual Orientation in Predicting Outcome Value and Anticipated Communication Behaviors."

33. APA Style.org, "Removing Bias in Language: Sexuality," www.apastyle.org/sexuality.html. Accessed March 2006.

34. *Random House Webster's Unabridged Dictionary* (New York: Random House, 1998), 1590.

35. R. Lewontin, "The Apportionment of Human Diversity," *Evolutionary Biology* 6 (1973): 381–97.

36. Matsumoto and Juang, *Culture and Psychology*, 16; also see H. A. Yee, H. H. Fairchild, F. Weizmann, and E. G. Wyatt, "Addressing Psychology's Problems with Race," *American Psychologist* 48 (1994): 1132–40.

37. B. J. Allen, *Differences Matter: Communicating Social Identity* (Long Grove, IL: Waveland Press, 2004), 68.

38. Allen, *Differences Matter*.

39. S. Grasmuck, J. Martin, and S. Zhao, "Ethno-Racial Identity Displays on Facebook," *Journal of Computer-Mediated Communication* 15 (2009): 158–88.

40. A. Williams and P. Garrett, "Communication Evaluations Across the Life Span: From Adolescent Storm and Stress to Elder Aches and Pains," *Journal of Language and Social Psychology* 21 (June 2002): 101–26; also see D. Cai, H. Giles, and K. Noels, "Elderly Perceptions of Communication with Older and Younger Adults in China: Implications for Mental Health," *Journal of Applied Communication Research* 26 (1998): 32–51.

41. J. Montepare, E. Koff, D. Zaitchik, and M. Albert, "The Use of Body Movements and Gestures as Cues to Emotions in Younger and Older Adults," *Journal of Nonverbal Behavior* 23 (Summer 1999): 133–52.

42. J. Harwood, E. B. Ryan, H. Giles, and S. Tysoski, "Evaluations of Patronizing Speech and Three Response Styles in a Non-Service-Providing Context," *Journal of Applied Communication Research* 25 (1997): 170–95.

43. C. Segrin, "Age Moderates the Relationship Between Social Support and Psychosocial Problems," paper presented at the International Communication Association, San Diego, California (2003).

44. N. Howe and W. Strauss, *Millennials Rising: The Next Great Generation* (New York: Vintage Books, 2000).

45. Howe and Strauss, *Millennials Rising*.

46. Our discussion of generational differences and communication is also based on J. Smith, "The Millennials Are Coming," workshop presented at Texas State University, San Marcos, TX (2006).

47. W. Wang, "The Rise of Intermarriage" Pew Research Center: Social & Geographic Trends, February, 2012 www.pewsocialtrends.org/2012/02/16/the-rise-of-intermarriage. Accessed, February 15, 2015; T. Agan, "Embracing the Millennials' Mind-Set at Work," *The New York Times* (November 9, 2013): 10.

48. K. Holt, E. Ljungberg, A. Shehata, and J. Stromback, "Age and the Effects of News Media Attention and Social Media Use on Political Interest and Participation: Do Social Media Function as Leveler?" *European Journal of Communication* 28.1 (2013): 19–34.

49. M. Booth-Butterfield, K. G. Odenweller, and K. Weber, "Investigating Helicopter Parenting, Family Environments, and Relational Outcomes for Millennials," *Communication Studies* 65 (2014): 407–425.

50. Howe and Strauss, *Millennials Rising*.

51. H. Karp, C. Fuller, and D. Sirias, *Bridging the Boomer-Xer Gap: Creating Authentic Teams for High Performance at Work*

(Palo Alto, CA: Davies-Black Publishing, 2002).

52. Howe and Strauss, *Millennials Rising*.

53. D. Bugental, R. Corpuz, and J. A. Hehman, "Patronizing Speech to Older Adults," *Journal of Nonverbal Behavior* 36 (2012): 249–61.

54. M. Argyle, *The Psychology of Social Class* (London: Routledge, 1994).

55. Allen, *Differences Matter*, 113.

56. P. Henry, "Modes of Thought That Vary Systematically with Both Social Class and Age," *Psychology & Marketing* 17 (2000): 421–40.

57. Argyle, *The Psychology of Social Class*, 62.

58. Allen, *Differences Matter*, 100.

59. G. Hofstede, *Culture's Consequences: International Differences in Work-Related Values* (Beverly Hills, CA: Sage, 1980); G. Hofstede and G. J. Hofstede, *Cultures and Organizations: Software of the Mind* (New York: McGraw-Hill, 2005); National Cultural Dimensions, http://geert-hofstede.com/national-culture.html. Accessed February 10, 2015.

60. R. Shuter and S. Chattopadhyay, "Emerging Interpersonal Norms of Text Messaging in India and the United States," *Journal of Intercultural Communication Research* 39, no. 2 (July 2010): 123–47.

61. http://www.quickfacts.census.gov/qfd/states/00000.html. Accessed May 9, 2012.

62. Lucic, "Use of Evaluative Devices by Youth for Sense-Making of Culturally Diverse Interpersonal Interactions."

63. Hofstede, *Culture's Consequences*.

64. W. B. Gudykunst, *Bridging Differences: Effective Intergroup Communication* (Newbury Park, CA: Sage, 1998), 45.

65. Gudykunst, *Bridging Differences*.

66. J. Boase and K. Ikeda, "Core Discussion Networks in Japan and America," *Human Communication Research* 38 (2012): 95–119.

67. J. M. Honeycutt, R. M. McCann, and H. Ota, "Inter-Asian Variability in Intergenerational Communication," *Human Communication Research* 38 (2012): 172–198.

68. E. T. Hall, *Beyond Culture* (Garden City, NY: Doubleday, 1976).

69. L. A. Samovar and R. E. Porter, *Communication Between Cultures* (Belmont, CA: Wadsworth, 2001), 234.

70. Hofstede, *Culture's Consequences*; also see G. Hofstede, "Cultural Dimensions in Management and Planning," *Asia Pacific Journal of Management* (January 1984): 81–98.

71. For an extensive review of communication gender differences see L. H. Turner, K. Dindia, and J. C. Pearson, "An Investigation of Female/Male Verbal Behaviors in Same-Sex and Mixed-Sex Conversations," *Communication Reports* 8 (Summer 1995): 86–96.

72. Hofstede and Hofstede, *Cultures and Organizations*.

73. S. Hofstede, "Cultural Dimensions in Management and Planning"; Hofstede and Hofstede, *Cultures and Organizations*.

74. For a discussion of long-and short-term oriented national cultures, see Hofstede and Hofstede, *Cultures and Organizations*, 210–38.

75. G. Hofstede, "Dimensionalizing Cultures: The Hofstede Model in Context," *Online Readings in Psychology and Culture* 2(1) (2011) http://dx.doi.org/10.9707/2307-0919.1014. Accessed February 10, 2015.

76. Hofstede, "Dimensionalizing Cultures."

77. Hofstede, "Dimensionalizing Cultures."

78. J. L. Allen, K. M. Long, J. O'Mara, and B. B. Judd, "Verbal and Nonverbal Orientations Toward Communication and the Development of Intracultural and Intercultural Relationships," *Journal of Intercultural Communication Research* 32 (2003): 129–60.

79. H. Z. Li, "Communicating Information in Conversations: A Cross-Cultural Comparison," *International Journal of Intercultural Relations* 23, no. 3 (1999): 387.

80. M. V. Redmond and J. M. Bunyi, "The Relationship of Intercultural Communication Competence with Stress and the Handling of Stress as Reported by International Students," *International Journal of Intercultural Relations* 17 (1993): 235–54; R. Brislen, *Cross-Cultural Encounters: Face-to-Face Interaction* (New York: Pergamon Press, 1981).

81. P. Coy, "The Future of Work," *Business Week* (August 20 and 27, 2007), 43.

82. U. Rohn, "Social Networking Sites Across Cultures and Countries: Proximity and Network Effects," *Qualitative Research Reports in Communication* 14 (2013): 28–34.

83. Adapted from Peter Rose, "Prejudice," in *Cultural Tapestry: Readings for a Pluralistic Society*, edited by F. B. Evans, B. Gleason, and M. Wiley (New York: HarperCollins, 1992), 420.

84. Lustig and Koester, *Intercultural Competence*.

85. J. W. Neuliep and J. C. McCroskey, "The Development of a U.S. and Generalized Ethnocentrism Scale," *Communication Research Reports* 14 (1997): 385–98.

86. W. B. Gudykunst, *Bridging Differences: Effective Intergroup Communication* (Newbury Park, CA: Sage, 1991), 2.

87. R. K. Dillon and N. J. McKenzie, "The Influence of Ethnicity on Listening, Communication Competence, Approach, and Avoidance," *International Journal of Listening* 12 (1998): 106–21.

88. R. E. Axtell, *Do's and Taboos of Hosting International Visitors* (New York: John Wiley & Sons, 1989), 118.

89. F. T. McAndrew, A. Akande, R. Bridgstock, L. Mealey, S. C. Gordon, J. E. Scheib, B. E. Akande-Adetoun, F. Odewale, A. Morakinyo, P. Nyahete, and G. Mubvakure, "A Multicultural Study of Stereotyping in English-Speaking Countries," *The Journal of Social Psychology* 140 (2000): 487–502.

90. J. A. Richeson and J. N. Shelton, "Brief Report: Thin Slices of Racial Bias," *Journal of Nonverbal Behavior* 29 (2005): 75–85.

91. M. M. Duguid and M. C. Thomas-Hunt, "Condoning Stereotyping?: How Awareness of Stereotyping Prevalence Impacts Expression of Stereotypes," *Journal of Applied Psychology* (October 2014).

92. B. Bratanova and Y. Kashima, "The 'Saying Is Repeating' Effect: Dyadic Communication Can Generate Cultural Stereotypes," *The Journal of Social Psychology* 154 (2014): 155–74.

93. C. Kluckhohn and H. A. Murray, 1953 as quoted by J. S. Caputo, H. C. Hazel, and C. McMahon, *Interpersonal Communication* (Boston: Allyn & Bacon, 1994), 304.

94. L. Mae and D. E. Carlston, "Hoist on Your Own Petard: When Prejudiced Remarks Are Recognized and Backfire on Speakers," *Journal of Experimental Social Psychology* 41 (2005): 240–55.

95. L. C. Aguilar, *Ouch! That Stereotype Hurts: Communicating Respectfully in a Diverse World* (Dallas, TX: Walk the Talk, 2006), 20–21.

96. S. Kamekar, M. B. Kolsawalla, and T. Mazareth, "Occupational Prestige as a Function of Occupant's Gender," *Journal of Applied Social Psychology* 19 (1988): 681–88.

97. F. F. Jordan-Jackson and K. A. Davis, "Men Talk: An Exploratory Study of Communication Patterns and Communication Apprehension of Black and White Males," *Journal of Men's Studies* 13 (2005): 347–67.

98. I. H. M. Hashim, S. Khodarahimi, and N. Mohd-Zaharim, "Factors Predicting Inter-Ethnic Friendships at the Workplace," *Interpersona* 6.2 (2012): 191–99.

99. D. E. Brown, "Human Universals and Their Implications," in *Being Humans: Anthropological Universality and Particularity in Transdisciplinary Perspectives*, edited by N. Roughley (New York: Walter de Gruyter, 2000). For an applied discussion of these universals, see Steven Pinker, *The Blank Slate: The Modern Denial of Human Nature* (London: Penguin Books, 2002).

100. D. W. Kale, "Ethics in Intercultural Communication," in *Intercultural Communication: A Reader*, 6th ed., edited by L. A. Samovar and R. E. Porter (Belmont, CA: Wadsworth, 1991).

101. Samovar and Porter, *Communication Between Cultures*, 29.

102. S. Pinker, "The Moral Instinct," *The New York Times Magazine* (January 13, 2008): 36–42.

103. M. Obernauer, "Lessons on Values to Go Beyond Schools," *Austin-American Statesman* (March 30, 2005): B1, B5.

104. Eleanor Roosevelt, as cited by Lustig and Koester, *Intercultural Competence*.

105. M. R. Hammer, M. J. Bennett, and R. Wiseman, "Measuring Intercultural Sensitivity: The Intercultural Development Inventory," *International Journal of Intercultural Relations* 27 (2003): 422.

106. B. H. Spitzberg and W. R. Cupach, "Interpersonal Skills," in *Handbook of Interpersonal Communication*, edited by M. L. Knapp and J. A. Daly (Thousand Oaks, CA: Sage, 2002), 564–611.

107. R. Plutchick, *Emotion: A Psychoevolutionary Synthesis* (New York: Harper & Row, 1980).

108. See, for example, M. Biehl, D. Matsumoto, P. Ekman, V. Hearn, K. Heider, T. Kudoh, and V. Ton, "Matsumoto and Ekman's Japanese and Caucasian Facial Expressions of Emotion (JACFEE): Reliability Data and Cross-National Differences," *Journal of Nonverbal Behavior* 21 (1997): 3–21; J. D. Boucher and G. E. Carlson, "Recognition of Facial Expressions in Three Cultures," *Journal of Cross-Cultural Psychology* 11 (1980): 263–80; D. Keltner and J. Haidt, "Social Functions of Emotions at Four Levels of Analysis," *Cognition and Emotion* 13 (1999): 505–21.

109. C. Darwin, with contributions by P. Ekman, *The Expression of the Emotions in Man and Animals*, 3rd ed. (London: Oxford University Press, 1998), 391.

110. M. D. Pell, L. Monetta, S. Paulmann, and S. A. Kotz, "Recognizing Emotions in a Foreign Language," *Journal of Nonverbal Behavior* 33 (2009): 107–20.

111. J. A. Russell, "Is There Universal Recognition of Emotion from Facial Expressions?: A Review of the Cross-Cultural Studies," *Psychological Bulletin* 115 (1994): 102–41.

112. E. Suh, E. Diener, S. Oishi, and H. C. Triandis, "The Shifting Basis of Life Satisfaction Judgments Across Cultures: Emotions versus Norms," *Journal of Personality and Social Psychology* 74 (1998): 482–93.

113. See B. Parkinson, A. H. Fischer, and A. S. R. Manstead, *Emotion in Social Relations: Cultural, Group, and Interpersonal Processes* (New York: Psychology Press, 2004).

114. S. L. Kline, B. Horton, and S. Zhang, "Communicating Love: Comparisons Between American and East Asian University Students," *International Journal of Intercultural Relations* 32 (2008): 200–14.

115. S. A. Myers and R. L. Knox, "The Relationship Between College Student Information Seeking Behaviors and Perceived Instructor Verbal Responses," *Communication Education* 50 (2001): 343–56; Baldwin and Hunt, "Information-Seeking Behavior."

116. For an excellent discussion of worldview and the implications for intercultural communication, see C. H. Dodd, *Dynamics of Intercultural Communication* (New York: McGraw-Hill, 2007).

117. T. F. Pettigrew and L. R. Tropp. "A Meta-Analytic Test of Intergroup Contact Theory," *Journal of Personality and Social Psychology* 90 (2006): 751–83.

118. U. Rohn, "Social Networking Sites Across Cultures and Countries: Proximity and Network Effects," *Qualitative Research Reports in Communication* 14 (2013): 28–34.

119. J. N. Martin, A. B. Trego, and T. K. Nakayama, "College Students' Racial Attitudes and Friendship Diversity," *The Howard Journal of Communications* 21 (2010): 97–118.

120. R. Berger and R. J. Calabrese, "Some Explorations in Initial Interactions and Beyond," *Human Communication Research* 1 (1975): 99–125.

121. B. J. Broome, "Building Shared Meaning: Implications of a Relational Approach to Empathy for Teaching Intercultural Communication," *Communication Education* 40 (1991): 235–49.

122. F. L. Casmir and N. C. Asuncion-Lande, "Intercultural Communication Revisited: Conceptualization, Paradigm Building, and Methodological Approaches," in *Communication Yearbook 12*, edited by J. A. Anderson (Newbury Park, CA: Sage, 1989): 278–309.

123. P. M. Sias, J. A. Drzewiecka, M. Meares, R. Bent, Y. Konomi, M. Ortega, and C. White, "Intercultural Friendship Development," *Communication Reports* 21, no. 1 (January–June 2008): 1–13.

124. Gudykunst and Kim, *Communicating with Strangers*; Gudykunst, *Bridging Differences*.

125. K. Luijters, K. I. van der Zee, and S. Otten, "Cultural Diversity in Organizations: Enhancing Identification by Valuing Differences," *International Journal of Intercultural Relations* 32 (2008): 154–163.

126. L. B. Szalay and G. H. Fisher, "Communication Overseas," in *Toward Internationalism: Readings in Cross-Cultural Communication,* edited by E. C. Smith and L. E Luce (Rowley, MA: Newbury House, 1979); also see P. E. King and C. R. Sawyer, "Mindfulness, Mindlessness and Communication Instruction," *Communication Education* 47 (October 1998): 326–36.

127. S. T. Mortenson, "Interpersonal Trust and Social Skill in Seeking Social Support Among Chinese and Americans," *Communication Research* 36, no. 1 (February 2009): 32–53.

128. C. S. Lewis, *The Abolition of Man* (New York: Macmillan Publishing Company, 1947).

129. R. F. Chapdelaine and L. R. Alexitch, "Social Skills Difficulty: Model of Culture Shock for International Graduate Students," *Journal of College Student Development* 45, no. 2 (March/April 2004): 16.

130. K. Domenici and S. Littlejohn, *Facework: Bridging Theory and Practice* (Thousand Oaks, CA: Sage, 2006), 159.

131. X. Guan, H. S. Park, and H. E. Lee, "Cross-Cultural Differences in Apology," *International Journal of Intercultural Relations* 33 (2009): 32–45.

132. S. DeTurk, "Intercultural Empathy: Myth, Competency, or Possibility for Alliance Building?" *Communication Education* 50 (October 2001): 374–84.

133. Also see J. B. Stiff, J. P. Dillard, L. Somera, H. Kim, and C. Sleight, "Empathy, Communication, and Prosocial Behavior," *Communication Monographs* (June 1988): 198–213.

134. D. Matsumoto, S. Nakagawa, and S. H. Yoo, "Culture, Emotion Regulation, and Adjustment," *Journal of Personality and Social Psychology* 94, no. 6 (2008): 925–37.

135. P. Sadler, G. R. Gunn, N. Ethier, D. Duong, and E. Woody, "Are We on the Same Wavelength? Interpersonal Complementarity as Shared Cyclical Patterns During Interactions," *Journal of Personality and Social Psychology* 97, no. 6 (2009): 1005–20.

136. See H. Giles, A. Mulack, J. J. Bradac, and P. Johnson, "Speech Accommodation Theory: The First Decade and Beyond," in *Communication Yearbook 10*, edited by M. L. McLaughlin (Newbury Park, CA: Sage, 1987), 13–48. For an excellent summary and application of accommodation theory, see R. West and L. H. Turner, *Introducing Communication Theory: Analysis and Application* (Mountain View, CA: Mayfield, 2000).

137. C. R. Glass, E. Gomez, and A. Urzua, "Recreation, Intercultural Friendship, and International Students' Adaptation to College by Region of Origin," *International Journal of Intercultural Relations* 42 (2014): 104–17.

138. L. J. Carrell, "Diversity in the Communication Curriculum: Impact on Student Empathy," *Communication Education* 46 (October 1997): 234–44.

139. R. Steves, "Travel Advice to Broaden Your Horizons," *The Orlando Sentinel*, Sunday, March 1, 2015: F5.

140. M. J. Bennett, "Overcoming the Golden Rule: Sympathy and Empathy," in *Communication Yearbook 3*, edited by D. Nimmo (Beverly Hills, CA: Sage, 1979), 407–22.

141. Bennett, "Overcoming the Golden Rule."

Chapter 5

1. H. J. M. Nouwen, *Bread for the Journey* (San Francisco: HarperCollins, 1997), entry for March 11.

2. Nouwen, *Bread for the Journey*, March 11.

3. "The Most Valued Workplace Skills," *The Wall Street Journal*, September 9, 2002: 1A.

4. R. W. Young and C. M. Cates, "Emotional and Directive Listening in Peer Mentoring," *International Journal of Listening* 18 (2004): 21–33; also see D. A. Romig, *Side by Side Leadership* (Marietta, GA: Bard, 2001).

5. M. L. Beall, J. Gill-Rosier, J. Tate, and A. Matten, "State of the Context: Listening in Education," *The International Journal of Listening* 22 (2008): 123–32.

6. P. Skaldeman, "Converging or Diverging View of Self and Other: Judgment of Relationship Quality in Married and Divorced Couples," *Journal of Divorce & Remarriage* 44 (2006): 145–60.

7. B. R. Brunner, "Listening, Communication & Trust: Practitioners' Perspectives of Business/Organizational Relationships," *The International Journal of Listening* 22 (2008): 73–82.

8. For a review of literature documenting the importance of listening in the health professions see D. L. Roter and J. A. Hall, *Doctors Talking with Patients/Patients Talking with Doctors: Improving Communication in Medical Visits* (Westport, CT: Praeger, 2006); J. Davis, C. R. Thompson, A. Foley, C. D. Bond, and J. DeWitt, "An Examination of Listening Concepts in the Healthcare Context: Differences Among Nurses, Physicians,

and Administrators," *The International Journal of Listening* 22 (2008): 152–67.

9. K. Wright, "Similarity, Network Convergence, and Availability of Emotional Support as Predictors of Strong-Tie/Weak-Tie Support Network Preference on Facebook," *Southern Communication Journal* 77.5 (2012): 389–402; M. Scott and S. Sale, "Consumers Use Smartphones for 195 Minutes Per Day, But Spend Only 25% of that Time on Communications," *Analysys Mason* (May 2014), accessed April 21, 2015, http://www.analysysmason.com/About-Us/News/Insight/consumers-smartphone-usage-May2014-RDMV0/.

10. L. Barker et al., "An Investigation of Proportional Time Spent in Various Communication Activities of College Students," *Journal of Applied Communication Research* 8 (1981): 101–09; K. Dindia and B. L. Kennedy, "Communication in Everyday Life: A Descriptive Study Using Mobile Electronic Data Collection," paper presented at the annual conference of the National Communication Association, Chicago, IL (November 2004); R. Emanuel, J. Adams, K. Baker, E. K. Daufin, C. Ellington, F. Fits, J. Himsel, L. Holladay, and D. Okeowo, "How College Students Spend Their Time Communicating," *International Journal of Listening* 22 (2008): 13–28; L. Cooper and T. Buchanan, "Listening Competency on Campus: A Psychometric Analysis of Student Learning," *The International Journal of Listening* 24 (2010): 141–63.

11. Adapted from the International Listening Association's definition of *listening*, which may be found on their website at www.listen.org; G. D. Bodie, "Issues in the Measurement of Listening," *Communication Research Reports* 30.1 (2013): 76–84.; S. D. Cohen and A. D. Wolvin, "An Inventory of Listening Competency Dimensions," *International Journal of Listening* 26.2 (2012): 64–66.

12. W. G. Powers and G. D. Bodie, "Listening Fidelity: Seeking Congruence Between Cognitions of the Listener and the Sender," *International Journal of Listening* 17 (2003): 20–31.

13. L. A. Janusik, "Listening and Cognitive Processing: Is There a Difference?" paper presented at the annual conference of the National Communication Association, New Orleans, LA (November 2002). Janusik suggests that it's important to include a behavioral component, such as responding to a message, in any definition of listening.

14. L. Lipari, "Listening, Thinking, Being," *Communication Theory* 20 (2010): 348–62.

15. L. A. Janusik, "Building Listening Theory: The Validation of the Conversational Listening Span," *Communication Studies* 58, no. 2 (June 2007): 139.

16. G. D. Bodie, C. C. Gearhart, and D. L. Worthington, "The Listening Styles Profile-Revised (LSP-R): A Scale of Revision and Evidence for Validity," *Communication Quarterly* 61.1 (2013): 72–90.; G. D. Bodie, J. P. Denham, and C. C. Gearhart, "Listening as a Goal-Directed Activity," *Western Journal of Communication* 78.5 (2014): 668–84.

17. G. D. Bodie and D. L. Worthington, "Revisiting the Listening Styles Profile (LSP-16): A Confirmatory Factor Analytic Approach to Scale Validation and Reliability Estimation," *International Journal of Listening* 24.2 (2010): 69–88.

18. D. L. Worthington, "Exploring the Relationship Between Listening Style Preference and Personality," *International Journal of Listening* 17 (2003): 68–87; D. L. Worthington, "Exploring Jurors' Listening Processes: The Effect of Listening Style Preference on Juror Decision Making," *International Journal of Listening* 17 (2003): 20–37.

19. J. B. Weaver III and M. Kirtlev, "Listening Styles and Empathy," *Southern Communication Journal* 2 (1995): 131–41.

20. G. D. Bodie and W. A. Villaume, "Aspects of Receiving Information: The Relationship Between Listening Preferences, Communication Apprehension, Receiver Apprehension, and Communicator Style," *International Journal of Listening* 17 (2003): 48–67.

21. Worthington, "Exploring Jurors' Listening Processes: The Effect of Listening Style Preference on Juror Decision Making."

22. Bodie and Villaume, "Aspects of Receiving Information."

23. S. L. Sargent and J. B. Weaver, "Correlates Between Communication Apprehension and Listening Style Preferences," *Communication Research Reports* 14 (1997): 74–78.

24. M. D. Kirtley and J. M. Honeycutt, "Listening Styles and Their Correspondence with Second Guessing," *Communication Research Reports* 13 (1996): 174–82.

25. Bodie, Denham, and Gearhart, "Listening as a Goal-Directed Activity."

26. Bodie and Villaume, "Aspects of Receiving Information."

27. See C. Kiewitz, J. B. Weaver III, B. Brosius, and G. Weimann, "Cultural Differences in Listening Style Preferences: A Comparison of Young Adults in Germany, Israel, and the United States," *International Journal of Public Opinion Research* 9 (1997): 233–48; N. Dragon and J. C. Sherblom, "The Influence of Cultural Individualism and Collectivism on U.S. and Post Soviet Listening Styles," *Human Communication* 11 (2008): 177–92.

28. A. K. Przybylski and N. Weinstein, "Can You Connect with Me Now? How the Presence of Mobile Communication Technology Influences Face-to-Face Conversation Quality," *Journal of Social and Personal Relationships* 30.3 (2012): 237–246.

29. W. Winter, A. J. Ferreira, and N. Bowers, "Decision-Making in Married and Unrelated Couples," *Family Process* 12 (1973): 83–94.

30. J. Stauffer, R. Frost, and W. Rybolt, "The Attention Fact of Recalling Network News," *Journal of Communication* 33, no. 1 (1983): 29–37.

31. O. E. Rankis, "The Effects of Message Structure, Sexual Gender, and Verbal Organizing Ability upon Learning Message Information," doctoral dissertation, Ohio University, 1981; C. H. Weaver, *Human Listening, Process and Behavior* (New York: Bobbs-Merrill, 1972); R. D. Halley, "Distractibility of Males and Females in Competing Aural Message Situations: A Research Note," *Human Communication Research* 2 (1975): 79–82. Our discussion of gender-based differences and listening is also based on a discussion by S. A. Beebe and J. T. Masterson, *Family Talk: Interpersonal Communication in the Family* (New York: Random House, 1986); J. Lurito, "Listening and Gender," paper presented to the Radiological Society of North America, Chicago (2000), as cited by L. Tanner, "Listening Study Finds Difference in the Sexes," *Austin American Statesman*, November 29, 2000: A11.; S. L. Sargent and J. B. Weaver III, "Listening Styles: Sex Differences in Perceptions of Self and Others," *International Journal of Listening* 17 (2003): 5–18; Rankis, "The Effects of Message Structure, Sexual Gender, and Verbal Organizing Ability upon Learning Message Information"; ABC News, 20/20, January 12,1998, featuring the research of communication researcher Kittie Watson.

32. S. L. Sargent and J. B. Weaver III, "Listening Styles: Sex Differences in Perceptions of Self and Others."

33. J. T. Wood, "A Critical Response to John Gray's Mars and Venus Portrayals of Men and Women," The Southern Communication Journal 67 (2002): 201–11.

34. This discussion is based on A. Vangelisti, M. Knapp, and J. Daly, "Conversational Narcissism," *Communication Monographs* 57 (1990): 251–74.

35. M. Gordon, "Listening as Embracing the Other: Martin Buber's Philosophy of Dialogue," *Educational Theory* 61, no. 2 (2011): 207–19.

36. B. L. Fredrickson and C. Branigan, "Positive Emotions Broaden the Scope of Attention and Thought-Action Repertoires," *Cognition and Emotion* 19, no. 3 (2005): 313–32.

37. R. Montgomery, *Listening Made Easy* (New York: Amacom, 1981); O. Hargie, C. Sanders, and D. Dickson, *Social Skills in Interpersonal Communication* (London: Routledge, 1994); O. Hargie, ed., *The Handbook of Communication Skills* (London: Routledge, 1997). Also see S. W. Littlejohn and K. Domenici, *Engaging Communication in Conflict: Systematic Practice* (Thousand Oaks, CA: Sage, 2001), 105–08.

38. R. G. Owens, "Handling Strong Emotions," in *A Handbook of Communication Skills*, edited by O. Hargie (London: Croom Helm/New York University Press, 1986).

39. R. G. Nichols, "Factors in Listening Comprehension," *Speech Monographs* 15 (1948): 154–1203; G. M. Goldhaber and

C. H. Weaver, "Listener Comprehension of Compressed Speech When the Difficulty, Rate of Presentation, and Sex of the Listener Are Varied," *Speech Monographs* 35 (1968): 20–25.

40. Przybylski and Weinstein, and "Can You Connect with Me Now?"

41. M. Fitch-Hauser, L. A. Barker, and A. Hughes, "Receiver Apprehension and Listening Comprehension: A Linear or Curvilinear Relationship?" *The Southern Communication Journal* (1988): 62–71; P. Schrodt and L. R. Wheeless, "Aggressive Communication and Informational Reception Apprehension: The Influence of Listening Anxiety and Intellectual Inflexibility on Trait Argumentativeness and Verbal Aggressiveness," *Communication Quarterly* 49 (Winter 2001): 53–69.

42. A. Mulanx and W. G. Powers, "Listening Fidelity Development and Relationship to Receiver Apprehension and Locus of Control," *International Journal of Listening* 17 (2003): 69–78.

43. K. Gayle, W. G. Powers, C. R. Sawyer, and A. Topa, "Listening Fidelity Among Native and Nonnative English-Speaking Undergraduates as a Function of Listening Apprehension and Gender," *Communication Research Reports* 31.1 (2014): 62–71.

44. Gayle, Powers, Sawyer, and Topa, "Listening Fidelity Among Native and Nonnative English-Speaking Undergraduates as a Function of Listening Apprehension and Gender."

45. D. Carnegie, *How to Win Friends and Influence People* (New York: Holiday House, 1937).

46. K. K. Halone and L. L. Pecchioni, "Relational Listening: A Grounded Theoretical Model," *Communication Reports* 14 (2001): 59–71.

47. Halone and Pecchioni, "Relational Listening."

48. K. Ruyter and M. G. Wetzels, "The Impact of Perceived Listening Behavior in Voice-to-Voice Service Encounters," *Journal of Service Research* 2 (February 2000): 276–84.

49. J. Harrigan, "Listeners' Body Movements and Speaking Turns," *Communication Research* 12 (1985): 233–50.

50. S. Strong et al., "Nonverbal Behavior and Perceived Counselor Characteristics," *Journal of Counseling Psychology* 18 (1971): 554–61.

51. Halone and Pecchioni, "Relational Listening."

52. K. Acheson, "Silence as Gesture: Rethinking the Nature of Communicative Silence," *Communication Theory* 18 (November 2008): 535–55.

53. Bodie, Denham, and Gearhart, "Listening as a Goal-Directed Activity."

54. M. Imhof, "How to Listen More Efficiently: Self-Monitoring Strategies in Listening," *International Journal of Listening* 17 (2003): 2–19.

55. See R. G. Nichols and L. A. Stevens, "Listening to People," *Harvard Business Review* 35 (September-October, 1957): 85–92.

56. W. T. Mickelson and S. A. Welch, "A Listening Competence Comparison of Working Professionals," *International Journal of Listening* 27.2 (2013): 85–99.

57. J. Hakansson and H. Montgomery, "Empathy as an Interpersonal Phenomenon," *Journal of Social and Personal Relationships* 20 (2003): 267–84.

58. Wright, "Similarity, Network Convergence, and Availability of Emotional Support as Predictors of Strong-Tie/Weak-Tie Support Network Preference on Facebook."

59. Wright, "Similarity, Network Convergence, and Availability of Emotional Support as Predictors of Strong-Tie/Weak-Tie Support Network Preference on Facebook."

60. For a review of literature about measuring empathy see: G. D. Bodie, "The Active-Empathic Listening Scale (AELS): Conceptualization and Validity Evidence," *Communication Quarterly* 59 (2011): 277–95; G. D. Bodie, J. P. Denham, C. C. Gearhart, and A. J. Vickery, "The Temporal of Stability and Situational Contingency of Active-Empathic Listening," *Western Journal of Communication* 77.2 (2013): 113–38.

61. M. V. Redmond, "The Functions of Empathy (Decentering) in Human Relations," *Human Relationships* 42 (1993): 593–606; also see M. V. Redmond, "A Multidimensional Theory and Measure of Social Decentering," *Journal of Research in Personality* 19 (1995): 35–58. For an excellent discussion of the role of emotions in establishing empathy, see D. Goleman, *Emotional Intelligence* (New York: Bantam, 1995).

62. Hakansson and Montgomery, "Empathy as an Interpersonal Phenomenon."

63. D. L. Rehling, "Compassionate Listening: A Framework for Listening to the Seriously Ill," *The International Journal of Listening* 22 (2008): 83–89.

64. For an excellent review of research about expressing affection and empathy, see K. Floyd, *Communicating Affection: Interpersonal Behavior and Social Context* (Cambridge, England: Cambridge University Press, 2006); also see K. Floyd and M. T. Morman, "Affection Received from Fathers as a Predictor of Men's Affection with Their Own Sons: Tests of the Modeling and Compensation Hypotheses," *Communication Monographs* 67, no. 4 (2000): 347–61.

65. Floyd, *Communicating Affection*.

66. Hargie, Sanders, and Dickson, *Social Skills in Interpersonal Communication*; Hargie, *The Handbook of Communication Skills*.

67. G. C. Bell, E. M. Minei, M. C. Robinson, and H. Weger Jr., "The Relative Effectiveness of Active Listening in Initial Interactions," *International Journal of Listening* 28.1 (2014): 13–31.

68. Bell, Minei, Robinson, and Weger Jr., "The Relative Effectiveness of Active Listening in Initial Interactions."

69. C. Alex, D. R. Castro, A. N. Kluger, and G. Tohar, "The Role of Active Listening in Teacher-Parent Relations and the Moderating Role of Attachment Style," *International Journal of Listening* 27.3 (2013): 136–145.

70. Bodie, Denham, Gearhart, and Vickery, "The Temporal of Stability and Situational Contingency of Active-Empathic Listening."

71. D. F. Barone, P. S. Hutchings, H. J. Kimmel, H. L Traub, J. T. Cooper, and C. M. Marshall, "Increasing Empathic Accuracy Through Practice and Feedback in a Clinical Interviewing Course," *Journal of Social and Clinical Psychology* 24 (2005): 156–71.

72. For a review of the role of empathy in enhancing the quality of interpersonal relationships as well as in addressing social and political problems see J. D. Trout, *The Empathy Cop: Building Bridges to the Good Life and Society* (New York: Viking, 2009).

73. Goleman, *Emotional Intelligence*.

74. For a comprehensive review of emotional intelligence that served as the basis for our summary of emotional intelligence, see D. Grewal and P. Salovey, "Feeling Smart: The Science of Social Intelligence," *American Scientist* 93 (July-August 2005): 330–39.

75. J. E. Barbuto, Jr. and M. E. Burbach, "The Emotional Intelligence of Transformational Leaders: A Field Study of Elected Officials," *The Journal of Social Psychology* 146, no. 1 (2006): 51–64.

76. H. Gardner, *Frames of Mind: The Theory of Multiple Intelligences* (New York: BasicBooks, 1983).

77. Goleman, *Emotional Intelligence*; Grewal and Salovey, "Feeling Smart."

78. Goleman, *Emotional Intelligence*.

79. J. B. Weaver and M. B. Kirtley, "Listening Styles and Empathy," *The Southern Communication Journal* 60 (1995): 131–40.

80. C. Rogers, *Client-Centered Therapy* (Boston: Houghton Mifflin, 1951).

81. J. B. Bavelas, L. Coates, and T. Johnson, "Listeners as Co-Narrators," *Journal of Personality and Social Psychology* 79, no. 6 (2000): 941–52.

82. W. R. Miller, K. E. Hedrick, and D. R. Orlofsky, "The Helufl Responses Questionnaire: A Procedure for Measuring Therapeutic Empathy," *Journal of Clinical Psychology* 47 (1991): 444–48; A. Paukert, B. Stagner, and K. Hope, "The Assessment of Active Listening Skills in Helpline Volunteers," *Stress, Trauma, and Crisis* 7 (2004): 61–76; D. H. Levitt, "Active Listening and Counselor Self-Efficacy: Emphasis on One Micro-Skill in Beginning Counselor Training," *The Clinical Supervisor* 20 (2001): 101–15; V. B. Van Hasselt, M. T. Baker, S. J. Romano, K. M. Schlessinger, M. Zuker, R. Dragone, and A. L. Perera, "Crisis (Hostage) Negotiation Training: A Preliminary Evaluation of Program Efficacy," *Criminal Justice and Behavior* 33 (2006): 56–69; H. Weger Jr., G. R. Castle, and M. C. Emmett, "Active Listening in Peer

Interviews: The Influence on Perceptions of Listening Skill," *The International Journal of Listening* 24 (2010): 34–49.

83. Weger Jr., Castle, and Emmett, "Active Listening in Peer Interviews."; also see M. R. Wood, "What Makes for Successful Speaker-Listener Technique? Two Case Studies," *Family Journal* 18, no. 1 (2010): 50–54.

84. C. W. Ellison and I. J. Fireston, "Developing Interpersonal Trust as a Function of Self-Esteem, Target Status and Target Style," *Journal of Personality and Social Psychology* 29 (1974): 655–63.

85. S. Gilbert, "Self-Disclosure, Intimacy, and Communication in Families," *Family Coordinator* (1975).

86. C. Gallois, T. Ogay, and H. Giles, "Communication Accommodation Theory: A Look Back and a Look Ahead," in *Theorizing about Intercultural Communication*, edited by W. B. Gudykunst (Thousand Oaks, CA: Sage, 2005): 121–48; H. Giles and T. Ogay, "Communication Accommodation Theory," in *Explaining Communication: Contemporary Theories and Exemplars*, edited by B. B. Whaley and W. Samter (Mahway, NJ: Erlbaum, 2006): 293–310.

87. T. T. Lineweaver, P. Hutman, C. Ketcham, and J. N. Bohannon III, "The Effect of Comprehension Feedback and Listener Age on Speech Complexity," *Journal of Language and Social Psychology* 30, no. 1 (2011): 46–65.

88. K. Floyd, "Empathetic Listening as an Expression of Interpersonal Affection," International Journal of Listening 28.1 (2014): 1–12.

89. J. Gottman and J. DeClaire, *The Relationship Cure* (New York: Crown, 2001), 198–201.

90. Hargie, Sanders, and Dickson, *Social Skills in Interpersonal Communication*; R. Boulton, *People Skills* (New York: Simon & Schuster, 1981).

91. R. Lemieuz and M. R. Tighe, "Attachment Styles and the Evaluation of Comforting Responses: A Receiver Perspective," *Communication Research Reports* 21 (2004): 144–53; also see W. Samter, "How Gender and Cognitive Complexity Influence the Provision of Emotional Support: A Study of Indirect Effects," *Communication Reports* 15 (2002): 5–16.

92. Our discussion of the appropriate and inappropriate social support responses is taken from B. D. Burleson, "Emotional Support Skill," in *Handbook of Communication and Social Interaction Skills*, edited by J. O. Greene and B. R. Burleson (Mahwah, NJ: Erlbaum, 2003), 566–68.

93. E. Sieburg and C. Larson, "Dimensions of Interpersonal Response," paper delivered at the annual conference of the International Communication Association, Phoenix, Arizona, (April 1971); K. Ellis, "Perceived Teacher Confirmation: The Development and Validation of an Instrument and Two Studies of the Relationship to Cognitive and Affective Learning," *Human Communication Research* 26 (2000): 264–91.

94. G. D. Bodie and S. M. Jones, "The Nature of Supportive Listening II: The Role of Verbal Person Centeredness and Nonverbal Immediacy," *Western Journal of Communication* 76.3 (2012): 250–269.

95. S. DeTurk, "Intercultural Empathy: Myth, Competency, or Possibility for Alliance Building," *Communication Education* 50 (October 2001): 374–84.

96. J. Gottman and J. DeClaire, The Relationship Cure (New York: Crown, 2001), 198–201. Boulton, *People Skills*. We also acknowledge others who have presented excellent applications of listening and responding skills in interpersonal and group contexts: D. A. Romig and L. J. Romig, *Structured Teamwork Guide* (Austin, TX: Performance Resources, 1990); S. Deep and L. Sussman, *Smart Moves* (Reading: MA. Addison-Wesley, 1990); P. R. Scholtes, *The Team Handbook* (Madison, WI: Joiner Associates, 1992); Hargie, Sanders, and Dickson, *Social Skills in Interpersonal Communication*; Littlejohn and Domenici, *Engaging Communication in Conflict*.

97. Lemieux and Tighe, "Attachment Styles and the Evaluation of Comforting Responses"; also see J. M. Gottman and J. S. Gottman, *10 Lessons to Transform Your Marriage* (New York: Crown Publishers, 2006).

98. J. Shotter, "Listening in a Way That Recognizes/Realizes the World of 'the Other,'" *The International Journal of Listening* 23 (2009): 21–43.

99. M. M. Bakhtin, *Problems of Dostoevsky's Poetics*, trans. and ed. C. Emerson (Minneapolis, MN: University of Minnesota Press, 1984): 292–93.

100. R. M. McLaren, D. H. Solomon, and J. S. Priem, "Explaining Variation in Contemporaneous Responses to Hurt in Premarital Romantic Relationships: A Relational Model of Perspective," *Communication Research* 38, no. 4 (2011): 543–64.

101. A. Bangerter, E. Chevalley, and S. Derouwaux, "Managing Third-Party Interruptions in Conversations: Effects of Duration and Conversational Role," *Journal of Language and Social Psychology* 29, no. 2 (2010): 235–44.

Chapter 6

1. B. Spitzberg and J. P. Dillard, "Social Skills and Communication," in *Interpersonal Communication Research: Advances Through Meta-Analysis*, edited by M. Allen, R. W. Preiss, B. M. Gayle, and N. Burrell (Mahwah, NJ: Erlbaum, 2002), 89–107.

2. K. Kellermann and N. A. Palomares, "Topical Profiling: Emergent, Co-Occurring, and Relationally Defining Topics in Talk," *Journal of Language and Social Psychology* 23 (2004): 308–37.

3. K. Maatta and S. Uusiautti, "Silence is Not Golden: Review of Studies of Couple Interaction," *Communication Studies* 4.1 (2013) 33–48.

4. R. Ling, "Texting as a Life Phase Medium," *Journal of Computer-Mediated Communication* 15 (2010): 277–92.; J. B. Walther, "Interaction Through Technological Lenses: Computer-Mediated Communication and Language," *Journal of Language and Social Psychology* 31.4 (2012): 397-414.

5. A. C. High and D. H. Solomon, "Communication Channel, Sex, and the Immediate and Longitudinal Outcomes of Verbal Person-Centered Support," *Communication Monographs* 81.4 (2014): 439–68.

6. S. A. Golder and M. W. Macy, "Diurnal and Seasonal Mood Vary with Work, Sleep, and Daylength Across Diverse Cultures," *Science* 333 (2011): 1878.

7. C. K. Ogden and L. A. Richards, *The Meaning of Meaning* (London: Kegan, Paul Trench, Trubner, 1923).

8. Merriam Webster Dictionary, www.merriam-webster.com/dictionary/school. Accessed July 2015.

9. A. Liptak, "Must It Always Be About Sex?" *The New York Times* (November 2, 2008): WK4.

10. S. I. Hayakawa and A. R. Hayakawa, *Language in Thought and Action* (New York: Harcourt, Brace, Jovanovich, 1990).

11. C. F. Hockett, *A Course in Modern Linguistics* (New York: Macmillan, 1958).

12. C. S. Lewis, *Studies in Words* (Cambridge, England: Cambridge University Press, 1960).

13. B. Towner, "What Are They Talking About: 50 Words That Kids Think You Don't Know," *Bulletin* (October 2008): 39.; nws.merriam-webster.com/opendictionary/. Accessed February 1, 2015.

14. See G. H. Mead, *Mind, Self and Society* (Chicago: University of Chicago Press, 1934); H. Blumer, *Symbolic Interactionism: Perspective and Method* (Englewood Cliffs, NJ: Prentice Hall, 1969).

15. D. Tannen, *You Just Don't Understand: Women and Men in Conversations* (New York: Morrow, 1990).

16. R. Edwards, "The Effects of Gender, Gender Role, and Values on the Interpretation of Messages," *Journal of Language and Social Psychology* 17 (1998): 52–71.

17. A. Korzybski, *Science and Sanity* (Lancaster, PA: Science Press, 1941).

18. G. Gusdorff, *Speaking* (Evanston, IL: Northwestern University Press, 1965), 9.

19. A. Ellis, *A New Guide to Rational Living* (North Hollywood, CA: Wilshire Books, 1977); also see W. Glaser, *Choice Theory* (New York: HarperCollins, 1998).

20. R. C. Martin and E. R. Dahlen, "Irrational Beliefs and the Experience and Expression of Anger," *Journal of Rational-Emotive & Cognitive-Behavior Therapy* 22 (2004): 3–20.

21. C. Peterson, M. E. P. Seligman, and G. E. Vaillant, "Pessimistic Explanatory Style Is a Risk Factor for Physical Illness: A 35-Year Longitudinal Study," *Journal of Personality and Social Psychology* 5 (1988): 23–7.

22. Ānandajoti Bhikkhu. "A Comparative Edition of the Dhammapada with Parallels from Sanskritised Prakrit," (2nd

revised edition, July 2007 -2551), www.ancient-buddhist-texts.net/Buddhist-Texts/C3-Comparative-Dhammapada. Accessed May 15, 2015.

23. See J. K. Barge and M. Little, "A Discursive Approach to Skillful Activity," *Communication Theory* 18 (2008): 505–34.

24. C. S. Areni and J. R. Sparks, "Language Power and Persuasion," *Psychology & Marketing* 22 (2005): 507–25.

25. W. M. O'Barr, *Linguistic Evidence* (New York: Academic Press, 1982).

26. B. L. Whorf, "Science and Linguistics," in *Language, Thought and Reality*, edited by J. B. Carroll (Cambridge, MA: MIT Press, 1956), 207. This discussion of the Sapir–Whorf hypothesis is based on D. Crystal, *The Cambridge Encyclopedia of Language* (Cambridge, England: Cambridge University Press, 1997).

27. We thank an anonymous reviewer for this example.

28. W. Johnson, *People in Quandaries* (New York: Harper & Row, 1946).

29. A fascinating article, "The Melting of a Mighty Myth" in *Newsweek* (July 22, 1991) explores the topic of the Eskimos' words for snow.

30. J. Coupland, "Small Talk: Social Function," *Research on Language and Social Interaction* 36 (2003): 1–6; M. M. Step and M. O. Finucane, "Interpersonal Communication Motives in Everyday Interactions," *Communication Quarterly* 50 (2002): 93–100.

31. M. McCarthy, "Talking Back: 'Small' Interactional Response Tokens in Everyday Conversation," *Research on Language and Social Interaction* 36 (2003): 33–63.

32. E. P. Lemay, Jr. and M. S. Clark, "'Walking on Eggshells': How Expressing Relationship Insecurities Perpetuates Them," *Journal of Personality and Social Psychology* 95, no. 2 (2008): 420–41.

33. S. Duck, "Talking Relationships into Being," *Journal of Social and Personal Relationships*" 12 (1995): 535–40.

34. J. K. Alberts, C. G. Yoshimura, M. Rabby, and R. Loschiavo, "Mapping the Topography of Couples' Daily Conversation," *Journal of Social and Personal Relationships* 22 (2005): 299–322.

35. K. Weber, A. K. Goodboy, and J. L. Cayanus, "Flirting Competence: An Experimental Study on Appropriate and Effective Opening Lines," *Communication Research Reports* 27, no. 2 (April–June 2010): 184–91.

36. K. Byron, "Carrying Too Heavy a Load? The Communication and Miscommunication of Emotion by Email," *Academy of Management Review* 33, no. 2 (2008): 309–27.

37. T. Parker-Pope, "Small Talk: Can Your Romantic Life Be Reduced to the Pronouns You Say (or Tweet or Post or Text)? Sort of," *The New York Times Magazine* (October 30, 2011): 18.

38. M. Booth-Butterfield and D. H. Mansson, "Grandparents' Expressions of Affection for Their Grandchildren: Examining Grandchildren's Relational Attitudes and Behaviors," *Southern Communication Journal* 76.5 (2011): 424–42.; D. H. Mansson, "Affectionate Communication and Relational Characteristics in the Grandparent–Grandchild Relationship," *Communication Reports* 26.2 (2013): 47–60.

39. A. M. Ledbetter, "Online Communication Attitude Similarity in Romantic Dyads: Predicting Couples' Frequency of E-Mail, Instant Messaging, and Social Networking Site Communication," *Communication Quarterly* 62.2 (2014): 233–52.

40. A. Kramer and C. K. Chung, "Dimensions of Self-Expression in Facebook Status," Paper presented at the ICWSM Conference, Barcelona, Spain (July 2011).

41. N. N. Bazarova, Y. H. Choi, D. Cosley, and J. G. Taft, "Managing Impressions and Relationships on Facebook: Self-Presentational and Relational Concerns Revealed Through the Analysis of Language Style," *Journal of Language and Social Psychology* 32.2 (2012): 131–41.

42. Bazarova, Choi, Cosley, and Taft, "Managing Impressions and Relationships on Facebook."

43. Bazarova, Choi, Cosley, and Taft, "Managing Impressions and Relationships on Facebook."

44. M. Dainton, A. K. Goodboy, and M. C. Stewart, "Maintaining Relationships on Facebook: Associations with Uncertainty, Jealousy, and Satisfaction," *Communication Reports* 27.1 (2014): 13–26.

45. R. L. Howe, *The Miracle of Dialogue* (New York: The Seabury Press, 1963), 23–24.

46. C. C. Kopecky and W. G. Powers, "Relational Development and Self-Image Communication Accuracy," *Communication Research Reports* 19 (2002): 283–90.

47. L. D. Rosen, J. Chang, L. Erwin, L. M. Carrier, and N. A. Cheever, "The Relationship Between 'Textism' and Formal and Informal Writing Among Young Adults," *Communication Research* 37, no. 3 (2010): 420–40.

48. S. Emling, "NuSrvc2 OffrGr8 Litr8tr On YrFon," *Austin American-Statesman* (November 26, 2005): A1, A6.

49. T. M. Karelitz and D. V. Budescu, "You Say 'Probable' and I Say 'Likely': Improving Interpersonal Communication with Verbal Probability Phrases," *Journal of Experimental Psychology* 10 (2004): 25–41.

50. See D. K. Ivy, *Exploring GenderSpeak* (Boston: Pearson, 2012).

51. J. Gray, *Men Are from Mars, Women Are from Venus* (New York: HarperCollins, 1992).

52. J. T. Wood, "A Critical Response to John Gray's Mars and Venus Portrayals of Men and Women," *The Southern Communication Journal* 67 (2002): 201–11.

53. J. Wood, *Gendered Lives: Communication, Gender, and Culture,* (Mason, OH: Cengage Learning, 2014).

54. V. B. Harper, Jr., "Differences Between Males and Females Concerning Perceived Electronic Mail Appropriateness," *The Quarterly Review of Distance Education* 9, no. 3 (2008): 311–16.

55. A. Colley and Z. Todd, "Gender-Linked Differences in the Style and Content of E-Mails to Friends," *Journal of Language and Social Psychology* 21 (2002): 380–92.

56. A. C. Knupsky and N. M. Hagy-Bell, "Dear Professor: The Influence of Recipient Sex and Status on Personalization and Politeness in E-Mail," *Journal of Language and Social Psychology* 30, no. 1 (2011): 103–13.

57. Wood, *Gendered Lives*.

58. Wood, *Gendered Lives*.

60. A. Mulac, "The Gender-Linked Language Effect: Do Language Differences Really Make A Difference?" In *Sex Differences and Similarities in Communication: Critical Essays and Empirical Investigations of Sex and Gender in Interaction*, edited by D. J. Canary and K. Dindia (Mahwah, NJ: Erlbaum, 1998), 127–55.

61. Tannen, *You Just Don't Understand*.

62. Jeffrey Jones, "U.S. Blacks, Hispanics Have No Preferences on Group Labels," Gallup Survey, www.gallup.com/poll/163706/blacks-hispanics-no-preferences-group-labels.aspx. Accessed February 2, 2015.

63. We acknowledge and appreciate D. K. Ivy's contribution to this section on biased language. For an expanded discussion on this topic, see Ivy, *Exploring Genderspeak*.

64. J. S. Seiter, J. Larsen, and J. Skinner, "'Handicapped' or 'Handi-capable'? The Effects of Language About Persons with Disabilities on Perceptions of Source Credibility and Persuasiveness," *Communication Reports* 11, no. 1 (1998): 21–31.

65. D. O. Braithwaite and C. A. Braithwaite, "Understanding Communication of Persons with Disabilities as Cultural Communication," in *Intercultural Communication: A Reader*, 8th ed., edited by L. A. Samovar and R. E. Porter (Belmont, CA: Wadsworth, 1997), 154–64.

66. G. D. Bodie, B. R. Burleson, and S. M. Jones, "Explaining the Relationships among Supportive Message Quality, Evaluations, and Outcomes: A Dual-Process Approach," *Communication Monographs* 79.1 (2012): 1–22.

67. For an excellent review of the supportive communication literature see E. L. MacGeorge, B. Feng, and B. R. Burleson, "Supportive Communication," in *The Sage Handbook of Interpersonal Communication*, edited by M. L. Knapp and J. A. Daly (Los Angeles: Sage, 2011), 317–54.

68. A. M. Hicks and L. M. Diamond, "How Was Your Day? Couples' Affect When Telling and Hearing Daily Events," *Personal Relationships* 15 (2008): 205–28.

69. J. R. Gibb, "Defensive Communication," *Journal of Communication* 11 (1961): 141–48. Also see R. Boulton, *People Skills* (New York: Simon & Schuster, 1979), 14–26; O. Hargie, C. Sanders, and D. Dickson, *Social Skills in Interpersonal Communication* (London: Routledge, 1994); O. Hargie, Ed., *The Handbook of Communication Skills* (London: Routledge, 1997); S. W. Littlejohn and K. Domenici, *Engaging Communication in Conflict* (Thousand Oaks, CA: Sage, 2001).

70. S. M. Yoshimura, "Emotional and Behavioral Responses to Romantic Jealousy Expressions," *Communication Reports* 17 (2004): 85–101.

71. G. L. Forward, K. Czech, and M. Lee, "Assessing Gibb's Supportive and Defensive Communication Climate: An Examination of Measurement and Construct Validity," *Communication Research Reports* 28 (2011): 1015.

72. L. K. Guerrero, L. Farinelli, and B. McEwan, "Attachment and Relational Satisfaction: The Mediating Effect of Emotional Communication," *Communication Monographs* 76, no. 4 (2009): 487–514.

73. K. Sereno, M. Welch, and D. Braaten, "Interpersonal Conflict: Effects of Variations in Manner of Expressing Anger and Justifications for Anger upon Perceptions of Appropriateness, Competence, and Satisfaction," *Journal of Applied Communication Research* 15 (1987): 128–43; J. Gottman, *A Couples Guide to Communication* (Champaign, IL: Research Press, 1976); E. S. Kubany, G. B. Bauer, M. E. Pangilinan, M. Y. Muraoka, and V. G. Enriquez, "Impact of Labeled Anger and Blame in Intimate Relationships: Cross-Cultural Extension of Findings," *Journal of Cross-Cultural Psychology* 26 (1995): 65–83; E. S. Kubany, G. B. Bauer, M. Muraoka, D. C. Richard, and P. Read, "Impact of Labeled Anger and Blame in Intimate Relationships," *Journal of Social and Clinical Psychology* 14 (1995): 53–60; M. R. Leary, C. Springer, L. Negel, E. Ansell, and K. Evans, "The Causes, Phenomenology, and Consequences of Hurt Feelings," *Journal of Personality and Social Psychology* 74 (1998): 1225–37.

74. A. M. Bippus and S. L. Young, "Owning Your Emotions: Reactions to Expressions of Self-versus Other-Attributed Positive and Negative Emotions," *Journal of Applied Communication Research* 33 (2005): 26–45.

75. K. J. Williams-Baucom, D. C. Atkins, M. Sevier, K. A. Eldridge, and A. Christensen, "'You' and 'I' Need to Talk About 'Us': Linguistic Patterns in Marital Interactions," *Personal Relationships* 17 (2010): 41–56.

76. R. B. Slatcher, S. Vazire, and J. W. Pennebaker, "Am 'I' More Important Than 'We'? Couples' Word Use in Instant Messages," *Personal Relationships* 15 (2008): 407–24.

77. J. M. Ackerman, N. P. Li, and V. Griskevicius, "Let's Get Serious: Communicating Commitment in Romantic Relationships," *Journal of Personality and Social Psychology* 100, no. 6 (2011): 1079–94.

78. A. Q. Gonzalez and R. Koestner, "What Valentine Announcements Reveal about the Romantic Emotions of Men and Women," *Sex Roles* 55 (2006): 767–73.

79. M. Grossman and W. Wood, "Sex Differences in Intensity of Emotional Experience: A Social Role Interpretation," *Journal of Personality and Social Psychology* 65 (1993): 1010–22.

80. B. S. Moran, "Intimacy of Disclosure Topics and Sex Differences in Self-Disclosure," *Sex Roles* 2 (1976): 161–67.

81. V. J. Derlega, B. A. Winstead, P. T. P. Wong, and S. Hunter, "Gender Effects in an Initial Encounter: A Case Where Men Exceed Women in Disclosure," *Journal of Social and Personal Relationships* 2 (1985): 25–44.

82. Ackerman, Li, and Griskevicius, "Let's Get Serious," 1090.

83. Ackerman, Li, and Griskevicius, "Let's Get Serious," 1091.

84. C. Rogers, *On Becoming a Person: A Therapist's View of Psychotherapy* (Boston: Houghton Mifflin, 1961); C. Rogers, *A Way of Being* (Boston: Houghton Mifflin, 1980); C. Rogers, "Comments on the Issue of Equality in Psychotherapy," *Journal of Humanistic Psychology* 27 (1987): 38–39.

85. D. I. Johnson, "Model Expressions in Refusals of Friends' Interpersonal Requests: Politeness and Effectiveness," *Communication Studies* 59, no. 2 (April–June 2008): 148–63.

86. A. M. Bippus, "Recipients' Criteria for Evaluating the Skillfulness of Comforting Communication and the Outcomes of Comforting Interactions," *Communication Monographs* 68 (2001): 301–13.

87. B. R. Burleson, "Comforting Messages: Features, Functions, and Outcomes," in *Strategic Interpersonal Communication*, edited by J. A. Daly and J. M. Wiemann (Hillsdale, NJ: Erlbaum, 1994), 135–61.

88. B. M. Gayle and R. W. Preiss, "An Overview of Interactional Processes in Interpersonal Communication," in *Interpersonal Communication Research: Advances Through Meta-Analysis*, edited by M. Allen, R. W. Preiss, B. M. Gayle, and N. Burrell (Mahwah, NJ: Erlbaum, 2002), 213–26.

89. M. Allen, "A Synthesis and Extension of Constructivist Comforting Research," in *Interpersonal Communication Research*, 237–45.

90. A. M. Bippus, "Human Usages in Comforting Episodes: Factors Predicting Outcomes," *Western Journal of Communication* 54 (Fall 2000): 359–84; A. M. Bippus, "Recipients' Criteria for Evaluating the Skillfulness of Comforting Communication and the Outcomes of Comforting Interactions," *Communication Monographs* 68 (September 2001): 301–13; A. M. Bippus, "Humor Motives, Qualities, and Reactions in Recalled Conflict Episodes," *Western Journal of Communication* 67 (2003): 413–26.

91. S. Turkle, "The Flight From Conversation," *The New York Times* (April 22, 2012): 1, 6.

92. "Funny, Cute, Flattering and Cheesy Pick-up Lines!," www.pickuplinesgalore.com/cheesy.html. Accessed May 13, 2015.

93. High and Solomon, "Communication Channel, Sex, and the Immediate and Longitudinal Outcomes of Verbal Person-Centered Support."

94. Turkle, "The Flight From Conversation."

95. D. Jones, "No. 37: Big Wedding or Small? Quiz: The 36 Questions That Lead to Love," http://www.nytimes.com/2015/01/11/fashion/no-37-big-wedding-or-small.html. Accessed

February 23, 2015. Print edition: *New York Times*, Styles, January 18, p.4.

96. M. L. Knapp, R. P. Hart, G. W. Friedrich & G. M. Shulman, "The Rhetoric of Goodbye: Verbal and Nonverbal Correlates of Human Leave-Taking," *Communication Monographs*, 40.3 (1973): 182–198.

97. K. Ohbuchi, M. Kameda, and N. Agarie, "Apology as Aggression Control: Its Role in Mediating Appraisal of and Response to Harm," *Journal of Personality and Social Psychology* 56 (1989): 219–27.

98. M. McCollough, K. Rachal, J. Steven, E. Worthington, S. Brown, and T. Hight, "Interpersonal Forgiving in Close Relationships II: Theoretical Elaboration and Measurement," *Journal of Personality and Social Psychology* 75 (1998): 1586–603.

99. J. R. Meyer and K. Rothenberg, "Repairing Regretted Messages: Effects of Emotional State, Relationship Type, and Seriousness of Offense," *Communication Research Reports* 21 (2005): 348–56.

100. B. W. Darby and B. R. Schlenker, "Children's Reactions to Transgressions: Effects of the Actor's Apology, Reputation and Remorse," *British Journal of Social Psychology* 28 (1989): 353–64.

101. S. J. Scher and J. M. Darley, "How Effective Are the Things People Say to Apologize? Effects of the Realization of the Apology Speech Act," *Journal of Psycholinguistic Research* 26 (1997): 127–40.

102. C. McPherson Frantz and C. Bennigson, "Better Late Than Early: The Influence of Timing on Apology Effectiveness," *Journal of Experimental Social Psychology* 41 (2005): 201–07.

103. L. S. Aloia and D. H. Solomon, "Perceptions of Verbal Aggression in Romantic Relationships: The Role of Family History and Motivational Systems," *Western Journal of Communications* 77.4 (2013): 411–423.

104. Our prescriptions for assertiveness are based on a discussion by R. Boulton, *People Skills* (New York: Simon and Schuster 1979). Also see J. S. St. Lawrence, "Situational Context: Effects on Perceptions of Assertive and Unassertive Behavior," *Behavior Therapy* 16 (1985): 51–62; D. Borisoff and D. A. Victor, *Conflict Management: A Communication Skills Approach* (Boston: Allyn & Bacon, 1999).

105. V. Boogart, "Discovering the Social Impacts of Facebook on a College Campus" (master's thesis, Kansas State University, 2006), 38, as cited in N. S. Baron, *Always On: Language in an Online and Mobile World* (New York: Oxford University Press), 97.

106. E. Craig and K. B. Wright, "Computer-Mediated Relational Development and Maintenance on Facebook," *Communication Research Reports* 29.2 (2012): 119–29.

107. K. B. Wright, "Emotional Support and Perceived Stress Among College Students Using Facebook.com: An Exploration of the Relationship Between Source Perceptions and Emotional Support," *Communication Research Reports* 29.3 (2012): 175–84.

108. F. Farina, L. Farrell, J. Hanney, F. Lyddy, and N. K. O'Neill, "An Analysis of Language in University Students' Text Messages," *Journal of Computer-Mediated Communication* 19 (2014): 546–61.

109. R. Wright, "E-Mail and Prozac," *The New York Times* (April 17, 2007): A23.

110. J. T. Hancock, L. E. Curry, S. Goorha, and M. Woodworth, "On Lying and Being Lied To: A Linguistic Analysis of Deception in Computer-Mediated Communication," *Discourse Processes* 45 (2008): 1–23.

111. D. Cloven and M. E. Roloff, "The Chilling Effect of Aggressive Potential on the Expression of Complaints in Intimate Relationships," *Communication Monographs* 60 (1993): 199–219.

CHAPTER 7

1. E. Lipton, "Faces, Too, Are Searched as U.S. Airports Try to Spot Terrorists," *The New York Times* (August 17, 2066): A1.

2. J. Kabat-Zinn, *Wherever You Go, There You Are: Mindfulness Meditation in Everyday Life* (New York: Hyperion Books, 1994).

3. G. Bente, S. Ruggenberg, N. C. Kramer, and F. Eschenburg, "Avatar-Mediated Networking: Increasing Social Presence and Interpersonal Trust in Net-Based Collaborations," *Human Communication Research* 34 (2008): 287–318.

4. A. Mehrabian, *Nonverbal Communication* (Chicago: Aldine Atherton, 1972), 108.

5. D. Lapakko, "Three Cheers for Language: A Closer Examination of a Widely Cited Study of Nonverbal Communication," *Communication Education* 46 (1997): 63–67. Although other researchers suggest that nonverbal messages may *not* carry as much as 93 percent of the emotional weight of our communication, *all* nonverbal communication researchers agree that nonverbal communication is the most significant means of expressing emotions to others.

6. D. Matsumoto, J. LeRoux, C. Wilson-Cohn, J. Raroque, K Kooken, P. Ekman, N. Yrizarry, S. Loewinger, H. Uchida, A. Yee, L. Arno, and A. Goh, "A New Test to Measure Emotion Recognition Ability: Matsumoto and Ekman's Japanese and Caucasian Brief Affect Recognition Test (JACBART)," *Journal of Nonverbal Behavior* 24 (Fall 2000): 179–209; J. K Burgoon and A. E. Bacue, "Nonverbal Communication Skills," in *Handbook of Communication and Social Interaction Skills*, edited by J. O. Greene and B. R. Burleson (Mahwah, NJ: Erlbaum, 2003), 179–219; B. H. Lafrance, A. D. Heisel, and M. J. Beatty, "Is There Empirical Evidence for a Nonverbal Profile of Extraversion? A Meta-Analysis and Critique of the Literature," *Communication Monographs* 71 (2004): 28–48.

7. M. Zuckerman, D. DePaulo, and R. Rosenal, "Verbal and Nonverbal Communication of Deception," *Advances in Experimental Social Psychology* 14 (1981): 1–59.

8. E. Hess, *The Tell-Tale Eye* (New York: Van Nostrand Reinhold, 1975).

9. P. Ekman, "Communication Through Nonverbal Behavior: A Source of Information About an Interpersonal Relationship," in *Affect Cognition and Personality*, edited by S. S. Tomkins and C. E. Izard (New York: Springer, 1965).

10. J. K. Burgoon, J. A. Bonito, A. Ramirez Jr., N. E. Dunbar, K Kam, and J. Fischer, "Testing the Interactivity Principle: Effects of Mediation, Propinquity, and Verbal and Nonverbal Modalities in Interpersonal Interaction," *Journal of Communication* 52, no. 3 (2002): 657–77.

11. J. K. Burgoon, L. A. Stern, and L. Dillman, *Interpersonal Adaptation: Dyadic Interaction Patterns* (Cambridge, England: Cambridge University Press, 1995).

12. A. S. E. Hubbard, "Interpersonal Coordination in Interactions: Evaluations and Social Skills," *Communication Research Reports* 17 (Winter 2000): 95–104.

13. R. L. Birdwhistell, *Kinesics and Context* (Philadelphia: University of Pennsylvania Press, 1970).

14. N. Zunin and M. Zunin, *Contact: The First Four Minutes* (New York: Signet, 1976).

15. J. H. Bert and K Piner, "Social Relationships and the Lack of Social Relations," in *Personal Relationships and Social Support*, edited by S. W. Duck with R. C. Silver (London: Sage, 1989).

16. D. J. Atkin, D. S. Hunt, and C. A. Lin, "Communication Social Relationships via the Use of Photo-Messaging," *Journal of Broadcasting & Electronic Media* 58.2 (2014) 234–52.

17. S. M. Jones and L. K Guerrero, "The Effects of Nonverbal Immediacy and Verbal Person Centeredness in the Emotional Support Process," *Human Communication Research* 27 (October 2001): 567–96.

18. J. A. Samp and J. L. Monahan, "Alcohol-Influenced Nonverbal Behaviors During Discussions About a Relationship Problem," *Journal of Nonverbal Behavior* 33 (2009): 193–211.

19. A. F. Koerner and M. A. Fitzpatrick, "Nonverbal Communication and Marital Adjustment and Satisfaction: The Role of Decoding Relationship Relevant and Relationship Irrelevant Affect," *Communication Monographs* 69 (2002): 33–51.

20. Koerner and Fitzpatrick, "Nonverbal Communication and Marital Adjustment and Satisfaction."

21. J. V. Cordova, C. B. Gee, and L. Z. Warren, "Emotional Skillfulness in Marriage: Intimacy as a Mediator of the Relationship Between Emotional Skillfulness and Marital Satisfaction," *Journal of Social and Clinical Psychology* 24 (2005): 218–35.

22. T. Docan-Morgan, J. Marvey, and V. Manusov, "When a Small Thing Means so Much: Nonverbal Cues as Turning Points in Relationships," *Interpersona* 7.1 (2013): 110–24.

23. This example originally appeared in P. Collett, "History and Study of Expressive Action," in *Historical Social Psychology*, edited by K. Gergen and M. Gergen (Hillsdale, NJ: Erlbaum, 1984).

24. Birdwhistell, *Kinesics and Context*. Also see D. G. Leathers, *Successful Nonverbal Communication: Principles and Applications* (Boston: Allyn & Bacon, 1997).

25. A. E. Scheflen, "Quasi-Courtship Behavior in Psychotherapy," *Psychiatry* 28 (1965): 245–57.

26. M. Moore, "Interpreting Nonverbal Messages," *Journal of Ethology and Sociology* (Summer 1994); also see D. Knox and K. Wilson, "Dating Behaviors of University Students," *Family Relations* 30 (1981): 255–58.

27. A. Mehrabian, *Silent Messages* (Belmont, CA: Wadsworth, 1972), 108.

28. M. Reece and R. Whitman, "Expressive Movements, Warmth, and Verbal Reinforcement," *Journal of Abnormal and Social Psychology* 64 (1962): 234–36.

29 P. Ekman and W. V. Friesen, "The Repertoire of Nonverbal Behavior: Categories, Origins, Usage and Coding," *Semiotica* 1 (1969): 49–98.

30. A. T. Dittman, "The Body Movement-Speech Rhythm Relationship as a Cue to Speech Encoding," in *Studies in Dyadic Communication*, edited by A. W. Siegman and B. Pope (New York: Pergamon, 1972).

31. A. A. Cohen and R. P. Harrison, "Intentionality in the Use of Hand Illustrators in Face-to-Face Communication Situations," *Journal of Personality and Social Psychology* 28 (1973): 276–79.

32. C. Darwin, *The Expression of the Emotions in Man and Animals* (Chicago: University of Chicago Press, 1965). Originally published 1872.

33. A. Mehrabian and M. Williams, "Nonverbal Concomitants of Perceived and Intended Persuasiveness," *Journal of Personality and Social Psychology* 13 (1969): 37–58.

34. M. Argyle, E. Alkema, and R. Gilmour, "The Communication of Friendly and Hostile Attitudes by Verbal and Nonverbal Signals," *European Journal of Social Psychology* 1 (1972): 385–402.

35. D. Morris, *People Watching* (London: Vanage Press, 2002), 104. For a review of eye contact and facial expression research in intercultural settings, see M. Yuki, W. M. Maddux, and T. Masuda, "Are the Windows to the Soul the Same in the East and West? Cultural Differences in Using the Eyes and Mouth as Cues to Recognize Emotions in Japan and the United States," *Journal of Experimental Social Psychology* 43 (2007): 303–11.

36. A. Kendon, "Some Functions of Gaze-Direction in Social Interaction," *Acta Psychologica* 26 (1967): 22–63.

37. These research conclusions were summarized by M. L. Knapp and J. A. Hall, *Nonverbal Communication in Human Interaction* (Belmont, CA: Wadsworth, 1997); also see D. K. Ivy and S. T. Wahl, *The Nonverbal Self: Communication for a Lifetime* (Boston: Allyn and Bacon, 2009), 221–37.

38. R. Petrican, T. Bielak, M. Moscovitch, C. T. Burris, and U. Schimmack, "For My Eyes Only: Gaze Control, Enmeshment, and Relationship Quality," *Journal of*

Personality and Social Psychology 100, no. 6 (2011): 1111–23.

39. P. Ekman, W. V. Friesen, and S. S. Tomkins, "Facial Affect Scoring Technique: A First Validity Study," *Semiotica* 3 (1971): 37–58; P. Ekman and W. V. Friesen, *Unmasking the Face* (Englewood Cliffs, NJ: Prentice Hall, 1975).

40. Associated Press, "Frowning Outlawed in Meeting Code of Conduct," retrieved May 7, 2003, from www.Boston.com.

41. V. M. Lammers, M. L. Patterson, and M. E. Tubbs, "Busy Signal: Effects of Mobile Device Usage on Pedestrian Encounters," *Journal of Nonverbal Behavior* 38 (2014): 313–24.

42. J. X. Goh and J. A. Hall, "Nonverbal and Verbal Expressions of Men's Sexism in Mixed-Gender Interactions," *Sex Roles*, 73 (2015): 1–10.

43. Ekman and Friesen, *Unmasking the Face*; Ekman, Friesen, and Tomkins, "Facial Affect Scoring Technique."

44. M. D. Weathers. E. M. Frank, and L. A. Spell, "Differences in the Communication of Affect: Members of the Same Race Versus Members of a Different Race," *Journal of Black Psychology* 28 (2002): 66–77.

45. S. A. Tabak and V. Zayas, "The Roles of Featural and Configural Face Processing in Snap Judgment of Sexual Orientation," *PloS ONE* 7.5 (May 2012): 1–7.

46. Ekman and Friesen, *Unmasking the Face*; Ekman, Friesen, and Tomkins, "Facial Affect Scoring Technique."

47. A. Buck, R. E. Miller, and C. F. William, "Sex, Personality, and Physiological Variables in the Communication of Affect via Facial Expression," *Journal of Personality and Social Psychology* 30 (1974): 587–89.

48. Ekman and Friesen, *Unmasking the Face.*

49. Ekman and Friesen, *Unmasking the Face.*

50. G. J. McHugo, "Emotional Reactions to a Political Leader's Expressive Displays," *Journal of Personality and Social Psychology* 49 (1985): 513–29.

51. K. Yamamoto and N. Suzuki, "The Effects of Social Interaction and Personal Relationships on Facial Expressions," *Journal of Nonverbal Behavior* 30 (2006): 211–25.

52. D. Matsumoto, A. Olide, J. Schug, B. Willingham, and M. Callan, "Cross-Cultural Judgments of Spontaneous Facial Expressions of Emotion," *Journal of Nonverbal Behavior* 33 (2009): 213–38.

53. D. LaPlante and N. Ambady, "Multiple Messages: Facial Recognition Advantage for Compound Expressions," *Journal of Nonverbal Behavior* 24 (Fall 2000): 211–25.

54. E. Krumhuber and A. Kappas, "Moving Smiles: The Role of Dynamic Components for the Perception of the Genuineness of Smiles," *Journal of Nonverbal Behavior* 29 (2005): 3–24.

55. J. Elliott, "If You're Happy and You Know It, You're a Buddhist," *The Sunday Times* [London], (May 25, 2003): 1.14.

56. B. Munson, E. C. McDonald, N. L. DeBoe, and A. R. White, "The Acoustic and Perceptual Bases of Judgment of Women and Men's Sexual Orientation from Read Speech," *Journal of Phonetics* 34 (2006): 202–40.

57. R. Smyth, G. Jacobs, and H. Rogers, "Male Voices and Perceived Sexual Orientation: An Experimental and Theoretical Approach," *Language in Society* 32 (2003): 329–50.

58. N. Singer, "In a Mood? Call Center Agents Can Tell," *The New York Times* (October 13, 2013): 3.

59. J. K. Burgoon, D. B. Buller, and W. G. Woodall, *Nonverbal Communication: The Unspoken Dialogue* (New York: McGraw-Hill, 1996).

60. R. Davitz, *The Communication of Emotional Meaning* (New York: McGraw-Hill, 1964).

61. M. J. Owren and J. Bachorowski, "Reconsidering the Evolution of Nonlinguistic Communication: The Case of Laughter," *Journal of Nonverbal Behavior* 27 (2003): 183–200.

62. B. Le Poire, C. Shepard, A. Duggan, and J. Burgoon, "Relational Messages Associated with Nonverbal Involvement, Pleasantness, and Expressiveness in Romantic Couples," *Communication Research Reports* 19 (2002): 195–206.

63. S. D. Farley, S. M. Hughes, and J. N. LaFayette, "People Will Know We Are in Love: Evidence of Differences Between Vocal Samples Directed Toward Lovers and Friends," *Journal of Nonverbal Behavior* 37 (2013): 128–38.

64. K. K. Sereno and G. J. Hawkins, "The Effect of Variations in Speakers' Nonfluency upon Audience Ratings of Attitude Toward the Speech Topic and Speakers' Credibility," *Speech Monographs* 34 (1967): 58–74; G. R. Miller and M. A. Hewgill, "The Effect of Variations in Nonfluency on Audience Ratings of Source Credibility," *Quarterly Journal of Speech* 50 (1964): 36–44; Mehrabian and Williams, "Nonverbal Concomitants of Perceived and Intended Persuasiveness."

65. R. L. Street, R. M. Brady, and W. B. Putman, "The Influence of Speech Rate Stereotypes and Rate Similarity on Listeners' Evaluations of Speakers," *Journal of Language and Social Psychology* 2 (1983): 37–56.

66. K. Acheson, "Silence as Gesture: Rethinking the Nature of Communicative Silence," *Communication Theory* 18 (2008): 535–55.

67. T. Bruneau, "Communicative Silences: Forms and Functions," *Journal of Communication* 23 (1973): 17–46.

68. Y. M. Kalman and S. Rafaeli, "Online Pause and Silence: Chronemic Expectancy Violations in Written Computer-Mediated Communication," *Communication Research* 38, no. 1 (2011): 54–69.

69. Our discussion of how to accurately interpret emotions in others is adapted from an excellent distillation of the research conducted by Burgoon and Bacue, "Nonverbal Communication Skills."

70. Burgoon, Buller, and Woodall, *Nonverbal Communication.*

71. N. Horatcsu and B. Ekinci, "Children's Reliance on Situational and Vocal Expression of Emotions: Consistent and Conflicting Cues," *Journal of Nonverbal Behavior* 16 (1992): 231–47.

72. R. Banse and K. R. Schere, "Acoustic Profiles in Vocal Emotion Expression," *Journal of Personality and Social Psychology* 70 (1996): 614–36.

73. N. Ambady, "Cross-Cultural Perspectives on Social Judgments and Behavior," paper presented at the annual meeting of the Society of Experimental Social Psychology, St. Louis, MO (1999), as cited by Burgoon and Bacue, "Nonverbal Communication Skills."

74. J. M. Montepare and J. S. Tucker, "Aging and Nonverbal Behavior: Current Perspectives and Future Directions," *Journal of Nonverbal Behavior* 23 (1999): 105–10.

75. R. E. Riggio, B. Throckmorton, and S. DePaola, "Social Skills and Self-Esteem," *Personality and Social Psychology Bulletin* 13 (1990): 568–77.

76. Burgoon and Bacue, "Nonverbal Communication Skills."

77. S. J. Baker, "The Theory of Silence," *Journal of General Psychology* 53 (1955): 145–67.

78. C. N. Wright and M. E. Roloff, "Relational Commitment and the Silent Treatment," *Communication Research Reports* 26, no. 1 (February 2009): 12–21.

79. J. M. Gottman with N. Silver, *Why Marriages Succeed or Fail* (New York: Simon and Schuster, 1994); J. M. Gottman and J. S. Gottman, *10 Lessons to Transform Your Marriage* (New York: Crown Publishers, 2006).

80. E. T. Hall, *The Hidden Dimension* (New York: Doubleday, 1966).

81. A. Sorokowska, "Assessing Personality Using Body Odor: Differences Between Children and Adults," *Journal of Nonverbal Behavior* 37 (2013): 153–63.

82. R. Sommer, "Studies in Personal Space," *Sociometry* 22 (1959): 247–60.

83. Sommer, "Studies in Personal Space."

84. D. Chandler and R. Munday, *A Dictionary of Media and Communication* (Oxford University Press, 2011).

85. See B. Stenzor, "The Spatial Factor in Face-to-Face Discussion Groups," *Journal of Abnormal and Social Psychology* 45 (1950): 552–55.

86. T. Prinsen and N. M. Punyanunt-Carter, "The Difference in Nonverbal Behaviors and How It Changes in Different Stages of a Relationship," *Texas Speech Communication Journal* 34 (Summer 2009): 1–7.

87. G. D. Bodie and W. Villaume, "Men and Women Holding Hands Revisited: Effects of Mutual Engagement and Hand Dominance on Attributions of Cross-Sex Handholding," *Communication Research Reports* 25, no. 4 (2008): 243–54.

88. A. Montague, *Touching: The Human Significance of the Skin* (New York: Harper & Row, 1978).

89. Montague, *Touching.*

90. N. M. Henley, *Body Politics:*

Power, Sex, and Nonverbal Communication (Englewood Cliffs, NJ: Prentice Hall, 1977).

91. K. Guerrero and P. A. Andersen, "Patterns of Matching and Initiation: Touch Behavior and Touch Avoidance Across Romantic Relationship Stages," *Journal of Nonverbal Behavior* 18 (1994): 137–53; M. M. Martin and C. M. Anderson, "Psychological and Biological Differences in Touch Avoidance," *Communication Research Reports* 10 (12993): 141–47.

92. A. Hanzal, C. Segrin, and S. M. Dorros, "The Role of Marital Status and Age on Men's and Women's Reactions to Touch from a Relational Partner," *Journal of Nonverbal Behavior* 32 (2008): 21–35.

93. L. K. Guerrero and P. A. Anderson, "The Waxing and Waning of Relational Intimacy: Touch as a Function of Relational Stage, Gender, and Touch Avoidance," *Journal of Social and Personal Relationships* 8 (1991): 147–65; Guerrero and Anderson, "Patterns of Matching and Initiation."

94. J. K. Burgoon, L. K. Guerrero, and V. Manusov, "Nonverbal Signals," in *The Sage Handbook of Interpersonal Communication*, edited by M. A. Knapp and J. A. Daly (Los Angeles: Sage, 2001), 239.

95. J. K. Burgoon, L. K. Guerrero, and V. Manusov, "Nonverbal Signals," 248.

96. P. Ekman and W. V Friesen, "Constants Across Cultures in the Face and Emotion," *Journal of Personality and Social Psychology* 17 (1971): 124–29; M. Argyle, *Bodily Communication,* (New York: Methuen, 1988), 157; I. Eibl-Eibesfeldt, "Similarities and Differences Between Cultures in Expressive Movements," in *Nonverbal Communication,* edited by R. A. Hinde (Cambridge, England: Royal Society & Cambridge University Press, 1972); Collett, "History and Study of Expressive Action"; E. T. Hall, *The Silent Language* (Garden City, NY: Doubleday, 1959); R. Shuter, "Gaze Behavior in Interracial and Intraracial Interaction," *International and Intercultural Communication Annual* 5 (1979): 48–55; R. Shuter, "Proxemics and Tactility in Latin America," *Journal of Communication* 26 (1976): 46–52; Hall, *The Hidden Dimension.* For an excellent discussion of worldview and the implications for intercultural communication, see C. H. Dodd, *Dynamics of Intercultural Communication* (Dubuque, IA: Brown & Benchmark, 1995); G. W. Beattie, *Talk: An Analysis of Speech and Nonverbal Behavior in Conversation* (Milton Keynes: Open University Press, 1983); O. Hargie, C. Sanders, and D. Dickson, *Social Skills in Interpersonal Communication* (London: Routledge, 1994); O. Hargie (Ed.), The *Handbook of Communication Skills* (London: Routledge, 1997); H. A. Elfenbein and N. Ambady, "On the Universality and Cultural Specificity of Emotion Recognition: A Meta-Analysis," *Psychological Bulletin* 128, no. 2 (2002): 203–35; P. Ekman, "Strong Evidence for Universals in Facial Expressions: A Reply to Russell's Mistaken Critique," *Psychological Bulletin* 115 (1994): 268–87; P. Ekman and W. Friesen, *Facial Action Coding System: Investigator's Guide* (Palo Alto, CA: Consulting Psycholo-

gists Press, 1978); P. Ekman and W. Friesen, "A New Pan-Cultural Facial Expression of Emotion," *Motivation & Emotion* 10 (1986): 159–68; P. Ekman, E. R. Sorenson, and W. Friesen, "Pancultural Elements in Facial Displays of Emotion," *Science* 164 (1969): 86–88; D. Matsumoto, "Scalar Ratings of Contempt Expressions," *Journal of Nonverbal Behavior* 29 (2005): 91–104.

97. C. M. J. Beaulieu, "Intercultural Study of Personal Space: A Case Study," *Journal of Applied Social Psychology* 34, no. 4 (2004): 794–805.

98. For an excellent review of gender and nonverbal cues, see J. Pearson, L. Turner, and W. Todd-Mancillas, *Gender and Communication* (Dubuque, IA: William C. Brown, 1991); D. K. Ivy and P. Backlund, *Exploring GenderSpeak: Personal Effectiveness in Gender Communication* (New York: McGraw-Hill, 1994). Also see Leathers, *Successful Nonverbal Communication.*

99. Beaulieu, "Intercultural Study of Personal Space."

100. For a review of culture and touch, see R. Dibiase and J. Gunnoe, "Gender and Cultural Differences in Touching Behavior," *The Journal of Social Psychology* 144, no. 1 (2004): 49–62.

101. J. Kelly, "Dress as Non-Verbal Communication," paper presented to the annual conference of the American Association for Public Opinion Research, May 1969.

102. J. C. Valentine, V. Blankenship, H. Cooper, and E. S. Sullins, "Interpersonal Expectancy Effects and the Preference for Consistency," *Representative Research in Social Psychology* 25 (2001): 26–33.

103. J. Lefkowitz, R. Blake, and J. Mouton, "Status Factors in Pedestrian Violation of Traffic Signals," *Journal of Abnormal and Social Psychology* 51 (1970): 4–6.

104. J. T. Molloy, *Dress for Success* (New York: Warner Books, 1975); J. T. Molloy, *The Woman's Dress for Success Book* (Chicago: Follett, 1977).

105. C. B. Murray and J. D. Meadors, "Measuring Nonverbal Bias Through Body Language Responses to Stereotypes," *Journal of Nonverbal Behavior* 38 (2014): 209–29.

106. Murray and Meadors, "Measuring Nonverbal Bias Through Body Language Responses to Stereotypes."

107. N. R. Toosi, L. G. Babbit, N. Ambady, and S. R. Sommers, "Dyadic Interacial Interactions: A Meta-Analysis," *Psychological Bulletin* 138 (2012): 1–27.

108. Murray and Meadors, "Measuring Nonverbal Bias Through Body Language Responses to Stereotypes."

109. R. R. Provine, R. J. Spencer, and D. L. Mandell, "Emotional Expression Online: Emoticons Punctuate Website Text Messages," *Journal of Language and Social Psychology* 26, no. 3 (September 2007): 299–307.

110. E. Dresner and S. C. Herring, "Functions of the Nonverbal in CMC: Emotions and Illocutionary Force," *Communication Theory* 20 (2010): 249–68.

111. A. Gronning, A. Kankaanranta, and K. Skovholt, "The Communicative Functions

of Emoticons in Workplace E-Mails: ☐*," *Journal of Computer-Mediated Communication* 19 (2014): 780–97.

112. Y. M. Baek, M. Cha, and J. Park, "Cross-Cultural Comparison of Nonverbal Cues in Emoticons on Twitter: Evidence from Big Data Analysis," *Journal of Communication* 64 (2014): 333–54.

113. V. O. Castella, A. M. Abad, F. P. Alonso, and J. M. P. Silla, "The Influence of Familiarity Among Group Members, Group Atmosphere and Assertiveness on Uninhibited Behavior Through Three Different Communication Media," *Computers in Human Behavior* 16 (2000): 141–59; also see A. N. Joinson, *Understanding the Psychology of Internet Behavior: Virtual Worlds, Real Lives* (New York: Palgrave MacMillan, 2003), 64–65.

114. P. Collett, *The Book of Tells* (London: Doubleday, 2003).

115. Mehrabian, *Nonverbal Communication.*

116. L. Hinkle, "Nonverbal Immediacy Communication Behaviors and Liking in Marital Relationships," *Communication Research Reports* 16, no. 1 (1999): 81–90.

117. J. K. Burgoon and B. A. Le Poire, "Nonverbal Cues and Interpersonal Judgments: Participant and Observer Perceptions of Intimacy, Dominance, Composure, and Formality," *Communication Monographs* 66 (1999): 105–24.

118. Jones and Guerrero, "The Effects of Nonverbal Immediacy"; also see D. J. Dolin and M. Booth-Butterfield, "Reach Out and Touch Someone: Analysis of Nonverbal Comforting Responses," *Communication Quarterly* 41 (1993): 383–93.

119. Argyle, *Bodily Communication.*

120. K. J. Tusing and J. P. Dillard, "The Sounds of Dominance: Vocal Precursors of Perceived Dominance During Interpersonal Influence," *Human Communication Research* 26 (January 2000): 148–71; N. E. Dunbar and J. K. Burgoon, "Perceptions of Power and Interactional Dominance in Interpersonal Relationships," *Journal of Social and Personal Relationships* 22 (2005): 207–33.

121. A. Mignault and A. Chaudhuri, "The Many Faces of a *Neutral* Face: Head Tilt and Perception of Dominance and Emotion," *Journal of Nonverbal Behavior* 27, no. 2 (Summer 2001): 111–32.

122. Mehrabian, *Nonverbal Communication.*

123. A. Pease and B. Pease, *The Definitive Book of Body Language* (London: Orion, 2005): 42.

124. Collett, *The Book of Tells.*

125. J. A. Hall, J. C. Rosip, L. Smith LeBeau, T. G. Horgan, and J. D. Carter, "Attributing the Sources of Accuracy in Unequal-Power Dyadic Communication: Who Is Better and Why?" *Journal of Experimental Social Psychology* 41 (2005): 1–10.

126. D. A. Carney, J. A. Hall, and L. Smith LeBeau, "Beliefs About the Nonverbal Expression of Social Power," *Journal of Nonverbal Behavior* 29 (2005): 105–23.

127. Argyle, *Bodily Communication.*

128. Burgoon, Stern, and Dillman, *Interpersonal Adaptation.*

129. B. A. Le Poire and S. M. Yoshirnura, "The Effects of Expectancies and Actual Communication on Nonverbal Adaptation and Communication Outcomes: A Test of Interaction Adaptation Theory," *Communication Monographs* 66 (1999): 1–30.

130. Burgoon and Bacue, "Nonverbal Communication Skills."

131. J. A. Hall, N. A. Murphy, and M. S. Mast, "Recall of Nonverbal Cues: Exploring a New Definition of Interpersonal Sensitivity," *Journal of Nonverbal Behavior* 30 (2006): 141–55.

132. See Birdwhistell, *Kinesics and Context.*

133. E. Hatfield, J. T. Cacioppo, and R. L. Rapson, *Emotional Contagion* (New York: Cambridge University Press, 1994).

134. Hubbard, "Interpersonal Coordination in Interactions."

135. B. Marsh, "The Voice Was Lying. The Face May Have Told the Truth," *The New York Times* (February 15, 2009): WK3.

136. J. K. Burgoon, J. P. Blair, and R. E. Strom, "Cognitive Biases and Nonverbal Cue Availability in Detecting Deception," *Human Communication Research* 34 (2008): 572–99.

137. For an excellent summary of deception and nonverbal communication, see Leathers, *Successful Nonverbal Communication*, 253–74. Also see P. Ekman, M. O' Sullivan, W. V. Friesen, and K. R. Scherer, "Invited Article: Face, Voice, and Body in Detecting Deceit," *Journal of Nonverbal Behavior* 15 (1991): 125–35; P. Ekman and W. Friesen, "Detecting Deception from the Body and Face," *Journal of Personality and Social Psychology* 29 (1974): 288–98; M. Millar and K. Millar, "Detection of Deception in Familiar and Unfamiliar Persons: The Effects of Information Restriction," *Journal of Nonverbal Behavior* 19 (1995): 69–84; D. B. Buller, J. K. Burgoon, A. Buslig, and J. F. Roiger, "Interpersonal Deception: VIII. Further Analysis of the Nonverbal Correlates of Equivocation from the Bavelas et a1. (1990) Research," *Journal of Language & Social Psychology* 13 (1994): 396–417.

138. Adapted from Leathers, *Successful Nonverbal Communication*, with supporting research from Ekman and Friesen, "Detecting Deception from the Face and Body"; M. Zuckerman, B. M. DePaulo, and R. Rosenthal, "Verbal and Nonverbal Communication of Deception," in *Advances in Experimental Social Psychology*, vol. 14, edited by L. Berkowitz (New York: Academic Press, 1981), 1–60.

139. J. T. Hancock, L. E. Curry, S. Goorha, and M. Woodworth, "On Lying and Being Lied To: A Linguistic Analysis of Deception in Computer-Mediated Communication," *Discourse Processes* 45 (2008): 1–23; also see J. F. George and A. Robb, "Deception and Computer-Mediated Communication in Daily Life," *Communication Reports* 21, no. 2 (July-December 2008): 92–103.

140. A. Vrij, K. Edward, K. P. Roberts, and R. Bull, "Detecting Deceit Via Analysis of Verbal and Nonverbal Behavior," *Journal of Nonverbal Communication* 24 (Winter 2000): 239–63; also see Burgoon and Bacue, "Nonverbal Communication Skills."

141. H. S. Park, T. R. Levine, S. A. McComack, K. Morrison, and M. Ferrara, "How People Really Detect Lies," *Communication Monographs* 69 (June 2002): 144–57.

142. Burgoon and Bacue, "Nonverbal Communication Skills."

143. B. M. DePaulo and H. S. Friedman, "Nonverbal Communication," in The *Handbook of Social Psychology*, edited by D. T. Gilbert, S. T. Fiske, and G. Lindzey (New York: McGraw-Hill, 1998).

144. Argyle, *Bodily Communication.*

145. W. G. Woodal and J. K. Burgoon, "The Effects of Nonverbal Synchrony on Message Comprehension and Persuasiveness," *Journal of Nonverbal Behavior* 5 (1981): 207–23.

146. Argyle, *Bodily Communication.*

147. K. N. Blurton-Jones and G. M. Leach, "Behavior of Children and Their Mothers at Separation and Parting," in *Ethological Studies of Child Behavior*, edited by N. Blurton-Jones (Cambridge, England: Cambridge University Press, 1972).

148. D. A. Friedman and B. S. Hasler, "Sociocultural Conventions in Avatar-Mediated Nonverbal Communication: A Cross-Cultural Analysis of Virtual Proxemics," *Journal of Intercultural Communication Research* 41.3 (2012): 238–59.

Chapter 8

1. S. A. Lloyd, "Conflict in Premarital Relationships: Differential Perceptions of Males and Females," *Family Relations* 36 (1987): 290–94.

2. M. Hicks and L. M. Diamond, "Don't Go To Bed Angry: Attachment, Conflict, and Affective and Physiological Reactivity," *Personal Relationships* 18 (2011): 266–84.

3. H. B. Braiker and H. H. Kelley, "Conflict in the Development of Close Relationships," in *Social Exchange in Developing Relationships*, edited by R. L Burgess and T. L Huston (New York: Academic Press, 1979), 135–68.

4. D. Cramer, "Relationship Satisfaction and Conflict Style in Romantic Relationships," *Journal of Psychology* 134 (2000): 337–41.

5. Our definition of conflict is adapted from W. Wilmot and J. Hocker, *Interpersonal Conflict* (New York: McGraw-Hill, 2007).

6. B. Fehr and C. Harasymchuk, "The Experience of Emotion in Close Relationships: Toward an Integration of the Emotion-in-Relationships and Interpersonal Script," *Personal Relationships* 12 (2005): 81–196; T. L. Zacchilli, C. Hendrick, and S. S. Hendrick, "The Romantic Partner Conflict Scale: A New Scale to Measure Relationship Conflict," *Journal of Social and Personal Relationships* 26, no. 8 (2009): 1073–96.

7. A. J. Johnson, "A Functional Approach to Interpersonal Argument: Differences Between Public-Issue and Personal-Issue Arguments," *Communication Reports* 22, no. 1 (2009): 13–28.

8. J. W. Keltner, *Mediation: Toward a Civilized System of Dispute Resolution* (Annandale, VA: Speech Communication Association, 1987); also see Wilmot and Hocker, *Interpersonal Conflict.*

9. For a review of literature about violence in relationships, see L. N. Olson and T. D. Golish, "Topics of Conflict and Patterns of Aggression in Romantic Relationships," *Southern Communication Journal* 67 (Winter 2002): 180–200.

10. D. J. Canary, W. R. Cupach, and R. T. Serpe, "A Competence-Based Approach to Examining Interpersonal Conflict: Test of a Longitudinal Model," *Communication Research* 29 (February 2001): 79–104; also see L. N. Olson and D. O. Braithwaite, "'If You Hit Me Again, I'll Hit You Back': Conflict Management Strategies of Individuals Experiencing Aggression During Conflicts," *Communication Studies* 55 (2004): 271–85; L. L. Marshall, "Physical and Psychological Abuse," in *The Dark Side of Interpersonal Communication*, edited by W. R. Cupach and B. H. Spitzberg (Hillsdale, NJ: Erlbaum, 1994), 281–311; Olson and Golish, "Topics of Conflict and Patterns of Aggression in Romantic Relationships," 41.

11. Wilmot and Hocker, *Interpersonal Conflict*, 8–15.

12. Olson and Braithwaite, "'If You Hit Me Again, I'll Hit You Back.'"

13. Y. B. Zhang and M. C. Lin, "Conflict-Initiating Factors in Intergenerational Relationships," *Journal of Language and Social Psychology* 28, no. 4 (2009): 343–63.

14. W. E. Schweinle, W. Ickes, and I. H. Bernstein, "Empathic Inaccuracy in Husband to Wife Aggression: The Overattribution Bias," *Personal Relationships* 9 (2002): 141–58; also see W. E. Schweinle and W. Ickes, "The Role of Men's Critical/Rejecting Overattribution Bias, Affect, and Attentional Disengagement in Marital Aggression," *Journal of Social and Clinical Psychology* 26, no. 2 (2007): 173–98.

15. A. M. Bippus, J. P. Boren, and S. Worsham, "Social Exchange Orientation and Conflict Communication in Romantic Relationships," *Communication Research Reports* 25, no. 3 (2008): 227–34.

16. L. A. Kurdek, "Areas of Conflict for Gay, Lesbian, and Heterosexual Couples: What Couples Argue About Influences Relationship Satisfaction," *Journal of Marriage and the Family* 56 (November 1994): 923–34; L. A. Kurdek, "Conflict Resolution Styles in Gay, Lesbian, Heterosexual Nonparent, and Heterosexual Parent Couples," *Journal of Marriage and the Family* 56 (August 1994): 705–22.

17. G. MacDonald, M. P. Zanna, and J. G. Imes, "An Experimental Test of the Role of Alcohol in Relationship Conflict," *Journal of Experimental Social Psychology* 36 (2000): 182–93.

18. L. A. Erbert, "Conflict and Dialectics: Perceptions of Dialectical

Contradictions in Marital Conflict," *Journal of Social and Personal Relationships* 17 (2000): 638–59.

19. A. C. Filley, *Interpersonal Conflict Resolution* (Glenview, IL: Scott Foresman, 1975); R. H. Turner, "Conflict and Harmony," *Family Interaction* (New York: Wiley, 1970); K. Galvin and B. J. Brommel, *Family Communication: Cohesion and Change* (New York: Addison Wesley Longman, 2000).

20. Olson and Golish, "Topics of Conflict and Patterns of Aggression in Romantic Relationships."

21. Wilmot and Hocker, *Interpersonal Conflict,* 10.

22. D. J. Canary, W. R. Cupach, and S. J. Messman, *Relationship Conflict: Conflict in Parent-Child, Friendship, and Romantic Relationships* (Thousand Oaks, CA: Sage, 1999).

23. Canary, Cupach, and Serpe, "A Competence-Based Approach to Examining Interpersonal Conflict."

24. Adapted from D. W. Johnson, *Reaching Out: Interpersonal Effectiveness and Self-Actualization* (Boston: Allyn & Bacon, 2000), 314.

25. M. Deutsch, *The Resolution of Conflict* (New Haven, CT: Yale University Press, 1973).

26. R. Dumlao and R. A. Botta, "Family Communication Patterns and the Conflict Styles Young Adults Use with Their Fathers," *Communication Quarterly* 48 (Spring 2000): 174–89; also see W. Aquilino, "From Adolescent to Young Adult: A Prospective Study of Parent-Child Relations During the Transition to Adulthood," *Journal of Marriage and the Family* 59 (1997): 670–86.

27. R. J. Doolittle, *Orientations of Communication and Conflict* (Chicago: Science Research Association 1976), 7–9.

28. Canary, Cupach, and Serpe, "A Competence-Based Approach to Examining Interpersonal Conflict."

29. D. H. Solomon, K. L. Knoblock, and M. A. Fitzpatrick, "Relational Power, Marital Schema, and Decisions to Withhold Complaints: An Investigation of the Chilling Effect of Confrontation in Marriage," *Communication Studies* 55 (2004): 146–67.

30. D. Canary, W. Cupach, and S. Messman, *Relationship Conflict* (Thousand Oaks, CA: Sage, 1995); J. Gottman, *What Predicts Divorce? The Relationship Between Marital Process and Marital Outcomes* (Hillsdale, NJ: Erlbaum, 1994).

31. Lloyd, "Conflict in Premarital Relationships."

32. E. H. Mudd, H. E. Mitchell, and J. W. Bullard, "Areas of Marital Conflict in Successfully Functioning and Unsuccessfully Functioning Families," *Journal of Health and Human Behavior* 3 (1962): 88–93; N. R. Vines, "Adult Unfolding and Marital Conflict," *Journal of Marital and Family Therapy* 5 (1979): 5–14.

33. B. A. Fisher, "Decision Emergence: Phases in Group Decision Making," *Speech Monographs* 37 (1970): 60.

34. G. R Miller and M. Steinberg, *Between People: A New Analysis of Interpersonal Communication* (Chicago: Science Research Associates, 1975), 264.

35. C. M. Hoppe, "Interpersonal Aggression as a Function of Subject's Sex Role Identification, Opponent's Sex, and Degree of Provocation," *Journal of Personality* 47 (1979): 317–29.

36. Wilmot and Hocker, *Interpersonal Conflict;* also see S. W. Littlejohn and K. Domenici, *Engaging Communication in Conflict: Systemic Practice* (Thousand Oaks, CA: Sage, 2001).

37. J. M. Olsen, *The Process of Social Organization* (New York: Holt, Rinehart and Winston, 1978).

38. N. C. Overall, C. G. Sibley, and R. Tan, "The Cost and Benefits of Sexism: Resistance to Influence During Relationship Conflict," *Journal of Personality and Social Psychology* 101, no. 2 (2011): 271–90.

39. G. Bodenmann, N. Meuwly, T. N. Bradbury, S. Gmelch, and T. Ledermann, "Stress, Anger, and Verbal Aggression in Intimate Relationships: Moderating Effects of Individual and Dyadic Coping," *Journal of Social and Personal Relationships* 27, no. 3 (2010): 408–24.

40. S. L. Young, "Factors That Influence Recipients' Appraisals of Hurtful Communication," *Journal of Social and Personal Relationships* 21 (2004): 291–303; S. L. Young, T. L. Kubicka, C. E. Tucker, D. Chavez-Appel, and J. S. Rex, "Communicative Responses to Hurtful Messages in Families," *The Journal of Family Communication* 5 (2005): 123–40.

41. M. S. Mast, J. A. Hall, and K. Jonas, "Give a Person Power and He or She Will Show Interpersonal Sensitivity: The Phenomenon and Its Why and When," *Journal of Personality and Social Psychology* 97, no. 5 (2009): 835–50.

42. J. M. Gottman, "Repair and the Core Triad of Balance," in *The Marriage Clinic: A Scientifically-Based Marital Therapy,* edited by J. M. Gottman (New York: W. W. Norton & Company, 1999), 31–86.

43. N. E. Dunbar, A. M. Bippus, and S. L. Young, "Interpersonal Dominance in Relational Conflict: A View From Dyadic Power Theory," *Interpersona* 2, no. 1 (2008): 1–33.

44. K. Kellerman, "A Goal-Directed Approach to Gaining Compliance: Relating Differences Among Goals to Differences in Behaviors." *Communication Research* 31 (2004): 397–445.

45. J. R. P. French and B. H. Raven, "The Bases of Social Power," in *Group Dynamics,* edited by J. D. Cartwright and A. Zander (Evanston, IL: Row, Peterson, 1962), 607–22.

46. K. Kellerman, "A Goal-Directed Approach to Gaining Compliance."

47. E. V. Wilson, "Perceived Effectiveness of Interpersonal Persuasion Strategies in Computer-Mediated Communication," *Computers in Human Behavior* 19 (2003): 537–52.

48. R. Kilmann and K. Thomas, "Interpersonal Conflict-Handling Behav-

ior as Reflections of Jungian Personality Dimensions," *Psychological Reports* 37 (1975): 971–80; K. W. Thomas and R. H. Kilmann, *Thomas-Kilmann Conflict Mode Instrument* (Tuxedo, NY: XICOM, 1974).

49. G. R. Miller and F. Boster, "Persuasion in Personal Relationships," in *A Handbook of Personal Relationships,* edited by S. Duck (New York: Wiley, 1988), 275–88; M. G. Garko, "Perspectives and Conceptualizations of Compliance and Compliance Gaining," *Communication Quarterly* 38, no. 2 (1990): 138–57.

50. M. G. Lawler and G. S. Risch, "Time, Sex and Money: The First Five Years of Marriage," *America* 184 (2001): 16–20.

51. M. A. Rahinn and N. R. Magner, "Confirmatory Factor Analysis of the Styles of Handling Interpersonal Conflict: First-Order Factor Model and Its Invariance Across Groups," *Journal of Applied Psychology* 80, no. 1 (1995): 122–32.

52. J. S. Aubrey, M. Fine, L. N. Olson, D. M. Rhea. "Conflict and Control: Examining the Association Between Exposure to Television Portraying Interpersonal Conflict and the Use of Controlling Behaviors in Romantic Relationships," *Communication Studies* 64 (March 2013): 106–24.

53. V. Satir, *Peoplemaking* (Palo Alto, CA: Science and Behavior Books, 1972).

54. A. F. Koerner and M. A. Fitzpatrick, "You Never Leave Your Family in a Fight: The Impact of Family of Origin on Conflict Behavior in Romantic Relationships," *Communication Studies* 53 (2002): 234–51.

55. C. Harrington, T. D. D. R. Schudlich, N. M. Stettler, and K. A. Stouder, "Adult Romantic Attachment and Couple Conflict Behaviors: Intimacy as a Multi-Dimensional Mediator," *Interpersonal* 7(1) (2013): 26–43.

56. Kilmann and Thomas, "Interpersonal Conflict-Handling Behavior as Reflections of Jungian Personality Dimensions"; Thomas and Kilmann, *Thomas-Kilmann Conflict Mode Instrument.*

57. C. W. Miller, R. M. Reznik, and M. E. Roloff, "Hopelessness and Interpersonal Conflict: Antecedents and Consequences of Losing Hope," *Western Journal of Communication* 78(5) (2014): 563–85.

58. A. Buysse, A. De Clercq, L. Verhofstadt, E. Heene, H. Roeyers, and P. Van Oost, "Dealing with Relational Conflict: A Picture in Milliseconds," *Journal of Social and Personal Relationships* 17 (2000): 574–79.

59. T. D. Afifi, T. McManus, K. Steuber, and A. Coho, "Verbal Avoidance and Dissatisfaction in Intimate Conflict Situations," *Human Communication Research* 35 (2009): 357–83.

60. N. A. Klinetob and D. A. Smith, "Demand-Withdraw Communication in Marital Interaction: Tests of Interspousal Contingency and Gender Role Hypotheses," *Journal of Marriage and the Family* 58 (November 1996): 945–57; also see J. P. Caughlin and A. L. Vangelisti, "Desire to Change in One's Partner as a Predictor of the Demand/Withdraw Pattern of

Marital Communication," *Communication Monographs* 66 (1999): 66–89.

61. Miller, Reznik, and Roloff, "Hopelessness and Interpersonal Conflict."

62. I. M. Papp, C. D. Kouros, and E. M. Cummings, "Demand-Withdraw Patterns in Marital Conflict in the Home," *Personal Relationships*, 16 (2009): 285–300.

63. Papp, Kouros, and Cummings, "Demand-Withdraw Patterns in Marital Conflict in the Home."

64. J. P. Caughlin and R. S. Malis, "Demand/Withdraw Communication Between Parents and Adolescents as a Correlate of Relational Satisfaction," *Communication Reports* 17 (2004): 59–71.

65. R. Bello and R. Edwards, "Interpretations of Messages: The Influence of Various Forms of Equivocation, Face Concerns, and Sex Differences," *Journal of Language and Social Psychology* 24 (2005): 160–81.

66. J. T. Tedeschi, "Threats and Promises," in *The Structure of Conflict*, edited by R. Swingle (New York: Academic Press, 1970).

67. A. M. Czopp, M. J. Monteith, and A. Y. Mark, "Standing Up for a Change: Reducing Bias Through Interpersonal Confrontation," *Journal of Personality and Social Psychology* 90, no. 5 (2006): 784–803.

68. S. Dincyurek and A. H. Civelek, "The Determination of the Conflict Resolution Strategies of University Students that They Use When They Have Conflicts with People," *The Behavior Analyst Today* 9 (2009): 215–33.

69. Our discussion of the advantages and disadvantages of using different conflict management styles is based on material in Wilmot and Hocker, *Interpersonal Conflict*.

70. For an excellent review of the literature on flaming, see A. N. Joinson, *Understanding the Psychology of Internet Behavior: Virtual Worlds, Real Lives* (Houndsmill, England: Palgrave Macmillan, 2003), 64–77.

71. K. K. Stephens and S. A. Rains, "Information and Communication Technology Sequences and Message Repetition in Interpersonal Interaction," *Communication Research* 38, no. 1 (2011): 101–22.

72. D. S. Ebersole, A. V. Middleton, and A. L. Vangelisti, "Couples' Online Cognitions during Conflict: Links between What Partners Think and their Relational Satisfaction," *Communication Monographs* 80:2 (2013): 125–49.

73. L. Powell and M. Hickson, "Power Imbalance and Anticipation of Conflict Resolution: Positive and Negative Attributes of Perceptual Recall," *Communication Research Reports* 17 (Spring 2000): 181–90.

74. D. Cramer, "Linking Conflict Management Behaviors and Relational Satisfaction: The Intervening Role of Conflict Outcome Satisfaction," *Journal of Social and Personal Relationships* 19 (2000): 425–32.

75. D. A. Cai and E. L. Fink, "Conflict Style Differences Between Individualists and Collectivists," *Communication Monographs* 69 (March 2002): 67–87.

76. R. Dominque and D. Mollen, "Attachment and Conflict Communication in Adult Romantic Relationships," *Journal of Social and Personal Relationships* 26, no. 5 (2009): 678–96.

77. M. R. Hammer, "The Intercultural Conflict Style Inventory: A Conceptual Framework and Measure of Intercultural Conflict Resolution Approaches," *International Journal of Intercultural Relations* 29 (2005): 675–95.

78. Hammer, "The Intercultural Conflict Style Inventory."

79. Canary, Cupach, and Serpe, "A Competence-Based Approach to Examining Interpersonal Conflict."

80. T. J. Burke, C. Segrin, and A. Woszidlo, "Social Skills, Family Conflict, and Loneliness in Families," *Communication Reports* 25:2 (2012): 75–87.

81. Our discussion of conflict management skills is based on several excellent discussions of conflict management prescriptions. We acknowledge R. Fisher and W. Ury, *Getting to Yes: Negotiating Agreement Without Giving In* (Boston: Houghton Mifflin, 1991); R. Boulton, *People Skills* (New York: Simon & Schuster, 1979); D. A. Romig and L. J. Romig, *Structured Teamwork Guide* (Austin, TX: Performance Resources, 1990); O. Hargie, C. Saunders, and D. Dickson, *Social Skills in Interpersonal Communication* (London: Routledge, 1994); S. Deep and L. Sussman, *Smart Moves* (Reading, MA: Addison-Wesley, 1990); Wilmot and Hocker, *Interpersonal Conflict*; M. D. Davis, E. L. Eshelman, and M. McKay, *The Relaxation and Stress Reduction Workbook* (Oakland, CA: New Harbinger Publications, 1982); W. A. Donohue and R. Kolt, *Managing Interpersonal Conflict* (Newbury Park: CA: Sage, 1992); O. Hargie (Ed.), *The Handbook of Communication Skills* (London: Routledge, 1997); Littlejohn and Domenici, *Engaging Communication in Conflict*; M. W. Isenhart and M. Spangle, *Collaborative Approaches to Resolving Conflict* (Thousand Oaks, CA: Sage, 2000); K. Sanford and A. J. Grace, "Emotion and Underlying Concerns During Couples' Conflict: An Investigation of Within-Person Change," *Personal Relationships* 18 (2011): 96–109.

82. Czopp, Monteith, and Mark, "Standing Up for a Change."

83. Boulton, *People Skills*, 217.

84. For additional strategies on managing emotion, see J. Gottman, *Why Marriages Succeed and Fail: And How You Can Make Yours Last* (New York: Simon & Schuster, 1994); J. Gottman, *The Seven Principles for Making Marriage Work* (New York: Crown, 1999). Also see Johnson, *Reaching Out*.

85. A. M. Hicks and L. M. Diamond, "Don't Go to Bed Angry: Attachment, Conflict, and Affective and Physiological Reactivity," *Personal Relationships* 18 (2011): 266–84.

86. J. A. Feeney, "Hurt Feelings in Couple Relationships: Towards Integrative Models of the Negative Effects of Hurtful Events," *Journal of Social and Personal Relationships* 21 (2004): 487–508.

87. Young, "Factors That Influence Recipients' Appraisals of Hurtful Communication."

88. H. Weger Jr., "Disconfirming Communication and Self-Verification in Marriage: Associations Among the Demand/Withdraw Interaction Pattern, Feeling Understood, and Marital Satisfaction." *Journal of Social and Personal Relationships* 22 (2005): 19–31.

89. Gottmann, *What Predicts Divorce?*

90. M. Morris, J. Nadler, T. Kurtzberg, and L. Thompson, "Schmooze or Lose: Social Friction and Lubrication in E-Mail Negotiations," *Group Dynamics: Theory, Research and Practice* 6 (2002): 89–100.

91. Dincyurek and Civelek, "The Determination of the Conflict Resolution Strategies of University Students that They Use When They Have Conflicts with People."

92. A. M. Bippus, S. L. Young, and N. E. Dunbar, "Humor in Conflict Discussions: Comparing Partners' Perceptions," *Humor* 24, no. 3 (2011): 287–303.

93. A. Ellis, *A New Guide to Rational Living* (North Hollywood, CA: Wilshire Books, 1977).

94. M. Sinaceau and L. Z. Tiedens, "Get Mad and Get More Than Even: When and Why Anger Expression Is Effective in Negotiations," *Journal of Experimental Social Psychology* 20 (2005): 1–9.

95. K. du Plessis and D. Clarke, "Couples' Helpful, Unhelpful and Ideal Conflict Resolution Strategies: Secure and Insecure Attachment Differences and Similarities," *Interpersona* 2, no. 1 (2008): 65–88.

96. A. M. Bippus and S. L. Young, "Your Emotions: Reactions to Expressions of Self-versus Other-Attributed Positive and Negative Emotions," *Journal of Applied Communication Research* 33 (2005): 26–45.

97. S. R. Covey, *The 7 Habits of Highly Effective People* (New York: Simon & Schuster, 1989), 235.

98. S. G. Lakey and D. J. Canary, "Actor Goal Achievement and Sensitivity to Partner as Critical Factors in Understanding Interpersonal Communication Competence and Conflict Strategies," *Communication Monographs* 69 (2002): 217–35.

99. Lakey and Canary, "Actor Goal Achievement and Sensitivity to Partner as Critical Factors in Understanding Interpersonal Communication Competence and Conflict Strategies."

100. For a review of goal setting and conflict management see J. L. Bevan, "Serial Argument Goals and Conflict Strategies: A Comparison Between Romantic Partners and Family Members," *Communication Reports* 23, no. 1 (2010): 52–64.

101. Fisher and Ury, *Getting to Yes.*

102. W. Ury, *Getting Past No* (New York: Bantam Books, 1993); also see S. Hackley, "When Life Gives You Lemons: How

to Deal with Difficult People," *Harvard Business School Publishing Corporation* (2004): 3–5.

103. For an excellent review and analysis of collaborative, side-by-side leadership research, see D. Romig, *Side by Side Leadership: Achieving Outstanding Results Together* (Marietta, GA: Bard Press, 2001).

104. Fisher and Ury, *Getting to Yes*; also see D. Yankelovich, *The Magic of Dialogue: Transforming Conflict into Cooperation* (New York: Simon & Schuster, 1999).

105. Fisher and Ury, *Getting to Yes*.

106. D. Romig, *Breakthrough Teamwork: Outstanding Results Using Structured Teamwork* (New York: Irwin, 1996).

107. Lakey and Canary, "Actor Goal Achievement and Sensitivity to Partner as Critical Factors in Understanding Interpersonal Communication Competence and Conflict Strategies."

108. E. Goffman, *Interaction Rituals: Essays on Face-to-Face Interaction* (Garden City, NY: Doubleday, 1967).

109. J. G. Oetzel, S. T. Toomey, and Q. Zhang, "Linking Emotion to the Conflict Face-Negotiation Theory: A U.S.–China Investigation of the Mediating Effects of Anger, Compassion, and Guilt in Interpersonal Conflict," *Human Communication Research* 40 (2014): 373–95.

110. S. Ting-Toomey, "Face and Facework: An Introduction," in *The Challenge of Facework*, edited by S. Ting-Toomey (Albany, NY: SUNY Press, 1994), 1–14; S. Ting-Toomey, "Managing Intercultural Conflicts Effectively," in *Intercultural Communication: A Reader*, edited by L. A Samovar and R. E. Porter (Belmont, CA: Wadsworth, 1994), 360–72; also see S. Ting-Toomey and L. Chung, "Cross-Cultural Interpersonal Communication: Theoretical Trends and Research Directions," in *Communication in Personal Relationships Across Cultures*, edited by W. B. Gudykunst, S. Ting-Toomey, and T. Nishida (Thousand Oaks, CA: Sage, 1996), 237; Isenhart and Spangle, *Collaborative Approaches to Resolving Conflict*, 19–20; Oetzel, Toomey, and Zhang, "Linking Emotion to the Conflict Face-Negotiation Theory."

111. V. Manusov, J. K. Kellas, and A. R. Trees, "Do Unto Others? Conversational Moves and Perceptions of Attentiveness Toward Other Face in Accounting Sequences Between Friends," *Human Communication Research* 30 (2004): 514–39.

112. M. L. McLaughlin, M. J. Cody, and H. D. O'Hair, "The Management of Failure Events: Some Contextual Determinants of Accounting Behavior," *Human Communication Research* 9 (1983): 102–25; Manusov, Kellas, and Trees, "Do Unto Others?"

113. R. M. McLaren and A. Sillars, "Human Episodes in Parent Adolescent Relationships: How Accounts and Attributions Contribute to the Difficulty of Talking about Hurt, "*Communication Monographs* 81(3) (2014): 359–85.

114. A. J. Merolla, "Communicating Forgiveness in Friendships and Dating Relationships," *Communication Studies* 59, no. 2 (April-June 2008): 114–31.

Chapter 9

1. S. L. Murray and J. G. Holmes, *Interdependent Minds: The Dynamics of Close Relationships* (New York: Guilford Press, 2011).

2. L. K. Knobloch and D. H. Solomon, "Information Seeking Beyond Initial Interaction: Negotiating Relational Uncertainty within Close Relationships," *Human Communication Research* 28 (April 2002): 243–57.

3. F. E. Millar and L. E. Rogers, "A Relational Approach to Interpersonal Communication," in *Explorations in Interpersonal Communication*, edited by G. R. Miller (Newbury Park, CA: Sage, 1976), 87–103.

4. D. Layer, *Intimacy and Power: The Dynamics of Personal Relationships in Modern Society* (New York, NY: Palgrave Macmillian, 2009).

5. J. K. Burgoon, L. K, Guerrero, and V. Manusov, "Nonverbal Signals," in *The Sage Handbook of Interpersonal Communication*, 4th ed., edited by M. L. Knapp and J. A. Daly (Thousand Oaks, CA: Sage, 2011), 239–80.

6. C. A. Lennon, A. L. Stewart, and T. Ledermman, "The Role of Power in Intimate Relationships," *Journal of Social and Personal Relationships* 30 (2012): 95–114.

7. F. E. Millar and L. E. Rogers, "Relational Dimensions of Interpersonal Dynamics," in *Interpersonal Processes: New Directions in Communication Research*, edited by M. E. Roloff and G. R. Miller (Newbury Park, CA: Sage, 1987), 117–39.

8. N. E. Dunbar and J. K. Burgoon, "Perceptions of Power and Interactional Dominance in Interpersonal Relationships," *Journal of Social and Personal Relationships* 22 (2005): 207–33.

9. M. Sunnafrank, "Predicted Outcome Value During Initial Interaction: A Reformulation of Uncertainty Reduction Theory," *Human Communication Research* 13 (1986): 3–33.

10. J. Deyo, P. Walt, and L. Davis, "Rapidly Recognizing Relationships: Observing Speed-Dating in the South," *Qualitative Research Reports in Communication*, 12.1 (2011): 71–8.

11. Sunnafrank, "Predicted Outcome Value During Initial Interaction."

12. H. T. Reis, M. R. Maniaci, and P. A. Caprariello, "Familiarity Does Indeed Promote Attraction in Live Interaction," *Journal of Personality and Social Psychology*,101 (2011): 557–70.

13. M. Sunnafrank, "Interpersonal Attraction and Attitude Similarity: A Communication Based Assessment," in *Communication Yearbook 14*, edited by J. A. Anderson (Newbury Park, CA: Sage, 1991), 451–83.

14. S. W. Duck, *Personal Relationships and Personal Constructs: A Study of Friendship Formation* (New York: Wiley, 1993).

15. S. S. Wang, S. Moon, K. H. Kwon, C. A. Evans, and M. A. Stefanone. "Face Off: Implications of Visual Cues on Initiating Relationships on Facebook," *Computers in Human Behavior* 26 (2010): 226–34.

16. K. F. Albada, M. L. Knapp, and K. E. Theune, "Interaction Appearance Theory: Changing Perceptions of Physical Attractiveness Through Social Interaction," *Communication Theory* 12 (2002): 8–40; B. Hendrickson and R. Goei, "Reciprocity and Dating: Explaining the Effects of Favor and Status on Compliance with a Date Request," *Communication Research* 36 (2009): 585–608.

17. P. A. Mongeau and K. L. Johnson, "Predicting Cross-Sex First-Date Sexual Expectations and Involvement: Contextual and Individual Difference Factors," *Personal Relationships* 2 (1995): 301–12.

18. P. C. Regan, L. Levin, S. Sprecher, F. S. Christopher, and R. Cate, "Partner Preferences: What Characteristics Do Men and Women Desire in Their Short-Term Sexual and Long-Term Romantic Partners?" *Journal of Psychology and Human Sexuality* 12 (2000): 1–21.

19. W. G. Graziano and J. W. Bruce, "Attraction and the Initiation of Relationships: A Review of the Empirical Literature," in *Handbook of Relationship Initiation*, edited by S. Sprecher, A. Wenzel, and J. Harvey (New York: Psychology Press, 2008), 269–95.

20. S. Sprecher, "Insiders' Perspectives on Reasons for Attraction to a Close Other," *Social Psychology Quarterly* 61 (1998): 287–300.

21. Sprecher, "Insiders' Perspectives."

22. N. L. Collins and L. C. Miller, "Self-Disclosure and Liking: A Meta-Analytic Review," *Psychological Bulletin* 116 (1994): 457–75.

23. R. A. Clark, M. Dockum, H. Hazeu, M. Huang, N. Luo, J. Ramsey, and A. Spyrou, "Initial Encounters of Young Men and Women: Impressions and Disclosure Estimates," *Sex Roles* 50 (2004): 699–709.

24. S. Sprecher and P. C. Regan, "Liking Some Things (in Some People) More Than Others: Partner Preferences in Romantic Relationships and Friendships," *Journal of Social and Personal Relationships* 19 (2002): 463–81.

25. Collins and Miller, "Self-Disclosure and Liking."

26. S. Sprecher, S. Teger, and J. D. Wondra, "Effects of Self-Disclosure Role on Liking, Closeness, and Other Impressions in Get-Acquainted Interactions," *Journal of Social and Personal Relationships* 30 (2013): 497–514.

27. Sprecher, "Insiders' Perspectives."

28. G. B. Ray and K. Floyd, "Nonverbal Expressions of Liking and Disliking in Initial Interaction: Encoding and Decoding Perspectives," *Southern Communication Journal* 71 (2006): 45–65.

29. P. W. Eastwick, E. J. Finkel, D. Mochon, and D. Ariely, "Selective versus Unselective Romantic Desire: Not All Reciprocity Is Created Equal," *Psychological Science* 18 (2007): 317–19.

30. M. V. Redmond and D. A. Vrchota, "The Effects of Varying Lengths of Initial

Interaction on Attraction and Uncertainty Reduction," paper presented at the annual meeting of the National Communication Association, New Orleans (1994).

31. Sprecher, "Insiders' Perspectives."

32. Sunnafrank, "Interpersonal Attraction and Attitude Similarity."

33. Sunnafrank, "Interpersonal Attraction and Attitude Similarity."

34. L. A. Baxter and L. West, "Couple Perceptions of Their Similarities and Differences: A Dialectical Perspective," *Journal of Social and Personal Relationships* 20 (2003): 491–514.

35. S. Sprecher, "Effects of Actual (Manipulated) and Perceived Similarity on Liking in Get-Acquainted Interactions: The Role of Communication." *Communication Monographs* 81 (2014): 4–29.

36. N. D. Tidwell, P. W. Eastwich, and E. J. Finkel, "Perceived, Not Actual, Similarity Predicts Initial Attraction in a Live Romantic Context: Evidence from the Speed-Dating Paradigm," *Personal Relationships* 20 (2013): 199–215.

37. Sprecher, "Effects of Actual (Manipulated) and Perceived Similarity on Liking in Get-Acquainted Interactions."

38. Baxter and West, "Couple Perceptions of Their Similarities and Differences."

39. Baxter and West, "Couple Perceptions of Their Similarities and Differences."

40. J. Fox and C. Anderegg, "Romantic Relationship Stages and Social Networking Sites: Uncertainty Reduction Strategies and Perceived Relational Norms on Facebook," *Cyberpsychology, Behavior, and Social Networking* 17 (2014): 685–91.

41. C. R. Berger and J. J. Bradac, *Language and Social Knowledge: Uncertainty and Interpersonal Relations* (Baltimore: Edward Arnold, 1982).

42. M. R. Cunningham and A. P. Barbee, "Prelude to a Kiss: Nonverbal Flirting, Opening Gambits, and Other Communication Dynamics of the Initiation of Romantic Relationships," in *Handbook of Relationship Initiation*, edited by S. Sprecher, A. Wenzel, and J. Harvey (New York: Psychology Press, 2008), 97–120.

43. D. Morgan, *Acquaintances: The Space between Intimates and Strangers.* (New York: Open University Press, 2009).

44. W. Douglas, "Question Asking in Same and Opposite Sex Initial Interactions: The Effects of Anticipated Future Interactions," *Human Communication Research* 14 (1987): 230–45.

45. Morgan, *Acquaintances: The Space between Intimates and Strangers.*

46. K. N. Dunleavy and M. Booth-Butterfield, "Idiomatic Communication in the Stages of Coming Together and Falling Apart." *Communication Quarterly,* 57 (2009): 416–32.

47. J. Fox, K. M. Warber, and D. C. Makstaller, "The Role of Facebook in Romantic Relationship Development: An Exploration of Knapp's Relational Stage Model," *Journal of Social and Personal Relationships* 30 (2013): 771–94.

48. M. Parks, *Personal Relationships and Personal Networks* (Mahwah, NJ: Erlbaum, 2007).

49. B. Laursen and C. A. Hafen, "Future Directions in the Study of Close Relationships: Conflict Is Bad (Except When It's Not)," *Social Development* 19 (2010): 858–72.

50. C. Harasymchuk and B. Fehr, "A Prototype Analysis of Relational Boredom," *Journal of Social and Personal Relationships* 30 (2012): 627–46.

51. J. K. Kellas, D. Bean, C. Cunningham, and K. Y. Cheng, "The Ex-Files: Trajectories, Turning Points, and Adjustment in the Development of Post-Dissolutional Relationships," *Journal of Social and Personal Relationships* 25 (2008): 23–50.

52. S. W. Duck, "A Topography of Relationship Disengagement and Dissolution," in *Personal Relationships 4: Dissolving Personal Relationships,* edited by S. W. Duck (London: Academic Press, 1982), 1–29.

53. L. A. Baxter and C. Bullis, "Turning Points in Developing Romantic Relationships," *Communication Research* 12 (1986): 469–93.

54. Baxter and Bullis, "Turning Points."

55. R. M. Dailey, N. Brody, L. LeFebvre, and B. Crook, "Charting Changes in Commitment: Trajectories of On-Again/Off-Again Relationships," *Journal of Social and Personal Relationships* 30 (2013): 1020–44.

56. A. J. Johnson, E. Wittenberg, E. M. Villagran, M. Mazur, and P. Villagran, "Relational Progression as a Dialectic: Examining Turning Points in Communication Among Friends," *Communication Monographs* 70 (2003): 230–49.

57. J. P. Dillard and L. K. Knobloch, "Interpersonal Influence," in *The Sage Handbook of Interpersonal Communication,* 4th ed., edited by M. L. Knapp and J. A. Daly (Thousand Oaks, CA: Sage, 2011): 389–422.

58. S. Duck, "Interpersonal Communication in Developing Relationships," in *Explorations in Interpersonal Communication,* edited by G. R. Miller (Newbury Park, CA: Sage, 1976), 127–47.

59. J. W. Thibaut and H. H. Kelley, *The Social Psychology of Groups* (New York: Wiley, 1959).

60. A. L. Busboom, D. M. Collins, M. D. Givertz, and L. A. Levin, "Can We Still Be Friends? Resources and Barriers to Friendship Quality after Romantic Relationship Dissolution," *Personal Relationships* 9 (2002): 215–23.

61. I. Altman and D. A. Taylor, *Social Penetration: The Development of Interpersonal Relationships* (New York: Holt, Rinehart and Winston, 1973).

62. L. Stafford, "Social Exchange Theories: Calculating the Rewards and Costs of Personal Relationships," in *Engaging Theories in Interpersonal Communication,* 2nd ed., edited by D. O. Braithwaite and P. Schrodt (Los Angeles: Sage, 2015), 403–36.

63. G. R. Miller and M. R. Parks, "Communicating in Dissolving Relationships," in *Personal Relationships 4: Dissolving Personal Relationships,* edited by S. W. Duck (London: Academic Press, 1982), 127–54.

64. A. J. Johnson, E. Wittenberg, M. M. Villagran, M. Mazur, and P. Villagran, "Relational Progression as a Dialectic: Examining Turning Points in Communication among Friends," *Communication Monographs* 70 (2003): 230–49.

65. L. A. Baxter, "Dialectical Contradictions in Relationship Development," in *Handbook of Personal Relationships,* edited by S. W. Duck (Chichester, England: Wiley, 1988), 257–73; L. A. Baxter and B. M. Montgomery, "Rethinking Communication in Personal Relationships from a Dialectical Perspective," in *Handbook of Personal Relationships,* 2nd ed., edited by S. W. Duck (Chichester, England: Wiley, 1997), 325–49.

66. D. R. Pawlowski, "Dialectical Tensions in Marital Partners' Accounts of Their Relationships," *Communication Quarterly* 46 (1998): 396–416.

67. Pawlowski, "Dialectical Tensions."

68. L. A. Baxter, "Interpersonal Communication as Dialogue: A Response to the 'Social Approaches' Forum," *Communication Theory* 2 (1992): 330–38.

69. A. Hoppe-Nagao and S. Ting-Toomey, "Relational Dialectics and Management Strategies in Marital Couples," *Southern Communication Journal* 67 (Winter 2002): 142–59.

70. Baxter, "Interpersonal Communication as Dialogue."

71. J. Fox, J. L. Osborn, and K. W. Warber, "Relational Dialectics and Social Networking Sites: The Role of Facebook in Romantic Relationship Escalation, Maintenance, Conflict, and Dissolution," *Computers in Human Behavior* 35 (2014): 527–34.

72. L. A. Baxter, "Dialectical Contradictions in Relationship Development," *Journal of Social and Personal Relationships* 7 (1990): 69–88; Baxter and Montgomery, "Rethinking Communication in Personal Relationships from a Dialectical Perspective."

73. A. Smith, "Americans and Text Messaging," Pew Internet and American Life Project, September 19, 2011, http://pewinternet.org/Reports/2011/ Cell-Phone-Texting-2011/Main-Report.aspx.

74. M. Duggan, "Cell Phone Activities 2013," Pew Internet and American Life Project, September 19, 2013, www.pewinternet.org/2013/09/19/cell-phone-activities-2013/

75. R. L. Duran, L. Kelly, and T. Rotaru, "Mobile Phones in Romantic Relationships and the Dialectic of Autonomy versus Connection." *Communication Quarterly* 59 (2011): 19–36.

76. J. L. Gibbs, N. B. Ellison, and C. Lai, "First Comes Love, Then Comes Google: An Investigation of Uncertainty Reduction Strategies and Self-Disclosure in Online Dating," *Communication Research* 38 (2011): 70–100.

77. I. Altman and D. A. Taylor, *Social Penetration: The Development of Interpersonal Relationships* (New York: Holt, Rinehart and Winston, 1973).

78. A. P. Bochner, "On the Efficacy of Openness in Close Relationships," in *Communication Yearbook 5*, edited by M. Burgoon (New Brunswick, NJ: Transaction Books, 1982), 109–24.

79. K. Dindia, "Self-Disclosure Research: Knowledge through Meta-Analysis," in *Interpersonal Communication Research: Analysis Through Meta-Analysis*, edited by M. Allen, R. W. Preiss, B. M. Gayle, and N. A. Burrell (Mahwah, NJ: Erlbaum, 2002), 169–85.

80. S. Petronio, *Boundaries of Privacy: Dialectics of Disclosure* (Albany: State University of New York Press, 2000).

81. J. P. Caughlin and T. D. Afifi, "When Is Topic Avoidance Unsatisfying? Examining Moderators of the Association Between Avoidance and Dissatisfaction," *Human Communication Research* 30 (2004): 479–513.

82. M. K. Venetis, K. Greene, K. Magsamen-Conrad, S. C. Banerjee, M. G. Checton, and Z. Bagdasarov, "'You Can't Tell Anyone but…': Exploring the Use of Privacy Rules and Revealing Behaviors," *Communication Monographs* 79 (2012): 344–65.

83. Venetis et al.,"'You Can't Tell Anyone but…'"

84. J. Powell, *Why Am I Afraid to Tell You Who I Am?* (Niles, IL: Argus Communications, 1969), 12.

85. W. B. Gudykunst and T. Nishida, "Social Penetration in Japanese and American Close Friendships," in *Communication Yearbook 7*, edited by R. N. Bostrom (Beverly Hills, CA: Sage, 1963), 592–611.

86. M. Kito, "Self-Disclosure in Romantic Relationships and Friendships Among American and Japanese College Students," *The Journal of Social Psychology* 145 (2005): 127–40.

87. J. C. Korn, "Friendship Formation and Development in Two Cultures: Universal Constructs in the United States and Korea," in *Interpersonal Communication in Friend and Mate Relationships*, edited by A. M. Nicotera (Albany: State University of New York Press, 1993), 61–78.

88. B. Fehr, "Friendship Formation," in *Handbook of Relationship Initiation*, edited by S. Sprecher, A. Wenzel, and J. Harvey (New York: Psychology Press, 2008), 29–54.

89. J. J. Weisel and P. E. King, "Involvement in a Conversation and Attributions Concerning Excessive Self-Disclosure," *Southern Communication Journal* 72 (2007) 345–54; Fehr, "Friendship Formation."

90. L. C. Jiang, N. N. Bazarova, and J. T. Hancock, "From Perception to Behavior: Disclosure Reciprocity and the Intensification of Intimacy in Computer-Mediated Communication," *Communication Research* 40 (2013): 125–43.

91. Fehr, "Friendship Formation."

92. Fehr, "Friendship Formation."

93. M. Argyle, M. Henderson, and A. Furnham, "The Rules of Social Relationships," *British Journal of Social Psychology* 24 (1985): 125–39.

94. A. L. Vangelisti, J. P. Caughlin, and L. Timmerman, "Criteria for Revealing Family Secrets," *Communication Monographs* 68 (March 2001): 1–27.

95. T. D. Afifi, L. N. Olson, and C. Armstrong, "The Chilling Effect and Family Secrets: Examining the Role of Self Protection, Other Protection, and Communication Efficacy," *Human Communication Research* 31 (2005): 564–98.

96. J. Walther, "Theories of Computer-Mediated Communication and Interpersonal Relations," in *The Sage Handbook of Interpersonal Communication*, 4th ed., edited by M. L. Knapp and J. A. Daly (Thousand Oaks, CA: Sage, 2011): 443–80.

97. J. Kim and K. Dindia, "Online Self-Disclosure: A Review of Research," in *Computer-Mediated Communication in Personal Relationships*, edited by K. B. Wright and L. M. Webb (New York: Peter Lang, 2011), 156–80.

Chapter 10

1. P. Noller, "Bringing It All Together: A Theoretical Approach," in *The Cambridge Handbook of Personal Relationships*, edited by A. L. Vangelisti and D. Perlman (New York: Cambridge University Press, 2006), 769–89.

2. S. Metts, "Relational Transgressions," in *The Dark Side of Interpersonal Communication*, edited by W. R. Cupach and B. H. Spitzberg (Hillsdale, NJ: Erlbaum, 1994), 217–39.

3. A. P. Buunk and P. Dijkstra, "Temptation and Threat: Extradyadic Relations and Jealousy," in *The Cambridge Handbook of Personal Relationships*, edited by A. L. Vangelisti and D. Perlman (New York: Cambridge University Press, 2006), 533–56.

4. M. R. Dillow, W.A. Afifi, and M. Matsunaga, "Perceived Partner Uniqueness and Communicative and Behavioral Transgression Outcomes in Romantic Relationships," *Journal of Social and Personal Relationships* 29 (2012): 28–51.

5. S. M. Horan, "Affection Exchange Theory and Perceptions of Relational Transgressions," *Western Journal of Communication* 76 (2012): 109–26.

6. F. D. Fincham, "The Account Episode in Close Relationships," in *Explaining One's Self to Others: Reason-Giving in a Social Context*, edited by M. L. McClaughlin, M. J. Cody, and S. J. Read (Hillsdale, NJ: Erlbaum, 1992), 167–82.

7. G. Makoul and M. E. Roloff, "The Role of Efficacy and Outcome Expectations in the Decision to Withhold Relational Complaints," *Communication Research* 25 (1998): 25–30.

8. R. M. McClaren and K. R. Steuber, "Emotions, Communicative Responses, and Relational Consequences of Boundary Turbulence," *Journal of Social and Personal Relationships* 30 (2013): 606–26.

9. M. L. McLaughlin, M. J. Cody, and H. D. O'Hair, "The Management of Failure Events: Some Contextual Determinants of Accounting Behavior," *Human Communication Research* 9 (1983): 208–24.

10. Fincham, "The Account Episode in Close Relationships."

11. J. W. Younger, R. L. Piferi, R. L. Jobe, and K. A. Lawler, "Dimensions of Forgiveness: The Views of Laypersons," *Journal of Social and Personal Relationships* 21 (2004): 837–55.

12. Younger, Piferi, Jobe, and Lawler, "Dimensions of Forgiveness."

13. B. M. Riek and E. W. Mania, "The Antecedents and Consequences of Interpersonal Forgiveness: A Meta-Analytic Review," *Personal Relationships* 19 (2012): 304–25.

14. Younger, Piferi, Jobe, and Lawler, "Dimensions of Forgiveness"; C. Pansera and J. La Guardia, "The Role of Sincere Amends and Perceived Partner Responsiveness to Forgiveness," *Personal Relationships* 19 (2012): 696–711.

15. A. J. Merolla, "Forgive like You Mean It: Sincerity of Forgiveness and the Experience of Negative Affect," *Communication Quarterly* 62 (2014): 36–56.

16. V. R. Waldron and D. L. Kelley, *Communicating Forgiveness* (Thousand Oaks, CA: Sage, 2008).

17. B. M. Reik, L. M. Root Luna, and C. A. Schnabelrauch, "Transgressors' Guilt and Shame: A Longitudinal Examination of Forgiveness Seeking," *Journal of Social and Personal Relationships* 31 (2014): 751–72.

18. V. R. Waldron and D. L. Kelley, "Forgiving Communication as a Response to Relational Transgressions," *Journal of Social and Personal Relationships* 22 (2005): 723–42.

19. S. Metts and W. R. Cupach, "Responses to Relational Transgressions: Hurt, Anger, and Sometimes Forgiveness," in *The Dark Side of Interpersonal Communication*, 2nd ed., edited by B. H. Spitzberg and W. R. Cupach (Mahwah, NJ: Erlbaum, 2007), 243–74; A. J. Merolla, and S. Zhang, "In the Wake of Transgressions: Examining Forgiveness Communication in Personal Relationships," *Personal Relationships* 18 (2010): 79–95.

20. C. R. Morse and S. Metts, "Situational and Communicative Predictors of Forgiveness Following a Relational Transgression." *Western Journal of Communication* 75 (2011): 239–58.

21. J. Eaton and C. B. Sanders, "A Little Help from Our Friends: Informal Third Parties and Interpersonal Conflict," *Personal Relationships*, 19 (2012): 623-643.

22. Eaton and Sanders, "A Little Help from Our Friends."

23. Eaton and Sanders, "A Little Help from Our Friends."

24. L. K. Guerrero and W. A. Afifi, "Toward a Goal-Oriented Approach for

Understanding Communicative Responses to Jealousy," *Western Journal of Communication* 63 (1999): 216–48.

25. M. A. Tofoya and B. H. Spitzberg, "The Dark Side of Infidelity: Its Nature, Prevalence, and Communicative Functions," in *The Dark Side of Interpersonal Communication*, 2nd ed., edited by B. H. Spitzberg and W. R. Cupach (Mahwah, NJ: Erlbaum, 2007), 201–42.

26. J. Fitness and J. Peterson, "Punishment and Forgiveness in Close Relationships: An Evolutionary, Social-Psychological Perspective," in *Social Relationships: Cognitive, Affective, and Motivational Processes*, edited by J. P. Forgas and J. Fitness (New York: Psychology Press, 2008), 255–69.

27. L. K. Guerrero and G. F. Bachman, "Forgiveness and Forgiving Communication in Dating Relationships: An Expectancy-Investment Explanation," *Journal of Social and Personal Relationships* 27 (2010): 801–23.

28. Noller, "Bringing It All Together"; Guerrero and Afifi, "Toward a Goal-Oriented Approach."

29. Adapted from Guerrero and Bachman, "Forgiveness and Forgiving Communication."

30. Guerrero and Bachman, "Forgiveness and Forgiving Communication."

31. H. L. Servaty-Seib and B. R. Burleson, "Bereaved Adolescents' Evaluations of the Helpfulness of Support-Intended Statements: Associations with Person Centeredness and Demographic, Personality, and Contextual Factors," *Journal of Social and Personal Relationships* 24 (2007): 207–23.

32. M. Booth-Butterfield, M. B. Wanzer, N. Weil, and E. Krezmien, "Communication of Humor During Bereavement: Intrapersonal and Interpersonal Emotion Management Strategies," *Communication Quarterly* 62 (2014): 436–54.

33. J. L. Dibble, "Breaking Good and Bad News: Face-Implicating Concerns as Mediating the Relationship Between News Valence and Hesitation to Share the News," *Communication Studies* 65 (2014): 223–43.

34. S. Rosen and A. Tesser, "On Reluctance to Communicate Undesirable Information: The MUM Effect," *Sociometry* 33 (1970): 253–63.

35. L. Sparks, M. M. Villagran, J. Parker-Raley, and C. B. Cunningham, "A Patient-Centered Approach to Breaking Bad News: Communication Guidelines for Health Care Providers." *Journal of Applied Communication* 35 (2007): 177–96.

36. A. S. B. Weiner and J. W. Hannum, "Differences in the Quantity of Social Support between Geographically Close and Long-Distance Friendships," *Journal of Social and Personal Relationships* 30 (2012): 662–72.

37. B. Le, T. J. Loving, G. W. Lewandowski, Jr. et al., "Missing a Romantic Partner: A Prototype Analysis," *Personal Relationships* 15 (2008): 511–32.

38. K. C. Macquire and S. L. Connaughton, "A Cross-Contextual Examination of Technologically Mediated Communication and Social Presence in Long-Distance Relationships," in *Computer-Mediated Communication in Personal Relationships*, edited by K. B. Wright and L. M. Webb (New York: Peter Lang, 2011), 244–65.

39. K. Rosetto, "Relational Coping during Deployment: Managing Communication and Connection in Relationships," *Personal Relationships* 20 (2013): 568–86.

40. L. Stafford, *Maintaining Long-Distance and Cross-Residential Relationships* (Mahwah, NJ: Erlbaum, 2005).

41. M. Dainton and B. Aylor, "A Relational Uncertainty Analysis of Jealousy, Trust, and Maintenance in Long-Distance versus Geographically Close Relationships," *Communication Quarterly* 49 (Spring 2001): 172–88.

42. Dainton and Aylor, "A Relational Uncertainty Analysis."

43. G. T. Guldner and C. H. Swensen, "Time Spent Together and Relationship Quality: Long-Distance Relationships as a Test Case," *Journal of Social and Personal Relationships* 12 (1995): 313–20; A. J. Johnson, "Examining the Maintenance of Friendships: Are There Differences Between Geographically Close and Long-Distance Friends?" *Communication Quarterly* 49 (Fall 2001): 424–35.

44. L. Stafford and J. R. Reske, "Idealization and Communication in Long-Distance Premarital Relationships," *Family Relations* 39 (July 1990): 274–79.

45. Stafford and Reske, "Idealization and Communication in Long-Distance Premarital Relationships."

46. Rosetto, "Relational Coping during Deployment."

47. Stafford, *Maintaining Long-Distance and Cross-Residential Relationships.*

48. B. Le and C. R. Agnew, "Need Fulfillment and Emotional Experience in Interdependent Romantic Relationships," *Journal of Social and Personal Relationships* 18 (2001): 423–40.

49. Lyndon, Pierce, and O'Regan, "Coping with Moral Commitment to Long-Distance Dating Relationships."

50. E. M. Sahlstein and T. Truong, "Proximal and Long-Distance Relations: A Web of Contradictions," paper presented at the annual meeting of the National Communication Association (2002).

51. Sahlstein and Truong, "Proximal and Long-Distance Relations."

52. E. M. Sahlstein, "Making Plans: Praxis Strategies for Negotiating Uncertainty-Certainty in Long-Distance Relationships," *Western Journal of Communication* 70 (2006): 147–65.

53. J. M. Bystydzienski, *Intercultural Couples: Crossing Boundaries, Negotiating Difference* (New York: New York University Press, 2011).

54. S. O. Gaines, Jr. and W. Ickes, "Perspectives on Interracial Relationships" in *The Social Psychology of Personal Relationships*, edited by W. Ickes and S. Duck, (New York: Wiley, 2000), 55–78.

55. Gaines and Ickes, "Perspectives on Interracial Relationships."

56. Gaines and Ickes, "Perspectives on Interracial Relationships."

57. M. J. Reiter and C. B. Gee, "Open Communication and Partner Support in Intercultural and Interfaith Romantic Relationships: A Relational Maintenance Approach," *Journal of Social and Personal Relationships* 25 (2008): 539–59.

58. Reiter and Gee, "Open Communication and Partner Support."

59. Bystydzienski, *Intercultural Couples: Crossing Boundaries, Negotiating Difference.*

60. Reiter and Gee, "Open Communication and Partner Support."

61. S. M. Haas and L. Stafford, "An Initial Examination of Maintenance Behaviors in Gay and Lesbian Relationships," *Journal of Social and Personal Relationships* 15 (1998): 846–55.

62. T. P. Mottet, "The Role of Sexual Orientation in Predicting Outcome Value and Anticipated Communication Behaviors," *Communication Quarterly* 48 (Summer 2000): 223–39.

63. Mottet, "The Role of Sexual Orientation in Predicting Outcome Value and Anticipated Communication Behaviors."

64. W. Cupach and B. Spitzberg (Eds.), *The Dark Side of Interpersonal Communication*, (Hillsdale, NJ: Erlbaum, 1994).

65. D. O'Hair and W. Cody, "Deception," in *The Dark Side of Interpersonal Communication*, edited by W. R. Cupach and B. H. Spitzberg (Hillsdale, NJ: Erlbaum, 1994), 181–213.

66. M. Knapp, "Lying and Deception in Close Relationships," in *The Cambridge Handbook of Personal Relationships*, edited by A. L. Vangelisti and D. Perlman (New York: Cambridge University Press, 2006), 517–32.

67. S. M. Horan and M. Booth-Butterfield, "Understanding the Routine Expression of Deceptive Affection in Romantic Relationships," *Communication Quarterly* 61 (2013): 195–216.

68. J. K. Burgoon and D. B. Buller, "Interpersonal Deception Theory: Purposive and Interdependent Behavior during Deception," in *Engaging Theories in Interpersonal Communication: Multiple Perspectives*, edited by L. A. Baxter and D. O. Braithwaite (Thousand Oaks, CA: Sage, 2008), 227–39.

69. N. E. Dunbar and M. Jensen, "Digital Deception in Personal Relationships," in *Computer-Mediated Communication in Personal Relationships* edited by K. B. Wright and L. M. Webb (New York: Peter Lang, 2011) 324–43.

70. A. E. Lucchetti, "Deception in Disclosing One's Sexual History: Safe-Sex Avoidance or Ignorance?" *Communication Quarterly* 47 (1999): 300–14.

71. O'Hair and Cody, "Deception."

72. T. R. Levine, K. J. K. Asada, and L. L. Massi Lindsey, "The Relative Impact of Violation Type and Lie Severity on Judgments of Message Deceitfulness," paper presented at the annual meeting of the National Communication Association (2002).

73. M. V. Redmond, *Human Communication: Theories and Applications* (Boston: Houghton Mifflin, 2000).

74. J. Guthrie and A. Kunkel, "Tell Me Sweet (And Not-So-Sweet) Little Lies: Deception in Romantic Relationships," *Communication Studies* 64 (2013): 141-157.

75. S. A. McCornack and T. R. Levine, "When Lies Are Uncovered: Emotional and Relational Outcomes of Discovered Deception," *Communication Monographs* 57 (1990): 119–38.

76. D. A. DePaulo and B. M. Kashy, "Everyday Lies in Close and Casual Relationships," *Journal of Personality and Social Psychology* 74 (1998): 63–80.

77. D. B. Buller and J. K. Burgoon, "Deception: Strategic and Nonstrategic Communication," in *Strategic Interpersonal Communication*, edited by J. A. Daly and J. M. Wiemann (Hillsdale, NJ: Erlbaum, 1994), 191–223; O'Hair and Cody, "Deception."

78. DePaulo and Kashy, "Everyday Lies in Close and Casual Relationships."

79. B. M. DePaulo, W. L. Morris, and R. W. Sternglanz, "When the Truth Hurts: Deception in the Name of Kindness," in *Feeling Hurt in Close Relationships* edited by A. L. Vangilisti (New York: Cambridge University Press, 2009): 167–90.

80. Horan and Booth-Butterfield, "Understanding the Routine Expression of Deceptive Affection in Romantic Relationships."

81. O'Hair and Cody, "Deception."

82. O'Hair and Cody, "Deception."

83. Knapp, "Lying and Deception in Close Relationships."

84. Knapp, "Lying and Deception in Close Relationships."

85. A. L. Vangelisti, "Messages That Hurt," in *The Dark Side of Interpersonal Communication*, edited by W. R. Cupach and B. H. Spitzberg (Hillsdale, NJ: Erlbaum, 1994), 181–213.

86. Vangelisti, "Messages That Hurt."

87. S. L. Young and A. M. Bippus, "Does It Make a Difference If They Hurt You in a Funny Way? Humorously and Non-Humorously Phrased Hurtful Messages in Personal Relationships," *Communication Quarterly* 49 (Winter 2001): 35–52.

88. P. E. Madlock and M. Booth-Butterfield, "Hurtful Teasing Between Romantic Couples: The Truth in Disguise?" paper presented at the annual meeting of the National Communication Association, San Diego (2008).

89. D. Hample, A. S. Richards, and C. Skubisz, "Blurting," *Communication Monographs* 80 (2013): 503–32.

90. Hample, Richards, and Skubisz. "Blurting."

91. J. A. Feeney, "Hurt Feelings in Couple Relationships: Towards Integrative Models of the Negative Effects of Hurtful Events," *Journal of Social and Personal Relationships* 21 (2004): 487–508.

92. A. L. Vangelisti and L. P. Crumley, "Reactions to Messages That Hurt: The Influence of Relational Contexts," *Communication Monographs* 65 (1998): 173–96.

93. Vangelisti and Crumley, "Reactions to Messages That Hurt."

94. S. Zhang and L. Stafford, "Perceived Face Threat of Honest but Hurtful Evaluative Messages in Romantic Relationships," *Western Journal of Communication* 72 (2008): 19–39.

95. Zhang and Stafford, "Perceived Face Threat of Honest but Hurtful Evaluative Messages."

96. S. L. Young, "Factors that Influence Recipients' Appraisals of Hurtful Communication," *Journal of Social and Personal Relationships* 21 (2004): 291–303.

97. R. M. McLaren, D. H. Solomon, and J. S. Priem. "Explaining Variation in Contemporaneous Responses to Hurt in Premarital Romantic Relationships: A Relational Turbulence Model Perspective," *Communication Research* 35 (2011): 543–64.

98. B. Jin, "Hurtful Texting in Friendships: Satisfaction Buffers the Distancing Effects of Intention," *Communication Research Reports* 30 (2013): 148–56.

99. L. K. Guerrero and P. A. Anderson, "Jealousy and Envy," in *The Dark Side of Close Relationships*, edited by W. R. Cupach and B. H. Spitzberg (Hillsdale, NJ: Erlbaum, 1994), 33–70.

100. L. K. Knobloch, "Evaluating a Contextual Model of Responses to Relational Uncertainty Increasing Events: The Role of Intimacy, Appraisals, and Emotions," *Human Communication Research* 31 (2005): 60–101.

101. J. L. Bevan and W. Samter, "Toward a Broader Conceptualization of Jealousy in Close Relationships: Two Exploratory Studies," *Communication Studies* 55 (2004): 14–28.

102. Guerrero and Anderson, "Jealousy and Envy."

103. J. L. Bevan and K. D. Tidgewell, "Relational Uncertainty as a Consequence of a Partner Jealousy Expressions," *Communication Studies* 60 (2009): 305–23.

104. Guerrero and Anderson, "Jealousy and Envy."

105. J. L. Bevan, "The Consequence Model of Jealousy Expression: Elaboration and Refinement," *Western Journal of Communication* 75 (2011): 525–40.

106. A. A. Fleishmann, B. H. Spitzberg, P. A. Anderson, and S. C. Roesch, "Tickling the Green Monster: Jealousy Induction in Relationships," *Journal of Social and Personal Relationships* 22 (2005): 49–73.

107. Fleishmann, Spitzberg, Anderson, and Roesch, "Tickling the Green Monster."

108. L. K. Guerrero, "Jealousy and Relational Satisfaction: Actor Effects, Partner Effects, and the Mediating Role of Destructive Communicative Responses to Jealousy," *Western Journal of Communication* 78 (2014): 586–611.

109. J. L. Bevan, "General Partner and Relational Uncertainty as Consequences of Another Jealousy Expression," *Western Journal of Communication* 68 (2004): 195–218.

110. S. M. Yoshimura, "Emotional and Behavioral Responses in Romantic Jealousy Expressions," *Communication Reports* 17 (2004): 85–102.

111. W. R. Cupach and B. H. Spitzberg, "Obsessive Relational Intrusion and Stalking," in *The Dark Side of Close Relationships*, edited by B. H. Spitzberg and W. R. Cupach (Mahwah, NJ: Erlbaum, 1998), 233–64.

112. W. R. Cupach and B. H. Spitzberg, *The Dark Side of Relationship Pursuit: From Attraction to Obsession and Stalking* (Mahwah, NJ: Erlbaum, 2004).

113. Cupach and Spitzberg, *The Dark Side of Relationship Pursuit*, 29–30.

114. Cupach and Spitzberg, "Obsessive Relational Intrusion and Stalking."

115. Cupach and Spitzberg, *The Dark Side of Relationship Pursuit*, 69–71.

116. K. Baum, S. Catalano, and M. Rand, "Stalking Victimization in the United States," Bureau of Justice Statistics, Special Report, January 2009.

117. C. L. McNamara and D. F. Marsil, "The Prevalence of Stalking Among College Students: The Disparity Between Researcher-and Self-Identified Victimization," *Journal of American College Health* 60 (2012): 168–74.

118. V. Ravensberg and C. Miller, "Stalking among Young Adults: A Review of the Preliminary Research," *Aggression and Violent Behavior* 8 (2003): 455–69; B. H. Spitzberg, A. M. Nicastro, and A. V. Cousins, "Exploring the Interactional Phenomenon of Stalking and Obsessive Relational Intrusion," *Communication Reports* 11 (1998): 33–48.

119. B. H. Spitzberg and W. R. Cupach, "Managing Unwanted Pursuit," in *Studies in Applied Interpersonal Communication*, edited by M. T. Motley (Thousand Oaks, CA: Sage, 2008), 3–26.

120. M. P. Johnson, "Violence and Abuse in Personal Relationships: Conflict, Terror, and Resistance in Intimate Partnerships," in *The Cambridge Handbook of Personal Relationships*, edited by A. L. Vangelisti, and D. Perlman (New York: Cambridge University Press, 2006), 557–76.

121. Centers for Disease Control and Prevention, "Intimate Partner Violence: Definitions," 2014, http://www.cdc.gov/violenceprevention/intimatepartnerviolence/definitions.html.

122. C. M. Feldman and C. A. Ridley, "The Role of Conflict-Based Communication Responses and Outcomes in Male Domestic Violence toward Female Partners," *Journal of Social and Personal Relationships* 17 (2000): 552–73.

123. B. W. Reyns, B. Henson, and B. S. Fisher, "Stalking in the Twilight Zone: Extent of Cyberstalking Victimization and Offending Among College Students," *Deviant Behavior* 33 (2012): 1–25.

124. A. J. Roberto, J. Eden, M. W. Savage, L. Ramos-Salazar, and D. M. Deiss, "Prevalence and Predictors of Cyberbullying Perpetration by High School Seniors," *Communication Quarterly* 62 (2014): 97–114.

125. Roberto et al., "Prevalence and Predictors of Cyberbullying Perpetration by High School Seniors."

126. K. Crosslin and M. Golman," 'Maybe You Don't Want to Face It' – College Student's

Perceptions of Cyberbullying," *Computers in Human Behavior* 41 (2014): 14–20; S. Vogl-Bauer," When Disgruntled Students Go to Extremes: The Cyberbullying of Instructors," *Communication Education* 63 (2014): 429–48.

127. H. Na, B. L. Dancy, and C. Park, "College Student Engaging in Cyberbullying Victimization: Cognitive Appraisals, Coping Strategies, and Psychological Adjustments," *Archives of Psychiatric Nursing* (2015), http://dx.doi.org/10.1016/j.apnu.2015.01.008.

128. Na, Dancy, and Park, "College Student Engaging in Cyberbullying Victimization."

129. R. S. Tokunaga, "Social Networking Site or Social Surveillance Site? Understanding the Use of Interpersonal Electronic Surveillance in Romantic Relationships," *Computers in Human Behavior* 27 (2011): 705–13.

130. Madden, "Privacy Management on Social Media Sites."

131. Madden, "Privacy Management on Social Media Sites."

132. M. Philips and B. H. Spitzberg, "Speculating about Spying on MySpace and Beyond: Social Network Surveillance and Obsessive Relational Intrusion," in *Computer-Mediated Communication in Personal Relationships* edited by K. B. Wright and L. M. Webb (New York: Peter Lang, 2011): 344–67.

133. Johnson, "Violence and Abuse in Personal Relationships."

134. Johnson, "Violence and Abuse in Personal Relationships."

135. Johnson, "Violence and Abuse in Personal Relationships."

136. B. H. Spitzberg, "Intimate Partner Violence and Aggression: Seeing the Light in a Dark Place," in *The Dark Side of Close Relationships II* edited by W. R. Cupach and B. H. Spitzberg (New York, NY: Routledge, 2011): 327–80.

137. G. R. Miller and M. R. Parks, "Communication in Dissolving Relationships," in *Personal Relationships 4: Dissolving Personal Relationships,* edited by S. W. Duck (London: Academic Press, 1982), 127–54.

138. J. Gottman with N. Silver, *Why Marriages Succeed or Fail* (New York: Simon and Schuster, 1994).

139. W. H. Denton and B. R. Burleson, "The Initiator Style Questionnaire: A Scale to Assess Initiator Tendency in Couples," *Personal Relationships* 14 (2007): 245–68.

140. R. J. Sidelinger, B. N. Frisby, and A. L. McMullen, "The Decision to Forgive: Sex, Gender, and the Likelihood to Forgive Partner Transgressions," *Communication Studies* 60 (2009): 164–79.

141. S. W. Duck, *Understanding Relationships* (New York: Guilford Press, 1991).

142. J. M. Gottman and S. Carrere, "Why Can't Men and Women Get Along? Developmental Roots and Marital Inequities," in *Communication and Relational Maintenance,* edited by D. J. Canary and L. Stafford (San Diego: Academic Press, 1991), 203–29.

143. C. Perilloux and D. M. Buss, "Breaking up Romantic Relationships: Costs Experienced and Coping Strategies Deployed," *Evolutionary Psychology* 6 (2008): 164–81.

144. Perilloux and Buss, "Breaking up Romantic Relationships."

145. Perilloux and Buss, "Breaking up Romantic Relationships."

146. G. O. Hagestad and M. A. Smyer, "Dissolving Long-Term Relationships: Patterns of Divorcing in Middle Age," in *Personal Relationships 4: Dissolving Personal Relationships,* edited by S. W. Duck (London: Academic Press, 1982), 155–88.

147. Gottman and Silver, *Why Marriages Succeed or Fail.*

148. B. Le, N. L. Dove, C. R. Agnew, M. S. Korn, and A. A. Mutso, "Predicting Nonmarital Romantic Dissolution: A Meta-Analytic Synthesis," *Personal Relationships* 17 (2010): 377–90.

149. W. W. Wilmot and D. C. Stevens, "Relationship Rejuvenation: Arresting Decline in Personal Relationships," in *Uses of "Structure" in Communication Studies,* edited by R. L. Conville (Westport, CT: Praeger, 1994), 103–24.

150. W. W. Wilmot, "Relationship Rejuvenation," in *Communication and Relational Maintenance,* edited by D. J. Canary and L. Stafford (San Diego, CA: Elsevier, 1994), 255–74.

151. S. A. Jang, S. W. Smith, and T. R. Levine, "To Stay or to Leave? The Role of Attachment Styles in Communication Patterns and Potential Termination of Romantic Relationships Following Discovery of Deception," *Communication Monographs* 69 (2002): 236–52.

152. Miller and Parks, "Communication in Dissolving Relationships."

153. S. W. Duck, "A Topography of Relationship Disengagement and Dissolution," in *Personal Relationships 4: Dissolving Personal Relationships,* edited by S. W. Duck (London: Academic Press, 1982), 1–29.

154. A. Weber, "Loving, Leaving, and Letting Go: Coping with Nonmarital Breakups," in *The Dark Side of Close Relationships,* edited by B. H. Spitzberg and W. R. Cupach (Mahwah, NJ: Erlbaum, 1998), 267–306.

155. M. J. Cody, "A Typology of Disengagement Strategies and an Examination of the Role Intimacy, Reactions to Inequity and Relational Problems Play in Strategy Selection," *Communication Monographs* 49 (1982): 148–70.

156. T. J. Wade, R. Palmer, M. Dimaria, C. Johnson, and M. Multack, "Deficits in Sexual Access versus Deficits in Emotional Access and Relationship Termination Decisions," *Journal of Evolutionary Psychology* 6 (2008): 309–19.

157. S. M. Rose, "How Friendships End: Patterns Among Young Adults," *Journal of Social and Personal Relationships* 1 (1984): 267–77.

158. M. Argyle and M. Henderson, *The Anatomy of Relationships* (New York: Guilford Press, 1991).

159. Duck, "A Topography of Relationship Disengagement and Dissolution"; S. Duck, "How Do You Tell Someone You're Letting Go?" *The Psychologist* 18 (2005): 210–13.

160. Miller and Parks, "Communication in Dissolving Relationships."

161. A. L. Alexander, "Relationship Resources for Coping with Unfulfilled Standards in Dating Relationships: Commitment, Satisfaction, and Closeness," *Journal of Social and Personal Relationships* 25 (2008): 725–47.

162. L. A. Baxter, "Accomplishing Relationship Disengagement," in *Understanding Personal Relationships: An Interdisciplinary Approach,* edited by S. Duck and D. Perlman (Beverly Hills, CA: Sage, 1984), 243–65.

163. T. J. Collins and O. Gillath, "Attachment, Breakup Strategies, and Associated Outcomes: The Effects of Security Enhancement on the Selection of Breakup Strategies," *Journal of Research in Personality* 46 (2012): 210–22.

164. Baxter, "Accomplishing Relationship Disengagement."

165. Collins and Gillath, "Attachment, Breakup Strategies, and Associated Outcome."

166. Cody, "A Typology of Disengagement Strategies."

167. P. W. Eastwick, E. J. Finkel, T. Krishnamurti, and G. Loewenstein, "Mispredicting Distress Following Romantic Breakup: Revealing the Time Course of the Affective Forecasting Error," *Journal of Experimental Social Psychology* 44 (2008): 800–07.

168. Weber, "Loving, Leaving, and Letting Go."

Chapter 11

1. L. K. Guerrero and P. A. Mongeau, "On Becoming 'More Than Friends': The Transition from Friendship to Romantic Relationship," in *Handbook of Relationship Initiation,* edited by S. Sprecher, A. Wenzel, and J. Harvey (New York: Psychology Press, 2008), 175–94.

2. A. M. Nicotera, "The Importance of Communication in Interpersonal Relationships," in *Interpersonal Communication in Friend and Mate Relationships,* edited by A. M. Nicotera and Associates (Albany: State University of New York Press, 1993), 3–12.

3. Nicotera, "The Importance of Communication in Interpersonal Relationships."

4. M. Argyle, *The Social Psychology of Everyday Life* (London: Routledge, 1991).

5. Nicotera, "The Importance of Communication in Interpersonal Relationships."

6. D. Felmlee, E. Sweet, H. C. Sinclair, "Gender Rules: Same-and Cross-Gender Friendship Norms," *Sex Roles* 66 (2012): 518–29.

7. P. M. Sias and H. Bartoo, "Friendship, Social Support, and Health," in *Low-Cost Approaches to Promote Physical and Mental Health,* edited by L. L'Abate (New York: Springer, 2007), 455–72.

8. Argyle, *The Social Psychology of Everyday Life,* 49.

9. Argyle, *The Social Psychology of Everyday Life.*

10. G. Allen, "Flexibility, Friendship, and Family," *Personal Relationships* 15 (2008): 1–16.

11. P. Marsh, *Eye to Eye: How People Interact* (Topsfield, MA: Salem House, 1988).

12. B. Fehr, "Friendship Formation," in *Handbook of Relationship Initiation*, edited by S. Sprecher, A. Wenzel, and J. Harvey (New York: Psychology Press, 2008), 29–54.

13. H. J. Markman, F. Floyd, and F. Dickson, "Towards a Model for the Prediction of Primary Prevention of Marital and Family Distress and Dissolution," in *Personal Relationships 4: Dissolving Personal Relationships*, edited by S. W. Duck and R. Gilmour (London: Academic Press, 1982).

14. J. F. Nussbaum, L. L. Pecchinoni, D. K. Baringer, and A. L. Kundrat, "Lifespan Communication," in *Communication Yearbook 26*, edited by W. B. Gudykunst (Mahwah, NJ: Erlbaum, 2002), 366–89.

15. W. J. Dickens and D. Perlman, "Friendship over the Life-Cycle," in *Personal Relationships 2: Developing Personal Relationships*, edited by S. W. Duck and R. Gilmour (London: Academic Press, 1981).

16. R. L. Selman, "Toward a Structural Analysis of Developing Interpersonal Relations Concepts: Research with Normal and Disturbed Preadolescent Boys," in *Minnesota Symposia on Child Psychology*, Vol. 10, edited by A. D. Pick (Minneapolis: University of Minnesota Press, 1976).

17. W. Rawlins, *Friendship Matters: Communication, Dialectics, and the Life Course* (New York: DeGruyter, 1992).

18. W. Samter, "Friendship Interaction Skills across the Life Span," in *Handbook of Communication and Social Interaction Skills*, edited by J. O. Greene and B. R. Burleson (Mahwah, NJ: Erlbaum, 2003), 637–84.

19. P. McDougall and S. Hymel, "Same-Gender Versus Cross-Gender Friendship Conceptions," *Merrill-Palmer Quarterly* 53 (2007): 347–80.

20. Dickens and Perlman, "Friendship over the Life-Cycle."

21. J. E. Benson, "Make New Friends but Keep the Old: Peers and the Transition to College," in *Advances in Life Course Research Vol. 12: Interpersonal Relations across the Life Course*, edited by T. J. Owens and J. J. Suitor (Boston: Elsevier, 2007), 309–34.

22. L. M. Swenson, A. Nordstrom, and M. Hiester, "The Role of Peer Relationships in Adjustment to College," *Journal of College Student Development* 49 (2008): 551–67.

23. A. J. Bahns, K. M. Pickett, and C. S. Crandall, "Social Ecology of Similarity: Big Schools, Small Schools, and Social Relationships," *Group Processes & Intergroup Relations* (2011): 1–13.

24. Rawlins, *Friendship Matters*, 105.

25. J. Stephenson-Abetz and A. Holman, "Home Is Where the Heart Is: Facebook and the Negotiation of "Old" and "New" During the Transition to College," *Western Journal of Communication* 76 (2012) 175–93.

26. Samter, "Friendship Interaction Skills across the Life Span."

27. Rawlins, *Friendship Matters*, 157.

28. M. Dainton, E. Zelley, and E. Langan, "Maintaining Friendships Throughout the Lifespan," in *Maintaining Relationships Through Communication*, edited by D. J. Canary and M. Dainton (Mahwah, NJ: Erlbaum, 2003), 79–102.

29. M. Kalmijn, "Shared Friendship Networks and the Life Course: An Analysis of Survey Data on Married and Cohabiting Couples," *Social Networks* 25 (2003): 231–49.

30. G. Luong, S. T. Charles, and K. L. Fingerman, "Better with Age: Social Relationships across Adulthood," *Journal of Social and Personal Relationships* 28 (2011): 9–23.

31. Luong, Charles, and Fingerman, "Better with Age."

32. N. Stevens, "Friendships in Late Adulthood," in *Encyclopedia of Human Relationships*, edited by H. T. Reis and S. Sprecher (Thousand Oaks, CA: Sage, 2009), 726–30.

33. Stevens, "Friendships in Late Adulthood."

34. J. M. Vigil, "Asymmetries in the Friendship Preferences and Social Styles of Men and Women," *Human Nature* 18 (2007): 143–61.

35. B. Fehr, "A Prototype Model of Intimacy Interactions in Same-Sex Friendships," in *Handbook of Closeness and Intimacy*, edited by D. J. Mahek and A. Aron (Mahwah, NJ: Erlbaum, 2004), 9–26.

36. Fehr, "A Prototype Model of Intimacy Interactions in Same-Sex Friendships."

37. P. H. Wright, "Toward an Expanded Orientation to the Comparative Study of Women's and Men's Same-Sex Friendships," in *Sex Differences and Similarities in Communication*, 2nd ed., edited by K. Dindia and D. J. Canary (Mahwah, NJ: Erlbaum, 2006), 37–57.

38. Wright, "Toward an Expanded Orientation."

39. Wright, "Toward an Expanded Orientation."

40. G. L. Greif, *Buddy System: Understanding Male Friendships* (New York: Oxford, 2009).

41. R. A. Singleton, Jr. and J. Vacca, "Interpersonal Competition in Friendships," *Sex Roles* 57 (2007): 617–27.

42. W. A. Collins and S. D. Madsen, "Personal Relationships in Adolescence and Early Adulthood," in *The Cambridge Handbook of Personal Relationships*, edited by A. L. Vangelisti and D. Perlman (New York: Cambridge University Press, 2006), 191–210.

43. Allen, "Flexibility, Friendship, and Family."

44. A. M. Ledbetter, M. A. Broeckelman-Post, and A. M. Krawsczyn, "Modeling Everyday Talk: Differences across Communication Media and Sex Composition of Friendship Dyads," *Journal of Social and Personal Relationships* 28 (2011): 223–31.

45. H. M. Reeder, "'I Like You … as a Friend': The Role of Attraction in Cross-Sex Friendship," *Journal of Social and Personal Relationships* 17 (2000): 329–48.

46. M. J. Miller, A. Denes, B. Diaz, and Y. Ranjit, "Touch Attitudes in Cross-Sex Friendships: We're Just Friends." *Personal Relationships* 21 (2014): 309–23.

47. Miller, Denes, Diaz, and Ranjit, "Touch Attitudes in Cross-Sex Friendships."

48. K. Knight, P. A. Mongeau, J. Eden, C. M. Shaw, and A. Ramirez, "The (Romantic) Relational Implication of Friends with Benefits Relationships," paper presented at the annual meeting of the National Communication Association (2008).

49. J. Owen, F. D. Fincham, and M. Manthos, "Friendship After a Friends with Benefits Relationship: Deception, Psychological Functioning, and Social Connectedness," *Archives of Sexual Behavior* 42 (2013): 1443–9.

50. M. Hughes, K. Morrison, and K. J. K. Asada, "What's Love Got to Do with It? Exploring the Impact of Maintenance Rules, Love Attitudes, and Network Support on Friends with Benefits Relationships," *Western Journal of Communication* 69 (2005): 49–66.

51. M. A. Bisson and T. R. Levine, "Negotiating a Friends with Benefits Relationship," *Archives of Sexual Behavior* 38 (2009): 66–73.

52. Hughes, Morrison, and Asada, "What's Love Got to Do with It?"

53. Bisson and Levine, "Negotiating a Friends with Benefits Relationship."

54. L. Rubin, *Just Friends: The Role of Friendship in Our Lives* (New York: Harper & Row, 1985).

55. S. H. Mathews, *Friendships Through the Life Course: Oral Biographies in Old Age* (Beverly Hills, CA: Sage, 1986).

56. S. J. Holladay and K. S. Kerns, "Do Age Differences Matter in Close and Casual Relationships? A Comparison of Age Discrepant and Age Peer Friendships," *Communication Reports* 12 (1999): 101–14.

57. M. J. Collier, "Communication Competence Problematics in Ethnic Relationships," *Communication Monographs* 63 (1996): 314–35.

58. Collier, "Communication Competence Problematics."

59. P. Lee, "Stages and Transitions of Relational Identity Formation in Intercultural Friendship: Implications for Identity Management Theory," *Journal of International and Intercultural Communication* 1 (2008): 51–69.

60. P. M. Sias, J. A Drzewiecka, M. Meares, R. Bent, Y. Konomi, M. Ortega, and C. White, "Intercultural Friendship Development," *Communication Reports* 21 (2008): 1–13.

61. X. de Souza Briggs, "'Some of My Best Friends Are …': Interracial Friendships, Class, and Segregation in America," *City & Community* 6 (2007): 263–90.

62. W. K. Rawlins, *The Compass of Friendship: Narratives, Identities, and Dialogues* (Thousand Oaks, CA: Sage, 2009).

63. Rawlins, *The Compass of Friendship*.

64. Rawlins, *The Compass of Friendship*, 149.

65. Rawlins, *The Compass of Friendship*, 151–52.

66. A. Aron and E. N. Aron, "Love," in *Perspectives on Close Relationships*, edited by

A. Weber and J. Harvey (Boston: Allyn & Bacon, 1994).

67. M. V. Redmond, "'We're Not dating. We're Just "Talking"': Meaning and Expectations Associated with Male–Female Relationship Labels," Unpublished Manuscript, 2015.

68. C. P. Fagundes and L. M. Diamond, "Intimate Relationships," in *Handbook of Social Psychology* edited by L. DeLamater and A. Ward (New York, NY: Springer, 2013): 371–411.

69. L. A. Kurdek, "Relationship Outcomes and Their Predictors: Longitudinal Evidence from Heterosexual Married, Gay Cohabiting, and Lesbian Cohabiting Couples," *Journal of Marriage and Family* 60 (1998): 553–68.

70. J. D. Cunningham and J. K. Antill, "Love in Developing Romantic Relationships," in *Personal Relationships 2: Developing Personal Relationships*, edited by S. W. Duck and R. Gilmour (London: Academic Press, 1981).

71. J. K. Rempel and C. T. Burris, "Let Me Count the Ways: An Integrative Theory of Love and Hate," *Personal Relationships* 12 (2005): 297–313; K. E. Hegi and R. M. Bergner, "What Is Love? An Empirically-Based Essentialist Account," *Journal of Social and Personal Relationships* 27 (2010): 620–36.

72. Z. Rubin, *Liking and Loving: An Invitation to Social Psychology* (New York: Holt, Rinehart and Winston, 1973).

73. R. J. Sternberg, "A Triangular Theory of Love," *Psychological Review* 93 (1986): 119–35.

74. E. Hatfield, L. Bensman, and R. L. Rapson, "A Brief History of Social Scientists' Attempts to Measure Passionate Love," *Journal of Social and Personal Relationships* 29 (2012): 143–64.

75. R. Lemieux and J. L. Hale, "Intimacy, Passion, and Commitment in Young Romantic Relationships: Successfully Measuring the Triangular Theory of Love," *Psychological Reports* 85 (1999): 497–504.

76. C. Hendrick and S. S. Hendrick, "Research on Love: Does It Measure Up?" *Journal of Personality and Social Psychology* 56 (1989): 784–94.

77. Bisson and Levine, "Negotiating Friends with Benefits Relationships."

78. S. Sprecher and B. Fehr, "Compassionate Love for Close Others and Humanity," *Journal of Social and Personal Relationships* 22 (2005): 629-51.

79. B. Fehr, C. Harasymchuk, and S. Sprecher, "Compassionate Love in Romantic Relationships: A Review and Some New Findings," *Journal of Social and Personal Relationships* 31 (2014): 575–600.

80. Fehr, Harasymchuk, and Sprecher, "Compassionate Love in Romantic Relationships."

81. S. Sprecher, C. Zimmerman, and B. Fehr, "The Influence of Compassionate Love on Strategies Used to End a Relationship," *Journal of Social and Personal Relationships* 31 (2014): 697–705.

82. J. A. Lee, "A Typology of Styles of Loving," *Personality and Social Psychology Bulletin* 3 (1977): 173–82.

83. T. B. Jamison and L. Ganong, "'We're Not Living Together': Stayover Relationships Among College-Educated Adults," *Journal of Social and Personal Relationships* 28 (2011): 536–57.

84. D. J. Weigel, "A Dyadic Assessment of How Couples Indicate Their Commitment to Each Other," *Personal Relationships* 15 (2008): 17–39.

85. D. J. Weigel and D. S. Ballard-Reisch, "Constructing Commitment in Intimate Relationships: Mapping Interdependence in the Everyday Expressions of Commitment, *Communication Research* 41 (2014): 311–32.

86. A. D. Hampel and A. L. Vangelisti, "Commitment Expectations in Romantic Relationships: Application of a Prototype Interaction-Pattern Model," *Personal Relationships* 15 (2008): 81–102.

87. D. J. Weigel and D. A. Weiser, "Commitment Messages Communicated in Families of Origin: Contributions to Relationship Commitment Attitudes," *Communication Quarterly* 62 (2014): 536–51.

88. M. Cui and F. D. Fincham, "The Differential Effects of Parental Divorce and Marital Conflict on Young Adult Romantic Relationships," *Personal Relationships* 17 (2010): 331–43.

89. P. A. Anderson, L. K. Guerrero, and S. M. Jones, "Nonverbal Behavior in Intimate Interactions and Intimate Relationships," *The Sage Handbook of Nonverbal Communication*, edited by V. Manusov and M. L. Patterson (Thousand Oaks, CA: Sage, 2006), 259–78.

90. S. M. Horan and M. Booth-Butterfield, "Investing in Affection: An Investigation of Affection Exchange Theory and Relational Outcomes," *Communication Quarterly*, 58, (2010): 394–413.

91. S. T. Carton and S. M. Horan, "A Diary Examination of Romantic and Sexual Partners Withholding Affectionate Messages," *Journal of Social and Personal Relationships* 31 (2014): 221–46.

92. C. A. Hill and L. K. Preston, "Individual Differences in the Experience of Sexual Motivation: Theory and Measurement of Dispositional Sexual Motives," *The Journal of Sex Research* 33 (1996): 27–45.

93. E. A. Impett, A. M. Gordon, and A. Strachman, "Attachment and Daily Sexual Goals: A Study of Dating Couples," *Personal Relationships* 15 (2008): 375–90.

94. Impett, Gordon, and Strachman, "Attachment and Daily Sexual Goals."

95. S. Sprecher, "Sexuality in Close Relationships," in *Close Relationships: Functions, Forms, and Processes*, edited by P. Noller and J. A. Feeney (New York: Psychology Press, 2006), 267–84.

96. J. A. Theiss, "Modeling Dyadic Effects in the Associations Between Relational Uncertainty, Sexual Communication, and Sexual Satisfaction for Husbands and Wives," *Communication Research* 38 (2011): 565–84.

97. J. L. Montesi, R. L. Fauber, E. A. Gordon, and R. G. Heimberg, "The Specific Importance of Communicating about Sex to Couples' Sexual and Overall Relationship Satisfaction," *Journal of Social and Personal Relationships* 28 (2011): 591–609.

98. J. A. Theiss and D. H. Solomon, "Communication and the Emotional, Cognitive, and Relational Consequences of First Sexual Encounters between Partners," *Communication Quarterly* 55 (2007): 179–206.

99. E. S. Byers and S. Demmons, "Sexual Satisfaction and Sexual Self-Disclosure within Dating Relationships," *The Journal of Sex Research* 36 (1999): 180–89.

100. T. A. Coffelt and J. A. Hess, "Sexual Goals-Plans-Actions: Toward a Sexual Script in Marriage," *Communication Quarterly* 63 (2015): 221–38.

101. Coffelt and Hess, "Sexual Goals-Plans-Actions."

102. Theiss and Soloman, "Communication and the Emotional, Cognitive, and Relational Consequences of First Sexual Encounters."

103. A. E. Lucchetti, "Deception in Disclosing One's Sexual History: Safe-Sex Avoidance or Ignorance?" *Communication Quarterly* 47 (1999): 300–14.

104. P. A. Mongeau, M. C. M. Serewicz, M. L. M. Henningsen, and K. L. Davis, "Sex Differences in the Transition to a Heterosexual Romantic Relationship," in *Sex Differences and Similarities in Communication*, 2nd ed., edited by K. Dindia and D. J. Canary (Mahwah, NJ: Erlbaum, 2006), 337–58.

105. H. Weger Jr. and M. C. Emmett, "Romantic Intent, Relationship Uncertainty, and Relationship Maintenance in Young Adults' Cross-Sex Friendships," *Journal of Social and Personal Relationships* 26 (2009): 964–88.

106. Guerrero and Mongeau, "On Becoming 'More Than Friends'."

107. Guerrero and Mongeau, "On Becoming 'More Than Friends'."

108. L. A. Baxter and W. W. Wilmot, "'Secret Tests': Social Strategies for Acquiring Information About the State of the Relationship," *Human Communication Research* 11 (1984): 171–202.

109. J. Fox and K. M. Warber, "Romantic Relationship Development in the Age of Facebook: An Exploratory Study of Emerging Adults' Perceptions, Motives, and Behaviors." *Cyberpsychology, Behavior, and Social Networking* 16 (2013): 3–7.

110. P. A. Mongeau, J. Jacobsen, and C. Donnerstein, "Defining Dates and First Date Goals: Generalizing from Undergraduates to Single Adults," *Communication Research* 34 (2007): 526–47.

111. Mongeau, Jacobsen, and Donnerstein, "Defining Dates and First Date Goals."

112. Mongeau, Jacobsen, and Donnerstein, "Defining Dates and First Date Goals."

113. Bogle, *Hooking Up,* 131.

114. A. D. Kunkel, S. R. Wilson, J. Olufowote, and S. J. Robson, "Identity Implications of Influence Goals: Initiating, Intensifying, and Ending Romantic Relationships,"

Western Journal of Communication 67 (2003): 382–412.

115. B. L. Wright and H. C. Sinclair, "Pulling the Strings: Effects of Friend and Parent Opinions on Dating Choices," *Personal Relationships* 19 (2012): 743–58.

116. P. C. Regan, *The Mating Game*, 2nd ed. (Thousand Oaks: CA, Sage, 2008).

117. Regan, *The Mating Game*.

118. M. C. M. Serewicz and E. Gale, "First-Date Scripts: Gender Roles, Context, and Relationship," *Sex Roles* 58 (2008): 149–64.

119. A. A. Eaton and S. Rose, "Has Dating Become More Egalitarian? A 35-Year Review Using Sex Roles," *Sex Roles* 64 (2011): 843–62.

120. K. A. Bogle, *Hooking Up: Sex, Dating and Relationships on Campus* (New York: New York University Press, 2008); K. A. Bogle, "The Shift from Dating to Hooking Up in College: What Scholars Have Missed," *Sociology Compass* 1/2 (2007): 775–88.

121. Bogle, *Hooking Up*, 42.

122. E. L. Paul, A. Wenzel, and J. Harvey, "Hookups: A Facilitator or a Barrier to Relationship Initiation and Intimacy Development?" in *Handbook of Relationship Initiation*, edited by S. Sprecher, A. Wenzel, and J. Harvey (New York: Psychology Press, 2008), 375–90.

123. M. T. Motley, L. J. Faulkner, and H. Reeder, "Conditions that Determine the Fate of Friendships after Unrequited Romantic Disclosures," in *Studies of Applied Interpersonal Communication*, edited by M. T. Motley (Thousand Oaks, CA: Sage, 2008): 27–50.

124. Motely, Faulkner, and Reeder, "Conditions that Determine the Fate of Friendships."

125. S. L. Young, C. G. Paxman, C. L. E. Koehring, and C. A. Anderson, "The Application of a Face Work Model of Disengagement to Unrequited Love," *Communication Research Reports* 25 (2008): 56–66.

126. Young, Paxman, Koehring, and Anderson, "The Application of a Face Work Model."

127. M. Duggan, N. B. Ellison, C. Lampe, A. Lenhart, and M. Madden, "Social Media Update 2014," Pew Research Center, January 2015, http://www.pewinternet.org/2015/01/09/social-media-update-2014/.

128. Pew Research Center, April, 2015, "The Smartphone Difference," available at: http://www.pewinternet.org/2015/04/01/us-smartphone-use-in-2015/.

129. Pew Research Center, February 2014, "Couples, the Internet, and Social Media," http://pewinternet.org/Reports/2014/Couples-and-the-internet.aspx.

130. S. T. Tong, B. Van Der Heide, L. Langwell, and J. B. Walther, "Too Much of a Good Thing? The Relationship Between Number of Friends and Interpersonal Impressions on Facebook," *Journal of Computer-Mediated Communication* 13 (2008): 531–49.

131. V. C. Sheer, "Teenagers' Use of MSN Features, Discussion Topics, and Online Friendship Development: The Impact of Media Richness and Communication Control," *Communication Quarterly* 59 (2011): 82–103.

132. J. Gorham and A. Fiore, "The Right Time for Love," https://www.facebook.com/notes/facebook-data-team/the-right-time-for-love-tracking-the-seasonality-of-relationship-formation/10150643989093859.

133. E. J. Finkel, P. W. Eastwick, B. R. Karney, H. T. Reis, and S. Sprecher, "Online Dating: A Critical Analysis from the Perspective of Psychological Science," *Psychological Science in the Public Interest* 13 (2012): 3–66.

134. C. L. Toma and J. T. Hancock, "A New Twist on Love's Labor: Self-Presentation in Online Dating Profiles," in *Computer-Mediated Communication in Personal Relationships* edited by K. B. Wright and L. M. Webb (New York, NY: Peter Lang, 2011), 41–55.

135. T. L. Anderson and T. M. Emmers-Sommer, "Predictors of Relationship Satisfaction in Online Romantic Relationships," *Communication Studies* 57 (2006): 153–72.

136. Anderson and Emmers-Sommer, "Predictors of Relationship Satisfaction."

137. Anderson and Emmers-Sommer, "Predictors of Relationship Satisfaction."

138. K. B. Wright, "On-Line Relational Maintenance Strategies and Perceptions of Partners within Exclusively Internet-Based and Primarily Internet-Based Relationships," *Communication Studies* 55 (2004): 239–53.

139. K. Dindia and L. Timmerman, "Accomplishing Romantic Relationships," in *Handbook of Communication and Social Interaction Skills*, edited by J. O. Greene and B. R. Burleson (Mahwah, NJ: Erlbaum, 2003), 685–22.

140. Adapted from K. Kellerman, S. Broatzman, T. S. Lim, and K. Kitao, "The Conversation MOP: Scenes in the Stream of Discourse," *Discourse Processes* 12 (1989): 27–61.

141. A. E. Lindsey and W. R. Zahaki, "Perceptions of Men and Women Departing from Conversational Sex Role Stereotypes During Initial Interaction," in *Sex Differences and Similarities in Communication*, edited by D. J. Canary and K. Dindia (Mahwah, NJ: Erlbaum, 1998), 393–412.

142. M. S. Clark and L. A. Beck, "Initiating and Evaluating Close Relationships: A Task Central to Emerging Adults," in *Romantic Relationships in Emerging Adulthood* edited by F. D. Fincham and M. Cui (New York: Cambridge Press, 2011), 190–212.

143. R. A. Bell and J. A. Daly, "The Affinity Seeking Function of Communication," *Communication Monographs* 51 (1984): 91–115.

144. K. Määttä and S. Uusiautti, "Silence is Not Golden: Review of Studies of Couple Interaction," *Communication Studies* 64 (2013): 33–48.

145. C. R. Berger and R. J. Calabrese, "Some Explorations in Initial Interaction and Beyond: Toward a Developmental Theory of Interpersonal Communication," *Human Communication Research* 1 (1975): 99–112; C. R. Berger and J. J. Bradac, *Language and Social Knowledge: Uncertainty in Interpersonal Relations* (Baltimore: Edward Arnold, 1982).

146. M. Sunnafrank, "Predicted Outcome Value During Initial Interactions," and "Interpersonal Attraction and Attitude Similarity," in *Communication Yearbook 14*, edited by J. A. Anderson (Newbury Park, CA: Sage, 1991), 451–83.

147. B. Jin and J. F. Peña, "Mobile Communication in Romantic Relationships: Mobile Phone Use, Relational Uncertainty, Love, Commitment, and Attachment Styles," *Communication Reports* 23 (2010): 39–51.

148. M. C. Stewart, M. Dainton, and A. K. Goodboy, "Maintaining Relationships on Facebook: Associations with Uncertainty, Jealousy, and Satisfaction," *Communication Reports* 27 (2014): 13–26.

149. L. K. Knobloch and J. A. Theiss, "Relational Uncertainty and Relationship Talk within Courtship: A Longitudinal Actor-Partner Interdependence Model," *Communication Monographs* 78 (2011): 3–26.

150. M. Dainton, "Equity and Uncertainty in Relational Maintenance," *Western Journal of Communication* 67 (2003): 164–86.

151. M. V. Redmond, "Relationship-Specific Social Decentering: Tapping Partner Specific Empathy and Partner Specific Perspective Taking," paper presented at the annual meeting of the National Communication Association (2006).

152. C. N. Wright and M. E. Roloff, "You Should Just Know Why I'm Upset: Expectancy Violation Theory and the Influence of Mind Reading Expectations (MRE) on Responses to Relational Problems," *Communication Research Reports*, 32 (2015): 10–19.

153. J. K. Kellas, E. K. Willer and A. R. Trees, "Communicated Perspective-Taking During Stories of Marital Stress: Spouses' Perceptions of One Another's Perspective-Taking Behaviors," *Southern Communication Journal* 78 (2013): 326–51.

154. R. M. Chory and S. Banfield, "Media Dependence and Relational Maintenance in Interpersonal Relationships," *Communication Reports* 22 (2009): 41–53.

155. A. L. Vangelisti, "Communication Problems in Committed Relationships: An Attributional Analysis," in *Attributions, Accounts, and Close Relationships*, edited by J. H. Harvey, T. L. Orbuch, and A. L. Weber (New York: Springer Verlag, 1992), 144–64.

156. G. Levinger and D. J. Senn, "Disclosure of Feelings in Marriage," *Merrill-Palmer Quarterly* 12 (1967): 237–49; A. Bochner, "On the Efficacy of Openness in Close Relationships," in *Communication Yearbook 5*, edited by M. Burgoon (New Brunswick, NJ: Transaction Books, 1982), 109–24.

157. A. B. Kelly, F. D. Fincham, and S. R. H. Beach, "Communication Skills in Couples: A Review and Discussion of Emerging Perspectives," in *Handbook of Communication and Social Interaction Skills*,

edited by J. O. Greene and B. R. Burleson (Mahwah, NJ: Erlbaum, 2003), 723–51.

158. N. M. Lambert, A. M. Gwinn, R. F. Baumeister, A. Stachman, I. J. Washburn, S. L Gable, and F. D. Fincham, "A Boost of Positive Affect: The Perks of Sharing Positive Experiences." *Journal of Social and Personal Relationships* 30 (2012): 24–43.

159. S. A. Westmyer and S. A. Myers, "Communication Skills and Social Support Messages across Friendship Levels," *Communication Research Reports* 13 (1996): 191–97.

160. B. R. Burleson and S. R. Mortenson, "Explaining Cultural Differences in Evaluations of Emotional Support Behaviors," *Communication Research* 30 (2003): 113–46; B. R. Burleson, "Comforting Messages: Features, Functions, and Outcomes," in *Strategic Interpersonal Communication,* edited by J. A. Daly and J. M. Weimann (Hillsdale, NJ: Erlbaum, 1994), 135–61.

161. A. M. Bippus, "Recipients' Criteria for Evaluating the Skillfulness of Comforting Communication and the Outcomes of Comforting Interactions," *Communication Monographs* 68 (2001): 301–13.

162. B. R. Sarason and I. G. Sarason, "Close Relationships and Social Support: Implications for the Measurement of Social Support," in *The Cambridge Handbook of Personal Relationships,* edited by A. L. Vangelisti and D. Perlman (New York: Cambridge University Press, 2006), 429–43.

163. E. Rafaeli and M. J. Gleason, "Skilled Support within Intimate Relationships," *Journal of Family Theory & Review* 1 (2009): 20–37.

164. R. A. Clark and J. G. Delia, "Individuals' Preferences for Friends' Approaches to Providing Support in Distressing Situations," *Communication Reports* 10 (1997): 115–21.

165. N. Miczo and J. K. Burgoon, "Facework and Nonverbal Behavior in Social Support Interactions within Romantic Dyads," in *Studies in Applied Interpersonal Communication,* edited by M. T. Motley (Thousand Oaks: CA, Sage, 2008), 246–66.

166. E. P. Lemay Jr. and K. L. Dudley, "Caution: Fragile! Regulating the Interpersonal Security of Chronically Insecure Partners," *Journal of Personality and Social Psychology* 100 (2011): 681–702.

167. Lemay and Dudley, "Caution: Fragile! Regulating Interpersonal Security."

168. Lemay and Dudley, "Caution: Fragile! Regulating Interpersonal Security."

169. J. M. Logan and R. J. Cobb, "Trajectories of Relationship Satisfaction: Independent Contributions of Capitalization and Support," *Personal Relationships* 20 (2013): 277–93.

170. E. M. Bryant and J. Marmo, "The Rules of Facebook Friendship: A Two-Stage Examination of Interaction Rules in Close, Casual, and Acquaintance Friendships," *Journal of Social and Personal Relationships* 29 (2012): 1013–35.

171. I. Shklovski, R. Kraut, and J. Cummings, "Keeping in Touch by Technology: Maintaining Friendships after a Residential Move," in *Proceedings of the Twenty-Sixth Annual SIGCHI Conference on Human Factors in Computing Systems* (New York: ACM, 2008): 807–16.

172. L. K. Guerrero and A. M. Chavez, "Relational Maintenance in Cross-Sex Friendships Characterized by Different Types of Romantic Intent: An Exploratory Study," *Western Journal of Communication* 69 (2005): 339–58.

173. L. K. Acitelli, "Knowing When to Shut Up: Do Relationship Reflections Help or Hurt Relationship Satisfaction?" in *Social Relationships: Cognitive, Affective, and Motivational Processes,* edited by J. P. Forgas and J. Fitness (New York: Psychology Press, 2008), 115–30.

174. J. F. Jensen and A. J. Rauer, "Turning Inward versus Outward: Relationship Work in Young Adults and Romantic Functioning," *Personal Relationships* 21 (2014): 451–67.

175. J. K. Alberts, "An Analysis of Couples' Conversational Complaints," *Communication Monographs* 55 (1988): 184–97.

176. N. C. Overall, G. J. O. Fletcher, J. A. Simpson, and C. G. Sibley, "Regulating Partners in Intimate Relationships: The Costs and Benefits of Different Communication Strategies," *Journal of Personality and Social Psychology* 96 (2009): 620–39.

177. M. A. Fitzpatrick and D. M. Badzinski, "All in the Family: Interpersonal Communication in Kin Relationships," in *Handbook of Interpersonal Communication,* edited by M. L. Knapp and G. R. Miller (Beverly Hills, CA: Sage, 1985), 687–736.

178. B. Laursen and C. A. Hafen, "Future Directions in the Study of Close Relationships: Conflict Is Bad (Except When It's Not)," *Social Development* 19 (2010): 858–72.

179. N. Epley, "Solving the (Real) Other Minds Problem," *Social and Personality Psychology Compass* 2/3 (2008): 1455–74.

Chapter 12

1. G. P. Murdock, *Social Structure* (New York: Free Press, 1965). Originally published 1949.

2. G. D. Nass and G. W. McDonald, *Marriage and the Family* (New York: Random House, 1982), 5.

3. G. Allan, "Flexibility, Friendship, and Family," *Personal Relationships* 18 (2008): 1–16.

4. J. Dixon and D. S. Dougherty, "A Language Convergence/Meaning Divergence Analysis Exploring How LGBTQ and Single Employees Manage Traditional Family Expectations in the Workplace," *Journal of Applied Communication Research* 42 (2014): 1–19

5. J. Koenig Kellas and E. A. Sutter, "Lesbian Mothers' Responses to Discursive Challenges," *Communication Monographs,* 79 (2013) 475–98.

6. P. Schrodt, J. Soliz, and D. O. Braithwaite, "A Social Relations Model of Everyday Talk and Relational Satisfaction in Stepfamilies," *Communication Monographs* 75 (2008): 190–217.

7. T. D. Golish, "Stepfamily Communication Strengths: Understanding the Ties That Bind," *Human Communication Research* 29 (2003): 41–80.

8. K. M. Galvin, "Joined by Hearts and Words: Adoptive Family Relationships," in *Widening the Family Circle: New Research on Family Communication,* edited by K. Floyd and M. T. Morman (Thousand Oaks, CA: Sage, 2006), 137–52.

9. Galvin, "Joined by Hearts and Words."

10. Galvin, "Joined by Hearts and Words."

11. K. A. Powell and T. D. Afifi, "Uncertainty Management and Adoptees' Ambiguous Loss of Their Birth Parents," *Journal of Social and Personal Relationships* 22 (2005): 129–51.

12. J. B. Kelly, "Children's Living Arrangements Following Separation and Divorce: Insights from Empirical and Clinical Research," *Family Process* 46 (2006): 35–52.

13. Kelly, "Children's Living Arrangements Following Separation and Divorce."

14. Kelly, "Children's Living Arrangements Following Separation and Divorce."

15. Kelly, "Children's Living Arrangements Following Separation and Divorce."

16. National Vital Statistics System, CDC, National Vital Statistics Report, 64 (2015), http://www.cdc.gov/nchs/data/nvsr/nvsr64/nvsr64_01.pdf.

17. Livermore and Powers, "Employment of Unwed Mothers."

18. D. O. Braithwaite, B. W. Bach, L. A. Baxter, et al., "Constructing Family: A Typology of Voluntary Kin," *Journal of Social and Personal Relationships* 27 (2010): 388–407.

19. T. J. Socha and J. Yingling, *Families Communicating with Children* (Malden, MA: Polity Press, 2010).

20. D. E. Beck and M. A. Jones, *Progress on Family Problems: A Nationwide Study of Clients' and Counselors' Views on Family Agency Services* (New York: Family Service Association of America, 1973).

21. H. J. Markman, "Prediction of Mental Distress: A 5-Year Follow-Up," *Journal of Consulting and Clinical Psychology* 49 (1981): 760–62.

22. D. H. L. Olson, H. L. McCubbin, H. L. Barnes, A. S. Larsen, M. J. Muxem, and M. A. Wilson, *Families: What Makes Them Work* (Beverly Hills, CA: Sage, 1983).

23. J. Koesten, "Family Communication Patterns, Sex of Subject, and Communication Competence," *Communication Monographs* 71 (2004): 226–44.

24. V. Satir, *Peoplemaking* (Palo Alto, CA: Science and Behavior Books, 1972), 30.

25. M. A. Fitzpatrick and L. D. Ritchie, "Communication Schemata within the Family: Multiple Perspectives on Family

Interaction." *Human Communication Research* 12 (1994): 275–301; A. F. Koerner and M. A. Fitzpatrick, "Toward a Theory of Family Communication," *Communication Theory* 12 (2002): 70–91.

26. A. F. Koerner and M. A. Fitzpatrick, "Family Communication Patterns Theory: A Social Cognitive Approach," in *Engaging Theories in Family Communication*, edited by D. O. Braithwaite and L. A. Baxter (Thousand Oaks, CA: Sage, 2006), 50–65.

27. A. F. Koerner and M. A. Fitzpatrick, "Family Type and Conflict: The Impact of Conversation Orientation and Conformity Orientation on Conflict in the Family," *Communication Studies* 48 (1997): 59–75.

28. Koerner and Fitzpatrick, "Family Communication Patterns Theory."

29. Koerner and Fitzpatrick, "Family Type and Conflict."

30. Koerner and Fitzpatrick, "Family Communication Patterns Theory."

31. Koerner and Fitzpatrick, "Family Type and Conflict."

32. Koerner and Fitzpatrick, "Family Communication Patterns Theory."

33. Koerner and Fitzpatrick, "Family Type and Conflict."

34. P. Schrodt, P. L. Witt, and A. S. Messersmith, "A Meta-Analytic Review of Family Communication Patterns and Their Associations with Information Processing, Behavioral, and Psychosocial Outcomes," *Communication Monographs* 75 (2008): 248–69.

35. J. Koesten, P. Schrodt, and D. J. Ford, "Cognitive Flexibility As a Mediator of Family Communication Environments and Young Adult's Well-Being," *Health Communication* 24 (2009): 82–94.

36. A. M. Ledbetter, "Family Communication Patterns and Relational Maintenance Behavior: Direct and Mediated Associations with Friendship Closeness," *Human Communication Research* 35 (2009): 130–47.

37. Ledbetter, "Family Communication Patterns."

38. P. Schrodt and K. Carr, "Trait Verbal Aggressiveness as a Function of Family Communication Patterns," *Communication Research Reports* 29 (2012): 54-63.

39. J. P. Caughlin, "Family Communication Standards: What Counts as Excellent Family Communication and How Are Such Standards Associated with Family Satisfaction?" *Human Communication Research* 29 (January 2003): 5–40.

40. K. M. Galvin and B. J. Brommel, *Family Communication: Cohesion and Change*, 5th ed. (New York: Longman, 2000).

41. J. Stachowiak, "Functional and Dysfunctional Families," in *Helping Families to Change*, edited by V. Satir, J. Stachowiak, and H. A. Taschman (New York: Jason Aronson, 1975).

42. M. E. Burns and J. C. Pearson, "An Exploration of Family Communication Environment, Everyday Talk, and Family Satisfaction," *Communication Studies* 62 (2011): 171–85.

43. Burns and Pearson, "An Exploration of Family Communication Environment."

44. A. Bochner and E. Eisenberg, "Family Process: Systems in Perspectives," in *Handbook of Communication Science*, edited by C. Berger and S. Chaffee (Beverly Hills, CA: Sage, 1987), 540–63.

45. D. M. Keating, J. C. Russell, J. Cornacchione, and S. W. Smith, "Family Communication Patterns and Difficult Family Conversations." *Journal of Applied Communication Research* 41 (2012): 160-80.

46. V. Satir, *The New Peoplemaking* (Mountain View, CA: Science and Behavior Books, 1988), 4.

47. P. Noller and M. A. Fitzpatrick, *Communication in Family Relationships* (Englewood Cliffs, NJ: Prentice Hall, 1993), 202.

48. J. Gottman with N. Silver, *Why Marriages Succeed or Fail* (New York: Simon and Schuster, 1994).

49. K. S. Birditt and T. C. Antonucci, "Relationship Quality Profiles and Well-Being Among Married Adults," *Journal of Family Psychology* 21 (2007): 595–604.

50. Birditt and Antonucci, "Relationship Quality Profiles."

51. M. A. Fitzpatrick, F. E. Jandt, F. L. Myrick, and T. Edgar, "Gay and Lesbian Couple Relationships," in *Queer Words, Queer Images*, edited by R.J. Ringer (New York: New York University Press, 1994), 265–77.

52. M. A. Fitzpatrick, *Between Husbands and Wives: Communication in Marriage* (Newbury Park, CA: Sage, 1988).

53. D. L. Kelly, "Relational Expectancy Fulfillment as an Explanatory Variable in Distinguishing Couple Types," *Human Communication Research* 25 (1999): 420–42.

54. Kelly, "Relational Expectancy Fulfillment."

55. P. Sheldon, E. Gilchrist-Petty, and J. A. Lessley, "You Did What? The Relationship Between Forgiveness Tendency, Communication of Forgiveness, and Relationship Satisfaction in Married and Dating Couples," *Communication Reports* 27 (2014): 78–90.

56. C. D. Kennedy-Lightsey and M. R. Dillow, "Initiating and Avoiding Communication with Mothers: Young Adult Children's Perceptions of Hurtfulness and Affirming Styles," *Southern Communication Journal* 76 (2011) 482–501.

57. M. M. Martin and C. M. Andersen, "Aggressive Communication Traits: How Similar Are Young Adults and Their Parents in Argumentativeness, Assertiveness, and Verbal Aggressiveness?" *Western Journal of Communication* 61 (1997): 299–314.

58. L. D. Ritchie and M. A. Fitzpatrick, "Family Communication Patterns: Measuring Intrapersonal Perceptions of Interpersonal Relationships," *Communication Research* 17 (1990): 523–44.

59. M. Booth-Butterfield and R. Sidelinger, "The Influence of Family Communication on the College-Aged Child: Openness, Attitudes, and Actions About Sex and Alcohol," *Communication Quarterly* 46 (1998): 295–308.

60. J. Koenig Kellas, "Transmitting Relational Worldviews: The Relationship between Mother–Daughter Memorable Messages and Adult Daughters' Romantic Relational Schemata," *Communication Quarterly* 58 (2010): 458–79.

61. S. C. Starcher, "Memorable Messages from Fathers to Children through Sports: Perspectives from Sons and Daughters," *Communication Quarterly* 63 (2015): 204–20.

62. S. M. Horan, M. L. Houser, and R. L. Cowan, "Are Children Communicated with Equally? An Investigation of Parent–Child Sex Composition and Gender Role Communication Differences," *Communication Research Reports* 24 (2007): 361–72.

63. K. McCoy, E. M. Cummings, and P. T. Davies, "Constructive and Destructive Marital Conflict, Emotional Security, and Children's Prosocial Behavior," *The Journal of Child Psychology and Psychiatry* 50 (2009): 270–79.

64. J. R. Shimkowski and P. Schrodt, "Coparental Communication as a Mediator of Interparental Conflict and Young Adult Children's Mental Well-Being," *Communication Monographs*, 79 (2012): 48–71.

65. Pew Research Center, February 2014, "Couples, the Internet, and Social Media," available at http://pewinternet.org/Reports/2014/Couples-and-the-internet.aspx.

66. G. S. Mesch, "Family Imbalance and Adjustment to Information and Communication Technologies," in *Computer-Mediated Communication in Personal Relationships* edited by K. B. Wright and L. M. Webb (New York: Peter Lang, 2011), 285–301.

67. J. H. Rudi, A. Walkner, and J. Dworkin, "Adolescent–Parent Communication in a Digital World: Differences by Family Communication Patterns," *Youth & Society* (forthcoming). Accessed online April 20, 2015.

68. A. E. Miller-Ott, L. Kelly, and R. L. Duran, "Cell Phone Usage Expectations, Closeness, and Relationship Satisfaction between Parents and Their Emerging Adults in College," *Emerging Adulthood* 2 (2014): 313–23.

69. Socha and Yingling, *Families Communicating with Children*.

70. A. Milevsky, M. J. Schelecter, and M. Machlev, "Effects of Parenting Style and Involvement in Sibling Conflict on Adolescent Sibling Relationships," *Journal of Social and Personal Relationships* 28 (2011): 1130–48.

71. S. A. Myers, "'I Have to Love Her, Even if Sometimes I May Not Like Her': The Reasons Why Adults Maintain Their Sibling Relationships," *North American Journal of Psychology*, (2011): 51–62.

72. C. Fowler, "Motives for Sibling Communication Across the Lifespan," *Communication Quarterly* 57 (2009): 51–66.

73. Fowler, "Motives for Sibling Communication."

74. A. Goetting, "The Developmental Tasks of Siblingship over the Life Cycle,"

Journal of Marriage and the Family 48 (1986): 703–14.

75. Fowler, "Motives for Sibling Communication."

76. P. Noller, "Sibling Relationships in Adolescence: Learning and Growing Together," *Personal Relationships* 12 (2005): 1–22.

77. L. K. Guerrero and W. A. Afifi, "Some Things Are Better Left Unsaid: Topic Avoidance in Family Relationships," *Communication Quarterly* 43 (1995): 276–96.

78. Guerrero and Afifi, "Some Things Are Better Left Unsaid."

79. P. A. Anderson and L. K. Guerrero, "Principles of Communication and Emotion in Social Interaction," in *Handbook of Communication and Emotion*, edited by P. A. Anderson and L. K. Guerrero (San Diego, CA: Academic Press, 1998), 49–96.

80. Anderson and Guerrero, "Principles of Communication and Emotion."

81. L. K. Guerrero, S. M. Jones, and R. R. Boburka, "Sex Differences in Emotional Communication," in *Sex Differences and Similarities in Communication*, 2nd ed., edited by K. Dindia and D. J. Canary (Mahwah, NJ: Erlbaum, 2006), 241–62.

82. L. Bloch, C. M. Haase, and R. W. Levenson, "Emotion Regulation Predicts Marital Satisfaction: More than a Wives' Tale," *Emotion* 14 (2014): 130–44.

83. K. Kitzmann, R. Cohen, and R. L. Lockwood, "Are Only Children Missing Out? Comparison of the Peer-Related Social Competence of Only Children and Siblings," *Journal of Social and Personal Relationships* 19 (2002): 299–316.

84. Noller, "Sibling Relationships in Adolescence."

85. A. C. Mikkelson, "Communication Among Peers: Adult Sibling Relationships," in *Widening the Family Circle: New Research on Family Communication*, edited by K. Floyd and M. T. Morman (Thousand Oaks, CA: Sage, 2006), 21–36.

86. S. Boland, "Social Support and Sibling Relationships in Middle Adulthood," paper presented to the Eastern Psychological Association (2007), http://www.lhup.edu/sboland/social_support_and_sibling_relat.htm. Accessed June 25, 2009.

87. Boland, "Social Support and Sibling Relationships in Middle Adulthood."

88. Mikkelson, "Communication Among Peers."

89. Mikkelson, "Communication Among Peers"; Goetting, "The Developmental Tasks of Siblingship."

90. M. Van Volkom, "Sibling Relationships in Middle and Older Adulthood: A Review of the Literature," *Marriage and Family Review* 40 (2006): 151–70.

91. Mikkelson, "Communication Among Peers."

92. P. M. Sias and D. J. Cahill, "From Coworkers to Friends: The Development of Peer Friendships in the Workplace," *Western Journal of Communication* 62 (1998): 273–99.

93. Sias and Cahill, "From Coworkers to Friends."

94. Sias and Cahill, "From Coworkers to Friends."

95. P. M. Sias, H. Pedersen, E. B. Gallagher, and I. Kopaneva, "Workplace Friendship in the Electronically Connected Organization," *Communication Research* 38 (2012): 253–79.

96. E. M. Berman, J. P. West, and M. N. Richter, Jr., "Workplace Relations: Friendship Patterns and Consequences (According to Managers)," *Public Administration Review* 62 (2002): 217–30.

97. P. Sias, G. Smith, and T. Avdeyeva, "Sex and Sex-Composition Differences and Similarities in Peer Workplace Friendship Development,"*Communication Studies* 54 (Fall 2003): 322–40.

98. P. Sias, *Organizing Relationships: Traditional and Emerging Perspectives on Workplace Relationships* (Thousand Oaks, CA: Sage, 2009), 93–94.

99. Sias, *Organizing Relationships*, 95–97.

100. P. S. Adler and S. Woon, "Social Capital: Prospects for a New Concept," *Academy of Management Review* 27 (2002): 17–40.

101. T. H. Feeley, J. Hwang, and G. A. Barnett, "Predicting Employee Turnover from Friendship Networks," *Journal of Applied Communication Research* 36 (2008): 56–73.

102. Sias, *Organizing Relationships*, 95.

103. P. M. Sias, R. G. Heath, T. Perry, D. Silva, and B. Fix, "Narratives of Workplace Friendship Deterioration," *Journal of Social and Personal Relationships* 21 (2004): 321–40.

104. P. M. Sias, E. B. Gallagher, I. Kopaneva, and H. Pederson, "Maintaining Workplace Friendships: Perceived Politeness and Predictors of Maintenance Tactic Choice," *Communication Research* (2011): 1–30.

105. Sias et al., "Narratives of Workplace Friendship Deterioration."

106. C. M. Schaefer and T. R. Tudor, "Managing Workplace Romances," *SAM Advanced Management Journal* 66 (2001): 4–11; Careerbuilder.com annual office romance survey, February, 10, 2009. careerbuilder.com. Accessed July 27, 2009.

107. J. Carson and J. Barling, "Romantic Relationships at Work: Old Issues, New Challenges," in *The Individual in the Changing Working Life*, edited by K K. Näswall, J. Hellgren, and M. Sverke (New York: Cambridge, 2008), 195–210; Sias, *Organizing Relationships*, 131–35.

108. CareerBuilder.com, "Nearly One-Third of Workers Who Had Office Romances Married Their Co-Worker, Finds Annual CareerBuilder CareerBuilder.com Valentine's Day Survey," February 9, 2012, http://www.careerbuilder.com/share/aboutus/pressreleasesdetail.aspx?id=pr678&sd=2%2F9%2F2012&ed=12%2F31%2F2012. Accessed May 24, 2012.

109. Carson and Barling, "Romantic Relationships at Work."

110. M. J. Lecker, "Workplace Romances: A Platonic Perspective," *Research in Ethical Issues in Organizations* 7 (2007): 253–79.

111. C. C. Malachowski, R. M. Chory, and C. J. Claus, "Mixing Pleasure with Work: Employee Perceptions of and Responses to Workplace Romance," *Western Journal of Communication* 76 (2012) 358–79.

112. K. Riach and F. Wilson, "Don't Screw the Crew: Exploring the Rules of Engagement in Organizational Romance," *British Journal of Management* 18 (2007): 79–92.

113. S. M. Horan and R. M. Chory, "Understanding Work/Life Blending: Credibility Implications for Those Who Date at Work," *Communication Studies* 62 (2011): 563–80.

114. Schaefer and Tudor, "Managing Workplace Romances."

115. F. Jablin, "Superior's Upward Influence, Satisfaction, and Openness in Superior-Subordinate Communication: A Reexamination of the 'Pelz Effect'," *Human Communication Research* 6 (1980): 210–20.

116. Jablin, "Superior's Upward Influence."

117. J. Gabarro and J. Kotter, "Managing Your Boss," *Harvard Business Review* 58 (1980): 92–100.

118. E. B. Meiners and V. D. Miller, "The Effect of Formality and Relational Tone on Supervisor/Subordinate Negotiation Episodes," *Western Journal of Communication* 68 (2004): 302–21.

119. B. L. S. Coker, "Freedom to Surf: The Positive Effects of Workplace Internet Leisure Browsing," *New Technology, Work, and Employment* 26 (2011): 238–47.

120. K. L. Fonner and M. E. Roloff, "Testing the Connectivity Paradox: Linking Teleworkers' Communication Media Use to Social Presence, Stress from Interruptions, and Organizational Identification," *Communication Monographs* 79 (2012): 205–31.

121. T. A. Domagalski and L A. Steelman, "The Impact of Gender and Organizational Status on Workplace Anger Expression," *Management Communication Quarterly* 20 (2007): 297–315.

122. Domagalski and Steelman, "The Impact of Gender and Organizational Status."

123. D. Katz and R. Kahn, *The Social Psychology of Organizations* (New York: Wiley, 1966).

124. V. R. Waldron and J. W. Kassing, *Managing Risk in Communication Encounters: Strategies for the Workplace* (Thousand Oaks, CA: Sage, 2011).

125. Sias, *Organizing Relationships*.

126. B. Fix and P. M. Sias, "Person-Centered Communication, Leader-Member Exchange, and Employee Job Satisfaction," *Communication Research Reports* 23 (2006): 35–44.

127. Fix and Sias, "Person-Centered Communication."

128. P. M. Sias, "Workplace Relationship Quality and Employee Information Experiences," *Communication Studies* 56 (2005): 375–96.

129. S. Kelly and C. Y. Kingsley Westerman, "Immediacy as an Influence on Supervisor–Subordinate Communication," *Communication Research Reports* 31 (2014) 252–61.

130. C. O. Longnecker and L. S. Fink, "Key Criteria in Twenty-First Century Management Promotional Decisions," *Career Development International* 13 (2008): 241–51.

131. D. A. Level, Jr., "Communication Effectiveness: Methods and Situation," *Journal of Business Communication* 10 (Fall 1972): 19–25.

132. Level, "Communication Effectiveness: Methods and Situation."

133. R. W. Pace and D. F. Faules, *Organizational Communication* (Englewood Cliffs, NJ: Prentice Hall, 1994).

134. S. Tye-Williams and K. J. Krone, "Chaos, Reports, and Quests: Narrative Agency and Co-Workers in Stories of Workplace Bullying," *Management Communication Quarterly*, 29 (2015): 3–27.

135. G. Namie, "2014 U.S. Workplace Bullying Survey," *Workplace Bullying Institute*, http://workplacebullying.org/multi/pdf/WBI-2014-US-Survey.pdf.

136. P. Lutgen-Sandvik, G. Namie, and R. Namie, "Workplace Bullying: Causes, Consequences, and Corrections," in *Destructive Organizational Communication* edited by P. Lutgen-Sandvik and B. D. Sypher (New York: Routledge Press, 2009) 27–52.

137. Tye-Williams and Krone, "Chaos, Reports, and Quests."

138. Lutgen-Sandvik, Namie, and Namie, "Workplace Bullying."

139. P. Malone and J. Hayes, "Backstabbing in Organizations: Employees' Perceptions of Incidents, Motives, and Communicative Responses," *Communication Studies* 63 (2012): 194–219.

140. N. A. Ploeger, K. M. Kelley, and R. S. Bisel, "Hierarchical Mum Effect: A New Investigation of Organizational Ethics," *Southern Communication Journal* 76 (2011): 465–81.

141. A. D. Galinsky, W. W. Maddux, D. Gilin, and J. B. White, "Why It Pays to Get Inside the Head of Your Opponent: The Differential Effects of Perspective Taking and Empathy in Negotiations," *Psychological Science* 19 (2008): 378–84.

142. Galinsky et al., "Why It Pays to Get Inside the Head of Your Opponent."

Glossary

A

accommodation   Conflict management style that involves giving in to the demands of others.

account   Response to a reproach.

acculturation   The process of transmitting a host culture's values, ideas, and beliefs to someone from outside that culture.

acquiescent responses   Crying, conceding, or apologizing in response to a hurtful message.

active listening   The process of being physically and mentally engaged in the listening process and letting the listener know that you are engaged.

active perception   Perception that occurs because you seek out specific information through intentional observation and questioning.

active verbal responses   Reactive statements made in response to a hurtful message.

adapt   To adjust one's behavior in accord with what someone else does. We can adapt based on the individual, the relationship, or the situation.

adaptability   A family's ability to modify and respond to changes in the family's power structure and roles.

adaptors   Nonverbal behaviors that satisfy a personal need and help a person adapt or respond to the immediate situation.

adapt predictively   To modify or change behavior in anticipation of an event.

adapt reactively   To modify or change behavior after an event.

affect displays   Nonverbal behaviors that communicate emotions.

affinity-seeking strategies   Strategies we use to increase others' liking us.

agape   Selfless love based on the giving of yourself for others.

aggressive   Expressing one's interests while denying the rights of others by blaming, judging, and evaluating other people.

agreeableness   A personality trait describing someone as friendly, compassionate, trusting, and cooperative.

allness   Tendency to use language to make unqualified, often untrue generalizations.

ambush listener   Person who is overly critical and judgmental when listening to others.

analytical listeners   Those who withhold judgment, listen to all sides of an issue, and wait until they hear the facts before reaching a conclusion.

androgynous role   Gender role that includes both masculine and feminine qualities.

anxious attachment style   The style of relating to others that is characteristic of those who experience anxiety in some intimate relationships and feel uncomfortable giving and receiving affection.

apology   Explicit admission of an error, along with a request for forgiveness.

arousal   Feelings of interest and excitement communicated by such nonverbal cues as vocal expression, facial expressions, and gestures.

assertive   Able to pursue one's own best interests without denying a partner's rights.

assertiveness   Tendency to make requests, ask for information, and generally pursue one's own rights and best interests.

asynchronous message   A message that is not read, heard, or seen exactly when it is sent; there is a time delay between the sending of the message and its receipt.

attachment style   A style of relating to others that develops early in life, based on the emotional bond one forms with one's parents or primary caregiver.

attending   Process of focusing on a particular sound or message.

attitude   Learned predisposition to respond to a person, object, or idea in a favorable or unfavorable way.

attribution theory   Theory that explains how you generate explanations for people's behaviors.

avoidance   Conflict management style that involves backing off and trying to side-step conflict.

avoidant attachment style   The style of relating to others that is characteristic of those who consistently experience discomfort and awkwardness in intimate relationships and who therefore avoid such relationships.

B

backchannel cues   Vocal cues that signal your wish to speak or stop speaking.

bald-faced lies   Deceptions by commission involving outright falsification of information intended to deceive the listener.

behavioral jealousy   Actions taken to monitor or alter a partner's jealousy-evoking activity.

belief   Way in which you structure your understanding of reality—what is true and what is false for you.

Big Five Personality Traits   Five personality traits that psychologists describe as constituting the major attributes of one's personality: extraversion, agreeableness, conscientiousness, neuroticism, and openness.

bilateral dissolution   Ending of a relationship by mutual agreement of both parties.

blended family   Two adults and their children. Because of divorce, separation, death, or adoption, the children are the offspring of other biological parents or of just one of the adults raising them.

breadth   The various pieces of self, like hobbies, beliefs, family, school, and fears, that can be potentially disclosed.

"but" messages   Statements using the word *but* that may communicate that whatever you've said prior to *but* is not really true.

bypassing   Confusion caused by the fact that the same word can mean different things to different people.

C

casual banter   Sub-stage of the acquaintance stage of relationship development, in which impersonal topics are discussed but very limited personal information is shared.

causal attribution theory   Theory of attribution that identifies the cause of a person's actions as circumstance, a stimulus, or the person himself or herself.

causal turning point   Event that brings about a change in a relationship.

channel   Pathway through which messages are sent.

circumplex model of family interaction   Model of the relationships among family adaptability, cohesion, and communication.

closure   Process of filling in missing information or gaps in what we perceive.

co-culture   A microculture; a distinct culture within a larger culture (such as the gay and lesbian co-culture).

coercive power   Power based on the use of sanctions or punishments to influence others.

cognitive jealousy   Thoughts about the loss of a partner, reflections on decreases in time spent with the partner, and analyses of behaviors or occurrences deemed suspicious.

cognitive schema   A mental framework used to organize and categorize human experiences.

cohesion   Emotional bonding and feelings of togetherness that families experience.

collaboration   Conflict management style that uses other-oriented strategies to achieve a positive solution for all involved.

commitment   Our intention to remain in a relationship.

communibiological approach   Perspective that suggests that genetic and biological influences play a major role in influencing communication behavior.

communication   Process of acting on information.

communication accommodation theory   Theory that all people adapt their behavior to others to some extent.

communication apprehension   Fear or anxiety associated with either real or anticipated communication with other people.

communication privacy management theory   Theory that suggests we each manage our own degree of privacy by means of personal boundaries and rules for sharing information.

communication social style   An identifiable way of habitually communicating with others.

compassionate listening   Nonjudgmental, nondefensive, empathic listening to confirm the worth of another person.

compassionate love   Feelings, cognitions, and behaviors that are focused on caring, concern, tenderness, and an orientation toward supporting, helping, and understanding the other.

competence   The quality of being skilled, intelligent, charismatic, and credible.

competition   Conflict management style that stresses winning a conflict at the expense of the other person involved.

competitive symmetrical relationship   Relationship in which both people vie for power and control of decision making.

complementary needs   Needs that match; each partner contributes something to the relationship that the other partner needs.

complementary relationship   Relationship in which power is divided unevenly, with one partner dominating and the other submitting.

compliance gaining   Taking persuasive actions to get others to comply with our goals.

compromise   Conflict management style that attempts to find the middle ground in a conflict.

confidant phase   Discussion and evaluation of a relationship, our concerns, and options with someone other than our partner (friends, family, or counselors).

confirming response   Statement that causes another person to value himself or herself more.

conflict management styles   Consistent patterns or approaches to manage disagreements with others.

conflict trigger   A common perceived cause of interpersonal conflict.

connotative meaning   Personal and subjective meaning of a word.

conscientiousness   A personality trait describing someone as efficient, organized, self-disciplined, dutiful, and methodical.

consensual families   Families with a high orientation toward both conversation and conformity.

construct   Bipolar quality or continuum used to classify people.

constructive conflict   Conflict that helps build new insights and establishes new patterns in a relationship.

contact hypothesis   The more contact you have with someone who is different from you, the more positive regard you will have for that person.

content   Information, ideas, or suggested actions that a speaker wishes to share.

context   Physical and psychological environment for communication.

conversation   The spontaneous, interactive exchange of messages with another person.

conversational narcissism   A focus on personal agendas and self-absorption rather than on the needs and ideas of others.

corrective facework   Efforts to correct what one perceives as a negative perception of oneself on the part of others.

critical listeners   Those who prefer to listen for the facts and evidence to support key ideas and an underlying logic; they also listen for errors, inconsistencies, and discrepancies.

critical listening   Listening to evaluate and assess the quality, appropriateness, value, or importance of information.

cues-filtered-out theory   Theory that suggests that communication of emotions is restricted when people send messages to others via text messages because nonverbal cues such as facial expression, gestures, and tone of voice are filtered out.

cultural context   Aspects of the environment and/or nonverbal cues that convey information not explicitly communicated through language.

culture   Learned system of knowledge, behavior, attitudes, beliefs, values, and norms shared by a group of people.

culture shock   Feelings of stress and anxiety a person experiences when encountering a culture different from his or her own.

cumulative rewards and costs   Total rewards and costs accrued during a relationship.

D

deception by commission (lying)   Deliberate presentation of false information.

deception by omission (concealment)   Intentionally holding back some of the information another person has requested or that you are expected to share.

decode   To interpret ideas, feelings, and thoughts that have been translated into a code.

demand-withdrawal pattern of conflict management   Pattern in which one person makes a demand and the other person avoids conflict by changing the subject or walking away.

denotative meaning   Restrictive or literal definition of a word.

dependent relationship   Relationship in which one partner has a greater desire for the other to meet his or her needs.

depth   How personal or intimate the information is that might be disclosed.

destructive conflict Conflict that dismantles rather than strengthens relationships.

dialectical tension Tension arising from a person's need for two things at the same time.

direct perception checking Asking for confirmation from the observed person of an interpretation or a perception about him or her.

direct termination strategies Explicit statements of a desire to break up a relationship.

disconfirming response Statement that causes another person to value himself or herself less.

discrimination Unfair or inappropriate treatment of people based on their group membership.

disinhibition effect The loss of inhibitions when interacting with someone online that leads to the tendency to escalate conflict.

dominance Power, status, and control communicated by such nonverbal cues as a relaxed posture, greater personal space, and protected personal space.

downward communication Communication that flows from superiors to subordinates.

dyadic effect The reciprocal nature of self-disclosure: "You disclose to me, and I'll disclose to you."

dyadic phase A phase in relationship termination, when the individual discusses termination with the partner.

E

egocentric communicator Person who creates messages without giving much thought to the person who is listening; a communicator who is self-focused and self-absorbed.

ego conflict Conflict in which the original issue is ignored as partners attack each other's self-esteem.

elaborated code Conversation that uses many words and various ways of describing an idea or concept to communicate its meaning.

electronically mediated communication (EMC) Messages that are sent via some electronic channel such as the phone, e-mail, text, or the Internet.

emblems Nonverbal cues that have specific, generally understood meanings in a given culture and may substitute for a word or phrase.

emotional contagion The process whereby people mimic the emotions of others after watching and hearing their emotional expressions.

emotional contagion theory Theory that emotional expression is contagious; people can "catch" emotions just by observing others' emotional expressions.

emotional intelligence The ability to be aware of, understand, and manage one's own emotions and those of other people.

emotional noise Form of communication interference caused by emotional arousal.

emotional or affective jealousy Feelings of anger, hurt, distrust, worry, or concern aroused by the threat of losing a relationship.

empathy Emotional reaction that is similar to the reaction being experienced by another person; empathizing is feeling what another person is feeling.

encode To translate ideas, feelings, and thoughts into code.

enculturation The process of transmitting a group's culture from one generation to the next.

envy A feeling of discontent arising from a desire for something someone else has.

episode Sequence of interactions between individuals, during which the message of one person influences the message of another.

eros Sexual, erotic love based on the pursuit of physical beauty and pleasure.

ethics The beliefs, values, and moral principles by which a person determines what is right or wrong.

ethnicity Social classification based on nationality, religion, language, and ancestral heritage, shared by a group of people who also share a common geographical origin.

ethnocentrism Belief that your cultural traditions and assumptions are superior to those of others.

euphemism A mild or indirect word that is substituted for one that describes something vulgar, profane, unpleasant, or embarrassing.

exaggeration Deception by commission involving "stretching the truth" or embellishing the facts.

expectancy violation theory Theory that you interpret the messages of others based on how you expect others to behave.

expected rewards and costs Expectation of how much reward we should get from a given relationship in comparison to its costs.

expert power Power based on a person's knowledge and experience.

extended family Relatives such as aunts, uncles, cousins, or grandparents and/or unrelated persons who are part of a family unit.

extended "I" language Brief preface to a feedback statement, intended to communicate that you don't want your listener to take your message in an overly critical way.

extraversion A personality trait describing someone as outgoing, talkative, positive, and sociable.

F

face A person's positive perception of himself or herself in interactions with others.

face-threatening acts Communication that undermines or challenges someone's positive face.

facework Using communication to maintain your own positive self-perception or to support, reinforce, or challenge someone else's self-perception.

fact Something that has been directly observed to be true and thus has been proven to be true.

fading away Ending a relationship by slowly drifting apart.

failure event or transgression An incident marked by the breaking or violating of a relational understanding or agreement.

family A self-defined unit made up of any number of persons who live or have lived in relationship with one another over time in a common living space and who are usually, but not always, united by marriage and kinship.

family communication patterns model A model of family communication based on two dimensions: conversation and conformity.

family of origin Family in which a person is raised.

feedback Response to a message.

feminine culture Culture in which people tend to value caring, sensitivity, and attention to quality of life.

filtering Process of reducing the number of partners at each stage of relational development by applying selection criteria.

flaming Sending an overly negative online message that personally attacks another person.

forecasted rewards and costs   Rewards and costs that an individual assumes will occur, based on projection and prediction.

friendship   A relationship of choice that exists over time between people who share a common history.

friendship-based intimacy   A type of intimacy based on feelings of warmth, understanding, and emotional connection.

fundamental attribution error   Error that arises from attributing another person's behavior to internal, controllable causes rather than to external, uncontrollable causes.

G

gender   Socially learned and reinforced characteristics that include one's biological sex and psychological characteristics (femininity, masculinity, androgyny).

grave-dressing phase   The phase in relationship termination, when the partners generate public explanations and move past the relationship.

gunny-sacking   Dredging up old problems and issues from the past to use against your partner.

H

halo effect   Attributing a variety of positive qualities to those you like.

hate speech   Words or phrases intended to offend or show disrespect for someone's race, ethnicity, cultural background, gender, or some other aspect of that person's identity.

hearing   Physiological process of decoding sounds.

high-contact cultures   Cultures in which people experience personal closeness and contact, often from warmer climates.

high-context culture   cultures in which people derive much information from nonverbal and environmental cues.

horizontal communication   Communication among colleagues or coworkers at the same level within an organization.

horn effect   Attributing a variety of negative qualities to those you dislike.

hostile environment   Type of harassment (often with a sexual component) in which an employee's rights are threatened through offensive working conditions or behavior on the part of other workers.

human communication   Process of making sense out of the world and sharing that sense with others by creating meaning through the use of verbal and nonverbal messages.

hyperpersonal relationship   A relationship formed primarily through electronically mediated communication that becomes more personal than an equivalent face-to-face relationship because of the absence of distracting external cues, smaller amounts of personal information, and idealization of the communication partner.

I

"I" language   Statements that use the word *I* to express how a speaker is feeling.

illustrators   Nonverbal behaviors that accompany a verbal message and either contradict, accent, or complement it.

immediacy   Feelings of liking, pleasure, and closeness communicated by such nonverbal cues as increased eye contact, forward lean, touch, and open body orientation.

immediate rewards and costs   Rewards and costs that are associated with a relationship at the present moment.

impersonal communication   Process that occurs when we treat others as objects or respond to their roles rather than to who they are as unique persons.

implicit personality theory   Your unique set of beliefs and hypotheses about what people are like.

impression formation theory   Theory that explains how you develop perceptions about people and how you maintain and use those perceptions to interpret their behaviors.

impressions   Collection of perceptions about others that you maintain and use to interpret their behaviors.

incrementalism   Systematic progression of a relationship through each of the de-escalation stages.

independent couples   Married partners who exhibit sharing and companionship and are psychologically interdependent but allow each other individual space.

indexing   Avoiding generalizations by using statements that separate one situation, person, or example from another.

indirect perception checking   Seeking through passive perception, such as observing and listening, additional information to confirm or refute interpretations you are making.

indirect termination strategies   Attempts to break up a relationship without explicitly stating the desire to do so.

inference   Conclusion based on speculation.

information triage   Process of evaluating information to sort good information from less useful or less valid information.

interaction adaptation theory   Theory suggesting that people interact with others by adapting to their communication behaviors.

interactional synchrony   Mirroring of each other's nonverbal behavior by communication partners.

intercultural communication   Communication between or among people who have different cultural traditions.

intercultural communication competence   Ability to adapt one's behavior toward another in ways that are appropriate to the other person's culture.

interdependent   Dependent on each other; one person's actions affect the other person.

interpersonal attraction   Degree to which you want to form or maintain an interpersonal relationship.

interpersonal communication   A distinctive, transactional form of human communication involving mutual influence, usually for the purpose of managing relationships.

interpersonal conflict   An expressed struggle between at least two interdependent people who perceive incompatible goals, scarce resources, or interference in the achievement of their goals.

interpersonal deception theory   An explanation of deception and detection as processes affected by the transactional nature of interpersonal interactions.

interpersonal intimacy   Degree to which relational partners mutually accept and confirm each other's sense of self.

interpersonal perception   Process of selecting, organizing, and interpreting your observations of other people.

interpersonal power   Degree to which a person is able to influence his or her partner.

interpersonal relationship   Perception shared by two people of an ongoing interdependent connection that results in the development of relational expectations and varies in interpersonal intimacy.

intimate space   Zone of space most often used for very personal or intimate interactions, ranging from 0 to 1½ feet between individuals.

intrapersonal communication Communication within yourself; self-talk.

intrapsychic phase First phase in relationship termination, when an individual engages in an internal evaluation of the partner.

introductions Sub-stage of the acquaintance stage of relationship development, in which interaction is routine and basic information is shared.

invulnerable responses Ignoring, laughing, or being silent in response to a hurtful message.

J

jargon Another name for restricted code; specialized terms or abbreviations whose meanings are known only to members of a specific group.

jealousy Reaction to the threat of losing a valued relationship.

Johari Window model Model of self-disclosure that summarizes how self-awareness is influenced by self-disclosure and information about yourself from others.

K

kinesics Study of human movement and gesture.

L

laissez-faire families Families with a low orientation toward both conversation and conformity.

leader-member exchange (LMX) theory Theory that supervisors develop different types of relationships with different subordinates and that seeks to explain those differences.

legitimate power Power that is based on respect for a person's position.

life position Feelings of regard for self and others, as reflected in one's sense of worth and self-esteem.

linguistic determinism Theory that describes how use of language determines or influences thoughts and perceptions.

linguistic relativity Theory that each language includes some unique features that are not found in other languages.

listener apprehension The fear of misunderstanding, misinterpreting, or being unable to adjust to the spoken messages of others.

listening Process of selecting, attending to, creating meaning from, remembering, and responding to verbal and nonverbal messages.

listening style Preferred way of making sense out of spoken messages.

long-term maintenance attraction Degree of liking or positive feelings that motivate us to maintain or escalate a relationship.

looking-glass self Concept that suggests you learn who you are based on your interactions with others, who reflect your self back to you.

low-contact cultures Cultures in which people experience less contact and personal closeness, often from cooler climates.

low-context culture Culture in which people derive much information from the words of a message and less information from nonverbal and environmental cues.

ludus Game-playing love based on the enjoyment of another.

M

malapropism Confusion of one word or phrase for another that sounds similar to it.

mania Obsessive love driven by mutual needs.

masculine culture Culture in which people tend to value traditional roles for men and women, achievement, assertiveness, heroism, and material wealth.

mass communication Process that occurs when one person issues the same message to many people at once; the creator of the message is usually not physically present, and listeners have virtually no opportunity to respond immediately to the speaker.

material self Concept of self as reflected in the total of all the tangible things you own.

media richness theory Theory that identifies the richness of a communication medium based on the amount of feedback it allows, the number of cues receivers can interpret, the variety of language it allows, and the potential for emotional expression.

message Written, spoken, and unspoken elements of communication to which people assign meaning.

metacommunication Verbal or nonverbal communication about communication.

meta-message A message about a message; the message a person is expressing via nonverbal means (such as by facial expression, eye contact, and posture) about the message articulated with words.

mindful Being conscious of what you are doing, thinking, and sensing at any given moment.

mindfulness The ability to consciously think about what you are doing and experiencing.

mixed couples Married couples in which the two partners each adopt a different perspective (traditional, independent, separate) on the marriage.

motivation Internal state of readiness to respond to something.

N

natural or nuclear family A mother, father, and their biological children.

need for affection Interpersonal need to give and receive love, support, warmth, and intimacy.

need for control Interpersonal need for some degree of influence in our relationships, as well as the need to be controlled.

need for inclusion Interpersonal need to be included and to include others in social activities.

neuroticism A personality trait describing someone as nervous, insecure, emotionally distressed, and anxious.

noise Anything literal or psychological that interferes with accurate reception of a message.

nonverbal communication Behavior other than written or spoken language that creates meaning for someone.

O

objective self-awareness Ability to be the object of one's own thoughts and attention—to be aware of one's state of mind and what one is thinking.

obsessive relational intrusion (ORI) Repeated invasion of a person's privacy by a stranger or acquaintance who desires or assumes a close relationship.

onomatopoeia A word that imitates a sound associated with what is named; also, the use of such a word.

openness A personality trait describing someone as curious, imaginative, creative, adventurous, and inventive.

other-oriented To be aware of the thoughts, needs, experiences, personality, emotions, motives, desires, culture, and goals of your communication partners while still maintaining your own integrity.

outward communication Communication that flows to those outside an organization (such as customers).

P

parallel relationship Relationship in which power shifts back and forth between the partners, depending on the situation.

paraphrase Verbal summary of the key ideas of your partner's message that helps you check the accuracy of your understanding.

passion-based intimacy A type of intimacy based on romantic and sexual feelings.

passive perception Perception that occurs without conscious effort, simply in response to one's surroundings.

Pelz effect Subordinates feel more satisfied in their jobs the more their supervisors are able to influence higher-level decisions.

perception Process of experiencing the world and making sense out of what you experience.

perception checking Asking someone whether your interpretation of his or her nonverbal behavior is accurate.

personality A set of enduring behavioral characteristics and internal predispositions for reacting to your environment.

personal space Zone of space most often used for conversations with family and friends, ranging from 1½ to 4 feet between individuals.

physical affection The use of touch to convey emotional feelings of love and caring for another person.

physical appearance Nonverbal cues that allow us to assess relationship potential.

pluralistic families Families with a high orientation toward conversation but a low orientation toward conformity.

polarization Description and evaluation of what you observe in terms of extremes such as good or bad, old or new, beautiful or ugly.

politeness theory Theory that people have positive perceptions of others who treat them politely and respectfully.

positive face An image of yourself that will be perceived as positive by others.

post-intimacy relationship Formerly intimate relationship that is maintained at a less intimate stage.

pragma Practical love based on mutual benefits.

predicted outcome value theory (POV) People predict the future of a relationship based on how they size up someone during their first interaction.

prejudice A judgment or opinion of someone, formed before you know all of the facts or the background of that person.

preventative facework Efforts to maintain and enhance one's positive self-perceptions.

primacy effect Tendency to attend to the first pieces of information observed about another person in order to form an impression.

profanity Words considered obscene, blasphemous, irreverent, rude, or insensitive.

protective families Families with a low orientation toward conversation but a high orientation toward conformity.

proxemics Study of how close or far away from people and objects people position themselves.

proximity Physical nearness to another that promotes communication and thus attraction.

pseudoconflict Conflict triggered by a lack of understanding and miscommunication.

psychology The study of how a person's thinking and emotional responses influence their behavior.

public communication Process that occurs when a speaker addresses an audience.

public space Zone of space most often used by public speakers or anyone speaking to many people, ranging beyond 12 feet from the individual.

punctuation Process of making sense out of stimuli by grouping, dividing, organizing, separating, and categorizing information.

Q

quid pro quo harassment Implied or explicit promise of reward in exchange for sexual favors or threat of retaliation if sexual favors are withheld, given to an employee by a coworker or a superior. The Latin phrase quid pro quo roughly means "You do something for me and I'll do something for you."

R

race A group of people with a common cultural history, nationality, or geographical location, as well as genetically transmitted physical attributes.

receiver Person who decodes a message and attempts to make sense of what the source has encoded.

recency effect Tendency to attend to the most recent information observed about another person in order to form or modify an impression.

reciprocation of liking Liking those who like us.

referent The thing that a symbol represents.

referent power Power that comes from our attraction to another person, or the charisma a person possesses.

reflective turning point Event that signals a change in the way a relationship is defined.

reframing Process of redefining events and experiences from a different point of view.

regulators Nonverbal messages that help to control the interaction or flow of communication between two people.

relational de-escalation Movement of a relationship away from intimacy through five stages: turmoil or stagnation, deintensification, individualization, separation, and post-separation.

relational development Movement of a relationship from one stage to another, either toward or away from greater intimacy.

relational dialectics theory Theory that views relational development as the management of tensions that are pulling us in two directions at the same time (connection–autonomy; predictability–novelty; openness–closedness).

relational escalation Movement of a relationship toward intimacy through five stages: preinteraction awareness, acquaintance, exploration, intensification, and intimacy.

relational listeners Those who prefer to focus on the emotions and feelings communicated verbally and nonverbally by others.

relational violence Range of destructive behaviors aimed at other people, including aggressiveness, threats, violent acts, and verbal, psychological, or physical abuse.

relationship Connection established when one person communicates with another.

relationship dimension The implied aspect of a communication message, which conveys information about emotions, attitudes, power, and control.

relationship of choice Interpersonal relationship you choose to initiate, maintain, and, perhaps, terminate.

relationship of circumstance   Interpersonal relationship that exists because of life circumstances (who your family members are, where you work or study, and so on).

relationship-specific social decentering   Other-oriented skills based on the knowledge and understanding gained in a specific intimate relationship.

relationship talk   Talk about the nature, quality, direction, or definition of a relationship.

remembering   Process of recalling information.

reproach   Message that a failure event has occurred.

responding   Process of confirming your understanding of a message.

responsiveness   Tendency to be sensitive to the needs of others, including being sympathetic to others' feelings and placing the feelings of others above one's own feelings.

restricted code   Set of words that have particular meaning to a person, group, or culture.

resurrection phase   Review and adjustment of our perspectives on self, others, and relationships while beginning the pursuit of new meaningful relationships.

reward power   Power based on a person's ability to satisfy our needs.

rule   Followable prescription that indicates what behavior is obligated, preferred, or prohibited in certain contexts.

S

Sapir–Whorf hypothesis   Based on the principles of linguistic determinism and linguistic relativity, the hypothesis that language shapes our thoughts and culture, and our culture and thoughts affect the language we use to describe our world.

second-guessing   Questioning the ideas and assumptions underlying a message; assessing whether the message is true or false.

secret test   Behavior designed to indirectly determine a partner's feelings.

secure attachment style   The style of relating to others that is characteristic of those who are comfortable giving and receiving affection, experiencing intimacy, and trusting other people.

selecting   Process of choosing one sound while sorting through various sounds competing for your attention.

selective attention   Process of focusing on specific stimuli, locking on to some things in the environment and ignoring others.

selective exposure   Tendency to put ourselves in situations that reinforce our attitudes, beliefs, values, or behaviors.

selective listening   Letting pre-formed biases, prejudices, expectations, and stereotypes cause us to hear what we want to hear, instead of listening to what a speaker actually said.

selective perception   Process of seeing, hearing, or making sense of the world around us based on such factors as our personality, beliefs, attitudes, hopes, fears, and culture, as well as what we like and don't like.

selective recall   Process that occurs when we remember things we want to remember and forget or repress things that are unpleasant, uncomfortable, or unimportant to us.

self   Sum total of who a person is; a person's central inner force.

self-awareness   A person's conscious understanding of who he or she is.

self-concept   A person's subjective description of who he or she is.

self-disclosure   Purposefully providing information about yourself to others that they would not learn if you did not tell them.

self-efficacy   A person's belief in his or her ability to perform a specific task in a particular situation.

self-fulfilling prophecy   Prediction about future actions that is likely to come true because the person believes that it will come true.

self-reflexiveness   Ability to think about what you are doing while you are doing it.

self-serving bias   Tendency to perceive our own behavior as more positive than others' behavior.

self-worth (self-esteem)   Your evaluation of your worth or value based on your perception of such things as your skills, abilities, talents, and appearance.

separate couples   Married partners who support the notion of marriage and family but stress the individual over the couple.

sex   Biologically based differences that determine whether one is male or female.

short-term initial attraction   Degree to which you sense a potential for developing an interpersonal relationship.

shyness   A behavioral tendency not to talk or interact with others.

similarity   Having comparable personalities, values, upbringing, personal experiences, attitudes, and interests.

simple conflict   Conflict that stems from different ideas, definitions, perceptions, or goals.

single-parent family   One parent raising one or more children.

skill   Behavior that improves the effectiveness or quality of communication with others.

small group communication   Process that occurs when a group of three to fifteen people meet to interact with a common purpose and mutually influence one another.

social comparison   Process of comparing yourself to others who are similar to you, to measure your worth and value.

social decentering   Cognitive process in which we take into account another person's thoughts, feelings, values, background, and perspective.

social exchange theory   Theory that claims people make relationship decisions by assessing and comparing the costs and rewards.

social identity model of deindividuation effects (SIDE)   Theory that people are more likely to stereotype others with whom they interact online, because such interactions provide fewer relationship cues and the cues take longer to emerge than they would in face-to-face interactions.

social information-processing theory   Theory that suggests people can communicate relational and emotional messages via the Internet, although such messages take longer to express without nonverbal cues.

social learning theory   A theory that suggests people can learn behavior that helps them adapt and adjust their behavior toward others.

social media   A variety of technological applications such as Facebook, Twitter, and Instagram that serve as channels to help people connect to one another.

social penetration model   A model of the self that reflects both the breadth and the depth of information that can potentially be disclosed.

social penetration theory   Theory of relational development that posits that increases in intimacy are connected to increases in self-disclosure.

social phase   A phase in relationship termination, in which members of the social network around both parties are informed of and become involved in the termination process.

social presence   The feeling that communicators have of engaging in unmediated, face-to-face interactions even though messages are being sent electronically.

social self   Concept of self as reflected in social interactions with others.

social space   Zone of space most often used for group interactions, ranging from 4 to 12 feet between individuals.

social support   Expression of empathy and concern for others that is communicated while listening to them and offering positive and encouraging words.

source   Originator of a thought or emotion, who puts it into a code that can be understood by a receiver.

spiritual self   Concept of self based on thoughts and introspections about personal values, moral standards, and beliefs.

stalking   Repeated, unwelcome intrusions that create concern for personal safety and fear in the target.

standpoint theory   Theory that a person's social position, power, or cultural background influences how the person perceives the behavior of others.

static evaluation   Pronouncement that does not take the possibility of change into consideration.

stereotype   To place a person or group of persons into an inflexible, all-encompassing category.

storge   Solid love found in friendships and family, based on trust and caring.

subjective self-awareness   Ability to differentiate the self from the social and physical environment.

submissive symmetrical relationship   Relationship in which neither partner wants to take control or make decisions.

sudden death   Abrupt and unplanned ending of a relationship.

superimpose   To place a familiar structure on information you select.

symbol   Word, sound, or visual image that represents something else, such as a thought, concept, or object.

symbolic interaction theory   Theory that people make sense of the world based on their interpretation of words or symbols used by others.

symbolic self-awareness   Uniquely human ability to think about oneself and use language (symbols) to represent oneself to others.

symmetrical relationship   Relationship in which both partners behave toward power in the same way, either both wanting power or both avoiding it.

sympathy   Acknowledgment of someone else's feelings.

synchronous message   A message that is sent and received simultaneously.

systems theory   Theory that describes the interconnected elements of a system in which a change in one element affects all of the other elements.

T

talk therapy   Technique in which a person describes his or her problems and concerns to a skilled listener in order to better understand the emotions and issues creating the problems.

task-oriented listeners   Those who look at the overall structure of the message to see what action needs to be taken; they also like efficient, clear, and brief messages.

tells   Nonverbal cues, such as facial expressions, body postures, or eye behaviors, that give away what we are thinking and feeling.

territoriality   Study of how animals and humans use space and objects to communicate occupancy or ownership of space.

territorial markers   Tangible objects that are used to signify that someone has claimed an area or space.

the Platinum Rule   Communicating or behaving toward another person as you assume he or she would like to be treated (as opposed to the "Golden Rule" which is treat someone as you would like to be treated).

thin slicing   Observing a small sample of someone's behavior and then making a generalization about what the person is like, based on the sample.

third culture   Common ground established when people from separate cultures create a third, "new," more comprehensive and inclusive culture.

thought   Mental process of creating an image, sound, concept, or experience triggered by a referent or symbol.

traditional couples   Married partners who are interdependent and who exhibit a lot of sharing and companionship.

triangular theory of love   Theory that suggests that all loving relationships can be described according to three dimensions: intimacy, commitment, and passion.

turning point   Specific event or interaction associated with a positive or negative change in a relationship.

U

uncertainty reduction theory   Theory that claims people seek information in order to reduce uncertainty, thus achieving control and predictability.

understanding   Process of assigning meaning to sounds.

unilateral dissolution   Ending of a relationship by one partner, even though the other partner wants it to continue.

unrequited romantic interest   Feelings created when one partner desires a more intimate, romantic relationship than the other partner would like.

upward communication   Communication that flows from subordinates to superiors.

V

value   Enduring concept of good and bad, right and wrong.

visualization   Technique of imagining that you are performing a particular task in a certain way; positive visualization can enhance self-esteem.

voluntary (fictive) kin   Individuals considered family regardless of their legal or blood connection.

W

warranting   Looking for clues to validate or invalidate an online claim.

white lies   Deceptions by commission involving only a slight degree of falsification that has a minimal consequence.

willingness to communicate   A behavioral trait that describes a person's comfortableness with and likelihood of initiating communication with other people.

word picture   Short statement or story that illustrates or describes an emotion; word pictures often use a simile (a comparison using the word like or as) to clarify the image.

worldview   Individual perceptions or perceptions by a culture or group of people about key beliefs and issues, such as death, God, and the meaning of life, which influence interaction with others.

Index

Credits

Text Credits

Page 1, Satir, V. (1976). *Making Contact* (Milbrae, CA: Celestial Arts); p. 6, V. Satir, *Peoplemaking* (Palo Alto, CA: Science and Behavior Books, 1972); p. 10, Duncan, H.D. (1967), "The Search for a Social Theory of Communication in American Sociology," in F. Dance (ed.), *Human Communication Theory*. New York: Holt, Rinehart and Winston, pp. 24–52; p. 11, © F. E. X. Dance, in *Human Communication Theory* (Holt, Rinehart and Winston, 1967, p. 294); p. 12; O. Wiio, *Wiio's Laws—and Some Others* (Espoo, Finland: WelinGoos, 1978); p. 13, S. B. Shimanoff, *Communication Rules: The Theory and Research* (Beverly Hills: Sage, 1980); M. Argyle, M. Hendershot, and A. Furnham "The Rules of Social Relationships," *British Journal of Social Psychology* 24 (1985): 125–39; p. 15, Sherry Turkle, TED Talk, March 2012 on ted.com/Turkle. Accessed April 5, 2012; p. 21; Based on L. K. Trevino, R. L. Draft, and R. H. Lengel, "Understanding Managers' Media Choices: A Symbolic Interactionist Perspective." In *Organizations and Communication Technology*, edited by J. Fulk and C. Steinfield (Newbury Park, CA: Sage, 1990), 71–94; p. 22; D. Crystal, *Txtng: The gr8 db8* (Oxford: Oxford University Press, 2008); p. 23; M. J. Collier, "Researching Cultural Identity: Reconciling Interpretive and Postcolonial Approaches," in *Communication and Identity Across Cultures*, edited by D. Tanno and A. Gonzalez (Thousand Oaks, CA: Sage, 1998), 142. Also see S. DeTurk, "Intercultural Empathy: Myth, Competency, or Possibility for Alliance Building?" *Communication Education* 50 (October 2001): 374–84; p. 24; M. Twenge, *Generation Me: Why Today's Young Americans Are More Confident, Assertive, Entitled—and More Miserable Than Ever Before* (New York: Free Press, 2006): 69; p. 30, Miguel de Cervantes, quoted in Madelene Victoria MacAdam, *Fortune in My Own Hands*. Christopher Publishing House, 1940; p. 31, K. Horney, *Neurosis and Human Growth* (New York: Norton, 1950), 17; p. 34, E. Goffman, *Frame Analysis: An Essay on the Organization of Experience* (Cambridge, MA: Harvard University Press, 1974), 508; p. 40, J. C. McCroskey and V. P. Richmond, *Fundamentals of Human Communication: An Interpersonal Perspective* (Prospect Heights, IL: Waveland Press, 1996); p. 44, K. Domenici and S. W. Littlejohn, *Facework: Bridging Theory and Practice* (Thousand Oaks CA: Sage, 2008); p. 46, Barbra Streisand as told to Oprah Winfrey, September 23, 2009. Accessed August 29, 2012 at http://www.oprah.com/oprahshow/Barbra-Streisands-Stage-Fright-Video; p. 48, F. E. X. Dance and C. Larson, *The Functions of Human Communication* (New York: Holt, Rinehart and Winston, 1976), 141; pp. 50–51, George Bernard Shaw, *Pygmalion*, 1913; Based on *Looking Out/Looking In*, edited by R. B. Adler and N. Towne (Fort Worth, TX: Harcourt Brace Jovanovich, 1993). Also see C. R. Berger, "Self Conception and Social Information Processing," in *Personality and Interpersonal Communication*, edited by J. C. McCroskey and J. A. Daly (1986): 275–303; Based on D. E. Harnachek, *Encounters with the Self* (New York: Holt, Rinehart and Winston, 1982); C. R. Berger, "Self Conception and Social Information Processing," in *Personality and Interpersonal Communication*, edited by J. C. McCroskey and J. A. Daly (1986): 275–303; p. 52, B. J. Bond, "He Posted, She Posted: Gender Differences in Self-Disclosure on Social Network Sites," *Rocky Mountain Communication Review* 6, no. 2 (October 2009): 29–37; p. 54, Based on Snavely and J. D. McNeill, "Communicator Style and Social Style: Testing a Theoretical Interface," *Journal of Leadership and Organizational Studies* 14, no. 3 (February 2008): 219–32; p. 55, McCroskey, James C. and Virgina P. Richmond. *Fundamentals of Human Communications: An Interpersonal Perspective*. Reprinted with permission of James C. McCroskey and Virgina P. Richmond; p. 56, R. Bolton and D. G. Bolton, *People Styles at Work: Making Bad Relationships Good and Good Relationships Better* (New York: AMACOM, 1996). 82; R. Bolton and D. G. Bolton, *People Styles at Work: Making Bad Relationships Good and Good Relationships Better* (New York: AMACOM, 1996). 83; p. 57, William Shakespeare, *Hamlet*, Act I, Scene iii; p. 60, C. S. Lewis, *The Magician's Nephew. The Bodley Head*, 1955; p. 71, Based on P. Cateora and J. Hess, *International Marketing* (Homewood, IL: Irwin, 1979), 89; as discussed by L. A. Samovar and R. E. Porter, *Communication Between Cultures* (Belmont, CA: Wadsworth, 2001), 52; p. 73, R. Nisbett and L. Ross, *Human Inference: Strategies and Shortcomings of Social Judgment* (Englewood Cliffs, NJ: Prentice Hall, 1980); p. 83, H. J. M. Nouwen, *Bread for the Journey* (San Francisco: HarperCollins, 1997), entry for March 11; p. 84, W. B. Gudykunst and Y. Y. Kim, *Communicating with Strangers: An Approach to Intercultural Communication* (New York: McGraw-Hill, Inc. 1997); p. 85, R. Bernstein, press release, Public Information Office, U.S. Census Bureau, www.census.gov/Press-Release/www/releases/archives/population/010048.html; p. 86, D. Tannen, *You Just Don't Understand* (New York: William Morrow, 1990); p. 88, J. Allen, *Differences Matter: Communicating Social Identity* (Long Grove, IL: Waveland Press, 2004), 68; p. 89, N. Howe and W. Strauss, *Millennials Rising: The Next Great Generation* (New York: Vintage Books, 2000); J. Smith, "The Millennials Are Coming," workshop presented at Texas State University, San Marcos, TX (2006); Data from Howe, N. and W. Strauss, *Millennials Rising: The Next Great Generation* (New York, Vintage Books, 2000); p. 90, B. J. Allen, *Differences Matter: Communicating Social*

Identity (Long Grove, IL: Waveland Press, 2004), 68; p. 92, G. Hofstede, *Culture's Consequences: International Differences in Work-Related Values* (Beverly Hills, CA: Sage, 1980); W. B. Gudykunst, *Bridging Differences: Effective Intergroup Communication* (Newbury Park, CA: Sage, 1998), 45; pp. 96–97, Rudyard Kipling, *Debits and Credits* (1923); p. 98, W. B. Gudykunst, *Bridging Differences: Effective Intergroup Communication* (Newbury Park, CA: Sage, 1991); R. E. Axtell, *Do's and Taboos of Hosting International Visitors* (New York: John Wiley & Sons, 1989), 118; p. 101, Based on Pinker, "The Moral Instinct," *The New York Times Magazine* (January 13, 2008): 36–42; Eleanor Roosevelt, as cited by M. W. Lustig and J. Koester, *Intercultural Competence: Interpersonal Communication Across Cultures* (Boston: Allyn & Bacon, 2009), 11; p. 102, C. Darwin, with contributions by P. Ekman, *The Expression of the Emotions in Man and Animals*, 3rd ed. (London: Oxford University Press, 1998), 391; p. 103, From Robert Plutchik, *Emotion: A Psychoevolutionary Synthesis*, 1st. ed. (Pearson Education, Inc., Upper Saddle River, New Jersey); p. 108, K. Domenici and S. Littlejohn, *Facework: Bridging Theory and Practice* (Thousand Oaks, CA: Sage, 2006), 159; p. 110, © Mark V. Redmond, "Interpersonal Content Adaptation In Everyday Interactions," paper presented at the annual meeting of the National Communication Association, Boston (2005); p. 112, M. J. Bennett, "Overcoming the Golden Rule: Sympathy and Empathy," in *Communication Yearbook* 3, edited by D. Nimmo (Beverly Hills, CA: Sage, 1979), 407–22; pp. 113–4, J. W. Neuliep and J. C. McCroskey, "The Development of a U.S. and Generalized Ethnocentrism Scale," *Communication Research Reports* 14 (1997): 393; p. 115, Larry King, in an interview to *Esquire* magazine; p. 116, H. J. M. Nouwen, *Bread for the Journey* (San Francisco: HarperCollins, 1997), entry for March 11; p. 124, Mother Teresa; p. 125, Franklin D. Roosevelt, First inauguration, 1933; p. 126, D. Carnegie, *How to Win Friends and Influence People* (New York: Holiday House, 1937); K. K. Halone and L. L. Pecchioni, "Relational Listening: A Grounded Theoretical Model," *Communication Reports* 14 (2001): 59–71; p. 133, Goleman, *Emotional Intelligence*, (New York: Bantam, 1994) p. 134, C. Rogers, *Client-Centered Therapy* (Boston: Houghton Mifflin, 1951); p. 139, J. Gottman and J. DeClaire, *The Relationship Cure* (New York: Crown, 2001), 198–201; Based on Hargie, Sanders, and Dickson, *Social Skills*; R. Boulton, *People Skills* (New York: Simon & Schuster, 1981); pp. 140–41, Based on B. D. Burleson, "Emotional Support Skill," in *Handbook of Communication and Social Interaction Skills*, edited by J. O. Greene and B. R. Burleson (Mahwah, NJ: Erlbaum, 2003), 566–68; p. 142, M. M. Bakhtin, *Problems of Dostoevsky's Poetics*, trans. and ed. C. Emerson (Minneapolis, MN: University of Minnesota Press, 1984): 292–93; p. 147, Jeane Kirkpatrick, *National and International Dimensions* (Transaction Publishers, 1988); p. 151, By permission. From Merriam-Webster Online (www.Merriam-Webster.com); p. 152, George Cupples, *Tappy's Chicks: And Other Links Between Nature and Human Nature* (Strahan & Co., 1872); Robert Browning, *Poetical Works* (Smith, Elder, 1899); G. Gusdorff, *Speaking* (Evanston, IL: Northwestern University Press, 1965), 9; p. 153, *The Dhammapada: The Sayings of the Buddha*, translated by Thomas Byrom (Boston: Shambhala, 1993), chapter 1, verses 1–2; Paraphrased from Proverbs 23:7; p. 156, George Carlin's monologue, 1972; p. 157, R. L. Howe, *The Miracle of Dialogue* (New York: The Seabury Press, 1963), 23–24; p. 159, Emling, "NuSrvc2 OffrGr8 Litr8tr On YrFon," *Austin American-Statesman* (November 26, 2005): A1, A6; William Shakespeare, *Hamlet*; William Shakespeare, *Richard III*; William Shakespeare, *Macbeth*; F. Scott Fitzgerald, *The Great Gatsby* (Charles Scribner's Sons, 1925); J. D. Salinger, *The Catcher in the Rye* (Little, Brown and Company), 1951; p. 160, T. M. Karelitz and D. V. Budescu, "You Say 'Probable' and I Say 'Likely': Improving Interpersonal Communication with Verbal Probability Phrases," *Journal of Experimental Psychology* 10 (2004): 25–41; p. 163, J. Wood, *Gendered Lives: Communication, Gender, and Culture* (Mason, OH: Cengage Learning, 2014); p. 165, D. O. Braithwaite and C. A. Braithwaite, "Understanding Communication of Persons with Disabilities as Cultural Communication," in *Intercultural Communication: A Reader*, 8th ed., edited by L. A. Samovar and R. E. Porter (Belmont, CA: Wadsworth, 1997), 154–64; p. 166, Winston Churchill; p. 167, J. M. Ackerman, N. P. Li, and V. Griskevicius, "Let's Get Serious: Communicating Commitment in Romantic Relationships," *Journal of Personality and Social Psychology* 100, no. 6 (2011): 1079–94; p. 170, Sherry Turkle, *Alone Together* (Cambridge, Mass.: Perseus Books, 2013); p. 171, S. Turkle, "The Flight From Conversation," *The New York Times* (April 22, 2012): 1, 6; D. Jones, "No. 37: Big Wedding or Small? Quiz: The 36 Questions That Lead to Love," http://www.nytimes.com/2015/01/11/fashion/no-37-big-wedding-or-small.html Accessed February 23, 2015. Print edition: *New York Times*, Styles, January 18, p. 4; p. 173, Proverbs 25:11, The Holy Bible, English Standard Version (ESV). Copyright © 2001 Crossway Bibles, a publishing ministry of Good News Publishers; p. 175, R. Wright, "E-Mail and Prozac," *The New York Times* (April 17, 2007): A23; p. 179, Ralph Waldo Emerson, "Social Aims," 1867; p. 184, Francis Bacon, *The Advancement of Learning*, 1605; p. 187, Based on A. Kendon, "Some Functions of Gaze-Direction in Social Interaction," *Acta Psychologica* 26 (1967): 22–63; Associated Press, "Frowning Outlawed in Meeting Code of Conduct." Retrieved May 7, 2003 from www.Boston.com; p. 188, Based on P. Ekman and W. V. Friesen, *Unmasking the Face* (Englewood Cliffs, NJ: Prentice

F Jo); p. 190, T. Brun, "Communicative Silences: Forms and Functions," Nommunication 1973): 17–46; p. 193, Robert Frost, "Mending Wall," in Powston, (David t, 1914); p. 194, Based on N. M. Henley, *Body Politics: Communication* (Englewood Cliffs, NJ: Prentice Hall, 1977); and Nonver cLuhan, *The Medium Is the Massage* (Penguin Books, 1967); p. Marsha . Argyle, *Bodily Communication* (New York: Methuen, 1988); p. Based verb from the book, *Moving Forward, Keeping Still* (MJF Books, 19 Chinese ted from W. Wilmot and J. Hocker, *Interpersonal Conflict* (New York 210 ll, 2007); National Communication Association; p. 214, Yogi Berra; G, *What Time Is It? You Mean Now?: Advice for Life from the Zennest Master* ll (New York: Simon & Schuster, 2002); p. 215, Adapted from D. W. Jo *aching Out: Interpersonal Effectiveness and Self-Actualization* (Boston: Ally , 2000), 314; p. 218, J. M. Olsen, *The Process of Social Organization* (New lt, Rinehart and Winston, 1978); p. 229, R. Boulton, *People Skills* (New on & Schuster, 1979); p. 230, William Blake, *A Poison Tree*, 1794; p. 232 Roosevelt, *This Is My Story* (Harper & Brothers, 1937); p. 233, S. R. Covey *bits of Highly Effective People* (New York: Simon & Schuster, 1989), 235; *Collection of Chinese Proverbs*, translated and arranged by William Scarbo merican Presbyterian Mission Press, 1815); p. 244, D. Layder, *Intimacy an The Dynamics of Personal Relationships in Modern Society* (New York rave Macmillian, 2009); p. 252, C. Harasymchuk and B. Fehr, "A Prototy sis of Relational Boredom," *Journal of Social and Personal Relationships*, 3 627–646; p. 262, Powell, John, *Why Am I Afraid to Tell You Who I Am?* (Ni rgus Communications, 1969); p. 271, A. J. Merolla, "Forgive Like You Sincerity of Forgiveness and the Experience of Negative Affect," C *ation Quarterly*, 62 (2014): 36–56; pp. 183–225, Jack W. Berry, Everett L. gton Jr., Lynn E. O'Connor, Les Parrott III, and Nathaniel G. Wade, "Fe ess, Vengeful Rumination, and Affective Traits," *Journal of Personality* 7 5). Reproduced with permission of BLACKWELL PUBLISHING, INC format Republish in a book via Copyright Clearance Center. Reprodu permission of Wiley; p. 273, Based on L. K. Guerrero, and G. F. Bachman eness and Forgiving Communication in Dating Relationships: An Expe vestment Explanation," *Journal of Social and Personal Relationships*, 27 1–823; p. 280, D. Hample, A. S. Richards, and C. Skubisz, "Blurting." Co *tion Monographs* 80 (2013): 503–32; p. 284, A. J. Roberto, J. Eden, M. W. S Ramos-Salazar, and D. M. Deiss, "Prevalence and Predictors of Cyberbu erpetration by High School Seniors." *Communication Quarterly* 62 (2014): p. 285, M. P. Johnson, "Violence and Abuse in Personal Relationships: C Terror, and Resistance in Intimate Partnerships," in *The Cambridge Handbo onal Relationships*, edited by A. L. Vangelisti and D. Perlman (New York: C e University Press, 2006), 557–76; p. 286, Based on J. Gottman with N *Why Marriages Succeed or Fail* (New York: Simon and Schuster, 1994); p Weber, "Loving, Leaving, and Letting Go: Coping with Nonmarital Bre in *The Dark Side of Close Relationships*, edited by B. H. Spitzberg and W pach (Mahwah, NJ: Erlbaum, 1998), 267–306; M. V. Redmond, *Human nication: Theories and Applications* (Boston: Houghton Mifflin, 2000); p. 290 yle and M. Henderson, *The Anatomy of Relationships* (New York: Guilfo , 1991); p. 291, Based on S. Duck, "A Typography of Relationship Disen nt and Dissolution," from *Personal Relationships, 4: Dissolving Relationsh* don: Academic Press, 1982), p. 16; p. 293, M. J. Cody, "A Typology of Disen nt Strategies and an Examination of the Role Intimacy, Reactions to Inequ Relational Problems Play in Strategy Selection," *Communication Mono* 49 (1982): 148–70; p. 297, Fr. Jerome Cummings; pp. 298–99, A. M. Nico he Importance of Communication in Interpersonal Relationships," in *Inter Communication in Friend and Mate Relationships*, edited by A. M. Nicotera ssociates (Albany: State University of New York Press, 1993), 3–12; p. 300, "Friendship Formation," in *Handbook of Relationship Initiation*, edited by S her, A. Wenzel, and J. Harvey (New York: Psychology Press, 2008), 29–5 1, R. L. Selman, "Toward a Structural Analysis of Developing Interpers elations Concepts: Research with Normal and Disturbed Preadolescent in *Minnesota Symposia on Child Psychology*, Vol. 10, edited by A. D. Pick (Mi lis: University of Minnesota Press, 1976); p. 303, *When Harry Met Sally*, 198 5, M. J. Collier, "Communication Competence Problematics in Ethnic Rel ips," *Communication Monographs* 63 (1996): 314–35; p. 306, Based on Fe erly, "Intimacy Expectations in Same-Sex Friendships: A Prototype Int n-Pattern Model," *Journal of Personality and Social Psychology* 86 (2004): 26 p. 308, C. P. Fagundes and L. M. Diamond, "Intimate Relationships," in *Ha of Social Psychology*, edited by L. DeLamater and A. Ward (New York, N nger, 2013): 371–411; p. 309, J. D. Cunningham and J. K. Antill, "Love in D ing Romantic Relationships," in *Personal Relationships 2: Developing Per so lationships*, edited by S. W. Duck and R. Gilmour (London: Academic P 981); E. Hatfield, L. Bensman, and R. L. Rapson, "A Brief History of Social S ts' Attempts to Measure Passionate Love," *Journal of Social and Personal R ships* 29 (2012): 143–64; p. 311, D. J. Weigel, "A Dyadic Assessment of How C s Indicate Their Commitment to Each Other," *Personal Relationships* 15 (2 17–39; p. 315, Based on P. A. Mongeau, J. L. Hale, K. L. Johnson, and J. D. H "Who's Wooing Whom? An Investigation of Female Initiated Dating," in P. J lesch, Ed., *Interpersonal Communication: Evolving Interpersonal Relationships* (Ha , NJ: Erlbaum, 1993), 51–68; p. 316, Based on M. T. Motley, L. J. Faulkner, a . leeder, "Conditions that Determine the Fate of Friendships after Unreq omantic Disclosures," in *Studies of Applied Interpersonal Communication*, ed M. T. Motley (Thousand Oaks, CA: Sage, 2008): 27–50; p. 320, Data from B A. and J. A. Daly, "The Affinity Seeking Function of Communication," C *mication Monographs* 51 (1984): 91–115; p. 328, Kyle, *South Park*; p. 330, G. P. Murdock, *Social Structure* (New York: Free Press, 1965). Originally published 1949; G. D. Nass and G. W. McDonald, *Marriage and the Family* (New York: Random House, 1982), 5; p. 332, D. O. Braithwaite, B. W. Bach, L. A. Baxter, et al., "Constructing Family: A Typology of Voluntary Kin," *Journal of Social and Personal Relationships* 27 (2010): 388–407; p. 334, Data from David H. L. Olson, Candyce S. Russell, and Douglas H. Sprenkle (Eds.), *Circumplex Model: Systemic Assessment and Treatment of Families* (New York: Haworth Press, 1989); V. Satir, *Peoplemaking* (Palo Alto, CA: Science and Behavior Books, 1972), 30; p. 337, J. P. Caughlin, "Family Communication Standards: What Counts as Excellent Family Communication and How Are Such Standards Associated with Family Satisfaction?" *Human Communication Research* 29 (January 2003): 5–40; K . M. Galvin and B. J. Brommel, *Family Communication: Cohesion and Change*, 5th ed. (New York: Longman, 2000); p. 342, Based on Pew Research Center, February 2014, "Couples, the Internet, and Social Media." Available at: http://pewinternet.org/Reports/2014/Couples-and-the-internet.aspx; p. 350, Based on C. M. Schaefer and T. R. Tudor, "Managing Workplace Romances," *SAM Advanced Management Journal* 66 (2001): 4–11. Careerbuilder.com, annual office romance survey, February, 10, 2009. Careerbuilder.com, retrieved July 27, 2009; p. 351, Excerpted from "Men & Women Communicating in the Workplace: Effective Strategies to Smooth Out Gender Differences," by Edward Leigh. Reprinted from the "Joy on the Job Newsletter," a complimentary electronic newsletter featuring informative and entertaining tips for creating positive workplaces. Subscribe at www.EdwardLeigh.com and receive the complimentary special report, 25 Ways to Create a Positive Workplace; p. 353, Based on Kristen Purcell, Lee Rainie. Pew Research Center, December 2014. "Technology's Impact on Workers." Available at: http://www.pewInternet.org/2014/12/30/technologys-impact-on-workers; p. 354, Katz and R. Kahn, *The Social Psychology of Organizations* (New York: Wiley, 1966); P. Sias, *Organizing Relationships: Traditional and Emerging Perspectives on Workplace Relationships* (Thousand Oaks, CA: Sage, 2009), 93–94; p. 355, Adapted primarily from Dan Blacharski, *The Savvy Business Traveler's Guide to Customs and Practices in Other Countries: The Dos and Don'ts to Impress Your Hosts and Make the Sale* (Ocala, FL: Atlantic Publishing Group, 2008

Photo Credits

Page vii, Diego Cervo/Shutterstock; p. viii, David Gilder/Shutterstock; p. x, StockLite/Shutterstock; p. xii, Susan Beebe; Mark V. Redmond; Texas State University p. 1, Diego Cervo/Shutterstock; p. 5, Monkey Business Images/Shutterstock; p. 13, Ian Shaw/Getty Images; p. 19, Wang Hsiu Hua/Fotolia; p. 21, (top to bottom) Shock/Fotolia, Robert Kneschke/Fotolia, SiSSen/Fotolia, Oleksiy Mark/Fotolia, Vladimir Voronin/Fotolia, Evgeniya_m/Fotolia, Chris Gloster/Fotolia, Myrleen Pearson/Alamy; p. 22, Pablocalvog/Fotolia; p. 24, PEANUTS © 1994 Peanuts Worldwide LLC. Dist. By UNIVERSAL UCLICK. Reprinted with permission. All rights reserved; p. 29, Edhar/Shutterstock; p. 33, Peter Nadolski/Shutterstock; p. 39, Gina Smith/Shutterstock; p. 42, Bruce Eric Kaplan/The New Yorker Collection/The Cartoon Bank; p. 44, B2M Productions/Getty Images; p. 46, Luis Louro/Fotolia; p. 50, Kzenon/Shutterstock; p. 60, Universal Images Group Limited/Alamy; p. 61, Disability Images/Alamy; p. 63, Kali Nine LLC/Getty Images; p. 66, Mika—Images/Alamy; p. 69, ZITS © 2000 Zits Partnership. Dist. by King Features Syndicate; p. 72, Paul Thuysbaert/Grapheast/Alamy; p. 75, Hurricane/Fotolia; p. 76, Don Bayley/Getty Images; p. 79, Golden Pixels LLC/Shutterstock; p. 83, Jasmin Merdan/Fotolia; p. 88, Yin Bogu/Xinhua/Alamy; p. 92, Zuma Press, Inc/Alamy; p. 94, Ilyas Dean/The Image Works; p. 97, Hideo Haga/The Image Works; p. 99, PEANUTS © 1999 Charles Schultz. Reprinted by permission of Universal UClick for UFS. All rights reserved; p. 104, Bob Mahoney/The Image Works; p. 107, Wesley Roberts/Alamy; p. 115, David Gilder/Shutterstock; p. 118 (top to bottom), © 2011 Stephan Pastis. Reprinted with permission of Universal UClick. All rights reserved, Dorothy Littell Greco/The Image Works, p. 124, Auremar/Fotolia; p. 130, Charles O. Cecil/Alamy, p. 134, Rachel Epstein/PhotoEdit; p. 136, JPC-PROD/Fotolia; 147, Creatista/Shutterstock; p. 149 (top to bottom), Edyta Pawlowska/Fotolia, Rita Kochmarjova/Fotolia; p. 154, Zac Macaulay/Getty Images; p. 156, Roz Chast/The New Yorker Collection/The Cartoon Bank; p. 161, Aijohn784/Fotolia; p. 166, Jason Stitt/Shutterstock; p. 172, Queerstock, Inc./Alamy; p. 179, JackF/Fotolia; p. 181; ZITS © 2006 Zits Partnership. Dist. by King Features Syndicate; p. 182, Scala/Art Resource, NY; p. 189, Monkey Business Images/Shutterstock; p. 192 (left to right), Wavebreakmedia/Shutterstock, David Gilder/Shutterstock, Phil Date/Shutterstock; p. 198, Nyul/Fotolia; p. 201, Monkey Business/Fotolia, Bonnie Kamin/PhotoEdit; p. 204, Hemera Technologies/Getty Images; p. 209, COSPV/Shutterstock; p. 211, Zulufoto/Shutterstock; p. 217, Theartofphoto/Fotolia; p. 220, Ingram Publishing/Alamy; p. 223 (left to right), MTomicic/Fotolia, Michael Flippo/Fotolia; p. 229, © 2015 Michael Maslin; p. 236 (top to bottom), Maria Sbytova/Fotolia, Anton Gvozdikov/Shutterstock; p. 241, StockLite/Shutterstock; p. 243, Jörg Carstensen/Pearson Education; p. 244 (left to right), Sean De Burca/Shutterstock, Conrado/Shutterstock; p. 247, AF archive/Alamy; p. 248, Chris Whitehead/Getty Images; p. 250, David Gilder/Shutterstock; p. 254, ZITS © 2000 Zits Partnership. Dist. by King Features Syndicate; p. 256, Jupiterimages/Getty Images; p. 262, Peter Bernik/Shutterstock; p. 267, Auremar/Fotolia; p. 271, Barbara Smaller/The New Yorker Collection/The Cartoon Bank; p. 274, Phil Boorman/Getty Images; p. 277, Monkeybusinessimages/Getty Images; p. 280, Monkey Business Images/Shutterstock; p.281, JGI/JamieGrill/GettyImages; p.283, AndyDeanPhotography/Shutterstock;